P9-CQG-202

DATE DUE

OCT 2 6 2006	
DEC - 7 2006	

DEMCO, INC. 38-2931

The Theory and Practice
of Concurrency

Series editors: Tony Hoare and Richard Bird

Series listing continued at back of book

The Theory and Practice of Concurrency

A.W. Roscoe

Oxford University Computing Laboratory

Prentice Hall

London   New York   Toronto   Sydney   Tokyo   Singapore
Madrid   Mexico City   Munich   Paris

First published 1998 by
Prentice Hall Europe
Campus 400, Maylands Avenue
Hemel Hempstead
Hertfordshire, HP2 7EZ
A division of
Simon & Schuster International Group

Printed and bound in Great Britain by
T.J. International Ltd, Cornwall

Library of Congress Cataloging-in-Publication Data

Roscoe, A. W.
    The theory and practice of concurrency / A.W. Roscoe.
      p. cm.—(Prentice Hall international series in computer science)
    Includes bibliographical references and index.
    ISBN 0-13-674409-5
    1. Parallel processing (Electronic computers)   I. Title.
  II. Series.
  QA76.58.R67   1997
  004´.35—dc21   97–31217
                                              CIP

British Library Cataloguing in Publication Data

A catalogue record for this book is available from the British Library

ISBN 0-13-674409-5 (pbk)

1 2 3 4 5   02 01 00 99 98

Contents

Preface

Since C.A.R. Hoare's text *Communicating Sequential Processes* was published in 1985, his notation has been extensively used for teaching and applying concurrency theory. This book is intended to provide a comprehensive text on CSP from the perspective that 12 more years of research and experience have brought.

By far the most significant development in this time has been the emergence of tools to support both the teaching and industrial application of CSP. This has turned CSP from a notation used mainly for describing 'toy' examples which could be understood and analyzed by hand, into one which can and does support the description of industrial-sized problems and which facilitates their automated analysis. As we will see, the FDR model checking tool can, over a wide range of application areas, perform analyses and solve problems that are beyond most, if not all, humans.

In order to use these tools effectively you need a good grasp of the fundamental concepts of CSP: the tools are most certainly not an *alternative* to gaining an understanding of the theory. Therefore this book is still, in the first instance, a text on the principles of the language rather than being a manual on how to apply its tools. Nevertheless the existence of the tools has heavily influenced both the choice and presentation of material. Most of the chapters have a section specifically on the way the material in them relates to tools, two of the appendices are tool-related, and there is an associated web site

http://www.comlab.ox.ac.uk/oucl/publications/books/concurrency/

on which readers can find

- a list of tools available for CSP

- demonstrations and details of some of the tools

- directories of example files containing most of the examples from the text and many other related ones

- practical exercises which can be used by those teaching and learning from this book

- a list of materials available to support teaching (overhead foils, solutions to exercises, etc.) and instructions for obtaining them

as well as supporting textual material. Contact information, etc., relating to those tools specifically mentioned in the text can be found in the Bibliography.

The Introduction (Chapter 0) gives an indication of the history, purpose and range of applications of CSP, as well as a brief survey of the classes of tools that are available. There is also a discussion of how to go about one of the major steps when using CSP to model a system: deciding what constitutes an *event*. It provides background reading which should be of interest to more experienced readers before beginning the rest of the book; those with no previous exposure to concurrency might find some parts of the Introduction of more benefit after looking at Part I.

The rest of the book is divided into three parts and structured to make it usable by as wide an audience as possible. It should be emphasized, however, that the quantity of material and the differing levels of sophistication required by various topics mean that I expect it will be relatively uncommon for people to attempt the whole book in a short space of time.

Part I (Chapters 1–6) is a foundation course on CSP, covering essentially the same ground as Hoare's text except that most of the mathematical theory is omitted. At an intuitive level, it introduces the ideas behind the operational (i.e., transition system), denotational (traces, failures and divergences) and algebraic models of CSP, but the formal development of these is delayed to Part II. Part I has its origins in a set of notes that I developed for an introductory 16-lecture course for Oxford undergraduates in Engineering and Computing Science. I would expect that all introductory courses would cover up to Section 5.1 (buffers), with the three topics beyond that (buffer tolerance, communications protocols and sequential composition[1]) being more optional.

Part II and Part III (Chapters 7–12 and 13–15, though Chapter 12 arguably belongs equally to both) respectively go into more detail on the theory and practice

---

[1]Instructors who are intending to deal at any length with the theory presented in Part II should consider carefully whether they want to include the treatment of sequential composition, since it can reasonably be argued that the special cases it creates are disproportionate to the usefulness of that operator in the language. Certainly it is well worth considering presenting the theory without these extra complications before going back to see how termination and sequencing fit in.

of CSP. Either of them would form the basis of a one-term graduate course as a follow-on to Part I, though some instructors will doubtless wish to mix the material and to include extracts from Parts II and III in a first course. (At Oxford, introductory courses for more mathematically sophisticated audiences have used parts of Chapters 8 and 9, on the denotational semantics and its applications, and some courses have used part of Chapter 13, on deadlock.) The chapters of Part III are independent of each other and of Part II.[2]

This book assumes no mathematical knowledge except for a basic understanding of sets, sequences and functions. I have endeavoured to keep the level of mathematical sophistication of Parts I and III to the minimum consistent with giving a proper explanation of the material. While Part II does not require any further basic knowledge other than what is contained in Appendix A (which gives an introduction to the ideas from the theory of partial orders and metric/restriction spaces required to understand the denotational models), the mathematical constructions and arguments used are sometimes significantly harder than in the other two parts.

Part II describes various approaches to the semantic analysis of CSP. Depending on your point of view, you can either regard its chapters as an introduction to semantic techniques for concurrency via the medium of CSP, or as a comprehensive treatment of the theory of this language. Each of the three complementary semantic approaches used – operational, denotational and algebraic – is directly relevant to an understanding of how the automated tools work. My aim in this part has been to give a sufficiently detailed presentation of the underlying mathematics and of the proofs of the main results to enable the reader to gain a thorough understanding of the semantics. Necessarily, though, the most complex and technical proofs are omitted.

Chapter 12 deserves a special mention, since it does not so much introduce semantic theory as apply it. It deals with the subject of *abstraction*: forming a view of what a process looks like to a user who can only see a subset of its alphabet. A full understanding of the methods used requires some knowledge of the denotational models described in Chapters 8, 9 and 10 (which accounts for the placing of Chapter 12 in Part II). However, their applications (to the formulation of specifications in general, and to the specification of fault tolerance and security in particular), are important and deserve attention by the 'practice' community as well as theoreticians.

Chapter 13, on deadlock avoidance, is included because deadlock is a much

---

[2]It follows that a course based primarily on Part III need not cover the material in order and that instructors can exercise considerable freedom in selecting what to teach. For example, the author has taught a tool-based graduate course based on Section 15.1, Chapter 5, Section 15.2, Appendix C, Chapter 14, Chapter 12 (Sections 12.3 and 12.4 in particular), the first half of Chapter 13 and Section 15.3.

feared phenomenon and there is an impressive range of techniques, both analytic and automated, for avoiding it. Chapter 14 describes how the untimed version of CSP (the one this book is about) can be used to describe and reason about timed systems by introducing a special event to represent the passage of time at regular intervals. This has become perhaps the most used dialect of CSP in industrial applications of FDR. Each of these two chapters contains extensive illustrative examples; Chapter 15 is based entirely around four case studies (two of which are related) chosen to show how CSP can successfully model, and FDR can solve, *interesting, difficult* problems from other application areas.

The first appendix, as described above, is an introduction to mathematical topics used in Part II. The second gives a brief description of the machine-readable version of CSP and the functional programming language it contains for manipulating process state. The third explains the operation of FDR in terms of the theory of CSP, and in particular describes the process-compression functions it uses.

At the end of each chapter in Parts II and III there is a section entitled 'Notes'. These endeavour, necessarily briefly, to put the material of the chapter in context and to give appropriate references to related work.

Exercises are included throughout the book. Those in Part I are mainly designed to test the reader's understanding of the preceding material; many of them have been used in class at Oxford over the past three years. Some of those in Parts II and III have the additional purpose of developing sidelines of the theory not otherwise covered.

Except for one important change (the decision not to use process alphabets, see page 76), I have endeavoured to remain faithful to the notation and ideas presented in Hoare's text. There are a few other places, particularly in my treatment of termination, variable usage and unbounded nondeterminism, where I have either tidied up or extended the language and/or its interpretation.

Acknowledgements

I had the good fortune to become Tony Hoare's research student in 1978, which gave me the opportunity to work with him on the development of the 'process algebra' version of CSP and its semantics from the first. I have constantly been impressed that the decisions he took in structuring the language have stood so well the twin tests of time and practical use in circumstances he could not have foreseen. The work in this book all results, either directly or indirectly, from his vision. Those familiar with his book will recognize that much of my presentation, and many of my examples, have been influenced by it.

Much of the theory set out in Chapters 7, 8, 9 and 11 was established by the early 1980s. The two people most responsible, together with Tony and myself, for the development of this basic theoretical framework for CSP were Steve Brookes and Ernst-Rudiger Olderog, and I am delighted to acknowledge their contributions. We were, naturally, much influenced by the work of those such as Robin Milner, Matthew Hennessy and Rocco de Nicola who were working at the same time on other process algebras.

Over the years, both CSP and my understanding of it have benefited from the work of too many people for me to list their individual contributions. I would like to thank the following present and former students, colleagues, collaborators and correspondents for their help and inspiration: Geoff Barrett, Stephen Blamey, Naiem Dathi, Jim Davies, Richard Forster, Paul Gardiner, Michael Goldsmith, Anthony Hall, Jifeng He, Jason Hulance, David Jackson, Lalita Jategoankar, Alan Jeffrey, Ranko Lazić, Gavin Lowe, Helen McCarthy, Jeremy Martin, Albert Meyer, Michael Mislove, David Park, Mike Reed, Bill Rounds, Peter Ryan, Jeff Sanders, Bryan Scattergood, Steve Schneider, Brian Scott, Karen Seidel, Antti Valmari, David Walker, Jim Woodcock, Lars Wulf, Jay Yantchev, Irfan Zakiuddin and Zhou Chao Chen. Many of them will recognize specific influences their work has had on my book. A few of these contributions are referred to in individual chapters.

Special thanks are due to the present and former staff of Formal Systems (some of whom are listed above) for their work in developing FDR, and latterly ProBE. The remarkable capabilities of FDR transformed my view of CSP and made me realize that writing this book had become essential. Bryan Scattergood was chiefly responsible for both the design and the implementation of the ASCII version of CSP used on these and other tools. I am grateful to him for writing Appendix B on this version of the language.

Many of the people mentioned above have read through drafts of my book and pointed out errors and obscurities, as have various students. The quality of the text has been greatly helped by this. I have had valuable assistance from Jim Davies in my use of LaTeX.

My work on CSP has benefited from funding from several bodies over the years, including EPSRC, DRA, ESPRIT, industry and the US Office of Naval Research. I am particularly grateful to Ralph Wachter from the last of these, without whom most of the research on CSP tools would not have happened, and who has specifically supported this book and the associated web site.

This book could never have been written without the support of my wife Coby. She read through hundreds of pages of text on a topic entirely foreign to her, expertly pointing out errors in spelling and style. More importantly, she put up with me writing it.

Bill Roscoe
May 1997

Introduction

CSP is a notation for describing *concurrent* systems (i.e., ones where there is more than one process existing at a time) whose component processes interact with each other by communication. Simultaneously, CSP is a collection of mathematical models and reasoning methods which help us understand and use this notation. In this chapter we discuss the reasons for needing a calculus like CSP and some of the historical background to its development.

0.1 Background

Parallel computers are starting to become common, thanks to developing technology and our seemingly insatiable demands for computing power. They provide the most obvious examples of concurrent systems, which can be characterized as systems where there are a number of different activities being carried out at the same time. But there are others: at one extreme we have loosely coupled networks of workstations, perhaps sharing some common file-server; and at the other we have single VLSI circuits, which are built from many subcomponents which will often do things concurrently. What all examples have in common is a number of separate components which need to communicate with each other. The theory of concurrency is about the study of such communicating systems and applies equally to all these examples and more. Though the motivation and most of the examples we see are drawn from areas related to computers and VLSI, other examples can be found in many fields.

CSP was designed to be a notation and theory for describing and analyzing systems whose primary interest arises from the ways in which different components interact *at the level of communication*. To understand this point, consider the design of what most programmers would probably think of first when parallelism is mentioned, namely parallel supercomputers and the programs that run on them. These computers are usually designed (though the details vary widely) so that parallel programming is as easy as possible, often by enforcing highly stylized communication which takes place in time to a global clock that also keeps the various parallel processing threads in step with each other. Though the design of the parallel programs that run on these machines – structuring computations so that calculations may be done in parallel and so that transfers of information required fit the model provided by the computer – is an extremely important subject, it is not what CSP or this book is about. For what is interesting there is understanding the structure of the problem or algorithm, not the concurrent behaviour (the clock and regimented communication having removed almost all interest here).

In short, we are developing a notation and calculus to help us understand interaction. Typically the interactions will be between the components of a concurrent system, but sometimes they will be between a computer and external human users. The primary applications will be areas where the main interest lies in the structure and consequences of interactions. These include aspects of VLSI design, communications protocols, real-time control systems, scheduling, computer security, fault tolerance, database and cache consistency, and telecommunications systems. Case studies from most of these can be found in this book: see the table of contents.

Concurrent systems are more difficult to understand than sequential ones for various reasons. Perhaps the most obvious is that, whereas a sequential program is only 'at' one line at a time, in a concurrent system all the different components are in (more or less) independent states. It is necessary to understand which combinations of states can arise and the consequences of each. This same observation means that there simply are more states to worry about in parallel code, because the total number of states grows exponentially (with the number of components) rather than linearly (in the length of code) as in sequential code. Aside from this state explosion there are a number of more specific misbehaviours which all create their own difficulties and which any theory for analyzing concurrent systems must be able to model.

Nondeterminism

A system exhibits *nondeterminism* if two different copies of it may behave differently when given exactly the same inputs. Parallel systems often behave in this way because of contention for communication: if there are three subprocesses P, Q and R where P and Q are competing to be the first to communicate with R, which in turn bases its future behaviour upon which wins the race, then the whole system may veer one way or the other in a manner that is uncontrollable and unobservable from the outside.

Nondeterministic systems are in principle untestable, since however many times one of them behaves correctly in development with a given set of data, it is impossible to be sure that it will still do so in the field (probably in subtly different conditions which might influence the way a nondeterministic decision is taken). Only by formal understanding and reasoning can one hope to establish any property of such a system. One property we might be able to prove of a given process is that it is deterministic (i.e., will always behave the same way when offered a given sequence of communications), and thus amenable to testing.

Deadlock

A concurrent system is *deadlocked* if no component can make any progress, generally because each is waiting for communication with others. The most famous example of a deadlocked system is the 'five dining philosophers', where the five philosophers are seated at a round table with a single fork between each pair (there is a picture of them on page 61). But each philosopher requires both neighbouring forks to eat, so if, as in the picture, all get hungry simultaneously and pick up their left-hand fork then they deadlock and starve to death. Even though this example is anthropomorphic, it actually captures one of the major causes of real deadlocks, namely competition for resources. There are numerous others, however, and deadlock (particularly nondeterministic deadlock) remains one of the most common and feared ills in parallel systems.

Livelock

All programmers are familiar with programs that go into infinite loops, never to interact with their environments again. In addition to the usual causes of this type of behaviour – properly called *divergence*, where a program performs an infinite unbroken sequence of internal actions – parallel systems can *livelock*. This occurs when a network communicates infinitely internally without any component communicating externally. As far as the user is concerned, a livelocked system looks similar to a deadlocked one, though perhaps worse since the user may be able to observe the presence of internal activity and so hope eternally that some output will emerge eventually. Operationally and, as it turns out, theoretically, the two phenomena are very different.

The above begin to show why it is essential to have both a good understanding of the way concurrent systems behave and practical methods for analyzing them. On encountering a language like CSP for the first time, many people ask why they have to study a new body of theory, and new specification/verification techniques, rather than just learning another programming language. The reason is that, unfortunately, mathematical models and software engineering techniques developed for sequential systems are usually inadequate for modelling the subtleties of concurrency so we have to develop these things alongside the language.

0.2   Perspective

As we indicated above, a system is said to exhibit concurrency when there can be several processes or subtasks making progress at the same time. These subtasks might be running on separate processors, or might be time-sharing on a single one. The crucial thing which makes concurrent systems different from sequential ones is the fact that their subprocesses communicate with each other. So while a sequential program can be thought of as progressing through its code a line at a time – usually with no external influences on its control-flow – in a concurrent system each component is at its own line, and without relying on a precise knowledge of the implementation we cannot know what sequence of states the system will go through. Since the different components are influencing each other, the complexities of the possible interactions are mind-boggling. The history of concurrency consists both of the construction of languages and concepts to make this complexity manageable, and the development of theories for describing and reasoning about interacting processes.

CSP has its origins in the mid 1970s, a time when the main practical problems driving work on concurrency arose out of areas such as multi-tasking and operating system design. The main problems in those areas are ones of maintaining an illusion of simultaneous execution in an environment where there are scarce resources. The nature of these systems frequently makes them ideally suited to the model of a concurrent system where all processes are able (at least potentially) to see the whole of memory, and where access to scarce resources (such as a peripheral) is controlled by *semaphores*. (A process seeks a semaphore by executing a claim, or P, operation, and after its need is over releases it with a V operation. The system must enforce the property that only one process 'has' the semaphore at a time. This is one solution to the so-called *mutual exclusion problem*.)

Perhaps the most superficially attractive feature of shared-variable concurrency is that it is hardly necessary to change a programming language to accommodate it. A piece of code writes to, or reads from, a shared variable in very much the same way as it would do with a private one. The concurrency is thus, from the point of view of a sequential program component, in some senses implicit. As with many things, the shared variable model of concurrency has its advantages and disadvantages. The main disadvantage from the point of view of modelling general interacting systems is that the communications between components, which are plainly vitally important, happen *too* implicitly. This effect also shows up when it comes to mathematical reasoning about system behaviour: when it is not made explicit in a program's semantics when it receives communications, one has to allow for the effects of any communication at any time.

In recent years, of course, the emphasis on parallel programming has moved to the situation where one is distributing a single task over a number of separate processors. If done wrongly, the communications between these can represent a real bottleneck, and certainly an unrestricted shared variable model can cause problems in this way. One of the most interesting developments to overcome this has been the BSP (Bulk Synchronous Parallelism) model [69, 114] in which the processors are synchronized by the beat of a relatively infrequent drum and where the communication/processing trade-off is carefully managed. The BSP model is appropriate for large parallel computations of numerical problems and similar; it does not give any insight into the way parallel systems interact at a low level. When you need this, a model in which the communications between processors are the essence of process behaviour is required. If you were developing a parallel system on which to run BSP programs, you could benefit from using a communication-based model at several different levels.

In his 1978 paper [49], C.A.R. Hoare introduced, with the language CSP (Communicating Sequential Processes), the concept of a system of processes, each with its own private set of variables, interacting only by sending messages to each other via *handshaken* communication. That language was, at least in appearance, very different from the one studied in this book. In many respects it was like the language OCCAM [52, 55] which was later to evolve from CSP, but it differed from OCCAM in one or two significant ways:

- Parallelism was only allowed into the program at the highest syntactic level. Thus the name Communicating *Sequential* Processes was appropriate in a far more literal way than with subsequent versions of CSP.

- One process communicated with another by name, as if there were a single channel from each process to every other. In OCCAM, processes communicate by named channels, so that a given pair might have none or many between them.

The first version of CSP was the starting point for a large proportion of the work on concurrency that has gone on since. Many researchers have continued to use it in its original form, and others have built upon its ideas to develop their own languages and notations.

The great majority of these languages have been notations for describing and reasoning about purely communicating systems: the computations internal to the component processes' state (variables, assignments, etc.) being forgotten about. They have come to be known as *process algebras*. The first of these were Milner's CCS [73, 75] and Hoare's second version of CSP, the one this book is about. It is somewhat confusing that both of Hoare's notations have the same name and acronym, since in all but the deepest sense they have little in common. Henceforth, for us, CSP will mean the second notation. Process algebra notations and theories of concurrency are useful because they bring the problems of concurrency into sharp focus. Using them it is possible to address the problems that arise, both at the high level of constructing theories of concurrency, and at the lower level of specifying and designing individual systems, without worrying about other issues. The purpose of this book is to describe the CSP notation and to help the reader to understand it and, especially, to use it in practical circumstances.

The design of process algebras and the building of theories around them has proved an immensely popular field over the past two decades. Concurrency proves to be an intellectually fascinating subject and there are many subtle distinctions which one can make, both at the level of choice of language constructs and in the subtleties of the theories used to model them. From a practical point of view the resulting tower of Babel has been unfortunate, since it has both created confusion and meant that perhaps less effort than ought to have been the case has been devoted to the practical use of these methods. It has obscured the fact that often the differences between the approaches were, to an outsider, insignificant.

Much of this work has, of course, strongly influenced the development of CSP and the theories which underlie it. This applies both to the *untimed* version of CSP, where one deliberately abstracts from the precise times when events occur, and to *Timed* CSP, where these times are recorded and used. Untimed theories tend to have the advantages of relative simplicity and abstraction, and are appropriate for many real circumstances. Indeed, the handshaken communication of CSP is to some extent a way of making precise timing of less concern, since, if one end of the communication is ready before the other, it will wait. Probably for these reasons the study of untimed theories generally preceded that of the timed ones. The timed ones are needed because, as we will see later on, one sometimes needs to rely upon timing details for the correctness of a system. This might either be at the level of overall (externally visible) behaviour, or for some internal reason. The realization of this, and the increasing maturity of the untimed theories, have led to a growing number of people working on real-time theories since the mid 1980s.

There are a number of reasons why it can be advantageous to combine timed and untimed reasoning. The major ones are listed below.

- Since timed reasoning is more detailed and complex than untimed, it is useful to be able to localize timed analysis to the parts of the system which really depend on it.

- In many cases proving a timed specification can be factored into proving a complex untimed one and a simple timed property. This is attractive for the same reasons as above.

- We might well want to develop a system meeting an untimed specification before refining it to meet detailed timing constraints.

There have been two distinct approaches to introducing time into CSP, and fortunately the above advantages are available in both. The first, usually known as *Timed CSP* (see, for example, [26, 28, 88, 89]), uses a continuous model of time and has a mathematical theory quite distinct to the untimed version. To do it justice would require more space than could reasonably be made available in this volume, and therefore we do not cover it. A complementary text by S.A. Schneider, based primarily round Timed CSP, is in preparation at the time of writing.

The continuous model of time, while elegant, makes the construction of automated tools very much harder. It was primarily for this reason that the author proposes (in Chapter 14) an alternative in which a timed interpretation is placed on the 'untimed' language. This represents the passage of time by the regular occurrence of a specific event (*tock*) and had the immediate advantage that the untimed tools were applicable. While less profound than Timed CSP, it does, for the time being at least, seem more practical. It has been used frequently in industrial applications of FDR.

0.3   Tools

For a long time CSP was an algebra that was reasoned about only manually. This certainly had a strong influence on the sort of examples people worked on – the lack of automated assistance led to a concentration on small, elegant examples that demonstrated theoretical niceties rather than practical problems.

In the last few years there has been an explosion of interest in the development of automated proof tools for CSP and similar languages. The chief proof and analytic tool for CSP at present is called FDR (standing for Failures/Divergences Refinement, a name which will be explained in Section 3.3), whose existence has led to a revolution in the way CSP is used. To a lesser extent it has also influenced the way CSP is modelled mathematically and the presentation of its models.

A number of other tools, with similar external functionality though based on very different algorithms, have been or are being developed. FDR appears to be the most powerful (for most purposes) and complete at the time of writing. Because of this, and because the author has played a leading role in its development and is therefore more familiar with it than other tools, this book is, so far as the use of tools is concerned, centred chiefly on FDR. Many of the examples and exercises have been designed so they can be 'run' on it.

Equally useful from the point of view of learning about the language are simulators and animators which allow the human user to experiment with CSP processes: interacting with them in reality instead of having to *imagine* doing so. The difference between this sort of tool and FDR is that simulations do not *prove* results about processes, merely providing a form of implementation that allows experimentation. At the time of writing the most capable such tool appears to be ProBE (used by the author in a preliminary version and due to be released later in 1997).

The above are general-purpose tools, in that they deal with more-or-less any program and desired property which you want to investigate. More specific tools are customized to perform analyses of restricted classes of system (such as protocols) or to check for specific conditions such as deadlock.

These and other tool developments have led to a restructuring and standard-ization of the CSP notation itself. The fact that the tools have allowed so many more practical-size examples to be developed has certainly influenced our percep-tion of the relative importance and, too, uses of various parts of the language, especially the parts which are at the level of describing data and operations over it (for building individual communications, and constructing a process's state). The presentation in this book has been influenced by this experience and is based on the standardized syntax with the important difference that (at the time of writing) the machine-readable syntax is ASCII, and the textual appearance of various con-structs therefore differs from the more elegantly typeset versions which appear here in print. The ASCII syntax is given in an appendix and is used in Chapter 15 (Case Studies).

On past experience it is reasonable to expect that the range and power of tools will increase markedly over the next few years. Thus a snap-shot from mid 1997 would soon get out of date. It is hoped to keep the web site associated with this book (see Preface) as up-to-date as possible on developments and to include appropriate references and demonstrations there.

It is only really since the advent of tools that CSP has been used to a sig-nificant extent for the development and analysis of practical and industrial-scale examples.

0.4   What is a communication?

CSP is a calculus for studying processes which interact with each other and their environment by means of communication. The most fundamental object in CSP is therefore a communication event. These events are assumed to be drawn from a set Σ (the Greek capital letter 'Sigma') which contains all possible communications for processes in the universe under consideration. Think of a communication as a transaction or synchronization between two or more processes rather than as necessarily being the transmission of data one way. A few possible events in very different examples of CSP descriptions are given below.

- In a railway system where the trains and signal boxes are communicating, a typical event might be a request to move onto a segment of track, the granting or refusing of permission for this, or the actual movement.

- If trying to model the interaction between a customer and a shop, we could either model a transaction as a single event, so that $\langle A, X, Y \rangle$ might mean A *buys* X *for* $\pounds Y$, or break it up into several (offer, acceptance, money, change, etc.). The choice of which of these two approaches to follow would depend on taste as well as the reason for writing the CSP description.

- The insertion of an electronic mail message into a system, the various internal transmissions of the message as it makes its way to its destination, and its final receipt would all be events in a description of a distributed network. Note that the user is probably not interested in the internal events, and so would probably like to be able to ignore, or *abstract away* their presence.

- If we were using CSP to describe the behaviour of VLSI circuits, an event might be a clock tick, seen by a large number of parallel communications, or the transmission of a word of data, or (at a lower level) the switching of some gate or transistor.

More than one component in a system may have to co-operate in the performance of an event, and the 'real' phenomenon modelled by the event might take some time. In CSP we assume firstly that an event only happens when all its participants are prepared to execute it (this is what is called *handshaken* communication), and secondly that the abstract event is instantaneous. The instantaneous event can be thought of as happening at the moment when it becomes inevitable because all its participants have agreed to execute it. These two related abstractions constitute perhaps the most fundamental steps in describing a system using CSP.

The only things that the environment can observe about a process are the events which the process communicates with it. The interaction between the environment and a process takes the same form as that between two processes: events only happen when both sides agree.

One of the fundamental features of CSP is that it can serve as a notation for writing programs which are close to implementation, as a way of constructing specifications which may be remote from implementation, and as a calculus for reasoning about both of these things – and often comparing the two. For this reason it contains a number of operators which would either be hard to implement in a truly parallel system, or which represent some 'bad' forms of behaviour, thus making them unlikely candidates for use in programs as such. The reason for having the bad forms of behaviour (deadlock, divergence and nondeterminism) represented explicitly and cleanly is to enable us to reason about them, hopefully proving them absent in practical examples.

Part I

A foundation course in CSP

Chapter 1

Fundamental concepts

A CSP process is completely described by the way it can communicate with its external environment. In constructing a process we first have to decide on an *alphabet* of communication events – the set of all events that the process (and any other related processes) might use. The choice of this alphabet is perhaps the most important modelling decision that is made when we are trying to represent a real system in CSP. The choice of these actions determines both the level of detail or abstraction in the final specification, and also whether it is possible to get a reasonable result at all. But this will only really become clear once we have a grasp of the basic notation and start to look at some examples, though some guidance is given in Section 0.4. So let us assume for now that the alphabet Σ of all events has been established.

The fundamental assumptions about communications in CSP are these:

- They are instantaneous: we abstract the real time intervals the performance of events takes into single moments – conceptually the moments when the event becomes inevitable.

- They only occur when both the process and its environment allow them; but at any moment when the process and its environment *do* agree on an event then it (or some other event) must happen.

CSP is about setting up and reasoning about processes that interact with their environments using this model of communication. Ultimately, of course, we will want to set up parallel systems of processes that communicate with each other, but in this chapter we will meet a basic collection of operators that allow us to create processes that simply describe (internally sequential) patterns of communication.

1.1   Fundamental operators

1.1.1   Prefixing

The simplest CSP process of them all is the one which can do nothing. It is written *STOP* and never communicates.

Given an event a in Σ and a process P, $a \to P$ is the process which is initially willing to communicate a and will wait indefinitely for this a to happen. After a it behaves like P. Thus

$$up \to down \to up \to down \to STOP$$

will communicate the cycle *up*, *down* twice before stopping.

Clearly *STOP* and prefixing, together, allow us to describe just the processes that make a fixed, finite sequence of communications before stopping.

1.1.2   Recursion

If we want to use a version of the process above which, instead of quickly stopping, can go on performing *up*, *down* indefinitely, we can use *recursion*. Two different processes which achieve this effect are defined by the equations

$$P_1 = up \to down \to P_1$$
$$P_2 = up \to down \to up \to down \to P_2$$

The idea is that any use of the recursively defined process's name (P_1 or P_2) on the right-hand side of the equations means exactly the same as the whole. It should be intuitively clear that any process satisfying either of these equations has the desired behaviour. The form of a recursive definition by a single equation is that an identifier representing the process being defined is at the left-hand side, and a process term, probably involving the identifier, is on the right. (If the identifier does not appear then the recursion is not really a recursion at all and simply defines the identifier on the left to be the process on the right.) We can draw a picture illustrating the behaviour of P_1 and P_2: see Figure 1.1

Instead of defining one process by a single equation we can define a number simultaneously by a *mutual* recursion. For example, if we set

$$P_u = up \to P_d$$
$$P_d = down \to P_u$$

then P_u should behave in just the same way as P_1 and P_2 defined earlier. The mutual recursions we meet later will be more interesting!

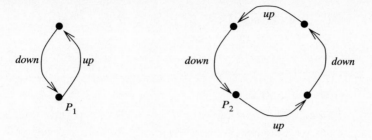

Figure 1.1 The behaviour of P_1 and P_2.

Most of the recursions in this book will be written in this equational style, but sometimes it is useful to have a way of writing down a recursive term without having to give it a name and a separate line. The single recursion $P = F(P)$ (where $F(P)$ is any CSP term involving P) defines exactly the same process as the 'nameless' term $\mu\, P.F(P)$. (μ is the Greek letter 'mu'.) Thus

$$up \to (\mu\, p.down \to up \to p)$$

defines yet another process alternating up's and $down$'s.

We have seen quite a few ways of defining recursive processes with all our examples having very similar behaviour – invariably rather dull since we still can only create processes whose sequence of communications is completely fixed. In fact all the theories we explain in this book will allow us to prove that the processes P_1, P_2 and P_u are equal. But that is a subject for later.

1.1.3   Guarded alternative

It is still only possible to define processes with a single thread of behaviour: all we can do so far is to define processes which execute a fixed finite or infinite sequence of actions. CSP provides a few ways of describing processes which offer a choice of actions to their environment. They are largely interchangeable from the point of view of what they can express, each being included because it has its distinct uses in programming.

The simplest of them takes a list of distinct initial actions paired with processes and extends the prefix operator by letting the environment choose any one of the events, with the subsequent behaviour being the corresponding process.

$$(a_1 \to P_1 \mid \ldots \mid a_n \to P_n)$$

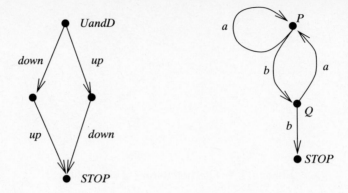

Figure 1.2 The behaviours of two processes with choice.

can do any of the events $a_1, \ldots, a_n$ on its first step and, if the event chosen is a_r, subsequently behaves like P_r. This construct is called *guarded alternative*. The process

$$UandD \;=\; (up \to down \to STOP \mid down \to up \to STOP)$$

can do the two events *up* and *down* in either order.

Combining this operator with recursion, it is now possible to define some complex behaviours. As a relatively simple example, consider the processes

$$P \;=\; (a \to P \mid b \to Q)$$
$$Q \;=\; (a \to P \mid b \to STOP)$$

where P will accept any sequence of a's and b's except that it stops if given two consecutive b's. Indeed, it should not be hard to see that any *deterministic finite state machine* – a finite collection of states, each of which has a finite set of actions available and the next state depends deterministically on which of this set occurs (i.e., only one possible state per action) – can be encoded using this operator and mutual recursion with finitely many equations. The behaviours of this P and of *UandD* are illustrated in Figure 1.2

Combining this construct with an *infinite* mutual recursion which defines one process $COUNT_n$ for every natural number $n \in \mathbb{N}$ we can define a system of counter processes as follows:

$$COUNT_0 \;=\; up \to COUNT_1$$
$$COUNT_n \;=\; (up \to COUNT_{n+1}$$
$$\mid down \to COUNT_{n-1}) \quad (n > 0)$$

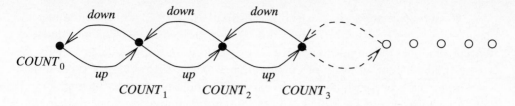

Figure 1.3 The behaviour of $COUNT_n$.

$COUNT_n$ is the process which will communicate any sequence of *up*'s and *down*'s, as long as there have never been $n + 1$ more *down*'s than *up*'s. These are not, of course, finite state machines: there are infinitely many fundamentally different states that any one of the $COUNT_n$ processes can pass through. The distinction between finite-state and non-finite-state CSP processes is extremely important for model checking, the term usually used for state exploration tools such as FDR (see Section 1.4), since that method relies on being able to visit every state. Of course the pictures of these processes are also infinite – see Figure 1.3.

If $A \subseteq \Sigma$ is any set of events and, for each $x \in A$, we have defined a process $P(x)$, then

$$?x : A \to P(x)$$

defines the process which accepts any element a of A and then behaves like the appropriate $P(a)$. This construct is known as *prefix choice* for obvious reasons. Clearly it generalizes the guarded alternative construction, since any guarded alternative can be recast in this form, but if A is infinite the reverse is not true. It *strictly* generalizes it in cases where A is infinite. $?x : \{\} \to P(x)$ means the same as $STOP$ and $?x : \{a\} \to P(x)$ means the same as $a \to P(a)$.

This operator *tends* to be used in cases where the dependency of $P(x)$ upon x is mainly through its use of the identifier x in constructing subsequent communications, in constructing the index of a mutual recursion, or similar. Thus we can write a process which simply repeats every communication which is sent to it:

$$REPEAT \quad = \quad ?x : \Sigma \to x \to REPEAT$$

or one which behaves like one of the counters defined above depending on what its first communication is:

$$Initialize \quad = \quad ?n : \mathbb{N} \to COUNT_n$$

In many situations it is useful to have an alphabet Σ which contains compound objects put together by an infix dot. So if c is the name of a 'channel' and T is the type of object communicated down it, we would have $c.T = \{c.x \mid x \in T\} \subseteq \Sigma$. It is natural to think of processes inputting and outputting values of type T over c: an inputting process would typically be able to communicate any element of $c.T$ and an outputting process would only be able to communicate one. Rather than write the input in the form $?y : c.T \to P(y)$, where the uses of y in $P(y)$ have to extract x from $c.x$, it is more elegant to use the 'pattern matching' form

$$c?x : T \to P'(x)$$

where the definition of P' is probably slightly simpler than that of P because it can refer to the value x input along c directly rather than having to recover it from a compound object. For example, the process $COPY$, which inputs elements of T on channel *left* and outputs them on channel *right* is defined

$$COPY = left?x : T \to right!x \to COPY$$

It is the simplest example of a *buffer* process: one which faithfully transfers the input sequence on one channel to its outputs on another.

Where we want to allow *any* communication over channel c, the set T can be omitted: $c?x \to P(x)$ means the same as $c?x : T \to P(x)$ where T is the *type* of c. In cases like this, one frequently writes the 'outputs' using an exclamation mark $c!x$ for symmetry or clarity, but this is usually a synonym for $c.x$. (The only cases where this does not apply arise where a communication is more highly structured than we have seen here and has both 'input' and 'output' components – see page 27 where this subject is discussed further.) So, where T is understood, we might write

$$COPY = left?x \to right!x \to COPY$$

It is important to remember that, even though this syntax allows us to model input and output over channels, the fundamental CSP model of communication still applies: neither an input nor an output can occur until the environment is willing to allow it.

We broaden the guarded alternative operator to encompass arguments of the form $c?x : T \to P(x)$ as well as ones guarded by single events. For now we will assume, as an extension of the earlier assumption of disjointness, that all of the events and input channels used in the guards are distinct and that none of the single events belongs to one of the input channels.

For example, we can define a buffer process which, unlike $COPY$, does not insist upon outputting one thing before inputting the next. If T is the type of objects being input and output, and $left.T \cup right.T \subseteq \Sigma$, we can define a process B_s^∞ for every $s \in T^*$ (the set of finite sequences of elements of T) as follows:

$$
\begin{aligned}
B_{\langle\rangle}^\infty &= \quad left?x : T \to B_{\langle x \rangle}^\infty \\
B_{s^\frown\langle y\rangle}^\infty &= \quad (left?x : T \to B_{\langle x \rangle^\frown s^\frown \langle y \rangle}^\infty \\
&\quad\ \ \mid right!y \to B_s^\infty)
\end{aligned}
$$

So B_s^∞ is the buffer presently containing the sequence s, and $B_{\langle\rangle}^\infty$ is the initially empty one. Notice the basic similarity between this recursive definition and the ones (particularly $COUNT$) seen earlier. This *tail recursive* style, particularly when each recursive call is guarded by exactly one communication (*one-step* tail recursion) shows the state space of a process extremely clearly. This style of definition is important both in presenting CSP specifications and in verification techniques.

The use of sequence notation should be self-explanatory here. We will, however, discuss the language of sequences in more detail in Section 1.3.

The example B^∞ above illustrates two important and related aspects of CSP style that have also been seen in earlier examples: the uses of parameterized mutual recursions and of identifiers representing 'data' values. The value of a parameterized recursion such as this one or $COUNT$ is that it allows the succinct presentation of a large (and even, as in both these cases, infinite) set of processes. We will think of the parameters as representing, in some sense, the *state* of such a process at the points of recursive call. In particular, even though the recursive call may be within the scope of an identifier x, this identifier cannot influence the value of the call unless it appears within one of the parameters. A parameterized process can have any fixed number of parameters, which can be numbers, events, tuples, sets, sequences etc., though they may not be processes (or tuples etc. that contain processes).

The parameters can be written as subscripts (as in B_s^∞ above), superscripts (e.g., $R^{(a,b)}$) or as 'functional arguments' (e.g., $R(n,x)$). The first two of these were the traditional style before the advent of machine-readable CSP, which only accepts the third. There is no formal difference between the different positions, the choice being up to the aesthetic taste of the programmer. Often, in more complex examples, they are combined.

The identifiers used for input (i.e., those following '?') are the second main contributor to process state. Each time an input is made it has the effect of creating a new binding to the identifier, whose scope is the process it enables (i.e., in $c?x \to P$ and $(c?x \to P \mid d \to Q)$ it is P). Both these identifiers and the ones introduced as parameters can be used freely in creating events and parameters, and in deciding conditionals (see later). They cannot, however, be assigned to: you should think of CSP as a *declarative* language in its use of identifiers. CSP 'programs' have a great deal in common with ones in a functional language such as Haskell.

EXAMPLE 1.1.1 (CASH-POINT MACHINE) Anyone who has read Hoare's book will be familiar with his use of vending machines as examples of CSP descriptions. This type of example is useful because it models a form of interaction with which the reader can identify – placing himself or herself in the role of one process communicating in parallel with another.

Cash-point machines (or Automated Teller Machines – ATMs) provide a related example where, because of the increased value of transactions and the need for different machines to co-operate with each other and with central databases, there is perhaps better reason to be interested in formal specification. It is also a good example later when we come to look at real time, since there are actually a good many real-time constraints on the operation of these machines.

At various points through this chapter and the rest of this book we will use examples drawn from this world to illustrate CSP constructs and ideas. For the moment we will only attempt to describe the interface between the machine and the customer.

We will have to imagine that the set Σ of all communications contains events such as *in.c* and *out.c* for all cards $c \in Card$, *pin.p* for all possible PIN numbers p, and *req.n*, *dispense.n* and *refuse* for all n drawn from possible withdrawal amounts (the set of which we denote by *WA*). In general we will simply assume that Σ contains all events which are used in our process descriptions.

We first describe a rather simple machine which goes through cycles of accepting any card, requiring its PIN number, and servicing one request for withdrawal which is always successful, before returning the card to the customer.

$$ATM1 \quad = \quad in?c : CARD \rightarrow pin.f_{pin}(c) \rightarrow req?n : WA \rightarrow$$
$$dispense!n \rightarrow out.c \rightarrow ATM1$$

Here $f_{pin}(c)$ is the function which determines the correct PIN number of card c. The set of all PIN numbers will be written *PIN*. It may appear from this description that we are assuming that the customer never makes a mistake with his PIN number. But this is not the case: what we are saying is (i) that the machine does not allow the customer to proceed with his request until he has inserted the right number and (ii) that we do not deem a 'handshaken' communication to have taken place until the customer has inserted this number. Incorrect numbers are not modelled in this treatment: they can be thought of in terms of one partner trying out successive communications until he finds one which is not refused.

This illustrates one of the most important principles which one should bear in mind when making a CSP abstraction of a system, whether a 'human' one like this, a parallel machine, or a VLSI chip. This is that we should understand clearly when an event or communication has taken place, but that it is often possible to abstract several apparent events (here the cycles of inserting numbers and acceptance or rejection) into a single one. Clearly in this case both parties can clearly tell when the communication has actually taken place – a PIN number has been entered and accepted – which is perhaps the most important fact making this a legitimate abstraction.

Despite these observations the model, in particular the abstraction surrounding the PIN number, is not ideal in the sense that it describes a system we probably would not want. The chief difficulty surrounding the PIN number insertion is that a customer who had forgotten his number would be able to 'deadlock' the system entirely with his card inside. In fact we will, in later examples, refine this single synchronization into multiple entry and acceptance/rejection phases. Later, when we deal with time, we will be able to model further features that there might be in the interface, such as a *time-out* (if no response is received within a set amount of time, the ATM will act accordingly). *(End of example)*

EXERCISE 1.1.1   A *bank account* is a process into which money can be deposited and from which it can be withdrawn. Define first a simple account $ACCT_0$ which has events *deposit* and *withdraw*, and which is always prepared to communicate either.

EXERCISE 1.1.2   Now extend the alphabet to include *open* and *close*. $ACCT_1$ behaves like $ACCT_0$ except that it allows no event before it has been opened, and allows no further event after it has been closed (and is always prepared to accept *close* while open). You might find it helpful to define a process $OPEN$ representing an open account.

EXERCISE 1.1.3 $ACCT_0$ and $ACCT_1$ have no concept of a balance. Introduce a parameter representing the balance of an $OPEN$ account. The alphabet is *open* and *close* as before, *deposit*.$\mathbb{N}$ and *withdraw*.$\mathbb{N}$ (which have now become channels indicating the amount of the deposit or withdrawal) plus *balance*.$\mathbb{Z}$ ($\mathbb{Z}$ is the set of positive and negative integers), a channel that can be used to find out the current balance. An account has zero balance when opened, and may only be closed when it has a zero balance. Define processes $ACCT_2$ and $ACCT_3$ which (respectively) allow *any* withdrawal and only those which would not overdraw the account (make the balance negative).

EXERCISE 1.1.4   Figure 1.4 shows the street map of a small town. Roads with arrows on are one-way. Define a mutually recursive set of CSP processes, one for each labelled corner, describing the ways traffic can move starting from each one. The alphabet is {*north, south, east, west*}, an action only being available when it is possible to move in the appropriate direction, and then having the effect of moving the traveller to the next label.

EXERCISE 1.1.5   Define a process SUM with two channels of integers: *in* and *sum*. It is always prepared to input (any integer) on *in* and to output on *sum*. The value appearing on *sum* is the sum of all the values input so far on *in*. Modify your process so that it can also output (on separate channels *prod* and *last*) the product of all the inputs and the most recent input.

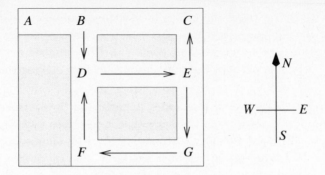

Figure 1.4 A town plan.

1.1.4   Further choice operators

External choice

The various ways of defining a choice of events set out in the last section all set out *as part of the operator* what the choice of initial events will be. In particular, in guarded alternatives such as $(a \to P \mid b \to Q)$, the a and b are an integral part of the operator even though it is tempting to think that this process is a choice between the processes $a \to P$ and $b \to Q$. From the point of view of possible implementations, the explicitness of the guarded alternative has many advantages[1] but from an algebraic standpoint and also for generality it is advantageous to have a choice operator which provides a simple choice between processes; this is what we will now meet.

$P \square Q$ is a process which offers the environment the choice of the first events of P and of Q and then behaves accordingly. This means that if the first event chosen is one from P only, then $P \square Q$ behaves like P, while if one is chosen from Q it behaves like Q. Thus $(a \to P) \square (b \to Q)$ means exactly the same as $(a \to P \mid b \to Q)$. This generalizes totally: any guarded alternative of the sorts described in the last section is equivalent to the process that is obtained by replacing all of the |'s of the alternative operator by $\square$'s.[2] Therefore we can regard $\square$ as strictly generalizing guarded alternative: for that reason we will henceforth tend to use only $\square$ even in cases where the other would have been sufficient. (In fact, in ordinary use it is rare to find a use of $\square$ which could not have been presented

---

[1]Note that guarded alternative is provided in OCCAM.

[2]This transformation is trivial textually, but less so syntactically since the prefixes move from being part of the operator to become part of the processes being combined, and also we are moving from a single operator of arbitrary 'arity' to the repeated use of the binary operator $\square$. The fact that $\square$ is associative (see later) means that the order of this composition is irrelevant.

as a guarded alternative, at least if one, as in OCCAM, extends the notation of a guard to include conditionals.)

The discussion above leaves out one important case that does not arise with guarded alternatives: the possibility that P and Q might have initial events in common so that there is no clear prescription as to which route is followed when one of these is chosen. We define it to be ambiguous: if we have written a program with an overlapping choice we should not mind which route is taken and the implementation may choose either. Thus, after the initial a, the process $(a \to a \to STOP) \square (a \to b \to STOP)$ is free to offer a or b *at its choice* but is not obliged to offer both. It is thus a rather different process to $a \to ((a \to STOP) \square (b \to STOP))$ which *is* obliged to offer the choice of a and b. This is the first example we have met of a *nondeterministic* process: one which is allowed to make internal decisions which affect the way it looks to its environment.

We will later find other examples of how nondeterminism can arise from natural constructions, more fundamentally – and inevitably – than this one.

A *deterministic* process is one where the range of events offered to the environment depends only on things it has seen (i.e., the sequence of communications so far). In other words, it is formally *nondeterministic* when some internal decision can lead to uncertainty about what will be offered. The distinction between deterministic and nondeterministic behaviour is an important one, and we will later (Section 3.3) be able to specify it exactly.

Nondeterministic choice

Since nondeterminism does appear in CSP whether we like it or not, it is necessary to be able to reason about it cleanly. Therefore, even though they are not constructs one would be likely to use in any program written for execution in the usual sense, CSP contains two closely related ways of presenting the nondeterministic choice of processes. These are

$$P \sqcap Q \qquad \text{and} \qquad \sqcap S$$

where P and Q are processes, and S is a non-empty set of processes. The first of these is a process which can behave like either P or Q, the second is one that can behave like any member of S.

Clearly we can represent $\sqcap S$ for finite S using $\sqcap$. The case where S is infinite leads to a number of difficulties in modelling since (obviously) it introduces infinite, or *unbounded*, nondeterminism. It turns out that this is somewhat harder to cope with than finite nondeterminism, so we will sometimes have to exclude it from consideration. Apart from the explicit operator $\sqcap S$ there are several other operators we will meet later which can introduce unbounded nondeterminism. We will mention this in each case where it can arise, and the precautions necessary to avoid it.

It is important to appreciate the difference between $P \,\square\, Q$ and $P \,\sqcap\, Q$. The process $(a \to STOP) \,\square\, (b \to STOP)$ is obliged to communicate a or b if offered only one of them, whereas $(a \to STOP) \,\sqcap\, (b \to STOP)$ may reject either. It is only obliged to communicate if the environment offers *both* a and b. In the first case, the choice of what happens is in the hands of the environment, in the second it is in the hands of the process. Some authors call these two forms of choice *external* and *internal* nondeterminism respectively, but we prefer to think of 'external nondeterminism' as 'environmental choice' and not to confuse it with a form of nondeterminism.

The process P can be used in any place where $P \,\sqcap\, Q$ would work, since there is nothing we can do to stop $P \,\sqcap\, Q$ behaving like P every time anyway. If R is such that $R = R \,\sqcap\, P$ we say that P is more deterministic than R, or that it *refines* R. Since $(P \,\sqcap\, Q) \,\sqcap\, P = P \,\sqcap\, Q$ for any P and Q, it follows that P is, as one would expect, always more deterministic than $P \,\sqcap\, Q$. This gives the basic notion of when one CSP process is 'better' than another, and forms the basis of the most important partial orders over CSP models. When $P \,\sqcap\, R = R$ we will write

$$R \sqsubseteq P$$

The concept of refinement will turn out to be exceptionally important.

EXAMPLE 1.1.2 (NONDETERMINISTIC ATM) From the point of view of the user of our cash-point machine, it will probably be nondeterministic whether his request for a withdrawal is accepted or not. We could therefore remodel his view of it as follows:

$$
\begin{aligned}
ATM2 \;=\; & in?c : CARD \to pin.f_{pin}(c) \to req?n : WA \to \\
& ((dispense.n \to out.c \to ATM2) \\
& \quad \sqcap (refuse \to (ATM2 \sqcap out.c \to ATM2)))
\end{aligned}
$$

Notice that it is also nondeterministic from the point of view of the user whether he gets his card back after a refusal.

Even if the machine's decision is entirely deterministic given the information it can see (such as how much money it has, the state of the network connecting it to central machines and the health of the customer's account) this does not reduce the validity of the above model. For the customer cannot know most of this information and chooses not to include the rest of it in modelling this interface. He has introduced an *abstraction* into the model and is paying for the simple model with some nondeterminism.

Abstraction is another important idea of which we will see much more later, especially Chapter 12. *(End of example)*

Conditional choice

Since we allow state identifiers into CSP processes through input and process parameters, a further form of choice is needed: conditional choice based on the value of a boolean expression. In the informal style of presenting CSP there is no need to be very prescriptive about how these choices are written down,[3] though obviously a tighter syntax will be required when we consider machine-readable CSP However a choice is written down, it must give a clear decision about which process the construct represents for any legitimate value of the state identifiers in scope, and only depend on these.

Conditionals can thus be presented as *if ... then ... else ...* constructs (as they are in the machine-readable syntax), as case statements, or in the following syntax which elegantly reduces the conditional to an algebraic operator: $P \triangleleft b \triangleright Q$ means exactly the same as *if b then P else Q*. Because it fits in well with the rest of CSP notation, we will tend to quote this last version when discussing or using conditionals. It is also legitimate to use conditionals in computing sub-process objects such as events. Thus the two processes

$$ABS_1 \quad = \quad left?x \rightarrow right!((-x) \triangleleft x > 0 \triangleright x) \rightarrow ABS_1$$

$$ABS_2 \quad = \quad left?x \rightarrow (\ (right!(-x) \rightarrow ABS_2)$$
$$\triangleleft x > 0 \triangleright (right!x \rightarrow ABS_2))$$

are equivalent: both input numbers and output the absolute values.

The use of conditionals can obviously reduce the number of cases of a parameterized mutual recursion that have to be treated separately to one (simply replacing each case by one clause in a conditional), but they can, used judiciously, frequently give a substantial simplification as well. Consider, for example, a two-dimensional version of our *COUNT* process which now represents a counter on a chess board. It will have two parameters, both restricted to the range $0 \leq i \leq 7$. One is changed by the events $\{up, down\}$, the other by $\{left, right\}$. There are no less than nine separate cases to be considered if we were to follow the style (used for *COUNT* earlier) of dealing with the different possible initial events one by one: see Figure 1.5. Fortunately these all reduce to a single one with the simple use of

---

[3]Indeed, in many presentations of CSP they seem to be considered so informal that they are not described as part of the language.

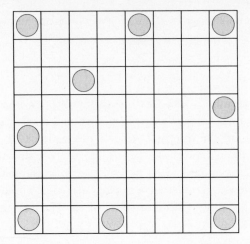

Figure 1.5 The nine case different sets of initial events in $Counter(i, j)$.

conditionals:

$$Counter(n, m) \quad = \quad \begin{array}{ll} (down & \to Counter(n - 1, m)) \triangleleft n > 0 \triangleright STOP \\ \square \quad (up & \to Counter(n + 1, m)) \triangleleft n < 7 \triangleright STOP \\ \square \quad (left & \to Counter(n, m - 1)) \triangleleft m > 0 \triangleright STOP \\ \square \quad (right & \to Counter(n, m + 1)) \triangleleft m < 7 \triangleright STOP \end{array}$$

Note that the availability of each event has been defined by a conditional, where the process produced when the event is not available is $STOP$, which of course makes no contribution to the initial choices available.[4]

Multi-part events: extending the notation of channels

Thus far all events we have used have been atomic (such as *up* and *down*) or have comprised a channel name plus one 'data' component (such as *left*.3). In general we allow events that have been constructed out of any finite number of parts using the infix dot '.' (which is assumed to be associative). In written CSP it is a convention, which is enforced as a rule in machine-readable CSP[5] (see Appendix B) that a

---

[4]This style of coding in CSP is essentially the same as the use of boolean guards on commu-nications in OCCAM alternatives. We could, of course, explicitly extend the guarded alternative in CSP to include a boolean component, but since the above style is possible there is little point from a formal point of view. The machine-readable form understood by FDR does include such a shorthand: `b & P` abbreviates `if b then P else STOP`.

[5]In machine-readable CSP all channels have to be declared explicitly

channel consists of an identifier (its name or tag) plus a finite (perhaps empty) sequence of data types, and that Σ then consists of all events of the form

$$c.x_1.\ldots.x_n$$

where c is such a name, $T_1, \ldots, T_n$ is its sequence of types, and $x_i \in T_i$ for each i.

The most common use for communications with more than two parts is when we want to set up what is effectively an array of channels for communication in a parallel array where the processes are probably similarly indexed. Thus if we had processes indexed $P(i)$ forming a one-dimensional array, we might well have a channel of type $\mathbb{N}.\mathbb{N}.T$ where T is a data type that these processes want to send to each other. If c were such a channel, then $c.i.j.x$ might represent the transmission of value x from $P(i)$ to $P(j)$. We will see many examples like this once we have introduced parallel operators.

They can also, however, be used to achieve multiple data transfers in a single action. This can even be in several directions at once, since the input (?) and output (!) modes of communication can be mixed in a multi-part communication. Thus

$$c?x : A!e \to P$$

represents a process whose first step allows all communications of the form $\{c.a.b \mid a \in A\}$ where b is the value of the expression e. The identifier x is then, of course, bound to the relevant member of a in the body of P. The advent of machine-readable CSP and FDR has proved the usefulness of this type of construct, and has led to the adoption of conventions to deal with various cases that can arise. One of these shows the subtle distinction between the use of the infix dot '.' and the output symbol ! in communications. For example, if d is a channel of type $A.B.C.D$ then if the communication $d?x.y!z.t$ appears in a process definition it is equivalent to $d?x?y!z!t$ because an infix dot following a ? is taken to be part of a pattern matched by the input. Thus one ? can bind multiple identifiers until overridden by a following !. None of the examples in this book uses this or any other related convention – in the rare examples where more than one data component follows a ? we will follow the good practice of using only ? or ! as appropriate for each successive one – but further details of them can be found in Appendix B and [35].

One very useful notation first introduced in machine-readable CSP, which we will use freely, allows us to turn any set of channels and partially defined events into the corresponding events. This the $\{| c_1, c_2 |\}$ notation which forms the appropriate set of events from one or more channels: it is formally defined as follows. If c has type $T_1.T_2 \ldots T_n$ as above, $0 \le k \le n$ and $a_i \in T_i$ for $1 \le i \le k$, then

$$events(c.a_1 \ldots a_k) = \{c.a_1 \ldots a_k.b_{k+1} \ldots b_n \mid b_{k+1} \in T_{k+1}, \ldots, b_n \in T_n\}$$

is the set of events which can be formed as extensions of $c.a_1 \ldots a_k$. We can then define

$$\{| \, e_1, \ldots, e_r \, |\} = events(e_1) \cup \ldots \cup events(e_r)$$

EXERCISE 1.1.6   Extend the definition of $COUNT_n$ so that it also has the events $up5$, $up10$, $down5$ and $down10$ which change the value in the register by the obvious amounts, and are only possible when they do not take the value below zero.

EXERCISE 1.1.7   A *change-giving* machine which takes in £1 coins and gives change in 5, 10 and 20 pence coins. It should have the following events: $in£1$, $out5p$, $out10p$, $out20p$. Define versions with the following behaviours:

(a) *CMA* gives the environment the choice of how it wants the change, and if an extra £1 is inserted while it still has a non-zero balance it increases the amount of change available accordingly.

(b) *CMB* behaves like *CMA* except that it will only accept a further £1 if its balance is less than 20p.

(c) *CMC* is allowed to choose any correct combination of change nondeterministically, only allowing the insertion of £1 when it has zero balance.

EXERCISE 1.1.8   *COPY* represents a one-place buffer and $B_{\langle\rangle}^{\infty}$ represents an unbounded one. These are just two examples of processes representing communication media for transmitting information from channel *left* to channel *right*. Describe ones with the following behaviours (except for the last one, their output streams must always copy the input ones without loss, and preserving order):

(a) *FCOPY* behaves like *COPY* except that it is allowed to input a second item when it already contains one, but if it does it breaks ($STOP$).

(b) *DELAY* can hold up to two items, but cannot output the first one unless it is full. Thus its outputs are (after the initial input) always one or two behind its inputs, unlike the case with *COPY* where they are always zero or one behind.

(c) $BUFF_{\langle\rangle}$ is a buffer that cannot be guaranteed to accept an input except when empty, but neither can it be guaranteed not to accept one. When non-empty, it never refuses to output the next item due.

(d) *LEAKY* behaves like *COPY* except that it loses every third item.

EXERCISE 1.1.9   Redesign the process $ATM1$ so that the action of accepting a PIN number is broken into the successive input of up to three numbers (any PIN numbers), with a correct or incorrect one being rewarded with *ok* or *wrong* respectively. After *ok* it carries on in the same way as the original $ATM1$, and after the third *wrong* it reverts to the initial state (without returning the card).

1.1.5   A few important processes

There are a few processes with very basic behaviour that it is useful to have standard names for. We have already met *STOP*, the process that does nothing at all. Two more are

$$RUN_A = ?x : A \to RUN_A$$

the process which, for a set of events $A \subseteq \Sigma$, can always communicate any member of A desired by the environment, and

$$Chaos_A = STOP \sqcap (?x : A \to Chaos_A)$$

which can always choose to communicate or reject any member of A. Evidently $Chaos_{\{\}}$ and $RUN_{\{\}}$ are both equivalent to *STOP*. If no alphabet is specified for one of these processes (*RUN* or *Chaos*) then we understand it (the alphabet) to be the whole of Σ. Clearly $Chaos_A$ is refined by both *STOP* and RUN_A.

Two other important constants (**div** and *SKIP*) will be introduced later (respectively Sections 3.1 and 6.1) once the concepts they involve have been established.

1.2   Algebra

One of our primary ways of understanding CSP will be to develop a set of algebraic laws which the operators satisfy. An algebraic law is the statement that two expressions, involving some operators and identifiers representing arbitrary processes (and perhaps other things such as events) are equal. By 'equal', we mean that the two sides are essentially the same: for CSP this means that their communicating behaviours are indistinguishable by the environment.

Everyone with the most basic knowledge of arithmetic or set theory is familiar with the sort of algebra we are now talking about. There are a number of basic patterns that many laws conform to; the following are a few familiar examples illustrating these:

$$
\begin{aligned}
x + y &= y + x &&\text{a } \textit{commutative, or symmetry} \text{ law} \\
x \times y &= y \times x &&\text{ditto} \\
x \cup y &= y \cup x &&\text{ditto} \\
(x + y) + z &= x + (y + z) &&\textit{associativity} \\
(x + y) \times z &= (x \times z) + (y \times z) &&\text{(right) } \textit{distributive} \text{ law} \\
0 + x &= x &&\textit{unit} \text{ law (0 is a left unit of } + \text{)} \\
\{\} \cap x &= \{\} &&\textit{zero} \text{ law (}\{\}\text{ is a left zero of } \cap \text{)} \\
x \cup x &= x &&\textit{idempotence}
\end{aligned}
$$

We will find all of these patterns and more amongst the laws of CSP. Let us now consider what laws ought to relate the CSP operators we have met so far: prefixing, external choice, nondeterministic choice, and conditionals.

We would expect the choice between P and itself to be the same as P, the choice between P and Q the same as that between Q and P, and the choice between three processes P, Q and R to be the same however bracketed. And this will all apply whether we are talking about internal (nondeterministic) choice or external choice. In other words, these properties all hold whether the environment or the process gets to choose which path is chosen. Thus there are idempotence, symmetry and associative laws for both $\square$ and $\sqcap$:

$$P \,\square\, P \;=\; P \qquad\qquad\qquad \langle\square\text{-idem}\rangle \quad (1.1$$

$$P \sqcap P \;=\; P \qquad\qquad\qquad \langle\sqcap\text{-idem}\rangle \quad (1.2$$

$$P \,\square\, Q \;=\; Q \,\square\, P \qquad\qquad \langle\square\text{-sym}\rangle \quad (1.3$$

$$P \sqcap Q \;=\; Q \sqcap P \qquad\qquad \langle\sqcap\text{-sym}\rangle \quad (1.4$$

$$P \,\square\, (Q \,\square\, R) \;=\; (P \,\square\, Q) \,\square\, R \qquad \langle\square\text{-assoc}\rangle \quad (1.5$$

$$P \sqcap (Q \sqcap R) \;=\; (P \sqcap Q) \sqcap R \qquad \langle\sqcap\text{-assoc}\rangle \quad (1.6$$

These three laws (idempotence, symmetry and associativity) are just what is needed to ensure that the nondeterministic choice operator over sets, $\bigsqcap S$, makes sense (see Exercise 1.2.5). For what we mean by this (for finite $S = \{P_1, \ldots, P_n\}$) must be the same as $P_1 \sqcap \ldots \sqcap P_n$, and since sets are oblivious to the repetition and order of their elements, we need $\sqcap$ to be idempotent (ignoring repetitions), symmetric (ignoring order) and associative (so that bracketing is not required). Clearly the operator $\bigsqcap S$ has laws that we could write down too, but these would not follow such conventional forms as it is not an ordinary binary operator. We will always feel at liberty to rewrite $\bigsqcap\{P_1, \ldots, P_n\}$ as

$$P_1 \sqcap \ldots \sqcap P_n$$

and similar without formal recourse to laws.

Notice that each law has been given a name and a number to help us refer to it later.

If we have any operator or construct $F(\cdot)$ which, in any 'run' takes at most one copy of its argument, then it is natural to expect that $F(\cdot)$ will be *distributive*, in that

$$F(P \sqcap Q) \;=\; F(P) \sqcap F(Q)$$

$$F(\textstyle\bigsqcap S) \;=\; \bigsqcap\{F(P) \mid P \in S\}$$

(i.e., the operator distributes over $\sqcap$ and distributes through $\bigsqcap$). In the first of these, this is because the argument on the left-hand side can act like P or like Q, so the effect of running $F(P \sqcap Q)$ must be either like running $F(P)$ or like running $F(Q)$. Since that is precisely the set of options open to $F(P) \sqcap F(Q)$, the two sides are equal. The second is just the same argument applied to an arbitrary, rather than two-way, choice. All of the operators, other than recursion, which we have described so far fall into this category. The distributive laws for some of the constructs seen to date are:

$$P \,\square\, (Q \sqcap R) \;=\; (P \,\square\, Q) \sqcap (P \,\square\, R) \qquad\qquad \langle\square\text{-dist}\rangle \qquad (1.7)$$

$$P \,\square\, \textstyle\bigsqcap S \;=\; \textstyle\bigsqcap\{P \,\square\, Q \mid Q \in S\} \qquad\qquad \langle\square\text{-Dist}\rangle \qquad (1.8)$$

$$a \rightarrow (P \sqcap Q) \;=\; (a \rightarrow P) \sqcap (a \rightarrow Q) \qquad\qquad \langle\text{prefix-dist}\rangle \qquad (1.9)$$

$$a \rightarrow \textstyle\bigsqcap S \;=\; \textstyle\bigsqcap\{a \rightarrow Q \mid Q \in S\} \qquad\qquad \langle\text{prefix-Dist}\rangle \qquad (1.10)$$

$$?x : A \rightarrow (P \sqcap Q) \;=\; (?x : A \rightarrow P) \sqcap (?x : A \rightarrow Q) \qquad\qquad \langle\text{input-dist}\rangle \qquad (1.11)$$

$$?x : A \rightarrow \textstyle\bigsqcap S \;=\; \textstyle\bigsqcap\{?x : A \rightarrow Q \mid Q \in S\} \qquad\qquad \langle\text{input-Dist}\rangle \qquad (1.12)$$

Note that there is a pair for each. In fact, of course, the second of each pair implies the other. An operator that distributes over $\bigsqcap S$ will be called *fully* distributive, whereas one that distributes over $\sqcap$ will be called *finitely* distributive. In future, we will generally only quote one of each pair of distributive laws explicitly, to save space. It may be assumed that they both hold if either does, except in the rare cases (always explicitly flagged) of operators that are finitely but not fully distributive.

You should, in general, expect an operator $F(P)$ to be distributive unless it has the chance, in a single run, to compare two different copies of P. If it can make such a comparison then $F(P \sqcap Q)$ may be different from $F(P) \sqcap F(Q)$ because the two copies it compares may be different (one P and one Q) whereas in the second case they must be the same (whichever they are). This is why recursion is not distributive. We only have to consider a simple example like

$$\mu\, p.((a \rightarrow p) \sqcap (b \rightarrow p)) \qquad \text{and} \qquad (\mu\, p.a \rightarrow p) \sqcap (\mu\, p.b \rightarrow p)$$

where the left-hand side can perform any sequence of a's and b's (at its own choice) while the right-hand side has to be consistent: once it has communicated one a it must keep on doing a's.

$\langle\square\text{-dist}\rangle$ is actually only one of the two distributive laws for $\square$ over $\sqcap$. The other one (the right distributive law) follows from this one and $\langle\square\text{-sym}\rangle$. There are also (left and right) distributive laws for $\sqcap$ over itself – provable from the existing set of laws for $\sqcap$ (see Exercise 1.2.1 below).

There is a further law relating the two forms of choice whose motivation is much more subtle. Consider the process $P \sqcap (Q \,\square\, R)$. It may *either* behave like P *or* offer the choice between Q and R. Now consider

$$(P \sqcap Q) \,\square\, (P \sqcap R)$$

a process which the distributive laws of $\square$ can expand to

$$(P \,\square\, P) \sqcap (P \,\square\, R) \sqcap (Q \,\square\, P) \sqcap (Q \,\square\, R)$$

The first of these four equals P by $\langle\square\text{-idem}\rangle$. It follows that the first and last alternatives provide all the options of the first process. Every behaviour of the second and third is possible for one of the other two: every set of events they reject initially is also rejected by P (for they offer the choice of the first actions of P and another process), and every subsequent behaviour belongs to one of P, Q and R. We therefore assert that these two processes are equal – in other words, $\sqcap$ distributes over $\square$.

$$P \sqcap (Q \,\square\, R) \;=\; (P \sqcap Q) \,\square\, (P \sqcap R) \qquad\qquad \langle\sqcap\text{-}\square\text{-dist}\rangle \quad (1.1\text{?})$$

The following is the chief law relating prefixing and external choice. It says that if we give the environment the choice between processes offering A and B, then we get a process offering $A \cup B$ whose subsequent behaviour depends on which of A and B the first event belongs to:

$$(?x : A \to P) \,\square\, (?x : B \to Q) \;=\; ?x : A \cup B \to \begin{array}{l} ((P \sqcap Q) \\ \langle\!\langle x \in A \cap B \rangle\!\rangle \qquad \langle\square\text{-step}\rangle \quad (1.1\text{?}) \\ (P \,\langle\!\langle x \in A \rangle\!\rangle\, Q)) \end{array}$$

We have called this a *step* law because it allows us to compute the first-step behaviour of the combination (i.e., the selection of initial actions plus the process that succeeds each action) from the first step behaviour of the processes we are combining.[6]

STOP is the process that offers no choice of initial actions. This can of course be written as the prefix choice over an empty set:

$$STOP \;=\; ?x : \{\} \to P \qquad\qquad\qquad \langle STOP\text{-step}\rangle \quad (1.1\text{?})$$

---

[6]From here on, in quoting laws about prefixed processes, we will usually refer only to the form $?x : A \to P$. The others, namely $a \to P$ and $c?x : A \to P$ (and the more complex forms for multi-part events discussed above) can be transformed into this form easily, and so quoting a lot of extra laws to deal with them would serve no particular purpose.

It is an immediate consequence of the last two laws that

$$STOP \ \Box \ (?x : A \to P) \ = \ ?x : A \to P$$

Of course we would expect that the external choice of *any* process with $STOP$ would have no effect. This gives us our first unit law:

$$STOP \ \Box \ P \ = \ P \qquad\qquad \langle\Box\text{-unit}\rangle \quad (1.16)$$

(There is no need for a right unit law as well as this one, since it is easily inferred from this one and the symmetry law $\langle\Box\text{-sym}\rangle$.)

Conditional choice is idempotent and distributive:

$$P \blacktriangleleft b \blacktriangleright P \ = \ P \qquad\qquad \langle\blacktriangleleft \cdot \blacktriangleright\text{-idem}\rangle \quad (1.17)$$

$$(P \sqcap Q) \blacktriangleleft b \blacktriangleright R \ = \ (P \blacktriangleleft b \blacktriangleright R) \sqcap (Q \blacktriangleleft b \blacktriangleright R) \qquad\qquad \langle\blacktriangleleft \cdot \blacktriangleright\text{-dist-l}\rangle \quad (1.18)$$

$$R \blacktriangleleft b \blacktriangleright (P \sqcap Q) \ = \ (R \blacktriangleleft b \blacktriangleright P) \sqcap (R \blacktriangleleft b \blacktriangleright Q) \qquad\qquad \langle\blacktriangleleft \cdot \blacktriangleright\text{-dist-r}\rangle \quad (1.19)$$

Left and right distributive laws are required here because conditional choice is not symmetric.

The conditional behaviour is brought out by the following pair of laws:

$$P \blacktriangleleft true \blacktriangleright Q \ = \ P \qquad\qquad \langle\blacktriangleleft true \blacktriangleright\text{-id}\rangle \quad (1.20)$$

$$P \blacktriangleleft false \blacktriangleright Q \ = \ Q \qquad\qquad \langle\blacktriangleleft false \blacktriangleright\text{-id}\rangle \quad (1.21)$$

There are other laws in which conditional choice interacts with boolean operators on the condition(s), but we do not attempt to enumerate them here (though see the exercises below). One interesting class of laws is that almost all operators distribute over this form of choice as well as $\sqcap$. The only ones that do not are ones (in particular prefix choice) that may modify the bindings of identifiers used in the boolean condition. An example of a law that does hold is

$$P \ \Box \ (Q \blacktriangleleft b \blacktriangleright R) \ = \ (P \ \Box \ Q) \blacktriangleleft b \blacktriangleright (P \ \Box \ R) \qquad\qquad \langle\blacktriangleleft \cdot \blacktriangleright\text{-}\Box\text{-dist}\rangle \quad (1.22)$$

while the failure of this distribution in the presence of binding constructs is illustrated by

$$?x : \mathbb{N} \to ?x : \mathbb{N} \to (P \blacktriangleleft x \text{ is even} \blacktriangleright Q) \neq$$
$$?x : \mathbb{N} \to ((?x : \mathbb{N} \to P) \blacktriangleleft x \text{ is even} \blacktriangleright (?x : \mathbb{N} \to Q))$$

since the distribution of ⦃*x* is even⦄ through the inner prefix choice results in *x* being bound to the first input rather than the second.

The fundamental law of *recursion* is that a recursively defined process satisfies the equation defining it. Thus the law is (in the case of equational definitions) just a part of the program. For the μ form of recursion this law is

$$\mu\, p.P \;=\; P[\mu\, p.P/p] \qquad\qquad\qquad \langle\mu\text{-unwind}\rangle \quad (1.23)$$

where the notation $Q[R/p]$ means the substitution of the process R for all free (i.e., not bound by some lower-level recursion) occurrences of the process identifier p.

We have already noted that recursion fails to be distributive.

Laws of the sort seen in this section serve several functions: they provide a useful way of gaining understanding and intuition about the intended meaning of constructs, they can (as we will see later) be useful in proofs about CSP processes, and finally, if presented and analyzed highly systematically, they can be shown to completely define the meaning, or *semantics* of language constructs (in a sense we are not yet in a position to appreciate but which is fully explained in Chapter 11). Whenever we introduce a new operator in later chapters, we will usually use some of its laws to help explain how it behaves.

EXERCISE 1.2.1   Using the laws quoted in the text for $\sqcap$, prove that it distributes over itself (i.e., that $P \sqcap (Q \sqcap R) = (P \sqcap Q) \sqcap (P \sqcap R)$).

EXERCISE 1.2.2   Suggest some laws for $\bigsqcap S$ and how it relates to $\sqcap$.

EXERCISE 1.2.3   Write down the left and right distributive laws of $\cdot$⦃*b*⦄$\cdot$ through $\sqcap$.

EXERCISE 1.2.4   Use $\langle\square\text{-step}\rangle$ and other laws given above to prove that

$$(?x : A \to P) \,\square\, (?x : A \to Q) = (?x : A \to P) \sqcap (?x : A \to Q)$$

EXERCISE 1.2.5   Suppose we try to extend the binary operator $\oplus$ (e.g. $\sqcap$) to finite non-empty sets by defining

$$\bigoplus\{P_1, \ldots, P_n\} = P_1 \oplus (P_2 \oplus \ldots (P_{n-1} \oplus P_n) \ldots)$$

Show that this makes sense (i.e., the value of $\bigoplus S$ is independent of the way S is written down) only if $\oplus$ is idempotent, symmetric and associative. For example, it must be idempotent because $\{P, P\} = \{P\}$, and hence $P \oplus P = \bigoplus\{P, P\} = \bigoplus\{P\} = P$.

In this case prove that $\bigoplus(A \cup B) = (\bigoplus A) \oplus (\bigoplus B)$ for any non-empty A and B.

What additional algebraic property must $\oplus$ have to make $\bigoplus\{\}$ well defined in such a way that this union law remains true? *[Hint:* $\square$ *has this property but* $\sqcap$ *does not.]* What is then the value of $\bigoplus\{\}$?

EXERCISE 1.2.6   Complete the following laws of the conditional construct by filling in the blank(s) (...) in each

(a) $P \triangleleft \neg b \triangleright Q = \ldots \triangleleft b \triangleright \ldots$

(b) $P \triangleleft b \triangleright (Q \triangleleft b \wedge c \triangleright R) = \ldots \triangleleft b \triangleright R$

(c) $(P \triangleleft c \triangleright Q) \triangleleft b \triangleright R = \ldots \triangleleft c \triangleright \ldots$

1.3   The traces model and traces refinement

Imagine you are interacting with a CSP process. The most basic record you might make of what happens is to write down the *trace* of events that occur: the sequence of communications between you (the environment) and the process. In general, a trace might be finite or infinite: finite either because the observation was terminated or because the process and environment reach a point where they cannot agree on any event, infinite when the observation goes on for ever and infinitely many events are transacted.

There are two basic levels of detail at which we might record traces: either we write down the events that occur in order or we write them down with the exact times when they happen. The choice of which of these is picked selects between the two main ways of looking at CSP. The version of CSP covered in this book is *untimed* CSP, where only the order of events matters. The more detailed version, *Timed* CSP, includes the time of each event in traces. A trace thus becomes a sequence of event/ time pairs (with the times increasing, of course). The basic principle of untimed CSP is that, while the relative order of what processes communicate *does* matter (and can be used to distinguish and specify them), the exact timing of events does not. (We will see a way of building a different model of time into 'untimed' CSP in Chapter 14. References to work on Timed CSP can be found in Section 14.8.)

It is natural to model an untimed CSP process by the set of all traces it can perform. It turns out that recording only *finite* traces is sufficient in the majority of cases – after all, if u is an infinite trace then all its finite *prefixes* (initial subsequences) are finite traces – and for the time being we will do this. In Section 8.3.2 and Chapter 10 we will see the subtle distinctions infinite traces can make in some cases – though at some cost in terms of theoretical difficulty.

1.3.1   Working out *traces*(*P*)

For any process P, we define $traces(P)$ to be the set of all its finite traces – members of Σ^*, the set of finite sequences of events. For example:

- $traces(STOP) = \{\langle\rangle\}$ – the only trace of the process that can perform no event is the empty trace;

- $traces(a \to b \to STOP) = \{\langle\rangle, \langle a\rangle, \langle a, b\rangle\}$ – this process may have communicated nothing yet, performed an a only, or an a and a b;

- $traces((a \to STOP) \,\square\, (b \to STOP)) = \{\langle\rangle, \langle a\rangle, \langle b\rangle\}$ – here there is a choice of first event, so there is more than one trace of length 1;

- $traces(\mu\, p.((a \to p) \,\square\, (b \to STOP))) = \{\langle a\rangle^n, \langle a\rangle^n{}^\smallfrown\langle b\rangle \mid n \in \mathbb{N}\}$ – this process can perform as many a's as its environment likes, followed by a b after which there can be no further communication.

Note the use of finite sequence notation here: $\langle a_1, a_2, \ldots, a_n\rangle$ is the sequence containing a_1, a_2 to a_n in that order. Unlike sets, the order of members of a sequence *does* matter, as does the number of times an element is repeated. Thus $\langle a, a, b\rangle$, $\langle a, b\rangle$ and $\langle b, a\rangle$ are all different. $\langle\rangle$ denotes the empty sequence. If s and t are two finite sequences, then $s^\smallfrown t$ is their *concatenation*: the members of s followed by those of t: for example $\langle a, b\rangle^\smallfrown\langle b, a\rangle = \langle a, b, b, a\rangle$. If s is a finite sequence and $n \in \mathbb{N}$, then s^n means the n-fold concatenation of s: $s^0 = \langle\rangle$ and $s^{n+1} = (s^n)^\smallfrown s$. If s is an initial subsequence, or *prefix* of t, in that there is a (possibly empty) sequence w with $t = s^\smallfrown w$, then we write $s \leq t$. We will meet more sequence notation later when it is required.

For any process P, $traces(P)$ will always have the following properties:

- $traces(P)$ is non-empty: it always contains the empty trace $\langle\rangle$;

- $traces(P)$ is prefix closed: if $s^\smallfrown t$ is a trace then at some earlier time during the recording of this, the trace was s.

There are two important things we can do with $traces(P)$: give a meaning, or semantics, to the CSP notation, and specify the behaviour required of processes. The set of all non-empty, prefix-closed subsets of Σ^* is called the *traces model* – the set of all possible representations of processes using traces. It is written $\mathcal{T}$ and is the first – and simplest – of a number of models for CSP processes we will be meeting in this book. The formal definitions of the rest of them can be found in Part II.

Hopefully, given the earlier explanations of what the various constructs of CSP 'meant', the example sets of traces are all obviously correct in the sense that they are the only possible sets of traces that the various processes might have. We can, in fact, *calculate* the trace-set of any CSP process by means of a set of simple rules – for in every case we can work out what the traces of a compound process (such as $a \to P$ or $P \,\square\, Q$) are in terms of those of its components (P and Q). Thus the traces of any process can be calculated by following its syntactic construction.

The rules for the prefixing and choice constructs are all very easy:

1. $traces(STOP) = \{\langle\rangle\}$

2. $traces(a \rightarrow P) = \{\langle\rangle\} \cup \{\langle a\rangle\hat{\ }s \mid s \in traces(P)\}$ – this process has either done nothing, or its first event was a followed by a trace of P.

3. $traces(?x : A \rightarrow P) = \{\langle\rangle\} \cup \{\langle a\rangle\hat{\ }s \mid a \in A \wedge s \in traces(P[a/x])\}$ – this is similar except that the initial event is now chosen from the set A and the subsequent behaviour depends on which is picked: $P[a/x]$ means the substitution of the value a for all free occurrences of the identifier x.

4. $traces(c?x : A \rightarrow P) = \{\langle\rangle\} \cup \{\langle c.a\rangle\hat{\ }s \mid a \in A \wedge s \in traces(P[a/x])\}$ – the same except for the use of the channel name.

5. $traces(P \mathbin{\square} Q) = traces(P) \cup traces(Q)$ – this process offers the traces of P and those of Q.

6. $traces(P \sqcap Q) = traces(P) \cup traces(Q)$ – since this process can behave like either P or Q, its traces are those of P and those of Q.

7. $traces(\sqcap S) = \bigcup\{traces(P) \mid P \in S\}$ for any non-empty set S of processes.

8. $traces(P \triangleleft b \triangleright Q) = traces(P)$ if b evaluates to *true*; and $traces(Q)$ if b evaluates to *false*.[7]

The traces of a guarded alternative can be computed by simply re-writing it as an external choice (i.e., replacing all |'s by $\square$'s).

Notice that the traces of internal and external choice are indistinguishable. What this should suggest to you is that $traces(P)$ does not give a complete description of P, since we certainly want to be able to tell $P \mathbin{\square} Q$ and $P \sqcap Q$ apart. We will see the solution to this problem later, but its existence should not prevent you from realizing that knowledge of its traces provides a great deal of information about a process.

The final construct we need to deal with is recursion. Think first about a single, non-parameterized, recursion $p = Q$ (or equivalently $\mu\,p.Q$, where Q is any process expression possibly involving the identifier p). This means the process which behaves like Q when the whole recursively defined object is substituted for

---

[7] *Technical note:* The treatment of identifiers representing input values and process parameters, and appearing in boolean expressions, is very lightweight here. This treatment implicitly assumes that the only terms for which we want to compute $traces(P)$ are those with no free identifiers – so that for example any boolean expression must evaluate to *true* or *false*. The advantage of this approach is that it frees us from the extra notation that would be needed to deal with the more general case, but there is certainly no reason why we could not deal with processes with free identifiers as 'first class objects' if desired.

the process identifier p in its body: $Q[\mu\, p.\, Q/p]$ as in the law $\langle\mu\text{-unwind}\rangle$. The way traces have been calculated through the other constructs means that a term, like Q, with a free process identifier p, represents a function F from sets of traces to sets of traces: if p has set of traces X, then Q has traces $F(X)$. For example, if Q is $a \to p$, $F(X) = \{\langle\rangle\} \cup \{\langle a\rangle\hat{}s \mid s \in X\}$. $traces(\mu\, p.\, Q)$ should be a set X that solves the equation $X = F(X)$.

Now it turns out that the functions F over $\mathcal{T}$ that can arise from CSP process descriptions always have a least *fixed point* in the sense that $X = F(X)$ and $X \subseteq Y$ whenever $Y = F(Y)$ – this least fixed point always being the appropriate value to pick for the recursion. Two separate mathematical theories can be used to demonstrate the existence of these fixed points – but we will leave the details of these till Chapter 8 and Appendix A.

The case of parameterized and other mutual recursions is little different, though the greater generality makes it somewhat harder to formulate. In this case we have a definition for a collection of processes, where the definition of each may invoke any or all of the others. This defines what we might term a *vector* of process names (where, in the case of a parameterized family, the parameter value is part of the name, meaning that there are as many names as there are parameter values) to be equal to a vector of process expressions. The problem of determining the trace-set of one of these mutually defined processes then comes down to solving an equation $\underline{X} = F(\underline{X})$ where $\underline{X}$ is a vector of trace-sets – one for each process name as above – and $F(\cdot)$ is now a function which both takes and delivers a vector of trace-sets. For example, in the mutual recursion

$$
\begin{aligned}
P &= (a \to P) \,\square\, (b \to Q) \\
Q &= (c \to Q) \,\square\, (b \to P)
\end{aligned}
$$

all the vectors have length 2 – one component corresponding to each of P and Q. Given a vector $\underline{X} = \langle X_P, X_Q\rangle$, the function F produces a vector, $\langle Y_P, Y_Q\rangle$ say, where

- $Y_P = \{\langle\rangle\}\cup\{\langle a\rangle\hat{}s \mid s \in X_P\}\cup\{\langle b\rangle\hat{}s \mid s \in X_Q\}$ i.e., the result of substituting $\underline{X}$ into the recursive definition of P, and

- $Y_Q = \{\langle\rangle\}\cup\{\langle c\rangle\hat{}s \mid s \in X_Q\}\cup\{\langle b\rangle\hat{}s \mid s \in X_P\}$ i.e., the result of substituting $\underline{X}$ into the recursive definition of Q.

In the case of $COUNT$, the vectors would be infinite – with one component for each natural number. B^∞ will also produce infinite vectors, but this time there is one component for each finite sequence of the type being transmitted.

The extraction of fixed points is mathematically the same whether the functions are on single trace-sets or on vectors. The only difference is that the intended process value in the case of a mutual recursion will be one of the components of the fixed point vector, rather than the fixed point itself.

All of the recursions we have seen to date (and almost all recursions one meets in practice) have a property that makes them easier to understand – and reason about. They are *guarded*, meaning that each recursive call comes after (i.e., is prefixed by) a communication that is introduced by the recursive definition[8] rather than being exposed immediately. Examples of *non*-guarded recursions are $\mu\, p.p$ (perhaps the archetypal one), $\mu\, p.p \;\square\; (a \to p)$, and the parameterized mutual recursion (over the natural numbers)[9]

$$P(n) \;\; = \;\; (a \to P(1)) \triangleleft n = 1 \triangleright P((3n+1) \text{ div } 2 \triangleleft n \text{ odd} \triangleright n \text{ div } 2)$$

The point about a guarded recursion is that the first-step behaviour does not depend at all on a recursive call, and when a recursive call is reached, the first step of its behaviour, in turn, can be computed without any deeper calls, and so on. In other words, we are guaranteed to have communicated at least n events before a recursive call is made at depth n.

1.3.2   Traces and laws

In Section 1.2 we introduced the notion of equality between processes provable by a series of laws. One can have two quite different processes, textually, which are provably equal by a series of these laws. Whatever the text of a process, the previous section gives us a recipe for computing its set of traces. We should realize that these two theories have to be squared with each other, since it would be a ridiculous situation if there were two processes, provably equal in the algebra, that turned out to have different trace-sets.

Of course this is not so, and all the laws quoted are easily shown to be valid in the sense that the traces of the processes on the left- and right-hand sides are always the same. For example, since the traces of $P \;\square\; Q$ and $P \;\sqcap\; Q$ are both given by union, the trace-validity of their idempotence, symmetry and associative laws follow directly from the same properties of set-theoretic union ($\cup$). Since $\sqcap$ and $\square$ are indistinguishable from each other in traces, their distributive laws over

---

[8]This definition will be modified later to take account of language constructs we have not met yet.

[9]The interesting thing about this particular example is that it is not known whether or not the series (of parameters) generated by an arbitrary starting value will always reach 1, so in fact we *do not know* whether all the components of this recursion will always be able to communicate an a. Of course not nearly this amount of subtlety is required to give unguarded mutual recursions!

each other are equally simple, for example

$$traces(P \sqcap (Q \square R)) = traces(P) \cup (traces(Q) \cup traces(R))$$
$$= (traces(P) \cup traces(Q))$$
$$\cup (traces(P) \cup traces(R))$$
$$= traces((P \sqcap Q) \square (P \sqcap R))$$

On the other hand, since there are distinctions we wish to make between processes that we know are not made by traces, we would expect that there are processes P and Q such that $traces(P) = traces(Q)$ (which we can abbreviate $P =_T Q$) but such that $P = Q$ is *not* provable using the laws. This is indeed so, as our investigations of more refined models in later chapters will show.

Clearly the validity of the various laws with respect to traces means we can prove the equality of $traces(P)$ and $traces(Q)$ by transforming P to Q by a series of laws. The rather limited set of operators we have seen to date means that the range of interesting examples of this phenomenon we can discuss yet is rather limited. However, there is one further proof rule which greatly extends what is possible: the principle of unique fixed points for guarded recursions.

Unique fixed points

If $Z = F(Z)$ is the fixed-point equation generated by any guarded recursion (single, parameterized or mutual) for trace-sets and Y is a process (or vector of processes) whose trace-sets satisfies this equation, then $X =_T Y$ where X is the process (or vector) defined by the recursion. In other words, the equation has precisely one solution over $\mathcal{T}$ or the appropriate space of vectors over $\mathcal{T}$. This rule is often abbreviated UFP; its theoretical justification of this rule will have to wait until we have developed the mathematics of fixed points.

For example, recalling the first two recursive processes we defined:

$$P_1 = up \rightarrow down \rightarrow P_1$$
$$P_2 = up \rightarrow down \rightarrow up \rightarrow down \rightarrow P_2$$

We know, by unwinding the first of these definitions twice, that

$$P_1 = up \rightarrow down \rightarrow up \rightarrow down \rightarrow P_1 \qquad (\dagger)$$

Thus it satisfies the equation defining P_2. Since P_2 is guarded we can deduce that $P_1 =_T P_2$ – in other words, $traces(P_1)$ is a solution to an equation with only one solution, namely $traces(P_2)$. Of course it was obvious that these two processes are equivalent, but it is nice to be able to prove this!

In applying this rule in future we will not usually explicitly extract the trace-sets of the process we are claiming is a fixed point. Instead, we will just apply laws to demonstrate, as in (†) above, that the syntactic process solves the recursive definition.

Most interesting examples of the UFP rule seem to derive from mutual recursions, where we set up a vector $\underline{Y}$ that satisfies some mutual recursion $\underline{X} = F(\underline{X})$. Indeed, the mutual recursion is usually in the form of a one-step tail recursion (precisely one event before each recursive call). The thing to concentrate on is how these vectors $\underline{Y}$ are constructed to model the state spaces that these tail recursions so clearly describe.

As an easy but otherwise typical example, suppose our *COUNT* process were extended so that the parameter now ranges over *all* the integers $\mathbb{Z}$ rather than just the non-negative ones:

$$ ZCOUNT_n \quad = \quad up \rightarrow ZCOUNT_{n+1} \;\square\; down \rightarrow ZCOUNT_{n-1} $$

The striking thing about this example, when you think about it, is that the value of the parameter n actually has no effect at all on the behaviour of $ZCOUNT_n$: whatever its value, this process can communicate any sequence of *up*'s and *down*'s. This might lead us to believe it was equal to the process

$$ AROUND \quad = \quad up \rightarrow AROUND \;\square\; down \rightarrow AROUND $$

and indeed we can use the UFP rule to prove $AROUND =_T ZCOUNT_n$ for all n. Let $\underline{A}$ be the vector of processes with structure matching the *ZCOUNT* recursion (i.e., it has one component for each $n \in \mathbb{Z}$) where every component equals *AROUND*. This is a natural choice since we conjecture that every $ZCOUNT_n$ equals *AROUND*. Applying the function F_{ZC} of the *ZCOUNT* recursion to this vector we get another whose nth component is

$$
\begin{aligned}
F_{ZC}(\underline{A})_n \quad &= \quad up \rightarrow A_{n+1} \;\square\; down \rightarrow A_{n-1} \\
&= \quad up \rightarrow AROUND \;\square\; down \rightarrow AROUND \\
&= \quad AROUND \\
&= \quad A_n
\end{aligned}
$$

(where the second line follows by definition of $\underline{A}$ and the third by definition of *AROUND*). Thus $\underline{A}$ is indeed a fixed point of F_{ZC}, proving our little result.

The basic principle at work here is that, in order to prove that some process P (in this case *AROUND*) is equivalent to a component of the tail recursion $\underline{X} = F(\underline{X})$ (in this case $\underline{ZCOUNT}$) you should work out what states P goes through as it evolves. Assuming it is possible to do so, you should then form a hypothesis about which of these states each component of $\underline{X}$ matches up with. In our case there is only one state of P, and *all* the components of $ZCOUNT$ match up with it. You then form the vector $\underline{Y}$ by replacing each component of $\underline{X}$ by the state of P conjectured to be equivalent, and then try to prove that this creates a solution to the tail recursion: if you can do this, you have completed the proof.

Both in the text and the exercises, there will be a number of examples following basically this argument through the rest of Part I (see, for example, pages 59, 85 and 142, and Exercises 2.3.3 and 6.3.1).

EXERCISE 1.3.1   Prove the validity in traces of the laws ⟨prefix-dist⟩ (1.9) and ⟨□-step⟩ (1.14).

EXERCISE 1.3.2   Recall the processes P_1, and P_u and P_d from Section 1.1.2. Prove that $P_u =_T P_1$ by the method above. *[Hint: show that a vector consisting of P_1 and one other process is a fixed point of the ⟨P_u, P_d⟩ recursion.]*

EXERCISE 1.3.3   Use laws and the UFP rule to prove that

$$Chaos_A \sqcap RUN_A =_T Chaos_A$$

for any alphabet A.

1.3.3   Specification and refinement

Traces are not just a dry and abstract model of processes to help us decide equality, but give a very usable language in *specification*. A specification is some condition that we wish a given process to satisfy. Since a CSP process is, by assumption, characterized completely by its communicating behaviour, it is obviously the case that we will be able to formulate many specifications in terms of $traces(P)$. In fact, most trace specifications one meets in practice are what we term *behavioural* specifications: the stipulation that each $s \in traces(P)$ meets some condition $R(s)$. This is termed a behavioural specification because what we are doing is 'lifting' the specification R on the individual recorded behaviours (i.e., traces) to the whole process.

There are two different approaches to behavioural specifications and their verification. The first (which is that adopted in Hoare's book, where you can find many more details than here) is to leave R explicitly as a specification of traces (generally using the special identifier tr to range over arbitrary traces of P). Then

$$P \text{ sat } R(tr) \quad \text{means} \quad \forall tr \in traces(P).R(tr)$$

This is meaningful however R is constructed, though usually it is expressed in predicate logic using trace notation.

In order to be able to express this sort of property it is useful to extend our range of trace notation:

- If s is a finite sequence, $\#s$ denotes the *length* of s (i.e., number of members).

- If $s \in \Sigma^*$ and $A \subseteq \Sigma$ then $s \upharpoonright A$ means the sequence s *restricted* to A: the sequence whose members are those of s which are in A. $\langle \rangle \upharpoonright A = \langle \rangle$ and $(s^\smallfrown\langle a \rangle) \upharpoonright A = (s \upharpoonright A)^\smallfrown\langle a \rangle$ if $a \in A$, $s \upharpoonright A$ otherwise.

- If $s \in \Sigma^*$ then $s \downarrow c$ can mean two things depending on what c is. If c is an *event* in Σ then it means the number of times c appears in s (i.e., $\#(s \upharpoonright \{c\})$), while if c is a *channel name* (associated with a non-trivial data type) it means the sequence of values (without the label c) that have been communicated along c in s. For example

$$\langle c.1, d.1, c.2, c.3, e.4 \rangle \downarrow c = \langle 1, 2, 3 \rangle$$

The following are some examples of specifications describing various features of some of the processes we have already met.

- The various processes in Section 1.1.2 all satisfy the condition:

$$tr \downarrow down \leq tr \downarrow up \leq tr \downarrow down + 1 \tag{$\ddagger$}$$

which states that they have never communicated more *down*'s than *up*'s, and neither do they fall more than one behind.

- The specification of $COUNT_n$ is similar but less restrictive:

$$tr \downarrow down \leq tr \downarrow up + n$$

- $B_{\langle \rangle}^\infty$ and $COPY$ both satisfy the basic *buffer* specification:

$$tr \downarrow right \leq tr \downarrow left$$

(noting that here $\leq$ means prefix and the things to its left and right are sequences of values). This is in fact the strongest specification that $B_{\langle \rangle}^\infty$ meets, but $COPY$ meets further ones.

Hoare gives a set of proof rules for establishing facts of the form P **sat** $R(tr)$ – essentially a re-coding into logic of the rules we have already seen for computing *traces*(P). The following rules cover the operators we have seen to date (bearing in mind the known equivalences between forms of prefixing).

$$STOP \textbf{ sat } (tr = \langle \rangle)$$

$$\frac{\forall\, a \in A.P(a) \textbf{ sat } R_a(tr)}{?a : A \to P \textbf{ sat } (tr = \langle\rangle \vee \exists\, a \in A.\, \exists\, tr'.\; tr = \langle a \rangle^\smallfrown tr' \wedge R_a(tr'))}$$

$$\frac{P \textbf{ sat } R(tr) \wedge Q \textbf{ sat } R(tr)}{P \;\Box\; Q \textbf{ sat } R(tr)}$$

$$\frac{P \textbf{ sat } R(tr) \wedge Q \textbf{ sat } R(tr)}{P \;\sqcap\; Q \textbf{ sat } R(tr)}$$

$$\frac{P \textbf{ sat } R(tr) \wedge \forall\, tr.R(tr) \Rightarrow R'(tr)}{P \textbf{ sat } R'(tr)}$$

$$\frac{P \textbf{ sat } R(tr) \wedge P \textbf{ sat } R'(tr)}{P \textbf{ sat } R(tr) \wedge R'(tr)}$$

The most interesting is that relating to recursion, and in fact Hoare's rule can usefully (and validly) be generalized in two ways: his assumption that the recursion is guarded is not necessary for this style of proof (though it is in many similar proof rules, some of which we will see later), and we can give a version for mutual recursion by attaching one proposed specification to each component of the vector of processes being defined.

PROOF RULE FOR RECURSION   *Suppose $\underline{X} = F(\underline{X})$ is the fixed point equation for (vectors of) trace-sets resulting from some recursive definition, and that $\underline{X}$ is the (least) fixed point which it defines. Let Λ be the indexing set of the vectors, so that $\underline{X} = \langle X_\lambda \mid \lambda \in \Lambda \rangle$. Suppose that for each λ there is a specification R_λ such that*

- *$STOP \textbf{ sat } R_\lambda(tr)$ for all $\lambda \in \Lambda$, and*
- *$\forall\, \lambda \in \Lambda.\, Y_\lambda \textbf{ sat } R_\lambda(tr) \Rightarrow \forall\, \lambda \in \Lambda.F(\underline{Y})_\lambda \textbf{ sat } R_\lambda(tr)$*

then $X_\lambda \textbf{ sat } R_\lambda(tr)$ for all $\lambda \in \Lambda$.

Paraphrasing this: we attach a specification R_λ to each component of the mutual recursion, and providing all of these are satisfied by $STOP$ and, on the assumption that they all hold of recursive calls they hold of the body of the recursion, then we can infer they hold of the actual process(es) defined by the recursion. This rule is formally justified in Section 9.2.

The above can be used to prove that the $COUNT$ processes meet the vector of specifications quoted for them above and, provided one can come up with appropriate specifications for the B_s^∞ processes for $s \neq \langle \rangle$, one can prove that $B_{\langle \rangle}^\infty$ meets its specification.

The most curious feature of this is the role played by $STOP$. It does not seem a very useful process and yet its satisfying R is a precondition to the above rule (and Hoare's). At first sight it seems unlikely that many useful specifications will be met by $STOP$, but in fact *any* behavioural trace specification which is satisfied by any process at all is satisfied by $STOP$. For $traces(STOP) = \{\langle\rangle\} \subseteq traces(P)$ for any P, and so if all the traces of P satisfy R, so do all those of $STOP$.

This shows precisely the limitation of trace specifications: while they can say that a process P cannot do anything stupid, they cannot force it to do anything at all. For this reason they are often termed *safety* or *partial correctness* conditions, while *liveness* or *total correctness* conditions are ones that additionally force a process to be able to do things. In later chapters we will develop models that allow us to build liveness specifications.

In order to satisfy 'sat $R(tr)$' a process's traces must be a *subset* of the traces which R allows. In fact, most of the example specifications given above have the property that the target process has the *largest possible* set of traces of any process satisfying it. This can be expressed in several different, but equivalent, ways (where P is the process and R the trace condition):

- $P =_T \sqcap\{Q \mid Q \text{ sat } R(tr)\}$ or, in other words, P is trace-equivalent to the nondeterministic choice over all processes meeting the specification.

- $Q \text{ sat } R(tr) \Rightarrow traces(Q) \subseteq traces(P)$

- $traces(P) = \{s \mid \forall t \leq s.R(t)\}$ the largest prefix-closed set of traces satisfying R. (It is worth noting that the set of traces satisfying each of the trace specifications on page 43 above is *not* prefix closed. For example, the trace $\langle down, up \rangle$ satisfies the specification ($\ddagger$) there, but since the prefix $\langle down \rangle$ does not, the longer trace is not possible for a process *all* of whose traces satisfy ($\ddagger$).)

Remember we defined that Q *refines* P, written $P \sqsubseteq Q$ if $P = Q \sqcap P$. Interpreted over the traces model, this leads to the slightly weaker concept of *traces refinement*

$$P \sqsubseteq_T Q \equiv P =_T Q \sqcap P \equiv traces(Q) \subseteq traces(P)$$

The above properties demonstrate that, for any satisfiable behavioural trace specification R there is always a process P_R (given by the formula in the first, and whose traces are the expression in the third) that is the most nondeterministic satisfying R and such that

$$Q \text{ sat } R(tr) \Leftrightarrow P_R \sqsubseteq_T Q$$

Let us say that P_R is the *characteristic* process of R. In other words, satisfaction (**sat**) can be replaced by deciding refinement against a suitably chosen process.

For example, $B_{\langle\rangle}^{\infty}$ is the (characteristic process of the) trace specification of a buffer, and a process will trace-refine it if, and only if, it meets the trace-based buffer specification. Thus $COPY \sqsupseteq_T B_{\langle\rangle}^{\infty}$, and all but the last of your answers to Exercise 1.1.8 should have the same property. (Here, we are taking the liberty of writing $P \sqsupseteq_T Q$ as the equivalent of $Q \sqsubseteq_T P$. We will do this for all order relations in future without comment, as the need arises.)

Which approach one *prefers* – abstract or process-based specification – will depend on both personal taste and, to some extent, the example being considered. Perhaps the major hurdle to overcome in adopting the latter is grasping the idea that a CSP process can be a specification as well as a model of an implementation. Of course, ideally, one should cultivate the ability to move backwards and forwards between the two approaches.

There are some major advantages in identifying each specification with the most nondeterministic process satisfying it.

- As we will see, this is the form in which the proof tool FDR codes specifications and allows them to be mechanically verified or refuted.

- Refinement has many properties that can be exploited, for example it is *transitive*:

$$P \sqsubseteq Q \wedge Q \sqsubseteq T \Rightarrow P \sqsubseteq T$$

and *monotone*: if $C[\cdot]$ is any process context, namely a process definition with a slot to put a process in, then

$$P \sqsubseteq Q \Rightarrow C[P] \sqsubseteq C[Q]$$

If $C[Q]$ is a process definition with component Q, with an overall target specification S, we might be able to factor the proof of $S \sqsubseteq C[Q]$ into two parts. First, find a specification P such that $S \sqsubseteq C[P]$. Second, prove $P \sqsubseteq Q$, which implies thanks to monotonicity that $C[P] \sqsubseteq C[Q]$. Transitivity then gives $S \sqsubseteq C[Q]$. This software engineering technique is known as *compositional development.*

Note how the identification of processes and specifications allowed us to consider the object $C[P]$, which we might read as '$C[Q]$, on the assumption that the process Q satisfies the specification P'.

- It allows one to move gradually from specification to implementation, using the transitivity property quoted above, creating a series of processes

$$Spec \sqsubseteq P_1 \sqsubseteq \ldots \sqsubseteq P_n \sqsubseteq Impl$$

where the first is the specification, and each is created by refining the previous one till an acceptable implementation is reached. This is known as *stepwise refinement.*

It is worth noting that, since the refinement $P \sqsubseteq Q$ is expressible as the equality $P \sqcap Q = P$, it makes sense to try to prove it algebraically. Recall Exercise 1.3.3.

Of course, the limitations of trace specification discussed earlier still apply here. It is worth noting that $STOP \sqsupseteq_T P$ and $RUN \sqsubseteq_T P$ for all processes P.

From here on this text will tend to emphasize the refinement-based approach to formulating and proving specifications. And while we will still sometimes formulate specifications abstractly in terms of traces and other behaviours we will see later, we will usually look to refinement-based (often automated) proofs based on their characteristic processes. Therefore we will not give any of the **sat** rules for the further operators and models we introduce later in this book; the interested reader can, of course, find many of them in Hoare's text.

1.3.4   Afters and initials

If P is any process, *initials*(P) (abbreviated P^0 in some publications on CSP) is the set of all its initial events

$$initials(P) = \{a \mid \langle a \rangle \in traces(P)\}$$

This set is often used in specifications and other definitions.

For example, *initials*$(STOP) = \{\}$ and *initials*$(?x : A \to P(x)) = A$.

If $s \in traces(P)$ then P/s (pronounced 'P *after* s') represents the behaviour of P after the trace s is complete. Over the traces model, P/s can be computed

$$traces(P/s) = \{t \mid s\hat{\ }t \in traces(P)\}$$

This operator should not be thought of as an ordinary part of the CSP language, rather as a notation for discussing behaviour of processes in fairly abstract contexts, to represent the behaviour of P on the *assumption* that s has occurred. The best reason for not including it as an operator you could use in programs is that it is not implementable in a conventional sense: the process

$$(STOP \sqcap a \to a \to STOP)/\langle a \rangle$$

is equivalent to $a \to STOP$, but no reasonable implementation acting on the non-deterministic choice here can force it to do anything.

Over the traces model it is true that

$$P =_T ?x : initials(P) \to P/\langle x \rangle$$

but we will find that this is not true over more discriminating models.

EXERCISE 1.3.4   (a)   Let $N \geq 0$. Give a trace specification for a process with events a, b and c which states that the difference between the number of a's and the total number of b's and c's is at most N.

(b)   Now find a CSP definition of a process D_N for which this is the strongest specification. *[Hint: give a parameterized recursion whose parameter is the present difference.]* D_0 is equivalent to a well-known simple process: what is it and why?

(c)   What traces refinements hold between the D_N?

EXERCISE 1.3.5   Give the strongest trace specification satisfied by $COPY = left?x \to right!x \to COPY$. Use the proof rules for **sat** given above to prove that $COPY$ meets it.

EXERCISE 1.3.6   See Exercise 1.1.7. Give a trace specification that a machine with events $\{in£1, out5p, out10p, out20p\}$ has never given out more money than it has received.

1.4   Tools

There are two types of tool available at the time of writing which will help the reader learn the ideas of this chapter: animators and refinement checkers.

With an *animator* such as ProBE you can write an arbitrary process description and interact with it much as described in the text. In other words, you can play at being 'the environment'. In fact, an animator may give you various options about how much control you want over the process (i.e., how much you want to be automatic) and, in particular, will give you the option of controlling the process more precisely than the real environment could. For example, if you like, it will let you make all its internal decisions: an internal choice $P \sqcap Q$ will be implemented as a process which can take an invisible τ (tau) action to each of P and Q. If you decide to take control over the τ actions, then you have the power to resolve the nondeterministic choices and can thus explore whichever avenue you desire. τ actions will be discussed properly in Chapter 3. In essence, an animator allows you to explore the transition picture of your process, like the simple examples shown in Figures 1.1 and 1.2.

Both ProBE and FDR work by loading in *scripts*: files of definitions (of processes and functions, etc., used within the process code). You then select processes defined within the current script to animate or prove things about. A file containing all the important examples in this chapter can be found on the web site associated with this book (see the Preface). You are, naturally, encouraged to try out your solutions to exercises on the tools. They must, of course, be written in the machine-readable (ASCII) version of CSP that these tools use. Full details of this version can be found in Appendix B. In this version, events and channels are written very much as in this chapter, but must all be declared.

Of the constructs defined in this chapter, two are not supported in the machine-readable version because their effects can easily be achieved in other ways. These are guarded alternative $(a \to P \mid \ldots \mid z \to Q)$ and the form of prefix choice without a channel name preceding the '?': one can write `c?x`, `c.n?x:T`, etc., but there is no direct equivalent of $?x : A \to P$. Both of these can be written in terms of the external choice operator (written `[]` rather than $\square$): the case of guarded choice has already been discussed in the text, and the prefix choice above can be written `[] a:A @ a -> P` which is the literal translation of $\square_{a \in A} a \to P$. `|~|` (the machine-readable version of $\sqcap$) and several other operators we will meet later also have indexed forms like this.

The machine-readable version of conditional is `if..then..else..` rather than $P \mathbin{\triangleleft} b \mathbin{\triangleright} Q$. Process parameters are written in 'argument' style `P(a,b,...,z)`. Look at the demonstration files for examples of all these things and more.

The alphabet Σ of all events is written `Events` in machine-readable CSP.

You will quickly appreciate the difference, once you have used them, between animators and refinement checkers like FDR. FDR does not let you interact with a process, rather it allows you to check assertions about them and will explore all of the states of a process necessary to verify these. It only shows you specific behaviours when you debug failures of refinement.

The checks for FDR to perform can be pre-loaded into FDR by including lines such as

`assert Spec [T= Imp`

in the scripts you write for it. (This represents the check of process `Imp` trace-refining process `Spec`.) Note that it gives you a choice of modes and models for checks; the only thing we are in a position to understand yet is *trace* checks in the *refinement* mode.

Finite-state machines

Thanks to the existence of infinite types it is all too easy to write process descriptions, such as $COUNT_0$ and $B_{\langle\rangle}^{\infty}$ which have infinitely many states. Since FDR works by expanding the state spaces of processes it will not terminate if asked to do much with one of these. There is nothing to stop you applying an animator to an infinite-state process, though obviously you will never be able to explore all of one of these!

One can usually get round this problem by restricting the range of the offending parameter(s) to that which will be encountered in the example being considered. Examples of this can be found in this chapter's demonstration file, and we have already seen one: the process $Counter(n, m)$ restricts both its parameters to the range $\{0, 1, \ldots, 7\}$ and thus has 64 states.

This restriction is most often annoying at the specification end of refinement, since it is sometimes the case that we would (as with buffers) like to have an infinite-state specification, since this is what best represents our requirements. All one can do at the time of writing is to choose a finite-state specification which we know refines the 'real' one (for example, the specification that a process is a buffer with capacity no greater than 5) and prove it. It is likely that future releases of the tool will be able to handle some infinite-state specifications (though not implementations), but you should always expect this to be less efficient.

You will, after using the tool, get a feel for the sizes of process it can handle comfortably. As a guide, with the syntax you have seen so far, the current version of FDR will deal comfortably with a few hundred states to a few thousand states. (This number will increase vastly as we meet the syntax of parallelism.)

Chapter 2

Parallel operators

All the processes defined so far have, at least in their obvious executions, only one thread of action. The whole idea of concurrency is to be able to reason about systems where there are a number of processes with independent control, interacting where necessary. In this chapter we see how to add operators which model this within our framework.

2.1   Synchronous parallel

We have already set down the principle that processes interact by agreeing, or handshaking, on communications. The simplest form of the CSP parallel operator insists that processes agree on *all* actions that occur. It is written $P \parallel Q$. For example, if $a \in \Sigma$, then

$$(a \to REPEAT) \parallel REPEAT$$

will have the same behaviour (except, perhaps, for precise timing details that we choose to ignore) as $\mu\, p.a \to p$. We can see this by following through how this combination works. Recall that

$$REPEAT = ?x : \Sigma \to x \to REPEAT$$

Since both sides have to agree on all events, it is clear that the only possible first event is a, and this indeed is a possible event for the right-hand process. The copy of $REPEAT$ on the right-hand side then forces the second event to be an a, which is accepted by $REPEAT$ on the left-hand side, forcing the third event to be a also, and so on for ever.

Perhaps the clearest description of this parallel operator is contained in the following law:

$$?x : A \to P \parallel ?x : B \to Q \ = ?x : A \cap B \to (P \parallel Q) \qquad \langle\parallel\text{-step}\rangle \qquad (2.1$$

$\parallel$ is also symmetric, associative and distributive. We do not quote these laws explicitly here since they will be subsumed later into laws for generalizations of $\parallel$.

Turning parallel processes into sequential ones

It is important to realize that CSP makes no fundamental distinction between 'parallel' and 'sequential' processes. There are just processes, and you can use any operator on any process. Indeed, any parallel CSP process is equivalent to sequential processes with the same pattern of communications.

The law $\langle\parallel\text{-step}\rangle$ (together with the other properties listed above, and the laws quoted in the previous chapter) can be used for this transformation. For example, if

$$\begin{aligned} P &= (a \to a \to STOP) \ \Box \ (b \to STOP) \\ Q &= (a \to STOP) \ \Box \ (c \to a \to STOP) \end{aligned}$$

these laws prove $P \parallel Q = a \to STOP$.

When the component processes are recursively defined, the algebraic laws alone will probably not be enough. In this case we use a combination of laws and the UFP rule: the parallel combination is expanded until we have a guarded expression for it and every other parallel combination discovered during the exploration. Consider, for example, the combination

$$(a \to REPEAT) \parallel REPEAT$$

discussed earlier:

$$\begin{aligned} &= \ (a \to REPEAT) \parallel (?x : \Sigma \to x \to REPEAT) \\ &= \ a \to \underline{(REPEAT \parallel (a \to REPEAT))} \end{aligned}$$

The underlining here indicates the parallel expression we have uncovered behind the guard a. Now we could use the symmetry of $\parallel$ to observe that this second combination equals the original one, so that

$$(a \to REPEAT) \parallel REPEAT = a \to (a \to REPEAT) \parallel REPEAT$$

showing that the process satisfies the guarded recursion $P = a \to P$. Alternatively (as would have been the only option if this example were not so symmetric) we could expand this second parallel combination in the same way that we did the first, and would find

$$REPEAT \parallel (a \rightarrow REPEAT) = a \rightarrow \underline{(a \rightarrow REPEAT) \parallel REPEAT}$$

At this point we notice that the parallel combination reached here is one we have seen before, so there is no need to expand it again (in general you should proceed by expanding each combination you find until there is none you have not seen before). We have thus expanded two processes and shown that they satisfy the guarded mutual recursion

$$
\begin{aligned}
R &= a \rightarrow Q \\
Q &= a \rightarrow R
\end{aligned}
$$

Depending on which route we have followed, this has proved via the UFP rule that the parallel combination is trace equivalent to one of the processes P and R above. Of course, the fact that P, Q and R are equivalent is itself an easy consequence of the UFP rule.

When the processes in parallel depend on a parameter introduced by recursion or input, it is likely that the family of processes uncovered by the exploration will be another parameterized one. Some examples can be found in the exercises below and in later sections.

EXAMPLE 2.1.1 (CUSTOMERS AND ATM'S) A customer of one of our cash-point machines might be described by the following expression.

$$
\begin{aligned}
CUST1 \quad = \quad & in.card \rightarrow pin?p : S \rightarrow req.50 \rightarrow \\
& dispense?x : \{y \in WA \mid y \geq 50\} \rightarrow out.card \rightarrow CUST1
\end{aligned}
$$

He only has one card (*card*), after which he remembers his PIN number belongs to the set $S \subseteq PIN$ and so will try these numbers. He always expects to withdraw £50, and get his card back. Notice that he is quite happy to accept *more* than £50 from the machine. Provided his memory is accurate and $f_{pin}(card) \in S$, the parallel combination $ATM1 \parallel CUST1$ is equivalent to

$$
\begin{aligned}
\mu\, q. \quad & in.card \rightarrow pin.f_{pin}(card) \rightarrow req.50 \rightarrow \\
& dispense.50 \rightarrow out.card \rightarrow q
\end{aligned}
$$

Since we are insisting that both parties must agree on all communications taking place in $P \parallel Q$, there is the unavoidable possibility that they might be unable to agree (even when each process has some events it could have performed if it were not forced to agree). This is illustrated by what happens when $f_{pin}(card) \notin S$, when the above combination becomes $in.card \rightarrow STOP$. This is known as *deadlock*. We discussed deadlock in general terms earlier, but this is the first proper example we have come across of a deadlocking CSP network. Note that $STOP$ behaves just like a deadlocked process – one of its main roles in CSP is to provide a clean representation of deadlock, just like $\sqcap$ provides one of nondeterminism.

If we force $CUST1$ to use $ATM2$ rather than $ATM1$, then it will deadlock as soon as the ATM decides to refuse a request – for this customer will not take no for an answer. It is important here that the decision of whether to accept or refuse a request is made by $\sqcap$ (nondeterminism) rather than $\square$ (external choice), for the latter would not have given rise to the deadlock. We can modify the customer to accept refusals more gracefully.

$$CUST2 \quad = \quad in.card \rightarrow pin?n : S \rightarrow req.50 \rightarrow$$
$$((dispense?x : \{y \in WA \mid y \geq 50\} \rightarrow out.card \rightarrow CUST2)$$
$$\square \ (refuse \rightarrow out.card \rightarrow CUST2))$$

But this combination still deadlocks if the customer does not get his card back. (Presumably the machine designer *wants* the customer to be deadlocked in this circumstance!)

$$\mu \, q. \quad (in.card \rightarrow pin.f_{pin}(card) \rightarrow req.50 \rightarrow$$
$$((dispense.50 \rightarrow out.card \rightarrow q)$$
$$\sqcap (refuse \rightarrow (out.card \rightarrow P) \sqcap STOP)))$$

(End of example)

The traces of $P \parallel Q$ are easy to compute: since this process can perform an action just when its two arguments can, it follows that

$$traces(P \parallel Q) = (traces(P)) \cap (traces(Q))$$

It is worth noting that, even though this implies $traces(P \parallel P) = traces(P)$, the existence of nondeterminism (which we know is not described fully by traces) makes it possible that $P \parallel P$ will not behave like P: for both sides may make different nondeterministic choices and so fail to agree on any communication. This means $\parallel$ is not idempotent. For example, if $P = (a \rightarrow STOP) \sqcap (b \rightarrow STOP)$, which cannot deadlock on its first step, then $P \parallel P = P \sqcap STOP$, which can. The reasons for this are closely connected with our discussion of distributivity in Section 1.2: $P \parallel P$ clearly requires two copies of P and so can compare them.

EXERCISE 2.1.1   How do $COUNT_0 \parallel COUNT_3$, $COUNT_0 \parallel Counter(0,0)$ and $COUNT_0 \parallel REPEAT$ behave, where they are all as described in the previous chapter?

For each either find an existing process that behaves like the appropriate combination, or define a new (sequential) process that does.

Prove trace equivalence in at least one case using the UFP rule.

EXERCISE 2.1.2   Construct a customer for $ATM2$ who has two cards, and whose reaction to *refuse* of the first card is to attempt to take money out with the second. He should do this whether or not the machine is prepared to give him the first card back. *Hint: you might find it easier to solve the problem of how the customer deals with an arbitrary list of cards (as a parameter to the process).*

2.2   Alphabetized parallel

The more processes we combine using $\|$, the more have to agree on every event. This is not what we will usually want (though it is a theme we will expand on in Section 2.5), and so we require a more general version of the parallel operator. What we need to reflect is the truth that, when two processes P and Q are placed in parallel, some of the communications of P are with Q, and some are not.

If X and Y are subsets of Σ, $P \ _X\|_Y\ Q$ is the combination where P is allowed to communicate in the set X, which we will call its *alphabet*, Q is allowed to communicate in its alphabet Y, and they must agree on events in the intersection $X \cap Y$. Thus $P \ _\Sigma\|_\Sigma\ Q = P \| Q$. So, for example,

$$(a \to b \to b \to STOP) \ _{\{a,b\}}\|_{\{b,c\}}\ (b \to c \to b \to STOP)$$

behaves like

$$a \to b \to c \to b \to STOP$$

since initially the only possible event is a (as the left-hand side blocks b); then both sides agree on b; then the right-hand side blocks b so only c is possible and finally they agree on b again. In most cases, as in this one, the alphabets of individual processes composed in parallel will be the sets of events which they can communicate. But they have to be given explicitly for a number of subtle reasons – for example, we often give processes strictly larger alphabets than the sets of events they actually use (frequently the process is then $STOP$). You should note that the same process can be used in different parallel compositions with different alphabets.[1]

---

[1] In allowing this we are giving a different presentation to that in Hoare's book, where a process has an intrinsic alphabet αP which makes the presentation of this particular parallel operator easier. See Section 2.7 for more details of this difference.

Figure 2.1 A parallel process.

A pantomime horse has two actors in it: one playing the front and one the back. You can think of it as a parallel composition of two processes showing that the two halves have to co-operate on moving, but each has control of some other activities.

$$Front \;_F\|_B\; Back$$

where $F = \{forward, backward, nod, neigh\}$
         $B = \{forward, backward, wag, kick\}$

If, in fact, *Front* will only nod the horse's head until it has moved forwards, and *Back* will only wag its tail until it has moved backwards:

$$Front \;=\; forward \to Front'$$
$$\quad\quad\quad \Box\; nod \to Front$$

$$Back \;=\; backward \to Back'$$
$$\quad\quad\quad \Box\; wag \to Back$$

then the composition will never move whatever the processes *Front'* and *Back'* are (since they are never reached), but it will simply nod and wag for ever. It will be equivalent to $RUN_{\{nod, wag\}}$.

When P can perform any of the events A (being equivalent to a process of the form $?x : A \to P'$) and Q can perform the events B (respectively $?x : B \to Q'$), then $P \,_X\|_Y\, Q$ can perform any of

$$C \;=\; (A \cap (X \setminus Y)) \cup (B \cap (Y \setminus X)) \cup (A \cap B \cap X \cap Y)$$

The first component of this union are the events P can perform on its own (because they are in X and not Y); similarly, the second are the events Q can do by itself. The final component are the events which they can synchronize on: the ones that they both can do and are in both their alphabets. The law expressing this is the following

$$P \,_X\|_Y\, Q \;=\; ?x : C \to (\; P' \,\langle\!\langle x \in X \rangle\!\rangle\, P$$
$$_X\|_Y$$
$$Q' \,\langle\!\langle x \in Y \rangle\!\rangle\, Q) \qquad\qquad \langle _X\|_Y\text{-step}\rangle \qquad (2.2)$$

where C is as above. $_X\|_Y$ is distributive, like most operators, over $\sqcap$ and $\langle\!\langle b \rangle\!\rangle$. The second of these can be used to give an alternative version of the above law:

$$P \,_X\|_Y\, Q \;=\; ?x : C \to ((P' \,_X\|_Y\, Q') \langle\!\langle x \in X \cap Y \rangle\!\rangle$$
$$(P' \,_X\|_Y\, Q \langle\!\langle x \in X \rangle\!\rangle P \,_X\|_Y\, Q'))$$

All we have done here is to distribute the two conditionals in $\langle _X\|_Y\text{-step}\rangle$ outside $_X\|_Y$ and to discard the one of four cases ($x \notin X \cup Y$) that cannot arise.

The rest of its basic laws are given below. It has symmetry and associativity laws that are slightly more complex than usual because of the alphabets.

$$P \,_X\|_Y\, (Q \sqcap R) = (P \,_X\|_Y\, Q) \sqcap (P \,_X\|_Y\, R) \qquad\qquad \langle _X\|_Y\text{-dist}\rangle \qquad (2.3)$$

$$P \,_X\|_Y\, Q = Q \,_Y\|_X\, P \qquad\qquad \langle _X\|_Y\text{-sym}\rangle \qquad (2.4)$$

$$(P \,_X\|_Y\, Q) \,_{X\cup Y}\|_Z\, R = P \,_X\|_{Y\cup Z}\, (Q \,_Y\|_Z\, R) \qquad\qquad \langle _X\|_Y\text{-assoc}\rangle \qquad (2.5)$$

As the last of these begins to show, composing a large network using this binary operator gets rather clumsy because of the bookkeeping required on the alphabets. We therefore include a better, indexed notation for n-way parallel composition:

$$\Big\|_{i=1}^{n}(P_i, X_i) \;=\; P_1 \,_{X_1}\|_{X_2 \cup \ldots \cup X_n}\, (\ldots (P_{n-1} \,_{X_{n-1}}\|_{X_n}\, P_n)\ldots)$$

So, for example, if

$$COPY'(c, d) \;=\; c?x : T \to d.x \to COPY'(c, d)$$

Figure 2.2 A simple chain connected in parallel.

and $X_r = c_r.T \cup c_{r+1}.T$ (with $c_0, c_1, \ldots, c_n$ all being distinct) then

$$\left\|_{r=0}^{n-1}(COPY'(c_r, c_{r+1}), X_r)\right.$$

represents a chain of n one-place buffer processes. $COPY'(c_0, c_1)$ can input a value on channel c_0 without requiring the co-operation of any other process in the network. This value is then communicated across the channels $c_1, \ldots, c_{n-1}$ in turn (each transfer requiring the agreement of the two processes involved) until it appears at the far end and $COPY'(c_{n-1}, c_n)$ is able to output it without needing any other process to agree. The network is shown in Figure 2.2. It is natural to think of the channels c_0 and c_n as external, because they are only in the alphabet of one process each, and the rest are internal.

The reason it is natural to think of the above network as a chain is because the alphabets $X_r = c_r.T \cup c_{r+1}.T$ of the processes only have non-empty intersection – corresponding to the possibility of communication between them – for consecutively numbered cells. By appropriate choices of alphabets it is possible to construct networks using $\|$ which have any chosen finite graph structure. The graph with one node per process and an edge between processes with non-empty intersection of alphabets is termed the *communication graph*. One might be tempted to put arrows on this graph to correspond to the direction of the channels, but this would be a mistake: you should remember that communication in CSP is symmetric and that channels are just a gloss on this.

Just as with the synchronous parallel operator, any system of sequential processes put in parallel with $_X\|_Y$ can be expanded into a (usually recursive) sequential one using the laws (predominantly $\langle_X\|_Y\text{-step}\rangle$) and the UFP rule. Consider, for example, the combination

$$COPY'(a, b)\ _{\{|a,b|\}}\|_{\{|b,c|\}}\ COPY'(b, c)$$

The initial events of the two processes are respectively $\{| a |\}$ and $\{| b |\}$ (since they are both ready to input). The initial events of the combination are therefore (showing the full calculation!)

$$(\{| a |\} \cap \{| b |\} \cap \{| a, b |\} \cap \{| b, c |\})$$
$$\cup (\{| a |\} \cap (\{| a, b |\} \setminus \{| b, c |\}))$$
$$\cup (\{| b |\} \cap (\{| b, c |\} \setminus \{| a, b |\}))$$

which reduces to $\{\} \cup \{|\ a\ |\} \cup \{\} = \{|\ a\ |\}$ (i.e., there is no shared event possible initially, no event possible for the right-hand process, but the left-hand one can input). This is, of course, exactly what one would have expected.

Thus the original process (which we will name CC_0) equals (by $\langle_X \|_Y\text{-step}\rangle$)

$$a?x \to ((b!x \to COPY'(a,b))\ {}_{\{|a,b|\}}\|_{\{|b,c|\}}\ COPY'(b,c))$$

Call the parallel combination here $CC_1(x)$ (the x is needed because it depends on the input value). Now both processes can only perform shared (b) events, and agree on one, so by another use of $\langle_X \|_Y\text{-step}\rangle$ turns $CC_1(x)$ into

$$b!x \to (COPY'(a,b)\ {}_{\{|a,b|\}}\|_{\{|b,c|\}}\ c!x \to COPY'(b,c))$$

If we similarly call the parallel combination here $CC_2(x)$, we find that neither process can perform any b action, but each can perform some of its own actions independently. It equals

$$a?y \to (b!y \to COPY'(a,b)\ {}_{\{|a,b|\}}\|_{\{|b,c|\}}\ c!x \to COPY'(b,c))$$
$$\square\ c!x \to (COPY'(a,b)\ {}_{\{|a,b|\}}\|_{\{|b,c|\}}\ COPY'(b,c))$$

which, naming the first parallel combination $CC_3(y,x)$, equals

$$a?y \to CC_3(y,x)$$
$$\square\ c!x \to CC_0$$

In $CC_3(y,x)$, the left-hand process can only perform the shared event $b!y$, while the right-hand one can only perform its own action $c!x$. It follows that this process equals

$$c!x \to ((b!y \to COPY'(a,b))\ {}_{\{|a,b|\}}\|_{\{|b,c|\}}\ COPY'(b,c))$$

which is $c!x \to CC_1(y)$. Since there are no more parallel combinations to expand, the state exploration is complete and we have shown that the processes CC_0, $CC_1(x)$, $CC_2(x)$ and $CC_3(y,x)$ satisfy a guarded mutual recursion:

$$
\begin{aligned}
CC_0' &= a?x \to CC_1'(x) \\
CC_1'(x) &= b!x \to CC_2'(x) \\
CC_2'(x) &= (c!x \to CC_0')\ \square\ (a?y \to CC_3'(y,x)) \\
CC_3'(y,x) &= c!x \to CC_1'(y)
\end{aligned}
$$

Thus these two systems are trace-equivalent by the UFP rule. A picture of this system of states is in Figure 2.3 (the picture over-simplifies the values input and

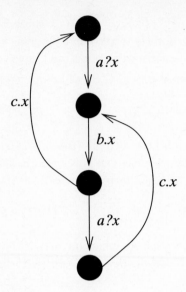

Figure 2.3 The states of two one-place buffers in parallel.

output in that it does not allow you to reconstruct the relationship between the values going in and those going out). Clearly this simple example is already getting a bit tedious to expand. Much larger examples are impractical by hand – fortunately, however, tools like FDR are much better able to deal with the expansion and bookkeeping than we are, and in fact a large part of what they do is precisely this.

The traces of $P \;_X\|_Y\; Q$ are just those which combine a trace of P and a trace of Q so that all communications in $X \cap Y$ are shared.

$$traces(P \;_X\|_Y\; Q) \;=\; \{s \in (X \cup Y)^* \mid s \upharpoonright X \in traces(P) \\ \land\; s \upharpoonright Y \in traces(Q)\}$$

EXAMPLE 2.2.1 (FIVE DINING PHILOSOPHERS) This is perhaps the best known of all examples in this field: it has already been briefly described in the introduction. As shown in Figure 2.4, five philosophers share a dining table at which they have allotted seats. In order to eat (in the figure, from a tangled bowl of spaghetti in the middle of the table!), a philosopher must pick up the forks on either side of him or her but, as you see, there are only five forks. A philosopher who cannot pick up one or other fork has to wait. We can model this story in various ways in CSP by choosing different episodes of philosophers' lives as events, but the essential things from the point of view of interaction are when they pick up or put down their forks.

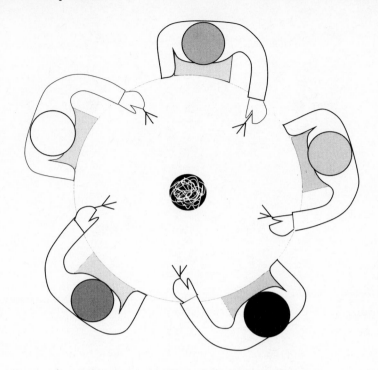

Figure 2.4 The five dining philosophers.

In order to make sure no fork can be held by two philosophers at once, we also require a process to represent each fork.

We will therefore describe two classes of process: $PHIL_i$ and $FORK_i$, in each case for $i \in \{0, 1, 2, 3, 4\}$. The events of $FORK_i$ are

- *picksup.i.i* and *picksup.i$\ominus$1.i* where $\ominus$ represents subtraction *modulo* 5 (with $\oplus$ being the corresponding addition operator). These respectively represent $FORK_i$ being picked up by $PHIL_i$ and $PHIL_{i\ominus 1}$.

- *putsdown.i.i* and *putsdown.i$\ominus$1.i*, representing the fork being put down again.

$$FORK_i \quad = \quad (picksup.i.i \rightarrow putsdown.i.i \rightarrow FORK_i)$$
$$\square \ (picksup.i\ominus 1.i \rightarrow putsdown.i\ominus 1.i \rightarrow FORK_i)$$

The philosophers have these same events, plus some individual ones. What turns out to be crucial in describing the philosophers is the order in which they pick up their forks. There are various options: either left-hand one first, right-hand one first, or some form of choice between the two. And of course different philosophers

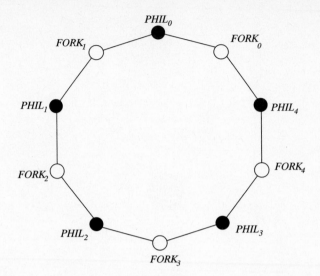

Figure 2.5 The communication network of the dining philosophers.

might have different preferences. For simplicity, the following definition asserts that each philosopher picks up the left fork first and puts it down last.

$$
\begin{aligned}
PHIL_i \quad = \quad & thinks.i \rightarrow sits.i \rightarrow picksup.i.i \rightarrow \\
& picksup.i.i{\oplus}1 \rightarrow eats.i \rightarrow putsdown.i.i{\oplus}1 \rightarrow \\
& putsdown.i.i \rightarrow getsup.i \rightarrow PHIL_i
\end{aligned}
$$

The complete system is then formed by putting all of these processes in parallel, each having as its alphabet the set of events it can use. If AF_i and AP_i are these sets for $FORK_i$ and $PHIL_i$ respectively, the network is formed by composing together the ten pairs

$$
\{(FORK_i, AF_i), (PHIL_i, AP_i) \mid i \in \{0, 1, 2, 3, 4\}\}
$$

in parallel. The communication graph of the resultant network, with an edge between two processes if their alphabets have non-empty intersection, is shown in Figure 2.5.

So how does this system behave? We have already noted that one philosopher might have to wait for a neighbour to put down a fork. The greatest danger, however, is that they might all get hungry at once and all manage to pick up their left-hand fork (as is about to happen in Figure 2.4). For then none can make any progress and the system is deadlocked. The philosophers starve to death. We will return to this example in Chapter 13 when we study the subject of deadlock in more detail. Amongst other things, we will examine the impact of different choices of fork-picking-up. *(End of example)*

As well as demonstrating the use of the parallel operator, this example also illustrates uses of events we have not seen before. Like many networks we will see, this one has numbers of processes which behave similarly except for the precise events they use. Of course the easy way to define these is to use parameterization: $PHIL_i$ rather than $PHIL_0, \ldots, PHIL_4$ separately. Notice, however, that unlike previous parameterized recursions, these processes do not depend on each other: $PHIL_2$ only makes recursive calls to $PHIL_2$, for example. To create the arrays of events that are needed to tie in with these arrays of processes, we use the channel notation to create arrays of events as anticipated on page 27. Sometimes, as with the *picksup* and *putsdown* events, we need a two-dimensional array (or even more).

One can mix the array and data-passing uses of channels. The best way of implementing the chain of $COPY'$ processes is to create an array of channels c whose communications look like $c.i!x$ or $c.i?x$. $COPY'(c.i, c.i + 1)$ would then be equivalent to the process

$$COPY''(i) = c.i?x \rightarrow c.i{+}1!x \rightarrow COPY''(i)$$

EXAMPLE 2.2.2 (CASH-POINT MACHINE WITH EXTENDED INTERFACE) The model of ATM and customer given above using synchronous parallel only gives their common interface. The new operator allows us to bring in the actions which they perform by themselves or at other interfaces. This has already been seen in the pantomime horse and dining philosopher examples.

We can, for example, bring in a component of an ATM's state to represent the amount of money it contains: it can always (except when full) be refilled when not in use by a customer, but rejects requests for more money than it has in; the customer spends nondeterministic amounts of money and goes back for more when he has none left. The *refill* and *spend* events only belong to one of the two alphabets.

If the capacity of the machine is £N, and the customer makes withdrawals of £M (where $M < N$), we need to define processes $ATM\,ref_n$ and $CUST\,spend_m$ for each integer $0 \le n \le N$ and $0 \le m \le M$. They are

$$
\begin{aligned}
ATM\,ref_n \;=\; & ((refill \rightarrow ATM\,ref_N) \triangleleft n < N \triangleright STOP) \\
& \square\; (in?c : CARD \rightarrow pin.f_{pin}(c) \rightarrow req?w : WA \rightarrow \\
& \qquad ((dispense.w \rightarrow out.c \rightarrow ATM\,ref_{n-w}) \\
& \qquad \triangleleft w \le n \triangleright \\
& \qquad (refuse \rightarrow out.c \rightarrow ATM\,ref_n)))
\end{aligned}
$$

$$CUST\,spend_0 \;=\; in.card \to pin?p : S \to req.M \to$$
$$((dispense?x : \{y \in WA \mid x \geq M\} \to$$
$$out.card \to CUST\,spend_M)$$
$$\square\,(refuse \to out.card \to CUST\,spend_0))$$

$$CUST\,spend_m \;=\; \bigsqcap\{spend.r \to CUST\,spend_{m-r} \mid 1 \leq r \leq m\}$$
$$(m > 0)$$

The alphabets of $ATM\,ref_n$ and $CUST\,spend_m$ are respectively X and Y, where

$$Z \;=\; in.CARD \cup out.CARD \cup pin.PIN \cup req.WA$$
$$\cup\, dispense.WA \cup \{refuse\}$$

$$X \;=\; Z \cup \{refill\}$$

$$Y \;=\; Z \cup spend.\mathbb{N}$$

(Z represents the common communications of the two processes; the others are their 'external' actions.) The combination $ATM\,ref_n\;_X\|_Y\;CUST\,spend_m$ then represents their interaction given initial capital £n and £m respectively. Note again that the customer has no control over refilling and the machine has none over spending. *(End of example)*

EXERCISE 2.2.1   Find pairs of actors ($Front_i, Back_i$) ($i = 1, 2, 3$) for the pantomime horse so that the overall behaviour is respectively (using the same alphabets for the parallel composition as on page 56)

$$PH_1 \;=\; neigh \to forward \to kick \to backward \to PH_1$$

$$PH_2 \;=\; forward \to neigh \to PH_2$$
$$\square\; backward \to kick \to PH_2$$

$$PH_3 \;=\; neigh \to wag \to forward \to PH_3$$
$$\square\; wag \to neigh \to forward \to PH_3$$

Find a process with alphabet $F \cup B$ which *cannot* be constructed in this way, and explain why it is impossible.

EXERCISE 2.2.2   Let $X = \{a, b, c, d\}$ and $Y = \{c, d\}$, and let

$$P \;=\; a \to c \to P$$
$$\square\; b \to d \to P$$

$$Q \;=\; c \to d \to Q$$

What are the traces of $P\;_X\|_Y\;Q$? Which of these traces are terminal, in the sense that they are not prefixes of any other trace? What can you say about the behaviour of a process after it has performed such a trace?

EXERCISE 2.2.3   Use the methods illustrated in this section to expand $P \ _X\|_Y\ Q$ to a sequential process (where P and Q are as in the previous question). You should find some states in this expansion equivalent to $STOP$ – corresponding to deadlock. Compare these states to the terminal traces.

Find a process R with alphabet $Z = \{a, b\}$ such that $R \ _Z\|_X\ (P \ _X\|_Y\ Q)$ is deadlock-free.

EXERCISE 2.2.4   Extend the definition of $ATMref_n$ by adding an additional pair of channels with which it communicates with a central computer. After a customer has requested a withdrawal the request is relayed by the ATM to the computer, which sends one of three responses: OK, OD or $retain$. These indicate, respectively:

- Issue the money, if there is enough in the ATM.

- The request is too large for the balance, refuse it but give the card back.

- Refuse the request and retain the card.

Your ATM should now be a process defined without nondeterministic choice which, from the customer's perspective (since he or she cannot see these other interactions), looks just like ATM_2.

EXERCISE 2.2.5   Formulate trace specifications of the following properties in the alphabets of the examples to which they refer.

(a) The numbers of times the pantomime horse has wagged its tail and neighed always differ (in absolute value) by at most one.

(b) The number of cards handed back by the ATM is never greater than the number inserted into it.

(c) Whenever $PHIL_i$ eats, $PHIL_{i\oplus 1}$ is not holding any fork.

Find the characteristic process (over the respective alphabet) for each. How do you deal with the events each system can do which are irrelevant to the specification? Which of these is finite state? If any is infinite state can you suggest a stronger, finite-state one which the appropriate network will still satisfy and which is as close in meaning to the original as possible? Prove (either manually or using FDR or a similar tool) that each holds of one or more of the systems we have already seen (in the first case in Exercise 2.2.1 (c)).

2.3 Interleaving

The parallel operators seen so far ($\|$ and $_X\|_Y$) have the property that all partners allowed to make a particular communication must synchronize on it for the event to occur. The opposite is true of parallel composition by *interleaving*, written $P \parallel\mid Q$. Here, the processes run completely independently of each other. Any event which the combination communicates arose in precisely one of P and Q. If they could both have communicated the same event then the choice of which one executed it is nondeterministic, but only one did. The law governing this is the following: if $P = ?x : A \to P'$ and $Q = ?x : B \to Q'$ then

$$P \parallel\parallel Q = ?x : A \cup B \to \quad (P' \parallel\parallel Q) \sqcap (P \parallel\parallel Q')$$
$$\blacktriangleleft x \in A \cap B \blacktriangleright$$
$$(P' \parallel\parallel Q) \blacktriangleleft x \in A \blacktriangleright (P \parallel\parallel Q')$$

$$\langle\parallel\parallel\text{-step}\rangle \quad (2.6)$$

As one would expect, $\parallel\parallel$ is symmetric, associative and distributive.

$$P \parallel\parallel Q = P \parallel\parallel Q \qquad\qquad \langle\parallel\parallel\text{-sym}\rangle \quad (2.7)$$

$$(P \parallel\parallel Q) \parallel\parallel R = P \parallel\parallel (Q \parallel\parallel R) \qquad\qquad \langle\parallel\parallel\text{-assoc}\rangle \quad (2.8)$$

$$P \parallel\parallel (Q \sqcap R) = (P \parallel\parallel Q) \sqcap (P \parallel\parallel R) \qquad\qquad \langle\parallel\parallel\text{-dist}\rangle \quad (2.9)$$

The process $L_1 = up \to down \to L_1$ keeps $tr \downarrow down$ (the number of $down$'s it has communicated to date) between $tr \downarrow up - 1$ and $tr \downarrow up$. By interleaving a number of these we can increase this margin:

$$L_n = L_1 \parallel\parallel L_1 \parallel\parallel \ldots \parallel\parallel L_1 \quad n \text{ copies of } L_1$$

keeps $tr \downarrow down$ between $tr \downarrow up - n$ and $tr \downarrow up$. Even though which of a number of processes performs a given event is usually nondeterministic, the overall effect here is actually deterministic.

Clearly $L_n \parallel\parallel L_m = L_{n+m}$, whereas $L_n \parallel L_m = L_{min\{n,m\}}$.

The combination of interleaving and recursion can allow us to describe complex behaviours which would otherwise need infinite mutual recursions. For example, we can simulate the infinite-state recursion $COUNT$ by a single line

$$Ctr \quad = \quad up \to (Ctr \parallel\parallel down \to STOP)$$

or, more subtly

$$Ctr' \quad = \quad up \to (Ctr' \parallel\parallel \mu P.down \to up \to P) \quad \text{or even}$$
$$Ctr'' \quad = \quad up \to (Ctr'' \parallel\parallel down \to Ctr'')$$

All of these behave the same as $COUNT_0$. In each case see if you can understand why.

The above uses of $\parallel\parallel$ have all involved combinations of processes that use the same events, creating nondeterminism about which side carries out an event. In practice such uses, though clever when they work, are rather rare except for the special case of an abstraction mechanism we will meet in Chapter 12. In creating practical networks, it is usual to find processes which use disjoint sets of events or perhaps soon come into a state where they do this. Think back to the five dining philosophers: the five philosophers do not (in our model!) talk to each other, and neither do the five forks. Therefore we can achieve exactly the same effect as previously by first composing these two groups by interleaving:

$$FORKS \ = \ FORK_0 \ ||| \ FORK_1 \ ||| \ldots ||| \ FORK_4$$

$$PHILS \ = \ PHIL_0 \ ||| \ PHIL_1 \ ||| \ldots ||| \ PHIL_4$$

and then, if $AFS = AF_0 \cup AF_1 \cup AF_2 \cup AF_3 \cup AF_4$, we can form the complete system

$$FORKS \ _{AFS}||_\Sigma \ PHILS$$

The traces of $P \ ||| \ Q$ are just the interleavings of traces of P and Q. We need to define an operator for producing the interleavings of a given pair of traces: this is defined recursively below

$$\langle \rangle \ ||| \ s \ = \ \{s\}$$

$$s \ ||| \ \langle \rangle \ = \ \{s\}$$

$$\langle a \rangle\hat{\ }s \ ||| \ \langle b \rangle\hat{\ }t \ = \ \{\langle a \rangle\hat{\ }u \mid u \in s \ ||| \ \langle b \rangle\hat{\ }t\}$$
$$\cup \{\langle b \rangle\hat{\ }u \mid u \in \langle a \rangle\hat{\ }s \ ||| \ t\}$$

Given this

$$traces(P \ ||| \ Q) \ = \ \bigcup \{s \ ||| \ t \mid s \in traces(P) \wedge t \in traces(Q)\}$$

EXERCISE 2.3.1   A *bag* is a process with channels *left* and *right* which behaves like a buffer except that the order in which things come out is not necessarily that in which they are put in. Use $|||$ and $COPY$ to define a bag with capacity N. Explain your definition. Now define an infinite capacity bag by following the style of recursion in the process Ctr above.

EXERCISE 2.3.2   Prove that $COUNT_0 \ ||| \ COUNT_0$ is trace-equivalent to $COUNT_0$. You should do this by calculating the sets of traces directly (bearing in mind what has already been established about $traces(COUNT_0)$).

EXERCISE 2.3.3   Consider the following mutual recursion indexed by pairs of natural numbers $\mathbb{N} \times \mathbb{N}$:

$$CT2(n, m) \ = \ up \rightarrow (CT2(n + 1, m) \sqcap CT2(n, m + 1))$$
$$\square \ ((down \rightarrow CT2(n - 1, m)) \ \triangleleft n > 0 \triangleright STOP)$$
$$\square \ ((down \rightarrow CT2(n, m - 1)) \ \triangleleft m > 0 \triangleright STOP)$$

Show that it is satisfied by the vectors $\langle COUNT_{n+m} \mid (n, m) \in \mathbb{N} \times \mathbb{N} \rangle$ and

$$\langle COUNT_n \mid\mid\mid COUNT_m \mid (n, m) \in \mathbb{N} \times \mathbb{N} \rangle$$

and deduce that $COUNT_n \mid\mid\mid COUNT_m$ and $COUNT_{n+m}$ are trace-equivalent for all $(n, m) \in \mathbb{N} \times \mathbb{N}$.

If you look at this question carefully, you will see that it shows a way of using the UFP rule to prove the equivalence to two systems where there is a many–one relation of equivalence between the underlying state spaces.

EXERCISE 2.3.4   Suppose we need multiple cash-point machines to cope with increased customer demand. Why is an interleaving of two or more of our existing machines (for example $ATM2 \mid\mid\mid ATM2$) not a good idea?

Hint: think what might happen in this model when two customers are using them simultaneously. How might you avoid this problem?

2.4   Generalized parallel

The effects of all the parallel operators we have seen so far, and more, can be achieved with a single operator which, for whatever reason, has become the most commonly used with FDR even though it does not appear in Hoare's book. In $P _X\|_Y Q$, we decide which events are synchronized and which are not by looking at X and Y. In the new operator, we simply give the interface: $P \underset{X}{\|} Q$ is the process where all events in X must be synchronized, and events outside X can proceed independently. It is called *generalized* or *interface* parallel. We will always have

$$P \mid\mid\mid Q = P \underset{\{\}}{\|} Q$$

and, provided P and Q never communicate outside X and Y,

$$P _X\|_Y Q = P \underset{X \cap Y}{\|} Q$$

(The case when P or Q do not satisfy this condition is left as an exercise.)

In almost all cases one meets, this new operator just gives a different presentation of something we could have written with $_X\|_Y$. However, you should realize there are new effects that could not have been achieved without it: if X is non-empty but does not cover all events that can be used by P and by Q then $P \underset{X}{\|} Q$ acts a little bit like the alphabetized parallel and a little bit like $P \mid\mid\mid Q$. There are some events that are synchronized and some which can ambiguously come from either side. For example, $COUNT_0 \underset{\{up\}}{\|} COUNT_0$ is a process that will allow *twice* as many *down*'s as *up*'s, since the *down* events proceed independently.

If $P = ?x : A \to P'$ and $Q = ?x : B \to Q'$ then the initial events of $P \underset{X}{\|} Q$ are $C = (X \cap A \cap B) \cup (A \setminus X) \cup (B \setminus X)$. The behaviour is shown by the following step law, whose complexity reflects the operator's generality: an event may now be synchronized, unsynchronized but ambiguous, or from one side only

$$
\begin{aligned}
P \underset{X}{\|} Q \; = \; ?x : C \to \;\; & (P' \underset{X}{\|} Q') \blacktriangleleft x \in X \blacktriangleright \\
& (((P' \underset{X}{\|} Q) \sqcap (P \underset{X}{\|} Q')) \blacktriangleleft x \in A \cap B \blacktriangleright \\
& ((P' \underset{X}{\|} Q) \blacktriangleleft x \in A \blacktriangleright (P \underset{X}{\|} Q')))
\end{aligned}
$$

$\langle \underset{X}{\|}\text{-step} \rangle$ (2.10)

It is symmetric and distributive:

$$P \underset{X}{\|} Q \; = \; Q \underset{X}{\|} P$$

$\langle \underset{X}{\|}\text{-sym} \rangle$ (2.11)

$$P \underset{X}{\|} (Q \sqcap R) \; = \; (P \underset{X}{\|} Q) \sqcap (P \underset{X}{\|} R)$$

$\langle \underset{X}{\|}\text{-dist} \rangle$ (2.12)

It has the following weak (in that both interfaces are the same) associativity property

$$P \underset{X}{\|} (Q \underset{X}{\|} R) \; = \; (P \underset{X}{\|} Q) \underset{X}{\|} R)$$

$\langle \underset{X}{\|}\text{-assoc} \rangle$ (2.13)

but the possibility, in $P \underset{X}{\|} (Q \underset{Y}{\|} R)$, of X containing an event not in Y that Q and R can both perform, makes it hard to construct a universally applicable and elegant associative law.

The traces of $P \underset{X}{\|} Q$ are simply combinations of traces of P and Q where actions in X are shared and all others occur independently. As with the interleaving operator, the best way to calculate the trace-set is in terms of an operator that maps each pair of traces to the set of possible results (which is always empty when they do not agree on X). The following clauses allow one to calculate $s \underset{X}{\|} t$ (a set of traces, like $s \;\||\; t$) for all $s, t \in \Sigma^*$; below x denotes a typical member of X and y a typical member of $\Sigma \setminus X$.

$$s \parallel_X t = t \parallel_X s$$

$$\langle\rangle \parallel_X \langle\rangle = \{\langle\rangle\}$$

$$\langle\rangle \parallel_X \langle x\rangle = \{\}$$

$$\langle\rangle \parallel_X \langle y\rangle = \{\langle y\rangle\}$$

$$\langle x\rangle^\frown s \parallel_X \langle y\rangle^\frown t = \{\langle y\rangle^\frown u \mid u \in \langle x\rangle^\frown s \parallel_X t\}$$

$$\langle x\rangle^\frown s \parallel_X \langle x\rangle^\frown t = \{\langle x\rangle^\frown u \mid u \in s \parallel_X t\}$$

$$\langle x\rangle^\frown s \parallel_X \langle x'\rangle^\frown t = \{\} \qquad \text{if } x \neq x'$$

$$\langle y\rangle^\frown s \parallel_X \langle y'\rangle^\frown t = \{\langle y\rangle^\frown u \mid u \in s \parallel_X \langle y'\rangle^\frown t\}$$
$$\cup \{\langle y'\rangle^\frown u \mid u \in \langle y\rangle^\frown s \parallel_X {}^\frown t\}$$

Given this, it is possible to define

$$traces(P \parallel_X Q) = \bigcup\{s \parallel_X t \mid s \in traces(P) \wedge t \in traces(Q)\}$$

EXERCISE 2.4.1   If we do not assume that P and Q never communicate outside X and Y, how can we express $P \,_X\|_Y\, Q$ in terms of $\|_Z$? *[Hint: use STOP.]*

EXERCISE 2.4.2   Describe the behaviours of the following processes; in each case find a tail-recursive process equivalent to it.

   (i) $COPY \parallel_{\{|left|\}} COPY$

  (ii) $COPY \parallel_{\{|right|\}} COPY$

EXERCISE 2.4.3   Show that $(P \,|||\, Q) \parallel R$ and $P \,|||\, (Q \parallel R)$ need not be equivalent. What does this tell you about the 'law'

$$P \parallel_X (Q \parallel_Y R) =? (P \parallel_X Q) \parallel_Y R$$

2.5   Parallel composition as conjunction

The uses seen so far of the synchronized parallel operator $\|$ and the alphabetized one $_X\|_Y$ have all had broadly the intuition one would have expected of a parallel operator, namely describing interactions between processes which might reasonably be expected to run concurrently and communicate with each other. But they can be used in a rather different way in situations where we are using CSP more in the manner of a *specification* language than as a method of describing systems as implemented.

It turns out to be very difficult, even impractical, to implement handshaken communication in anything like the generality implied by the CSP parallel operators, at least if a genuinely parallel implementation is required. In particular, handshakes involving more than two parties come into this 'impractical' category. Except in special circumstances, CSP descriptions which are intended to model the construction of parallel systems tend to respect this restriction.

Multi-way handshaking is nevertheless an extremely useful construct in CSP: it is used to build up specifications of intended behaviour (i.e., processes that are probably going to be used on the left-hand side of a refinement check). For parallel composition turns out to be equivalent to the conjunction (i.e. logical 'and') of trace specifications. In this style of use, you should view parallel as belonging to the category of CSP operators (for example $\sqcap$) whose main role is in constructing specifications rather than implementations.

Suppose Q is a process using only events from Y. In $P \mathbin{{}_\Sigma\|_Y} Q = P \mathbin{\underset{Y}{\|}} Q$, it can be thought of as adding to P, since every communication of P in Y must be possible for Q. As P participates in all of the combination's events, we can think of Q's role as simply being to restrict P's behaviour. If P represents a trace specification, then $P \mathbin{{}_\Sigma\|_Y} Q$ is a stronger one.

As a simple example, consider a robot which roams around the plane by making movements in the four directions $\{N, S, E, W\}$. It can also report its position. If its initial co-ordinates are $(0,0)$, it becomes the process $ROBOT_{0,0}$ where

$$
\begin{aligned}
ROBOT_{n,m} \quad=\quad & position.(n,m) \to ROBOT_{n,m} \\
& \square\; N \to ROBOT_{n+1,m} \\
& \square\; S \to ROBOT_{n-1,m} \\
& \square\; E \to ROBOT_{n,m+1} \\
& \square\; W \to ROBOT_{n,m-1}
\end{aligned}
$$

We can restrict the area it can roam over by placing it parallel with processes stopping it entering forbidden areas. For example, if it is actually sitting on a rectangular table whose corners are $\{(0,0), (n,0), (n,m), (0,m)\}$ then we can enforce this either by putting it in parallel with four $COUNT$-like processes:

$CT(E,W)_0$	alphabet $\{E, W\}$
$CT(W,E)_m$	alphabet $\{E, W\}$
$CT(N,S)_0$	alphabet $\{N, S\}$
$CT(S,N)_n$	alphabet $\{N, S\}$

where

$$CT(a, b)_0 = a \to CT(a, b)_1$$
$$CT(a, b)_r = a \to CT(a, b)_{r+1}$$
$$\square\ b \to CT(a, b)_{r-1} \quad \text{if } r > 0$$

or by using two processes (each imposing both limits in one dimension) or just one (imposing all four limits). We could prevent it entering a specific square, (r, s), say, by placing it in parallel with the following process with alphabet $\{N, S, E, W\}$:

$$BLOCK(r, s)_{n,m} =$$
$$(N \to BLOCK(r, s)_{n+1,m}) \blacktriangleleft n \neq r-1 \vee m \neq s \blacktriangleright STOP$$
$$\square\ (S \to BLOCK(r, s)_{n-1,m}) \blacktriangleleft n \neq r+1 \vee m \neq s \blacktriangleright STOP$$
$$\square\ (E \to BLOCK(r, s)_{n,m-1}) \blacktriangleleft n \neq r \vee m \neq s+1 \blacktriangleright STOP$$
$$\square\ (W \to BLOCK(r, s)_{n,m+1}) \blacktriangleleft n \neq r \vee m \neq s-1 \blacktriangleright STOP$$

Note the use we have again made here of the conditional construct to reduce the number of clauses. Clearly we can use as many of these as we like to ban any finite region of space. Notice that $BLOCK(0,0)$ stops the robot from re-entering the origin once it has left it – it cannot be prevented from being there initially!

Other things we could do would be to stop it doing more than K actions in total say, representing its fuel capacity, or from communicating its position when in specified areas.

One of the simplest and most useful examples of this style is the banning of events: $P\ _\Sigma\|_X\ STOP = P\ \|_X\ STOP$ is the process which behaves like P except that events in X are banned.

This style of use of the parallel operator amounts to building up a complex behaviour by adding together a number of simple constraints. Clearly the number of participants in a given action in this example might get very large. But this need not worry us since, as we already know, it is quite possible to have a parallel process equivalent to a sequential one, and the eventual implementation of our specification will almost certainly be very different from the combination of the parallel constraints.

The exercises below illustrate this style well, and we will see further examples at various points in this book, especially in Section 15.1.

EXERCISE 2.5.1   We can describe a bank as a process that simply opens and closes:

$$BANK = bank\_open \to bank\_close \to BANK$$

Interleave this with the process that records what day of the week it is:

$$DAYS = Monday \to Tuesday \to \ldots \to Sunday \to DAYS$$

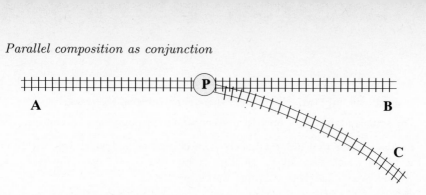

Figure 2.6 Some railway track (see Exercise 2.5.3).

Express the following as parallel constraints to this system:

(i) It opens no more than once per day.

(ii) It is always closed at midnight (when the day events occur).

(iii) It is never open on a Sunday.

(iv) It is always open at least two times per week.

EXERCISE 2.5.2   Put your solutions to the previous exercise and Exercise 1.1.3 in parallel via interleaving. Impose the following constraints:

(i) An account can only be opened or closed when the bank is open.

(ii) Balance enquiries may not be made on Sundays.

EXERCISE 2.5.3   Figure 2.6 shows a section of a railway network. There are signals at A, B, C governing entry to the section, and points at P which connect the line from A to either B or C. The alphabet is as follows:

signal.X.Y   for $X \in \{A, B, C\}$ and $Y \in \{red, green\}$ indicate the change of the signal at X to colour Y

point.X   for $X \in \{B, C\}$ represents the points being switched to connect A to X

enter.X.t   for $X \in \{A, B, C\}$ and $t \in$ *Trains* represents train t entering the section at X

leave.X.t   (X and t as above) represents t leaving at X.

Assume that initially all signals are red, the points connect A to B, and the track is empty.

Give trace specifications for each of the following properties:

(i) Each signal alternates between turning green and red.

(ii) Only one signal can be green at any time.

(iii) The points alternate between the two directions.

(iv) The points only switch when all signals are red and there is no train on the track.

(v) A signal can only turn green when there is no train on the track.

(vi) The signals at B and C only turn green when the points are appropriately set.

Build a process that meets all of these specifications and which has, within reason, all of the traces which they allow. Do this by building one or more processes for each constraint and combining them appropriately in parallel.

The above specifications allow a train to enter against a red signal. Introduce an extra event *alarm* which occurs (before anything else) if this happens, and modify your process definition appropriately.

2.6   Tools

The last three binary parallel operators we have seen are supported in machine-readable CSP. They are written as follows:

$P \ _X\|_Y \ Q$ is written P [X||Y] Q

$P \ ||| \ Q$ is written P ||| Q

$P \ \|_X \ Q$ is written P [|X|] Q

($P \| Q$ can easily be modelled using the others, for example P[|Events|] Q.)

Indexed versions are written as follows:

$\left\|\right\|_{i=1}^{N}(P_i, A_i)$ is written|| i:{1..N} @ [A(i)] P(i)

$\left\|\right\|\right\|_{i=1}^{N} P_i$ is written||| i:{1..N} @ P(i)

$\left\|\right\|_{X\ i=1}^{N} P_i$ is written[|X|] i:{1..N} @ P(i)

Note that the last of these assumes that all the P_i synchronize on the set X, and that no other event is synchronized at all.

The addition of parallel operators has an enormous effect on the expressive power of the language, in the sense that it becomes possible to describe many complex and interesting systems concisely and naturally. One effect that is very noticeable is the exponential *state explosion* that can, and frequently does, occur when we put a lot of processes in parallel. If each P_i has just two states, then $\left\|\right\|\right\|_{i=1}^{N} P_i$ has 2^N. Synchronizing events, as in $\left\|\right\|_{i=1}^{N}(P_i, A_i)$, usually prevents the combination reaching *some* arrangements of component states; it often leaves enough of them to leave a lot of work.

With an animator this state explosion only shows up if you seek to cover all the states, but with a model checker[2] you usually have to visit each reachable state, and so it is common experience (one each reader who uses these techniques will doubtless share) that the time and space taken for refinement checks frequently increases exponentially with the size of a parallel system.

Overcoming this complexity barrier is a major active research topic at the time of writing. It seems most unlikely that it can be got around for *every* parallel combination and specification; the objective is to do so for as many classes of useful problems as possible. We will discuss the techniques FDR uses at several later points in this book, especially Section C.2, when we understand enough of the theory.

The existence of this barrier does not prevent one from modelling many systems which are both non-trivial and practical without any attempt to get around it at all other than by making the enumeration of states as efficient as possible in both space and time, and sometimes careful coding of the CSP to avoid *unnecessary* states. Thus at the time of writing FDR can, even on the author's laptop computer, deal entirely explicitly with combinations with order 10^7 states at several million states per hour.

In order to achieve this efficiency, FDR uses very different techniques for computing the state spaces of *low-level* processes (broadly speaking, ones definable in the syntax introduced in Chapter 1) and *high-level* ones (broadly speaking, parallel combinations of low-level ones). When FDR says it is *compiling* a system it is using relatively slow symbolic techniques for turning low-level components into explicit state-machines. This does not enumerate the states of the entire system (assuming it involves a high-level construct), but rather gives efficient rules for computing the initial actions and next states of any combination of low-level states that might arise.

A process structured as the parallel combination of reasonably-sized low-level components will thus tend to be explored much more efficiently by FDR than an equivalent one which is structured so that it is entirely compiled at low level. Certainly one of the keys to the successful use of FDR is an understanding of this fact and the division into high- and low-level syntax that lies behind it. This is explained in more detail in Appendix C.

---

[2] *Model checker* is the name for the class of tools to which FDR belongs in a broad sense: one can define a model checker as a tool which seeks to verify that a system which is defined by transitions between (sometimes very large) finite sets of states satisfies some specification and which performs the verification by traversing the entire state space. (This traversal might be one-state-at-a-time or use some way of dealing with many at once.) In other classes of model checkers, the specification is usually defined in a language other than that used for the implementation (often a specially defined logic). What characterizes a refinement checker like FDR is that the specification is another process in the same language.

2.7   Postscript: On alphabets

The most significant difference between the version of CSP used in this book and
that in Hoare's text is the treatment of *alphabets*. Hoare stipulates that every
process P has its own associated alphabet αP. One can think of the alphabet of a
process as representing its type. A process may only communicate events from its
alphabet, but there may be events in its alphabet which it can never communicate
and which do not even appear in its description. The presence of alphabets makes
the parallel operator more elegant, since by writing $P \parallel Q$ we know immediately
that P has control over αP and Q has control over αQ, and so they interact in, and
must co-operate on, $\alpha P \cap \alpha Q$. This is in contrast with our version where alphabets
are given explicitly: $P \ _X\|_Y \ Q$. Hoare makes a number of stipulations about the
alphabets of the processes that are composed together; most of the operators require
that all processes combined have the same alphabet and that the result is the same
again. Others, such as $\parallel$ and hiding, have special rules. The CSP operators in the
alphabetized theory are thus *polymorphic* in a sense very close to the usual one.

The disadvantages of the alphabetized version of CSP are firstly the need
to give *all* processes alphabets (which can clutter definitions, especially recursions),
the occasional need for special language constructs to get the 'typing' right, and
additional theoretical complexity. The main manifestation of the last of these is the
need to construct separate mathematical models for every different alphabet where
we can get away with just one.

The choice of one version or the other is largely a matter of taste, though it
is certainly the case that the balance changes from application to application. We
do not regard this as an important issue, since everything done in one version of
CSP can be done in the other with trivial changes.

In this book we sometimes refer to the 'alphabet' of a process. This, in an
informal sense, means the same as Hoare's, namely the set of communications it
might use. However, whenever *we* need such an alphabet to have semantic significance (as in the set of events a P controls in a parallel combination), it has to be
defined and used explicitly.

Chapter 3

Hiding and renaming

It is often useful either to remove certain actions from the view of the environment or to apply mappings to a process's events. In this chapter we introduce the operators that allow us to do these things.

3.1   Hiding

Consider the parallel combination of $COPY'(c_r, c_{r+1})$ processes we saw on page 58. We said there that it would be natural to think of c_0 and c_n as being external channels, and the others as internal ones. If they really are internal then the fact that we can still see the communications passing along them is unfortunate from several points of view.

- Seeing these communications clutters up our picture of the process and makes it impossible to show that this system behaves like an n-place buffer implemented some other way. We should not have to see unnecessary internal details of a system.

- By leaving the internal communications visible we are leaving open the possibility that another process might be put in parallel with the currently defined network, with some of these internal events in its alphabet. Thus, it would be able to stop these events from happening. In this case, and in many like it, we would expect 'internal' communications such as these to proceed without requiring further control from outside.

Both of these difficulties can be avoided by *hiding* the internal events, making them invisible to and uncontrollable by the environment.

Given any process P and any set of events X, the process $P \setminus X$ behaves like P except that the events from X have been internalized in this way. If we want to hide a single event or channel a then we will sometimes write $P \setminus a$ rather than $P \setminus \{a\}$ or $P \setminus \{| a |\}$.

Thus, if we want to hide all the communication between a pair of parallel processes we would write $(P \ _X\|_Y \ Q) \setminus (X \cap Y)$ or $(P \ \|_Z \ Q) \setminus Z$. This creates point-to-point, invisible communication, which is arguably closest to the 'natural' parallel operator of implementations such as OCCAM. In specifying a real parallel communicating system, rather than one devised as a specification where the parallel operator takes the role of conjunction as described in Section 2.5, one almost always uses a combination of the parallel and hiding operators.[1] The natural view of the chain of buffers would be

$$(\|_{r=0}^{n-1} (COPY'(c_r, c_{r+1}), \{| c_r, c_{r+1} |\})) \setminus (\{| c_1, \ldots, c_{n-1} |\})$$

The only communications visible in this system are its inputs and outputs, namely $\{| c_0, c_n |\}$. Since we are no longer seeing the internal workings, we can potentially prove this equivalent to a totally different one which might have different internal channels or none at all, or to another CSP description intended as a specification.

Perhaps the easiest way of understanding the effect of the hiding operator is to see how it transforms the picture of a process's transitions. We saw a few of these in previous chapters (Figures 1.1, 1.2, etc.). Any process can be given such a *transition system*, which provides a much less abstract view of how it behaves than its set of traces[2]. The shape of the transition system remains exactly the same, but hidden actions are transformed into *invisible* actions, which we label τ (the Greek letter 'tau'). An example is shown in Figure 3.1. Invisible (or internal) actions are to be thought of as ones which (a) do not contribute to the trace, because the environment cannot see them and (b) the process can perform by itself. τ is a special event that is never in Σ.

Since it is a unary (one-place) rather than binary operator (on processes), the only one of the 'usual' sorts of algebraic laws that apply to it is the distributive law. There is a rich collection of laws, nevertheless, of which the following are a few:

$$(P \sqcap Q) \setminus X = (P \setminus X) \sqcap (Q \setminus X) \qquad \langle \text{hide-dist} \rangle \qquad (3.1$$

---

[1] Some other process algebras, notably CCS, combine parallel and hiding into a single operator: they do not factor the 'natural' operator into two parts like CSP.

[2] A complete set of recipes for deriving these transition systems is given in Chapter 7, where it is the method of presenting the operational semantics of CSP.

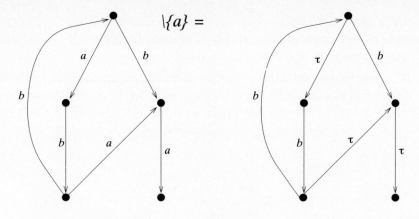

Figure 3.1 The effects of hiding on a transition system.

$$(P \setminus Y) \setminus X \;=\; (P \setminus X) \setminus Y \qquad\qquad \langle\text{hide-sym}\rangle \quad (3.2)$$

$$(P \setminus Y) \setminus X \;=\; P \setminus (X \cup Y) \qquad\qquad \langle\text{hide-combine}\rangle \quad (3.3)$$

$$P \setminus \{\} \;=\; P \qquad\qquad \langle\text{null hiding}\rangle \quad (3.4)$$

$$(a \to P) \setminus X \;=\; \left\{ \begin{array}{ll} P \setminus X & \text{if } a \in X \\ a \to (P \setminus X) & \text{if } a \notin X \end{array} \right. \qquad \langle\text{hide-step 1}\rangle \quad (3.5)$$

The second of these is an easy consequence of the third. The final law above shows the hiding actually happening: the a disappears when it is an element of X. Note that this shows that a process whose only initial action is a single τ is equivalent to whatever state follows the τ.

This is not a full 'step' law, in the sense we have already used to describe other operators, since that requires the process to have an arbitrary set of initial actions. The full version is more complex because it has to deal with what happens when (i) there is a choice of hidden actions and (ii) there is a choice between hidden and visible actions. Rather than writing down the whole law immediately let us look at each of these two situations separately.

$$(a \to P \,\square\, b \to Q) \setminus \{a, b\}$$

has two hidden actions possible. Now only one happens, and we cannot be sure which, so in fact this equates to $(P \setminus \{a, b\}) \sqcap (Q \setminus \{a, b\})$. This creates the first principle we are looking for here: when there is more than one hidden action possible, it is nondeterministic which occurs. And in fact the usual[3] way of creating a transition picture of the process $P \sqcap Q$ is by creating one whose initial state has two τ actions: one to P and one to Q.

It is tempting to think that we should either give hidden actions the ability to exclude visible ones from the same choice – because the hidden action occurs as soon as it is possible – or perhaps the reverse. In fact, neither of these views is consistent with what we already know. Consider the process

$$(a \to P \,\square\, b \to Q) \setminus b$$

(the same as above except that only one of the two events is hidden). If either the unhidden or the hidden event were preferred, this would equal

$$a \to P \setminus b \qquad \text{or} \qquad Q \setminus b$$

which, if we then hid a, would in either case give a different answer from hiding $\{a, b\}$ together, in contradiction to the law $\langle$hide-combine$\rangle$. Thus both the hidden and unhidden actions must remain possible. The right way to think about how this type of process behaves is that as soon as an internal action becomes available then *something* must happen, but it might be a visible action rather than a hidden one. Unless we do manage to get a visible communication, a hidden one must occur. The right answer to what the above process equals turns out to be

$$((a \to (P \setminus b)) \sqcap STOP) \,\square\, (Q \setminus b)$$

We must get the options of $Q \setminus b$ if we wait long enough, but may also get the chance of the a if we are quick enough. The principle underlying this is that, in a choice between visible and hidden actions, we *may* get the chance of communicating one of the visible ones, but given a long enough wait, one of the hidden ones *must* occur. It is perhaps easiest to understand this by considering transition pictures like Figure 3.2.

The combination $(P \sqcap STOP) \,\square\, Q$ arises frequently in theoretical work on CSP because of this phenomenon with hiding. It is convenient to introduce an extra, asymmetric choice operator to represent it directly: $P \rhd Q$. This can be thought of as a 'time-out' or 'sliding choice' operator in which, as above, the options of P are offered for a short time before it opts to behave like Q. For obvious reasons the representation of a time-out is very imperfect in a model without time – we will see how to make them more realistic in Chapter 14. There is no need to quote $P \rhd Q$'s

---

[3]This is exactly how FDR and ProBE represent nondeterministic choice, as previously described in Section 1.4.

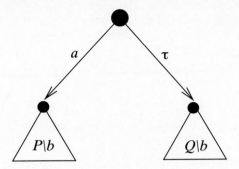

Figure 3.2 Hiding creating a 'time-out'.

algebraic laws, etc., formally because they can all be derived from those of $\sqcap$, $\square$ and *STOP*. See Exercise 3.1.6, for example.

The complete step law for hiding is given below:

$$(?x : A \to P) \setminus X \ =$$

$$\begin{cases} ?x : A \to (P \setminus X) & \text{if } A \cap X = \{\} \\ (?x : (A \setminus X) \to (P \setminus X)) \\ \quad \rhd \sqcap \{(P[a/x]) \setminus X \mid a \in A \cap X\} & \text{if } A \cap X \neq \{\} \end{cases} \qquad \langle \text{hide-step} \rangle \quad (3.6)$$

It should be noticed that this 'step' law is unlike all of the ones we have seen before, in that, while it obviously uses one step of the process it is applied *to*, it does not necessarily give us the first visible action of the *result*. Of course this is perfectly natural with a hiding operator, but it does mean that one might never come to a conclusion from it about what the initial actions of $P \setminus X$ are: just think what would happen if you were to apply it to $(\mu\, p.a \to p) \setminus a$.

Notice that in the buffer example above we hid all the internal communications at once, at the outermost level, where we could have combined the cells in steps hiding the internal channels as we go. This is represented by the complex expression

$$((\ldots(COPY'(c_0, c_1)\ {}_{\{|c_0,c_1|\}}\|_{\{|c_1,c_2|\}}\ COPY'(c_1, c_2)) \setminus \{|\ c_1\ |\} \ldots)$$

$${}_{\{|c_0,c_{n-1}|\}}\|_{\{|c_{n-1},c_n|\}}\ COPY'(c_{n-1}, c_n)) \setminus \{|\ c_{n-1}\ |\}$$

(We will see a much more convenient way of writing this down in Section 4.1.) Provided that moving the hiding does not influence the number of processes that have to agree on an action, it should not matter whether we hide that action at an inner or an outer level of a parallel combination. Thus, we can expect

$$(P \,_X\|_Y\, Q) \setminus Z = (P \setminus Z \cap X) \,_X\|_Y\, (Q \setminus Z \cap Y)$$
$$\text{provided } X \cap Y \cap Z = \{\}$$

$\langle \text{hide-}_X\|_Y\text{-dist} \rangle$ (3.

$$(P \,\underset{X}{\|}\, Q) \setminus Z = (P \setminus Z) \,\underset{X}{\|}\, (Q \setminus Z)$$
$$\text{provided } X \cap Z = \{\}$$

$\langle \text{hide-}\underset{X}{\|}\text{-dist} \rangle$ (3.

These laws are helpful in understanding how a network put together with parallel and hiding operators behaves: we can move all the hiding to the outermost level so we can 'see' all of the communications in the network at once before applying a single hiding operator to get rid of the ones we don't want to see. As we will see in later chapters, these laws are vital in support of reasoning about deadlock, and are crucial in advanced model-checking techniques.

Hiding can remove other details aside from communications between partners. For example, we might want to conceal the spending of *CUST spend* and the refilling of *ATM ref* in order to concentrate on their common interface.

$$CUST\,spend_r \setminus spend.\mathbb{N}$$

can be expected to behave exactly like $CUST2$, while $ATM\,ref_r \setminus refill$ behaves like an *implementation* of $ATM2$: it is strictly more deterministic because it never swallows the card. It is nevertheless nondeterministic, even though $ATM\,ref_r$ is deterministic, because since we cannot see when the machine is being refilled, we get imperfect knowledge of when a request for funds is refused. Notice how this hiding of details actually invisible to the customer makes the ATM exhibit nondeterminism, just as he or she observes. We will study the process of *abstracting* like this from a subset of a process's events in Chapter 12.

Hiding is the most common source of nondeterminism in CSP descriptions. It often shows up in real systems where one parallel partner has to arbitrate between two others. For example, we know that the process

$$P = a \rightarrow c \rightarrow STOP \,\square\, b \rightarrow d \rightarrow STOP$$

offers the environment the choice between a and b, with subsequent behaviour depending on which option is chosen. If we give it the alphabet $X = \{a, b, c, d\}$ of all events it can perform, then simply putting it in parallel with processes which choose a and b respectively does not change the way it looks to the outside world:

$$N = P \,_X\|_{\{a,b\}}\, (a \rightarrow STOP \,_{\{a\}}\|_{\{b\}}\, b \rightarrow STOP)$$

N can be expected to behave in the same way as P. If, however, we 'complete' the parallel composition by hiding the internal events $N \setminus \{a, b\}$ then we introduce nondeterminism. The result will behave like

$$(c \to STOP) \sqcap (d \to STOP)$$

This type of behaviour is what makes nondeterminism an inevitable constituent of any theory describing concurrency where arbitration is present in some form.

If we had allowed our ATM to be refilled when full, or the customer to spend a zero sum, then the hiding above would have introduced *divergence*, which is the possibility of a process entering into an infinite sequence of internal actions. For then the ATM would allow an infinite sequence of hidden *refill* actions without ever interacting with the user, and the customer could perform an infinite number of hidden *spend*.0's. Clearly a process which is diverging is useless, and arguably more useless than $STOP$, since we can never detect by the lack of internal activity that a diverging state will never do anything. A common source of divergence in CSP occurs in parallel networks with internal communications hidden, where the processes can communicate infinitely with each other without ever communicating externally. This is sometimes termed 'livelock' or 'infinite internal chatter'.

On the same principle that led us to introduce an operator for nondeterminism (i.e., that it is useful to have a clean representation of it) we will use a special symbol for a divergent process: **div** is the process that does nothing but diverge.[4] The only way of introducing divergence except through hiding and the symbol **div** is by ill-formed recursions. The simplest recursive definition of them all, $\mu\, p.p$ is an example: clearly evaluating it will lead to an infinite unwinding without getting anywhere. Divergence plays an important role in the mathematical modelling of CSP, so we will meet **div** frequently in later chapters.

Particular care has to be exercised in dealing with *infinite* hiding, i.e., $P \setminus X$ for infinite sets of events X. For it can introduce unbounded nondeterminism in just the same way as the unconstrained use of $\sqcap$. That this is so is readily demonstrated: if $S = \{P_\lambda \mid \lambda \in \Lambda\}$ for a set of events Λ chosen to be disjoint from those which the P_λ themselves can communicate, then clearly

$$\bigsqcap S \;=\; (\lambda : \Lambda \to P_\lambda) \setminus \Lambda$$

---

[4]In Hoare's text, the process $CHAOS$ is assumed to be able to diverge as well as everything else it can do, and there is no special representation for a simply diverging process. We distinguish the special process **div** because it represents an important concept and, as we will see in later chapters, different mathematical theories of CSP treat it in widely varying ways. For us, *Chaos* is not a divergent process and is in every model equivalent to its definition on page 29.

The traces of $P \setminus X$ are very easy to compute: if we define $\dot{s} \setminus X$, for any trace s, to be $s \restriction (\Sigma \setminus X)$, then

$$traces(P \setminus X) = \{s \setminus X \mid s \in traces(P)\}$$

Hiding *versus* constructiveness

It must be pointed out that the very useful notion of a guarded recursion fits uneasily with hiding. For the meaning of 'guarded' is that information – in the sense of communications – is added by a recursion. Another (and, in general, more accurate) term we can use is 'constructive'. Hiding deletes events: consider the recursion

$$P = a \rightarrow (P \setminus a)$$

which, according to our earlier definition, is guarded because the recursive call is prefixed by an event. The problem is that communications are deleted by the hiding, so that what the recursion gives with one hand it takes away with the other. In fact this recursion does not have a unique fixed point over the traces model $\mathcal{T}$: if S is any member of $\mathcal{T}$ at all (possibly able to communicate events other than a), then

$$\{\langle\rangle\} \cup \{\langle a\rangle^\frown(s \setminus a) \mid s \in S\}$$

is a solution to the fixed point equation we get from the recursion. The least and natural solution is, of course, $\{\langle\rangle, \langle a\rangle\}$. After the trace $\langle a\rangle$ we would expect that this process would diverge, since it would perform a sequence of increasingly deeply hidden a's. Our intuition, therefore, is that this $P = a \rightarrow \mathbf{div}$.

This behaviour forces us to add a caveat to the definition of guardedness: no recursion in which the hiding operator is applied (directly or indirectly) to a recursive call should be considered guarded (at least, without a careful analysis based on mathematical models).

Of course, this restriction applies equally to the *derived* operators we will meet later that use hiding in their definition. In a few cases it is possible to assert that recursions involving hiding are constructive, but to do this we will have to understand the mathematics of constructiveness a great deal better: see an example on page 103 and Sections 8.2 and 9.2 for some of the theory.

It is easy to think that the above restriction prevents us from applying the UFP rule to any process involving hiding: this is not so, it is only the recursion to which the rule is applied that has to be constructive. A good example is the process we get when we hide the internal channel of the combination we studied in the last chapter:

$$(COPY'(a, b) \;_{\{|a,b|\}}\|_{\{|b,c|\}}\; COPY'(b, c)) \setminus \{| \; b \; |\}$$

Now of course we already know that the process inside the hiding is equivalent to CC_0', where

$$
\begin{aligned}
CC_0' &= a?x \rightarrow CC_1'(x) \\
CC_1'(x) &= b!x \rightarrow CC_2'(x) \\
CC_2'(x) &= (c!x \rightarrow CC_0') \;\square\; (a?y \rightarrow CC_3'(y, x)) \\
CC_3'(y, x) &= c!x \rightarrow CC_1'(y)
\end{aligned}
$$

When we hide $\{| \; b \; |\}$ in this we find (applying $\langle$hide-step$\rangle$) that

$$
\begin{aligned}
CC_0' \setminus b &= a?x \rightarrow CC_1'(x) \setminus b \\
CC_1'(x) \setminus b &= CC_2'(x) \setminus b \\
CC_2'(x) \setminus b &= (c!x \rightarrow CC_0' \setminus b) \;\square\; (a?y \rightarrow CC_3'(y, x) \setminus b) \\
CC_3'(y, x) \setminus b &= c!x \rightarrow CC_1'(y) \setminus b
\end{aligned}
$$

which is not (applying the usual trick of replacing each term on the left-hand side by a new recursive variable) guarded. However, the above equations imply trivially that $CC_0' \setminus b$, $CC_1'(x) \setminus b$ and $CC_3'(y, x) \setminus b$ satisfy the recursive definition

$$
\begin{aligned}
B_0^2 &= a?x \rightarrow B_1^2(x) \\
B_1^2(x) &= a?y \rightarrow B_2^2(y, x) \\
&\quad\;\;\square\; c!x \rightarrow B_0^2 \\
B_2^2(y, x) &= c!x \rightarrow B_2^1(y)
\end{aligned}
$$

which *is* guarded. So we have shown that our original processes satisfy this guarded recursion and therefore equal its unique fixed point. It is quite irrelevant that the definition of the original processes involved hiding. There was, we should point out, no need to go through the intermediate step of discovering the C' recursion: it would have been just as good to prove that a vector of parallel/hiding combinations satisfy the B^2 recursion.

Note that what we actually proved here was that the parallel combination of two one-place buffers, placed in parallel with the middle channel hidden, behaves like a two-place buffer – clearly something we would expect.

EXERCISE 3.1.1   Take the dining philosophers network from pages 61 and 67 with the *picksup* and *putsdown* events hidden (after the entire network has been combined). Can this system still deadlock? Do you think hiding can ever affect deadlock? *Think carefully and write down your conclusions – we will later develop theories that will answer this question definitively.*

EXERCISE 3.1.2   If $P = (a \rightarrow P) \; \Box \; (b \rightarrow a \rightarrow P)$, we would expect that $P \setminus b$ is equivalent to $\mu \, p.a \rightarrow p$. Use $\langle \mathsf{hide\text{-}step} \rangle$ (3.6) and the laws of choice to show that

$$P \setminus b \; = \; a \rightarrow (P \setminus b)$$

and hence that this equivalence is true by the UFP rule. *Make sure you understand why the rule is valid here when it was invalid on the very similar equation $P = a \rightarrow (P \setminus a)$.*

EXERCISE 3.1.3   If $P = a?x \rightarrow b!x \rightarrow b!x \rightarrow P$ then it is possible to find a process Q such that

$$(P \; {}_{\{|a,b|\}}\|_{\{|b,c|\}} \; Q) \setminus \{| \, b \, |\} \; =_T \; COPY'(a,c)$$

(i.e., a one-place buffer). Find Q and use the UFP rule to prove the equivalence.

EXERCISE 3.1.4   Give a CSP expression defining the process equivalent to the one on the left-hand side of Figure 3.1. Use the step law and laws about the choice operators to prove that the hidden process $P \setminus \{a\}$ satisfies the equation

$$P \setminus \{a\} \; = \; b \rightarrow (STOP \sqcap b \rightarrow P \setminus \{a\})$$

EXERCISE 3.1.5   Use $\langle \sqcap\text{-}\Box\text{-dist} \rangle$, $\langle \Box\text{-dist} \rangle$ and other standard laws to prove that

$$(Q \; \Box \; R) \sqcap STOP \; = \; (Q \; \Box \; R) \sqcap Q \sqcap R \sqcap STOP \quad \text{and hence}$$

$$(P \; \Box \; Q \; \Box \; R) \sqcap P \; = \; (P \; \Box \; Q \; \Box \; R) \sqcap (P \; \Box \; Q) \sqcap P$$

EXERCISE 3.1.6   Prove, using the laws set out in Section 1.2, that $\rhd$ is distributive in each argument and is associative. *Hint: for associativity, use the result of the previous exercise.*

Can you find any other laws it satisfies (perhaps in relation to other operators)?

3.2   Renaming and alphabet transformations

In the previous section we saw how to remove certain events from sight. A less drastic effect is achieved by *renaming*, which means applying a map that changes which (visible) member of Σ a process is performing.

While one can imagine that the alphabet transformation thus accomplished might change through the life of a process – perhaps event a maps to b if it appears before the 12th event and to c later – in practice we rarely want to do this. Thus, our renaming operators apply the same transformation throughout a process's life: in this section we see three increasingly general ways of doing this.[5]

3.2.1   Injective functions

Suppose P is a CSP process and $f : \Sigma \to \Sigma$ is an injective, or 1–1, function (simply meaning that $f(x) = f(y)$ implies $x = y$) from Σ to itself. f can be a *partial* function provided its domain contains every event possible for P. Then $f[P]$ is the process which can communicate $f(a)$ whenever P can communicate a. The communications of P have been *renamed*, or equivalently P has been subjected to an *alphabet transformation*. The transition system of $f[P]$ is that of P with the function f applied to the arcs.

All of this works whether f is injective or not. The reason why we want to distinguish this case is because it is both simpler to understand and is used most often in CSP descriptions of real systems. The point is that, in this case, $f[P]$ works *exactly* like P except for the names of its events. (The sense in which this is not true when f is not 1–1 will be seen later.)

If f is the function that swaps the events *down* and *up*, then $f[COUNT_0]$ will behave like a counter through the negative numbers, since it will never allow any more *up*'s than *down*'s.

If g is a function that maps (for any $x \in T$) *left.x* to *a.x* and *right.x* to *b.x* then $g[COPY]$ is the same as the parameterized process $COPY'(a, b)$ (assuming, of course, that *left*, *right*, a and b are all channels of type T). One could similarly devise a renaming that would map a single $FORK_i$ from the dining philosophers to any other $FORK_j$, and likewise for the philosopher processes. In each case this is possible because, except for the names of their events, the target process always behaves identically to the original: evidently no renaming could make $FORK_i$ into $PHIL_i$!

Thus, renaming is an alternative to parameterization as a way of creating many similar processes to put into a network. Which method is better depends on the example and the taste of the programmer.

One form of renaming that is useful when we want to create copies of a process with entirely disjoint alphabets is *process naming*. If the compound event $a.x$ is in Σ for each event communicable by P, then $a.P$ is the process which communicates

---

[5]In Section 14.4.1 we will see how the variable renaming can be constructed by combining constant renaming with other constructs; see also Exercise 3.2.5 below.

$a.x$ whenever P communicates x. The renaming function here is clear, but this form of use is sufficiently common that the shorthand $a.P$ is commonly used. If $a_1, a_2, \ldots, a_n$ are distinct names, we can get n copies of P running independently in parallel by naming them:

$$\Big\|_{r=1}^{n} (a_r.P, a_r.X) \quad \text{or equivalently} \quad \big\||\big|_{r=1}^{n} a_r.P$$

where X is whatever alphabet is natural for P and $a.X = \{a.x \mid x \in X\}$. Since these processes have disjoint alphabets they do not interact at all. If either the environment or another process wants to communicate with one of them it has to select the one by name, since the communications all include the given name.

Since injective renaming leaves the behaviour of a process unchanged except for the names of actions, it has an extremely rich set of laws – too many to write down conveniently! Essentially it distributes over all operators. We will give a list of laws that apply to any sort of renaming later, but three that apply specifically to this one are

$$f[P \parallel_{X} Q] = f[P] \parallel_{f(X)} f[Q] \quad \text{if } f \text{ is 1–1} \qquad \langle f[\cdot]\text{-}\|\text{-dist}\rangle_{X} \qquad (3.$$

$$f[P \ _X\|_Y \ Q] = f[P] \ _{f(X)}\|_{f(Y)} \ f[Q] \quad \text{if } f \text{ is 1–1} \qquad \langle f[\cdot]\text{-}_X\|_Y\text{-dist}\rangle \quad (3.1$$

$$f[P \setminus X] = f[P] \setminus f(X) \quad \text{if } f \text{ is 1–1} \qquad \langle f[\cdot]\text{-hide-sym}\rangle \quad (3.1$$

The third of these is frequently used, in combination with the following, to change the name of hidden actions. This might be done to prevent a clash of names for the subsequent application of other laws. An example may be found in Section 13.7.

$$f[P \setminus X] = P \setminus X \quad \text{if } f(y) = y \text{ for all } y \in \Sigma \setminus X \qquad \langle f[\cdot]\text{-hide-null}\rangle \quad (3.1$$

3.2.2   Non-injective functions

The most common use of renaming $f[P]$ when f is not injective on the events of P is when we want to forget about some level of detail in a process. Consider a splitting process which accepts inputs on channel *in* and, depending on what the input is, sends it either to *out1* or to *out2*.

$$SPLIT \ = \ in?x : T \to$$
$$((out1.x \to SPLIT) \triangleleft x \in S \triangleright (out2.x \to SPLIT))$$

For some purposes the composition of messages may be unimportant. If we forget that detail by using the renaming function *forget* which remembers only the channel name, the process *forget*[*SPLIT*] we get is equivalent to *SPLIT'*, where

$$SPLIT' \quad = \quad in \to (out1 \to SPLIT' \sqcap out2 \to SPLIT')$$

This has introduced nondeterminism because we have deliberately forgotten the information which allowed us to know whether *out1* or *out2* occurs. Though this might appear a retrograde step, this type of abstraction is frequently beneficial, for

- it allows us to demonstrate that some aspect of the correctness of the system does not depend on precisely how decisions are made, and

- in cases where this is true the details of decision making frequently clutter proofs.

Several examples of this type of abstraction in deadlock analysis can be found later, on pages 348 and 363, for example.

Non-injective renaming becomes more dangerous when the alphabet transformation f in use maps an infinite set of events to a single one (i.e., f is not finite-to-one). This, like $\sqcap S$ for infinite S, and $P \setminus X$ for infinite X, is a construct which can introduce unbounded nondeterminism.

3.2.3   Relational renaming

Various treatments of CSP have included a second sort of renaming, using *inverse* functions: $f^{-1}[P]$ can communicate a whenever P can communicate $f(a)$. This is equivalent in expressive power to the direct image renaming we have already seen when f is 1–1, but it can produce some interesting effects when f is many-to-one. For a single event in P can be transformed into the choice between many different ones – though all leading to the same place. What we will now describe here is a more general form of renaming that encompasses both direct and inverse functions, and at the same time corresponds most closely to the notation for renaming used in machine-readable CSP.

A function can be thought of as a set of ordered pairs: (x, y) is in the set if $f(x) = y$. A set of pairs is a function if no x is mapped to more than one y. A *relation* on the other hand, is any set of ordered pairs, with no restriction as to how many things a given object can be related to. If $(x, y) \in R$ we write $x \, R \, y$. If R is a relation, its *domain* and *range* are respectively

$$\begin{aligned} dom(R) \quad &= \quad \{x \mid \exists \, y.x \, R \, y\} \\ ran(R) \quad &= \quad \{y \mid \exists \, x.x \, R \, y\} \end{aligned}$$

The composition of two relations $R \circ S$ is

$$\{(x, z) \mid \exists\, y.\, x\, R\, y \wedge y\, S\, z\}$$

(confusingly, because of a clash of conventions, this is the opposite way round to the way composition of functions works). The *relational image* $R(x)$ of x under R is $\{y \mid x\, R\, y\}$.

If R is a relation whose domain includes all the events of P, then $P[\![R]\!]$ is the process that can perform each event in $R(a)$ whenever P can perform a. If R is a function then this is identical to the renaming $R[P]$. If f is a function then its inverse f^{-1} is the relation $\{(y, x) \mid (x, y) \in f\}$. The operator $f^{-1}[P]$ is then identical to $P[\![f^{-1}]\!]$. For example, if D is the relation which relates a to both itself and b, then

$$(a \to STOP)[\![D]\!] = (a \to STOP) \,\square\, (b \to STOP)$$

If U is the universal relation $\Sigma \times \Sigma$, then $P[\![U]\!] = RUN$ if and only if the divergence-free process P is deadlock-free.

The following laws, etc., are thus all true (suitably translated) for the functional form of renaming. Renaming distributes over both choice operators:

$$(P \sqcap Q)[\![R]\!] = P[\![R]\!] \sqcap Q[\![R]\!] \qquad\qquad \langle[\![R]\!]\text{-dist}\rangle \quad (3.1$$
$$(P \,\square\, Q)[\![R]\!] = P[\![R]\!] \,\square\, Q[\![R]\!] \qquad\qquad \langle[\![R]\!]\text{-}\square\text{-dist}\rangle \quad (3.1$$

If the initials of P' are A, then those of $P'[\![R]\!]$ are $R(A) = \{y \mid \exists\, x \in A.\, (x, y) \in R\}$:

$$(?x : A \to P)[\![R]\!] = ?y : R(A) \to \textstyle\bigsqcap\{(P[z/x])[\![R]\!] \mid z \in A \wedge z\, R\, y\} \; \langle[\![R]\!]\text{-step}\rangle \quad (3.1$$

This shows that renaming can introduce nondeterminism when more than one event in A maps under R to the same thing. This cannot happen when R is either an injective function or f^{-1} for any function: in these cases the nondeterministic choice is over a set of one process – no choice at all – as there is then only ever one z such that $z\, R\, y$.

Renaming by one relation and then another is equivalent to renaming by the composition of these relations:

$$(P[\![R]\!])[\![R']\!] = P[\![R \circ R']\!] \qquad\qquad \langle[\![R]\!]\text{-combine}\rangle \quad (3.1$$

This law is one reason why relations are written on the right of a process rather than (as with functions) on the left. It implies the following law for functional renaming, where the opposite sense of composition is used

$$f[g[P]] = (f \circ g)[P] \qquad\qquad \langle f[\cdot]\text{-combine}\rangle \quad (3.1$$

Renaming in this most general form is such a powerful operator that most of the useful distribution laws that held for 1–1 renaming are no longer true. (In most cases versions can be found, but these tend to come with an unfortunately complex set of side conditions.)

The traces of $P[\![R]\!]$ are just the images of those of P under the obvious extension of R to traces:

$$\langle a_1, \ldots a_n \rangle R^* \langle b_1, \ldots, b_m \rangle \quad \Leftrightarrow \quad n = m \wedge \forall\, i \le n.a_i\, R\, b_i$$

$$traces(P[\![R]\!]) \quad = \quad \{t \mid \exists\, s \in traces(P).s\, R^* t\}$$

A good way of defining relations for use as alphabet transformations is to use a notation like substitution: we can write $P[\![^a/b]\!]$ to mean that the event or channel b in P is replaced by a. (Note that all others remain the same – including any a that is already there.) To modify more than one thing, or to send one thing to more than one place, we write something like

$$P[\![^{a,\,b}/b,\,a]\!] \qquad \text{or} \qquad P[\![^{b,\,c}/a,\,a]\!]$$

Note that the first of these *swaps* a and b and the second maps a to both b and c.

EXERCISE 3.2.1   Recall that $COPY = left?x \to right!x \to COPY$. Suppose we want, instead, a process $CELL_f$ which inputs values v on channel $left$ and immediately outputs $f(v)$ on $right$. Find an appropriate alphabet transformation g_f so that $CELL_f = g_f[COPY]$. Under what conditions is g_f injective?

EXERCISE 3.2.2   Use an alphabet transformation to connect the output channel of $COPY$ to the input channel of $CELL_f$ and *vice-versa* (i.e., there are two processes running in parallel). How does this process behave? How does it behave if $COPY$ is replaced by $right!x \to COPY$?

Add an extra channel *in* to $COPY$ so that the resulting process can be initialized along this channel and thereafter behaves as before, so achieving the effect of the second case in the last paragraph for any x.

EXERCISE 3.2.3   Find renaming relations R_i which, applied to the process $COUNT_0$, achieve the following effects:

(i) A process with events a, b and c, where the number of c's is always less than or equal to the total of the a's and b's.

(ii) A process that can always communicate either *up* or *down*.

(iii) A process that has the same traces as $COUNT_0$ but may nondeterministically sometimes refuse to communicate *down* when $COUNT_0$ would have accepted it.

EXERCISE 3.2.4   Find examples to show that the laws for distributing *injective* renaming over hiding and general parallel composition do not work when the function f is not injective.

What weaker restrictions on the renamings could you make so that these laws become valid again? *You might find thinking about the laws for distributing hiding over parallel helpful here.*

EXERCISE 3.2.5   Remember the possibility quoted at the start of this section of mapping a to b if it is before the 12th event and to c thereafter. Use a combination of a relational renaming and parallel composition with a process you define to achieve this effect. (Assume that the process P does not itself use events b and c.)

3.3   A basic guide to failures and divergences

Though we knew this well enough already, our exposure to nondeterminism and divergence in this chapter has shown that traces alone give a far from complete picture of the way a process behaves. Whether or not you intend to study the details of how these phenomena are modelled in detail – this is done in Chapter 8 – you should at least gain a basic understanding of the two main tools that are used, in addition to traces.

Traces tell us about what a process *can* do, but nothing about what it *must* do. The processes $\mu\, p.a \to p$ and $(\mu\, p.a \to p) \sqcap STOP$ have the same traces, even though the second is allowed to do nothing at all no matter what we offer it. In order to distinguish these processes we need to record not only what a process *can* do, but also what it can *refuse* to do. A *refusal set* is a set of events that a process can fail to accept anything from however long it is offered. (It is *not* enough for it simply to be refused for a finite time.) *refusals*(P) is the set of P's initial refusals.

In fact, we need to know not only what P can refuse to do after the empty trace, but also what it can refuse after any of its traces. A *failure* is a pair (s, X), where $s \in traces(P)$ and $X \in refusals(P/s)$. (Recall that P/s represents process P *after* the trace s.) *failures*(P) is the set of all P's failures.

One can calculate the failures of a process P in exactly the same way as we have already shown how to calculate the traces of P: by induction on P's syntax. For details of this you should see Chapter 8. But they can be calculated just as easily from the transition diagram of a process: you simply collect together all of the routes through this diagram which (ignoring τ's) result in a given trace. If the node you end up at is *stable* – i.e., has no τ action leading out of it – then it gives rise to a failure, since it can (and must) refuse all actions which do not lead out of it. On the other hand, a node with one or more τ's (an *unstable* node) does not give rise to a refusal since the internal action will eventually happen: as we cannot

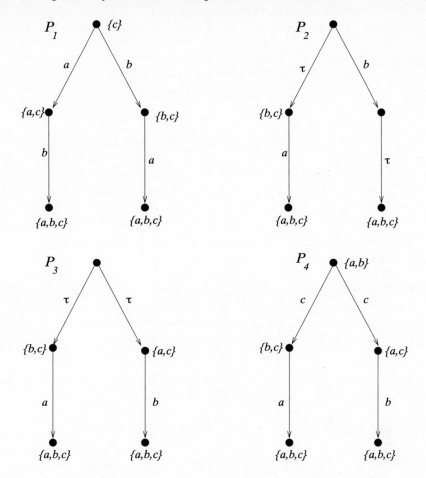

Figure 3.3 The refusal sets of some transition systems.

sit at this node for ever it cannot give rise to a refusal. In other words, we have to wait for the τ's to run out before we get refusals. In Figure 3.3 we see how to calculate the failures of a few simple processes in this way. Assuming the alphabet is $\{a, b, c\}$, each stable node is labelled with its maximal refusal. (If a node can refuse X, then it can clearly refuse $Y \subseteq X$.)

P_1 is $(a \to b \to STOP) \;\Box\; (b \to a \to STOP)$ (or equivalently $(a \to STOP) \;|||\;$ $(b \to STOP)$). It has a *deterministic* transition system (as it has no τ's, and no ambiguous branching on any visible actions). It follows that there is a unique path through the tree for any trace. Thus, there will be just one maximal refusal for any trace s: the complement of *initials*(P/s). Examples of this process's failures are $(\langle\rangle, \{\})$, $(\langle\rangle, \{c\})$, $(\langle a\rangle, \{a, c\})$ and $(\langle b, a\rangle, \{a, b, c\})$.

P_2 shows how internal actions can introduce nondeterminism. It could have arisen as $((c \rightarrow a \rightarrow STOP) \square (b \rightarrow c \rightarrow STOP)) \setminus c$. Its initial refusals are the subsets of $\{b, c\}$ but it can also accept b initially. Its complete failures are

$$\{(\langle\rangle, X) \mid X \subseteq \{b, c\}\} \cup \{(\langle a\rangle, X), (\langle b\rangle, X) \mid X \subseteq \{a, b, c\}\}$$

P_3 could be $(a \rightarrow STOP) \sqcap (b \rightarrow STOP)$. It has two initial τ's to choose from. Its initial refusals are $\{X \mid \{a, b\} \not\subseteq X\}$. It can refuse either a or b separately but must accept something if $\{a, b\}$ is offered. Notice how this is different from the initial behaviours of both P_1 (which must accept either) and P_2 (which must accept a), even though all three have exactly the same initial events possible.

P_4 which could be $(c \rightarrow a \rightarrow STOP) \square (c \rightarrow b \rightarrow STOP)$ shows how ambiguous branching on a visible action can lead to nondeterminism. Its refusals after the trace $\langle c \rangle$ are $\{X \mid \{a, b\} \not\subseteq X\}$. The similarity to the initial refusals of P_3 is no accident: we know this process is equivalent to $c \rightarrow (a \rightarrow STOP \sqcap b \rightarrow STOP)$ and the equality simply reflects this fact.

One process *failures*-refines another: $P \sqsubseteq_F Q$ if and only if

$$traces(P) \supseteq traces(Q) \qquad \text{and} \qquad failures(P) \supseteq failures(Q)$$

or, in other words, if every trace s of Q is possible for P and every refusal after this trace is possible for P. Q can neither accept an event nor refuse one unless P does. Among the processes of Figure 3.3, P_2 and P_3 are trace equivalent and both trace-refine P_1. The only failures refinement that holds is that P_2 refines P_3. Make sure you understand why this is. We can define two processes to be *failures*-equivalent ($=_F$) if each failures-refines the other.

Failures allow us to distinguish between internal and external choice, something we could not do with traces alone. This is shown by the examples in Figure 3.3, but comes across more clearly when we consider the failures of

$$Q_1 = (a \rightarrow STOP) \square (b \rightarrow STOP) \qquad \text{and}$$
$$Q_2 = (a \rightarrow STOP) \sqcap (b \rightarrow STOP)$$

If $\Sigma = \{a, b\}$, the only refusal on $\langle\rangle$ of the first of these processes is $\{\}$: the only time it will not communicate is if it is offered nothing at all! Q_2 can additionally refuse

$\{a\}$ and $\{b\}$, but cannot refuse $\{a, b\}$ since whichever way the nondeterministic choice is resolved it has to accept one or the other. On the other hand, the process

$$Q_3 \quad = \quad STOP \sqcap ((a \to STOP) \,\square\, (b \to STOP))$$

can refuse any set of events, because it can behave like $STOP$. In general, a process can deadlock if, and only if, it can refuse the whole of Σ. The failures specification of deadlock freedom is thus that, for all traces s, $(s, \Sigma) \notin failures(P)$.

Full calculation of the failures of Q_1, Q_2 and Q_3 would reveal that

$$Q_3 \sqsubseteq_F Q_2 \sqsubseteq_F Q_1$$

Failures refinement gets very close to the natural notion of what refinement 'ought' to mean for CSP processes. The only real problem comes from the phenomenon of divergence that we noticed earlier in this chapter. A diverging process such as $(\mu\,p.a \to p) \setminus a$ is neither doing anything useful nor is it refusing anything in the sense discussed above. The only really satisfactory way of dealing with divergence is to record the set of traces on which a process can diverge. We can calculate this from one of our transition systems, since divergence here is simply an infinite path of τ's (if this graph is finite, this implies the existence of a τ-loop: a path of τ's from a node back to itself).

When we look into the mathematical theory of how divergences are calculated, it turns out that seeing accurately what a process can do after it has already been able to diverge is very difficult, and not really worth the effort.[6] (This can happen, for example, if a process has a nondeterministic choice between diverging or doing something else.) For once we take a process up to the point where it can diverge, there is no way we can rely on it doing anything. Therefore, the standard mathematical model of CSP, the *failures/divergences model*, takes the decision that any two processes that can diverge immediately (whatever else they can do) are (i) equivalent and (ii) completely useless. Specifically, once a process can diverge, we assume (whether it is true or not) that it can then perform any trace, refuse anything, and always diverge on any later trace. $divergences(P)$ thus contains not only the traces s on which P can diverge, but also all extensions $s\hat{\ }t$ of such traces. We also need extended, *strict* sets of traces and failures when working with divergences:

$$traces_{\perp}(P) \quad = \quad traces(P) \cup divergences(P)$$
$$failures_{\perp}(P) \quad = \quad failures(P) \cup \{(s, X) \mid s \in divergences(P)\}$$

---

[6]On the other hand, the traces model and a refinement of it we will be meeting in Section 8.4, the *stable failures model*, allow one to see beyond any divergence by ignoring divergence altogether.

You can think of the second of these as saying that a process which is diverging is, in effect, refusing everything. The representation of a process P in this model is

$$(failures_\perp(P), divergences(P))$$

This can either be extracted from the transition graph by simply recording which behaviours it can perform, as in Figure 3.3, or via clauses like those seen earlier for $traces(P)$. The latter can be found in Section 8.3, as can further details of the model, but for now it is quite sufficient for you to think primarily in terms of the former. That is, after all, essentially how FDR works out the failures and divergences of a process. Your main aim in reading this section should, perhaps, be to understand what failures and divergence are, so that you know what it means when FDR does the calculations involving them for you.

Because of the closure under divergence, over this model *any* process that can diverge immediately (i.e., without any visible communication) is equivalent to **div**, no matter what else it may also be able to do.

One process *failures/divergences-refines* another, written $P \sqsubseteq_{FD} Q$ (or just $P \sqsubseteq Q$ when the context is clear), if and only if

$$failures_\perp(P) \supseteq failures_\perp(Q) \land divergences(P) \supseteq divergences(Q)$$

(it turns out that this implies the corresponding relation for traces, so there is no need to include that clause). **div** is the *least* refined process under $\sqsubseteq_{FD}$: **div** $\sqsubseteq_{FD} P$ for all P.

The corresponding notion $=_{FD}$ of equivalence in the failures/divergences model is the standard notion of equivalence for CSP processes over most of the literature.[7]

Even though almost all of the correct processes one ever writes are divergence-free, we often need to be able to demonstrate that this is indeed so for ones we have constructed. This is why we need to go to the trouble of including divergence in our model of refinement: if it were not there, we would have no way of telling if a process could diverge or not.

It is only when we know the failures and divergences of a process that we can definitively tell whether it is *deterministic* or not. A process P is defined to be deterministic if, and only if, $divergences(P) = \{\}$ and $s^\smallfrown\langle a\rangle \in traces(P) \Rightarrow (s, \{a\}) \notin failures(P)$. In other words, it cannot diverge, and never has the choice of both accepting and refusing any action. It turns out that the deterministic processes are exactly the maximal ones under $\sqsubseteq_{FD}$ – the processes that have no

---

[7]Though one needs to be careful with unboundedly nondeterministic ones.

proper refinements. $P \sqsubseteq_{FD} Q$ means, rather precisely, that Q is more deterministic than P. Of the processes in Figure 3.3, only P_1 is deterministic (as any process with a deterministic transition system is, though the reverse is not true). We will study the class of deterministic processes further in Part II of this book, especially in Section 9.1. The unique fixed point (UFP) rule is valid with respect to both failures and failures/divergences equivalence.

Failures and divergences in specifications

These three levels of refinement – traces, failures, and failures/divergences – are what FDR allows you to check. Indeed, FDR stands for *Failures/Divergences Refinement.*

The two new modes of refinement $\sqsubseteq_F$ and $\sqsubseteq_{FD}$ allow us to formulate stronger specifications of processes than are possible with traces refinement, since you can now make assertions about what a process can refuse and when it can diverge as well as what traces it can perform. Just as with trace specifications, they can be formulated either as behavioural specifications or, directly, as their characteristic processes. Thus deadlock freedom (either as a failures or failures/divergences specification) becomes the behavioural specification

$$\forall s.(s, \Sigma) \notin \textit{failures}(P) \qquad \text{or} \qquad \textit{ref} \neq \Sigma$$

In other words, P can never refuse all events; so there is always something it can do. The right-hand form extends the convention seen on page 42, that tr represents an arbitrary trace, to the assumption that (tr, ref) is an arbitrary failure. tr does not appear in the above simply because this specification is independent of traces. Its characteristic process is DF_Σ, where

$$DF_A \ = \ \sqcap \{a \to DF_A \mid a \in A\}$$

DF_Σ is, of course, the most nondeterministic deadlock-free process for, just as over the traces model, the characteristic process of any behavioural specification is equivalent to the nondeterministic choice of all processes that meet it. In similar vein, the most nondeterministic divergence-free process (in the failures/divergences model) is *Chaos*.

A specification can be extremely abstract like the above, can be highly specific and attempt to define all the behaviour of one's implementation – for example if Q is a deterministic process such as B_0^2 on page 85 then $Q \sqsubseteq_{FD} P$ is equivalent to $P =_{FD} Q$ and so P must be a complete description of intended functional behaviour – or can be somewhere in between. A good example of the latter is the *buffer* specification which we will study in Section 5.1.

Divergence checking is a more complex activity than the rest of what FDR does in its 'checking' phase, and therefore $\sqsubseteq_{FD}$ checks are slower. In practice we often know that processes are divergence-free for independent reasons. The most common use of failures checks is for proving full refinements $P \sqsubseteq_{FD} Q$ for processes P and Q that are already known (or are assumed) to be divergence-free. Indeed, at the time of writing, the author almost always structures a substantial failures/ divergences check this way. We will see some more sophisticated circumstances where one has to check $\sqsubseteq_F$ rather than $\sqsubseteq_{FD}$ in later chapters.

EXERCISE 3.3.1   What failures/divergences refinements hold between the following processes: div, $Chaos_{\{a,b\}}$, $Chaos_{\{a\}}$, $DF_{\{a,b\}}$, $RUN_{\{a,b\}}$, $RUN_{\{a\}}$, $STOP$, $a \to$ div and $a \to STOP$? Which of them are deterministic?

EXERCISE 3.3.2   Formulate a behavioural failures specification (using the variables tr and ref as discussed above) which asserts that a process must always accept the event a if the number of a's in tr is less than that of b's in tr. What is the characteristic process (i) on the assumption that $\Sigma = \{a, b\}$ and (ii) on the assumption that it is larger?

3.4   Tools

The notation for hiding in machine-readable CSP is almost exactly the same as we have used already: P\X, where X must be a *set of events*. While it is often convenient to have X a single event or channel, or a set of channels, in written text, you must convert it to the proper type for running. This is made easier by the {|a,b|} notation, which corresponds to the notation $\{| a, b |\}$ we have already defined.

There is only one way of writing renaming, which (apart from the precise way it is written) is a simple extension of the 'substitution' style renaming we saw at the end of the section: you create a relation by using variations on the notation

P[[b <- a, d <- c]]

This relation maps b to a, d to c and leaves all other events alone. a,b,c,d can be simple events or channel names. If you want to map one event to many (as in inverse function renaming) this can be done by using the same event on the left-hand side of <- more than once: P[[a <- a, a <- b]] 'shadows' each a with the alternative of a b. More sophisticated forms of this notation exist, in which the renamed pairs are generated rather than explicitly listed: see Appendix B.

Process naming in the $a.P$ style is not defined in machine-readable CSP at the time of writing. The reasons for this, which are connected with the type-theory of channels, are discussed on page 110 (in connection with the main application of process naming), together with how to get around this restriction.

Chapter 4

Piping and enslavement

In the previous chapter we pointed out that the most natural model of a real parallel system is probably to have a collection of processes synchronizing pairwise on their communications, and with these internal communications hidden. In this chapter we see two operators which model common ways in which such systems are put together. They are both *derived* operators, in the sense that they are both built out of – and can thus be thought of as abbreviations for – other ones.

4.1 Piping

A common and simple form of parallel composition is *pipelining*: taking a sequence of processes which input on one channel and output on another, and connecting them in sequence, the outputs of the rth process being fed into the inputs of the $(r+1)$th. We have already seen one example of this, namely the chain of *COPY* processes.

If it has been decided to use this form of network and furthermore to hide the internal communications, then the careful assignment of distinct labels to the individual channels can be a little tiresome. The *piping* or *chaining* operator $\gg$ provides a more convenient way of creating such systems. It assumes that the processes have all been defined so that their input channels are all called *left* and their output channels are all called *right*.[1] If we combine two or more of them together then it is natural that the input and output channels of the whole should retain these names. Thus, $P \gg Q$ connects the *right* channel of P to the *left* channel of Q and hides these internal communications. This leaves the *left* channel

---

[1] Of course the choice of this pair of names is somewhat arbitrary. Sometimes one sees *in* and *out* used instead.

of P and the *right* channel of Q visible externally.

We can now write the sequence of *COPY* processes with hidden internal communication as

$$COPY \gg COPY \gg \ldots \gg COPY$$

where the input and output channels are now *left* and *right* rather than c_0 and c_n of the previous example.

The piping operator can be expressed in terms of renaming, parallel and hiding: $P \gg Q =$

$$(P[\![{}^{right,\,mid} / {}_{mid,\,right}]\!] \; {}_{\{|left,mid|\}} \|{}_{\{|mid,right|\}}$$

$$Q[\![{}^{mid,\,left} / {}_{left,\,mid}]\!]) \setminus \{| \; mid \; |\}$$

where it is assumed *left*, *right* and the new channel name *mid* all have the same type T. The reason for *swapping* the pairs $(left, mid)$ and $(mid, right)$ rather than simply using $P[\![{}^{mid}/{}_{right}]\!]$ and $Q[\![{}^{mid}/{}_{left}]\!]$ is to guard against the possibility that P or Q might already have been able to communicate on the *mid* chosen. It makes absolutely sure that the renamings we are using in this definition are 1–1.

Though this definition is actually symmetrical between *left* and *right*, the piping operator is always used so that *left* is an 'input' channel (in the sense that it accepts any element of $\{| \; left \; |\}$ whenever it accepts any) and *right* is an 'output' channel. In other words, communications usually take the forms '*left?x*' and '*right!e*'.

The piping operator is distributive in both its arguments (a fact that follows from the distributivity of the operators used above to construct it) and associative.

$$(P \sqcap Q) \gg R = (P \gg R) \sqcap (Q \gg R) \qquad \langle \gg\text{-dist-l} \rangle \qquad (4.1$$

$$P \gg (Q \sqcap R) = (P \gg Q) \sqcap (P \gg R) \qquad \langle \gg\text{-dist-r} \rangle \qquad (4.2$$

$$(P \gg Q) \gg R = P \gg (Q \gg R) \qquad \langle \gg\text{-assoc} \rangle \qquad (4.3$$

This last fact, which is so intuitively obvious that we have already taken advantage of it without thinking in the *COPY*-chain, is actually rather subtle mathematically.[2] In the left-hand side of the law, the communications between P and Q are hidden before those between Q and R, and *vice-versa* on the right-hand side. It is intimately tied up with the laws for interchanging parallel and hiding ($\langle \text{hide-}_X \|_Y\text{-dist} \rangle$ (3.7) and $\langle \text{hide-}\|_X\text{-dist} \rangle$ (3.8)).

---

[2] A number of mathematical models have been discarded because they failed this test!

There is also a range of laws for allowing us to compute the first-step behaviour of $P \gg Q$ in common cases. These special forms are more easily applicable than coding the entire set into a single law: in all of these it is assumed that x is not free in Q nor y in P.

$$left?x \to P \gg left?y \to Q \;=\; left?x \to (P \gg left?y \to Q) \qquad \langle\gg\text{-step 1}\rangle \qquad (4.4)$$

$$right!x \to P \gg right!y \to Q \;=\; right!y \to (right!x \to P \gg Q) \qquad \langle\gg\text{-step 2}\rangle \qquad (4.5)$$

$$right!x \to P \gg left?y \to Q \;=\; P \gg Q[x/y] \qquad \langle\gg\text{-step 3}\rangle \qquad (4.6)$$

$$left?x \to P \gg right!y \to Q \;=\; \begin{aligned}&left?x \to (P \gg right!y \to Q)\\ &\square\; right!y \to (left?x \to P \gg Q)\end{aligned} \qquad \langle\gg\text{-step 4}\rangle \qquad (4.7)$$

The first two correspond to the situation where only the left- or right-hand sides can move because the other is stuck waiting for it. The third is what happens when each is willing to communicate across the hidden channel, and the final one shows the choice that appears when both are able to talk externally.

We can see these in operation if we consider the process $COPY \gg COPY$. This equals

$$
\begin{aligned}
&\ (left?x \to\ right!x \to COPY) \gg\\
&\ (left?y \to\ right!y \to COPY)\\
=&\ \ left?x \to\ ((right!x \to COPY) \gg & (\langle\gg\text{-step 1}\rangle)\\
&\qquad\qquad (left?y \to right!y \to COPY))\\
=&\ \ left?x \to\ (COPY \gg (right!x \to COPY)) & (\langle\gg\text{-step 3}\rangle)\\
=&\ \ left?x \to\ (left?y \to right!y \to COPY \gg\\
&\qquad\qquad (right!x \to COPY))\\
=&\ \ left?x \to\ (right!x \to (COPY \gg COPY)\\
&\qquad\qquad \square\; left?y \to\\
&\qquad\qquad (right!y \to COPY \gg right!x \to COPY)) & (\langle\gg\text{-step 4}\rangle)\\
&\ \text{etc.}
\end{aligned}
$$

(By naming the various parallel terms, as we have done previously, this could have been shown equivalent by this unfolding to a very similar mutual recursion that essentially the same process was proved equivalent to in the previous chapter.)

While the above laws deal with all the cases where the process at either end of $\gg$ is able to communicate exactly one of input and output, and we have the obvious cases of any input ($left?x$) and only one output ($right!x$) being possible, it can of course happen that more complex situations arise. The following law accounts for all of these cases: it is found by combining the step laws for parallel, renaming and hiding (to the last of which it bears an obvious resemblance). If

$$
\begin{aligned}
P &= (left?x : A \to P') \ \Box \ (right?x : B \to P'') \\
Q &= (left?y : C \to Q') \ \Box \ (right?y : D \to Q'')
\end{aligned}
$$

(where any of A, B, C, D can be empty and, if not, A, C are likely to be the whole of T and B, D are probably singletons), and x, y are respectively not free in Q, P, then

$$
\begin{aligned}
P \gg Q &= (left?x : A \to (P' \gg Q)) \ \Box \ (right?y : D \to (P \gg Q'')) \\
&\quad\quad \langle\!\langle B \cap C = \{\} \rangle\!\rangle \\
&\quad (left?x : A \to (P' \gg Q)) \ \Box \ (right?y : D \to (P \gg Q'')) \\
&\quad \rhd \ \sqcap\{P''[z/x] \gg Q'[z/y] \mid z \in B \cap C\}
\end{aligned}
$$

$\langle\gg\text{-step}\rangle$ (4.8

The traces of $P \gg Q$ are simple to compute: assuming, for a slight simplification, P and Q only communicate in the set $\{| \ left, right \ |\}$ they are

$$
\begin{aligned}
traces(P \gg Q) &= \\
\{u \in \{| \ left, right \ |\}^* &\mid \exists s \in traces(P), t \in traces(Q). \\
u \downarrow left = s \downarrow left &\wedge s \downarrow right = t \downarrow left \wedge t \downarrow right = u \downarrow right\}
\end{aligned}
$$

Clearly this operator has its main uses modelling applications where information is passed along a sequence of processes. For example,

$$
ITER \ = \ left?(data, input) \to right!(data, F(data, input)) \to ITER
$$

is a process for performing one step of an iteration on some data. So if *data* is a number and

$$
F(d, x) \ = \ \left(x + \frac{d}{x}\right) / 2
$$

then it carries one step of the Newton's method approximation to a square root. By piping N copies of *ITER* together we apply this number of iterations to each data and starting value:

$$
ITER \gg ITER \gg \ldots \gg ITER
$$

Of course there is no reason why all the processes have to perform the same task.

The other primary application of the piping operator is in the study of communications mechanisms and protocols. A typical application here might be dealing with a faulty communication channel, or simply one which uses a different representation of information than the one we wish to deal with (encrypted, perhaps). Suppose, therefore, that we wish to create a transparent channel of four-byte words W, allowing a certain amount of *buffering* between two processes, when what we are supplied with is an unreliable channel M of bytes *Byte* which might lose or corrupt some proportion of its throughput. A good way of modelling this is to design processes T and R (transmitter and receiver) such that

$$T \gg M \gg R$$

is a *buffer* of type W. A buffer is a process which, like $COPY$ and $B_{\langle\rangle}^{\infty}$ (page 19) copies information from its input to its output, preserving order and without loss, and such that it never refuses to output an item it contains and will not refuse to input when empty. We will give a formal specification of this later (page 114).

The difficulty of defining T and R will depend on just how bad we allow M to be. Our task might be made easier by splitting each of the processes into two: $T = T_1 \gg T_2$ and $R = R_2 \gg R_1$ should be such that $T_2 \gg M \gg R_2$ is a buffer of some type which it is easier to correct than W over the medium M (probably *Byte* or bits $\{0, 1\}$) and $T_1 \gg B \gg R_1$ a is a buffer of type W whenever B is one of the intermediate type. This modularization could be taken further by dividing the problem into yet more layers. See Exercises 4.1.3 and 4.1.4 for details of what the processes we have been discussing might look like. The idea of dividing communications protocols into layers like this is of great practical importance since it allows a separation of concerns (e.g., dealing with security, error correction, and message structuring separately).

There is a natural relationship between the piping operator and buffers. It will generally be true, for example, that $P \gg Q$ is a buffer if P and Q are. This will be discussed more in the next chapter.

By combining $\gg$ with recursions, we can define dynamically expanding chains of processes. For example, we can define an infinite-capacity buffer with the same behaviour as $B_{\langle\rangle}^{\infty}$ without using infinite mutual recursion, just as $|||$ allowed us to do this with $COUNT$.

$$B^{+} = left?x \rightarrow (B^{+} \gg right!x \rightarrow COPY)$$

Since the definition of piping involves hiding, we are not trivially able to assert that this recursion is constructive or guarded. In fact it is, and a formal proof of this (for which we will need further mathematical machinery) follows the pattern of the informal argument below.

A recursion $P = F(P)$ is constructive if, in order to see $n + 1$ steps of the behaviour of $F(P)$, we need only explore n steps of the behaviour of P. In other words, if P and P' are indistinguishable up to and including n communications, then $F(P)$ and $F(P')$ are indistinguishable up to and including $n + 1$. Now the initial input of the B^+ recursion clearly gives one step of behaviour without referring at all to the recursive call, so it will be enough to show that the process

$$B^+ \gg right!x \to COPY$$

that follows it is *non-destructive*: has always communicated as many actions as it has used of B^+. But this is actually rather obvious, since every communication of B^+ is either visible (contributing to the length of the trace) or an output to $right!x \to COPY$. But this latter process has always output at least as many things as it has input, so every communication of B^+ that gets hidden is compensated for by one of these outputs. For the mathematics underpinning this argument, see Section 8.2.

EXERCISE 4.1.1   Show that if P and Q satisfy the trace specification of a buffer: $tr \in \{| \, left, right \, |\}^* \wedge tr \downarrow right \leq tr \downarrow left$, then so does $P \gg Q$.

EXERCISE 4.1.2   Newton's method of approximating the square root of a positive number x is, starting with an arbitrary guess r_0, to set $r_{n+1} = (r_n + x/r_n)/2$.

(i) Devise processes *INIT* and *FINAL* such that

$$INIT \gg ITER \gg ITER \ldots \gg ITER \gg FINAL$$

inputs a number and outputs the Nth iteration (there being N copies of the *ITER* process defined earlier). Choose $x/2$ as the first guess at the square root.

(ii) Now, by using the pattern of recursion

$$P \quad = \quad left?(d, r) \to ((right!r \to P) \triangleleft b \triangleright (I(d, x) \gg P))$$

where you should specify what b and I are, create a system which iterates as many times as it has to so that $|\, r^2 - x \,| < \epsilon$ (ϵ is a small positive constant). What happens if the second number input to this dynamic network takes less, the same, or more iterations than the first?

EXERCISE 4.1.3   Devise processes T_1 and R_1 that unpack a word of four bytes into its individual 32 bits, and pack them up again. Thus, $T_1 \gg R_1$ should be a buffer for words, though the internal channel should be passing bits. (The best way to represent a word is as a sequence of 32 bits.)

EXERCISE 4.1.4 M is to be a model of an unreliable medium which transmits values in the set $\{0, 1, 2\}$. It sometimes loses data, but must transmit at least one out of every N. Define the processes M_i for $i = 0, 1, \ldots, N-1$, where M_i behaves like M_0 except that it may lose i values before being obliged to transmit one correctly. Which of these is the appropriate definition of M?

Now define processes $T^\dagger$ and $R^\dagger$ such that $T^\dagger \gg M \gg R^\dagger$ is a buffer of type $\{0, 1\}$, and explain informally why your definition works. *Hint: use the value 2 as a punctuation mark between transmitted values, using sufficient repetition to ensure one of each block gets through.*

Harder: do the same thing when the type of the medium is only $\{0, 1\}$.

4.2   Enslavement

It is useful to have an operator representing the situation where one process acts as the *slave* of another. The slave is only allowed to communicate with its master, and all communications between master and slave are hidden. The general case of this operation is written

$$P /\!\!/_Y Q$$

which means the same as $(P \;_\Sigma\|_Y\; Q) \setminus Y$. It is usual to use it in the case where the slave has some name, m say, and the master's communications with the slave are just those with the name m in the same sense we saw it applied in process naming earlier. This special form is written

$$P /\!\!/ m{:}Q$$

which means the same as $P /\!\!/_M m.Q$ where M is the set of all elements of Σ of the form $m.a$.

As with $\gg$, the laws and trace-set of $P /\!\!/_Y Q$ can be deduced from those of the operators it is built from. Just as $\gg$ is associative, meaning that we can introduce and hide the internal communications in either order, enslavement satisfies the following law, which one might term a symmetry principle: if $Y \cap Z = \{\}$ then

$$(P /\!\!/_Y Q) /\!\!/_Z R \;=\; (P /\!\!/_Z R) /\!\!/_Y Q \qquad\qquad \langle /\!\!/\text{-sym}\rangle \qquad (4.9)$$

so, in particular, if m and n are distinct names then

$$(P /\!\!/ m{:}Q) /\!\!/ n{:}R \;=\; (P /\!\!/ n{:}R) /\!\!/ m{:}Q$$

Enslavement is, of course, distributive in each argument and, like $\gg$, it is best in most cases to divide the step law into a number of commonly-occurring cases rather than dealing with the most general one all the time. These are left as an exercise.

One common use of enslavement is to represent one process providing a computational service to another, analogous to a (remote) procedure call. For example, if we were modelling a microprocessor, it might well be appropriate to represent the floating-point unit (FPU) as a slave to the CPU. The FPU might then be abstractly modelled by the process

$$FPU \; = \; fpreq?(data, op) \rightarrow fpout!fpu(data, op) \rightarrow FPU$$

where *fpu* is a function defining the appropriate result for each floating-point calculation. In the combination $CPU /\!\!/ fp{:}FPU$ the CPU would then send requests to the FPU by a communication such as $fp.fpreq!((a, b), +)$, and could then carry out some more operations before it required the result of this combination, which it could get by inputting $fp.fpout?x$.

If the designer required a higher MFLOP rate (i.e., floating point speed) than was obtainable from this simple server, there are at least two approaches he could take to get greater performance. One would simply be to provide more FPUs, so that with two of them the combination might look like

$$(CPU /\!\!/ fp1{:}FPU) /\!\!/ fp2{:}FPU$$

Rather than provide two entirely separate boxes, he might prefer to split one into several phases by pipelining, so that it is able to handle more than one operation at a time. If there were three of these (perhaps denormalizing and aligning in $FPU1$, arithmetic in $FPU2$ and normalizing, error detection and handling in $FPU3$), the FPU might then become something like

$$(FPU1 \gg FPU2 \gg FPU3)[\![^{fpreq, fpout}/_{left, right}]\!]$$

and able to deal with three computations at once. This approach has the advantage that it probably requires less extra silicon than providing three independent units, but the disadvantages that one must always take the results in the order in which the data was entered and that unless the three phases are well-balanced in the time they take (probably not true in this case) the performance would not be so good.

Another use of enslavement is to provide a CSP process with access to a state which can be assigned to, read from, or have other similar operations applied to it. A slave process representing a simple variable might be written

$$VAR(x) \; = \; assign?y \rightarrow VAR(y) \; \square \; read!x \rightarrow VAR(x)$$

The starting value of the variable could be dealt with by introducing a special error value, or by making the initial state

$$\bigsqcap \{ VAR(x) \mid x \in T \}$$

We can take this idea further and provide more complex data structures with different operations. These can, of course, be represented as a non-parallel CSP process with appropriate internal state. In the case of some dynamic structures there are interesting ways of modelling them via a combination of enslavement and recursion.

EXAMPLE 4.2.1 (SETS VIA ENSLAVEMENT) If we want to model a finite set to which we can add elements, remove them, and test for membership, then this can be done with the recursive process defined

$$
\begin{aligned}
SET \;\; = \;\; & add?x \rightarrow (C_x /\!/ m{:}SET) \\
& \square \; del?x \rightarrow SET \\
& \square \; isin?x \rightarrow no \rightarrow SET, \quad \text{where}
\end{aligned}
$$

$$
\begin{aligned}
C_x \;\; = \;\; & add?y \rightarrow (C_x \blacktriangleleft y = x \blacktriangleright m.add!y \rightarrow C_x) \\
& \square \; del?y \rightarrow (E \blacktriangleleft y = x \blacktriangleright m.del!y \rightarrow C_x) \\
& \square \; isin?y \rightarrow (yes \rightarrow C_x \blacktriangleleft y = x \blacktriangleright \\
& \qquad\qquad m.isin!y \rightarrow m?a : \{yes, no\} \rightarrow a \rightarrow C_x)
\end{aligned}
$$

$$
\begin{aligned}
E \;\; = \;\; & add?y \rightarrow m.del!y \rightarrow C_y \\
& \square \; del?y \rightarrow m.del!y \rightarrow E \\
& \square \; isin?y \rightarrow m.isin!y \rightarrow m?a : \{yes, no\} \rightarrow a \rightarrow E
\end{aligned}
$$

This works by holding the first object entered and storing the rest of the set in a recursively called slave set. C_x represents one cell of the resultant network which contains x, while E is one which is empty because the last thing it held has been deleted. Notice that when E is refilled (which it is by the first new element to come along) then the same element is deleted from E's slave. This is necessary to get the system to work correctly – see if you can work out why.

The essential feature of this recursion is that it creates a network composed of a lot of simple cells, each of which was generated by one recursive call and which can in turn make similar recursive calls. In the case above the network is always a chain (though rather different from the sort created by $\gg$ since it does all its external communication at one end), because each cell only has one potential slave. If there are two then we get a binary tree, and so on.[3] *(End of example)*

Using a similar strategy we can create an interesting version of the much-used example of a counter, in which each cell either knows that it and its slave are

---

[3] No network created using enslavement alone can be anything other than a tree – a connected network with no cycles. We will find that trees play an important role in our discussion of deadlock in Chapter 13.

set to zero (and communicating the event *iszero*) or that its slave is set to exactly one less than itself.

$$Zero_{/\!/} \;=\; up \to (Succ_{/\!/}\, m{:}Zero_{/\!/})$$
$$\qquad\qquad \Box\; iszero \to Zero_{/\!/}$$

$$Succ \;=\; down \to (m.iszero \to NoSucc)$$
$$\qquad\qquad\qquad \Box\; m.down \to Succ)$$
$$\qquad up \to m.up \to Succ$$

$$NoSucc \;=\; iszero \to NoSucc$$
$$\qquad\qquad \Box\; up \to Succ$$

This is well-defined and is equivalent to the obvious sequential counter process with the *iszero* event added to the zero state. An interesting variant can be found in Section 8.2, where we study how fixed points of recursions like this evolve and can be regarded as constructive despite the presence of hiding in the enslavement operator.

EXAMPLE 4.2.2 (QUICKSORT) Many divide-and-conquer algorithms can be implemented as parallel CSP 'programs' using recursive enslavement. For example, the following gives a version of quicksort.

$$Qsort \;=\; last \to end \to Qsort$$
$$\qquad\qquad \Box\; in?x \to ((IN_x /\!/ up{:}Qsort) /\!/ down{:}Qsort)$$

$$IN_x \;=\; in?y \to ((up.in!y \to IN_x) \mathbin{\triangleleft} y > x \mathbin{\triangleright} (down.in!y \to IN_x))$$
$$\qquad\qquad \Box\; last \to up.last \to down.last \to OUTA_x$$

$$OUTA_x \;=\; up.out?y \to out!y \to OUTA_x$$
$$\qquad\qquad \Box\; up.end \to out!x \to OUTB$$

$$OUTB \;=\; down.out?y \to out!y \to OUTB$$
$$\qquad\qquad \Box\; down.end \to end \to X$$

$$X \;=\; last \to end \to X$$
$$\qquad\qquad \Box\; in?x \to IN_x$$

Qsort takes a sequence of values on channel *in*, the end of which is signalled by *last*. It then sorts these into descending order and outputs them on *out*, indicating the end of the output phase by *end*. The first element of the input list is used as the pivot for quicksort, which is applied recursively to the elements of the remainder of the input which are respectively greater than, or less-than-or-equal-to, the pivot. The state X is present so that the network can be re-used: see if you can understand what happens when this occurs. *(End of example)*

EXERCISE 4.2.1   Create case-by-case step laws for $(?x : A \to P')/\!\!/_Y(?x : B \to Q')$. You should deal (at least) with the cases $A \cap Y = \{\}$ and $A \subseteq Y \wedge (Y \cap A \cap B) \neq \{\}$. What is the general step law (recalling $\langle \gg\text{-step}\rangle$ (4.8))?

EXERCISE 4.2.2   Define a one-step tail recursion $\underline{COUNT}^\dagger$ that behaves equivalently to $Zero_{/\!\!/}$ and prove this equivalence using the UFP rule and the laws you defined in the previous exercise. You can assume, if required, that the $Zero_{/\!\!/}$ recursion is constructive.

Hint: the most elegant way to prove this equivalence is probably in two applications of UFP. The first shows that a vector whose $(n+1)th$ component is $Succ_{/\!\!/}m : COUNT_n^\dagger$ (you should define the 0th component) is equivalent to $\underline{COUNT}^\dagger$. The second uses this to justify an application of UFP to the $Zero_{/\!\!/}$ recursion. It can also be done directly but you then have to be careful with the fact that $Zero_{/\!\!/}$ has many states corresponding to each $n \in \mathbb{N}$.

EXERCISE 4.2.3   *Mergesort* is another divide-and-conquer sorting algorithm. It works by dividing the input list into two parts (as equal as possible in length), recursively sorting these, and then merging the two sorted results into a single sorted list. Adapt the strategy used above for quicksort, copying the recursive structure of a master and two slaves, to give a CSP version of this.

Hints: split the input by sending odd- and even-numbered elements of the input, respectively, to the two slaves. Be careful that your design does not diverge for an input list of length 1.

EXERCISE 4.2.4   Produce a modified version of the process *SET* which does all of the following.

(a) The elements are stored in increasing order: if a cell receives an *add.x* with x less than its current value y, then y is pushed on and x retained.

(b) The invariant preserved by (a) is exploited when deciding whether to send a *del* or *isin* message to the slave.

(c) It is possible for the element held by a slave to drop down into its immediate master if the master has become empty (via a *del* or by doing this new function with its own master).

(d) The set can always communicate on one of two new channels: *least.x* outputs the least element from the set (the one held in the lowest cell) and removes it from the set, and *isempty* can be communicated whenever it is empty.

In what ways is this new version more efficient than the original? How would you convert it into a process (externally) equivalent to the original?

4.3   Tools

The piping and enslavement operators are not directly supported by machine-readable CSP. The reasons for this are both related to the way this version of the notation treats its channels.

The problem with the piping operator is the way it gives special importance to the two channels *left* and *right*. There is nothing wrong with that in itself, but many (perhaps most) large examples of pipes will involve a series of processes

$$P_1 \gg P_2 \gg \ldots \gg P_{n-1} \gg P_n$$

where the interfaces do not all have the same type. (Consider, for example, the layered protocol idea described on page 103.) In order to make sense of such an example it is necessary to be able to think of the channels *left* and *right* as having different types at different points in the program: for obvious reasons this clashes with the type discipline which says that each channel is declared with a single type.

There is no problem with the enslavement operator $P /\!\!/_X Q$ itself: it does not mention any specific channel and it is easy to define in terms of other constructs which are supported. The problem comes because this operator is most often used (as it was in this chapter) in its 'named slave' form $P /\!\!/ a : Q$. Machine-readable CSP presently insists that each channel comprises an atomic name and a type. Adding an extra name onto the beginning of an event does not preserve this discipline. It is easy to achieve the same effect of a named version of a process by using parameterization and adding the name as a component of the type of each channel, thus

```
B(n) = in.n?x -> out.n!x -> B(n)
       [] halt.n -> STOP
```

might replace $n.B$, where

$$
\begin{aligned}
B \;\; = \;\; & in?x \to out!x \to B \\
& \square\, halt \to STOP
\end{aligned}
$$

Since this is a significantly different style and it is easy to achieve the effect of enslavement via other constructs, it was decided not to include it directly in the machine-readable syntax.

One should also bear in mind that many of the most interesting examples of the use of enslavement are dynamic networks (i.e., recursions through enslavement). In their most natural forms these, being infinite state, will not work on FDR, though it can be entertaining to apply an animator such as ProBE to them.

It is, in fact, straightforward to re-create any network that comes out of a pen-and-paper use of $\gg$ and $/\!\!/$. This can either be done with the standard parallel, renaming and hiding operators (in much the same way as these operators were derived in the first place) or using a recently-added construct specific to the machine-readable language. If (a1,b1), (a2,b2), ..., (an,bn) are pairs of channels where the two in each pair have the same type, then

```
P [a1 <-> b1, a2 <-> b2, ... , an <-> bn] Q
```

puts P and Q in parallel, joining the given pairs of channels together (with left- and right-hand ones of each pair being treated as a channel of P and Q respectively) and hides the resulting communications. Thus we can, if P and Q are two processes that do not communicate outside $\{| \ left, right \ |\}$, implement $P \gg Q$ as P [right <-> left] Q.

Unlike $\gg$, this is not an associative operator and therefore must be fully bracketed. The main cases where it fails to associate are where the different uses of it mention different but overlapping sets of channels. We can, for example, achieve a result very close to enslavement: suppose P is a process with arrays of channels call.i and return.i (for $i \in \{1, \ldots, n\}$) and that Slave is a process with channels call' and return' designed to perform some subroutine. One can enslave n copies of Slave to P by the construct

```
(...(P [call.1 <-> call', return.1 <-> return'] Slave)
      [call.2 <-> call', return.2 <-> return'] Slave)
       ...
      [call.n <-> call', return.n <-> return'] Slave)
```

Note how the same channels of the various copies of Slave are attached to different channels of P. Other bracketings of this would mean very different (and generally nonsensical in this context) things.

There are also extensions to allow the pairs of tied channels to be defined by a comprehension (as for sets and renamings, for example) and for combining a list of processes under a replicated version of the operator.

The example files on the web site that illustrate this chapter use this new construct.

Chapter 5

Buffers and communication

We have already met buffer processes on numerous occasions. They are ones which input data on one channel and output it in the same order on another. While this may seem to be an extremely simple thing to achieve, you should bear in mind that we might have to do so between two nodes of a complex and perhaps unreliable network. Communications protocols are an extremely important application of CSP, and it is almost certain that the appropriate specification for such a protocol will either simply be that it is a buffer, or be closely related to this. For that reason, and also because they provide an excellent example of how to build and reason about a CSP specification, we will look in detail in this chapter at buffers, their relationship to the piping operator $\gg$, and discuss some of the more elementary communications protocol topics.

5.1 Pipes and buffers

The trace specification of a buffer is that its alphabet is $left.T \cup right.T$ for some type T, and that for any trace s, $s \downarrow right \leq s \downarrow left$.[1] This is as much as we can usefully say with a trace specification. This does, like any trace specification, pass some unlikely processes, such as

- $STOP$ which never does anything

- $\mu\, p.left?x \to p$ which accepts inputs, but never gives them back

---

[1]Invariably T will be the type of $left$ and $right$ so that, for example $\{|\ left\ |\} = left.T$. We will use whichever of these notations is most appropriate in future discussions of buffers, though the one on the left is problematic in cases where $left$ and $right$ may be used with different types in the internal and external channels of a buffer constructed as a chain.

- $\mu\, p.left.0 \rightarrow right.0 \rightarrow p$ which transmits only 0's
- $STOP \sqcap COPY$, which may behave perfectly, but may also deadlock.

All of these fall short, in one way or another, because they either may, or must, refuse some communication we might reasonably expect a buffer to agree to. What we need is to use a failures/divergences specification stating:

(i) All a buffer does is input on *left* and output on *right*. It correctly copies all its inputs to its output channel, without loss or reordering.

(ii) Whenever it is empty (i.e., it has output everything it has input) then it must accept any input.

(iii) Whenever it is non-empty, then it cannot refuse to output.

This can easily be translated into a specification in terms of failures and divergences. Since a diverging process is not responding to its environment; whether an input or output is expected of it, it is clear that we cannot allow a buffer to diverge. We therefore stipulate that, for any buffer B, $divergences(B) = \{\}$. The rest of the specification is then:

(i) $s \in traces(B) \Rightarrow s \in (left.T \cup right.T)^* \wedge s \downarrow right \leq s \downarrow left$

(ii) $(s, X) \in failures(B) \wedge s \downarrow right = s \downarrow left \Rightarrow X \cap left.T = \{\}$

(iii) $(s, X) \in failures(B) \wedge s \downarrow right < s \downarrow left \Rightarrow right.T \not\subseteq X$

These conditions simply translate the corresponding English clauses into mathematics. You should note, in particular, the statements that (ii) and (iii) make about the refusal set X: (ii) asserts that $X \cap left.T = \{\}$, or in other words there is no element of *left.T* that the process can refuse; (iii), on the other hand, states $right.T \not\subseteq X$, a much weaker statement simply saying that there is *some* output available (if we give it the opportunity to choose any output, it cannot refuse). This reflects the asymmetry between input and output, for we expect the environment to choose what happens on *left*, but the process to choose what is output on *right*. In fact, of course, we can predict exactly which output will appear from (i) – if any output other than what we would expect then the trace specification would fail. It would have been equivalent to have stated the following in place of (iii), which 'looks up' the next output:

(iii)' $(s, X) \in failures(B) \wedge (s \downarrow right)^\smallfrown\langle a \rangle \leq s \downarrow left \Rightarrow right.a \notin X$

Any behavioural specification based on failures will follow a pattern somewhat like the above, with a (possibly vacuous) condition on traces combined with various assertions about what the process may refuse after various classes of trace. Newcomers to this field are frequently over-optimisstic about how much one can deduce about the traces from what is stated about refusals. It is tempting to believe that statements like (iii)$'$, which state that a particular thing must be offered, imply that the next event will be that one. This is not so, and even if we were to state that $refusals(P/s) = \{X \mid a \notin X\}$, this would not imply that the next event is a – for the process might be able to nondeterministically accept or refuse some other b. The principle to follow here is that, if you want to limit what traces a process can do, then you should do so with a trace specification like (i) above.

Examples of processes that satisfy the above specification are $COPY$ and $B_{\langle\rangle}^{\infty}$. Just as with behavioural trace specifications, any satisfiable behavioural failures or failures/divergences specification has a most nondeterministic process satisfying it: $\sqcap S$, where S is the set of all processes meeting the specification. In most practical cases this process can be expressed elegantly in CSP in a way that reflects the structure of the specification. We have already seen the specifications for deadlock freedom (DF) and divergence freedom ($Chaos$) amongst many others.

The characteristic process of the buffer specification is $BUFF_{\langle\rangle}$ where

$$
\begin{aligned}
BUFF_{\langle\rangle} &= left?x \rightarrow BUFF_{\langle x\rangle} \\
BUFF_{s^{\frown}\langle a\rangle} &= ((left?x \rightarrow BUFF_{\langle x\rangle^{\frown}s^{\frown}\langle a\rangle}) \sqcap STOP) \\
&\quad \Box\ right!a \rightarrow BUFF_s
\end{aligned}
$$

This, like $B_{\langle\rangle}^{\infty}$, keeps a record of its current contents. However, what it can refuse is governed by the specification above: it cannot refuse to input when empty, but can either accept or refuse an input when non-empty; it cannot refuse to output when non-empty. In general, a process B is a buffer if, and only if, $BUFF_{\langle\rangle} \sqsubseteq_{FD} B$.

Like $B_{\langle\rangle}^{\infty}$, $BUFF_{\langle\rangle}$ is infinite state and therefore its usefulness for automated checking is limited (see Section 5.4 for more details). If you are trying to establish that a process B is a buffer by proving $BUFF_{\langle\rangle} \sqsubseteq_{FD} B$ with FDR, then if this is possible there is (as B must certainly be finite state itself for this to be a reasonable proposition) some limit N on the buffering capacity of B. If using a tool where it is either impossible or inefficient to deal with infinite-state specifications, in order to prove B is a buffer you can make an estimate of N, and attempt to prove $BUFF_{\langle\rangle}^{N} \sqsubseteq_{FD} B$, where $BUFF_{\langle\rangle}^{N}$ is the most nondeterministic N-place buffer:

$$
\begin{aligned}
BUFF_{\langle\rangle}^{N} &= left?x \rightarrow BUFF_{\langle x\rangle}^{N} \\
BUFF_{s^{\frown}\langle a\rangle}^{N} &= (((left?x \rightarrow BUFF_{\langle x\rangle^{\frown}s^{\frown}\langle a\rangle}^{N}) \sqcap STOP) \\
&\qquad\quad \triangleleft \#s < N{-}1 \triangleright STOP) \\
&\quad \Box\ right!a \rightarrow BUFF_s^{N}
\end{aligned}
$$

If the attempt to prove refinement fails this will be for one of two reasons: either your estimate of N was too low, or B is not a buffer. You can tell which one of these is the problem either by inspecting the counter-example behaviour provided by the tool, or by checking against the following process, which we will call an N-place *weak buffer*: it behaves like a buffer provided the environment does not over-fill it (with more than N things) but breaks if this does happen

$$
\begin{aligned}
WBUFF_{\langle\rangle}^N &= left?x \to WBUFF_{\langle x\rangle}^N \\
WBUFF_{s^\frown\langle a\rangle}^N &= ((left?x \to (WBUFF_{\langle x\rangle^\frown s^\frown\langle a\rangle}^N \mathbin{\langle\!\langle} \#s < N-1 \mathbin{\rangle\!\rangle} \mathbf{div})) \\
&\quad \sqcap STOP) \\
&\quad \square\ right!a \to WBUFF_s^N
\end{aligned}
$$

If your process refines $WBUFF_{\langle\rangle}^N$ this does not mean it is a buffer, but does mean that the reason why it failed $BUFF_{\langle\rangle}^N$ was because it could take in more than N things at once. The strategy should then be repeated with a larger value of N.

If your process fails to refine $WBUFF_{\langle\rangle}^N$ then it certainly is not a buffer. The specifications $WBUFF_{\langle\rangle}^N$ and $BUFF_{\langle\rangle}^N$ have a 'sandwiching' effect on $BUFF_{\langle\rangle}$: for any N

$$
WBUFF_{\langle\rangle}^N \sqsubseteq_{FD} WBUFF_{\langle\rangle}^{N+1} \sqsubseteq_{FD} BUFF_{\langle\rangle} \sqsubseteq_{FD} BUFF_{\langle\rangle}^{N+1} \sqsubseteq_{FD} BUFF_{\langle\rangle}^N
$$

Furthermore, one can show that any finite-state process that refines $BUFF_{\langle\rangle}$ will refine $BUFF_{\langle\rangle}^N$ for sufficiently large N, and a finite-state process that *fails* to refine $BUFF_{\langle\rangle}$ will fail to refine $WBUFF_{\langle\rangle}^N$ for sufficiently large N.[2]

The piping operator $\gg$ is intimately connected with the buffer specification, as is shown by the following *buffer laws*.

BL1. If P and Q are buffers, then so is $P \gg Q$. Note that this statement is equivalent to the fact that

$$
BUFF_{\langle\rangle} \sqsubseteq_{FD} BUFF_{\langle\rangle} \gg BUFF_{\langle\rangle}
$$

since the (monotonic) properties of refinement mean that this single refinement implies our law.

BL2. If Q uses only the events $left.T \cup right.T$, and P and $P \gg Q$ are both buffers, then Q is a buffer. This law represents a kind of quotient result compared with the product in BL1. It is also true on the other side, as shown by the next law.

---

[2]This is in part because the process $BUFF_{\langle\rangle}$ is the *least upper bound* of $\{WBUFF_{\langle\rangle}^N \mid N \in \mathbb{N}\}$. See Chapter 8 and Appendix A for more details.

BL3. If P uses only the events $left.T \cup right.T$, and Q and $P \gg Q$ are both buffers, then P is a buffer.

BL4. If $P \gg Q$ is a buffer and x is not free in either P or Q, then the following process is also a buffer:

$$left?x \to (P \gg right!x \to Q)$$

This process makes an arbitrary input (as any buffer must as its first step), and then behaves like the buffer $P \gg Q$ with the additional ability to output what was input. While this result is a sometimes useful technical fact, the next law, which is a kind of inverse to it, is the main analytic technique used to prove that piped systems that are not entirely composed of smaller buffers, are themselves buffers.

BL5. If x is free in neither P nor Q, which are such that

$$P \gg Q \sqsupseteq_{FD} left?x \to (P \gg right!x \to Q)$$

then $P \gg Q$ is a buffer. This is a sort of inductive principle which, very loosely paraphrased, says: if what the process does at first is OK, and it then refines an earlier view of itself, then everything it does is OK. Sometimes when applying this law one finds that it is not general enough because $P \gg Q$ evaluates to $left?x \to (P' \gg right!x \to Q')$ for some other processes P' and Q' for which you suspect $P' \gg Q'$ is also a buffer. By doing this repeatedly one might find a set $\{P_\lambda \gg Q_\lambda \mid \lambda \in \Lambda\}$ of piped combinations and find oneself using the following rather more complex generalization of BL5.

BL5'. If x is free in neither P_λ nor Q_λ for any λ in Λ, a non-empty indexing set, and for each $\lambda \in \Lambda$

$$P_\lambda \gg Q_\lambda \sqsupseteq_{FD} left?x \to \bigsqcap\{(P_\lambda \gg right!x \to Q_\lambda) \mid \lambda \in \Lambda\}$$

then each $P_\lambda \gg Q_\lambda$ is a buffer.

The applications of BL1 are many and obvious: for example, it shows that any chaining-together of any finite number of buffers using $\gg$ is still a buffer. BL2 and BL3 are more subtle properties. They might well be used in combination with BL5: if that rule can show $P \gg Q$ is a buffer and we already know that one of P and Q is, then so is the other by BL2 or BL3 (see Exercise 5.1.3). We will see an application of BL4 a little later. But our main examples for this section will be on the use of BL5 and BL5', for these are both the most complex of the laws and the ones that can establish the strongest-seeming results.

The form of BL1–BL3 ensures that all the visible uses of the channels *left* and *right* have the same type. However, in BL4–BL5', there is nothing to prevent the internal channel of the pipe having a different type to the external one, and indeed these laws are frequently used when this is the case. See Exercise 5.1.2, for example.

As an extremely simple example of BL5, suppose $T = \mathbb{N}$, the natural numbers and that

$$
\begin{aligned}
P &= \; left?x \to right!(2 \times x) \to P \\
Q &= \; left?x \to right!(x/2) \to Q
\end{aligned}
$$

then $P \gg Q$ is a buffer by BL5 because of the following simple calculation:

$$
\begin{aligned}
P \gg Q &= \; left?x \to (right!(2 \times x) \to P \gg Q) &&\text{by } \langle \gg\text{-step 1}\rangle \\
&= \; left?x \to (P \gg right!((2 \times x)/2) \to Q) &&\text{by } \langle \gg\text{-step 3}\rangle \\
&= \; left?x \to (P \gg right!x \to Q)
\end{aligned}
$$

EXAMPLE 5.1.1 (OVERCOMING MESSAGE CORRUPTION) For a larger example, suppose we are faced with a communication medium E that corrupts occasional messages. We want to overcome these errors by constructing processes S and R such that $S \gg E \gg R$ is a buffer. To do this we have to make some sort of assumption about how bad E is: our task would be impossible if it could corrupt any or all messages. Let us assume it can store only one message at a time, can corrupt at most one out of any three consecutive messages and, for simplicity, that the messages being passed are simple bits (0 or 1). We can build a CSP process that represents the medium: namely the most nondeterministic one that satisfies our assumptions about its behaviour. $E = E_0$, where

$$
\begin{aligned}
E_0 &= \; left?x \to (right!x \to E_0 \sqcap right!(1-x) \to E_2) \\
E_{n+1} &= \; left?x \to right!x \to E_n \qquad \text{for } n = 0, 1
\end{aligned}
$$

Here, E_n is the process that is obliged to transmit n values correctly before being allowed to corrupt another. Notice that though E_0 *can* corrupt the first bit it receives, it does not have to, and only becomes obliged to transmit two properly when it does in fact corrupt one. A process that reliably corrupted every third bit would be much easier to overcome than this one. Notice that (as $P \sqcap Q \sqsubseteq P$)

$$
\begin{aligned}
E_0 &= \; left?x \to (right!x \to E_0 \sqcap right!(1-x) \to E_2) \\
&\sqsubseteq \; left?x \to right!x \to E_0 = E_1
\end{aligned}
$$

and hence

$$
E_1 = \; left?x \to right!x \to E_0 \sqsubseteq left?x \to right!x \to E_1 = E_2
$$

In other words, $E_0 \sqsubseteq E_1 \sqsubseteq E_2$, which should not be very surprising given that the only difference between these processes is how long they have to wait before *being allowed to* corrupt a bit.

Notice how the fact that CSP can describe nondeterministic systems (having the $\sqcap$ operator) means we can describe system components over which we have no control and which might be nondeterministic. While it would be a strange decision to use operators like $\sqcap$ a in a process we are designing to build, having them is useful in cases like this. What we are in fact doing is to use for E the specification we are assuming it meets. Of course if, in reality, E fails to satisfy this specification then any results you may have proved are invalidated.

The obvious technique for overcoming the sort of error displayed by this E is to transmit each message three times through E and to take a majority vote. The process descriptions for the sender and receiver process are

$$S_{maj} \quad = \quad left?x \rightarrow right!x \rightarrow right!x \rightarrow right!x \rightarrow S_{maj}$$

$$R_{maj} \quad = \quad left?x \rightarrow left?y \rightarrow left?z \rightarrow right!(x \triangleleft x = y \triangleright z) \rightarrow R_{maj}$$

We can use BL5 to prove $S_{maj} \gg E \gg R_{maj}$ is a buffer using the decomposition $(S_{maj} \gg E) \gg R_{maj}$ (i.e., the 'P' of BL5 is $S_{maj} \gg E$). Denote by R_{maj}^{a}, $R_{maj}^{a,b}$ and $R_{maj}^{a,b,c}$ the process R_{maj} after inputting the values a, a and b, or a and b and c respectively (in the given order). $S_{maj} \gg E \gg R_{maj}$ equals the following series of processes, derived methodically using the step and distributive laws of $\gg$.

$$
\begin{aligned}
&\quad left?x \rightarrow \\
&\quad (((right!x \rightarrow right!x \rightarrow right!x \rightarrow S_{maj}) \\
&\qquad \gg E_0) \gg R_{maj}) && \text{by } \langle \gg\text{-step 1}\rangle \text{ twice} \\
={} &\quad left?x \rightarrow \\
&\quad ((right!x \rightarrow right!x \rightarrow S_{maj}) \\
&\qquad \gg (right!x \rightarrow E_0 \sqcap right!(1{-}x) \rightarrow E_2) \\
&\qquad \gg R_{maj}) && \text{by } \langle \gg\text{-step 3}\rangle \\
={} &\quad left?x \rightarrow \\
&\quad ((right!x \rightarrow right!x \rightarrow S_{maj}) \\
&\qquad \gg ((E_0 \gg R_{maj}^{x}) \sqcap (E_2 \gg R_{maj}^{1-x}))) && \text{by } \langle \gg\text{-step 3}\rangle \text{ and } \langle \gg\text{-dist-l}\rangle \\
={} &\quad left?x \rightarrow \\
&\quad (((right!x \rightarrow right!x \rightarrow S_{maj}) \\
&\qquad \gg (E_0 \gg R_{maj}^{x})) \\
&\quad \sqcap ((right!x \rightarrow right!x \rightarrow S_{maj}) \\
&\qquad \gg (E_2 \gg R_{maj}^{1-x}))) && \text{by distributivity}
\end{aligned}
$$

This represents its 'state' after the first of the triple communications has taken place. Similar derivations shows that after the second communication it is

$$left?x \rightarrow$$
$$(((right!x \rightarrow S_{maj}) \gg (E_0 \gg R_{maj}^{x,x}))$$
$$\sqcap ((right!x \rightarrow S_{maj}) \gg (E_2 \gg R_{maj}^{x,1-x})))$$
$$\sqcap ((right!x \rightarrow right!x \rightarrow S_{maj}) \gg (E_1 \gg R_{maj}^{1-x,x})))$$

and that when all three communications are taken account of it is equivalent to

$$left?x \rightarrow$$
$$((S_{maj} \gg (E_0 \gg R_{maj}^{x,x,x}))$$
$$\sqcap (S_{maj} \gg (E_2 \gg R_{maj}^{x,x,1-x}))$$
$$\sqcap (S_{maj} \gg (E_1 \gg R_{maj}^{x,1-x,x}))$$
$$\sqcap (S_{maj} \gg (E_0 \gg R_{maj}^{1-x,x,x})))$$

Since $R_{maj}^{x,x,x}$, $R_{maj}^{x,x,1-x}$, $R_{maj}^{x,1-x,x}$ and $R_{maj}^{1-x,x,x}$ all equal $right!x \rightarrow R_{maj}$, distributivity implies this equals

$$left?x \rightarrow (S_{maj} \gg (E_0 \sqcap E_2 \sqcap E_1 \sqcap E_0) \gg right!x \rightarrow R_{maj})$$

which, since $E_0 \sqsubseteq E_1 \sqsubseteq E_2$, equals

$$left?x \rightarrow (S_{maj} \gg E_0 \gg right!x \rightarrow R_{maj})$$

which is exactly what is required to prove our result using BL5. *(End of example)*

In the above example we took advantage of the properties of $\sqcap$ and refinement to convert what was rather a complex expression for the 'final' state – we were left with the possibility of any one of E_0, E_1 and E_2 in the middle – into what we wanted for the basic form of BL5. The more complex second form BL5′ exists for cases where we are not so lucky and where the states our system gets into after transmitting the first communication cannot be reconciled into the original one. It can be applied both in cases where the choice is nondeterministic, as above, or in cases where the system simply goes through an evolutionary cycle. As an example of the latter, consider the following.

EXAMPLE 5.1.2 (PARITY BITS) A pair of processes IP and CP, again transmitting bits, insert an extra parity bit after each group of 8, and respectively check and discard this bit. We might describe these processes as follows: $IP = IP(0,0)$ and

$CP = CP(0,0)$ where

$$
\begin{aligned}
IP(b,n) &= left?x \rightarrow right!x \rightarrow IP(b \oplus x, n+1) &&\text{for } n < 8 \\
&= right!b \rightarrow IP(0,0) &&\text{for } n = 8 \\
CP(b,n) &= left?x \rightarrow right!x \rightarrow CP(b \oplus x, n+1) &&\text{for } n < 8 \\
&= left.b \rightarrow CP(0,0) &&\text{for } n = 8
\end{aligned}
$$

Note that the combination will deadlock if CP is offered the wrong parity bit at any stage.

To prove that $IP \gg CP$ is a buffer, it is necessary to consider all the pairs

$$\{IP(b,n) \gg CP(b,n) \mid b \in \{0,1\}, n \in \{0,1,\ldots,8\}\}$$

If $n < 8$, it is easy to show that

$$
\begin{aligned}
IP(b,n) \gg CP(b,n) = \;& left?x \rightarrow (IP(b \oplus x, n+1) \gg \\
& right!x \rightarrow CP(b \oplus x, n+1))
\end{aligned}
$$

while $IP(b,8) \gg CP(b,8) = IP(0,0) \gg CP(0,0)$ which in turn equals

$$left?x \rightarrow (IP(x,1) \gg right!x \rightarrow CP(x,1))$$

It follows trivially that, for each b and $n \leq 8$,

$$
\begin{aligned}
IP(b,n) \gg CP(b,n) \quad \sqsupseteq \quad & left?x \rightarrow \\
& \textstyle\bigsqcap \{IP(b',m) \gg right!x \rightarrow CP(b',m) \mid \\
& \quad b' \in \{0,1\}, m \in \{0,1,\ldots,8\}\}
\end{aligned}
$$

which is what is needed to show that each of these combinations is a buffer by BL5$'$. *(End of example)*

Applying BL5$'$ has much in common with applying the UFP rule: you need to identify the set of states the system under consideration can go through, and show that each of them behaves properly. In the present case each state is a pair of processes (P, Q) (corresponding to $P \gg Q$): the way the right-hand side of the rule separates these makes this very important. You should note that it is possible to have P, Q, P', Q' such that

$$P \gg Q = P' \gg Q', \quad \text{but}$$

$$left?x \rightarrow (P \gg right!x \rightarrow Q) \neq left?x \rightarrow (P' \gg right!x \rightarrow Q')$$

Examples are $P = Q = COPY$, $P' = right!0 \rightarrow COPY$, $Q' = left?x \rightarrow COPY$.

Fixed-point induction

The following principle – which we will call *fixed-point induction* – can be used to prove that a recursive definition meets a specification. It has similarities both with laws BL5 and BL5′ above, and also with the principle of unique fixed points. As with both of these, we can state a simple version for a single process, and a more involved one for vectors of processes defined by mutual recursion.

FIXED-POINT INDUCTION (SINGLE RECURSION)[3] *If $P = F(P)$ is any recursive definition such that either it is guarded/constructive or it defines a divergence-free process, and Q is such that $Q \sqsubseteq_{FD} F(Q)$, then we may conclude $Q \sqsubseteq_{FD} P$. In the cases of $\sqsubseteq_F$ and $\sqsubseteq_T$ this principle holds without the need to assume the either/or condition of the recursion.*

Note that, since F is always monotone, $Q \sqsubseteq F(Q)$ is equivalent to the statement

$$Q \sqsubseteq P \implies Q \sqsubseteq F(P)$$

'if P satisfies (the specification) Q, then so does $F(P)$'.

For example, if $F(BUFF_{\langle\rangle}) \sqsupseteq_{FD} BUFF_{\langle\rangle}$ for a well-behaved function $F(\cdot)$, then the process defined by $P = F(P)$ is a buffer. Consider the process

$$B^+ = left?x \to (B^+ \gg right!x \to COPY)$$

defined in the previous chapter. If we accept the argument given there that this recursion is constructive, then fixed-point induction and our buffer laws easily prove it to be a buffer. Suppose P is a buffer, then

- $P \gg COPY$ is a buffer by BL1, which implies

- $left?x \to (P \gg right!x \to COPY)$ is a buffer by BL4.

- This proves what is required for fixed-point induction; we can infer that B^+ is a buffer.

FIXED-POINT INDUCTION (MUTUAL RECURSION)   *If $\underline{P} = F(\underline{P})$ is any recursive definition of a vector of processes which, as above, is either guarded/constructive or makes each component divergence-free, with indexing set Λ, and $\underline{Q}$ is such that $Q_\lambda \sqsubseteq_{FD} F(\underline{Q})_\lambda$ for all $\lambda \in \Lambda$, then we may conclude that $Q_\lambda \sqsubseteq_{FD} P_\lambda$ for all $\lambda \in \Lambda$. Again, in the cases of $\sqsubseteq_F$ and $\sqsubseteq_T$ this principle holds without the need to assume one of the definedness conditions of the recursion.*

---

[3]For the proof that this and similar rules are valid, see Section 9.2.

As an example of this rule in action, consider the mutual recursive process $B_{\langle\rangle}^{\infty}$ defined in Section 1.1.3. We asserted earlier that this is a buffer, a claim that can now easily be justified. We prove that

$$B_s^{\infty} \sqsupseteq BUFF_s \quad \text{for all finite sequences } s.$$

To do this (since the B^{∞} recursion is guarded) it is sufficient to prove that

$$\underline{BUFF} \sqsubseteq F(\underline{BUFF})$$

where F is the function of the B^{∞} recursion. This is verified by examining the definition of $BUFF$, copied here from page 115

$$
\begin{aligned}
BUFF_{\langle\rangle} &= left?x \rightarrow BUFF_{\langle x \rangle} \\
BUFF_{s^\frown\langle a \rangle} &= ((left?x \rightarrow BUFF_{\langle x \rangle^\frown s^\frown\langle a \rangle}) \sqcap \underline{STOP}) \\
&\quad \Box \; right!a \rightarrow BUFF_s
\end{aligned}
$$

Since removing nondeterministic options leads to a refinement, we can conclude that taking away the underlined option above leads to the inference that

$$
\begin{aligned}
BUFF_{\langle\rangle} &\sqsubseteq left?x \rightarrow BUFF_{\langle x \rangle} \\
BUFF_{s^\frown\langle a \rangle} &\sqsubseteq (left?x \rightarrow BUFF_{\langle x \rangle^\frown s^\frown\langle a \rangle}) \\
&\quad \Box \; right!a \rightarrow BUFF_s
\end{aligned}
$$

which is precisely what was required (since the right-hand side is $F(\underline{BUFF})$).

It should be emphasized that fixed point induction is a very general technique and is certainly not just restricted to proving things are buffers.

EXERCISE 5.1.1   Re-formulate the buffer specification in terms of the variables tr and ref (as used in Exercise 3.3.2).

EXERCISE 5.1.2   Take your answer to Exercise 4.1.3 and prove that it works. *This is probably an application of BL5.*

EXERCISE 5.1.3   Show, using the buffer laws, that if

$$B \gg COPY = left?x \rightarrow (B \gg right!x \rightarrow COPY)$$

then B is a buffer.

Now show that $B^+ \gg COPY$ satisfies the recursive definition of B^+ and deduce that $B^+ = B^+ \gg COPY$. Thus complete an alternative proof that B^+ is a buffer.

EXERCISE 5.1.4   A buffer works on the FIFO (first in, first out) principle. A *stack*, on the other hand, is LIFO (last in, first out): when non-empty, it will output the object it contains that was most recently input. Give a failures specification of a stack in the same style as that of a buffer: like a buffer it should not be able to reject input when empty or to refuse to output when non-empty. *Hint: you might find it helpful to define the concept of a stack trace recursively, based on the principle that whenever a stack outputs, the value output was input as the first member of a final subsequence (suffix) s of the trace containing equal numbers of inputs and outputs, and where s without its first and last elements is itself a stack trace.*

Show that *COPY* is a stack as well as a buffer. Are there any other processes satisfying both specifications?

EXERCISE 5.1.5   Implement an infinite stack using the enslavement-based recursive scheme used for the *SET* recursion. It is easiest to do this using an *isempty* event in a similar way. Since the stack specification does not allow such an event, it must be banned *at the outermost level of the recursion only* by parallel composition with *STOP*. Thus, your result should look like

$$STACK' \quad \underset{\{isempty\}}{\|} \quad STOP \quad \text{where } STACK' \text{ is recursively defined.}$$

Do the same thing without the *isempty* event: you should end up with a program that is no longer but perhaps a little more subtle. You might or might not find it helps here to think about how one might eliminate the *iszero* event from the process $Zero_{/\!/}$ defined on page 108.

EXERCISE 5.1.6   A *bag* is a process that behaves in the same general way as buffers and stacks, except that it can always output *any* object it contains (rather than being restricted to FIFO or LIFO, for example). Give a failures specification of a bag, and show it is refined by those for buffers and stacks. *Hint: you will find it helpful to construct or assume a function $bag(t)$ that maps a sequence $t \in T^*$ to the bag or multiset of elements in it: the order of t is lost in $bag(t)$ but the multiplicity of elements is retained. There are obvious analogues of the usual set-theoretic operations over bags.*

EXERCISE 5.1.7   If P_1 and P_2 are (i) buffers, (ii) stacks and (iii) bags, which of the following compositions must have the same property? (a) $P_1 \;|||\; P_2$, (b) $P_1 \gg P_2$, and (c) $P_1 \underset{\{|left,right|\}}{\|} P_2$. Give brief reasons for your answers.

EXERCISE 5.1.8   Suggest analogues of BL1–BL5 for bags using $|||$ rather than $\gg$. Which of them do you think is true?

EXERCISE 5.1.9   Suppose $\mu\, p.F(p)$ is a constructive recursion and it is conjectured that $F(P)$ is deadlock-free whenever P is. What refinement check is necessary to establish this fact? Why would this prove that the recursive process is deadlock-free?

EXERCISE 5.1.10   Consider the two different combinations of *COPY* with itself under the generalized parallel operator considered in Exercise 2.4.2. These can be chained together in two ways: prove that one is a buffer and show that the other is not.

5.2   Buffer tolerance

Consider the effect of placing a buffer on a channel connecting two CSP processes. It makes sense to do this on any channel which is used for communicating information one way, though it may very well alter the behaviour of the overall system even in this case: for example a buffer placed on the internal channel in *COPY* $\gg$ *COPY* will still be a buffer (as is easily proved by BL1) but with increased capacity. This is a relatively subtle effect which one probably would not mind in most circumstances, but (i) clearly it should not be allowed in any context where we are relying on a buffer capacity of two or less and (ii) there are other examples where inserting a buffer in this way would have a much more significant effect.

The extent to which a given channel is *buffer tolerant* is a measure of whether, and how much, it relies on the CSP model of handshaken communication. It is frequently desirable to make any channel that has to operate over a long distance buffer tolerant since implementing the flow-control necessary to avoid introducing some buffering can be expensive.

A given channel may be buffer tolerant in an absolute sense, meaning that the semantics of the overall process does not change at all, or more likely, *relative* to some overall specification. Thus, *COPY* $\gg$ *COPY* is buffer tolerant relative to the specification of being a buffer! Sometimes a channel may be tolerant of buffering up to some given limit or of any *finite* buffer but not infinite capacity ones.

In the *COPY* $\gg$ *COPY* example any buffer which is placed on the internal channels can clearly become full however large it is. Other examples, however, only use a fixed finite quantity of buffering no matter how much is provided. You can characterize such behaviour by testing whether one of the weak buffer processes $WBUFF_{\langle\rangle}^{n}$ can safely be placed on the channel (the parameter n, of course, capturing the maximum amount of buffering ever used). If more than n buffer places were ever used, this experiment would produce a divergent process. For an example of this type of behaviour, see Exercise 5.2.2.

It is easier to understand the concept of buffer tolerance than to provide general criteria under which it is true. Usually it is possible, with experience, to get a feel for whether a given system has this property: specific instances, at least for small buffer sizes, can often be checked using tools like FDR.

The type of circumstances in which it does and does not tend to hold are well illustrated by attempting to generalize the *COPY* $\gg$ *COPY* example to the following general rule. It would be very convenient if the following plausible 'buffer law' were true:

> If $P \gg R$ and Q are both buffers, with the type of Q matching the 'internal' type of $P \gg R$, then $P \gg Q \gg R$ is also a buffer.

Unfortunately, this is not universally valid because of the possibility that R might input selectively from P. As a simple example, suppose $COPY_2$ and $COPY_3$ are respectively defined over the types $T_2 = \{0, 1\}$ and $T_3 = \{0, 1, 2\}$. Then setting

$$
\begin{aligned}
P &= COPY_2 \,\square\, (right!2 \to STOP) \\
Q &= COPY_3 \\
R &= COPY_2
\end{aligned}
$$

gives a counter-example to the above (the internal type being T_3): R has the good sense to reject the offer of 2 in the combination $P \gg R$, which therefore behaves exactly like $COPY_2 \gg COPY_2$. Putting Q in the middle, however, allows P to make its fatal output and deadlock. If we take away the possibility of R controlling what P outputs to it, the law becomes true:

BL6. Suppose $P \gg R$ is a buffer, where the internal type is T (i.e., the type communicated by *right* in P and *left* in R), and that

    (a) Q is a buffer of type T,

    (b) if $s^\frown\langle left.x \rangle \in traces(R)$ and $y \in T$, then $s^\frown\langle left.y \rangle \in traces(R)$, and

    (c) if $(s, X) \in failures(R)$ then $\{| \, right \, |\} \subseteq X \Rightarrow left.T \cap X = \{\}$,

then $P \gg Q \gg R$ is a buffer.

The side conditions (b) and (c) here avoid the possibility that we are relying on influence passing backwards (via handshaking) along the channel in question in order to get the original system to work. They will automatically be satisfied provided R is deadlock-free and the only way it can communicate on *left* is by unrestricted input. Influence of this sort more or less excludes the possibility of buffer tolerance in any example. When looking to see whether there is such influence, you should bear mind that it can be much more subtle than in the $COPY_2/COPY_3$ example above, especially when there are other communication routes between the processes connected by the channel in question: see Exercise 5.2.1. (Needless to say, buffer tolerance makes sense over a much wider range of ways of connecting channels than just the $\gg$ operator.)

    Notice how BL6 supports the concept of a layered protocol discussed on page 103. If we have designed some pairs of processes (T_i, R_i) such that each

$T_i \gg R_i$ $(i > 0)$ is a buffer, and it can be shown that $T_0 \gg M \gg R_0$ is a buffer for some communication medium M, then BL6 and induction imply that

$$T_n \gg T_{n-1} \gg \ldots \gg T_1 \gg T_0 \gg M \gg R_0 \gg R_1 \gg \ldots \gg R_{n-1} \gg R_n$$

is one too, provided the R_i satisfy the no-selective-input criteria of BL6 and the types match up in the obvious way.

EXERCISE 5.2.1   (a)   We can define a pair of processes that alternately use two channels to communicate as follows:

$$
\begin{aligned}
Divide &= \quad left?x \to mid.1!x \to Divide' \\
Divide' &= \quad left?x \to mid.2!x \to Divide \\[4pt]
Merge &= \quad mid?n?x \to right!x \to Merge \\[4pt]
DandM &= \quad (Divide \underset{\{|mid|\}}{\|} Merge) \setminus \{| \ mid \ |\}
\end{aligned}
$$

Plainly *DandM* acts as a two-place buffer: you can prove this easily with BL5$'$ if you interpret *mid* as a single channel and note that the above combination is then equivalent to

$$Divide[\![right/mid]\!] \gg Merge[\![left/mid]\!]$$

Do this and hence show that *DandM* is (relative to the buffer specification) tolerant of buffer of type $\{| \ mid \ |\}$.

(b)   What would happen if we were to re-interpret *mid* as an array of two separate channels and place buffers on each? Show clearly why the result need not be a buffer.

(c)   Replace *Merge* with another process with the same alphabet so that the new system is still a two-place buffer but is tolerant of separate buffers on *mid*.1 and *mid*.2.

EXERCISE 5.2.2   The following processes carry messages alternately between two users:

$$
\begin{aligned}
SwapL &= \quad leftin?x \to to!x \to SwapL' \\
SwapL' &= \quad fro?x \to leftout!x \to SwapL \\[4pt]
SwapR &= \quad to?x \to rightout!x \to SwapR' \\
SwapR' &= \quad rightin?x \to fro!x \to SwapR \\[4pt]
LandR &= \quad (SwapL \underset{\{|to,fro|\}}{\|} SwapR) \setminus \{| \ to, \ fro \ |\}
\end{aligned}
$$

Find a sequential process that *LandR* is equivalent to, and show that a copy of $WBUFF^1_{\langle\rangle}$ can be inserted onto both the internal channels without changing this value.

By adapting this example, find a pair of processes connected by a pair of channels, one in each direction, that implement a buffer which is tolerant of the insertion of $WBUFF^1_{\langle\rangle}$ onto both channels.

How does your answer to Exercise 5.2.1 (c) react to having this weak buffer inserted onto either or both channels?

EXERCISE 5.2.3   Show that if a channel is tolerant of $WBUFF^n_{\langle\rangle}$ then it is tolerant of $WBUFF^{n+1}_{\langle\rangle}$ (relative to any behavioural specification). Find an example of a system that is tolerant of $WBUFF^2_{\langle\rangle}$ but not of $WBUFF^1_{\langle\rangle}$.

5.3   The alternating bit protocol

Earlier in this chapter we saw how to overcome the corruption of at most one in every three messages. It is similarly possible (though harder, particularly in the case where the 'messages' are just bits: see Exercise 4.1.4) to overcome bounded loss, duplication or even a combination of all three together. By 'similarly' here, we mean that the overall system maintains the structure $S \gg E \gg R$.

In practical terms the sort of techniques used in these cases probably only make sense in cases where very low level information (i.e., bits or little more) is being transmitted, almost certainly between hardware components. Since there is only a one-way passage of information there is no way R can let S know that a particular message has got through, and so S must put as much redundancy into the transmission of every message as is necessary to overcome the worst assumed behaviour of the communication medium.

There are more advanced techniques that can be used in cases where larger and more structured values can be passed as messages, and particularly where it is possible to implement an acknowledgement channel (albeit faulty in the same sense as the forward channel) back from R to S. When this channel cannot be implemented (or is impractical because of time delay – for example with the transmission delay, due to the finite speed of light, back from a remote space probe) the appropriate technology is a branch of mathematics called *error correcting codes* which is beyond the scope of this book but which allows one to get the same sort of error correction under corruption as was illustrated earlier, only with much greater efficiency. For various values of (n, k, d) (for example $(23, 12, 3)$) one can find ways of coding a k-bit message into $n > k$ bits in such a way that the result can be decoded even after up to e bits are corrupted. See [81] for a comprehensive introduction to this subject.

When we can implement the acknowledgement channel there are a number of protocols that can be used to exploit it. It is usual to restrict attention in that case to

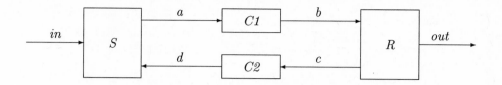

Figure 5.1 The process structure of the alternating bit protocol.

a medium that can lose messages, or perhaps duplicate them, but cannot corrupt them. This is, like so much else, an abstraction of what is really implemented: it is likely that the protocols we are looking at are built on top of mechanisms for inserting checksum-like information into messages and rejecting (i.e., 'losing') messages which fail the corresponding tests when delivered.

We might want to implement a buffer between two distant points but only have unreliable channels available. By this, we mean error-prone channels that can lose or duplicate as many messages as they wish – though not an infinite consecutive sequence – but preserve the value and order of those they do transmit. There are a number of protocols available to overcome this sort of error, the simplest of which is known as the *alternating bit protocol* (ABP). In fact, there are (as we will see in this and later chapters, where we will frequently use it as an example to illustrate new ideas) a number of variants of this protocol, but the basic idea is the same in all of them. The structure of the network used is shown in Figure 5.1, where the two error-prone channels are $C1$ and $C2$.

The basic idea is to add an extra bit to each message sent along the leaky channels which alternates between 0 and 1. The sending process sends multiple copies of each message until it is acknowledged. As soon as the receiving process gets a new message it sends repeated acknowledgements of it until the next message arrives. The two ends can always spot a new message or acknowledgement because of the alternating bit.

This is usually described using real-time features such as time-outs (for deciding when to re-send messages and acknowledgements; we will return to this in Section 14.5), but in fact with a little care it is possible to construct a version whose correctness is independent of timing details. Below we present sender (S) and receiver (R) processes which can readily be proved to work, in the sense that if $C1$ and $C2$ behave as described above, then the complete system behaves like a reliable buffer.

Very general error-prone channel processes are described by the following, where no limit is placed on the number of losses or duplications:

$$C(in, out) \quad = \quad in?x \rightarrow C'(in, out, x)$$

$$
\begin{aligned}
C'(in, out, x) \quad = \quad & out!x \rightarrow C(in, out) && \text{(correct transmission)} \\
& \sqcap out!x \rightarrow C'(in, out, x) && \text{(potential duplication)} \\
& \sqcap C(in, out) && \text{(loss of message)}
\end{aligned}
$$

With the channels implied by Figure 5.1, we get $C1 = C(a, b)$ and $C2 = C(c, d)$.

This sort of erroneous medium may lose as many messages as it likes, and repeat any message as often as it wishes. While we can reasonably hope to create a system using such media which works as long as they do not commit an infinite unbroken series of errors (so that only finitely many messages actually get through in an infinite time), any such system will inevitably be subject to divergence caused by infinite message loss or repetition. One can easily change the definition so that at least one correct action is performed every N as follows:

$$
\begin{aligned}
C_N(in, out, r) \quad = \quad & in?x \rightarrow C'(in, out, x, r) \\[4pt]
C'_N(in, out, x, 0) \quad = \quad & out!x \rightarrow C_N(in, out, N) \\[4pt]
C'_N(in, out, x, r) \quad = \quad & out!x \rightarrow C_N(in, out, N) && \text{if } r > 0 \\
& \sqcap out!x \rightarrow C'_N(in, out, x, r-1) \\
& \sqcap C_N(in, out, r-1)
\end{aligned}
$$

While this definition looks (and is!) very similar to that of E_0 in the previous section, there is the significant difference that this time we are designing a protocol that works independently of which N is chosen. The only function the limit N actually performs should be to prevent divergences. In Chapters 10 and 12 we will meet techniques that allow us to assume what we really want here, namely that neither of the medium processes ever commits an infinite sequence of errors.

The sender and receiver processes are now defined as follows: $S = S(0)$ and $R = R(0) \underset{\{|b,c|\}}{\|} Q$, where for $s \in \{0,1\}$ and x in the set of messages:

$$
S(s) \quad = \quad in?x \rightarrow S'(s, x)
$$

$$
\begin{aligned}
S'(s, x) \quad = \quad & a.s.x \rightarrow S'(s, x) \\
& \Box\, d.s \rightarrow S(1-s) \\
& \Box\, d.(1-s) \rightarrow S'(s, x)
\end{aligned}
$$

$$
\begin{aligned}
R(s) \quad = \quad & b.s?x \rightarrow out!x \rightarrow R(1-s) \\
& \Box\, b.(1-s)?x \rightarrow R(s) \\
& \Box\, c!(1-s) \rightarrow R(s)
\end{aligned}
$$

If we were simply to set $R = R(0)$ then the system could diverge even when $C1$ and $C2$ were error-free, because it could get stuck communicating over $C1$ or $C2$

exclusively. (For example, the transmission of some message might happen infinitely without it ever getting acknowledged.) Therefore we have introduced the extra process Q, with alphabet $\{|\ b, c\ |\}$, in parallel with it to ensure it is sufficiently well-behaved to avoid these types of divergence. Because of the way the two processes are combined in parallel, its effect is to restrict $R(0)$'s possible behaviours. Q is any process that is always either willing to perform any input on b or any output on c (or both) but which will not allow an infinite sequence of communications on one channel to the exclusion of the other (a *fairness* condition). The most obvious such Q is $\mu\, q.b?x \to c?x \to q$, which makes the two channels of R alternate. This illustrates a use of the parallel operator to impose constraints, and is related to the discussion in Section 2.5 about the use of parallel operators as conjunction over trace specifications.

There is no implication that R would be implemented as a parallel process – we would refine the parallel combination into a sequential one. (One satisfactory sequential R, equivalent to the parallel composition of $R(0)$ and the alternating process above, is one that accepts messages on b and sends appropriate acknowledgements on c in strict alternation.)

We will argue the correctness of this protocol informally but sufficiently rigorously that it should be clear how a formal proof would go. Let ABP denote the composition of S, $C1$, $C2$ and R (with R being any version well-behaved in the sense described above and $C1$ and $C2$ being of the form that avoids the simple infinite-error divergences).

Livelock is impossible because of the introduction of Q and because neither $C1$ nor $C2$ commits an infinite series of errors. The latter means that each of $C1$ and $C2$ eventually transmits any message that is input to it repeatedly, and that provided they are not blocked from outputting they will eventually accept any input they are offered. In short, since any divergence clearly involves an infinite number of communications by either $C1$ or $C2$, infinitely many messages must (in the divergence) be either getting through from S to R or *vice-versa*. But R can neither receive infinitely many messages without transmitting one, nor send infinitely many without receiving one. We can therefore conclude that R both sends and receives infinitely many messages in the divergence and (by the properties of $C1$ and $C2$) so does S – all this in a sequence where neither S nor R communicates externally. It easily follows from the definition of S that all the messages from S to R are repetitions of $s.x$ for some fixed bit s and packet x. The fact that R ignores these (as it must, for it does not generate any external communication) means it must be in state $1 - s$ and therefore that the acknowledgements it is sending back are all s. But, of course, since these are received by S they would necessarily interrupt the transmission of the $s.x$'s. Thus the system cannot diverge.

Nor can it deadlock. We will study deadlock in much more depth in Chapter

13 (and see Exercise 13.2.1), but the basic argument for this system rests on the fact that, except when it can communicate externally (which certainly precludes deadlock), S will always both accept any incoming communication on d and be willing to output on a. Hence neither $C1$ nor $C2$ can be waiting for S in a deadlock state, and it follows they are both waiting for R. But unless R is willing to communicate externally it can always communicate with $C1$ or $C2$, so one (at least) of the two requests coming into it is accepted, meaning that the system is not deadlocked. Because it can neither deadlock nor diverge, it follows that, whatever state it reaches, it always eventually comes into a stable state where all it can do is to communicate externally (input on *left*, output on *right* or perhaps both).

In order to study the transmission of messages it is easiest to consider the sequences of messages on a, b, c and d in which any message following another with the same tag bit is removed, as are any initial messages on c and d with tag bit 1. Call these stripped sequences $\overline{a}$, $\overline{b}$, $\overline{c}$ and $\overline{d}$. The structures of the processes involved then imply the following facts:

- $C1$ implies that $\#\overline{a} \geq \#\overline{b}$: the stripping process clearly removes any duplication.

- R implies that $\#\overline{b} \geq \#\overline{c}$: R can only change the bit it outputs along c in response to a change in the input bit on b. It only initiates the first member of $\overline{c}$ in response to the first 0 in $\overline{b}$.

- $C2$ implies that $\#\overline{c} \geq \#\overline{d}$.

- S implies that $\#\overline{d} \geq \#\overline{a} - 1$: S can only change the bit it outputs along a in response to a change in the input bit on d.

We can piece all of these together to get

$$\#\overline{a} \geq \#\overline{b} \geq \#\overline{c} \geq \#\overline{d} \geq \#\overline{a} - 1$$

or, in other words, these four sequences are, in length, all within one of each other. From this it is implied that $C1$ must, at each moment, have transmitted at least one of each equal-bit block of outputs sent by S except perhaps the current one (for it to have completely lost one would imply that $\#\overline{b}$ is at least two less than $\#\overline{a}$). This, the structure of S, and the fact that R outputs a member of each block it receives on *right*, imply that each trace s of the protocol satisfies

$$s \downarrow right \leq s \downarrow left \quad \text{and} \quad \#(s \downarrow left) \leq \#(s \downarrow right) + 1$$

or, in other words,

$$COPY \sqsubseteq_T ABP$$

The facts that *ABP* is deadlock- and divergence-free, and clearly never selects between its inputs, combine with this to imply that it is failures/divergences equivalent to *COPY*.

It can be shown fairly easily by modifying the above arguments that *ABP* is tolerant of any finite buffer on its internal channels. Placing an infinite buffer on one or more of them could lead to divergence.

The alternating bit protocol is too simple and inefficient to be used much in practice. The ideas it uses are, however, to be found in many that are. The interested reader can find some more advanced protocols both in the example files on the web site accompanying this book and in texts such as [24].

EXERCISE 5.3.1   Assume that *R* is the version of the receiver in which received messages and acknowledgements alternate. Estimate the worst-case performance of the resulting ABP when *C*1 and *C*2 are each obliged to commit no more than *N* consecutive errors (in terms of internal communications per message transmitted). Can you improve this by modifying *R*? Would the answer to this last question be changed if *C*1 and *C*2 lost the ability to duplicate messages (retaining the possibility of loss)?

EXERCISE 5.3.2   The version of the protocol in the text leaves *S* free to send and receive messages arbitrarily, but restricts *R* to behave 'fairly'. What would happen (i) if these roles were reversed and (ii) if they were both restricted to be fair?

5.4   Tools

It is usually much easier to analyze and prove things about the sort of systems we have seen in this chapter using a mechanical tool like FDR rather than by hand. The examples we have dealt with here are extremely simple compared to those that can be handled mechanically. Notice that laws like BL5 and BL5′ essentially work by enumerating the states of a chained system, and it is certainly true that computers do this sort of work better than humans.

As with the work in the previous chapter, the absence of direct support for $\gg$ in the machine-readable version of CSP means that the 'plumbing' of such networks has to be done in other ways such as the P[c <-> d]Q construct.

You should bear in mind, though, that current tools can only prove things about specific processes, and then only ones that are finite state.[4] Thus, we cannot

---

[4]With the version of FDR available at the time of writing it is not possible to have an infinite-state process like $BUFF_{\langle\rangle}$ as a specification. It is likely that future versions will be able to deal with these, by exploring only those parts of the specification that are necessary – employing *lazy* exploration and normalization. It will therefore be possible to prove that a finite-state process is a buffer without guessing its maximum size. However, this is likely to carry a performance penalty so it will probably remain a good idea to keep most specifications finite state.

use FDR to prove laws like BL1–BL6 and cannot directly prove that B^+ (an infinite-state process) is a buffer. Nor can it prove general buffer tolerance except where some $WBUFF_{\langle\rangle}^n$ works. Remember, however, that it may be required that the specification be finite state also, implying the need to use some of the restricted or approximate specifications discussed in the first section of this chapter.

An exception to the rule that one can only prove things about finite state implementations arises from fixed-point induction. The point is that, even though the process defined by a recursion $P = F(P)$ (like that of B^+) may be infinite state, it is quite likely that $F(Q)$ will be finite state if Q is. Thus, if the characteristic process of the specification Q we are trying to prove of P is finite state, the main proof obligation of fixed-point induction, namely

$$Q \sqsubseteq F(Q)$$

is likely to be something one can verify automatically.

For example, one can prove for any chosen N (that is small enough to allow FDR to deal with the resultant state spaces) that B^+ satisfies any of the weak buffer specifications $WBUFF_{\langle\rangle}^N$. You cannot ask the same question about the full specification $BUFF_{\langle\rangle}$ because the resulting right-hand side is infinite state. An attempt to prove any of the finite buffer specifications $BUFF_{\langle\rangle}^N$ will fail because B^+ does not satisfy these (but it would nevertheless be interesting to reassure yourself that this is so by attempting the checks).

It is an obvious limitation on this type of tool that they cannot take the step from proving that B^+ satisfies $WBUFF_{\langle\rangle}^N$ for any chosen N to proving it is true for *all N*. (This comes under the category of 'general results' that are unobtainable as discussed above.)

It is worth while pointing out one category of 'general results' that are obtainable using finite-state checking which tends to be particularly relevant to communications protocols. This relates to the notion of 'data-independence'. Many of the process definitions in this chapter were, or could have been, defined so that they transmitted data values taken from a completely arbitrary type. These values are input and passed around and manipulated uninspected within the program: the nature of the underlying data type is completely irrelevant to the operation of the program. It is frequently possible to infer results about how such a program behaves for general types based on their behaviour for very small ones (often size one or two). This concept is developed, together with two case studies, in Section 15.2.

Chapter 6

Termination and sequential composition

6.1 What is termination?

In many programming languages there is a sequential composition operator: P; Q runs P until it *terminates* and then runs Q. In CSP we would expect to see all of P's communications until it terminates, and for it then to behave like Q. There is no conceptual problem with this provided we understand just what termination means.

So far we have come across two sorts of process which can communicate no more: on the one hand, a deadlocked process such as $STOP$ or a deadlocked parallel network; on the other, the divergent process **div**. Neither of these can be said to have terminated *successfully*, since both represent error states. Indeed, divergence is in principle undetectable in a finite time in general, as a result of the unsolvability of the halting problem. It is natural to want to associate P; Q with a form of termination which happens positively rather than by default.

The process which terminates immediately will be written $SKIP$. We will think of the act of terminating as producing the special event $\checkmark$ (usually pronounced 'tick'). Thus, $SKIP$ can be identified with the process $\checkmark \to STOP$. You can think of a process communicating $\checkmark$ as saying 'I have terminated successfully'. The identification of termination with an event is often convenient, but the analogy should not be taken too far – for example, $\checkmark$ is always the final event a process performs. $\checkmark$ is not (in this presentation of CSP) a member of Σ – emphasizing that it is very special. It is not permitted to introduce $\checkmark$ directly: $SKIP$ is the only way it arises; for example the syntax $\checkmark \to STOP$ used above is illegal because it mentions $\checkmark$. $\Sigma^{\checkmark}$ will denote the extended alphabet $\Sigma \cup \{\checkmark\}$.

Thus $SKIP$; $P = P$ for all P, since all $SKIP$ does is terminate successfully and pass control over to P. In contrast, $STOP$; $P = STOP$, since $STOP$ does not terminate, merely come to an ungraceful halt. Similarly **div**; $P = $ **div**. Notice that the $\checkmark$ of the *SKIP* in *SKIP*; P is hidden from the environment – this simply means that we cannot see where the join occurs from the outside, and means that we do not confuse the occurrence of the first $\checkmark$ with overall termination. Because of this concealment parts of the theory of sequential composition bear some similarity to that of hiding and, in particular, it turns the final $\checkmark$ of the first process into a τ (invisible action).

A formal tabulation of the laws of these new constructs is delayed to a later section. However, we would expect ; (sequential composition) to be associative and distributive, and

$$(?x : A \rightarrow P);\ Q\ =\ ?x : A \rightarrow (P;\ Q)$$

amongst other laws (noting that $\checkmark$ cannot, by the assumptions above, be an element of A).

This 'law' brings up an interesting point in the interpretation of 'state' identifiers in CSP processes, the identifiers that represent objects input or used in parameterized recursions such as *COUNT* or B^∞. For consider the 'identity'

$$(?x : A \rightarrow SKIP);\ x \rightarrow STOP\ =\ ?x : A \rightarrow (SKIP;\ (x \rightarrow STOP))$$

In the right-hand side, it is quite clear that the second x must be the same event as the first, while on the left-hand side this would require the value of x communicated first to be remembered outside the prefix choice construct that introduced it, and across the sequential composition ; . This raises the important question of how the values and scopes of identifiers are to be interpreted. The real question we need to resolve in order to decide this is whether CSP is an *imperative* language, where the value of an identifier can be modified (and the input $?x : A$ is taken to modify an existing value), or a *declarative* language, where it cannot. We take the declarative view that a construct like $?x : A \rightarrow P$ creates a new identifier called x to hold the input value in P and that this value is not remembered once P has terminated, since we have left x's *scope*. An identifier gets its value at the point where it is declared and keeps the same value throughout that scope. If there are any other identifiers called x created by input or otherwise within P, then these simply create a hole in scope in the same way as in many programming languages. Thus, the final x in the term

$$?x : A \rightarrow ((?x : A \rightarrow SKIP);\ (x \rightarrow STOP))$$

will always be the one created by the first input.

It is this decision which allows us to identify all terminations with the single event $\checkmark$, and also allows us to avoid the question of how an assignable state is shared over a parallel construct. Note how this decision is consistent with the observation made in the Introduction (Chapter 0) about process algebras discarding standard programming language constructs such as assignment.

In conclusion, the law above is only valid if the term Q does not contain an unbound (i.e., free) reference to an identifier called x. If it does, then it would simply be necessary to change the name of the bound identifier so that it no longer clashes with any free in Q.

In examples, sequential composition can be used to improve the modularity of descriptions – allowing one to separate out different phases of behaviour. It also permits us to express some definitions finitely which normally require infinite mutual recursion. Recall the infinite mutual recursion defining $COUNT_n$ for $n \in \mathbb{N}$. There is a very clear sense in which this describes an infinite-state system, for all the different values that n can take lead to essentially different $COUNT_n$. We can simulate this behaviour using sequential composition as follows:

$$
\begin{aligned}
ZERO &= up \to POS;\ ZERO, \quad \text{where} \\
POS &= up \to POS;\ POS \\
&\quad \Box\ down \to SKIP
\end{aligned}
$$

The intuition here is that POS is a process that terminates as soon as it has communicated one more $down$'s than up's. Thus $ZERO$, which is intended to behave like $COUNT_0$, initially only accepts an up, and returns to that state.as soon as the number of subsequent $down$'s has brought the overall tally into balance.

We will prove this equivalence when we are equipped with enough laws.

Iteration

Now that we have a sequential composition operator it is natural to want ways of repeating a process. The simplest repetition operator is infinite iteration: P^* means the repetition of P for ever with no way of escaping. This is not a construct that makes sense in many programming languages, since in a standard language an infinitely repeated program would simply send one's computer into a useless loop (divergence). In CSP, of course, a process is measured by what it communicates as it goes along, so that the definition

$$P^* = P;\ P^*$$

makes sense. For example, $(a \to SKIP)^*$ is simply a process that communicates an infinite sequence of a's; it is indistinguishable from $\mu\, p.a \to p$. We can similarly write

$$COPY = (left?x \to right!x \to SKIP)^*$$

However, the declarative semantics of identifiers means that no information can be 'remembered' from an input in one P to a later one in P^*. Thus a two-place buffer cannot be written as neatly: the best we can do is to create a two-place temporary buffer that terminates when emptied:

$$
\begin{aligned}
TB &= left?x \to TB'(x) \\
TB'(x) &= right!x \to SKIP \\
&\quad \Box\ left?y \to right!x \to TB'(y) \\[4pt]
IterBuff_2 &= TB^*
\end{aligned}
$$

Because of the way the values x and y are intertwined in this definition, there is no hope of writing TB or $TB'(x)$ as an iteration. To do so we would require an external place to store values: see Exercise 6.1.2.

The declarative semantics also means that there can be no direct analogue of a WHILE loop: this depends on being able to evaluate a boolean whose value changes with the state of the process – something that makes no sense when an identifier's value does not change within its scope.

It would, however, be possible to define an analogue of a FOR loop: this might be

$$
FOR\ n = a, b\ DO\ P\ =\ \begin{array}{l} SKIP \triangleleft a > b \triangleright \\ P[a/n];\ (FOR\ n = a + 1, b\ DO\ P) \end{array}
$$

since the identifier of this type of loop is declared in the construct itself. Indeed many of the traditional inelegancies of imperative programming with FOR loops (such as assigning to the loop identifier or changing the values of the bounds within the body) become impossible in a declarative semantics. The FOR loop is not, however, part of usual CSP syntax.

EXERCISE 6.1.1   Define a process *PHOLE* representing a pigeon-hole: it can communicate *empty* when empty, when it will also accept *in?x* and become full. When full it can only accept *out.x* for the appropriate x, which empties it. You should give both a definition as an ordinary recursion and one as Q^* where Q contains no recursion.

Show that the two processes you have defined are equivalent.

EXERCISE 6.1.2   Find a process P such that the two-place buffer equals

$$
(P^* \mathbin{\|}_{\{|in, out, empty|\}} PHOLE)
$$

and P contains no form of recursion. [*Hint: P should, on each of its cycles, communicate first with its slave.*]

6.2   Distributed termination

Having introduced the concept of termination we have to understand how it relates to the other CSP operators, and in particular the parallel operators. If we treated $\checkmark$ like any other event, then we would say that $P \ _X\|_Y \ Q$ has the following cases for determining termination:

- If $\checkmark \notin X \cup Y$ then it can never terminate.
- If $\checkmark \in X \setminus Y$ then it will terminate whenever P does.
- If $\checkmark \in Y \setminus X$ then it will terminate whenever Q does.
- If $\checkmark \in X \cap Y$ then it terminates when both P and Q do.

The middle two of these are somewhat problematic, for they leave behind the question of what to do with the process which has not terminated. We might assert that it is closed down by some powerful mechanism which, if we are really expecting a distributed parallel implementation, seems to have to act instantaneously over a distance. On the other hand, the other process might continue, creating the embarrassment of a system which communicates after 'terminating'. Realizing that termination is really something that the environment observes rather than controls, the first case (and the non-terminating halves of the second and third) cannot realistically prevent the arguments from terminating, but can only fail to report this to the outer environment. Given this observation, there is really no sensible use of the first item ($\checkmark \notin X \cup Y$) above, since all that it can achieve is to turn what would have been termination into deadlock.

The route we take is to assert that the final clause always holds implicitly: there is no need to include $\checkmark$ in the alphabets X or Y, for after all $\checkmark$ is not a member of Σ, but the combination $P \ _X\|_Y \ Q$ always behaves as though it were in both. In other words, a parallel combination terminates when all of the combined processes terminate. This is known as *distributed termination*. This reading makes it sound as though the various processes have to synchronize on termination, as they do on normal events in $X \cap Y$. In fact the best way of thinking about distributed termination is that all of the processes are allowed to terminate when they want to, and that the overall combination terminates when the last one does. The fact that termination is the last thing a process does means that these two views are consistent with each other: in $P \ _X\|_Y \ Q$, neither process can communicate after it has terminated but the other has not.

If A is a set of events which we wish to communicate in any order and then terminate, then this can be expressed

$$\Big\|_{a \in A}(a \to SKIP, \{a\})$$

We will see in Section 13.2.2 that this method of combining communications can be useful in avoiding deadlock.

The principle of distributed termination is extended to all other parallel operators.[1] The view that distributed termination means waiting for all processes to terminate, rather than actively synchronizing $\checkmark$'s fits far better with the notion that ||| has distributed termination.

The fact that $\checkmark$ is being interpreted differently from other events – mainly in its finality – means that we must protect it from confusion with other events. This is helped by our assumption that $\checkmark \notin \Sigma$, but we should explicitly mention that $\checkmark$ may not be hidden by the usual hiding operator, and nor may it be affected by renaming. Any renaming affects only members of Σ, and implicitly maps $\checkmark$ and only $\checkmark$ to $\checkmark$.

6.3   Laws

We will present two sections of laws: one which could be said to describe how *SKIP* and sequential composition behave in themselves, while the other shows how they interact with other (mainly parallel) operators.

Sequential composition is distributive and associative, and has unit *SKIP*.

$$(P \sqcap Q); \ R \ = \ (P; \ R) \sqcap (Q; \ R) \qquad\qquad \langle ;\text{-dist-l} \rangle \quad (6.1)$$

$$P; \ (Q \sqcap R) \ = \ (P; \ Q) \sqcap (P; \ R) \qquad\qquad \langle ;\text{-dist-r} \rangle \quad (6.2)$$

$$P; \ (Q; \ R) \ = \ (P; \ Q); \ R \qquad\qquad \langle ;\text{-assoc} \rangle \quad (6.3)$$

$$SKIP; \ P \ = \ P \qquad\qquad \langle ;\text{-unit-l} \rangle \quad (6.4)$$

$$P; \ SKIP \ = \ P \qquad\qquad \langle ;\text{-unit-r} \rangle \quad (6.5)$$

The last of the above laws, though intuitively obvious, requires a good deal of care in modelling to make it true. A consequence of this care is the next law, which at first sight is far less obvious. Normally one would not write a process like $P \ \square \ SKIP$,[2] since the concept of offering the environment the choice of the process terminating

---

[1] There are good arguments for doing something different with enslavement. We might think that, when P terminates, $P /\!/_X Q$ should terminate irrespective of Q's state. This would have the disadvantage that enslavement would no longer be expressible in terms of other operators, and would also (arguably) be an opportunity for untidy programming: insisting on distributed termination of $P /\!/_X Q$ essentially means that P has to tidy up after itself before it terminates.

[2] It looks so unnatural that Hoare banned it, something I am reluctant to do because (i) even if it is banned, it is impractical to ban more elaborate processes that happen to equal it such as $(a \to SKIP) \setminus \{a\} \ \square \ Q$ and (ii) it is hard to make the algebraic semantics work without it.

or not is both strange in itself, and fits most uneasily with the principle that $\checkmark$ is something a process signals to say it *has* terminated. The best way to deal with this process, given that we are forced to consider it, is

$$P \square SKIP = P \rhd SKIP \qquad\qquad \langle \square\text{-}SKIP \text{ resolve} \rangle \qquad (6.6)$$

Remember that $P \rhd Q$ (equivalent to $(P \sqcap STOP) \square Q$ and $Q \sqcap (P \square Q)$) is the process that can choose to act like Q but can offer the initial choices of P. This law says that any process that has the option to terminate may choose to do so and there is nothing the environment can do to stop it: it is refined by $SKIP$.

It is not too hard to show the link between this law and $\langle; \text{-unit-r} \rangle$. If $P = (a \to STOP) \square SKIP$ meant one had the choice of a and $\checkmark$ – so by offering only a we could be sure that would be accepted and that the process would not terminate – then $P; SKIP$ would behave differently from P (invalidating the law). For, in $P; SKIP$, the $\checkmark$ from P is allowed to proceed without the agreement of the environment, which cannot stop it happening. The effect of this composition would be just like

$$((a \to STOP) \square (b \to SKIP)) \setminus b$$

since the hidden b here is exactly like the $\checkmark$ from P that gets hidden by ; . While this process *might* accept a it need not.

When a process cannot offer an initial $\checkmark$, the situation about how it acts under sequential composition is simple, we just get the law already discussed: provided x is not free in Q,

$$(?x : A \to P); \ Q = ?x : A \to (P; \ Q) \qquad\qquad \langle; \text{-step} \rangle \qquad (6.7)$$

We need a law that extends this and $\langle; \text{-unit-l} \rangle$ to take account of processes that can either terminate or offer other events. We can assume that such a process has already had the law $\langle \square\text{-}SKIP \text{ resolve} \rangle$ applied to change this choice into the $\rhd$ form. Thus the appropriate law is that, when x is not free in Q,

$$((?x : A \to P) \rhd SKIP); \ Q = (?x : A \to (P; \ Q)) \rhd Q \qquad \langle SKIP\text{-}; \text{-step} \rangle \qquad (6.8)$$

Sequential composition has many left 'zeros': if P is any process that can never terminate then $P; \ Q = P$ for any Q.

Since we are not allowed to hide or rename $\checkmark$, $SKIP$ is unchanged by any hiding or renaming construct.

$$SKIP \setminus X = SKIP \qquad\qquad \langle SKIP\text{-hide-Id} \rangle \qquad (6.9)$$

$$SKIP[\![R]\!] = SKIP \qquad\qquad\qquad \langle SKIP\text{-}[\![R]\!]\text{-Id}\rangle \quad (6.10$$

In order to deal with distributed termination, we need two extra laws for each parallel construct: one to deal with the case when both operands are *SKIP*, and one to deal with the case where one of them is. The first group are remarkably similar.

$$SKIP \;_X\|_Y\; SKIP = SKIP \qquad\qquad \langle _X\|_Y\text{-termination}\rangle \quad (6.11$$

$$SKIP \;\|_X\; SKIP = SKIP \qquad\qquad \langle \|_X\text{-termination}\rangle \quad (6.12$$

$$SKIP \gg SKIP = SKIP \qquad\qquad \langle \gg\text{-termination}\rangle \quad (6.13$$

$$SKIP \,/\!/_X\, SKIP = SKIP \qquad\qquad \langle /\!/\text{-termination}\rangle \quad (6.14$$

The other group reflect the differing modes of synchronization in the operators. Since the asymmetry of these operators makes the laws more numerous, and in any case the required laws can be derived from the ones relating to the operators out of which they are built, we omit the laws for $_X\|_Y$, $\gg$ and $/\!/_X$ here.

$$SKIP \;\|_X\; (?x : A \rightarrow P) = ?x : A \setminus X \rightarrow (SKIP \;\|_X\; P) \qquad \langle \|_X\text{-preterm}\rangle \quad (6.15$$

$$SKIP \;|\!|\!|\; P = P \qquad\qquad\qquad\qquad \langle |\!|\!|\text{-unit}\rangle \quad (6.16$$

Note the particularly simple law for interleaving – *SKIP* is the unit of $|\!|\!|$.

As an application of the laws we will prove, by the principle of unique fixed points, that the process *ZERO* defined earlier is equivalent to $COUNT_0$. To do this we prove that the vector of processes $\langle Z_n \mid n \in \mathbb{N}\rangle$, defined

$$Z_0 = ZERO \quad \text{and} \quad Z_{n+1} = POS; Z_n$$

(an inductive definition rather than a recursive one), has the property that $Z_n = COUNT_n$ for all n. We will demonstrate that $\underline{Z}$ is a fixed point of the constructive recursion defining $\underline{COUNT}$, proving this claim. Trivially $Z_0 = up \rightarrow POS; Z_0 = up \rightarrow Z_1$, and

$$
\begin{aligned}
Z_{n+1} \;&=\; (up \rightarrow POS; POS \\
&\qquad \Box\; down \rightarrow SKIP); Z_n \\[4pt]
&=\; (up \rightarrow POS; POS; Z_n) \\
&\qquad \Box\, (down \rightarrow SKIP; Z_n) \qquad \text{by } \langle ;\text{-step}\rangle \text{ etc.} \\[4pt]
&=\; (up \rightarrow POS; POS; Z_n) \\
&\qquad \Box\, (down \rightarrow Z_n) \qquad\qquad \text{by } \langle ;\text{-unit-l}\rangle \\[4pt]
&=\; up \rightarrow Z_{n+2} \\
&\qquad \Box\; down \rightarrow Z_n
\end{aligned}
$$

EXERCISE 6.3.1   The recursive definition of *POS* and *ZERO* can be modified easily to represent, instead, an unbounded *stack* process. The process S_x behaves like a temporary stack containing (only) the value x (i.e., it can have any value pushed onto it, or x popped off it) and terminates when all its contents are removed; while *Empty* is an empty stack which never terminates.

Define an unbounded, tail recursive, stack process $Stack_{\langle\rangle}$ as a parameterized recursion very like B_s^∞, which behaves like *Empty*. Prove $Empty = Stack_{\langle\rangle}$, modelling your proof on the one that *ZERO* is equivalent to $COUNT_0$.

6.4   Effects on the traces model

The presence of the special object $\checkmark$ in traces, subtly different from other events, means that some of the traces definitions given up to this point have to be extended to deal with $\checkmark$. In the traces model $\mathcal{T}$ we will now identify a process with a non-empty, prefix-closed subset of

$$\Sigma^{*\checkmark} = \Sigma^* \cup \{s^\smallfrown\langle\checkmark\rangle \mid s \in \Sigma^*\}$$

simply reflecting our assumption that any $\checkmark$ in a trace is final.

The earlier definitions of the traces of *STOP*, prefixing and prefix choice, internal and external choice, hiding and synchronous parallel remain unaltered. Obviously we need definitions for the two new constructs:

$$\begin{aligned}
traces(SKIP) &= \{\langle\rangle, \langle\checkmark\rangle\} \\
traces(P;\, Q) &= (traces(P) \cap \Sigma^*) \\
&\quad \cup \{s^\smallfrown t \mid s^\smallfrown\langle\checkmark\rangle \in traces(P) \land t \in traces(Q)\}
\end{aligned}$$

Notice how the second of these conceals the $\checkmark$ which terminates P and starts Q, leaving only any final $\checkmark$ of Q visible.

The semantics of the various renaming operators only needs modifying to make sure that $\checkmark$'s are preserved. Since both the functions and relations used are purely over Σ, we need to extend the 'liftings' of these to traces to deal with $\checkmark$'s. In each case this takes the obvious form, for example

$$f(\langle a_1, \ldots, a_n, \checkmark\rangle) = \langle f(a_1), \ldots, f(a_n), \checkmark\rangle$$

Most of the parallel operators have to be changed to reflect distributed termination. In alphabetized parallel we simply 'add' $\checkmark$ to the alphabets of both processes from the point of view of the definition:

$$\begin{aligned}
traces(P \ {}_X\|_Y\ Q) &= \{s \in (X \cup Y)^{*\checkmark} \mid s \restriction (X \cup \{\checkmark\}) \in traces(P) \\
&\qquad\qquad \land\, s \restriction (Y \cup \{\checkmark\}) \in traces(Q)\}
\end{aligned}$$

while in the other two we extend the definitions of the underlying operators on traces: if $s, t \in \Sigma^*$, then $s \mathrel{|||} t$ and $s \mathrel{\underset{X}{\|}} t$ are as before, and

$$
\begin{aligned}
s \mathrel{|||} t\hat{\ }\langle\checkmark\rangle &= \{\} \\
s \mathrel{\underset{X}{\|}} t\hat{\ }\langle\checkmark\rangle &= \{\} \\
s\hat{\ }\langle\checkmark\rangle \mathrel{|||} t\hat{\ }\langle\checkmark\rangle &= \{u\hat{\ }\langle\checkmark\rangle \mid u \in s \mathrel{|||} t\} \\
s\hat{\ }\langle\checkmark\rangle \mathrel{\underset{X}{\|}} t\hat{\ }\langle\checkmark\rangle &= \{u\hat{\ }\langle\checkmark\rangle \mid u \in s \mathrel{\underset{X}{\|}} t\}
\end{aligned}
$$

The definitions of the process-level parallel operators then remain as before (using the modified trace-level ones).

EXERCISE 6.4.1   Calculate the traces of the process

$$(a \to SKIP \mathrel{|||} a \to b \to SKIP)^*$$

Use the laws to find a tail-recursive process equivalent to it.

6.5   Effects on the failures/divergences model

The introduction of $\checkmark$ means that we have to look carefully at what a process can refuse (immediately) before and after this special event, and similarly at its effect on possible divergence.

The easy part of this is what goes on after $\checkmark$: nothing. In the last section we made the assumption that a process communicates nothing after $\checkmark$ (since its traces are in $\Sigma^{*\checkmark}$). It therefore makes sense to assume it refuses everything (i.e., $\Sigma^{\checkmark}$) after any trace of the form $s\hat{\ }\langle\checkmark\rangle$, and cannot diverge. We will make these assumptions, with the modification that we allow divergence traces of the form $s\hat{\ }\langle\checkmark\rangle$ provided they are implied by the assumption that all extensions of divergences are divergences. What really matters, in fact, is that all processes look alike after $\checkmark$, rather than the precise value we put them all equal to. The essential thing is that once a process has terminated by communicating $\checkmark$, we should be free to turn our attention elsewhere.[3]

We certainly want to distinguish between the processes *SKIP* and *SKIP* $\sqcap$ *STOP*, even though they have the same traces. The first one certainly terminates

---

[3]In some ways the best approach would be not to bother to include *any* refusals after a $\checkmark$. The only problem with this (and the reason why we have not followed it) is that, since even a divergence-free process's traces would not then be the trace-components of its failures, a process could not be represented by its failures and divergences: the termination traces (at least) would have to be included as a separate component.

successfully, the second one only might. If we put them in sequence with a second process P, the first one gives P, while the second might deadlock immediately whatever P is. The obvious way to make this distinction is to include $\checkmark$ in refusal sets: then the failure $(\langle\rangle, \{\checkmark\})$ belongs to $SKIP \sqcap STOP$ (because it belongs to $STOP$) but not $SKIP$, which cannot refuse to terminate. Thus, when recording a process's failures we will take note of when it can refuse to terminate as well as other events.

It turns out, however, that $\checkmark$ is not quite on a par with other potential members of refusal sets (i.e., ones that are members of Σ). This is because, as discussed earlier in this chapter, $\checkmark$ is not something a process expects its environment to agree to, it is simply a signal to the environment that it is terminating. Thus no process will ever offer its environment the choice of $\checkmark$ or events in Σ. In other words, any process that can terminate must be able (on the appropriate trace) to refuse every event other than $\checkmark$; if a process has the trace $s^\smallfrown\langle\checkmark\rangle$, it has the failure (s, Σ). This is discussed further in Chapters 7 and 8.

The unnatural process $SKIP \;\square\; Q$ – the subject of law $\langle\square\text{-}SKIP \text{ resolve}\rangle$ (6.6) – apparently offers its environment the choice of $\checkmark$ and the initial events of Q, in contravention of the above principle. In fact, since the environment's co-operation is not required for the event $\checkmark$, this process can decide to terminate whatever the environment. In other words, it can refuse all events other than $\checkmark$ despite the way it is built. For example, $SKIP \;\square\; a \to STOP$ has failures

$$\{(\langle\rangle, X) \mid \checkmark \notin X\} \cup \{(\langle a\rangle, X), (\langle\checkmark\rangle, X) \mid X \subseteq \Sigma^\checkmark\}$$

You can view this as a consequence of $\langle\square\text{-}SKIP \text{ resolve}\rangle$, since this law proves the above combination equivalent to

$$(SKIP \;\square\; a \to STOP) \sqcap SKIP$$

which can clearly refuse everything other than $\checkmark$.

The precise way in which failures are extracted from a process's transition system, allowing for possible $\checkmark$ actions, is described in Section 7.4.1. See Section 8.3 for full details of the way the failures/divergences semantics of processes composes, including taking account of the $SKIP \;\square\; Q$ issue.

Part II

Theory

Chapter 7

Operational semantics

7.1 A survey of semantic approaches to CSP

There are at least three distinct ways of gaining a rigorous mathematical understanding of what a CSP program 'means'. These are *operational, denotational,* and *algebraic* semantics. We have already seen all of these in action:

- The operational semantics interprets programs as transition diagrams, with visible and invisible actions for moving between various program states: we have frequently used these to describe informally how processes (and operators over them) behave. Operational semantics, as the name suggests, are relatively close to implementations: we might define an operational semantics as a mathematical formalization of some implementation strategy.

- A denotational semantics maps a language into some abstract model in such a way that the value (in the model) of any compound program is determinable directly from the values of its immediate parts. Usually, denotational semantics attempt to distance themselves from any specific implementation strategy, describing the language at a level intended to capture the 'inner meaning' of a program. There are several denotational semantics of CSP, all based on things like traces, failures and divergences; the value of any program just being some combination of its sets of these things.

- An algebraic semantics is defined by a set of algebraic laws like the ones quoted for the various operators in this book. Instead of being derived theorems (as they would be in a denotational semantics), the laws are the basic axioms of an algebraic semantics, and process equivalence is defined in terms of what equalities can be proved using them. In some ways it is reasonable to regard an algebraic semantics as the most abstract type (where 'abstract' is meant in its informal, rather than its formal, sense).

While any one of these flavours of semantics is enough to describe CSP, it is far preferable to understand something of them all and how they complement each other. This is why we have used all three, sometimes informally, to describe it in the preceding chapters. For most people using CSP there is no need to delve deeply into the sometimes difficult mathematics which underpins it, but for those who are interested this chapter and the following four give formal expositions of the three semantic styles, and show how they relate to each other.

Of these, the material in the rest of this chapter is probably the easiest for a non-mathematician to follow and the most important for using existing tools. Many of the ideas in it have already been seen in earlier chapters, at a lower level of formality.

The main purpose of CSP is, of course, to describe communicating and interacting processes. But in order to make it useful in practice we have added quite a rich language of sub-process objects: anyone who has used FDR will realize that CSP contains a functional programming language to describe and manipulate things like events and process parameters. Of course, any complete semantics of the language would have to take account of this other facet: in effect, we would need to give this sublanguage a semantics too. But this would take a lot of extra space, taking the focus off the main thing we want to do which is to understand the semantics of communication, and is complex in its own right. Thus, just as in the rest of this book we have focused on the main purpose of CSP, in this and the other chapters on semantics we will deliberately ignore the details of how the calculation of sub-process objects fits in.[1] Therefore we will tend to ignore the detailed syntax and evaluation of sub-process objects, just treating them as values. This 'glossing-over' is made a good deal less dangerous because we are assuming CSP has a declarative (pure functional) semantics, meaning that values are never changed by assignment. The only real problem occurs when the evaluation of a sub-process object fails to terminate or produces some other sort of error. Error-handling is an important, if occasionally irritating, part of the construction of any formal semantics, but in the spirit of our simplified treatment of sub-process objects we will not deal with these types of error in this book. These also are discussed in [110].

---

[1]Operational and denotational semantics taking these details into account can be found in Scattergood's thesis [110] and (in a more sophisticated form), in Lazić's work [59, 62].

7.2   Transition systems and state machines

In Part I we frequently referred to the *transition system* of a process: a graph showing the states it can go through and actions from $\Sigma^{\checkmark,\tau}$ that it takes to get from one to another. The operational semantics presented in this chapter is just a formal way of computing these graphs. In this section we investigate the behaviour of transition systems, whether or not derived from a process.

Formally speaking, a *labelled transition system* (LTS) is a set of nodes and, for each event a in some set, a relation $\xrightarrow{a}$ between nodes. It is a directed graph with a label on each edge representing what happens when we take the action which the edge represents. Most LTSs have a distinguished node n_0 which is the one we are assumed to start from.

The operational interpretation of an LTS is that, starting from any node such as n_0, the process state is always one of the nodes, and we make progress by performing one of the actions possible (on outward-pointing edges) for that node. This set of the initial actions of node P will be denoted P^0. The only things that matter are the actions each node has: if the nodes do carry some annotation then this cannot be observed during a run.

In interpreting CSP we usually take the set of possible labels to be $\Sigma^{\checkmark,\tau} = \Sigma \cup \{\checkmark, \tau\}$. Actions in Σ are visible to the external environment, and can only happen with its co-operation. The special action τ cannot be seen from the outside and happens automatically. Thus, if the process is in a state with no actions outside Σ (a *stable* state) it might have to wait there for ever; when it is in an *unstable* state ($\tau \in P^0$) we assume that some action must occur within a short time. (The event that occurs may be visible or τ.)

$\checkmark$, as discussed in Chapter 6, is a special signal representing the successful termination. It is – as we saw in Chapter 6 – different from other events, not least because it is presumably always the last event that happens. It is certainly visible to the environment, but it is better to think of it as an event that does not require the environment's co-operation: it is in one way like τ and in another like ordinary members of Σ. A state P that has $\checkmark \in P^0$ is not stable, because the environment cannot prevent it from happening. (Note that the previous discussion of stable states, in Section 3.3, was before we had met $\checkmark$.) We will be careful to give $\checkmark$ this intermediate interpretation, unlike most earlier works (where it has been treated like a member of Σ).[2]

Where a state has a range of visible actions we assume, especially when the

---

[2]This means that a few of the operational semantic rules in this book are different from earlier versions. Our more careful treatment of $\checkmark$ is designed to make the law $\langle$; -unit-r $\rangle$ (6.5) (P; *SKIP* = P) true, which it is not if $\checkmark$ is assumed to be like any other event. The implications of this decision for the structure of failure-sets were discussed in Section 6.5.

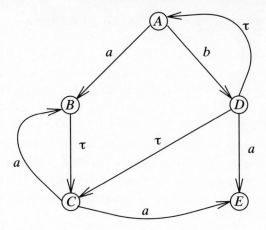

Figure 7.1 Example of a labelled transition system.

state is stable, that the environment has a free choice of which (if any) of the events (i.e., distinct labels) to choose. If there is more than one action with a given label a, the environment has no control over which is followed if it chooses a. In other words, this is a source of nondeterminism.

We assume that only finitely many actions (visible or invisible) can happen in a finite time.

To explain these ideas we will consider two LTSs. The one shown in Figure 7.1 displays most of the possible types of behaviour without $\checkmark$.

- In state A, the environment has the choice of either a or b, and since this is a stable state, nothing can happen until one of these is selected. The process then moves into state B or D, this being determined by which event is chosen.

- The only action available to state B is an internal one. Therefore the process takes this action and moves to state C.

- In state C, there is only one event available, a, and the process must wait until the environment communicates it. There are two possible states that can then arise, and the environment has no control over which one the process moves to.

- In state D, internal and external actions are both possible. The environment might be able to communicate the a action, but cannot rely on this. It can, however rely on the process moving to either A or C if this a does not happen. As in the previous case, the environment has no control over which.

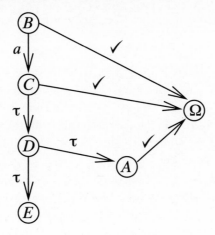

Figure 7.2 A labelled transition system with ✓ actions.

- State E has no actions: it is deadlocked. Once the process reaches this state it is doomed to remain there for ever.

The one in Figure 7.2 enables us to see the effects of ✓. This transition system follows the obvious convention that ✓ is always the last event and leads to an end state Ω. (If forced to interpret a transition system where this was not true we would just ignore anything that could happen after ✓.)

- The easiest state to understand is A: the only thing it can do is terminate. It behaves like the process *SKIP*.

- B can either terminate or perform the event a. Since it does not need the environment's co-operation to terminate, this is certain to happen unless the environment quickly offers a, in which case either can happen (nondeterministically).

- C either terminates or performs a τ, the choice being nondeterministic.

- D has a τ action to A, which gives it the ability to terminate. Indeed a τ action to a state that can only terminate like A is *always* equivalent, from the point of view of externally observable behaviour, to its having a ✓ action of its own. Either can be chosen, from any state that has it, independently of the environment and leads to inevitable termination.

  Even though the only visible action that can ever happen to a process in state D is ✓, its behaviour is different from A since it can follow the τ action to E and become deadlocked. In other words, D can refuse to terminate while A cannot.

An LTS can be finite or infinite (in terms of its set of nodes), and it is clearly the case that only those parts reachable from a node n (via finite sequences of actions) are relevant when we are describing the behaviour of n. In particular, we will usually assume that all the nodes are reachable from the distinguished node n_0. A process is said to be *finite state* if it can be represented by a finite LTS.

An LTS is not – by itself – a very good way to describe a process if you want to capture the essence of its behaviour, since there are many different ways of representing what any reasonable person would agree is essentially the same behaviour. For example, any LTS can be expanded into a special sort of LTS, a *synchronization tree*, where there are no cycles and a unique route from the root to every other node, in the manner illustrated in Figure 7.3. (The distinguished root nodes are indicated by open circles.) But notice that even two synchronization trees can easily represent the same behaviour, as all the original LTSs – and hence all their different expansions – represent behaviours we might suspect are essentially the same. If one does want to use operational semantics as a vehicle for deciding process equivalence, some sort of theory is required which allows us to analyze which process descriptions as an LTS represent the same behaviour.

In CSP, the main mode of deciding process equivalence is via failures, divergences etc., which are not primarily based on transition systems, but some other process algebras (most notably CCS) take the approach of defining the basic meaning of a process to be an LTS and then deciding equivalence by developing a theory of which LTSs are essentially the same. Thus, getting this analysis right can be extremely important.

Many different equivalences over LTSs (and the nodes thereof) have been proposed, most of which are specific to a given view, but the most fundamental one is valid in them all (in the sense that if it defines two nodes to be equivalent then so do the others). This is the notion of *strong bisimulation*, which takes the view that the only thing we can detect about a given process state is what events it can do, and that to be equivalent two processes must have the same set of events available immediately, with these events leading to processes that are themselves equivalent. Another way of looking at this is that no experiment which is based on exploring the behaviour of two nodes by examining and performing available events (including τ and $\checkmark$ on an equal basis to all the others) can tell them apart.

Since the notion of *weak* bisimulation (a weaker notion of equivalence used for CCS) is less relevant to CSP,[3] we will usually drop the word 'strong'.

_____

[3] This is because weak bisimulation fails to make enough distinctions about divergent processes.

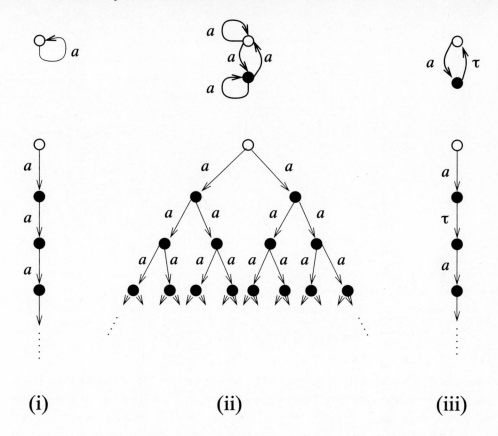

Figure 7.3 Unfolding LTSs to synchronization trees.

DEFINITION   If S is an LTS, the relation R on the set of nodes $\hat{S}$ of S is said to be a *(strong) bisimulation* if, and only if, both the following hold:

$$\forall\, n_1, n_2, m_1 \in \hat{S}.\, \forall\, x \in \Sigma^{\checkmark,\tau}.$$
$$n_1\, R\, n_2 \wedge n_1 \xrightarrow{\ x\ } m_1 \Rightarrow \exists\, m_2 \in \hat{S}.n_2 \xrightarrow{\ x\ } m_2 \wedge m_1\, R\, m_2$$

$$\forall\, n_1, n_2, m_2 \in \hat{S}.\, \forall\, x \in \Sigma^{\checkmark,\tau}.$$
$$n_1\, R\, n_2 \wedge n_2 \xrightarrow{\ x\ } m_2 \Rightarrow \exists\, m_1 \in \hat{S}.n_1 \xrightarrow{\ x\ } m_1 \wedge m_1\, R\, m_2$$

(Note that, though there is no requirement that a bisimulation is symmetric, the above definition is symmetric so that R^{-1} is a bisimulation if R is.)   ∎

   Two nodes in $\hat{S}$ are said to be *bisimilar* if there is any bisimulation which relates them. It is a theorem (see Exercise 7.2.4) that the relation this defines on the nodes of an LTS is *itself* a bisimulation: the maximal one. This is always an

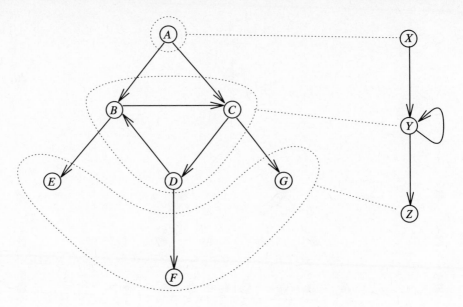

Figure 7.4 Bisimulation equivalence.

equivalence relation: reflexive, symmetric and transitive – it partitions the nodes into the sets whose members' behaviours are indistinguishable from each other (see Exercise 7.2.5).

Consider the systems in Figure 7.4, where for simplicity all the actions have the same label (a, say). In the left-hand system, it should not come as a surprise that E, F and G are all bisimilar, since none of them can perform any action at all. All the others can perform the event a, and are therefore *not* bisimilar to these three. This means that A cannot be bisimilar to any of B, C, D, as all of these can become one of E, F, G after a and A cannot: the definition of bisimulation states that if A is bisimilar to B then it must be able to move under a to something bisimilar to E. On the other hand, all of B, C and D are bisimilar – each of them can perform an a either to a member of the same set or to one of E, F, G. The partition produced by the maximal bisimulation is shown in the figure.

It makes sense to say that two nodes in different LTSs (with the same underlying alphabet) are bisimilar, because we can embed the two systems in one larger one (whose nodes are the union of disjoint copies of the nodes of the two we are summing). In this sense all the nodes of both versions of systems (i) and (ii) of Figure 7.3 are bisimilar. They are not, however, bisimilar to those in the right-hand ones – since the latter can perform τ actions. This shows the chief weakness of (strong) bisimulation as a technique for analyzing process behaviour: its inability

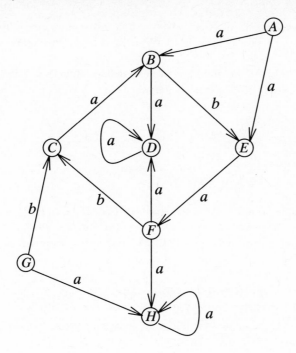

Figure 7.5 Which nodes are bisimilar (see Exercise 7.2.2)?

to distinguish between the different effects of visible and invisible actions.

Having found the maximal bisimulation on an LTS, we can produce another LTS with one node for each equivalence class, and an action a from class C_1 to class C_2 just when the nodes in C_1 have a actions to C_2 (they all will if and only if one does). This factoring process is shown in Figure 7.4, with the system on the right being the one derived from the one we have already examined. It is always the case that the nodes of the new system are bisimilar to the members of the classes they represent, and that no pair of the new system's nodes are bisimilar (see Exercise 7.2.6).

EXERCISE 7.2.1   No pair of nodes in the LTS of Figure 7.1 are bisimilar. Prove this.

EXERCISE 7.2.2   Which pairs of nodes are bisimilar in the LTS shown in Figure 7.5?

EXERCISE 7.2.3   Draw an LTS describing a game of tennis between players A and B, with the alphabet $\{point.A, point.B, game.A, game.B\}$. (The intention is that the appropriate event $game.X$ occurs when player X has won.) Recall that successive points take either player through the scores $\langle 0, 15, 30, 40, game \rangle$ except that the game is not won

if a player scores a point from 40-all (deuce), but rather goes to an 'advantage'–'deuce'
cycle until one player is two points ahead. Which scores are bisimilar?

EXERCISE 7.2.4   Let V be any LTS. We can define a function Ψ from $\mathbb{P}(\hat{V} \times \hat{V})$ (the
relations on the nodes of V) to itself as follows: $(n, m) \in \Psi(R)$ if and only if

$$\forall n' \in \hat{S}. \forall x \in \Sigma^{\checkmark, \tau}.$$
$$n \xrightarrow{x} n' \Rightarrow \exists m' \in \hat{V}. m \xrightarrow{x} m' \wedge n' R m' \qquad \text{and}$$

$$\forall m' \in \hat{S}. \forall x \in \Sigma^{\checkmark, \tau}.$$
$$m \xrightarrow{x} m' \Rightarrow \exists n' \in \hat{V}. n \xrightarrow{x} n' \wedge n' R m'$$

Show that Ψ is monotonic and that its pre-fixed points (i.e., relations R such that $R \subseteq$
$\Psi(R)$) are precisely the bisimulations. Deduce from Tarski's theorem (see Appendix A)
that there is a maximal bisimulation on V (i.e., one that contains all others) and that it
is a fixed point of Ψ.

EXERCISE 7.2.5   Show that the equality relation '=' is a bisimulation, and that if R
and R' are bisimulations then so is their relational composition $R \circ R'$.

Deduce that the maximal bisimulation is an equivalence relation.

EXERCISE 7.2.6   Let S be any LTS, let $\equiv$ be the maximal bisimulation over it, and
let $S/\equiv$ be the factored version of S described on page 157 and illustrated in Figure 7.4.
Show that if we form an LTS S^+ consisting of separate copies of S and $S/\equiv$, then the
equivalence relation on $\hat{S^+}$ in which each equivalence class of S (i.e., a node of $S/\equiv$) is
deemed equivalent to each of its members and nothing else, is the maximal bisimulation
on S^+.

7.3   Firing rules for CSP

The operational semantics of CSP treats the CSP language itself as a (large!) LTS.
It allows us to compute the initial events of any process, and what processes it
might become after each such event. By selecting one of these actions and repeating
the procedure, we can explore the state space of the process we started with. The
operational semantics gives a one-state-at-a-time recipe for computing the transition
system picture of any process.

It is now traditional to present operational semantics as a logical inference
system: we use this system to infer what the actions of a given process are. A
process has a given action if and only if that is deducible from the rules given.
There are separate rules for each CSP operator, to allow us to deduce what the
actions of a process are in terms of its top-level operator (often depending on the
actions of its syntactic parts).

The rules themselves are all simple, and correspond closely to our existing intuition about the operators they relate to.

Because the process *STOP* has no actions, there are no inference rules for it. It has no actions in the operational semantics because there is no possibility of proving it has any.

SKIP, on the other hand, can perform the single action ✓, after which it does nothing more.

$$\overline{SKIP \xrightarrow{\checkmark} \Omega}$$

The fact that there is nothing above the horizontal bar here means that no assumptions are required to infer the action described. The special process term Ω (which we are adding to the language/LTS for convenience) is intended to denote any process that *already has* terminated. The result state after a ✓ action is never important (its behaviour is never looked at) and it is sometimes helpful to have a standardized way of representing the result of termination in the LTS of processes.

The main way communications are *introduced* into the operational semantics is via the prefixing operation $e \to P$. In general, e may be a complex object, perhaps involving much computation to work out what it represents. There is a choice in what to do about computations like this in an 'operational' semantics. Clearly a real implementation would, in general, have to go through a procedure to work out this and other types of sub-process objects. One could include these steps (as τ actions or perhaps some other sort of invisible action) in the operational semantics, but this would make them much more complex both to define and to analyze. In the spirit of the discussion at the start of this chapter, we will ignore these computation steps (taking the values as given) and concentrate only on 'actions' which arise directly from CSP rather than from lower-level behaviour.

The prefix e may represent a range of possible communications and bind one or more identifiers in P, as in the examples

$$?x : A \to P \qquad c?x?y \to P \qquad c?x!e \to P$$

This leads to one of the main decisions we have to make when constructing an operational semantics for CSP (and many other languages): how do we deal with the identifiers in programs that represent data values, other processes, etc.? For it is clearly the case that the behaviour of a program with a free identifier (one whose value is not created within the program itself) might depend on the value of the identifier. The simple answer to this problem is to deal only with *closed* terms: processes with no free identifiers. Using this it is possible to handle most of the situations that can arise, making sure that each identifier has been substituted by a concrete value by the time we need to know it. Because of its simplicity, this is the approach we will take.

This simple approach does create some problems when handling some more advanced aspects of CSP, which means that another style is preferable if one wishes to give a complete operational semantics covering every nuance of the language. This is to introduce the concept of an *environment*[4]: a mapping from identifiers to the values (which might either be data or processes) they represent. Environments are then added to the state space of the LTS we are defining with the operational semantics: instead of transitions being between processes, we now have transitions between process/environment pairs. This alternative style makes very few differences to the individual semantic clauses except where a value is being looked up in the environment. Full details can be found in [110].

To implement the simpler approach we will assume the existence of functions *comms* and *subs*.

- *comms*(e) is the set of communications described by e. For example, $d.3$ represents $\{d.3\}$ and $c?x{:}A?y$ represents $\{c.a.b \mid a.b \in type(c), a \in A\}$.

- For $a \in comms(e)$, $subs(a, e, P)$ is the result of substituting the appropriate part of a for each identifier in P bound by e. This equals P if there are no identifiers bound (as when e is $d.3$). For example,

$$subs(c.1.2, c?x?y, d!x \to P(x, y)) = d!1 \to P(1, 2)$$

The transition rule for prefix is then easy to state:

$$\frac{}{e \to P \xrightarrow{\ a\ } subs(a, e, P)} \ (a \in comms(e))$$

It says what we might expect: that the initial events of $e \to P$ are *comms*(e) and that the process then moves into the state where the effects of any inputs in the communication have been accounted for. Note the way the limitation on events was introduced: via a *side condition* to the inference rule. A side condition simply means that the deduction is only valid under the stated restriction.

This is the only transition rule for prefixing, which means that the only actions of the process $e \to P$ are those deducible from it. The *initial* actions of $e \to P$ are thus independent of whatever P can or cannot do (in that *initials*$(e \to P) =$ *comms*(e) and this process is always stable). There are only two other operators of which this can be said. One of these is nondeterministic choice, which is modelled by a choice of τ actions, one to each process we are choosing between:

$$\frac{}{P \sqcap Q \xrightarrow{\ \tau\ } P} \qquad \frac{}{P \sqcap Q \xrightarrow{\ \tau\ } Q}$$

---

[4]This use of the word 'environment' has an entirely different meaning to the idea of an environment that the process communicates with, discussed elsewhere.

This easily translates to the generalized notion of choice over a non-empty set of processes:

$$\frac{}{\bigsqcap S \stackrel{\tau}{\longrightarrow} P} \quad (P \in S)$$

It is important to remember the restriction that S is non-empty since even though the above rule makes sense, in itself, when $S = \{\}$ the value of $\bigsqcap\{\}$ it predicts does not (no value makes sense in the failures/divergences model for this object, since it would have to (i) be a unit for $\bigsqcap$ in the sense that $P \sqcap X = P$ for all P, and (ii) refine every process even though, as we will see in the next chapter, the failures/divergences model does not have a greatest element).

The only other case where the initial actions are determined completely by the operator itself is recursion. It is a good idea to introduce a τ action to represent the 'effort' of unfolding a recursive definition via the following rule[5]

$$\frac{}{\mu\, p.P \stackrel{\tau}{\longrightarrow} P[\mu\, p.P/p]}$$

This τ action never causes any harm, since the externally visible behaviour of any process P is unchanged by the addition of an extra starting state with a τ action to P. This process has no option but to take this invisible action and behave like P. The τ action in recursion is there to avoid the difficulties caused by under-defined recursions such as $\mu\, p.p$ and $\mu\, p.(p \,\square\, Q)$. The most natural symptom of this type of process is divergence, and this is exactly what the introduction of the τ achieves. In fact, for well-constructed recursions, the τ is not really needed, though it still makes the mathematical analysis of the operational semantics good deal easier.[6]

All the other operators have rules that allow us to deduce what actions a process of the given form has from the actions of the sub-processes. Imagine that the operators have some of their arguments 'switched on' and some 'switched off'. The former are the ones whose actions are immediately relevant, the latter the ones which are not needed to deduce the first actions of the combination. (All the arguments of the operators seen above are initially switched off.)

---

[5]The $\mu\, p.P$ style of recursion is the only one we will deal with in this operational semantics, since a proper treatment of the more common style of using names in a script to represent (perhaps parameterized, and perhaps mutual) recursive processes requires the introduction of environments. The rule we are introducing here extends simply to that context: it is then the act of looking up a process identifier that generates a τ.

[6]FDR does not introduce τ actions of this sort because the only effect they have on well-constructed definitions is to increase the size of the state space. If you are using a tool where such actions are not used, the result is likely to be that an attempt to use a recursion like $\mu\, p.p$ will make the tool diverge. Thus, if you need to create a representation of **div** in such a tool where it is not built in as primitive, it is necessary to use a term like $(\mu\, p.a \rightarrow p) \setminus a$ or $\mu\, p.SKIP;\ p$.

Both the arguments of external choice ($\Box$) are switched on, since a visible action of either must be allowed. Once an argument is switched on, it must be allowed to perform any τ or $\checkmark$ action it is capable of, since the argument's environment (in this case the operator) is, by assumption, incapable of stopping them. There is, however, a difference between these two cases since a τ action is invisible to the operator, which means that there are always rules like the following

$$\frac{P \xrightarrow{\tau} P'}{P \Box Q \xrightarrow{\tau} P' \Box Q} \qquad \frac{Q \xrightarrow{\tau} Q'}{P \Box Q \xrightarrow{\tau} P \Box Q'}$$

which simply allow the τ to happen without otherwise affecting the process state. (In some cases these rules are implied by more general ones.) These rules simply *promote* the τ action of the arguments to τ actions of the whole process. On the other hand, the $\checkmark$ event is visible, so (as with other visible actions) the operator can take notice and, for example, resolve a choice. With $\Box$, there is no difference in how $\checkmark$ and other visible events are handled:

$$\frac{P \xrightarrow{a} P'}{P \Box Q \xrightarrow{a} P'}(a \neq \tau) \qquad \frac{Q \xrightarrow{a} Q'}{P \Box Q \xrightarrow{a} Q'}(a \neq \tau)$$

Of course, the place where $\checkmark$ is most important is in the sequential composition operator ; . Here, the first operand is necessarily switched on, while the second is not. In $P; Q$, P is allowed to perform any action at all, and unless that action is $\checkmark$ it has no effect on the overall configuration.

$$\frac{P \xrightarrow{x} P'}{P; Q \xrightarrow{x} P'; Q} \quad (x \neq \checkmark)$$

If P does perform $\checkmark$, indicating it is terminating, this simply starts up Q, with the action itself being hidden from the outside – becoming τ.

$$\frac{\exists P'.P \xrightarrow{\checkmark} P'}{P; Q \xrightarrow{\tau} Q}$$

It is semantically important that the second argument of ; and the process argument of $e \to P$ are switched off, for if they were not, they would be allowed to perform any τ actions so that if they could diverge, so could the overall process. And the process $STOP$; **div** could never get into a stable state even though it is supposed to be equivalent to $STOP$. This shows that any argument which is switched on is always one in which the operator is divergence-strict (i.e., maps immediately divergent processes to immediately divergent processes). There is, of course, a considerable interplay here between what is reasonable in the operational semantics and what is possible in the denotational semantics.

The rules for hiding and renaming have much in common, since both simply allow all the actions of the underlying process but change some of the names of the events. Any event not being hidden retains its own name under $\setminus B$, but when this event is $\checkmark$ we need a separate rule to respect our convention that the result process is always then Ω.

$$\frac{P \xrightarrow{x} P'}{P \setminus B \xrightarrow{x} P' \setminus B} \quad (x \notin B \cup \{\checkmark\}) \qquad \frac{P \xrightarrow{\checkmark} P'}{P \setminus B \xrightarrow{\checkmark} \Omega}$$

Events in B are, on the other hand, mapped to τ.

$$\frac{P \xrightarrow{a} P'}{P \setminus B \xrightarrow{\tau} P' \setminus B} \quad (a \in B)$$

Renaming has no effect on either τ or $\checkmark$ actions:

$$\frac{P \xrightarrow{\tau} P'}{P[\![R]\!] \xrightarrow{\tau} P'[\![R]\!]} \qquad \frac{P \xrightarrow{\checkmark} P'}{P[\![R]\!] \xrightarrow{\checkmark} \Omega}$$

Other actions are simply acted on by the renaming:

$$\frac{P \xrightarrow{a} P'}{P[\![R]\!] \xrightarrow{b} P'[\![R]\!]} \quad (a \, R \, b)$$

We have seen a wide range of parallel operators, but they could all be expressed in terms of the operator $\underset{X}{\|}$, which takes two processes and enforces synchronization on the set $X \subseteq \Sigma$. Because of this we will only give operational semantics for $\underset{X}{\|}$ – all the others being deducible. Since both the arguments are necessarily switched on, we need rules to promote τ actions:

$$\frac{P \xrightarrow{\tau} P'}{P \underset{X}{\|} Q \xrightarrow{\tau} P' \underset{X}{\|} Q} \qquad \frac{Q \xrightarrow{\tau} Q'}{P \underset{X}{\|} Q \xrightarrow{\tau} P \underset{X}{\|} Q'}$$

There are three rules for ordinary visible events: two symmetric ones for $a \notin X$

$$\frac{P \xrightarrow{a} P'}{P \underset{X}{\|} Q \xrightarrow{a} P' \underset{X}{\|} Q} \quad (a \in \Sigma \setminus X)$$

$$\frac{Q \xrightarrow{a} Q'}{P \underset{X}{\|} Q \xrightarrow{a} P \underset{X}{\|} Q'} \quad (a \in \Sigma \setminus X)$$

and one to show $a \in X$ requiring both participants to synchronize

$$\frac{P \xrightarrow{a} P' \quad Q \xrightarrow{a} Q'}{P \parallel_X Q \xrightarrow{a} P' \parallel_X Q'} \quad (a \in X)$$

The handling of $\checkmark$ events in the parallel operator[7] requires care, because of the following two facts:

- We decided earlier that this operator must have *distributed termination*: the combination $P \parallel_X Q$ terminates when both P and Q do.

- Since both arguments are switched on in $P \parallel_X Q$, the parallel operator cannot prevent either P or Q terminating if it wants to. Thus, the left-hand argument of $SKIP \parallel_X Q$ can terminate even if Q cannot.

The way to handle this is for the parallel operator to communicate $\checkmark$ when both its arguments have – the intuition we developed when introducing the idea of distributed termination. The terminations of the two arguments are turned into τ's much as in the first argument of $P;\ Q$.

$$\frac{P \xrightarrow{\checkmark} P'}{P \parallel_X Q \xrightarrow{\tau} \Omega \parallel_X Q} \qquad \frac{Q \xrightarrow{\checkmark} Q'}{P \parallel_X Q \xrightarrow{\tau} P \parallel_X \Omega}$$

Once one of its arguments has terminated and become Ω, all the rules above for $\parallel_X$ still apply, bearing mind that Ω itself has no transitions (being basically equivalent to $STOP$) so that $P \parallel_X \Omega$ can only do those of P's actions not in X. After the second argument has terminated the composition will have become $\Omega \parallel_X \Omega$: it can now terminate using the following rule.

$$\frac{}{\Omega \parallel_X \Omega \xrightarrow{\checkmark} \Omega}$$

That completes the operational semantics of the main operators of CSP. All the other operators we have seen can have their operational semantics derived from

---

[7]This is the only place where the operational semantics in this book differs significantly from earlier operational semantics for CSP. Previous treatments have considered $\checkmark$ to be an event that the environment can refuse from a process, and therefore simply required synchronization on the $\checkmark$ event between the two processes. Some simply allowed the termination of one of either process (especially under $\vert\vert\vert$) to terminate the combination.

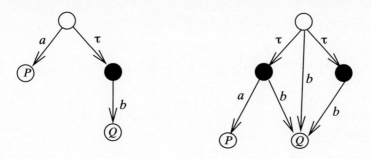

Figure 7.6 Operational semantics of $P' \vartriangleright Q'$ and $(P' \sqcap STOP) \mathbin{\square} Q'$.

the ways they can be written in terms of the operators above. The only case this produces an unnatural answer to is the time-out operator $P \vartriangleright Q$, defined as being equivalent to $(P \sqcap STOP) \mathbin{\square} Q$. A better operational semantics is produced by the following three rules, which more accurately refect our intuition about how this operator works: allowing P to decide the choice with any visible action, but with the certainty of a transition to Q if this does not happen. Since P is initially switched on, we need to promote any τ it performs. (Since it is natural to expect Q to be initially off, there is no need to do this for the second argument.)

$$\frac{P \xrightarrow{\tau} P'}{P \vartriangleright Q \xrightarrow{\tau} P' \vartriangleright Q}$$

Any visible action from P decides the choice in its favour

$$\frac{P \xrightarrow{a} P'}{P \vartriangleright Q \xrightarrow{a} P'} \quad (a \neq \tau)$$

while at any moment (as we have no way of modelling time directly in this semantics) the combination can time out and become Q.

$$\frac{}{P \vartriangleright Q \xrightarrow{\tau} Q}$$

This definition always produces a process with the same traces, failures and divergences as the derived definition but gives a much more natural transition diagram, as is shown by Figure 7.6 which contrasts the operational semantics of $P' \vartriangleright Q'$ with those of $(P' \sqcap STOP) \mathbin{\square} Q'$, where $P' = a \rightarrow P$ and $Q' = b \rightarrow Q$.

EXAMPLE 7.3.1   To show the operational semantics in action we will see how to derive the transitions of a simple process, namely

$$COPY \gg COPY =$$
$$(COPY \llbracket right, mid \,/\, mid, right \rrbracket \underset{\{|mid|\}}{\|} COPY \llbracket left, mid \,/\, mid, left \rrbracket) \setminus \{|\ mid\ |\}$$

where

$$COPY = \mu\, p.left?x \to right!x \to p$$

and the type of the various channels is $\{0, 1\}$, meaning that we can assume

$$\Sigma = \{left.x, mid.x, right.x \mid x \in \{0, 1\}\}$$

- Consider first the initial state $P_0 = COPY \gg COPY$. Since none of the rules associated with the operators $\underset{X}{\|}$, $\setminus B$ or renaming allows us to infer any action not produced by an action of an argument process, the only initial actions of P_0 are those associated with progress by the two $COPY$ processes. These, in turn, can each perform only a τ action to become

$$COPY^\tau = left?x \to right!x \to COPY$$

This τ action is promoted by each of renaming, parallel (both arguments) and hiding, so two τ actions are possible for P_0, to the processes

$$P_1 = COPY^\tau \gg COPY$$
$$P_2 = COPY \gg COPY^\tau$$

- In P_1, the second argument has exactly the same τ available as it did in P_0 (because it was not used in the move to P_1), so this can still be promoted to a τ action from P_1 to

$$P_3 = COPY^\tau \gg COPY^\tau$$

$COPY^\tau$ has initial actions $left.0$ and $left.1$ leading respectively to the states

$$COPY(0) = right!0 \to COPY$$
$$COPY(1) = right!1 \to COPY$$

These are promoted unchanged by the renaming $\llbracket right, mid \,/\, mid, right \rrbracket$. They are allowed by the parallel operator $\underset{\{|mid|\}}{\|}$ because they do not belong to $\{|\ mid\ |\}$, and by the hiding operator $\setminus \{|\ mid\ |\}$, so P_1 has actions $left.0$ and $left.1$ to

$$P_4(0) = COPY(0) \gg COPY$$
$$P_4(1) = COPY(1) \gg COPY$$

- In P_2, the first argument still has the same τ available as it did in P_0, so this can be promoted to a τ action from P_2 to P_3. The actions available to the right-hand argument are the same ones ($\{| \ left \ |\}$) as were available to the left-hand one in P_1. This time they are promoted to *mid* actions by the renaming operator, and prevented by the parallel operator since actions on *mid* require a synchronization (which is not possible). Thus P_2 only has the single τ action.

- In $P_3 = COPY^\tau \gg COPY^\tau$, the actions of the two arguments are obviously the same. As in P_1, the two *left* actions of the left-hand one are promoted to actions with the same name leading to respectively

$$P_5(0) \quad = \quad COPY(0) \gg COPY^\tau$$
$$P_5(1) \quad = \quad COPY(1) \gg COPY^\tau$$

  while the corresponding actions of the right-hand one are prevented as in P_2.

- In $P_4(x)$, the right-hand argument only has a τ action available, which is promoted by the rules to a τ action to $P_5(x)$. The left-hand argument has only the action *right.x*, which is renamed to *mid.x* and prevented by the parallel operator since the right-hand process cannot synchronize.

- The unique action of $COPY(x)$ is promoted by renaming, in $P_5(x)$, to *mid.x*. The two *left* actions of the right-hand argument are also promoted to *mid*. This time synchronization is possible (under $\underset{\{|mid|\}}{\|}$) on the action *mid.x*, which becomes a τ action of the overall process because of the hiding operator. The resulting process is

$$P_6(x) \quad = \quad COPY \gg COPY(x)$$

- In $P_6(x)$, the left-hand process has a τ to $COPY^\tau$, which can be promoted to a τ action to

$$P_7(x) \quad = \quad COPY^\tau \gg COPY(x)$$

  and the right-hand one has the action *right.x* to $COPY$, which promotes to the same action leading back to P_0.

- In $P_7(x)$, the right-hand process can communicate *right.x*, which again promotes to the same action, leading to $COPY^\tau \gg COPY$, in other words, P_1. The left-hand process can communicate *left.0* or *left.1*, which promote to the same events and the overall state

$$P_8(y, x) \quad = \quad COPY(y) \gg COPY(x)$$

  for the chosen y.

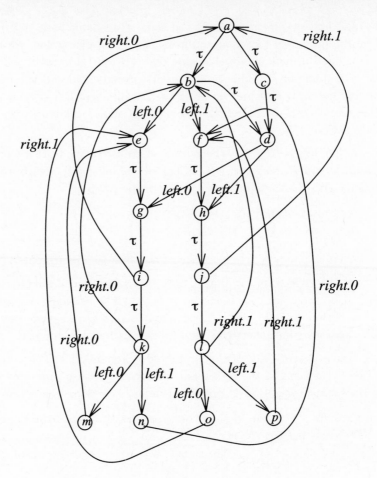

Figure 7.7 The full state space of $COPY \gg COPY$.

- The final state we have to consider is $P_8(y, x)$, where both components can only output. The right-hand one's *right.x* communication promotes to the same action externally leading to $P_4(y)$. The *reason* why no more states have to be considered is simply that all the states discovered during our exploration have already been examined.

Taking account of all the variation in x and y, there are 16 states altogether in the resulting LTS, which is shown in Figure 7.7. The states that the labels a–p in the figure denote are shown in Table 7.1. You should compare the LTS derived carefully here with the one, for essentially the same system, described in Figure 2.2

a	P_0		i	$P_6(0)$
b	P_1		j	$P_6(1)$
c	P_2		k	$P_7(0)$
d	P_3		l	$P_7(1)$
e	$P_4(0)$		m	$P_8(0,0)$
f	$P_4(1)$		n	$P_8(0,1)$
g	$P_5(0)$		o	$P_8(1,0)$
h	$P_5(1)$		p	$P_8(1,1)$

Table 7.1 States of Figure 7.7.

on page 58. The only differences are hiding the intermediate communications, the presence of the τ actions produced by unfolding recursions, and the fact that we have taken individual account of the values held in the buffer rather than showing them symbolically. Evidently this creates considerably more complexity! *(End of example)*

EXERCISE 7.3.1   Compute the LTSs resulting from evaluating the operational semantics of the following processes:

(a) $(a \to b \to STOP) \,\square\, (c \to d \to STOP)$

(b) $((a \to b \to STOP) \,\square\, (c \to d \to STOP)) \setminus \{a, c\}$

(c) $(a \to b \to STOP) \setminus \{a\} \,\square\, (c \to d \to STOP) \setminus \{c\}$

Your answers to (b) and (c) should show rather different externally observed behaviour. What is it about the rules for $\square$ that causes this?

EXERCISE 7.3.2   Draw the LTSs corresponding to the recursively defined processes

(a) $(\mu\, p.(a \to SKIP) \,\square\, (b \to p));\ (a \to SKIP)$

(b) $\mu\, p.(a \to STOP) \,\rhd\, ((b \to STOP) \,\rhd\, p)$

(c) $ZERO$ (see page 137)

EXERCISE 7.3.3   Give a set of rules for computing the operational semantics of $P \,|||\, Q$, derived from those of $\underset{X}{\|}$. Describe the LTS resulting from the process

$$(a \to b \to SKIP) \,|||\, (a \to c \to SKIP)$$

Give a set of rules for the operational semantics of $P \gg Q$ directly, rather than going through the series of inferences through renaming, parallel and hiding illustrated in the example above.

7.4   Relationships with abstract models

7.4.1   Extracting failures and divergences

It was already pointed out in Section 3.3 that there are two quite separate ways to work out a process's traces, failures and divergences: either by using the inductive semantic rules for piecing these together (and which we will be studying in the next chapter), or by examining the process's transition system.

It is easy to formalize the extraction of these values from an LTS C.

We first define two multi-step versions of the transition relation. The first just allows us to glue a series of actions together into a single sequence. If $P, Q \in \hat{C}$ and $s = \langle x_i \mid 0 \le i < n \rangle \in (\Sigma^\tau)^{*\checkmark}$ we say $P \overset{s}{\longmapsto} Q$ if there exist $P_0 = P, P_1, \ldots, P_n = Q$ such that $P_k \overset{x_k}{\longrightarrow} P_{k+1}$ for $k \in \{0, 1, \ldots, n-1\}$.

This first version includes τ actions (invisible to environment) in the sequence shown. The second ignores these τ's: for $s \in \Sigma^{*\checkmark}$ we write $P \overset{s}{\Longrightarrow} Q$ if there exists $s' \in (\Sigma^\tau)^{*\checkmark}$ such that $P \overset{s'}{\longmapsto} Q$ and $s' \setminus \tau = s$. The following properties of $\overset{s}{\Longrightarrow}$ and $\overset{s}{\longmapsto}$ are all obvious.

(a) $P \overset{\langle\rangle}{\Longrightarrow} P \wedge P \overset{\langle\rangle}{\longmapsto} P$

(b) $P \overset{s}{\Longrightarrow} Q \wedge Q \overset{t}{\Longrightarrow} R \Rightarrow P \overset{s\hat{\ }t}{\Longrightarrow} R$

(c) $P \overset{s}{\longmapsto} Q \wedge Q \overset{t}{\longmapsto} R \Rightarrow P \overset{s\hat{\ }t}{\longmapsto} R$

(d) $P \overset{s\hat{\ }t}{\Longrightarrow} R \Rightarrow \exists\, Q.P \overset{s}{\Longrightarrow} Q \wedge Q \overset{t}{\Longrightarrow} R$

(e) $P \overset{s\hat{\ }t}{\longmapsto} R \Rightarrow \exists\, Q.P \overset{s}{\longmapsto} Q \wedge Q \overset{t}{\longmapsto} R$

It is easy to extract the set of a node's finite traces using the above relations:

$$traces(P) \;=\; \{s \in \Sigma^{*\checkmark} \mid \exists\, Q.P \overset{s}{\Longrightarrow} Q\}$$

Suppose C is a transition system and $P \in \hat{C}$. We say P can *diverge*, written $P\ div$, if there exist $P_0 = P, P_1, P_2, \ldots$ such that, for all $n \in \mathbb{N}$, $P_n \overset{\tau}{\longrightarrow} P_{n+1}$.

$$divergences(P) \;=\; \{s\hat{\ }t \mid s \in \Sigma^* \wedge t \in \Sigma^{*\checkmark} \wedge \exists\, Q.P \overset{s}{\Longrightarrow} Q \wedge Q\ div\}$$

Notice that we have said that $s\hat{\ }t$ is a divergence trace whenever s is. This is a reflection of the decision, discussed in Section 3.3, not to try to distinguish what can happen after possible divergence. It would, of course, be easy to avoid this here, but it is much harder to get things right in the denotational semantics without it. Notice that *minimal* divergences (i.e., ones with no proper prefix that is a divergence) do not contain $\checkmark$. This is because we are not concerned with what a process does after it terminates. Our inclusion of divergences of the form $s^\frown\langle\checkmark\rangle$, where s is one, is simply a matter of taste.

In Section 3.3, we said that the only states that give rise to refusals are stable ones, since a τ action might lead to anything, in particular to a state that accepts an action from whatever set is on offer. Since then the notion of a stable state has been complicated a little by the intermediate nature of $\checkmark$, and so, inevitably, are the criteria for extracting refusals.

- A stable state (one without τ or $\checkmark$ events) refuses any set of visible events (perhaps including $\checkmark$) that does not intersect with the state's initial actions.

- We are interpreting $\checkmark$ as an event that cannot be resisted by the environment. Thus *any* state with this event amongst its initial actions can decide to terminate, plainly refusing all events other than $\checkmark$. So any state with a $\checkmark$ action (even such a state with τ actions) can be held to be able to refuse any subset of Σ. To help understand this, remember the discussion of Figure 7.2, where we commented that any state with a $\checkmark$ action is equivalent, so far as external observation is concerned, to one with a τ to state A (one with only a $\checkmark$ action). If we made this transformation, it would be this 'A' state that introduces this refusal.

We can formally define $P\ ref\ B\ (B \subseteq \Sigma^\checkmark)$ if and only if *either* P is stable and $B \cap P^0 = \{\}$ *or* there is Q with $P \xrightarrow{\checkmark} Q$ and $B \subseteq \Sigma$.

We can then extract the failures by combining this with the traces, taking account of the convention that a process refuses anything after $\checkmark$.

$$failures(P) \quad = \quad \{(s, X) \mid \exists\, Q.P \xRightarrow{s} Q \wedge Q\ ref\ X\}$$
$$\cup\{(s^\frown\langle\checkmark\rangle, X) \mid \exists\, Q.P \xRightarrow{s^\frown\langle\checkmark\rangle} Q\}$$

As we saw briefly in Chapter 3, and will study more in Section 8.3.1, it is sometimes necessary to ignore details of what a process does after possible divergence. Sets of traces and failures with post-divergence detail obscured are given by the definitions

$$traces_\bot(P) \quad = \quad traces(P) \cup divergences(P)$$
$$failures_\bot(P) \quad = \quad failures(P) \cup \{(s, X) \mid s \in divergences(P)\}$$

7.4.2   Infinite traces and infinite branching

There is one further important type of process behaviour that can be extracted from LTSs in much the same way that we have seen done for finite traces, divergences and failures. This is the *infinite traces*, the infinite sequences of communications a process can engage in – an obvious extension of the idea of finite traces. The notations $\xmapsto{u}$ and $\xLongrightarrow{u}$ can be extended to infinite u, though they now become unary rather than binary relations on the nodes in an LTS:

- If $u = \langle x_i \mid i \in \mathbb{N} \rangle \in (\Sigma^\tau)^\omega$ (the set of infinite sequences of members of Σ^τ), we say that $P \xmapsto{u}$ if there exist $P_0 = P, P_1, P_2, \ldots$ such that $P_i \xmapsto{x_i} P_{i+1}$ for all i.

- If $u \in \Sigma^\omega$ then $P \xLongrightarrow{u}$ if and only if there exists $u' \in (\Sigma^\tau)^\omega$ such that $P \xmapsto{u'}$ and $u = u' \setminus \tau$.

$\checkmark$'s, being final, play no part in infinite traces. Note that not all $u' \in (\Sigma^\tau)^\omega$ have $u' \setminus \tau$ infinite – the others all have the form $s \hat{\ } \langle \tau \rangle^\omega$ and give rise to divergences.

Infinite traces have more in common with divergences than with finite traces, in the sense that both take an infinite amount of time to unfold and result from the process performing infinitely many actions (in the case of divergence, all but finitely many being τ's). This means that, as with the set of divergences, there is no reasonable way to model, in the denotational semantics, what goes on in the infinite traces after potential divergence. The set of infinite traces we extract from an LTS therefore closes up after potential divergence, rather than offering a choice of two functions as with finite traces and failures.

$$infinites(P) \;=\; \{u \mid P \xLongrightarrow{u}\} \cup \{s \hat{\ } u \mid s \in divergences(P) \cap \Sigma^* \wedge u \in \Sigma^\omega\}$$

It makes a lot of sense, of course, to combine finite and infinite traces into a single set

$$Traces(P) \;=\; traces_\perp(P) \cup infinites(P)$$

This set is, naturally, always prefix closed like $traces(P)$ and $traces_\perp(P)$. Thus, every finite prefix of an infinite trace is also in this set. Studying infinite traces only conveys *extra* information about a process if the reverse of this can fail: if there can be u *not* in $infinites(P)$ all of whose finite prefixes are in $Traces(P)$, for otherwise

$$Traces(P) \;=\; \overline{traces_\perp(P)}$$

where $\overline{A} = A \cup \{u \in \Sigma^\omega \mid \{s \mid s < u\} \subseteq A\}$. We will say that $Traces(P)$ is *closed* when this happens.

There is a large and important class of LTSs where this identity always holds: ones with the following property:

DEFINITION   The LTS C is said to be *finitely branching* if for all nodes P and each $x \in \Sigma^{\checkmark,\tau}$, the set

$$\{Q \mid P \xrightarrow{x} Q\}$$

is finite.   ∎

This says that there are only finitely many nodes we can reach from a given one under a single action. This means that, if we know what action or sequence of actions have occurred, there is only finite uncertainty, or nondeterminism, about what state the process has reached. If Σ is infinite, because the above condition only restricts the size of the set that is reached after a single event, it is possible that a node of a finitely-branching LTS might have infinitely many successors.

The *proof* that nodes in finitely-branching LTSs have closed *Traces*(P) is a corollary of the following standard result, which we will want to use a number of times in the mathematical analysis of CSP.

THEOREM 7.4.1 (KÖNIG'S LEMMA) *Suppose X_i is, for each $i \in \mathbb{N}$, a non-empty finite set and that $f_i : X_{i+1} \to X_i$ is a (total) function. Then there is a sequence $\langle x_i \mid i \in \mathbb{N} \rangle$ such that $x_i \in X_i$ and $f_i(x_{i+1}) = x_i$.*

PROOF   We can compose the individual functions together to get, for $r > s$, functions $f_{r,s} : X_r \to X_s$:

$$f_{r,s} = f_s \circ \ldots \circ f_{r-1}$$

Fix s in $\mathbb{N}$. It is easy to see that $f_{r,s}(X_r)$ is a decreasing series of subsets of X_s for $r > s$ (i.e., $f_{r,s}(X_r) \supseteq f_{r+1,s}(X_{r+1})$ for all r), since

$$
\begin{aligned}
f_{r+1,s}(X_{r+1}) &= f_{r,s}(f_r(X_{r+1})) \\
&\subseteq f_{r,s}(X_r)
\end{aligned}
$$

But any decreasing sequence of finite sets must be eventually constant, and since the members of the sequence are all non-empty we have that

$$X_s^* = \bigcap_{r>s} f_{r,s}(X_r)$$

is non-empty and equals $f_{r,s}(X_r)$ for all sufficiently large r.

From this it follows that when we vary s, we have $f_s(X_{s+1}^*) = X_s^*$. The X_s^*, and the functions f_s restricted to these sets, thus satisfy the assumptions of the lemma and have the additional property that the restricted f_s are onto.

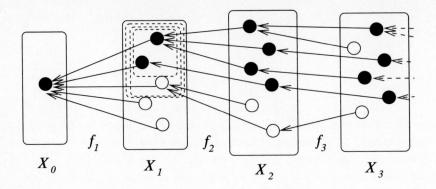

Figure 7.8 The proof of König's lemma.

Now simply pick $x_0 \in X_0^*$, and for each s let x_{s+1} be any member of X_{s+1}^* such that $f_s(x_{s+1}) = x_s$. This must exist by what we observed above.

Figure 7.8 illustrates a simple example of this proof. A few of the decreasing subsets $f_{r,1}(X_r)$ of X_1 are illustrated. The elements in black are those which, on the evidence before us, are candidates for the X_r^*. ∎

König's lemma is often stated in graph-theoretic terms: a finitely-branching tree with nodes at every (natural number) depth below a root r has an infinite path from r. The sets X_i just become the nodes reachable in i steps from r, and the functions f_i map each node to the one from which it was reached.

We can now use this result to establish the result about finitely-branching LTSs.

THEOREM 7.4.2 *If C is a finitely-branching LTS, and $P \in \hat{C}$, then Traces(P) is closed.*

PROOF   Let $u \in \Sigma^\omega$ be such that $\{s \in \Sigma^* \mid s < u\} \subseteq traces_\perp(P)$. We can assume that none of these s's is in $divergences(P)$, for then $u \in infinites(P)$ by definition. The proof works by applying König's lemma to the nodes reachable from P on traces that are prefixes of u. We can formally define sets and functions for the lemma as follows:

- $X_n = \{(Q,s) \mid Q \in C \wedge s \in (\Sigma^\tau)^n \wedge P \stackrel{s}{\longmapsto} Q \wedge s \setminus \tau < u\}$
- If $(Q, s\hat{}\langle x \rangle) \in X_{n+1}$ then there must be $R \in C$ such that $P \stackrel{s}{\longmapsto} R$ and $R \stackrel{x}{\longrightarrow} Q$. Necessarily $(R, s) \in X_n$. Let $f_n(Q, s\hat{}\langle x\rangle)$ be any such (R, s) (R is not necessarily unique, but this does not matter).

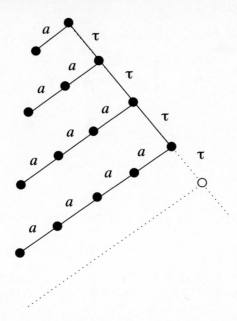

Figure 7.9 The role of divergence in Theorem 7.4.2.

The sets X_n are all finite by induction on n, using the assumption that C is finitely branching: if $(Q, s) \in X_n$, then the set of its successors in X_{n+1} is contained in the finite set

$$\{(R, s^\frown\langle\tau\rangle) \mid Q \xrightarrow{\tau} R\} \cup \{(R, s^\frown\langle a\rangle) \mid Q \xrightarrow{a} R\}$$

where a is the unique element of Σ such that $(s \setminus \tau)^\frown\langle a\rangle < u$. That the X_n are all non-empty is an easy consequence of the assumption that $s \in traces_\perp(P)$ for all $s < u$.

König's lemma then gives a sequence (P_i, s_i) such that $f_i(P_{i+1}, s_{i+1}) = (P_i, s_i)$. The structure of the X_i and the f_i imply that there is an infinite sequence $u' = \langle x_i \mid i \in \mathbb{N}\rangle \in (\Sigma^\tau)^\omega$ such that $s_i = \langle x_0, \ldots, x_{i-1}\rangle$ and $P_i \xrightarrow{x_i} P_{i+1}$. The fact that $s_i \setminus \tau < u$ for all i implies $u' \setminus \tau \leq u$. In fact, $u' \setminus \tau = u$ since otherwise (contrary to our assumption) a prefix of u is in $divergences(P)$.

Figure 7.9 shows how a finitely nondeterministic system can (for the infinite trace $\langle a, a, a, \ldots\rangle$) depend on the divergence-closure of $infinites(P)$ to make this result true. ∎

On the other hand, as soon as we allow infinite branching, the set of infinite traces does convey important information. For example, consider the two systems

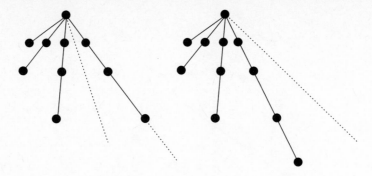

Figure 7.10   Infinite branching makes infinite traces significant. (All actions are *a*.)

in Figure 7.10: they clearly have the same sets of failures, divergences and finite traces, but the one on the left has the infinite trace $\langle a \rangle^\omega$ while the other does not. We will study the consequences of distinctions like this, and the extra power infinite traces give us for specifications, in Chapter 10.

The above result makes it important that we understand which CSP terms produce finitely-branching operational semantics. Every one of the operators, if *applied* to a term that already has infinite branching, is capable of producing infinite branching itself. But fortunately only three operators are capable of *introducing* infinite branching, or unbounded nondeterminism as it is often called.

- The choice operator $\sqcap S$ clearly introduces infinite branching (of τ actions) when S is infinite.

- If the set X is infinite, then $P \setminus X$ can branch infinitely (on τ) even if P does not. For example, the process $Q = (?n : \mathbb{N} \rightarrow P(n)) \setminus \mathbb{N}$ is operationally equivalent to $\sqcap \{P(n) \setminus \mathbb{N} \mid n \in \mathbb{N}\}$.

- If the relation R is such that $\{x \mid x \, R \, y\}$ is infinite for any y, then the renamed process $P[\![R]\!]$ can branch infinitely on y when P is finitely branching. For example, the functional renaming $f[Q]$ where $f(n) = 0$ for all $n \in \mathbb{N}$ introduces infinite branching.

The last two of these can only happen when Σ is infinite, but there is no such limitation on the first.

We could easily prove that avoiding these three things guarantees finite branching. The proof comes in two parts:

- Show by structural induction[8] that the initial actions of any CSP term not involving one of these three constructs are finitely branching.

- Show that if P does not involve them, and $P \xrightarrow{x} Q$, then neither does Q.

EXERCISE 7.4.1   Use your answer to Exercise 7.3.2 and the functions defined in this section to determine $traces(P)$, $failures(P)$ and $divergences(P)$ for each of the processes refered to in that earlier exercise. Is any of them infinitely nondeterministic?

EXERCISE 7.4.2   Can $(\bigsqcap\{COUNT_n \mid n \in \mathbb{N}\}) \setminus down$ diverge? What are its failures?

7.5   Tools

The role of an animator like ProBE is to bring the operational semantics to life: it will let you carry out the actions of a process as derived from the operational semantics. It may well allow you to see how the rules of the operational semantics have derived each action of a compound process from the actions of its parts.

---

[8] *Structural induction* is a technique for proving properties of objects in syntactically-defined sets such as the set of all CSP terms **CSP**. It says that if you can prove a property R of each term T of a syntax on the assumption that R holds of all the immediate subterms that T is built from (e.g., assuming it holds of P and Q to prove it holds of $P \,\square\, Q$) then it holds for all members of the syntax. Over most programming languages one can justify this principle easily, because structural induction is implied by ordinary mathematical induction over the size of programs. But a careful examination of what we allow as CSP terms reveals this argument does not work here, since we have infinite mutual recursion as well as the infinitary constructs $\bigsqcap S$ and $?x : A \to P$, meaning that there are terms with no finite 'size' in the ordinary sense. Structural induction can still be justified provided we assume that the syntax is *well-founded*, meaning that there is no infinite sequence of terms each of which is a subterm of its predecessor. This means we cannot have terms like

$$a_1 \to a_2 \to \ldots \to a_i \to \ldots$$

actually in the language, though there is nothing wrong with achieving the same effect using an infinite mutual recursion $P_i = a_i \to P_{i+1}$.

Well-foundedness corresponds to the natural assumption that the language generated by a syntax is the smallest set of terms which is closed under all the constructs of the syntax. This leads to a trivial proof of the principle of structural induction: the assumptions of that rule imply that the set of terms in the language that satisfy R is itself closed under all the constructs, and therefore contains the smallest set.

Readers with the necessary mathematical background might like to note that, in order to make the infinitary syntax of CSP well defined, it is necessary to put some bound on the size of sets that can have $\bigsqcap$ applied to them. This can be any infinite cardinal number κ, which can be chosen to accommodate all the nondeterministic choices required for a given theory. (The necessity of this bound is tied up with Russell's paradox and the non-existence of a set of all sets.)

You can use a tool like this both to help you understand the operational semantics and to apply these semantics to allow you to experiment with complex process definitions.

FDR is heavily dependent on the operational semantics. This is discussed in Appendix C.

7.6   Notes

Historically, the operational semantics of CSP was created to give an alternative view to the already existing denotational models rather than providing the intuition in the original design as it has with some other process algebras such as CCS.

The style of presenting an operational semantics as an inference system evolved at about the same time as CSP, the main influence being Plotkin's notes [84] which set out the general style used here. The operational semantics of CSP first appeared in something like their present form in Brookes's thesis [14], though essentially the same semantics in LTSs using different notations (more remote from Plotkin's) were present in [17, 91]. In providing CSP with an operational semantics of this form we were certainly heavily influenced by the earlier work on CCS, the standard treatment of which is now [75].

The version in [14] did not use the τ-expansion rule for recursion unfolding. This first seems to have appeared in print in [79], though it had certainly been in use for several years by then. This rule is interesting because it shows up one of the major differences between CSP and those other process algebras which, like CCS, give semantic significance to a single τ action. If it were not the case that, for any node P, another node Q whose only action is $Q \xrightarrow{\tau} P$ is equivalent to P, then the unwinding rule would be much more controversial.

The semantics presented in this book differ from the earlier versions in the way ✓, and hence the distributed termination of parallel constructs, are interpreted.

Chapter 8

Denotational semantics

8.1 Introduction

CSP has been given a number of denotational semantics, mainly based on sets of behaviours such as traces, failures and divergences. It is not necessary to understand a lot of difficult mathematics to use the behaviours as a tool for describing or specifying processes, especially when equipped with automated tools for evaluating which behaviours a process has. Indeed, the sets of behaviours of processes can equally and equivalently (thanks to congruence theorems) be extracted from operational semantics. However, it is possible to gain a much deeper insight into the language by investigating these notions of equivalence and the properties of the models they generate. In this chapter we set out the main ideas and methods of denotational semantics, or at least the ones important to CSP, and show how three models for CSP each give an interesting semantics.

In building a denotational semantics – a function[1] $\mathcal{S}[\![\cdot]\!]$ from a programming language $\mathcal{L}$ into a mathematical model $\mathcal{M}$ – there are a number of things we must always seek to do. The following paragraphs set out these aims.

Natural but abstract relationship between model and language
Ideally the construction of $\mathcal{M}$ should have a close relationship to a natural language for describing the 'essence' of programs in $\mathcal{L}$. This makes it easier to devise and justify the semantic clauses for the different operators and to use the semantic value of a program as a vehicle for specifying properties of it.

---

[1] The special style of brackets $[\![\cdot]\!]$ is commonly used in denotational semantics to separate program syntax from abstract semantics. They have no formal significance, but give a useful visual signal. In fact we will not generally use them when it comes to dealing with CSP except in places where a clear distinction between syntax and semantics is vital.

Natural notion of process equivalence

The equivalence over process terms induced by the semantics should be a natural one, in the sense that for all terms P and Q, $\mathcal{S}[\![P]\!] = \mathcal{S}[\![Q]\!]$ if and only if P and Q behave equivalently in some clearly defined sense. Depending on the way the model is built this may be obvious, or it may be rather more subtle. One of the best ways of demonstrating this is to identify a very few (rarely more than one or two) simple tests based on simple specifications (such as 'does not immediately deadlock', 'does not immediately diverge' or 'does not have the trace $\langle fail \rangle$') which are uncontroversial reasons for deciding two processes are different, and then showing that $\mathcal{S}[\![P]\!] = \mathcal{S}[\![Q]\!]$ if and only if, for all process contexts $C[\cdot]$, $C[P]$ and $C[Q]$ satisfy the same selection of these tests. If one can prove a result like this we say that the semantics $\mathcal{S}[\![\cdot]\!]$ is *fully abstract* with respect to the chosen selection of properties. We will study this idea in depth in the next chapter.

Model must be a congruence

The semantics has to be a *congruence*, in that for each operator $\oplus$ in the language, it is possible to compute $\mathcal{S}[\![P \oplus Q]\!]$ in terms of $\mathcal{S}[\![P]\!]$ and $\mathcal{S}[\![Q]\!]$ (with obvious modifications for non-binary operators). It is quite possible to propose what looks like a good model for a language only to discover that this property fails for some operator. For example, we might design a model for CSP in which a process was modelled by $(traces(P), deadlocks(P))$, where $deadlocks(P)$ is the set of traces on which P can deadlock, as a simplification of the failures model. We would then find it possible to give semantic clauses for $deadlocks(P)$ for most CSP operators, for example

$$
\begin{aligned}
deadlocks(STOP) &= \{\langle\rangle\} \\
deadlocks(a \to P) &= \{\langle a\rangle{}^\frown s \mid s \in deadlocks(P)\} \\
deadlocks(P \,\square\, Q) &= ((deadlocks(P) \cup deadlocks(Q)) \cap \{s \mid s \neq \langle\rangle\}) \\
&\quad \cup (deadlocks(P) \cap deadlocks(Q)) \\
deadlocks(P \,\sqcap\, Q) &= deadlocks(P) \cup deadlocks(Q) \\
deadlocks(P;\ Q) &= (deadlocks(P) \cap \Sigma^*) \\
&\quad \cup \{s{}^\frown t \mid s{}^\frown\langle\checkmark\rangle \in traces(P) \wedge t \in deadlocks(Q)\}
\end{aligned}
$$

But this breaks down for parallel operators involving synchronization, such as $\underset{X}{\|}$. If, for example

$$
\begin{aligned}
P &= (a \to P) \sqcap (b \to P) \\
R &= (a \to R) \,\square\, (b \to R)
\end{aligned}
$$

P and R have exactly the same sets of traces $(\{a, b\}^*)$ and deadlock traces $(\{\})$. But, while $R \underset{\{a,b\}}{\|} R$ still cannot deadlock, the process $P \underset{\{a,b\}}{\|} P$ can (on any trace) because the left-hand P can opt only to accept a and the right-hand one can opt only to accept b. Thus it is impossible, in general, to predict the semantics of $S \underset{X}{\|} T$ from those of processes S and T, so our proposed semantics is not a congruence and must be rejected.

Fixed-point theory

Just as we need to be able to combine semantic values accurately under all of the basic operators of our language, we also need to be able to compute the values of recursively defined processes. While you can think of recursion as just another operator that is applied to process terms (turning P into $\mu\,p.P$), it is conceptually a quite different thing to operators like $a \rightarrow$, $\square$ and $\underset{X}{\|}$. What $\mu\,p.P$ represents is a solution to the equation

$$A \;=\; P[A/p]$$

Since the denotational semantics is a congruence, the semantic value $\mathcal{S}[\![P[A/p]]\!]$ is a function of the value $\mathcal{S}[\![A]\!]$, in the sense that if $\mathcal{S}[\![A]\!] = \mathcal{S}[\![B]\!]$, then $\mathcal{S}[\![P[A/p]]\!] = \mathcal{S}[\![P[B/p]]\!]$. Thus $\mathcal{S}[\![\mu\,p.P]\!]$ is a *fixed point* of this function. You can think of the term P as a context in which the identifier p represents the process argument.

Giving a denotational semantics to recursively defined processes thus reduces to finding fixed points of the functions from $\mathcal{M}$ to itself that are generated by process contexts. This means that every appropriate function over $\mathcal{M}$ must have a fixed point – not something that is true for most mathematical structures. And, of course, there may be more than one fixed point, in which case we have to make a rational choice of which one to select.

Just as the semantics of recursion is stylistically very different from the semantic clauses of more ordinary operators, so too are the methods available for proving properties of recursively defined process. We need ways of proving properties of the objects extracted by whatever mechanism is chosen to pick fixed points. Such proof methods, the main ones seen so far being the UFP rule and fixed-point induction, are inevitably intimately tied up with whatever mathematical theory is used to prove the existence of the fixed points.

In the later sections of this chapter we formalize several denotational semantics for CSP and show how they meet the aims set out above.

Two different theories, partial orders (with Tarski's theorem) and metric spaces (with the contraction mapping theorem) for proving the existence of fixed points are commonly used in denotational semantics. Both of these are used in CSP and we use them widely in this and subsequent chapters. A tutorial introduction to both can be found in Appendix A, and readers not familiar with one or both should study that before continuing with the present chapter.

8.2   The traces model

We have already defined the traces model and the semantics of each individual operator over it. $\mathcal{T}$ is the set of non-empty, prefix-closed subsets of $\Sigma^{*\checkmark}$. This, as is shown in Section A.1.1, is a complete lattice under the refinement order $\sqsubseteq_T$ (which equates to reverse containment). But, since any complete lattice is also a complete lattice when turned upside down, we actually have three different choices of theories to get us the fixed points required for recursions: the two senses of the order, or metric spaces. In this section we discover which of these is the right answer by looking carefully at the properties of the model and the CSP operators over it.

It is instructive to examine the ways that the various operators are defined over $\mathcal{T}$. (Their definitions can be found in Section 1.3.1 and with later definitions of operators.) In every case, it is possible to restructure them so that instead of being functions from sets of traces to sets of traces, they are lifted in a natural way from relations over traces. This is well illustrated by considering the sequential composition operator $P; Q$. We can derive its traces from two relations: one (binary) between traces of P and output traces and one (ternary) between traces of P, traces of Q and output traces. These are described

$$
\begin{aligned}
s[;]_1 u &\;\Leftrightarrow\; s \in \Sigma^* \wedge u = s \\
(s, t)[;]_{1,2} u &\;\Leftrightarrow\; \exists s_0. s = s_0\hat{\ }\langle\checkmark\rangle \wedge u = s_0\hat{\ }t
\end{aligned}
$$

Thus, we get one relation describing the overall behaviours that the first argument can produce without the help of the second, and one describing the behaviours in which both arguments are active. There are two further relations we might need for a binary operator $\oplus$: $[\oplus]_2$ for the second argument acting alone and $[\oplus]_\bullet$ for the set of behaviours that can be produced without either playing a part; but in the case of ';' these are both empty. In general we then get

$$
\begin{aligned}
traces(P \oplus Q) \;=\; & \{u \mid \exists s \in traces(P), t \in traces(Q).(s, t, u) \in [\oplus]_{1,2}\} \\
& \cup \{u \mid \exists s \in traces(P).(s, u) \in [\oplus]_1\} \\
& \cup \{u \mid \exists t \in traces(Q).(t, u) \in [\oplus]_2\} \\
& \cup [\oplus]_\bullet
\end{aligned}
$$

For a unary operator we similarly need two relations: one for behaviours involving its argument and another for those that do not. The following give clauses for most of the other main CSP operators. Where a relation is not specified it is empty.

$$[a \to]_\bullet = \{\langle\rangle\}$$
$$[a \to]_1 = \{(s, \langle a\rangle\hat{\ }s) \mid s \in \Sigma^{*\checkmark}\}$$

$$[\Box]_{1,2} = \{(s, \langle\rangle, s), (\langle\rangle, s, s) \mid s \in \Sigma^{*\checkmark}\}$$

$$[\sqcap]_\bullet = \{\langle\rangle\}$$
$$[\sqcap]_1 = \{(s, s) \mid s \in \Sigma^{*\checkmark}\}$$
$$[\sqcap]_2 = \{(s, s) \mid s \in \Sigma^{*\checkmark}\}$$

$[\|]_{1,2} = \{(s, t, u) \mid u \in s \underset{X}{\|} t\}$ where $s \underset{X}{\|} t$ is as defined in Section 2.4 and
extended to deal with $\checkmark$ on page 143.

$$[\backslash\, X]_1 = \{(s, s \setminus X) \mid s \in \Sigma^{*\checkmark}\}$$

$$[[\![R]\!]]_1 = \{((\langle a_1, \ldots, a_n\rangle, \langle b_1, \ldots, b_n\rangle), (\langle a_1, \ldots, a_n, \checkmark\rangle, \langle b_1, \ldots, b_n, \checkmark\rangle)) \mid \forall\, i.a_i R b_i\}$$

It is interesting to note that the relations given above for $\sqcap$ and $\Box$ are different, even though these operators are identical over trace sets. On one hand, this shows that the choice of relations to achieve a given effect is not unique. On the other, the precise forms chosen have been influenced by the very different operational semantics of the two (see Section 7.3): in $P \sqcap Q$ it is never the case that both P and Q have 'run', while in $P \;\Box\; Q$ they may both have executed internal actions before the choice was resolved.

Perhaps the most important consequence of this relational representation is that it automatically yields important structural results about the semantics.

THEOREM 8.2.1 *Any operator $\oplus$ over $\mathcal{T}$ definable as the lifting of a family of trace relations is fully distributive in each of its arguments, in the sense that $F(\sqcap S) = \sqcap\{F(P) \mid P \in S\}$ for each non-empty S (where $F(\cdot)$ represents any unary function produced by fixing all arguments of $\oplus$ other than the one we are studying).*

PROOF   Suppose first that $\oplus$ is unary. Then there are no other arguments to fix, and so

$$
\begin{aligned}
F(\sqcap S) &= [\oplus]_\bullet \cup \{u \mid \exists\, s \in \bigcup S.(s, u) \in [\oplus]_1\} \\
&= [\oplus]_\bullet \cup \bigcup\{\{u \mid \exists\, s \in P.(s, u) \in [\oplus]_1\} \mid P \in S\} \\
&= \bigcup\{[\oplus]_\bullet \cup \{u \mid \exists\, s \in P.(s, u) \in [\oplus]_1\} \mid P \in S\} \\
&= \sqcap\{F(P) \mid P \in S\}
\end{aligned}
$$

the equality between the second and third lines following because S is non-empty.

If $\oplus$ were not unary then fixing all arguments but one means we can divide the relations into those which involve the chosen one and those that do not, and derive a unary and a binary relation to use in the above proof. For example, if we are studying the first argument of a binary operator and fix the second argument to be $Q \in \mathcal{T}$ then the cross-section $F(P) = P \oplus Q$ gives relations

$$
\begin{aligned}
[\oplus Q]_\bullet &= [\oplus]_\bullet \cup \{u \mid \exists\, t \in Q.(t, u) \in [\oplus]_2\} \\
[\oplus Q]_1 &= [\oplus]_1 \cup \{(s, u) \mid \exists\, t \in Q.(s, t, u) \in [\oplus]_{1,2}\}
\end{aligned}
$$

This completes the proof.   ∎

This gives another view of the distributive laws that hold of CSP operators and also proves (i) that they are all monotonic with respect to the refinement order and (ii) that under the subset order (i.e., the reverse of refinement) they are all continuous. The former is because we know $P \sqsubseteq Q$ is equivalent to $P \sqcap Q = P$, and so $F(P) \sqcap F(Q) = F(Q)$ for distributive $F(\cdot)$. The latter is because continuity under that order is equivalent to distributivity over directed sets.

It is also informative to consider continuity in the other direction. Now, it turns out, not all operators are continuous. An example that fails is hiding an infinite set $X = \{a_1, a_2, \ldots\}$, since, if we pick $b \notin X$, the processes

$$
P_n = STOP \sqcap \bigsqcap\{a_i \to b \to STOP \mid i \geq n\}
$$

form an increasing sequence under $\sqsubseteq_T$ with limit $STOP$. However, for every n,

$$
P_n \setminus X = STOP \sqcap b \to STOP
$$

so that the limit of applying $\setminus X$ to the sequence:

$$
\bigsqcup\{P_n \setminus X \mid n \in \mathbb{N}\}
$$

equals this value, which of course is not equal to $STOP \setminus X$.

The key to which operators are continuous lies in the relations that represent them. The crucial feature of $\setminus X$ (whether or not X is infinite, though it may not be empty) is that for any trace u not including a member of X, the set $\{s \in \Sigma^{*\checkmark} \mid (s, u) \in [\setminus X]_1\}$ is infinite: if we are told that $s \in traces(P \setminus X)$, there are infinitely many potential reasons for this and as we go through an infinite refining sequence of processes these reasons can disappear just as in the example above until there are none left in the limit.

Except for hiding, the only relation described above that can have this infinitary property is the one for renaming $P[\![R]\!]$ when the R used is infinite-to-one (i.e., it relates an infinite set of before-renaming events to a single after-renaming one).

Consider, for example, the case of ;. The fact that there are two[2] different relations generating traces is irrelevant since if there were an infinity of different reasons for a given trace, infinitely many of these would have to come from one or other. [;]$_1$ is obviously finitary since it is a subset of the identity relation – each trace has at most one precursor here. [;]$_{1,2}$ is more interesting since the trace $\langle a_1, \ldots, a_n \rangle$ has precursors

$$\{(\langle a_1, \ldots, a_k, \checkmark \rangle, \langle a_{k+1}, \ldots, a_n \rangle) \mid k \in \{0, \ldots, n\}\}$$

which, though always a finite set, grows in size with the length of trace.

Formally, we define an n-ary relation R to be *finitary* if, for all v in the domain of its final component,

$$\{(x_1, \ldots, x_{n-1}) \mid (x_1, \ldots, x_{n-1}, v) \in R\} \quad \text{is finite}$$

The following result shows the importance of these ideas to continuity.

THEOREM 8.2.2 *If $\oplus$ is any operator of finite arity, which can be represented by a family of relations all of which are finitary, then it is $\sqsubseteq_T$-continuous in each argument.*

PROOF   The reduction of this problem to the case where $\oplus$ is unary is essentially the same as in the previous proof, its finite arity being needed simply so that the number of representing relations is also finite. So we will restrict out attention to that case, so that $\oplus$ is generated by the relations $[\oplus]_\bullet$ and $[\oplus]_1$ where the latter is finitary (there being no question that a unary relation like $[\oplus]_\bullet$ can fail to be). We are therefore considering the function

$$F(P) = [\oplus]_\bullet \cup \{u \mid \exists\, s \in P.(s, u) \in [\oplus]_1\}$$

To prove it is continuous it is sufficient (thanks to its known monotonicity) to show

$$F(\bigsqcup \Delta) \sqsubseteq_T \bigsqcup \{F(P) \mid P \in \Delta\}$$

or, equivalently,

$$F(\bigcap \Delta) \supseteq \bigcap \{F(P) \mid P \in \Delta\}$$

for any directed $\Delta \subseteq \mathcal{T}$. So suppose u is a trace belonging to the right-hand side. We can dispose of it immediately if $u \in [\oplus]_\bullet$ for it is then trivially in the left-hand

---

[2]In the case of there being *infinitely* many relations, as there would be for $\bigsqcap S$ with S infinite, this would be of concern if the ranges of the relations overlap.

side; so we can assume $u \notin [\oplus]_\bullet$. If u did not belong to the left-hand side, it follows that each member of the finite set

$$pre_\oplus(u) = \{s \mid (s, u) \in [\oplus]_1\}$$

is absent from $\bigcap \Delta$. For each such s we can choose $P_s \in \Delta$ such that $s \notin P_s$. Finiteness and the fact that Δ is directed then implies that there is a $P^* \in \Delta$ such that $P_s \sqsubseteq_T P^*$ for all such s. Necessarily then, $P^* \cap pre_\oplus(u) = \{\}$ and hence $u \notin F(P^*)$ contradicting what we assumed above. This completes the proof. ∎

This, of course, only proves continuity for each individual CSP operator. As you will find in studying Appendix A, the composition of continuous (monotone) operators is itself continuous (monotone), which means that the above result easily yields the continuity of any expression built out of continuous operators. One important point that is often forgotten about in this type of explanation is the possibility of there being one recursion inside another, as in

$$\mu\, p.(a \to (\mu\, q.p \,\square\, b \to q))$$

The fact here is that, in order to define the meaning of the $\mu\, p$ recursion, we have to think of the inner recursion as a function of p (i.e., the fixed point varies with p). Fortunately Lemma A.1.8 (page 484) tells us that this causes no problems, but it is important that you understand clearly why it is needed.

$\mathcal{T}$ can be given a metric structure based on the system of restriction functions

$$P \downarrow n = \{s \in P \mid \#s \leq n\}$$

which are closely analogous to, and satisfy the same collection of properties as, the family introduced in Section A.2 for individual traces. Following the same approach set out there gives the distance function

$$d(P, Q) = inf\{2^{-n} \mid P \downarrow n = Q \downarrow n\}$$

If the sequence

$$\langle P_0, P_1, P_2, \ldots \rangle$$

satisfies $P_{n+1} \downarrow n = P_n$, then it is easy to see that $P^* = \bigcup \{P_n \mid n \in \mathbb{N}\}$ satisfies $P^* \downarrow n = P_n$. Thus $\mathcal{T}$ is (following the definitions in Section A.2) a complete restriction space and so the metric is complete.

The restriction functions, and hence the complete metric structure, extend easily to the product spaces used to reason about mutual recursions. If Λ is any non-empty indexing set, we restrict a vector $\underline{P} \in \mathcal{T}^{\Lambda}$ componentwise:

$$(\underline{P} \downarrow n)_{\lambda} = P_{\lambda} \downarrow n$$

It is the metric/restriction structure which is at the heart of the theory of guardedness/constructiveness that we first met in Chapter 1. For we can now precisely define what it means for a function F to be constructive with respect to $\mathcal{T}$: for all processes P, Q and $n \in \mathbb{N}$

$$P \downarrow n = Q \downarrow n \Rightarrow F(P) \downarrow (n+1) = F(Q) \downarrow (n+1)$$

As discussed in Section A.2, it is useful to define a corresponding concept of *non-destructive* function:

$$P \downarrow n = Q \downarrow n \Rightarrow F(P) \downarrow n = F(Q) \downarrow n$$

As shown in there, a function is constructive if and only if it is a contraction mapping with respect to the associated metric and is non-destructive when it is non-expanding in the metric space.

This immediately means that a constructive function has a unique fixed point (thus justifying the UFP rule for analyzing recursions that we have used frequently through this book).

In Section 1.3.1 we declared that a recursion was 'guarded' if every recursive call was directly or indirectly guarded by a communication, but when we met the hiding operator in Section 3.1 we had to exclude recursions in which hiding was used. Both of these steps are easily explained when we examine how the individual operators behave with respect to the restriction functions. The following result summarizes the position and is easy to establish; combining it with the compositional rules for constructive/non-destructive functions justifies the earlier claims.

LEMMA 8.2.3 *Each of the operators* $\sqcap$, $\square$, $\underset{X}{\|}$, *renaming and* ; *is non-destructive over* $\mathcal{T}$ *in each argument. The prefix operators* $a \rightarrow$ *and* $?x : A \rightarrow$ *are constructive.*

We could prove most of these in terms of the relational representations of the operators: if an operator can be represented by relations that are all non-destructive in the sense that the result trace of each tuple is never shorter than any of the others, then it is easily shown to be non-destructive, and if the other traces are always strictly shorter then it is constructive. The only relations amongst those defined above that are not non-destructive are $[\backslash X]_1$ (as one might expect) and $[;]_{1,2}$ which contains tuples like $(\langle a, \checkmark \rangle, \langle \rangle, \langle a \rangle)$. That ; is non-destructive despite this observation follows because any trace that results from such a 'destructive' triple also results from $[;]_1$ as the contribution of the second process to $[;]_{1,2}$ must be $\langle \rangle$ in such a case.

There are, as we saw in Chapter 4, useful classes of recursion that do involve hiding because of the way they create dynamic networks using piping and enslavement. It is possible to find ones that actually behave properly despite not being constructive at all, but most can be shown constructive using careful analysis. Recall the recursive definition of an infinite buffer:

$$B^+ = left?x \to (B^+ \gg right!x \to COPY)$$

When we introduced this on page 103 we saw an informal argument for the composition $(P \gg right!x \to COPY)$ being non-destructive as a function of P because the process on the right of the $\gg$ is built so that it compensates for all the events that get hidden. We now have the mathematics to analyze this situation, in clause (a) of the following lemma, whose proof is left as an exercise.

LEMMA 8.2.4 (a) *If Q satisfies*

$$s \in traces(Q) \implies \#(s \downarrow left) \leq \#(s \downarrow right)$$

then the function $F(P) = P \gg Q$ is non-destructive.

(b) *If Q satisfies*

$$s \in traces(Q) \implies \#(s \downarrow right) \leq \#(s \downarrow left)$$

then the function $F(P) = Q \gg P$ is non-destructive.

(c) *If, for each $s \in traces(Q)$ and $i \in \{1, \ldots, k\}$, we have*

$$\#(s \setminus \{\!| \, m_1, \ldots, m_k \, |\!\}) \geq \#(s \downarrow m_i)$$

then the function $F(P_1, \ldots, P_k) = Q \,/\!\!/\, m_1{:}P_1 \,/\!\!/\, \ldots \,/\!\!/\, m_k{:}P_k$ is non-destructive in each of its arguments.

Where the metric fixed point theory works it is, by virtue of the uniqueness of the fixed points it produces, certain to agree with those produced by both directions of the partial order (which, of course, then agree with each other). Virtually all well-behaved recursions fit within it, and in Section 9.2 we will see evidence that all other well-behaved ones (ones not introducing divergence) force there to be a unique fixed point. Nevertheless it is preferable to be in a position to interpret badly-behaved ones too, such as the three set out below.

- $Z_0 = Z_0$

- $Z_1 = a \to (Z_1 \setminus \{a\})$

- $Z_2 = (up \to (AZ \,/\!/\, u{:}Z_2)) \;\square\; (iszero \to Z_2)$, where

$$
\begin{aligned}
AZ \;\; &= \;\; down \;\; \to \;\; (u.iszero \to AZ' \\
&\qquad\qquad\qquad\; \square\; u.down \to u.down \to AZ) \\
&\quad\;\;\square\; up \;\; \to \;\; u.up \to u.up \to AZ \\
AZ' \;\; &= \;\; iszero \;\; \to \;\; AZ' \\
&\quad\;\;\square\; up \;\; \to \;\; AZ
\end{aligned}
$$

Z_2 is an interesting recursion closely modelled on the enslavement version of the counter process, seen on page 108, but which increments and decrements its slave by two rather than one. This violates Lemma 8.2.4 (c) since it frequently requires its slave to have communicated a longer trace than it has, and though the well-behaved counter is a fixed point, it is not the only one. Others are $BCOUNT$ and $PCOUNT$, where

$$
\begin{aligned}
BCOUNT \;\; &= \;\; iszero \to BCOUNT \\
&\quad\;\;\square\; up \to (down \to BCOUNT \\
&\qquad\qquad\qquad\;\; \square\; up \to (up \to STOP \;\square\; down \to STOP)) \\[1em]
PCOUNT \;\; &= \;\; iszero \to PCOUNT \\
&\quad\;\;\square\; up \to (down \to PCOUNT \\
&\qquad\qquad\qquad\;\; \square\; up \to MANY) \\[1em]
MANY \;\; &= \;\; down \to MANY \\
&\quad\;\;\square\; up \to MANY
\end{aligned}
$$

Both of these get confused when they reach the number 2 (which is the point where the slave counter gets raised to the same level as the overall one, leading to ill-definedness). $BCOUNT$ reacts by deadlocking soon after, while $PCOUNT$ loses track and accepts any number of *down* events.

And we are in a position to interpret arbitrary CSP-defined recursions, for we have both the $\sqsubseteq_T$ and $\subseteq$ orders. The only problem is to decide which, if either, is the right one to use.

- If we identify a recursion with the least fixed point with respect to $\sqsubseteq_T$ then we have to accept that the simple formula

$$
\bigsqcup_{r=0}^{\infty} F^r(\bot)
$$

for the least fixed point does not always hold because F is not always continuous. In this order, $\perp$ is $\Sigma^{*\checkmark}$. The fixed point produced will always be the one with as many traces as possible, consistent with its being a fixed point. Essentially, with this choice, we start out with the assumption that all behaviours are possible for a recursively defined process, and the construction of the fixed point is the determination of which of these traces are impossible based solely on the information that it *is* a fixed point.

- If we identify a recursion with the $\subseteq$-least fixed point then the above formula (with $\perp$ now being $STOP = \{\langle\rangle\}$) will always hold and we will always get the process with as few traces as possible. With this choice, the construction of the fixed point establishes which traces are certainly in any fixed point.

Now, in fact, the operational semantics given in Chapter 7 gives precisely the traces corresponding to the second choice (we will examine this fact further in Section 9.4). The only reasons to pick the first option would be (i) if one were proposing an alternative operational semantics in which some under-defined recursion could produce some other trace and (ii) somehow to express our disapproval of under-defined recursions by cluttering up their semantics with traces that may well make the process fail some safety specification. The first of these seems unlikely to the author, and the second really represents muddled thinking: in the traces model we can only expect to reason about safety properties and it is not possible accurately to model divergence (the natural way in which an under-defined recursion such as any of the above manifests itself at the point where the under-definedness 'bites') without expressly including it in the model.

Therefore the correct choice for $\mathcal{T}$ is to identify every recursion $\mu\, p.F(p)$ with its $\subseteq$-least fixed point which, because of the continuity of all operators with respect to this order, is just the set of all traces which some $F^n(STOP)$ can perform. For the examples Z_0, Z_1 and Z_2 above these are respectively $\{\langle\rangle\}$, $\{\langle\rangle, \langle a\rangle\}$ and the traces of $BCOUNT$.

The identification of a diverging process like Z_0 (or, indeed, a straightforward example like $(\mu\, q.a \to q) \setminus \{a\}$, about which there is no ambiguity in the calculation of the fixed point) with the most refined process of $\mathcal{T}$ is simply a reflection of the deficiencies of this model for reasoning about anything other than safety properties. This is similar to the phenomenon that identifies the deadlocked process $STOP$ with the same value. As we will see in the next section, as soon as we model both safety and liveness in the same model, there is no *most* refined process.

EXERCISE 8.2.1   Find sequences of processes of the form $P_0 \sqsubseteq_T P_1 \sqsubseteq_T P_2 \sqsubseteq_T \ldots$ illustrating failures of $\sqsubseteq_T$-continuity of (i) hiding a single event $\setminus \{a\}$ and (ii) infinite-to-one renaming.

EXERCISE 8.2.2   Prove that the relation $[\|]_{1,2}$ is finitary.
$$X$$

EXERCISE 8.2.3   Show that if a unary operator $\oplus$ satisfies $(s, t) \in [\oplus]_1 \Rightarrow \#t > \#s$, then $\oplus$ is constructive.

EXERCISE 8.2.4   Prove Lemma 8.2.4 (c), and hence show that the quicksort recursion via enslavement given on page 108 is constructive.

EXERCISE 8.2.5   Suppose Σ is infinite. Use renaming to find a CSP-definable function that is constructive but not continuous with respect to $\sqsubseteq_T$.

8.3   The failures/divergences model

8.3.1   Building the model

As we have already specified in Section 3.3, in the failures/divergences model each process is modelled by the pair $(failures_\perp(P), divergences(P))$, where, as formally set out in Section 7.4.1,

- $divergences(P)$ is the (extension-closed) set of traces s on which P can diverge, in the sense that an infinite unbroken sequence of τ actions can occur after some $s' \leq s$.

- $failures_\perp(P)$ consists of all stable failures (s, X) (where s is a trace of P and X is a set of actions P can refuse in some stable (unable to perform a τ or $\checkmark$) state after s, or results from a state after s which can perform $\checkmark$ and $X \subseteq \Sigma$), together with all pairs of the form (s, X) for $s \in divergences(P)$.

This model has long been taken as the 'standard' equivalence for CSP, and with good reason. It allows us to describe safety properties (via traces) and to assert that a process must eventually accept some event from a set that is offered to it (since stable refusal and divergence are the two ways it could avoid doing this, and we can specify in this model that neither of these can happen). Although, as we will see in Sections 8.4 and 10.1, it is possible to reason about either (stable) failures or divergences in the absence of the other, neither alone provides a sufficiently complete picture of how processes behave.

It is important to notice that if s is a trace that process P can perform then certainly either P diverges after s or reaches a stable state or one that can perform $\checkmark$. Thus, the failure $(s, \{\})$ always belongs to $failures_\perp(P)$, either because of the closure under divergence or because any stable (or $\checkmark$) state obviously refuses the empty set of events. It is, therefore, in general true that $traces_\perp(P) = \{s \mid (s, \{\}) \in failures_\perp(P)\}$, and we will use this identity without comment in what follows.

Recall that in the traces model we identified processes with non-empty, prefix-closed sets of traces in $\Sigma^{*\checkmark}$. Similarly, in the failures/divergences model we need a number of 'healthiness' conditions to identify which pairs of the form (F, D) ($F \subseteq \Sigma^{*\checkmark} \times \mathbb{P}(\Sigma^{\checkmark})$ and $D \subseteq \Sigma^{*\checkmark}$) can reasonably be regarded as processes. We formally define the model $\mathcal{N}$ to be the pairs $P = (F, D)$ of this form satisfying the following (where s, t range over $\Sigma^{*\checkmark}$ and X, Y over $\mathbb{P}(\Sigma^{\checkmark})$):

F1. $traces_\perp(P) = \{t \mid (t, X) \in F\}$ is non-empty and prefix closed.

F2. $(s, X) \in F \wedge Y \subseteq X \implies (s, Y) \in F$
This simply says that if a process can refuse the set X, then it can also refuse any subset.

F3. $(s, X) \in F \wedge \forall a \in Y . s^\smallfrown \langle a \rangle \notin traces_\perp(P) \implies (s, X \cup Y) \in F$
This says that if P can refuse the set X of events in some state then that same state must also refuse any set of events Y that the process can never perform after s.

F4. $s^\smallfrown \langle \checkmark \rangle \in traces_\perp(P) \implies (s, \Sigma) \in F$
This reflects the special role of the termination event/signal $\checkmark$ (see Section 7.2) and says that if a process can terminate then it can refuse to do anything but terminate.

D1. $s \in D \cap \Sigma^* \wedge t \in \Sigma^{*\checkmark} \implies s^\smallfrown t \in D$
This ensures the extension-closure of divergences as discussed briefly above.

D2. $s \in D \implies (s, X) \in F$
This adds all divergence-related failures to F.

D3. $s^\smallfrown \langle \checkmark \rangle \in D \implies s \in D$
The effect of this axiom is to ensure that we do not distinguish between how processes behave after successful termination. Already obliged not to communicate again (as $\checkmark$ is always final) and therefore to refuse all events (by F3), D3 states that the only way a trace $s^\smallfrown \langle \checkmark \rangle$ can get into D is via the implication in D1. Since $\checkmark$ is a signal indicating termination, after that event there is no possibility of the process carrying on and diverging.

Our earlier assertion that the set of traces of any process is just the set $\{s \in \Sigma^{*\checkmark} \mid (s, \{\}) \in F\}$ is justified for any pair (F, D) satisfying the above, because of F2.

It is fairly easy to see that the abstraction functions defined in Section 7.4.1 for deducing $(failures_\perp(P), divergences(P))$ for a member P of an LTS give a pair satisfying the above. That these conditions cannot be strengthened any further is demonstrated

(a) by the fact that, as demonstrated in Exercise 9.4.3, there is a member of an LTS mapping to any pair (F, D) that satisfies them, and

(b) by the facts that, under various sets of assumptions, it can be shown that every member of $\mathcal{N}$ is the image of a CSP process: see Sections 9.3 and 10.2.

Recall that refinement is defined over this model by reverse containment:

$$(F, D) \sqsubseteq_{FD} (F', D') \equiv F \supseteq F' \wedge D \supseteq D'$$

Any immediately divergent process such as **div** is identified with the bottom element of $\mathcal{N}$:

$$\bot_{\mathcal{N}} = (\Sigma^{*\checkmark} \times \mathbb{P}(\Sigma^{\checkmark}), \Sigma^{*\checkmark})$$

for notice that, thanks to conditions D1 and D2, $\langle\rangle \in divergences(P)$ implies that all of these behaviours are present.

The greatest lower bound for any non-empty subset of $\mathcal{N}$ is just given by componentwise union:

$$\sqcap S = (\bigcup\{F \mid (F, D) \in S\}, \bigcup\{D \mid (F, D) \in S\})$$

which is naturally identified with the nondeterministic choice over S and easily shown to be a member of $\mathcal{N}$ (see Exercise 8.3.3).

If s is a trace of $P = (F, D)$, then P/s (P *after* s) is the pair

$$(\{(t, X) \mid (s\hat{}t, X) \in F\}, \{t \mid s\hat{}t \in D\})$$

which simply represents the possible behaviour of P after s has been observed. Conditions D1 and D2 ensure that if $s \in D \cap \Sigma^*$ then $P/s = \bot_{\mathcal{N}}$. We can similarly extract the *initials* and *refusals* of P from its failures/divergence representation:

$$
\begin{aligned}
initials(P) &= \{a \in \Sigma^{\checkmark} \mid \langle a \rangle \in traces_{\bot}(P)\} \\
refusals(P) &= \{X \subseteq \Sigma^{\checkmark} \mid (\langle\rangle, X) \in F\}
\end{aligned}
$$

Clearly $\bot_{\mathcal{N}} \sqsubseteq_{FD} P$ for all P, so this process is the least refined under failures/divergences refinement. There is no single *most* refined process, unlike $\mathcal{T}$ where $STOP$ was most refined. It would have been worrying if there had been one, since $P \sqsubseteq_{FD} Q$ can be interpreted as saying that Q is more deterministic than P, and it is implausible for there to be a single most refined process in a model that claims to provide a complete description of processes. If there were we could put programmers out of a job and use it every time! The maximal processes of $\mathcal{N}$ are those that cannot diverge and can only refuse those sets implied by condition F3. These, satisfying the following

$$divergences(P) = \{\} \wedge$$

$$\forall s, a. \neg(s^\smallfrown\langle a\rangle \in traces_\perp(P) \wedge (s, \{a\}) \in failures(P))$$

are the *deterministic* processes we met in Section 3.3. Let $\mathcal{D}$ denote the set of deterministic processes. We will discuss these in Section 9.1, including showing that they are, indeed, the maximal elements of $\mathcal{N}$.

When Σ is finite, $\mathcal{N}$ is significantly easier to analyze and better-behaved. The following result illustrates this.

THEOREM 8.3.1 *If Σ is finite then $\mathcal{N}$ is a complete partial order (cpo) under the refinement order and the least upper bound of any directed set Δ of processes is simply the componentwise intersection*

$$P^\dagger = (F^\dagger, D^\dagger) = (\bigcap\{F \mid (F, D) \in \Delta\}, \bigcap\{D \mid (F, D) \in \Delta\})$$

PROOF   To prove this we have to show that $(F^\dagger, D^\dagger)$ satisfies all of F1–D3. All of these other than F3, which is the only one actually requiring the directedness of Δ, are straightforward, so we will concentrate on that one.

If (s, X) and Y meet the conditions of F3 for the failure-set $F^\dagger$, we have to show that $(s, X \cup Y) \in F$ for every $(F, D) \in \Delta$ as that would imply it is in the intersection $F^\dagger$. Let us fix on a specific $P_0 = (F_0, D_0)$. As P varies over Δ, the set

$$initials(P/s) = \{a \mid s^\smallfrown\langle a\rangle \in traces_\perp(P)\}$$

varies in such a way that

$$P \sqsubseteq_{FD} P' \Rightarrow initials(P/s) \supseteq initials(P'/s)$$

As we are assuming Σ (and hence $\mathbb{P}(\Sigma^\smallsmile)$) to be finite, it follows that the above sets form a finite directed set under reverse containment, which means that there is a $P^\ddagger = (F^\ddagger, D^\ddagger) \in \Delta$ such that it is minimum in the sense that $(P^\ddagger/s)^0 \subseteq (P/s)^0$ for all $P \in \Delta$. Directedness of Δ also lets us assume that $P^\ddagger \sqsupseteq P_0$ for if the one we pick first does not satisfy this we may pick one which refines both the original and P_0. It follows easily that $initials(P^\dagger/s) = initials(P^\ddagger/s)$ and so $(s, X \cup Y) \in F^\ddagger \subseteq F_0$ as required.

The use of directed finite sets in this proof is essentially a re-working in rather different language of the argument in Theorem 7.4.1 (König's lemma). It is interesting to compare them.   ∎

This proof depends crucially on the finiteness of Σ, for the result does not hold when Σ is infinite. We should not be too surprised at this, since moving from a finite to an infinite alphabet means that $\mathcal{N}$ contains processes that are fundamentally infinitely, or unboundedly, nondeterministic in the sense that they cannot be represented by a finitely nondeterministic LTS or by CSP syntax without one of the constructs ($\sqcap S$ for infinite S, infinite hiding and infinite-to-one renaming – note that the last two of these can only exist in the context of infinite Σ) known to introduce it. Since refinement is equated with the restriction of nondeterministic choice, if we start off (at some point in a process) with a finite range of options then – as shown in the proof above – any directed set of refinements must eventually settle down to a fixed non-empty subrange of these options, for a directed (under reverse inclusion) set of non-empty finite sets always has non-empty intersection. On the other hand, a similar directed set of infinite non-empty sets may have empty intersection, the simplest example being, perhaps,

$$\{\{0,1,2,\ldots\},\{1,2,3,\ldots\},\{2,3,4,\ldots\},\ldots,\{n,n+1,\ldots\},\ldots\}$$

This example can be translated directly to one showing that $\mathcal{N}$ is not a cpo when Σ is infinite; assume we have identified a distinct element $a_i \in \Sigma$ for each $i \in \mathbb{N}$. Now let

$$P_n = \sqcap\{a_i \to STOP \mid i \geq n\}$$

Clearly $P_n \sqsubseteq_{FD} P_{n+1}$ for all n and $(\langle\rangle, \Sigma) \notin \mathit{failures}_\perp(P_n)$ for any n. If this increasing sequence were to have an upper bound $P^\dagger$, it would have to have the following properties:

- $(\langle\rangle, \Sigma) \notin \mathit{failures}_\perp(P^\dagger)$ because $P^\dagger$ must refine the P_i, and
- $\mathit{traces}(P^\dagger) = \{\langle\rangle\}$ since every trace other than $\langle\rangle$ is absent from P_n for sufficiently large n.

But these two properties are inconsistent because of condition F3.

This, of course, means that it is easier to justify the existence of fixed points for recursive definitions when Σ is finite. A number of techniques[3] have been developed for establishing their existence over the type of incomplete order caused

---

[3]In this case it is possible to find a different and stronger partial order which is complete and with respect to which the operators of CSP are all monotonic. This order asserts that $P \leq Q$ only when $\mathit{divergences}(Q) \subseteq \mathit{divergences}(P)$ and whenever $s \in \mathit{traces}(P) \setminus \mathit{divergences}(P)$ then

by considering unbounded nondeterminism. These can be used to show that any CSP-definable function over $\mathcal{N}$ always has a least fixed point whether Σ is finite or not.

Thus, the incompleteness arising from infinite alphabets is more a mathematical inconvenience than a real problem. Nevertheless, the possibility of infinite nondeterminism (whatever the size of Σ) does create a real difficulty with the accuracy of $\mathcal{N}$ as we will see in the next section.

In order to extend the notions of constructiveness and non-destructiveness to $\mathcal{N}$ we need to define restrictions $P \downarrow n$ with the same properties as those already studied over $\mathcal{T}$. Various definitions would work, but the following one is perhaps the best since it identifies $P \downarrow n$ with the $\sqsubseteq_{FD}$-minimal process in the subset of $\mathcal{N}$ we would wish to identify with P based on n-step behaviour. $(F, D) \downarrow n = (F', D')$, where

$$
\begin{aligned}
D' &= D \cup \{s \hat{\ } t \mid (s, \{\}) \in F \wedge s \in \Sigma^n\} \\
F' &= F \cup \{(s, X) \mid s \in D'\}
\end{aligned}
$$

In other words, $P \downarrow n$ behaves exactly like P until exactly n events have occurred, at which point it diverges unless it has already terminated.

LEMMA 8.3.2 *These functions form a restriction sequence satisfying the conditions laid out on page 488, and furthermore*

(i) *For each $P \in \mathcal{N}$, $P = \bigsqcup\{P \downarrow n \mid n \in \mathbb{N}\}$.*

(ii) *If P_n is a sequence of processes such that $P_{n+1} \downarrow n = P_n$ for all n, then $P^\dagger = \bigsqcup\{P_n \mid n \in \mathbb{N}\}$ exists and is such that $P^\dagger \downarrow n = P_n$.*

Hence the metric generated by these functions is complete.

EXERCISE 8.3.1 List all the members of $\mathcal{N}$ whose traces are $\{\langle\rangle, \langle a \rangle, \langle b \rangle\}$, and find a CSP process corresponding to each.

EXERCISE 8.3.2 Axiom D3 states that any divergence must appear before successful termination. Reformulate the model so that divergence-sets are now subsets of Σ^* (i.e., do not contain $\checkmark$), in such a way that the new version is order-isomorphic to the original.

$refusals(P/s) = refusals(Q/s)$ and $initials(P/s) = initials(Q/s)$. Thus, non-divergent behaviour of P cannot be 'refined' any further and the divergence-free processes are all maximal in the order. For details of this order, the reader should consult [94]. We will see further applications of this order in Section 9.2. Other techniques for proving the existence of fixed points, with more general applicability, include comparison with the operational semantics [95] and the identification and manipulation of a complete sub-order [5, 7]. We will discuss these further in Chapter 10.

It is a somewhat arbitrary decision which version to choose. We have chosen the version in which ✓'s can appear in divergences because it simplifies some operator definitions in the next section slightly.

EXERCISE 8.3.3   Show that componentwise union of any non-empty subset S of $\mathcal{N}$ is a member of $\mathcal{N}$.

Find an example to show that the intersection of two members of $\mathcal{N}$ need not be in the model. What can you say about the intersection of two processes with the same traces?

EXERCISE 8.3.4   Prove Lemma 8.3.2 above (establishing that $\mathcal{N}$ is a complete restriction space).

8.3.2   Calculating the semantics of processes

Throughout Part I we generally gave the trace semantics of each operator as we introduced it. In this section we show how to calculate the failures/divergences semantics in the same way, thereby giving the building blocks of another denotational semantics.

The following clauses show how to calculate the failures and divergences of combinations under a number of operators where the definitions are all fairly obvious extensions of the corresponding traces definitions.

$$failures_\perp(STOP) = \{(\langle\rangle, X) \mid X \subseteq \Sigma^{\checkmark}\}$$

$$divergences(STOP) = \{\}$$

$$failures_\perp(SKIP) = \{(\langle\rangle, X) \mid X \subseteq \Sigma\} \cup \{(\langle\checkmark\rangle, X) \mid X \subseteq \Sigma^{\checkmark}\}$$

$$divergences(SKIP) = \{\}$$

$$\begin{aligned} failures_\perp(a \rightarrow P) \;=\; & \{(\langle\rangle, X) \mid a \notin X\} \\ & \cup \{(\langle a\rangle\hat{\ }s, X) \mid (s, X) \in failures_\perp(P)\} \end{aligned}$$

$$divergences(a \rightarrow P) = \{\langle a\rangle\hat{\ }s \mid s \in divergences(P)\}$$

$$\begin{aligned} failures_\perp(?x : A \rightarrow P) \;=\; & \{(\langle\rangle, X) \mid X \cap A = \{\}\} \\ & \cup \{(\langle a\rangle\hat{\ }s, X) \mid a \in A \wedge \\ & \quad (s, X) \in failures_\perp(P[a/x])\} \end{aligned}$$

$$divergences(?x : A \rightarrow P) = \{\langle a\rangle\hat{\ }s \mid a \in A \wedge s \in divergences(P[a/x])\}$$

$$failures_\perp(P \sqcap Q) = failures_\perp(P) \cup failures_\perp(Q)$$

$$divergences(P \sqcap Q) = divergences(P) \cup divergences(Q)$$

$$failures_\perp(\sqcap S) = \bigcup\{failures_\perp(P) \mid P \in S\} \text{ for any non-empty set } S \subseteq \mathcal{N}$$

$$divergences(\sqcap S) = \bigcup\{divergences(P) \mid P \in S\}$$

$$failures_\perp(P \mathbin{\triangleleft} b \mathbin{\triangleright} Q) = \begin{cases} failures_\perp(P) & \text{if } b \text{ evaluates to } true \\ failures_\perp(Q) & \text{if } b \text{ evaluates to } false \end{cases}$$

$$divergences(P \mathbin{\triangleleft} b \mathbin{\triangleright} Q) = \begin{cases} divergences(P) & \text{if } b \text{ evaluates to } true \\ divergences(Q) & \text{if } b \text{ evaluates to } false \end{cases}$$

As one would expect, in this model we can distinguish $P \sqcap Q$ from $P \mathbin{\square} Q$. The difference is, that on $\langle\rangle$, $P \mathbin{\square} Q$ cannot refuse a set of events just because P or Q does, they *both* have to. The obvious definitions are

$$divergences(P \mathbin{\square} Q) = divergences(P) \cup divergences(Q)$$

$$\mathsf{X} \quad failures_\perp(P \mathbin{\square} Q) = \{(\langle\rangle, X) \mid (\langle\rangle, X) \in failures_\perp(P) \cap failures_\perp(Q)\}$$
$$\cup \{(s, X) \mid (s, X) \in failures_\perp(P)$$
$$\cup failures_\perp(Q) \wedge s \neq \langle\rangle\}$$

The *divergences* clause is correct, but the failures one potentially breaches conditions D2 and F4. D2 fails, for example, on **div** $\mathbin{\square}$ $a \to STOP$, since the above definitions tell us that this process can diverge immediately but cannot refuse $\{a\}$ after the empty trace. Of course this process does not have the *stable* refusal $\{a\}$, but we have to remember that $failures_\perp(P)$ does not just contain the stable failures. F4 fails because in compositions like $SKIP \mathbin{\square} a \to P$ the definition does not take account of the special status of $\checkmark$: we decided in Section 6.3 that $SKIP \mathbin{\square} P$ had to be specially interpreted, and this must be reflected in the semantics. We can correct these two flaws by fairly obvious additions to the above definition

$$divergences(P \mathbin{\square} Q) = divergences(P) \cup divergences(Q)$$

$$failures_\perp(P \mathbin{\square} Q) = \{(\langle\rangle, X) \mid (\langle\rangle, X) \in failures_\perp(P) \cap failures_\perp(Q)\}$$
$$\cup \{(s, X) \mid (s, X) \in failures_\perp(P)$$
$$\cup failures_\perp(Q) \wedge s \neq \langle\rangle\}$$
$$\cup \{(\langle\rangle, X) \mid \langle\rangle \in divergences(P) \cup divergences(Q)\}$$
$$\cup \{(\langle\rangle, X) \mid X \subseteq \Sigma \wedge \langle\checkmark\rangle \in traces_\perp(P) \cup traces_\perp(Q)\}$$

Several later definitions will need similar additions to preserve the divergence conditions D1 and/or D2, but this is the only place the special treatment of F4 is required.

Since the parallel operators can all be defined in terms of the interface parallel operator $\parallel$, we only have a formal need to give the definition for that one. $P \parallel_X Q$ can refuse an event in X when either P or Q can because they both have to participate in it. On the other hand, since they can independently perform events outside X, these can only be refused when both P and Q do, much as on the empty trace in

$P \square Q$. $\checkmark$ is, for the purposes of calculating refusals, treated as though it were in X because of distributed termination (Section 6.2; recall that this is built into the definition of the trace-level parallel operator $s \parallel_X t$ which produces the set of all traces that could arise if P and Q respectively communicate s and t).

$$
\begin{aligned}
divergences(P \parallel_X Q) \; = \; & \{u^\frown v \mid \exists\, s \in traces_\perp(P), t \in traces_\perp(Q). \\
& u \in (s \parallel_X t) \cap \Sigma^* \\
& \wedge\, (s \in divergences(P) \vee t \in divergences(Q))\} \\[4pt]
failures_\perp(P \parallel_X Q) \; = \; & \{(u, Y \cup Z) \mid Y \setminus (X \cup \{\checkmark\}) = Z \setminus (X \cup \{\checkmark\}) \\
& \wedge\, \exists\, s, t.(s, Y) \in failures_\perp(P) \\
& \wedge\, (t, Z) \in failures_\perp(Q) \\
& \wedge\, u \in s \parallel_X t\} \\
& \cup \{(u, Y) \mid u \in divergences(P \parallel_X Q)\}
\end{aligned}
$$

The hiding operator is the most subtle and difficult one to deal with in the failures/divergences model; this is because it turns visible actions into τ's and thus (i) removes stable states and (ii) potentially introduces divergences. It is straightforward to deal with the first of these difficulties once we observe that the stable states of $P \setminus X$ correspond precisely to stable states of P that cannot perform any element of X, which is equivalent to saying that they can refuse the whole of X. In general,

$$
\begin{aligned}
failures_\perp(P \setminus X) \; = \; & \{(s \setminus X, Y) \mid (s, Y \cup X) \in failures_\perp(P)\} \\
& \cup \{(s, X) \mid s \in divergences(P \setminus X)\}
\end{aligned}
$$

It is the second problem that presents the greater difficulty and which will ultimately impose a bound on the accuracy of the semantics. Hiding introduces a divergence in $P \setminus X$ when P can perform an infinite consecutive sequence of events in X. The difficulty we have is that our model only tells us about *finite* traces of P, not about infinite ones. Our only option is to try to infer what the infinite traces are in terms of the information to hand. As we saw in Section 7.4.2, thanks to König's lemma, if P has a finitely-branching LTS as its operational semantics then $Traces(P)$ (P's finite and infinite traces $traces_\perp(P) \cup infinites(P)$) equals $\overline{traces_\perp(P)}$ (the closure which includes those infinite traces whose finite prefixes are all there). In that case we therefore know that

$$
\begin{aligned}
divergences(P \setminus X) \; = \; & \{(s \setminus X)^\frown t \mid s \in divergences(P)\} \\
& \cup \{(u \setminus X)^\frown t \mid u \in \Sigma^\omega \wedge (u \setminus X) \text{ finite} \\
& \qquad \wedge\, \forall\, s < u.s \in traces_\perp(P)\}
\end{aligned}
$$

If P's LTS is *not* finitely branching then it simply is not possible to be sure what the infinite traces are when we are told the finite ones, and therefore what the divergences of $P \setminus X$ are. The simplest example is provided by the two processes

$$
\begin{aligned}
A^* &= \ \sqcap\{A_n \mid n \in \mathbb{N}\} \quad \text{and} \\
A^\infty &= \ AS \sqcap \sqcap\{A_n \mid n \in \mathbb{N}\}
\end{aligned}
$$

where $A_0 = STOP$, $A_{n+1} = a \to A_n$ and $AS = a \to AS$. A^* and A^∞ have identical representations in $\mathcal{N}$, but clearly only one of them can actually perform an infinite sequence of a's and hence diverge when we hide $\{a\}$.

We must therefore conclude that it is not, in general, possible to determine the correct value in $\mathcal{N}$ of $P \setminus X$ from that of P when P is unboundedly nondeterministic. In other words, $\mathcal{N}$ unfortunately fails to be a *congruence* for the full CSP language, though it is when we forbid the operators that can introduce unbounded nondeterminism. All we can do in the general case is to assert

$$
\begin{aligned}
divergences(P \setminus X) \ \subseteq \ &\{(s \setminus X)\hat{\ }t \mid s \in divergences(P)\} \\
&\cup \{(u \setminus X)\hat{\ }t \mid u \in \Sigma^\omega \wedge (u \setminus X) \text{ finite} \\
&\wedge \forall s < u.s \in traces_\perp(P)\}
\end{aligned}
$$

so that a denotational semantics that uses the right-hand side as its definition of $divergences(P \setminus X)$ will give a conservative approximation of the true value, in the sense that the true value always refines it.

As we will see in Chapter 10, there is a straightforward solution to the problems we have just encountered, namely to include infinite traces explicitly in the representation of a process. Given this, the author recommends the adoption of the following principle:

> $\mathcal{N}$ *should be regarded as the standard model for giving semantics to finitely nondeterministic CSP (that is, for processes not involving infinite hiding, infinite-to-one renaming or infinite nondeterministic choices). It should not be used for giving denotational semantics to processes that do use these constructs.*

Before leaving this topic, it is worth considering briefly an example which illustrates one of the arguments for including axioms D1 and D2 (the ones that say that we do not attempt to distinguish behaviour after potential divergence). Consider the process P_0, where

$$
\begin{aligned}
P_n \ = \ &b \to P_{n+1} \\
&\Box \ c \to A_n
\end{aligned}
$$

and the A_n are as above. Plainly $P_0 \setminus \{b\}$ (a process that uses no infinitely nondeterministic construction) can diverge and so D1 and D2 force us to identify it with $\bot_{\mathcal{N}}$. If, however, we were tempted to use a version of the model without D1 then the only divergence of $P_0 \setminus \{b\}$ would presumably be $\langle\rangle$. It would have, as finite traces,

$$\{\langle\rangle\} \cup \{\langle c\rangle^\frown\langle a\rangle^n \mid n \in \mathbb{N}\}$$

in other words, all finite prefixes of $\langle c, a, a, a, a, \ldots\rangle$, so that applying the above definition of hiding would predict that $(P_0 \setminus \{b\}) \setminus \{a\}$ could diverge after $\langle c\rangle$. In fact, it cannot, since P_0 plainly cannot perform an infinite consecutive sequence of a's. Thus, discarding axiom D1 would lead us to a position where the semantics of hiding is not even accurate for finitely nondeterministic CSP. What is, if anything, more disturbing about this example is that the semantics would (correctly) not predict that $(P_0 \setminus \{a\}) \setminus \{b\}$ could diverge after $\langle c\rangle$; this means that the standard and obvious laws $\langle$hide-sym$\rangle$ (3.2) and $\langle$hide-combine$\rangle$ (3.3):

$$(P \setminus X) \setminus Y = (P \setminus Y) \setminus X = P \setminus (X \cup Y)$$

would fail. The real problem we are encountering here is that even finitely-branching LTSs can exhibit unbounded nondeterminism after potential divergence when we take into account the invisibility of τ actions. As $P_0 \setminus \{b\}$ diverges it gives the infinite choice of how many a's follow any c. In Theorem 7.4.2, we did not prove that an infinite trace was possible in a finitely branching LTS where every finite prefix was possible, rather that either it was possible or a finite prefix was a divergence. Note the similarity between the present example and Figure 7.9.

There are still two operators waiting to be given their failures/divergences semantics. The first of these is renaming. This creates few problems, though we do have to close up under D1 and D2 since not all traces may be in the image of the renaming relation.

$$\begin{aligned} divergences(P[\![R]\!]) &= \{s'^\frown t \mid \exists s \in divergences(P) \cap \Sigma^*.s \; R \; s'\} \\ failures_\bot(P[\![R]\!]) &= \{(s', X) \mid \exists s.s \; R \; s' \wedge (s, R^{-1}(X)) \in failures_\bot(P)\} \\ &\quad \cup \{(s, X) \mid s \in divergences(P[\![R]\!])\} \end{aligned}$$

Here, $R^{-1}(X) = \{a \mid \exists a' \in X.(a, a') \in X\}$ is the set of all events that map to X under R. In the above we use R extended to traces and so that $\checkmark R \checkmark$, as previously discussed.

If and when P terminates in $P; Q$, the $\checkmark$ signalled by P is hidden from the environment since the overall process has not yet terminated. This means that it is treated in essentially the same way for the calculation of failures as an event hidden in $P \setminus X$. We do not get into the same trouble with divergence because there is never more than one hidden $\checkmark$ in any run of P; Q.

$$
\begin{aligned}
divergences(P;\ Q) \quad &=\quad divergences(P)\ \cup\\
&\qquad \{s\hat{\ }t \mid s\hat{\ }\langle\checkmark\rangle \in traces_\bot(P) \wedge t \in divergences(Q)\}\\[4pt]
failures_\bot(P;\ Q) \quad &=\quad \{(s,X) \mid s \in \Sigma^* \wedge (s, X \cup \{\checkmark\}) \in failures_\bot(P)\}\\
&\qquad \cup\, \{(s\hat{\ }t,X) \mid s\hat{\ }\langle\checkmark\rangle \in traces_\bot(P) \wedge (t,X) \in failures_\bot(Q)\}\\
&\qquad \cup\, \{(s,X) \mid s \in divergences(P;\ Q)\}
\end{aligned}
$$

The properties of these operators over the refinement order are, as over $\mathcal{T}$, largely viewable as consequences of the fact that they can be reformulated as relations over behaviours. Actually defining the relations is rather dull, since we now have to worry about the interplay between two different types of behaviour as well as the combinations of different arguments. For example, consider renaming $P[\![R]\!]$, where we get a relation from failures to failures

$$\{((s, R^{-1}(X)),(s',X)) \mid s\, R\, s'\}$$

one from divergences to divergences

$$\{(s, s'\hat{\ }t) \mid s \in \Sigma^* \wedge s\, R\, s'\}$$

and one from divergences to failures

$$\{(s,(s'\hat{\ }t,X)) \mid s\, R\, s' \wedge (s \in \Sigma^* \vee t = \langle\rangle)\}$$

In every case except one this is possible, simply because each behaviour that results from applying an operator is inferred from at most one behaviour from each of the arguments. The exception is, of course, hiding because we had to infer the presence of a hiding-induced divergence from an infinite set of traces. Thus, we generally have to use a different type of argument when reasoning about hiding.

LEMMA 8.3.3 *Each of the operators other than* $\setminus X$ *is fully distributive (and hence monotonic) over* $\mathcal{N}$ *in every argument.* $\setminus X$ *is not fully distributive but does satisfy* $(P \sqcap Q) \setminus X = (P \setminus X) \sqcap (Q \setminus X)$ *(which also implies monotonicity).*

PROOF   In every case except hiding, the distributivity follows from the existence of a relational representation, as it did over $\mathcal{T}$.

We should not be surprised at the failure of full (i.e., infinite) distributivity for $\setminus X$, because we have already noted that $\mathcal{N}$ loses accuracy for infinitely nondeterministic processes. That it does fail can be seen from

$$(\sqcap\{A_n \mid n \in \mathbb{N}\}) \setminus \{a\} \neq \sqcap\{A_n \setminus \{a\} \mid n \in \mathbb{N}\}$$

where the A_n are as on page 200.

   It is finitely distributive because if each finite prefix of the infinite trace u is a trace of $P \sqcap Q$, then *either* infinitely many come from P *or* infinitely many come from Q. Whichever of these happens, it then follows by prefix closure of trace-sets that they *all* come from the chosen argument (though this does not, of course, preclude the possibility that some or all of them might also come from the other one).   ∎

   We again have to decide on the semantics of recursion, in other words how to extract fixed points. The status of the metric theory (of constructive recursions) is exactly the same as over $\mathcal{T}$, namely that it works for at least 99% of well-behaved recursions one typically meets, and, when it does, it says that there was not really a choice at all. Again, the only issue is what value to give to badly constructed recursions such as those on page 188. Whether or not Σ is finite meaning that $\mathcal{N}$ is complete, it can, as we discussed earlier, be shown that every CSP-definable function has a least fixed point in the refinement order $\sqsubseteq_{FD}$.

   It is, at first sight, by no means obvious that this will give the right answer since we ended up choosing the opposite order in $\mathcal{T}$ – a choice we no longer have since there is no least element of $\mathcal{N}$ under the subset or anti-refinement order. In particular, it will definitely give us a different set of traces for most under-defined recursions like $\mu\, p.p$ (mapped to $\{\langle\rangle\}$ in $\mathcal{T}$ and to $\perp_{\mathcal{N}}$ over $\mathcal{N}$ which has all traces). The crucial point is the distinction between $traces(P)$ (the value computed over $\mathcal{T}$) and $traces_{\perp}(P)$ (the traces of P's representation in $\mathcal{N}$), since the latter includes all extensions of divergent traces. Now the only thing (the operational semantics of) $\mu\, p.p$ does is diverge, which accounts precisely for the difference here, and. *in general*, you can characterize an ill-defined recursion as being one where, after some specified trace, the next step behaviour is not resolved no matter how often the recursion is unwound. In other words, an ill-defined recursion is one where the unwinding of the recursion creates a divergence, which means that the right value for it (after the given trace) is $\perp_{\mathcal{N}}$.

   Recall that on page 190 we characterized the two possible choices of order to use for computing least fixed points in terms of the existence of a proof that a given behaviour was not in any fixed point ($\sqsubseteq$) or had to be in any fixed point ($\subseteq$). The latter works for $\mathcal{T}$ because all the behaviours recorded in the model occur in a finite time, so some finite number of unwindings of a recursion are bound to demonstrate their presence (if a given behaviour over the operational semantics of a recursive process contains n actions, then its derivation never requires more than n unwindings simply because each unwinding introduces a τ action). It would not work for a behaviour that, like a divergence, takes an infinite amount of time to appear. The proof-of-absence idea still makes sense, however. Consider the recursion $\mu\, p.a \to p$: after unfolding this recursion n times we have a proof that divergence can never begin before the trace $\langle a \rangle^n$, so that for any finite trace there is a proof of absence of divergence. A trace of $\mu\, p.F(p)$ will thus be considered a divergence if there is no proof that it cannot be one. This always gives the right answer because an infinitely unfolding recursion results in divergence (see Section 9.4 where these arguments are explored in more detail).

We might therefore suspect that a CSP model in which all behaviours reveal themselves finitely will have a *positive* ($\subseteq$) fixed-point theory, whereas a model which has some infinite observations like divergences will require the *negative* ($\sqsubseteq$) theory. Perhaps the most persuasive argument for the principle of ignoring post-divergent behaviour (axioms D1 and D2) is that it makes this negative fixed-point theory work.

The least fixed point of the under-defined counter recursion Z_2 on page 188 is

$$
\begin{aligned}
Z_2 \;&=\; iszero \to Z_2 \\
&\quad \Box\; up \to Z_2' \\
Z_2' \;&=\; down \to Z_2 \\
&\quad \Box\; up \to \bot_{\mathcal{N}}
\end{aligned}
$$

which is exactly what you might expect operationally. After $\langle up, up \rangle$ the recursion unfolds infinitely since as soon as one of the cells AZ reaches this point it promptly drives its slave to exactly the same one, creating a divergence as this cascades down the infinite master/slave chain. All three of the processes identified earlier as trace fixed points of this recursion are actually failures/divergences fixed points as well. All are maximal since they are deterministic; and, as we would expect, they all refine the value Z_2 defined above.

Since we are using the $\sqsubseteq$ order for fixed points over $\mathcal{N}$, it makes the question of which operators are continuous with respect to that order more important[4] than over $\mathcal{T}$. Since $\mathcal{N}$ is not even a cpo when Σ is infinite, we will only consider the case when it is finite.

For operators represented as relations over behaviours, the continuity analysis closely parallels that over the refinement order over $\mathcal{T}$, namely any operator represented by finitary relations is automatically continuous thanks to essentially the same proof as that seen on page 185. Our assumption that Σ is finite greatly simplifies this analysis, since it means that the number of possible refusal sets attaching to a given trace is also finite. Thus any relational representation of an operator that is finitary on traces is *automatically* finitary on failures.

---

[4]Except for making the fixed-point formula simpler and perhaps more believable, the difference between monotonic and continuous has surprisingly little impact, given the importance that is usually placed on continuity.

Using this fact, and the observation that the relations which introduce divergences/failures based on a divergent prefix are finitary because each trace only has finitely many prefixes, it is straightforward to derive the following result.

LEMMA 8.3.4 *If Σ is finite, then each of the operators $a \to \cdot$, $\Box$, $\sqcap$, $\underset{X}{\|}$, ; and renaming is continuous.*

In fact, hiding (necessarily finite because of the restriction on Σ) is also continuous under this assumption, though the proof is rather different. This is interesting because it did not hold over $\mathcal{T}$ for the $\sqsubseteq$ order; the difference lies in our treatment of divergence. Close examination of the following proof, as well as the behaviour over $\mathcal{N}$ of any example which demonstrates the lack of continuity over $\mathcal{T}$, reveals that any failure of continuity over $\mathcal{T}$ is masked by axioms D1 and D2.

LEMMA 8.3.5 *If Σ is finite, then the hiding operator $\setminus X$ is continuous over $\mathcal{N}$.*

PROOF   The main components of the proof are as follows. Firstly, whenever P is such that the set $pre_{\setminus X}(P, t) = \{s \in traces_{\perp}(P) \mid s \setminus X \leq t\}$ is infinite, then $t \in divergences(P \setminus X)$ since by an application of König's lemma very like that on page 175 this set of traces must contain all the prefixes of some infinite trace.

Secondly, if Δ is a directed set of processes and $t \in \bigcap\{divergences(P \setminus X) \mid P \in \Delta\}$, then $t \in divergences(\bigsqcup \Delta \setminus X)$, because if this were not so then (by the last observation) we would have that

$$M = pre_{\setminus X}(\bigsqcup \Delta, t)$$

is finite, and clearly contains no element of $divergences(\bigsqcup \Delta)$. Let

$$M' = \{s^\smallfrown\langle a\rangle \mid s \in M \wedge s^\smallfrown\langle a\rangle \setminus X \leq t\} \setminus M$$

the set of all extensions of elements of M by either an element of X, or the next member of t, that are not themselves in M. For each $s \in M$ there is certainly $P_s \in \Delta$ such that $s \notin divergences(P_s)$, and for each $s \in M'$ there is $P'_s \in \Delta$ such that $s \notin traces_{\perp}(P'_s)$. But M and M' are both finite sets, so following the usual directed set argument yields a $\sqsubseteq_{FD}$ upper bound $P^\dagger \in \Delta$ for all the P_s and P'_s. This must satisfy

$$pre_{\setminus X}(P^\dagger, t) = M$$

for if not there would be a prefix-minimal element s in $pre_{\setminus X}(P^\dagger, t) \setminus M$. But then $s \in M'$, contradicting the construction of $P^\dagger$. Since plainly, then, we have

$t \notin divergences(P^\dagger \setminus X)$, this contradicts our original assumptions. We can thus conclude that $t \in divergences(\bigsqcup \Delta \setminus X)$.

Thirdly and finally, when $t \notin divergences(\bigsqcup \Delta \setminus X)$, the arguments in the previous paragraphs show that sufficiently far through Δ the behaviour of the hiding operator is effectively finitary. The proof that it preserves the limit of this Δ (for trace t) then follows more-or-less the same pattern as those for operators with finitary relational representations.   ∎

Thus every[5] function definable in finitely nondeterministic CSP is continuous over $\mathcal{N}$ for finite Σ.

The lists of operators that are constructive and non-destructive over $\mathcal{N}$ are identical to those that applied over $\mathcal{T}$.

LEMMA 8.3.6 *Each of the operators $\sqcap$, $\square$, $\underset{X}{\|}$, renaming and ; is non-destructive over $\mathcal{N}$ in each argument. The prefix operators $a \to$ and $?x : A \to$ are constructive.*

Again these facts are usually elementary consequences of relational representations, and the only one to be interesting is the left-hand side of sequencing (;) because of the effective hiding of $\checkmark$. For this, the precise form of the restriction operator $P \downarrow n$ is moderately important. If s is a trace of length n, then whether $s \in traces_\perp(P)$ can be established by looking at $P \downarrow n$, but the further details about s, namely whether a pair $(s, X) \in failures_\perp(P)$ or whether $s \in divergences(P)$, can only be established by looking at $P \downarrow (n + 1)$. This means that all failures and divergences of $P; Q$ that can be created by P performing the trace $s^\smallfrown\langle\checkmark\rangle$ have depth, in this sense, of at least $n + 1$ (the length of $s^\smallfrown\langle\checkmark\rangle$).

EXERCISE 8.3.5   (a)   Prove carefully that $\mathcal{N}$ is closed under (i) the prefix operator $a \to P$ and (ii) external choice $P \square Q$. (For the model to be closed under an operation means that, if the arguments to the operator belong to the model then so does the result. Another way of stating this is to say that the operator is *well-defined* over the model. While it is plainly tedious to have to prove such results for all operators, they are clearly a basic well-formedness check that has to be done either by someone or some theorem prover!)

(b)   Give direct proofs, for the same operators, that they are distributive (over $\sqcap$) and continuous.

EXERCISE 8.3.6   Prove that the following laws are valid over $\mathcal{N}$:

(a) $\langle\sqcap\text{-}\square\text{-dist}\rangle$ (1.13)

---

[5]The properties of continuous operators detailed in Appendix A are needed to combine the results about the basic operations into this general statement, in particular their closure under composition.

(b) ⟨|||-step⟩ (2.6)

(c) ⟨; -step⟩ (6.7)

EXERCISE 8.3.7   Give relational representations of the following operators over $\mathcal{N}$:

(a) Prefixing $a \to P$.

(b) Nondeterministic choice $P \sqcap Q$

(c) External choice $P \,\square\, Q$

In each case you will need relations to generate both failures and divergences; in the last case the set of relations generating failures have to take account of divergences.

EXERCISE 8.3.8   Find expressions, in the style of those on page 197 for the failures and divergences of $P \gg Q$ for any P and Q all of whose non-divergent traces lie in the set $\{| \, left, right \, |\}$. (You can find an expression for the traces on page 102.)

Use this to prove BL1 (if P and Q are buffers, so is $P \gg Q$). (All of the buffer laws except BL5 and BL5′ can be proved fairly straightforwardly from the failures/divergences semantics of $\gg$. These other two require rather sophisticated versions of the recursion induction rule.)

8.4   The stable failures model

The failures/divergences model gives us perhaps the most satisfactory representation of a process for deciding questions of liveness, since by excluding both divergence and the stable refusal of a set of events we can guarantee that a member of the set will eventually be accepted. It is possible to devise models which combine traces either only with divergences or only with stable refusals, but it must be emphasized that, in using either, one must appreciate the important information one is leaving out. There is not much to say about the finite traces/divergences model, except the obvious fact that the representation of any process can be found by dropping the refusal components in the failures from its representation in $\mathcal{N}$. The semantic clauses for the CSP operators are similarly derived from those over $\mathcal{N}$, noting that since refusal (as opposed to trace and divergence) information never influences the traces or divergences of any of the operators over $\mathcal{N}$, there is no problem in computing the values accurately. This model, like $\mathcal{N}$, uses the refinement order to compute the values of recursions, and needs to adopt axioms like D1 and D2. It has the same restriction to finitely nondeterministic CSP to make the semantics accurate.

The model in which we record traces and stable refusals (where 'stable' refusals include the ones generated by states that can perform $\checkmark$, or, in other words, the ones postulated by axiom F4) is more interesting for three reasons.

- Firstly, some authors have long considered the imposition of axioms D1 and D2 on $\mathcal{N}$ unfortunate because they have an obscuring effect. It turns out that by ignoring divergences completely one can, to some extent, satisfy their desires.

- Secondly, the calculations required to determine if a process diverges are significantly more costly than those for deciding other aspects of refinement. Therefore it is advantageous if tools like FDR have a model they can use that does not force the calculation of divergences.[6]

- Thirdly, it is sometimes advantageous to analyze a divergence-free process P by placing it in a context $C[P]$ in which it may diverge as the result of hiding some set of actions. This only works when the traces and stable failures that result are not obscured by D1 and D2.

The first thing to appreciate about only recording stable failures is that it is by no means inevitable that every trace of a process has one: it may never stop performing τ actions. Therefore, unlike the case with $\mathcal{N}$, it is necessary to record the traces separately, and so each process is represented as the pair $(traces(P), failures(P))$ rather than just $failures(P)$. The *stable failures model*, $\mathcal{F}$, thus consists of those pairs (T, F) ($T \subseteq \Sigma^{*\checkmark}$ and $F \subseteq \Sigma^{*\checkmark} \times \mathbb{P}(\Sigma^{\checkmark})$) satisfying the following healthiness conditions

T1. T is non-empty and prefix closed.

T2. $(s, X) \in F \Rightarrow s \in T$

plus conditions F2, F3, and F4 (with T replacing $traces_\perp(P)$) as for $\mathcal{N}$. We need a further condition which, like D3, serves to standardize how processes look after $\checkmark$:

T3. $s^\frown\langle\checkmark\rangle \in T \Rightarrow (s^\frown\langle\checkmark\rangle, X) \in F$

All of these are obvious, given our previous discussions. The fact that they are sufficient to characterize what processes look like will be shown in Section 9.3. $\mathcal{F}$ has both top and bottom elements with respect to the refinement order

$$P \sqsubseteq_F Q \equiv traces(P) \supseteq traces(Q) \wedge failures(P) \supseteq failures(Q)$$

The minimal, or least-defined process, is $\perp_\mathcal{F} = (\Sigma^{*\checkmark}, \Sigma^{*\checkmark} \times \mathbb{P}(\Sigma^{\checkmark}))$: as one would expect, the process that can perform any behaviour within the domain under consideration. The maximal process is a more surprising object, $\top_\mathcal{F} = (\{\langle\rangle\}, \{\})$, which

---

[6]In most cases one will combine such a check with a proof of divergence freedom, from which one can infer that refinement holds over $\mathcal{N}$.

satisfies all the axioms above. A little thought reveals that this represents the process **div** which simply diverges immediately without the possibility to do anything else. What has happened is that by omitting to model divergence, we have pushed processes that do diverge (as opposed to other things) upwards under the refinement order. Rather like the case with $\mathcal{T}$ (and the traces/divergences model, which also has $STOP$ as its maximal element), you should regard the existence of a top element under refinement as a strong indication that the model only presents a partial picture of processes.

As with $\mathcal{T}$ and $\mathcal{N}$, any non-empty subset of $\mathcal{F}$ has a greatest lower bound under $\sqsubseteq_F$ given by componentwise union: $\bigsqcap S = (T^+, F^+)$, where

$$
\begin{aligned}
T^+ &= \bigcup \{T \mid (T, F) \in S\} \\
F^+ &= \bigcup \{F \mid (T, F) \in S\}
\end{aligned}
$$

Since $\top_{\mathcal{F}}$ is the greatest lower bound of the empty set, this means that *every* subset has one, and hence (thanks to Lemma A.1.1) we immediately get the following.

THEOREM 8.4.1 *$\mathcal{F}$ is a complete lattice under both the refinement order and the subset order.*

This is a much stronger result than with $\mathcal{N}$, particularly since it applies whether or not Σ is finite. The least upper bounds generated under the refinement order are not always particularly intuitive, since this new model can and does create its upper bounds for sets of processes that are inconsistent over $\mathcal{N}$ by introducing behaviour like the top element $\top_{\mathcal{F}}$. Thus, the least upper bound of

$$\{a \to a \to STOP, a \to STOP\}$$

is $a \to \top_{\mathcal{F}} = (\{\langle\rangle, \langle a\rangle\}, \{(\langle\rangle, X) \mid a \notin X\})$; the inconsistent behaviour after $\langle a\rangle$ being resolved to $\top_{\mathcal{F}}$.

Noticing that the first component of a process's representation in $\mathcal{F}$ is its representation in $\mathcal{T}$, it follows:

- that the clauses for calculating that component of each operator are identical to the corresponding clauses in $\mathcal{T}$, and

- that to get the right value for recursively defined processes we should take fixed points with respect to $\subseteq$ rather than $\sqsubseteq$. Note that the existence of the $\sqsubseteq_F$ top, which is the bottom under $\subseteq$, supports this, as does the simple form of least upper bounds under $\subseteq$.

The latter may seem surprising since it is the opposite to $\mathcal{N}$, but the crucial distinction between $\mathcal{F}$ and $\mathcal{N}$ is that the former, like $\mathcal{T}$, only records finitely observable behaviours so (bearing in mind our discussions about the calculation of fixed points over $\mathcal{N}$) we neither need reverse-inclusion to allow infinite behaviours into fixed points, nor have the special properties of divergence to make the reverse-inclusion fixed point accurate.

As one might expect, the clauses for calculating the failures component are essentially the same as those over $\mathcal{N}$ except that there is no need to close under axioms D1 and D2.

$$failures(STOP) = \{(\langle\rangle, X) \mid X \subseteq \Sigma^\checkmark\}$$

$$failures(SKIP) = \{(\langle\rangle, X) \mid X \subseteq \Sigma\} \cup \{(\langle\checkmark\rangle, X) \mid S \subseteq \Sigma^\checkmark\}$$

$$failures(a \to P) = \{(\langle\rangle, X) \mid a \notin X\}$$
$$\cup \{(\langle a\rangle\hat{\ }s, X) \mid (s, X) \in failures(P)\}$$

$$failures(?x : A \to P) = \{(\langle\rangle, X) \mid X \cap A = \{\}\}$$
$$\cup \{(\langle a\rangle\hat{\ }s, X) \mid a \in A$$
$$\wedge \ (s, X) \in failures(P[a/x])\}$$

$$failures(P \sqcap Q) = failures(P) \cup failures(Q)$$

$$failures(\sqcap S) = \bigcup\{failures(P) \mid P \in S\} \text{ for } S \text{ a non-empty set of processes}$$

$$failures(P \mathbin{\triangleleft b \triangleright} Q) = \begin{cases} failures(P) & \text{if } b \text{ evaluates to } \textit{true} \\ failures(Q) & \text{if } b \text{ evaluates to } \textit{false} \end{cases}$$

$$failures(P \ \Box \ Q) = \{(\langle\rangle, X) \mid (\langle\rangle, X) \in failures(P) \cap failures(Q)\}$$
$$\cup \{(s, X) \mid (s, X) \in failures(P) \cup failures(Q) \wedge s \neq \langle\rangle\}$$
$$\cup \{(\langle\rangle, X) \mid X \subseteq \Sigma \wedge \langle\checkmark\rangle \in traces(P) \cup traces(Q)\}$$

$$failures(P \ \underset{X}{\|} \ Q) = \{(u, Y \cup Z) \mid Y \backslash (X \cup \{\checkmark\}) = Z \backslash (X \cup \{\checkmark\})$$
$$\wedge \ \exists s, t.(s, Y) \in failures(P)$$
$$\wedge \ (t, Z) \in failures(Q)$$
$$\wedge \ u \in s \ \underset{X}{\|} \ t\}$$

$$failures(P \setminus X) = \{(s \setminus X, Y) \mid (s, Y \cup X) \in failures(P)\}$$

$$failures(P[\![R]\!]) = \{(s', X) \mid \exists s.s \ R \ s' \wedge (s, R^{-1}(X)) \in failures(P)\}$$

$$failures(P; \ Q) = \{(s, X) \mid s \in \Sigma^* \wedge (s, X \cup \{\checkmark\}) \in failures(P)\}$$
$$\cup \{(s\hat{\ }t, X) \mid s\hat{\ }\langle\checkmark\rangle \in traces(P) \wedge (t, X) \in failures(Q)\}$$

We have lost the clause that caused difficulty over $\mathcal{N}$ (namely the inference of divergence under hiding), and all the operators thus have relational representations that are simplifications of those for $\mathcal{N}$. The arguments in Section 8.2 thus apply to yield the following result.

THEOREM 8.4.2 *All CSP operators are monotonic and continuous over $\mathcal{F}$ with respect to the subset order, and are fully distributive.*

In some ways $\mathcal{F}$ is better thought of as a refinement of $\mathcal{T}$ than as an approximation to $\mathcal{N}$: equivalence of processes over $\mathcal{F}$ implies equivalence over $\mathcal{T}$, whereas no such relationship exists between $\mathcal{N}$ and $\mathcal{F}$. It is, however, vital that we understand how a process's representations in $\mathcal{N}$ and $\mathcal{F}$ are related. The following paragraphs attempt to set this out.

- It is important to realize that, while you can sometimes tell from the shape of a member of $\mathcal{F}$ that it *must* diverge after a trace (specifically, when there are no failures associated with the trace), you can never infer that it must not. In particular, any simply divergent process like **div**, $\mu\,p.p$ or $\mu\,p.SKIP$; p is identified with $\top_{\mathcal{F}}$, and $P \sqcap \top_{\mathcal{F}} = P$ for all P.

- This same example shows the type of process for which $\mathcal{F}$ gives more distinctions than $\mathcal{N}$: since $P \sqcap \mathbf{div}$ can diverge immediately it is identified with $\bot_{\mathcal{N}}$ over $\mathcal{N}$. In other words, $\mathcal{F}$ lets us see the details of behaviour after possible divergence, whereas axioms D1 and D2 force us to obscure this in $\mathcal{N}$.

- We previously noted that the denotational semantics for CSP over $\mathcal{N}$ is only accurate for finitely nondeterministic processes. Since the problem which caused that restriction does not arise over $\mathcal{F}$, neither does the restriction.

- Since, for divergence-free processes, $failures(P) = failures_{\perp}(P)$, it follows that the representations of such processes in the two models are congruent in the obvious sense. It is this fact that leads to the most common use of $\mathcal{F}$ with FDR, namely that if the processes *Spec* and *Imp* are known, or postulated, to be divergence-free, then the refinement check *Spec* $\sqsubseteq_F$ *Imp* is equivalent to the less efficient *Spec* $\sqsubseteq_{FD}$ *Imp*.

It is the fact that $\mathcal{F}$ lets us see past potential divergence that gives it some uses which are more interesting than as a way of speeding up certain checks over $\mathcal{N}$. The first is in situations where divergence is difficult to exclude, and it is natural to build a system which is correct in other respects before addressing it. Here it may be natural to formulate and establish correctness conditions over $\mathcal{F}$ (dealing with safety properties and stable refusals), before making some final refinement to exclude divergence. (This is another application of the idea of *stepwise refinement*: see page 47.)   A good example of this is in dealing with communications protocols which, like the Alternating Bit Protocol (Section 5.3), are designed to deal with arbitrary message loss, and perhaps duplication. In our earlier presentation of that protocol we built a model of the lossy communication medium which placed a fixed bound on how many consecutive messages can be lost and how many times one can be duplicated, using the processes $C_N(in, out)$ to model the channels. Even though the protocol is designed to work for arbitrary but finite loss or duplication. For any N, the above medium is obviously a refinement of the process $C(in, out)$ as defined on page 130 which can misbehave as much as it likes. An alternative and equivalent definition of this is:

$$
\begin{aligned}
C(in, out) \;&=\; in?x \rightarrow C'(in, out, x) \\
C'(in, out, x) \;&=\; out!x \rightarrow C'(in, out, x) \\
&\;\; \sqcap\; in?y \rightarrow C'(in, out, y)
\end{aligned}
$$

If you replace the C_N medium processes by C in the system, which we can term ABP_N, defined in Section 5.3 (constrained, as described there, to avoid divergence in the absence of error), the result is a process ABP_∞ that can diverge, but which satisfies the specification $COPY$ (i.e., a one-place buffer) over $\mathcal{F}$:

$$COPY \sqsubseteq_F ABP_\infty$$

If checked on FDR, this will have substantially fewer states than does ABP_N for even small values of N.

This proves very cleanly that *unless ABP_∞ diverges*, it does what we want. The monotonic and transitive properties of refinement imply that this remains true whenever the C_∞ processes are replaced by refinements such as C_N. So

(i) all that remains to be proved for such a refinement is divergence freedom, and

(ii) it demonstrates that the only reason any limit is needed on the misbehaviour of the medium processes in the ABP is to avoid divergence.

The steps we have gone through in the above argument are summarized below, hopefully showing how it should be reworked for other examples.

- First build a system ABP_∞ such that

$$COPY \sqsubseteq_F ABP_\infty$$

- Then find a divergence-free ABP' such that

$$ABP_\infty \sqsubseteq_F ABP'$$

(established in this case by properties of refinement)

- This allows us to infer that

$$COPY \sqsubseteq_{FD} ABP'$$

The second distinctive use of $\mathcal{F}$ arises when we want to establish a property of a divergence-free process P by analyzing not the process itself, but some context $C[P]$ which involves hiding and can therefore potentially introduce divergence. As long as you are well aware of the existence of such divergences and what they mean, they frequently do not represent an undesirable behaviour of the underlying process P. Usually the context and hiding represent some mechanism whereby events irrelevant to the specification can be abstracted away. Abstraction is a very important subject, and Chapter 12 is devoted to it, including some uses of the idea we are now investigating. We will therefore content ourselves with a simple but important one here.

In Section 13.1.1 it is stated that a process P is deadlock-free if and only if $P \setminus X$ is, though the hiding can introduce divergence. Operationally, this is clearly true since all we care about there for deadlock freedom is that each reachable state has an action available: it does not matter what the name of the action is. Nevertheless this result is not one of $\mathcal{N}$, since in that model the introduction of divergence results in the assumption of deadlock via D2. It is, however, true in $\mathcal{F}$ and should therefore be regarded as a statement in that model. The most interesting X to try in the above statement is Σ. No matter what P is, there are four possible values for $P \setminus \Sigma$:

- $\top_{\mathcal{F}}$, indicating that $P \setminus \Sigma$ must diverge, or in other words P can neither deadlock nor terminate;

- $(\{\langle\rangle\}, \{(\langle\rangle, X) \mid X \subseteq \Sigma^{\checkmark}\})$ (equivalent in $\mathcal{F}$ to $STOP$) indicating that P cannot terminate, but can reach a deadlock state;

- $SKIP$, indicating that P can terminate and cannot deadlock before it has done so (though since $P \setminus \Sigma$ might diverge, this does not imply that it *must* eventually terminate); and

- $SKIP \sqcap STOP$, meaning that P can deadlock and can terminate.

The statement 'P is deadlock-free' is thus equivalent to the assertion $SKIP \sqsubseteq_F P \setminus \Sigma$. In the majority of cases where there is no possibility of P terminating, this can be replaced by $\top_{\mathcal{F}} \sqsubseteq_F P \setminus \Sigma$. Of course, this is curious since what we are in effect doing here is stipulating that a process $(P \setminus \Sigma)$ *must* diverge, so we have moved a long way from the treatment of divergence over $\mathcal{N}$. It is also of great practical importance since in FDR one usually gets much better compression of processes when events are hidden than without the hiding (see Section C.2).

The definition and theory of restriction operators over $\mathcal{F}$ are similar to those over $\mathcal{N}$: $(T, F) \downarrow n = (T', F')$, where

$$
\begin{aligned}
T' &= \{s \in T \mid \#s \le n\} \\
F' &= \{(s, X) \in F \mid \#s < n \lor (s = s'^\frown\langle\checkmark\rangle \land \#s = n)\}
\end{aligned}
$$

$P \downarrow n$ thus contains all the traces of length $\le n$ and, like with $\mathcal{N}$, only identifies the refusals of strictly shorter traces except for the special case dealing with condition T3.

EXERCISE 8.4.1   Find an example of a process such that $\{s \mid (s, X) \in \text{failures}(P)\}$ is not prefix closed.

EXERCISE 8.4.2   Find a singe CSP process which is mapped to the bottoms (under $\sqsubseteq$) of $\mathcal{T}$, $\mathcal{N}$ and $\mathcal{F}$ by the respective semantics.

EXERCISE 8.4.3   Find the least upper bound in $\mathcal{F}$ of the processes

$$(a \to STOP) \,\Box\, (b \to STOP) \quad \text{and} \quad a \to STOP$$

Find its representation in the model and a CSP expression with the given value.

EXERCISE 8.4.4   Suppose P is any process whose traces are contained in Σ^* (i.e., it is $\checkmark$-free). What can you say about the traces and failures of the process $P \,|||\, \text{div}$?

Harder: Achieve the same effect for a process P that can terminate (though, if it helps, you can assume there is a given $a \in \Sigma$ that P never communicates).

8.5   Notes

The central role given to semantic models such as those seen in this chapter is the thing that most characterizes the theoretical treatment of CSP in relation to those of other process algebras. In a sense that will be made formal in the next chapter, the CSP semantic models each define a congruence which is the coarsest possible subject to some natural criterion. Other process algebras have found their own way to capture failures-style equivalences, most notably the *testing equivalences* for CCS described by Hennessy and de Nicola [29, 46].

The traces model of CSP was introduced by Hoare in [50]. This was refined into the failures model developed by Hoare, the author and Brookes in [17]. That model was basically $\mathcal{N}$ without the divergence component, and used the refinement (reverse containment) order to compute fixed points: it identified $\mu\, p.p$ with *Chaos*. That model failed to give a consistent model of divergent processes, leading, for example, to the failure of a few of the basic laws. This was corrected with the introduction of the divergences component in [91], [14] and [18].

The formulation of the model in this book is different in two ways from that in these papers (the latter also being essentially the same one that Hoare used in his text [51]). The first is that the early version either specified that all refusal sets are finite (even over infinite Σ) or specified that an infinite refusal set was present whenever all its finite subsets were (which was, of course, effectively the same assumption). This was necessary to make the model a cpo under the refinement order (corresponding to the observation we made on page 195 that $\mathcal{N}$ over infinite Σ is incomplete). It meant that the model could not handle unboundedly nondeterministic operators like infinite hiding *at all*. This assumption has been dropped in this book (i) because the later development [94] of the strong order referred to on page 195 means that we do not need $\mathcal{N}$ to be complete under $\sqsubseteq$ to get fixed points and (ii) the development of the infinite traces extension of $\mathcal{N}$ that we will meet in Chapter 10 means that we can now unequivocally deal with unbounded nondeterminism and it is nice to have the projection function from the richer model cleanly defined. (Neither of the two equivalently powered restrictions on refusal sets mentioned above makes any sense over the infinite traces model. So to use them over $\mathcal{N}$ would leave us with a real problem when it came to deciding which member of $\mathcal{N}$ was the image of a general member of the other model.)

The second change is in the handling of termination $\checkmark$. The early models and CSP semantics did not special-case this nearly so much as we have done. The consequences of this were that sequential composition did not have some desirable properties such as $P; \ SKIP = P$ and that some semantics did not make all $\checkmark$'s final. So axioms F4 and D3 are new here. It has long been recognized that the treatment of termination in CSP was something of a compromise: the recent paper [113] points out one problem with the old approach (as well as providing a most interesting study of the automated proof of many theorems about CSP models and semantics). See [1] for an alternative approach to representing termination in a another process algebra.

The effects on the semantics and models of a move to an imperative (i.e., non-declarative) view of process state can be seen in [92] (where OCCAM is considered). The primary effect is on the representation of termination, since a process now has to be able to pass its state to its successors upon terminating.

The stable failures model $\mathcal{F}$ is a much more recent development. The author has seen a number of attempts (generally unsuccessful) over the years at eliminating the divergence-strictness of $\mathcal{N}$. Characteristically this involved interpreting a divergence as equivalent to a refusal of the whole alphabet, but discarding the axiom D1 which enforces extension-closure of divergence sets. That approach does not work because it is hard to compute fixed points accurately and various standard laws are invalidated. The idea of simply ignoring divergence was suggested to the author in 1992 by Lalita Jategoankar and Albert Meyer, and the model $\mathcal{F}$ as described in this book is a result of that conversation and subsequent collaboration between the author and these two people. A very similar model was described by Valmari in [116].

Chapter 9

Analyzing the denotational models

In this chapter we look in a bit more detail at the structure of the denotational models we saw in the previous chapter, especially that of $\mathcal{N}$. The aim is to convey somewhat deeper understanding of the models and how they represent CSP.

9.1   Deterministic processes

The deterministic processes $\mathcal{D}$, (as a subset of $\mathcal{N}$) are important both for practical and theoretical reasons. The most obvious practical benefit from having a deterministic process is that it is, in some sense, testable because its behaviours, when used over and over again, do not vary unless it is given different external stimuli. We will see in Section 12.4 that the concept can be applied in characterizing such properties as information flow.

The full expressive power of $\mathcal{N}$ is required to judge whether or not a process is deterministic. Practically no useful information can be obtained from the traces model $\mathcal{T}$, and the stable failures model $\mathcal{F}$ is inadequate because it does not model divergence and will equate $P \sqcap \top_{\mathcal{F}}$ with P whether P is deterministic or not. Of course, for processes known to be divergence-free, one can[1] test for determinism in $\mathcal{F}$ since the representation is then effectively the same as the one in $\mathcal{N}$. More generally, we can define a process to be $\mathcal{F}$-deterministic if its representation in $\mathcal{F}$ satisfies the obvious condition:

$$t^\frown\langle a\rangle \in traces(P) \Rightarrow (t, \{a\}) \notin failures(P))$$

This set of processes is closed under refinement and includes $\top_{\mathcal{F}}$. Since it does allow

---

[1]In practice it is usually better to test a process for divergence freedom and then (assuming this works) for determinism over $\mathcal{F}$.

some usually undesirable processes, this condition is mainly of technical interest, but it does have at least one practical use – see page 326.

We have already seen that members of $\mathcal{D}$ play a special role in $\mathcal{N}$ because, as stated in Section 8.3.1, they are the maximal elements under the refinement order. In this section we establish this and other important properties of $\mathcal{D}$. We first show that every member of $\mathcal{D}$ is maximal; the proof that they are the *only* maximal elements will follow later.

LEMMA 9.1.1 *Every member of $\mathcal{D}$ is maximal (under $\sqsubseteq$) in $\mathcal{N}$.*

PROOF   Suppose F are the failures of one member of $\mathcal{D}$, and $F' \subseteq F$ are the failures of another process (we do not have to worry about divergences since deterministic processes do not have any). We have to show that $F' = F$; first we show $traces(F) = traces(F')$. If not, there is $s\hat{\ }\langle a \rangle$ of minimal length in $traces(F) \setminus traces(F')$ (noting that thanks to condition F1 the empty trace does not have this property); by this minimality we have $(s, \{\}) \in F'$, so by condition F3 of F' we then have $(s, \{a\}) \in F'$; but since $F' \subseteq F$ we also have $(s, \{a\}) \in F$, contradicting determinism of F. Thus the trace-sets are equal; it follows by F2 that if $F \neq F'$ there is (s, X) with $X \neq \{\}$ such that $(s, X) \in F \setminus F'$. We know $(s, \{\}) \in F'$; if $a \in X$ then $(s, \{a\}) \in F$ by F2 and hence $s\hat{\ }\langle a \rangle \notin traces(F)$ by determinism. It follows that $X \subseteq \{a \mid s\hat{\ }\langle a \rangle \notin traces(F')\}$ which together with condition F3 yields a contradiction to our assumption that $(s, X) \notin F'$.   ∎

A deterministic process is completely characterized by its traces, because once we know $initials(P/s)$ we know $refusals(P/s)$. Not quite all members of $\mathcal{T}$ give rise to a deterministic process, because of the special treatment of $\checkmark$: a deterministic process that can decide to terminate immediately *must* do so, and so cannot offer any other choices of event.

LEMMA 9.1.2 *The deterministic processes are in 1–1 correspondence with the subset $\mathcal{T}^d$ of $\mathcal{T}$ consisting of those members satisfying*

$$s\hat{\ }\langle \checkmark \rangle \in P \Rightarrow \neg \exists\, a \in \Sigma.s\hat{\ }\langle a \rangle \in P$$

in the sense that $traces_\perp(P) \in \mathcal{T}^d$ for every $P \in \mathcal{D}$, and there is exactly one such P for every member of $\mathcal{T}^d$.

PROOF   The fact that $traces_\perp(P) \in \mathcal{T}^d$ is an immediate consequence of the axioms of $\mathcal{N}$: if $s\hat{\ }\langle \checkmark \rangle$ and $s\hat{\ }\langle a \rangle$ were both members of $traces_\perp(P)$ (for $s \in \Sigma^*$ and $a \in \Sigma$) then $(s, \{a\}) \in failures_\perp(P)$ by axioms F4 and F2, in contradiction to determinacy of P.

If $Q \in \mathcal{T}^d$, we have to find a member of $\mathcal{D}$ with this as its set of traces. This is $det(Q) = (F, \{\})$, where

$$F = \{(s, X) \mid s \in Q \wedge X \subseteq \Sigma^{\checkmark} \setminus \{a \mid s^\frown \langle a \rangle \in Q\}\}$$

It is easy to show that this has the required property. Since the failures in $det(Q)$ are precisely the ones implied by axiom F3 for the given set of traces, it follows that any other process P' with the same set of traces satisfies $P' \sqsubseteq det(Q)$. Since we know that deterministic processes are maximal, it follows that $P' \not\in \mathcal{D}$, establishing that $det(Q)$ is the only one with the given set of traces.   ∎

Now, if P is any member of $\mathcal{N}$, it is not hard to see that

$$P \sqsubseteq det(\{s \in traces_\perp(P) \mid (s' < s \wedge s'^\frown \langle \checkmark \rangle \in traces_\perp(P)) \Rightarrow s = s'^\frown \langle \checkmark \rangle\})$$

The set of traces on the right above are those of P which do not result as continuations of traces on which P could also terminate. Thus every process has a deterministic refinement, and in particular we can easily deduce the following.

LEMMA 9.1.3 *If P is a $\sqsubseteq$-maximal element of $\mathcal{N}$, then $P \in \mathcal{D}$.*

When we introduced CSP operators in earlier chapters we often said either that they could, or could not, introduce nondeterminism. This idea can now be given a precise meaning: an operator can introduce nondeterminism just when it can produce nondeterministic results when applied to member(s) of $\mathcal{D}$. In each case the result corresponds to the intuition we developed earlier: prefixing $(a \to \cdot)$ and prefix choice $(?x : A \to \cdot)$ both preserve determinism, as do 1–1 renaming, alphabetized parallel $(P \;_X\|_Y\; Q)$ and sequential composition $(P; \; Q)$. The last of these holds because a deterministic P never has any alternative to the event $\checkmark$ when the latter is possible. The rest of the standard operators can introduce nondeterminism:

- $(a \to STOP) \,\square\, (a \to a \to STOP)$ is nondeterministic because the initials of the two deterministic arguments are not disjoint. In general, if P and Q are deterministic, $\checkmark \not\in initials(P) \cup initials(Q)$ and $initials(P) \cap initials(Q) = \{\}$, then $P \,\square\, Q$ is deterministic.

- The nondeterministic choice operator $\sqcap$ obviously introduces nondeterminism!

- A non-injective renaming can introduce nondeterminism when it identifies two visible actions from some state: for example, if $f(a) = f(b) = a$ then

$$f((a \to STOP) \,\square\, (b \to b \to STOP))$$

is nondeterministic.

- A parallel operator that, for any event a, allows either argument to perform a independently of the other, can introduce nondeterminism because when we see a we cannot be sure which side it came from. Thus, for example,

$$(a \to STOP) \ ||| \ (a \to b \to STOP)$$

is nondeterministic because, after the trace $\langle a \rangle$, the event b may be either accepted or refused.

- Hiding introduces nondeterminism because it turns visible choices into internal actions, and can thus, amongst other things, emulate the behaviour of $\sqcap$:

$$\left(\begin{array}{l} (a \to c \to STOP) \\ \square \ (b \to d \to STOP) \end{array} \right) \setminus \{a, b\} = \begin{array}{l} c \to STOP \\ \sqcap \ d \to STOP \end{array}$$

$\mathcal{D}$ is a closed subset of the metric space $\mathcal{N}$, because whenever a process P fails to be deterministic, there is some trace s which is either a divergence or, after which, P has the choice of accepting or refusing some action a. Thus if $n = \#s + 1$ then

$$Q \downarrow n = P \downarrow n \quad \Rightarrow \quad Q \text{ is nondeterministic}$$

The rule of *metric fixed point induction*, which we will meet shortly (page 225) can then be applied to deduce the following result.

LEMMA 9.1.4 *If $\mu\, p.F(p)$ is a constructive recursion such that, whenever Q is deterministic then so is $F(Q)$, then the unique fixed point of F is also deterministic.*

Furthermore, any constructive mutual recursion $\underline{P} = F(\underline{P})$ such that each component of $F(\underline{Q})$ is deterministic when all components of $\underline{Q}$ are, has all components of its fixed point deterministic.

What this basically shows is that guarded recursion does not introduce nondeterminism. Thus, any process definition using only

- deterministic constant processes (such as $STOP$ and $SKIP$),

- operators that preserve determinism,

- other operators in cases that do not introduce nondeterminism, and

- constructive recursions

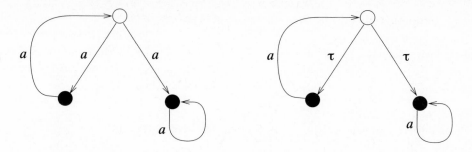

Figure 9.1   Two examples of 'nondeterministic' LTSs whose behaviour is deterministic.

is guaranteed to create a deterministic process.

The definition of determinism over $\mathcal{N}$ takes a broad view of a process, in the sense that it looks at its set of observable behaviours rather than the way it evolves operationally. It is easy to devise rules which ensure that a labelled transition system behaves deterministically, and one such set follows. Except for the last condition you can determine their truth or falsity by examining the transitions of individual nodes.

- No node has multiple branching on any action (visible or invisible); thus $P \xrightarrow{x} Q$ and $P \xrightarrow{x} Q'$ implies $Q = Q'$.

- If a node P has a τ or $\checkmark$ action, then it is the only action of P.

- There is no infinite sequence P_i of nodes such that $P_i \xrightarrow{\tau} P_{i+1}$.

The result of mapping any node of such a system to $\mathcal{N}$ is certain to be deterministic, but the reverse is far from the truth. In other words, there are LTSs whose local structure looks nondeterministic but which actually create processes that behave deterministically. Trivial examples are shown in Figure 9.1. A much more complex one is provided by communication protocols such as the Alternating Bit Protocol (Section 5.3) in which the effects of a nondeterministic communication medium are factored out by the way it is used, creating an overall deterministic effect. An important application of this possibility will be found in Section 12.4.

So it is not possible to decide whether a process is deterministic or not just by looking at the individual nodes of an LTS. There is an interesting algorithm for deciding this question, however, which takes advantage of the maximality of deterministic processes under refinement. This is set out below, both for its intrinsic importance and because it helps to illustrate some of the other ideas in this section.

Suppose we have a process P, presented as a finite-state LTS $(V, \rightarrow, P_0)$, and we want to know whether or not it is deterministic. By (perhaps partially) exploring the LTS we attempt to select a subsystem $(V', \rightarrow', P_0)$ (with the same root node) representing a process P' which refines P and which meets the conditions quoted above for being a deterministic LTS. This is done as follows:

- Initially we place P_0 in V' and begin the search there.

- If we have to explore the node Q, then if it is stable (has no τ or $\checkmark$ action) we select for each action $a \in initials(Q)$ a single node Q' such that $Q \xrightarrow{a} Q'$, add this transition to the subsystem and add Q' to the search if it is not already in V'. This choice means that the initial actions of Q in the subsystem are the same as they were in the original, but that all possibility of nondeterminism arising from ambiguity has been removed.

- If a node Q is not stable then select a single τ or $\checkmark$ action $Q \xrightarrow{x} Q'$ and make this action the only action of Q in the subsystem. This Q' is added to the search if not already in V'.

- If a loop of τ actions is thus encountered, we have discovered a divergence and so can abandon the search since P is not deterministic.

This search will either eventually be abandoned because the last case arises, or terminate because all the nodes added to V' have been explored. If it does terminate then the subsystem it produces is deterministic by construction and the process represented by each node refines the corresponding node in $(V, \rightarrow, P_0)$.

The algorithm above sometimes leaves a great many choices open about how to resolve a process's nondeterminism, meaning that from a given system $(V, \rightarrow, P_0)$ it might choose many different subsystems, perhaps with large differences in size and shape. This is illustrated in Figure 9.2, where two different selections (B and C) are made from a process (A) that is, in fact, deterministic. Thus the existence of these choices does not indicate that the original process P was nondeterministic. What we can guarantee, in any case, is that we have a deterministic process P' such that $P \sqsubseteq_{FD} P'$.

If P is deterministic then $P = P'$ (even though the transition systems representing these members of $\mathcal{N}$ may be very different) because deterministic processes are maximal. If P is not deterministic then $P \neq P'$ and hence $P' \not\sqsubseteq_{FD} P$. Thus P is deterministic if, and only if, $P' \sqsubseteq_{FD} P$, something we can decide with a refinement checker like FDR. Indeed, this is the method FDR uses to decide whether a process is deterministic.

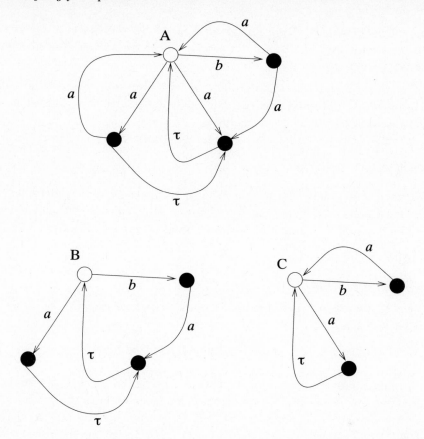

Figure 9.2   Two different 'deterministic' LTSs extracted from a 'nondeterministic' one.

9.2   Analyzing fixed points

In this section we see how understanding the structure of semantic models allows us to justify existing rules for proving properties of recursions and derive new rules.

At various points we have found it useful to be able to apply rules such as fixed point induction and UFP for inferring properties of processes. We have already seen how UFP is justified using metric spaces, but have not proved the fixed point induction rule set introduced in Section 5.1.

FIXED-POINT INDUCTION   *If $\underline{P} = F(\underline{P})$ is any recursive definition of a vector of processes which is either constructive or makes each component divergence-free, with indexing set Λ and $\underline{Q} \in \mathcal{N}^\Lambda$ is such that $Q_\lambda \sqsubseteq_{FD} F(\underline{Q})_\lambda$ for all $\lambda \in \Lambda$, then* we may conclude that $Q_\lambda \sqsubseteq_{FD} P_\lambda$ for all $\lambda \in \Lambda$. In the cases of $\sqsubseteq_F$ and $\sqsubseteq_T$ this principle holds without the need to assume the constructiveness or divergence-freedom of the recursion.

The above is a good starting point for our discussion, since it is really a combination of several results requiring quite different proofs. We will look at three different approaches to fixed point analysis.

Order-theoretic analysis

Sometimes one can simply use the fact that a recursive process is identified with the least fixed point of a monotonic function f in some cpo $(M, \leq)$. The following is a list of a few simple arguments which can often be applied. See Appendix A for more discussion and their proofs.

- If $x \geq f(x)$ then $\mu f \leq x$.

- If $x \leq f(x)$ then f has some fixed point y (not necessarily the least) such that $x \leq y$.

- If μf is maximal in M, then it is the unique fixed point.

An immediate application of the first of these is the proof of the fixed point induction rule for $\mathcal{T}$ and $\mathcal{F}$. For there the refinement order is the reverse of the one used to compute fixed points, so $\underline{Q} \sqsubseteq F(\underline{Q})$ is equivalent to $\underline{Q} \geq F(\underline{Q})$. This implies $\mu F \leq \underline{Q}$, which is equivalent to $\mu F \sqsupseteq \underline{Q}$, justifying the rule for these models.

Metric methods

The Banach fixed point theorem, with its ability to force convergence to the unique fixed point from any point in the underlying space, often makes it possible to achieve more powerful results about constructive recursions than about general ones. In the case of fixed point induction, it allows us to formulate a rule which applies to a much wider class of properties than that specified in the definition of the rule above.

Let X be any space with a family of restriction operators defined over it that give a complete metric (a complete restriction space). In general, a *predicate* $R(\cdot)$ on X (i.e., a function from X to $\{true, false\}$) can be thought of as a subset Y of X (the members of X satisfying it). If Y is both closed (in the metric space) and non-empty, then it is a complete metric subspace of X. If $f : X \to X$ is constructive, and $f(Y) \subseteq Y$, then we can regard f as being a contraction map from Y to itself, which implies that f has a fixed point in Y. But since f only has one fixed point in the whole of X, it must be the same one. (See Exercises A.2.1 and A.2.2 for another view of this.)

The subset Y is closed (see the Appendix) if and only if any $x \notin Y$ can be seen not to be a member by some finite depth of the restriction process. This can be paraphrased as follows:

DEFINITION   The predicate $R(\cdot)$ on the complete restriction space X is *continuous* if, whenever $\neg R(x)$, there exists $n \in \mathbb{N}$ such that, for all $y \in X$, $y \downarrow n = x \downarrow n$ implies $\neg R(y)$. ∎

The demonstration that the fixed point of f, under suitable assumptions, belongs to Y then immediately implies the truth of the following rule:

METRIC FIXED POINT INDUCTION   *Suppose R is a continuous, satisfiable (i.e., $\{x \mid R(x)\}$ is non-empty) predicate on the complete restriction space X. Then if the constructive function f is inductive in the sense that, for all $x \in X$,*

$$R(x) \;\Rightarrow\; R(f(x))$$

then $R(y)$, where y is the unique fixed point of f.

This justifies the 'constructive' case of the original fixed point rule, since, for any $\underline{Q} \in \mathcal{N}^{\Lambda}$ the predicate

$$R(\underline{P'}) \;\equiv\; \underline{Q} \sqsubseteq_{FD} \underline{P'}$$

is continuous. To see this, notice that if $\underline{Q} \not\sqsubseteq_{FD} \underline{P'}$ there must be a $\lambda \in \Lambda$ and a behaviour of P'_λ not belonging to Q_λ; you can choose any n larger than the length of this behaviour. Note that the predicate above is always satisfiable (being satisfied by $\underline{Q}$) and inductive by the assumptions of the rule and monotonicity.

Whereas the standard fixed point induction rule only allows us to prove behavioural properties, the metric rule allows us to address properties that do not have a characteristic process. This generalization is frequently unnecessary since most properties one typically wants to prove *are* behavioural, but it does allow us to deal with abstract specifications such as 'deterministic', as we saw on page 220.

EXERCISE 9.2.1   Suppose R and f satisfy the conditions of the metric fixed point induction rule and that Q is the fixed point of f. Let P be any process satisfying R. Prove by induction that $f^n(P) \downarrow n = Q \downarrow n$, and hence use the definition of a continuous predicate to show that $R(Q)$ holds. *(This gives a more direct proof of the validity of the rule than the one which explicitly uses the properties of metric spaces.)*

EXERCISE 9.2.2   Fixed-point induction, stated informally, might be 'if a recursive process meets some specification R on the assumptions that all recursive calls do, then it meets the specification unconditionally'. There are, however, three conditions that are required of the recursion/specification pair to make this valid: the specification must be satisfiable, the specification must satisfy some continuity condition, and the recursion must satisfy some well-formedness condition (such as being constructive).

The first of these is trivially necessary: without it, the rule would prove the predicate '*false*' true of any recursion! Find examples to show that the other two are needed as well.

EXERCISE 9.2.3   Show that, over $\mathcal{N}$, the predicates $R_1(P) \equiv P \sqsupseteq Q$, $R_2(P) \equiv P \sqsubseteq Q$ and $R_3(P) \equiv P = Q$ are all continuous when Q is any process. Show that $R_4(P) \equiv P \neq Q$ is only continuous if $Q = Q \downarrow n$ for some n.

EXERCISE 9.2.4

(a) Suppose that R is a continuous predicate and that G and G' are non-destructive functions (all over one of the models $\mathcal{T}$, $\mathcal{N}$ or $\mathcal{F}$). Show that the predicates $R(G(P))$ and $G(P) \sqsubseteq G'(P)$ are continuous.

(b) Hence show that if F is a constructive function, and H a subset of Σ, such that

$$P \ ||| \ RUN_H \in \mathcal{D} \Rightarrow F(P) \ ||| \ RUN_H \in \mathcal{D}$$

(remembering that $\mathcal{D}$ is the set of deterministic processes) then $Q \ ||| \ RUN_H \in \mathcal{D}$, where Q is the fixed point of F. *An important application of this result will become apparent in Sections 12.4 and 12.6: we will find that the predicate being used here can be read 'P is secure'.*

(c) Similarly show that the predicate on P

$$(P \underset{E}{\ ||\ } STOP) \ ||| \ RUN_E \sqsubseteq P \ ||| \ RUN_E$$

is continuous. *In Chapter 12 this predicate will be interpreted as 'P is fault tolerant': see Sections 12.3 and 12.6.*

The specifications quoted in parts (b) and (c) share with pure determinism the property of not being behavioural specifications. You may like to convince yourself of this now, or wait until studying them properly in Chapter 12.

The strong order on $\mathcal{N}$

When we discovered in Section 8.3.1 that $\mathcal{N}$ over an infinite Σ is not a complete partial order, it was stated in a footnote that you could use an alternative and stronger order, which was complete, to calculate the fixed points. Given (i) that $\mathcal{N}$ cannot model infinite nondeterminism properly, (ii) that infinite nondeterminism is unnatural to avoid with infinite Σ (because of hiding) and (iii) that there is no problem modelling these things in the infinite traces model that we will see in

Chapter 10, it can be argued that this application of the strong order is mainly of academic interest. However, the existence of the order is worthy of note, particularly since it both reveals much about how recursions converge to their fixed points in $\mathcal{N}$ and allows us to prove, *inter alia*, the final part of the fixed point induction rule. Much more detail on the strong order, as well as proofs of results quoted in this section, can be found in [94].

The strong order on $\mathcal{N}$ asserts that $P \leq Q$ only when $divergences(Q) \subseteq divergences(P)$ and whenever $s \in traces(P) \setminus divergences(P)$ then $refusals(P/s) = refusals(Q/s)$ and $initials(P/s) = initials(Q/s)$. Plainly $P \leq Q$ implies $P \sqsubseteq_{FD} Q$, because the only traces on which the two processes can differ are ones where P can diverge and thus has *all* behaviours, though there are many cases where the reverse does not hold. In a sense, this order takes the principles enshrined in axioms D1 and D2 to the extreme and says that not only is divergent behaviour undefined but that it is the *only* behaviour that can be 'refined' in moving up the order. One can replace any divergence with non-divergent behaviour, but cannot subsequently alter the result. The following summarizes some results about $\leq$.

LEMMA 9.2.1   *(a) $\leq$ is a partial order on $\mathcal{N}$ which is stronger than $\sqsubseteq_{FD}$ in the sense that $P \leq Q \Rightarrow P \sqsubseteq_{FD} Q$.*

(b) $\perp_{\mathcal{N}}$ is the least element of $\mathcal{N}$ under $\leq$.

(c)   If Δ is a $\leq$-directed set, then $\bigsqcup_{\leq} \Delta$ exists; in this case $\bigsqcup_{\sqsubseteq} \Delta$ also exists and the two are equal.

(d)   The maximal elements of $\mathcal{N}$ under $\leq$ are precisely the divergence-free processes.

The most curious feature of $\leq$ is that it turns out to be interchangeable with $\sqsubseteq_{FD}$ for the purpose of calculating fixed points: all CSP operators are monotone, the finitely nondeterministic ones are continuous, and each CSP-definable function has identical least fixed points in the two orders. For details, see [94]. An immediate consequence of this (using (d) above) is the following result:

LEMMA 9.2.2   *If $\underline{P} = F(\underline{P})$ is a CSP-defined recursion with indexing set Λ, and each component of the least fixed point $\underline{P}$ is divergence-free, then it is the unique fixed point.*

This extends the class of recursions where you can use the UFP rule to essentially all well-behaved ones.

This lemma easily disposes of the last part of the fixed point induction rule in the case where Σ is finite, since if $\underline{Q} \sqsubseteq_{FD} F(\underline{Q})$ then F must have a fixed point $\underline{P}'$ such that $\underline{Q} \sqsubseteq_{FD} \underline{P}'$. Obviously it must be the unique fixed point.

The case where Σ is infinite is more difficult since we cannot argue that since the set

$$\{\underline{P'} \in \mathcal{N}^\Lambda \mid \underline{Q} \sqsubseteq_{FD} \underline{P'}\}$$

is a cpo under $\sqsubseteq_{FD}$, and F preserves this set, there must be a fixed point in it – for it is no longer complete.

It can still be justified, but (so far as the author is aware) only using arguments based on topology. The predicate $R(\underline{P'}) = \underline{Q} \sqsubseteq_{FD} \underline{P'}$ represents a closed set with respect to the δ-topology defined in [94, 97] Results in those papers establish the rule. These same two papers, especially the second, give a rather fuller exposition of the mathematics and methods of fixed point induction.

9.3   Full abstraction

The concept of full abstraction addresses the question of how good a semantics is for a programming language. The definition is frequently divided into two aspects.

- The semantics $\mathcal{S}[\![\cdot]\!]$ should distinguish two programs P and Q if, and only if, they are distinguished by some natural criterion. Usually this criterion is the existence of some context such that one of $C[P]$ and $C[Q]$ passes, and the other fails, some simple test.

- The model $\mathcal{M}$ being used should not contain large classes of elements that are not in the image of $\mathcal{S}$. Specifically, the aim is usually to show that the expressible elements of the model are *dense*, in the sense that every element is the limit of a directed set of expressible ones.

While the second of these is clearly a desirable aim in itself – the existence of identifiable classes of inexpressible elements in a semantic model would seem to imply a mis-match with the language – the main reason for incorporating it under the heading of full abstraction is that it is frequently important in establishing the first. For having classes of elements of $\mathcal{M}$ that are distinct from all expressible ones can result in problems for program terms with free process identifiers because they might create functions only different on inexpressible values. We will study the two aspects below.

Of necessity the constructions used in this section often get rather detailed. The author hopes that even though some readers may not want to study all the intricacies involved, they will try to understand what full abstraction is and what the roles of the various constructions are.

Expressibility

Provided we take a reasonably liberal view of what the CSP language contains, demonstrating the expressibility of the members of our semantic models usually presents no problem.

The liberality referred to is in using rather non-constructive mathematical objects to do things like index mutual recursions and use as input sets. Thus the CSP we create here falls well outside the domain of 'effective computability'. We are thinking here of CSP as a mathematical language for describing communicating processes rather than a programming language.

Proving an expressibility result like those that follow establishes that the axioms (such as F1–F4 and D1–D3, in the case of $\mathcal{N}$) used to define the model are strong enough, because they do not allow anything to be considered a process which should not be. Let us deal with each of our models in turn.

Traces model

If s is any trace in $\Sigma^{*\checkmark}$, it is straightforward to define a CSP process T_s which has trace s and as few others as possible:

$$traces(T_s) \;=\; \{t \in \Sigma^{*\checkmark} \mid t \leq s\}$$

This is done by giving T_s one of the forms

$$a_1 \to a_2 \to \ldots \to a_k \to STOP \qquad \text{and} \qquad a_1 \to a_2 \to \ldots \to a_{k-1} \to SKIP$$

depending on whether s has last member $\checkmark$.

It follows that if $S \in \mathcal{T}$, then $S \,=\, traces(\sqcap\{T_s \mid s \in S\})$ which means that *every* member of $\mathcal{T}$ is represented by a CSP process, albeit one using a rather artificial and infinitary nondeterministic choice construct.

We will term the process constructed above $Int_S^{\mathcal{T}}$, because in some sense it interprets the process S.

Stable failures model

Suppose $(T, F) \in \mathcal{F}$. A similar, though slightly more involved, construction creates a CSP process with this value.

The trace component T can be dealt with in much the same way as in $\mathcal{T}$, except that we cannot use the simple T_s processes used above since they give rise to stable failures that will not, in most cases, be appropriate. They need to be adapted so that $failures(T_s)$ contains nothing that is not implied by the presence of s. In other words, we need to create processes T_s' that are maximal under $\sqsubseteq_F$

subject to containing s. These are as below, bearing in mind that we can express the value $\top_{\mathcal{F}}$ as any simply divergent process.

$$
\begin{aligned}
T'_{\langle\rangle} &= \top_{\mathcal{F}} \\
T'_{\langle\checkmark\rangle} &= SKIP \\
T'_{\langle a\rangle^\frown s} &= \top_{\mathcal{F}} \square\, a \to T'_s \quad (a \neq \checkmark)
\end{aligned}
$$

The situation with the failures component is slightly trickier, since there is usually no maximal process containing a failure (s, X). For example, consider the failure $(\langle a\rangle, \{\})$ in the context of the processes $a \to STOP$ and $a \to a \to STOP$ discussed on page 209. They both have this failure, but they have no common refinement that does.

It is necessary to concentrate on the failures which are complete in the sense that axiom F3 does not add anything (i.e., (s, X) such that $\{a \in \Sigma^\checkmark \mid s^\frown\langle a\rangle \notin T\} \subseteq X$). The structure of the processes $T'_{t^\frown\langle\checkmark\rangle}$ created above mean that we can assume that $s \in \Sigma^*$ and that $\checkmark \in X$. (All other complete members of F are failures of $T'_{s^\frown\langle\checkmark\rangle}$.) For such (s, X) we can define processes $F_{(s,X)}$ inductively as follows:

$$
\begin{aligned}
F_{(\langle\rangle, X)} &= ?x : \Sigma \setminus X \to \top_{\mathcal{F}} \\
F_{(\langle a\rangle^\frown s, X)} &= \top_{\mathcal{F}} \square\, a \to F_{(s, X)}
\end{aligned}
$$

Notice that the only failures of $F_{(s,X)}$ occur on trace s and are of subsets of X, and that its traces are all in T..

It is then always true that $(T, F) = (traces(\sqcap S_{(T,F)}), failures(\sqcap S_{(T,F)}))$, where $S_{(T,F)}$ is the following set of processes (noting that the first component is always non-empty because T is):

$$
\begin{aligned}
\{T'_s \mid s \in T\} \cup \{F_{(s,X)} \mid (s, X) \in F \wedge \{a \in \Sigma \mid s^\frown\langle a\rangle \notin T\} \subseteq X \\
\wedge\, s \in \Sigma^* \wedge \checkmark \in X\}
\end{aligned}
$$

We will term this nondeterministic choice $Int^{\mathcal{F}}_{(T,F)}$.

So, again, every element of $\mathcal{F}$ is expressible as the nondeterministic choice of a rather artificially created set of processes.

Standing back from the constructions used for $\mathcal{T}$ and $\mathcal{F}$, and looking at just how the processes we have constructed to model arbitrary elements of them actually behave, is an excellent way of understanding the limitations of these models. After all, these processes must be considered useless for any practical purpose! This will be illustrated shortly.

The failures/divergences model

With $\mathcal{T}$ and $\mathcal{F}$ we were able to deal with each constituent behaviour very nearly on an individual basis and form a process as a nondeterministic choice at the end. This was possible largely because of judicious use of the $\sqsubseteq$-top processes in the two models ($STOP$ and $\top_{\mathcal{F}}$), something that is not possible over $\mathcal{N}$. The use of an infinite nondeterministic choice operator would, in any case, be of questionable taste over $\mathcal{N}$ since we have already seen that this model does not treat unbounded nondeterminism accurately.

It turns out that, without $\sqcap$ and the other infinitely nondeterministic operators, it is impossible to model every member of $\mathcal{N}$ in CSP when Σ is infinite. There are some patterns of refusal behaviour which are allowed by the model axioms that cannot be created without infinite nondeterminism. In fact the only ones that can be created with finite nondeterminism are ones where, for every trace s,

$$refusals(P/s) \;=\; \{X \mid \exists\, Y \in \mathcal{R}.X \subseteq Y\}$$

for some non-empty finite subset[2] $\mathcal{R}$ of $\mathbb{P}(\Sigma^{\checkmark})$ (which can vary with s).

Therefore we will only deal with the case of finite Σ here. What we can then do is to define a mutual recursion over the whole of $\mathcal{N}$: in other words, we define one process for each $(F, D) \in \mathcal{N}$.

$$Int^{\mathcal{N}}_{(F,D)} \;=\; \begin{cases} \bot_{\mathcal{N}} & \text{if } \langle\rangle \in D, \text{ and otherwise} \\ \sqcap(\{?x : \Sigma \setminus X \to Int^{\mathcal{N}}_{(F,D)/\langle x\rangle} \mid \\ \qquad X \text{ maximal in } refusals(F, D) \wedge \checkmark \in X\} \\ \qquad \cup \{(SKIP \lhd (\langle\checkmark\rangle, \{\}) \in F \rhd STOP) \\ \qquad\qquad \Box\, ?x : initials(F, D) \setminus \{\checkmark\} \to Int^{\mathcal{N}}_{(F,D)/\langle x\rangle}\}) \end{cases}$$

where 'maximal' means maximal under $\subseteq$ (noting that any such refusal set is complete in the sense described earlier that it includes all impossible events, and that maximal refusals must be present because of our assumption that Σ is finite). In the interest of brevity, the above definition uses the general nondeterministic choice operator $\sqcap$, but only over finite sets of processes where it could have been replaced by the binary $\sqcap$.

---

[2]Obviously this condition has to be satisfied when Σ is finite, since then $\mathbb{P}(\Sigma^{\checkmark})$ is also finite. We could, of course, have included the above property as an additional axiom for $\mathcal{N}$. This would have made it a cleaner model for finitely nondeterministic CSP at the expense of losing the ability to model unboundedly nondeterministic CSP at all and making $\mathcal{N}$'s links with other models a little more obscure.

The special properties of $\checkmark$ and axiom F4 mean that not all such $\mathcal{R}$ produce an allowable set of refusal sets.

You can think of this curious recursion as an 'interpreter' of members of $\mathcal{N}$ into CSP: at any stage the process's state is $(F, D)/s$, where (F, D) is the initial value of the process and s is the current trace. The recursion is constructive, which leads to the following remarkable argument for its correctness. We can form a vector $Id_{\mathcal{N}}$ of processes, indexed by $\mathcal{N}$ itself (i.e., a member of $\mathcal{N}^{\mathcal{N}}$), in which each member is mapped to itself. This vector is easily seen to be a fixed point of the recursion and hence, by the UFP rule, equals $\langle Int^{\mathcal{N}}_{(F, D)} \mid (F, D) \in \mathcal{N} \rangle$, and so

$$(failures_{\perp}(Int^{\mathcal{N}}_{(F, D)}), divergences(Int^{\mathcal{N}}_{(F, D)})) = (F, D)$$

In contrast to the two models dealt with earlier, the processes $Int^{\mathcal{N}}_{(F, D)}$ are usually a reasonable reflection of how one would expect a process with the given value to behave. As a simple example, consider the process $P = a \rightarrow P$. If this were interpreted in the three models and we then applied the three constructions to the results, the processes obtained would behave as follows.

- $Int^{\mathcal{T}}_{T}$ gives a process which performs any number of a's and then stops. It is the same as the process A^* seen on page 200.

- $Int^{\mathcal{F}}_{(T, F)}$ gives a process which makes a choice, over all n, of offering n a's unstably in turn and then offering a again, stably, before finally simply diverging, and additionally has the option of offering any finite number of a's and *never* becoming stable (again, diverging after the last).

- $Int^{\mathcal{N}}_{(F, D)}$ behaves identically to the original P, simply offering a's stably for ever.

Distinguishing processes

The second thing we have to do is find what criteria for distinguishing processes best characterize each of our models. It is certainly reasonable to argue that the simple construction of the models from process behaviours makes this unnecessary[3]: the sets of behaviours are easy to understand and processes are identified if and only if they have the same ones. But these criteria can be simplified yet further if we use the full power of how full abstraction is formulated: P must equal Q if and only if $C[P]$ and $C[Q]$ always (i.e., for all contexts $C[\cdot]$) either both satisfy or both fail the tests.

---

[3]The concept of full abstraction is more vital on semantics using models which have a more sophisticated structure than simple sets of behaviours, frequently being applied to ones recursively defined using domain theory. There are some languages, such as the typed λ-calculus, for which it is famously difficult to find a fully abstract semantics.

Hopefully the following arguments will help the reader to understand the concept of full abstraction, as well as further exploring the expressive power of CSP.

Traces model

Select any member of Σ. It is convenient to give it a suggestive name such as *fail*. We can then formulate a simple test on processes: they fail it when they have the trace $\langle fail \rangle$ and pass it otherwise. Call this test $\mathbf{T}_1$.

Since $\mathbf{T}_1$ is formulated in terms of traces, and the traces model calculates the traces of any CSP process accurately, it is obvious that if $traces(P) = traces(Q)$ then $C[P]$ and $C[Q]$ either both pass or both fail it. In order to establish that the test is strong enough to distinguish all pairs of processes, we need to show that whenever $traces(P) \neq traces(Q)$ there is a context $C[\cdot]$ such that one of $C[P]$ and $C[Q]$ passes, and the other fails, it. We can achieve this by finding, for any trace s, a context $CT_s[\cdot]$ such that $CT_s[P]$ fails $\mathbf{T}_1$ precisely when $s \in traces(P)$. There are various ways to do this; one is set out below.

- When $s = s'^\frown\langle\checkmark\rangle$, a simple context that does what we want is

$$CT_s[V] \;\; = \;\; (V \underset{\Sigma}{\|} T_s) \setminus \Sigma; \; (fail \rightarrow STOP)$$

  where T_s is the same process used on page 229 in exploring expressibility. The point is that the process on the left-hand side of the sequential composition can only terminate when V has completed the trace s.

- For $s \in \Sigma^*$, we can use the context

$$CT_s[V] \;\; = \;\; ((V \underset{\Sigma}{\|} T_s)[\![a/x \mid x \in \Sigma]\!] \underset{\{a\}}{\|} FAIL(\#s)) \setminus \{a\}$$

  where again T_s is as used for expressibility, a is any member of Σ distinct from *fail*, and $FAIL(m)$ is defined

$$FAIL(m) \;\; = \;\; (fail \rightarrow STOP) \triangleleft m = 0 \triangleright (a \rightarrow FAIL(m - 1))$$

  This context, much as with the more obvious first case, works by only allowing the trace s to occur in V and, like the first one, communicating *fail* only when it is complete and its contents hidden.

This establishes that the traces model is, indeed, fully abstract with respect to the simple test chosen.

Stable failures model

One might expect the tests used for $\mathcal{F}$ to be a refinement of the method used above, and in order to distinguish processes on the basis of refusals it is clearly necessary that some aspect of the tests involves more than observing traces. We have two types of behaviour to handle: traces and failures. It is possible to combine two separate forms of test, one for each type, into one by disjoining them: let us define test $\mathbf{T}_2$ to fail if a process *either* can communicate *fail* as its first action *or* deadlocks immediately (i.e., stably refuses the whole of $\Sigma^\checkmark$).

Clearly the semantics of CSP in $\mathcal{F}$ can accurately calculate whether any process fails $\mathbf{T}_2$, and so all we have to do to establish full abstraction is to show that if $(T, F) \neq (T', F')$ are the representations of processes P and Q then there is a context that distinguishes them (with respect to $\mathbf{T}_2$).

Suppose first that $T \neq T'$. Then the context we use is a slightly modified version of the one used for $\mathcal{T}$. For any trace $s \in \Sigma^{*\checkmark}$, let

$$CT'_s[V] = CT_s[V] \,|||\, \top_\mathcal{F}$$

This has identical traces but, since it is never stable, will never fail $\mathbf{T}_2$ because of deadlock. Thus $CT'_s[Q]$ fails $\mathbf{T}_2$ exactly when $CT_s[Q]$ fails $\mathbf{T}_1$, which is when $s \in traces(Q)$. This form of context thus allows us to distinguish two processes with unequal trace sets.

We can thus assume that $T = T'$ and $F \neq F'$. So let s be a trace such that $refusals(P/s) \neq refusals(Q/s)$. It is easy to show that s is not of the form $s'^\frown\langle\checkmark\rangle$.

Without loss of generality we can assert there is a refusal set X such that

- $(s, X) \in F \setminus F'$

- $\{a \in \Sigma \mid s^\frown\langle a\rangle \notin T\} \subseteq X$

- $\checkmark \in X$, because if $s^\frown\langle\checkmark\rangle \in T$, then by F4 the sets of refusals of P and Q not containing $\checkmark$ are identical.

Consider the context

$$CF_{(s,X)}[V] = ((V; \top_\mathcal{F}) \underset{\Sigma}{\|} F_{(s,\Sigma^\checkmark \setminus X)}) \setminus \Sigma$$

where $F_{(t,Y)}$ is the process used when investigating expressibility that has the failures (t, Y') for $Y' \subseteq Y$ and no other. Since we are hiding the entire alphabet in a process that cannot terminate, there are only two possible values for $CF_{(s,X)}[V]$: $\top_\mathcal{F}$ or $STOP$, the latter being one that can deadlock and hence fail $\mathbf{T}_2$. $CF_{(s,X)}[P]$ can fail $\mathbf{T}_2$ because P has the failure (s, X), hence so does P; $\top_\mathcal{F}$ (using $\checkmark \in X$), and so the parallel combination has the failure $(s, \Sigma^{\checkmark})$. If $CF_{(s,X)}[Q]$ could fail it then you can argue in reverse to show Q must have a failure (s, X') for $X' \supseteq X$, but it cannot by our assumptions and axiom F2. Thus contexts of the form $CF_{(s,X)}[V]$ allow $\mathbf{T}_2$ to detect differences between failure-sets.

It is reasonable to hope that $\mathbf{T}_2$ might be simplified further to just testing for immediate deadlock, but unfortunately the standard CSP language does not allow us to construct contexts that are strong enough to tell differences between trace-sets by this means. The problem is that if P and Q are two members of $\mathcal{N}$, neither of which can either terminate or become stable (i.e., they both have the form $(T, \{\})$ for $T \subseteq \Sigma^*$) then there is no context that can distinguish them on the basis of deadlock. There is no way for P to make a significant contribution to the behaviour of $C[P]$, and for the context subsequently to become stable, for none of the standard operators of CSP can 'switch off' P.

It is easy to add an operator to CSP which rectifies this situation: an *interrupt* operator which allows one process Q to take over from another P. This is easiest to understand for a specified event i being the signal for Q to start: $P \triangle_i Q$. The semantics of this operator over $\mathcal{F}$ are:

$$
\begin{aligned}
traces(P \triangle_i Q) \;=\; & traces(P) \\
& \cup \{s^\frown \langle i \rangle^\frown t \mid s \in traces(P) \cap \Sigma^* \wedge t \in traces(Q)\} \\[6pt]
failures(P \triangle_i Q) \;=\; & \{(s, X) \in failures(P) \mid s \in \Sigma^* \wedge i \notin X\} \\
& \cup \{(s, X) \mid s^\frown \langle \checkmark \rangle \in traces(P) \wedge \checkmark \notin X\} \\
& \cup \{(s^\frown \langle \checkmark \rangle, X) \mid s^\frown \langle \checkmark \rangle \in traces(P)\} \\
& \cup \{(s^\frown \langle i \rangle^\frown t, X) \mid s \in traces(P) \cap \Sigma^* \\
& \qquad\qquad \wedge (t, X) \in failures(Q)\}
\end{aligned}
$$

Given this operator, it is not too hard to devise a context that will allow $C[P]$ to deadlock immediately, precisely when P has a specified trace $s \in \Sigma^*$, and to deal with traces of the form $s^\frown \langle \checkmark \rangle$ using sequential composition in a similar way. This then leads quickly to the aimed-for full abstraction result. The details are left as an exercise. See Exercise 9.3.2 for an investigation of a related result.

We can learn an important lesson from this: adding or removing constructs from a language, even when the semantic model is unchanged, can greatly affect full abstraction properties.

Failures/divergences model

With $\mathcal{N}$ there seems to be no option but to use a disjunctive test in the same spirit as $\mathbf{T}_2$. This is $\mathbf{T}_3$, which a process fails if it either immediately diverges or immediately deadlocks. Following in the footsteps of the earlier models, to show that $\mathbf{T}_3$ is strong enough we need to find a context to distinguish any pair P, P' of different elements of $\mathcal{N}$.

Let a be any member of Σ. For $s \in \Sigma^*$, then the context

$$CT''_s[V] \;\; = \;\; (V \parallel_{\Sigma} T''_s) \setminus \Sigma \;|||\; (a \to STOP)$$

can diverge immediately if and only if $s \in traces_\perp(V)$, where

$$
\begin{aligned}
T''_{\langle\rangle} &= \bot_\mathcal{N} \\
T''_{\langle b\rangle^\frown s} &= b \to T''_s
\end{aligned}
$$

The role of the event a in this definition is to prevent the process deadlocking immediately and thereby failing $\mathbf{T}_3$ in an unexpected way.

Thus, if P and P' differ in whether they have this trace, they can be distinguished. Traces of the form $s'^\frown\langle\checkmark\rangle$ can be dealt with similarly (see Exercise 9.3.1). We can thus use $\mathbf{T}_3$ to distinguish P and P' if their trace-sets differ.

If s is a divergence of one process and not the other, then by D3 we can assume $s \in \Sigma^*$. After replacing the process $\bot_\mathcal{N}$ by $STOP$ in the definition of T''_s, we can use the same context as for traces, since the divergence that trips the test then comes from V rather than T''_s.

So we can assume that our two processes have identical trace and divergence sets, and (without loss of generality) $(s, X) \in failures_\perp(P) \setminus failures_\perp(P')$. Clearly no prefix of s is a divergence, and exactly as over $\mathcal{F}$ we can assume $\checkmark \in X$ and that X includes all impossible events. We use a context similar to that used for failures over $\mathcal{F}$, the important difference being that we have to use a different method to avoid it deadlocking until the chosen failure is reached. It is built in two stages.

We have to deal separately with the cases $X = \{\checkmark\}$ and $X \neq \{\checkmark\}$. In the first case let

$$C_{(s,X)}[V] \;\; = \;\; (V \parallel T_{s^\frown\langle\checkmark\rangle}); (a \to STOP)$$

where again a is any member of Σ.

In the second case let $a \in X \setminus \{\checkmark\}$ and define $AS = a \to AS$. The following is a simplified version of the $F_{(s,X)}$ seen earlier:

$$
\begin{aligned}
F'_{(\langle\rangle,X)} &= \;?x : \Sigma \setminus X \to STOP \\
F'_{(\langle b\rangle^\frown s,X)} &= b \to F'_{(s,X)}
\end{aligned}
$$

Now define

$$C_{(s,X)}[V] \;\; = \;\; (V;\; AS) \parallel_{\Sigma} F'_{(s,\Sigma \setminus X)}$$

In either case $C_{(s,X)}[V]$ behaves as follows:

- Until it has completed s (or diverged in the process, something which will not happen when s is not a divergence of V) its trace is always a prefix of s.

- It may or may not be able to deadlock on proper prefixes of s.

- On the complete trace s it can deadlock if, and only if, V has the refusal (s, X).

What we have to do is place this process in a context which generates an immediate deadlock from any deadlock of the above after s, but not from any other trace, and does not introduce a divergence. One way of doing this is

$$CFD_{(s,X)}[V] = ((C_{(s,X)}[V][b/x \mid x \in \Sigma]) \parallel_{\{b\}} W(\#s)) \setminus \{b\}$$

where

$$
\begin{aligned}
W(0) &= b \to CS \\
W(n) &= (b \to W(n-1)) \mathbin{\square} CS \quad (n > 0) \\
CS &= c \to CS
\end{aligned}
$$

and b, c are arbitrary members of Σ. The process $W(\#s)$ keeps track of how many events $C_{(s,X)}[V]$ has performed, and only allows it to deadlock the combination when this number is exactly $\#s$, meaning that $C_{(s,X)}[V]$ has actually performed s. (The renaming is necessary here in case all the events of Σ are used in s.) Because the number of b's is limited, the hiding used in the context cannot introduce divergence. It follows that $CFD_{(s,X)}[V]$ fails $\mathbf{T}_3$ if and only if $(s, X) \in failures_\perp(V)$.

$CFD_{(s,X)}[V]$ can then be used to distinguish P and P', as desired.

We can summarize the results of this section in the following result:

THEOREM 9.3.1 *(i)   The traces $(\mathcal{T})$ semantics of CSP is fully abstract with respect to $\mathbf{T}_1$ (failed on the immediate occurrence of a chosen event).*

(ii)   The stable failures $(\mathcal{F})$ semantics is fully abstract with respect to $\mathbf{T}_2$ (failed on immediate occurrence of a chosen event or immediate deadlock), and with the addition of an interrupt operator this test can be weakened to immediate deadlock.

(iii)   The failures/divergences $(\mathcal{N})$ semantics of finitely nondeterministic CSP is fully abstract with respect to $\mathbf{T}_3$ (failed on the process immediately deadlocking or diverging) provided Σ is finite.

Another consequence of full abstraction properties like these is that each model generates the weakest congruence (i.e., identifies most processes) which allows us to tell whether a process satisfies the relevant test. Thus $\mathcal{T}$ gives the weakest congruence on CSP allowing us to tell whether a process has the trace $\langle fail \rangle$, and so on.

EXERCISE 9.3.1   Recall that the context $CT_s''[\cdot]$ is used to distinguish processes in $\mathcal{N}$ on the basis of traces. The version defined on page 236 was only for $s \in \Sigma^*$. Find a definition that works for traces of the form $s^\frown\langle\checkmark\rangle$.

EXERCISE 9.3.2   Notice that axiom T3 implies that all traces of the form $s^\frown\langle\checkmark\rangle$ are traces of failures. The only semantic clause for standard CSP operators over $\mathcal{F}$ in which the failures component depends on the input traces is $P; Q$, in which only traces of this form are used. Show that this means it is possible to give a semantics for CSP in a *pure* stable failures model in which a process is represented only by $failures(P)$ rather than $(traces(P), failures(P))$.

(a) Show that axioms F2, F3 and F4 (the failure axioms of $\mathcal{F}$) suffice to create a model whose members are exactly the failure-sets that arise in $\mathcal{F}$.

(b) Prove that this model is fully abstract for the standard CSP language with respect to the test for immediate deadlock.

(c) Find two processes that are identified over this new model but distinguished over both $\mathcal{T}$ and $\mathcal{F}$. What are the advantages of using $\mathcal{F}$ rather than the pure version? Are there any disadvantages?

9.4   Relations with operational semantics

We have two methods of working out the representations of CSP processes in our abstract models: either following the route of Chapter 7 and calculating the operational semantics and then extracting behaviours via abstraction functions, or that of Chapter 8 and doing it by directly using denotational semantics. There is a claim implicit in this, namely that both ways calculate the same value. We are, in other words, claiming that the operational semantics is *congruent* with each of the denotational ones. This is something that needs to be proved, and in this section we outline some of the methods that can be used to do this.

Firstly, one must remark that in order to keep the discussion clear we will have to be a little more formal than hitherto about the distinctions between the syntax of CSP and functions defined over it. The language of terms in CSP (i.e., the set of well-formed terms in the language that may contain free process identifiers) will be denoted **CSP**, and the closed terms (ones with no free identifiers) will be denoted $\overline{\textbf{CSP}}$. Naturally, when referring to a function like $failures_\perp(P)$ we will have to make it clear which of the two supposedly equal values this is.

The operationally-based versions of these functions defined in Section 7.4.1 provide us with functions to the models from any LTS V: for each node σ of V

$$
\begin{aligned}
\Phi_{\mathcal{T}}(\sigma) &= traces(\sigma) \\
\Phi_{\mathcal{F}}(\sigma) &= (traces(\sigma), failures(\sigma)) \\
\Phi_{\mathcal{N}}(\sigma) &= (failures_\perp(\sigma), divergences(\sigma))
\end{aligned}
$$

These can, of course, be used to compute one set of interpretations of CSP from the LTS generated by the operational semantics. The second set are produced by the denotational semantics given in Chapter 8: let us call these $\mathcal{S}_{\mathcal{T}}[\![\cdot]\!]$, $\mathcal{S}_{\mathcal{F}}[\![\cdot]\!]$ and $\mathcal{S}_{\mathcal{N}}[\![\cdot]\!]$.

A variety of techniques have been used over the years to establish the equivalence of pairs of these interpretations. Invariably the proofs have been by some sort of structural induction over the syntax of a CSP program and come in three parts: a series of lemmas dealing with basic operators other than recursion, a more difficult argument to handle the recursive case, and overall 'glue' to put all these pieces together. Presenting detailed arguments for each of the models here would be much too long and complex, so we will concentrate on the simplest model, $\mathcal{T}$, and indicate briefly at the end how things change for the others.

A CSP term can, in general, have free process identifiers. Even if we start with a closed term (one with none), if we want to establish results about it by structural induction we may well have to consider sub-terms which are not closed. In proving congruence between an operational and a denotational semantics it is therefore necessary to use notation capable of interpreting general terms[4] and to formulate our inductive congruence results accordingly.

It is mathematically superior to formulate each of the denotational semantics with *environments* giving a binding of each free process identifier to an element of the underlying semantic model. (This type of environment was previously discussed on page 160.) Thus, we can define

$$
Env_{\mathcal{T}} = Ide \rightarrow \mathcal{T}
$$

to be the set of $\mathcal{T}$-environments, so that the type of the semantic function becomes

$$
\mathcal{S}_{\mathcal{T}} : \textbf{CSP} \rightarrow Env_{\mathcal{T}} \rightarrow \mathcal{T}
$$

---

[4]As remarked previously (for example in Chapter 7), we have avoided doing this formally up to now. This was because the gain in terms of completeness and making the semantics of recursion tidier would have been outweighed by the notational and conceptual clutter.

and, for a process term P and environment $\rho \in Env_{\mathcal{T}}$, $\mathcal{S}_{\mathcal{T}}[\![P]\!]\rho$ is the value of P when its free identifiers have the trace sets assigned to them by ρ. The reason why it is superior is because, when we are faced with a recursive term such as $\mu\, p.P$, we can present the function that P represents cleanly: in a given environment ρ it maps $\alpha \in \mathcal{T}$ to $\mathcal{S}_{\mathcal{T}}[\![P]\!]\rho[\alpha/p]$.

The natural operational semantic analogue of an environment is a substitution ξ that maps each identifier to a closed CSP term:

$$\xi \in Subst : Ide \to \overline{\mathbf{CSP}}$$

ξ then converts any CSP term P into a closed one $subst(P, \xi)$ by replacing each free identifier p by $\xi(p)$. The full statement of the congruence result is now that, for all $\xi \in Subst$ and all terms $P \in \mathbf{CSP}$,

$$\Phi_{\mathcal{T}}(subst(P, \xi)) \;=\; \mathcal{S}_{\mathcal{T}}[\![P]\!]\overline{\xi}^{\mathcal{T}}$$

where $\overline{\xi}^{\mathcal{T}}$ is the member of $Env_{\mathcal{T}}$ produced by applying $\Phi_{\mathcal{T}}$ to each component of ξ:

$$\overline{\xi}^{\mathcal{T}}(p) \;=\; \Phi_{\mathcal{T}}(\xi(p))$$

It is this result we prove by structural induction over P (for all ξ simultaneously).

The claim is trivially true for all 'base' cases of the induction: P being either a process identifier p or one of the constant processes $STOP$ and $SKIP$.

The proof then follows the same pattern for each non-recursive operator. Consider, for example, $\Box$. We can assume P and Q are two terms both satisfying the claim for all ξ. We have

$$subst(P \,\Box\, Q, \xi) \;=\; (subst(P, \xi)) \,\Box\, (subst(Q, \xi)), \quad \text{and}$$
$$\mathcal{S}_{\mathcal{T}}[\![P \,\Box\, Q]\!]\overline{\xi}^{\mathcal{T}} \;=\; \mathcal{S}_{\mathcal{T}}[\![P]\!]\overline{\xi}^{\mathcal{T}} \,\Box_{\mathcal{T}}\, \mathcal{S}_{\mathcal{T}}[\![Q]\!]\overline{\xi}^{\mathcal{T}}$$

where $\Box_{\mathcal{T}}$ is the representation of this operator over $\mathcal{T}$, in this case $\cup$ (union). Thus, by induction, it is sufficient to prove that for any closed CSP terms R and S,

$$\Phi_{\mathcal{T}}(R \,\Box\, S) \;=\; \Phi_{\mathcal{T}}(R) \,\Box_{\mathcal{T}}\, \Phi_{\mathcal{T}}(S)$$

This result, and corresponding ones for all the other operators, can be proved by analyzing how the operational semantics behaves. Specifically, in this case, it is easy to show that, for any R and S,

- If $R \overset{\langle\rangle}{\Longrightarrow} R'$ and $S \overset{\langle\rangle}{\Longrightarrow} S'$ then $R \,\Box\, S \overset{\langle\rangle}{\Longrightarrow} R' \,\Box\, S'$.

- If $s \neq \langle \rangle$ and either $R \stackrel{s}{\Longrightarrow} T$ or $S \stackrel{s}{\Longrightarrow} T$ then $R \,\square\, S \stackrel{s}{\Longrightarrow} T$.

- The above are the only pairs (s, V) such that $R \,\square\, S \stackrel{s}{\Longrightarrow} V$.

This, of course, establishes what we want.

Now consider the case of a recursion $\mu p.P$. What we have to show is that, for any ξ, $\Phi_{\mathcal{T}}(subst(\mu p.P, \xi))$ is the least fixed point of the function Υ mapping $\alpha \in \mathcal{T}$ to $\mathcal{S}_{\mathcal{T}}[\![P]\!](\overline{\xi}^{\mathcal{T}}[\alpha/p])$. The inductive assumption makes it easy to show that it is a fixed point. Let P' be the term in which all free identifiers of P other than p have been substituted by ξ, so that $subst(\mu p.P, \xi) = \mu p.P'$. Then

$$
\begin{aligned}
\Phi_{\mathcal{T}}(subst(\mu p.P, \xi)) &= \Phi_{\mathcal{T}}(\mu p.P') \\
&= \Phi_{\mathcal{T}}(P'[\mu p.P'/p]) & \text{(a)} \\
&= \Phi_{\mathcal{T}}(subst(P, \xi[\mu p.P'/p])) & \text{(b)} \\
&= \mathcal{S}_{\mathcal{T}}[\![P]\!]\overline{\xi[\mu p.P'/p]}^{\mathcal{T}} & \text{(c)} \\
&= \mathcal{S}_{\mathcal{T}}[\![P]\!](\overline{\xi}^{\mathcal{T}}[\Phi_{\mathcal{T}}(\mu p.P')/p]) & \text{(d)} \\
&= \Upsilon(\Phi_{\mathcal{T}}(subst(\mu p.P, \xi)))
\end{aligned}
$$

(a) follows because of the operational semantics of recursion:

$$
\mu p.P' \stackrel{\tau}{\longrightarrow} P'[\mu p.P'/p]
$$

and because if A is a node of an LTS whose only action is $A \stackrel{\tau}{\longrightarrow} B$ then $\Phi_{\mathcal{T}}(A) = \Phi_{\mathcal{T}}(B)$. (b) follows by definition of P', (c) comes by induction on the term P which is simpler than $\mu p.P$, and (d) by definition of $\overline{\xi}^{\mathcal{T}}$.

Recall that, for $\mathcal{T}$, we chose to identify recursions with the subset-least fixed points of the associated functions, arguing that this was natural because all the behaviours recorded in this model always appear finitely. To show that this was the right decision, given the above argument, it is sufficient to show that every trace of $\Phi_{\mathcal{T}}(subst(\mu p.P, \xi))$ belongs to $\Upsilon^n(\{\langle \rangle\})$ for some n. (Containment in the other direction comes from the fact that $\Phi_{\mathcal{T}}(subst(\mu p.P, \xi))$ is a fixed point of Υ, and so is greater than the least one.)

If s is such a trace then there must be some $s' \in (\Sigma^\tau)^{*\checkmark}$ and Q such that $s' \setminus \tau = s$ and $subst(\mu p.P, \xi) \stackrel{s'}{\longmapsto} Q$. If $N = \#s'$, then during the derivation of the behaviour s', the recursion cannot possibly be unfolded more than N times, since every time it is unfolded a τ action is generated which must be present in s'. Consider the following two mutual recursions defining the processes p_0 and q_0.

$$
\begin{aligned}
p_n &= P'[p_{n+1}/p] & n \in \mathbb{N}
\end{aligned}
$$

$$
\begin{aligned}
q_n &= P'[q_{n+1}/p] & n \in \{0, \ldots, N-1\} \\
q_N &= STOP
\end{aligned}
$$

where P' is as above. The first of these clearly has exactly the same behaviour as $subst(\mu\,p.P, \xi)$, in the sense that the operational semantics are exactly alike except that the multiple names of the identifiers in the mutual version keeps track of how many times the recursion has been unfolded. The process q_0 behaves exactly like p_0 until after the Nth unfolding, which means that it has the behaviour s'; this means that $s \in \Phi_{\mathcal{T}}(q_0)$.

On the other hand, $\Phi_{\mathcal{T}}(q_N) = \{\langle\rangle\}$, $\Phi_{\mathcal{T}}(q_{N-1}) = \Upsilon(\{\langle\rangle\})$ etc., until $\Phi_{\mathcal{T}}(q_0) = \Upsilon^N(\{\langle\rangle\})$, because $\Phi_{\mathcal{T}}(subst(P, \xi[Q/p])) = \mathcal{S}_{\mathcal{T}}[\![P]\!]\bar{\xi}^{\mathcal{T}}[\Phi_{\mathcal{T}}(Q)/p]$ for every closed term Q. Hence $s \in \Upsilon^N(\{\langle\rangle\})$, which is what we wanted to show.

This completes our sketch of the proof of congruence between the operational semantics and the trace semantics. The proof for $\mathcal{F}$ goes through exactly the same steps, except that one obviously has to keep track of failures as well as traces and it is necessary to allow the q_0 recursion to unfold $N + 1$ times rather than N.

With $\mathcal{N}$ there is little difference with the overall structure of the proof or the cases for non-recursive operators. The recursive case is different because we have to handle infinite behaviours (divergences) and use what is really the opposite fixed point. We have to show that the effects of divergence lead to the operational semantics mapping under $\Phi_{\mathcal{N}}$ to the $\sqsubseteq_{\mathcal{N}}$-least fixed point, bearing in mind that the same basic argument applied over $\mathcal{T}$ (page 241) shows that any recursive term maps to *a* fixed point of the associated function.

Perhaps the easiest way of proving minimality uses König's lemma (applicable since we are in any case restricted to finitely nondeterministic CSP). For any trace $s \in \Sigma^{*\checkmark}$, one shows that *either* the tree of states reachable from a process such as $R = subst(\mu\,p.P, \xi)$ on prefixes of s is finite, *or* there is a divergence in the tree. In the second case, axioms D1 and D2 mean that every behaviour on s gets into $\Phi_{\mathcal{N}}(R)$, while in the first case you can limit the number N of times the recursion has to be unfolded to be the depth of the finite tree, and then a similar argument to that applied over $\mathcal{T}$ can be used to show that the operational and denotational semantics must agree on behaviours that are prefixes of s.

EXERCISE 9.4.1   Prove that, for any closed term P, $\Phi_{\mathcal{T}}(P \setminus X) = \Phi_{\mathcal{T}}(P) \setminus_{\mathcal{T}} X$.

EXERCISE 9.4.2   Repeat the previous exercise for (i) the stable failures model $\mathcal{F}$ and (ii) the failures/divergences model $\mathcal{N}$, the latter under the assumptions that the term P is finitely nondeterministic and X is finite.

EXERCISE 9.4.3   The results on expressibility in Section 9.3 imply that, in each of the cases considered, the function $\Phi_{\mathcal{M}}$ is surjective as a function from the closed CSP terms $\overline{\mathbf{CSP}}$ to the model $\mathcal{M}$. Show that there is a transition system V on which the function $\Phi_{\mathcal{N}}$ is surjective when Σ is infinite (i.e., the one case not dealt with by the previous remark).

9.5   Notes

The main properties of deterministic processes have been well known since failures-type models were first developed [14, 17, 18, 91].

The results of Section 9.2 are derived mainly from [91, 94, 97]. The last two of these contain the details omitted here of the purely topological approach to CSP fixed-point induction.

The notion of full abstraction evolved in the 1970s and early 1980s: see [72, 82] for example. The full abstraction result for $\mathcal{N}$ has been known for many years: it is implicitly present in [46], for example (which also contains mush other material on full abstraction). The full abstraction results for $\mathcal{F}$, like the other results about this model, arose from the collaboration between the author, Jategoankar and Meyer, and are closely related to independent results of Valmari [116].

The first congruence proof between operational and denotational semantics of CSP appears (rather briefly) in Olderog's important paper [79] with Hoare. A more complete presentation of a proof appears in [119] and [21]. The difficulty in such proofs comes mainly from the radically different ways in which denotational and operational semantics handle recursions. The above two references handle this in different ways; the author later developed a further way of handling this (encompassing unbounded nondeterminism and discontinuous functions) in [95] – the later is the style of proof he presently prefers.

Chapter 10

Infinite traces

We have seen (Section 8.3.2) that the failures/divergences model is deficient in the way it models infinitely nondeterministic processes. The solution is to include the set of a process's infinite traces in the model. An infinite trace is a member of Σ^ω, the sequences of the form $\langle a_i \mid i \in \mathbb{N} \rangle$. It represents a complete (i.e., throughout all time) communication history of a process that neither pauses indefinitely without communicating nor terminates.

In this chapter we see how this is done and get an idea of the extra expressive power it gives us.

10.1   Calculating infinite traces

Our aim is to represent each process by the triple

$$(failures_\perp(P), divergences(P), infinites(P))$$

recalling that $infinites(P)$ already, by definition, contains all extensions of divergences.

Bear in mind that we know (thanks to the argument in the proof of Theorem 7.4.2 on page 174) that for any finitely nondeterministic process

$$infinites(P) \;=\; \overline{traces_\perp(P)} \setminus traces_\perp(P)$$

where $\overline{S} = S \cup \{u \in \Sigma^\omega \mid \forall t < u.t \in S\}$. Thus, the extra component will only convey extra information outside this category of process.

If we are to follow the route taken in Chapter 8 we should now axiomatize which triples (F, D, I) are allowable, investigate the model's properties (order-theoretic and otherwise) and then use it to give the semantics. It is entirely possible to build such a model, and indeed we will do so later in this chapter, but it turns out that the relationship in it between failures and infinite traces is remarkably subtle and creates problems which there is no overriding need for us to meet yet.

One can, at least temporarily, avoid these difficulties thanks to the following observations:

- The stable failures $failures(P)$ are accurately calculated, even for infinitely nondeterministic CSP, by the semantics over the stable failures model $\mathcal{F}$.

- If one examines the way that CSP operators generate behaviours, it turns out that the stable failures of component processes never influence any of finite or infinite traces or divergences.

It therefore makes sense to introduce infinite traces via a simpler model in which a process is modelled as

$$(traces_{\perp}(P),\, divergences(P),\, infinites(P))$$

We can still work out $failures_{\perp}(P)$ from a combination of the second components of this representation and the semantics over $\mathcal{F}$.

$\mathcal{I}$, the infinite traces/divergences model, consists of the triples (T, D, I), where $T, D \subseteq \Sigma^{*\checkmark}$ and $I \subseteq \Sigma^{\omega}$, meeting the following conditions:

T1. T is non-empty and prefix closed.

D1. $s \in D \cap \Sigma^* \wedge t \in \Sigma^{*\checkmark} \Rightarrow s\hat{\ }t \in D$

D2'. $D \subseteq T$

D3. $s\hat{\ }\langle\checkmark\rangle \in D \Rightarrow s \in D$

D4. $s \in D \cap \Sigma^* \wedge u \in \Sigma^{\omega} \Rightarrow s\hat{\ }u \in I$

I1'. $u \in I \wedge s < u \Rightarrow s \in T$

$\mathcal{I}$ is a complete lattice under both $\sqsubseteq_{\mathcal{I}}$ (defined, of course, to mean reverse inclusion on all three components) and its reverse, the subset order. For $\top_{\mathcal{I}} = (\{\langle\rangle\}, \{\}, \{\})$ (the representation of $STOP$) is the greatest $\sqsubseteq_{\mathcal{I}}$-lower bound of the empty set, and the greatest lower bound of any non-empty set is given, as usual, by componentwise union: $\bigsqcap S = (T^*, D^*, I^*)$, where

$$
\begin{aligned}
T^* &= \bigcup\{T \mid (T, D, I) \in S\} \\
D^* &= \bigcup\{D \mid (T, D, I) \in S\} \\
I^* &= \bigcup\{I \mid (T, D, I) \in S\}
\end{aligned}
$$

The least refined element is $\perp_{\mathcal{I}} = (\Sigma^{*\checkmark}, \Sigma^{*\checkmark}, \Sigma^{\omega})$, representing any process that can diverge immediately.

It is easy to give clauses for calculating *infinites*(P) for all the standard CSP operators.

$$
\begin{aligned}
\textit{infinites}(STOP) &= \{\} \\
\textit{infinites}(SKIP) &= \{\} \\
\textit{infinites}(a \to P) &= \{\langle a \rangle ^\frown u \mid u \in \textit{infinites}(P)\} \\
\textit{infinites}(?x : A \to P) &= \{\langle a \rangle ^\frown u \mid a \in A \wedge u \in \textit{infinites}(P[a/x])\} \\
\textit{infinites}(P \ \Box \ Q) &= \textit{infinites}(P) \cup \textit{infinites}(Q) \\
\textit{infinites}(P \sqcap Q) &= \textit{infinites}(P) \cup \textit{infinites}(Q) \\
\textit{infinites}(P \underset{X}{\|} Q) &= \{u \in \Sigma^{\omega} \mid \exists s \in \textit{Traces}(P), \\
&\qquad t \in \textit{Traces}(Q).u \in s \underset{X}{\|} t\} \\
&\quad \cup \{s^\frown u \mid s \in \textit{divergences}(P \underset{X}{\|} Q) \cap \Sigma^* \wedge u \in \Sigma^{\omega}\} \\
\textit{infinites}(P; \ Q) &= \textit{infinites}(P) \\
&\quad \cup \{s^\frown u \mid s^\frown\langle\checkmark\rangle \in \textit{traces}_{\perp}(P) \wedge u \in \textit{infinites}(Q)\} \\
\textit{infinites}(P[\![R]\!]) &= \{u' \mid \exists u \in \textit{infinites}(P).u \ R \ u'\} \\
&\quad \cup \{s^\frown u \mid s \in \textit{divergences}(P[\![R]\!]) \cap \Sigma^* \wedge u \in \Sigma^{\omega}\} \\
\textit{infinites}(P \setminus X) &= \{u' \in \Sigma^{\omega} \mid \exists u \in \textit{infinites}(P).u \setminus X = u'\} \\
&\quad \cup \{s^\frown u \mid s \in \textit{divergences}(P \setminus X) \cap \Sigma^* \wedge u \in \Sigma^{\omega}\}
\end{aligned}
$$

Recall that *Traces*(P) is an abbreviation for $\textit{traces}_{\perp}(P) \cup \textit{infinites}(P)$. The trace constructs $\underset{X}{\|}, \setminus X$ and renaming have been extended in the natural ways to encompass infinite traces. Of course, to give a denotational semantics to CSP you need clauses for the other components, $\textit{traces}_{\perp}(P)$ and $\textit{divergences}(P)$, of the representation. In all but one case, the clauses for $\textit{divergences}(P)$ are the same as they were over $\mathcal{N}$ because knowledge of a process's infinite traces does not affect what the divergences are when applying the respective operators. The exception is hiding, since we no longer have to attempt to infer what the infinite traces are from the finite ones and can directly define:

$$
\begin{aligned}
\textit{divergences}(P \setminus X) &= \{(u \setminus X)^\frown t \mid u \in \textit{infinites}(P) \wedge \\
&\qquad t \in \Sigma^{*\checkmark} \wedge u \setminus X \text{ is finite}\} \\
&\quad \cup \{(s \setminus X)^\frown t \mid s \in \textit{divergences}(P) \cap \Sigma^* \wedge t \in \Sigma^{*\checkmark}\}
\end{aligned}
$$

The definitions for the finite traces component $\textit{traces}_{\perp}(P)$ are identical to the mappings on traces that can be extracted from the failures clauses for $\mathcal{N}$. These differ from the clauses for the finite traces model $\mathcal{T}$ only in the cases where it is necessary to close up to preserve axiom D2/D2′, so for example

$$
\begin{aligned}
traces_\perp(P \setminus X) \ &= \ \{s \setminus X \mid s \in traces_\perp(P)\} \\
&\cup \{s\hat{\ }t \mid s \in divergences(P \setminus X) \cap \Sigma^* \wedge t \in \Sigma^{*\checkmark}\}
\end{aligned}
$$

All the resulting semantic clauses are both universally accurate and representable as relations over behaviours: we have eliminated the problem which caused the semantics over $\mathcal{N}$ to break down for infinitely nondeterministic CSP. It is now possible to prove the lemmas of an operational/denotational congruence proof (like that for $\Box$ and $\mathcal{T}$ on page 240) for every one of the operators. For example, the processes A^* and A^∞ defined on page 200 are now clearly distinguished by the semantics, which correctly predict that $A^\infty \setminus \{a\}$ can diverge and that $A^* \setminus \{a\}$ cannot.

The fact that they are representable by relations implies (as in Section 8.2) that they are all monotonic, fully distributive, and continuous in the $\subseteq$ order. Let us consider the question of continuity in the $\sqsubseteq$ order. The argument for the continuity of hiding over $\mathcal{N}$ no longer applies because of the different way we are calculating divergence. One would not expect the argument to apply when we reason about infinitely nondeterministic CSP, since it relied on König's lemma, which in turn requires finite branching. And, in fact, hiding is not continuous over $\mathcal{I}$. When Σ is infinite, the same example as used on page 184 works. An example for finite Σ is provided by the processes Q_n defined below (hiding $\{a, b\}$ makes each Q_n diverge, but not their limit A^*). Indeed, the incorporation of infinite traces, which each contain an infinite amount of information, leads to several other relations becoming infinitary and the corresponding operators discontinuous. This applies to sequential composition, parallel and finitary renaming.

For example, let R be a renaming that maps events a and b to b, and let P_n be the process that performs n a's and then an infinite sequence of b's:

$$
\begin{aligned}
P_n \ &= \ a \to \ldots \to a \to BS \\
BS \ &= \ b \to BS
\end{aligned}
$$

Obviously $P_n[\![R]\!] = BS$ for all n. If we define $Q_n = \bigsqcap\{P_m \mid m \geq n\}$ then these form an increasing sequence under $\sqsubseteq_\mathcal{I}$ whose limit is actually A^* (it can perform any finite sequence of a's, but has no infinite trace). But we then have

$$
\bigsqcup\{Q_n[\![R]\!] \mid n \in \mathbb{N}\} = BS \neq (\bigsqcup\{Q_n \mid n \in \mathbb{N}\})[\![R]\!]
$$

demonstrating the failure of continuity.

In Chapter 8 we established a rule of thumb that one should identify a recursion with either the $\sqsubseteq$ or $\subseteq$ least fixed point depending on whether or not one's model incorporates infinite behaviours. On this principle we must expect the right answer for $\mathcal{I}$ to be $\sqsubseteq$, and indeed it is, despite the fact that it means a large-scale abandonment of continuity and the resulting simple formula for fixed points. The need to use $\sqsubseteq$ rather than $\subseteq$ can now be demonstrated not only from under-defined recursions such as $\mu\,p.p$, (which diverges and so must be mapped to $\bot_{\mathcal{I}}$ rather than to $\top_{\mathcal{I}}$), but also from very ordinary ones such as $\mu\,p.a \to p$.

For $(\{\langle a\rangle^n \mid n \in \mathbb{N}\}, \{\}, \{\})$ (which is the value in $\mathcal{I}$ of the process A^*), is the $\subseteq$-least fixed point of the function $F(\cdot)$ derived from the recursion $\mu\,p.a \to p$. This is plainly not the right value, since it does not contain the infinite trace that the process self-evidently has. The problem is that $F(P)$ can never have an infinite trace when P does not, so starting an iteration from $\top_{\mathcal{I}}$ (which itself has no infinite traces) will never yield one. On the other hand, the $\sqsubseteq$-least fixed point (and greatest $\subseteq$ one) is $(\{\langle a\rangle^n \mid n \in \mathbb{N}\}, \{\}, \{\langle a\rangle^\omega\})$, the correct answer.

In the case of $\mu\,p.a \to p$, there are only the two fixed points quoted above, but in only slightly more complex cases, such as $\mu\,p.(a \to p) \sqcap (b \to p)$, there can be infinitely many. In this second example also it is clear that the correct answer is the $\sqsubseteq$-least one, which contains all infinite traces made up of a's and b's.

Even 'constructive' recursions can fail to reach their least fixed points via the simple formula

$$\mu f \;=\; \bigsqcup_{n=0}^{\infty} f^n(\bot)$$

This is illustrated by the recursion

$$\mu\,q.\,((a \to q) \underset{\{a\}}{\parallel} A^*)$$

where A^* is as above. For this recursion, $F^n(\bot_{\mathcal{I}})$ has the infinite trace $\langle a\rangle^\omega$ for all n (because $\langle a\rangle^n$ is a divergence), and hence so does $\bigsqcup_{n=0}^{\infty} F^n(\bot_{\mathcal{I}})$ which equals

$$(\{\langle a\rangle^n \mid n \in \mathbb{N}\}, \{\}, \{\langle a\rangle^\omega\})$$

However, this value is neither a fixed point of this recursion, nor does the operational semantics of the recursion have the infinite trace $\langle a\rangle^\omega$. The least fixed point, which is also the operationally correct value, is A^*. It is clear, both from this and the multiplicity of fixed points we saw above, that the proof that you always get the operationally right answer is more critical than over previous models.

The argument we saw for $\mathcal{T}$ in Section 9.4 still applies when it comes to proving that the operational semantics of any recursion maps to *some* fixed point of the associated function. But the proof that it is always the *least* one seems to require subtlety and mathematical machinery well beyond what we can present here. The interested reader can consult [95].

But the important thing is that the result, and hence the congruence theorem with the operational semantics, can be proved and so is true. This establishes that the denotational semantics for CSP, derived from the above operator definitions and $\sqsubseteq$ least fixed points for recursions, does give the correct value for every process.

The demise of metrics

The major gain we have made from the move to incorporate infinite traces in our model is the ability to calculate a satisfactory semantics for general CSP (i.e., incorporating unbounded nondeterminism) denotationally. The attentive reader may already have noticed what is the greatest practical loss, and one of the best reasons for not using infinite traces all the time. The recursions $\mu\,p.a \rightarrow p$ and $\mu\,p.(a \rightarrow p) \sqcap (b \rightarrow p)$ are certainly constructive in every reasonable sense, and yet we have seen that they do not have unique fixed points. This is because no family of restriction functions based (as all those for other models have been) on describing what a process does up to some finite length of trace, can discriminate between a pair P, P' which only differ in infinite traces.

Thus the UFP rule, and the fixed point induction principles relying on constructiveness as defined in Section A.2, are not in general valid over $\mathcal{I}$ or other models using infinite traces. We will be able to repair the damage somewhat, but it is better to do this after we have studied the incorporation of failures information into our model as this can significantly affect the situation.

EXERCISE 10.1.1   Suppose Σ is infinite (containing, say, $\{a_i \mid i \in \mathbb{N}\}$). Find finitely nondeterministic processes P_1, P_2, Q_1 and Q_2, a set X and a renaming relation R such that

- $traces_\perp(P_1 \setminus X) = traces_\perp(P_2 \setminus X)$ but $infinites(P_1 \setminus X) \neq infinites(P_2 \setminus X)$.
- $traces_\perp(Q_1[\![R]\!]) = traces_\perp(Q_2[\![R]\!])$ but $infinites(Q_1[\![R]\!]) \neq infinites(Q_2[\![R]\!])$.

The existence of such examples demonstrates that infinite hiding and infinitary renaming can introduce unbounded nondeterminism.

EXERCISE 10.1.2   Find the relations which generate $infinites(P;\ Q)$ in the relational representation of this operator. Show by means of example that they are not all finitary.

Find a process Q and a directed subset Δ of $\mathcal{I}$ (with respect to $\sqsubseteq$) such that

$$(\bigsqcup \Delta);\ Q \neq \bigsqcup\{P;\ Q \mid P \in \Delta\}$$

This shows ; to be discontinuous in its first argument; is it also discontinuous in its second argument?

10.2   Adding failures

We now know that, for any CSP process, we can calculate its divergences, traces both finite and infinite, and (stable) failures. In fact, we know how to do these things two ways since we can either get them from the operational semantics or by using a combination of two denotational models. It is nevertheless interesting to try to combine all of these types of behaviour into a single model, because only by doing this can we understand what 'the space of all processes' looks like, and establish results like full abstraction. We want to build the failures/divergences/infinite traces model $\mathcal{U}$ consisting of sets of triples (F, D, I).

The main issue in understanding which (F, D, I) can represent the

$$(failures_\perp(P), divergences(P), infinites(P))$$

of some process P is the way in which failures and infinite traces interact, for the other relationships have all been established in studying $\mathcal{I}$ and $\mathcal{N}$.

Their relationship is analogous to axiom F3, which can be read as stating that when an event a is not refusable after trace s, then $s^\smallfrown\langle a\rangle$ is a finite trace. Carrying on this argument to infinity will lead to infinite traces; we will investigate this by studying the two recursions used as examples in the previous section:

$$
\begin{aligned}
R_a &= a \to R_a \\
R_{ab} &= (a \to R_{ab}) \sqcap (b \to R_{ab})
\end{aligned}
$$

It is easy to see that

$$
\begin{aligned}
F_a &= failures_\perp(R_a) &&= \{(\langle a\rangle^n, X) \mid a \notin X\} \\
F_{ab} &= failures_\perp(R_{ab}) &&= \{(s, X) \mid s \in \{a, b\}^* \wedge \{a, b\} \not\subseteq X\}
\end{aligned}
$$

In the model $\mathcal{I}$, both of the recursions have solutions with no infinite traces, but that would be inconsistent with the failure information since, if we always offer either process the set $\{a, b\}$, then it is certain to perform an infinite trace. A process with no infinite trace is certain, if we always offer it the whole of Σ, eventually to deadlock or terminate; neither of these processes can do either.

So in fact the R_a recursion does have a unique fixed point when we take into account the additional information from failures, since the set of infinite traces from the 'wrong' one of the pair seen on page 249 can now be discounted.

We can be sure that any set of infinite traces to be paired with F_a has the trace $\langle a\rangle^\omega$ because this infinite trace can be *forced* from a known finite one. Specifically, if s is a finite trace of the process P, and $u > s$ is in Σ^ω, and whenever $s < t^\smallfrown\langle a\rangle < u$ we have $(t, \{a\}) \notin failures_\perp(P)$, then u must belong to *infinites*(P). This implies that whenever F is the failure-set of a deterministic process in $\mathcal{N}$ then there is only one set of infinite traces consistent with F, namely $\overline{traces_\perp(F)} \setminus traces_\perp(F)$.

As infinite traces tell us nothing interesting about processes in $\mathcal{U}$ whose projection into $\mathcal{N}$ (the first two components) appear deterministic, we can take exactly the same definition for 'deterministic' over $\mathcal{U}$ as over $\mathcal{N}$.

Unfortunately the story is not quite as simple with R_{ab}, for there are still infinitely many sets of infinite traces consistent with the failures. Furthermore, there is no specific infinite trace you can be sure is there. If I is any subset of $\{a, b\}^\omega$ with the property that for all $s \in \{a, b\}^*$ there is $u \in I$ with $s < u$, it turns out that we can create a CSP process with value $(F_{ab}, \{\}, I)$.

If v is any infinite trace, let T_v be the process that simply communicates the members of v in turn (akin to the processes T_s for finite traces used on page 229). Then

$$N_I = \bigsqcap \{ T_v \mid v \in I \}$$

is the process we want: it obviously has the correct infinite traces, and our assumption implies it has the right failures since if $s \in \{a, b\}^*$ then there are v_a and v_b in I with $s^\smallfrown \langle a \rangle < v_a$ and $s^\smallfrown \langle b \rangle < v_b$. The processes T_{v_a} and T_{v_b} give to N_I all the failures of F_{ab} for this s.

These are *precisely* the sets of infinite traces consistent with F_{ab}. For we know that every finite trace is possible, and if after the trace you offer a process with failures F_{ab} the set $\{a, b\}$ for ever, you are bound to get an infinite extension of s. Not all I of this form give rise to fixed points of our recursion, though infinitely many of them do (see Exercise 10.2.3), but that is not relevant to the issue of determining what it means for a set of infinite traces to be consistent with a set of failures.

Whatever formula captures the general relationship between infinite traces and failures is inevitably going to be more complex than previous axioms such as F1–F4 since it evidently relates the entire sets of these behaviours rather than individual ones. A variety of formulations of an axiom relating F and I have been discovered, but all of them rest ultimately on something very like the following ideas.

Imagine that you are about to experiment on a process. Now there may well be some nondeterminism in the implementation, and on any run it will then have to make decisions to resolve this. From the experimenter's point of view there is no way of telling whether the decisions are being made in 'real time' as the experiment proceeds, or have all been pre-ordained. If all the decisions have been made in advance, then the process you are actually dealing with is a refinement P' of P that is at least nearly deterministic.[1] The reasons why the procedure in the footnote may not deliver a deterministic result are divergence and the events that are left as alternatives to an internal action. It is certainly closed in the sense that

$$Traces(P') \; = \; \overline{traces_{\perp}(P')}$$

Since every recordable behaviour of P is present in one of these P' it follows that

$$P \; = \; \bigsqcap \{P' \mid P \sqsubseteq P' \wedge P' \text{ is closed}\}$$

This identity is the key to deciding when sets of failures and infinite traces are consistent. For there can be no doubt that if (F, D) is a member of $\mathcal{N}$ then its closure

$$\overline{(F, D)} \; = \; (F, D, \overline{traces(F)} \setminus traces(F))$$

must be included in the failures/divergences/infinite traces model $\mathcal{U}$. A construction identical to that for $\mathcal{N}$ on page 231 (which now requires unbounded choice since Σ may be infinite) creates a process with these behaviours. And it is clear that for any $(F, D, I) \in \mathcal{U}$, (F, D) is a member of $\mathcal{N}$, so that the closed processes are precisely $\overline{\mathcal{N}}$, the set of closures of members of $\mathcal{N}$.

Thus the model $\mathcal{U}$ equals

$$\{\bigsqcap S \mid \{\} \neq S \subseteq \{\overline{(F, D)} \mid (F, D) \in \mathcal{N}\}\}$$

and the way we have derived this fact equips $\mathcal{U}$ with the expressibility half of a full abstraction result.

There is no reason, of course, why you should not take the above as the definition of $\mathcal{U}$. But one can get back to the earlier, directly axiomatized, style by extracting what this says about infinite traces into a suitable formula.

We can thus define $\mathcal{U}$ to consist of those triples (F, D, I) satisfying F1–F4, D1–D4, the following property slightly reformulated from I1$'$ of $\mathcal{I}$

---

[1]You can imagine this choice procedure as being applied to an LTS which has been unrolled into a tree, as in Figure 7.3 on page 155, so that no node is visited more than once, recognizing that different decisions may be made each time a node is visited. There is then an 'implementation' of it that is produced by a method like the algorithm for extracting a deterministic refinement described on page 221, except that you should select one representative for each label leading from a node irrespective of whether it is stable or not. This is because we have to recognize that the process is allowed to accept visible alternatives to internal actions and that if such alternatives were always ignored then there would be legitimate behaviours of the LTS which would not appear in any of the 'implementations'.

I1. $u \in I \wedge s < u$ (for $s \in \Sigma^*$) implies $s \in traces(F)$

and one more property, I2. A wide range of formulations, as well as some plausible alternatives that fail, can be found in [95] and especially in [12]. The axiom can be stated in terms of game theory and via logical formulae with infinitely deeply nested quantifications, but the most understandable are probably those closer in spirit to the discussion above. The following version simply states that from any point a process can reach, we can pre-resolve the nondeterministic choices it will make thereafter so that it acts deterministically:

I2. $s \in traces(F) \quad \Rightarrow \quad \exists\, T \in \mathcal{T}^d.(F, D)/s \sqsubseteq_{FD} det(T)$
$$\wedge \{s\hat{\ }u \mid u \in \overline{T}\} \subseteq I$$

The more refusal sets a process has (relative to a fixed set of finite traces), the less infinite traces it need have. This is because, in the above, the sets T can be smaller when F is able to refuse more. Thus, for the failure-set $\Sigma^{*\checkmark} \times \mathbb{P}(\Sigma^{\checkmark})$ and divergence-set $\{\}$, any set of infinite traces is permissible. In particular, you can have the empty set of infinite traces, creating the interesting process $FINITE_\Sigma$ which can be written

$$\sqcap\{T_s \mid s \in \Sigma^{*\checkmark}\}$$

with T_s, as before, being the process which simply communicates the trace s.

The semantic clauses for computing how CSP operators behave over $\mathcal{U}$ can easily be put together from those of earlier models. Those for divergences and infinite traces are identical to those over $\mathcal{I}$, while those for failures are identical[2] to those over $\mathcal{N}$. Every one has a relational representation and so is monotonic and fully distributive. Just as over $\mathcal{I}$, many fail to be continuous.

You should always remember that if P is a finitely nondeterministic term (or, indeed, a node in a finitely nondeterministic LTS) then its value in $\mathcal{U}$ is always simply the closure of its value in $\mathcal{N}$.

Full abstraction

Our first expression for $\mathcal{U}$ as a set of nondeterministic compositions equips it with the expressibility half of its full abstraction result.

The second half serves to emphasize that $\mathcal{U}$ is the natural extension to unboundedly nondeterministic CSP of the failures/divergences model $\mathcal{N}$, since except

---

[2]Those, especially $\setminus X$, that refer to divergence-sets, of course now mean the ones derived from $\mathcal{I}$.

for the larger language the testing criterion is identical. $\mathcal{U}$ is fully abstract with respect to the test for immediate deadlock or divergence ($\mathbf{T}_3$, see page 235). Exactly the same contexts as over $\mathcal{N}$ distinguish processes on the bases of finite traces, failures and divergences, so all we need is to find contexts that distinguish them on the basis of infinite traces. If T_u is, as above, the process that simply performs the trace u then

$$C_u[V] = ((V \underset{\Sigma}{\|} T_u) \setminus \Sigma) \ ||| \ a \to STOP$$

can diverge if and only if $u \in \mathit{infinites}(V)$. As with finite traces, the last part of the context is included to avoid any possibility of immediate deadlock and so 'diverge' can be replaced by 'fail $\mathbf{T}_3$' here.

Partial order properties

The refinement order on $\mathcal{U}$ is exactly what we would expect:

$$(F, D, I) \sqsubseteq_{\mathcal{U}} (F', D', I') \equiv F \supseteq F' \wedge D \supseteq D' \wedge I \supseteq I'$$

This order has a bottom element, the one representing any process that can diverge immediately:

$$\bot_{\mathcal{U}} = (\Sigma^{*\checkmark} \times \mathbb{P}(\Sigma^{\checkmark}), \Sigma^{*\checkmark}, \Sigma^{\omega})$$

Like $\mathcal{N}$, it has no top element but many maximal elements which are exactly the deterministic processes

$$\{\overline{\mathit{det}(T)} \mid T \in \mathcal{T}^d\}$$

The nondeterministic choice operator, as over other models, corresponds to the greatest lower bound operator over arbitrary non-empty subsets of $\mathcal{U}$ and to componentwise union.

It should not come as a great surprise that the refinement order fails to be complete over $\mathcal{U}$, since we have seen there is a close correspondence between finite nondeterminism and the attractive properties of completeness and continuity. If A^* is, as before, the process that can perform any finite number of a's but not infinitely many, then the following series of refinements hold:

$$A^* \sqsubseteq_{\mathcal{U}} a \to A^* \sqsubseteq_{\mathcal{U}} a \to a \to A^* \sqsubseteq_{\mathcal{U}} \dots$$

since prefixing A^* with a simply removes its ability to perform *no* a's. However, this sequence has no upper bound since any such bound could never refuse a but would be unable (as all the members of the sequence are) to perform the forceable trace $\langle a \rangle^{\omega}$.

Whereas over $\mathcal{N}$ for infinite Σ the incompleteness of $\sqsubseteq$ could be got round by introducing the strong order $\leq$, no such remedy exists[3] here since one can actually prove (see [95]) that *any* order which makes CSP operators monotone and which finds the same fixed points for them as $\sqsubseteq_{\mathcal{U}}$ is incomplete.

Nevertheless, it turns out that every CSP definable function does have a least fixed point, and that fixed point is the correct (judged by congruence with operational semantics) value for it. There are two known ways of proving this result, the outlines of which are sketched below.

It is this difficulty in finding fixed points, added to the subtlety needed to build and understand the model in the first place, that led us to look at the infinite traces/divergences model $\mathcal{I}$ before $\mathcal{U}$. We observed there that a failures/divergences/infinite traces representation for every process could be computed from its values in $\mathcal{I}$ and $\mathcal{F}$ (see page 246). There is no guarantee, just because we have pieced together a member of $\mathcal{I}$ and one of $\mathcal{F}$ that the result will be one of $\mathcal{U}$, since in general the failures and infinite sets produced need not satisfy I2. However, the congruence theorems of the two models with the operational semantics do imply it is in $\mathcal{U}$, since the combined value is guaranteed by these to be the abstraction into $\mathcal{U}$ of (the operational semantics of) the process in question. A little analysis then shows it is a fixed point, and indeed the least fixed point, of the corresponding operator over $\mathcal{U}$.

This is a simple proof given the earlier congruence theorems, and indeed it establishes the extremely important congruence theorem for $\mathcal{U}$ as a bonus. It is, however, worth bearing in mind (i) that the results on which it rests, especially the congruence for $\mathcal{I}$, are highly non-trivial and (ii) that it has the curious property of being a proof entirely stated in one domain (the denotational semantics in $\mathcal{U}$) which rests on detailed analysis of another one (the operational semantics).

There is an elegant proof, discovered by Geoff Barrett [5, 7], whose overall difficulty is considerably less and which does not rely on analyzing the operational model. The following is an outline of his work.

Say a process $(F, D, I) \in \mathcal{U}$ is *pre-deterministic* if it behaves deterministically whenever it does not diverge. In other words,

$$s \in traces(F) \backslash D \wedge s\hat{\ }\langle a \rangle \in traces(F) \Rightarrow (s, \{a\}) \notin F$$

---

[3]The strong order can be defined on $\mathcal{U}$: $(F, D, I) \leq (F', D', I')$ if and only if $(F, D) \leq (F', D')$ in $\mathcal{N}$ and $I \supseteq I'$. All CSP operators are monotone with respect to this order, but it fails to be complete.

The combination of axioms D1, D2, I1 and I2 ensures that each pre-deterministic process is closed. In fact, the pre-deterministic processes $\mathcal{P}$ form a complete partial order under $\sqsubseteq_\mathcal{U}$, and have the property that every member of $\mathcal{U}$ is refined by one of them. The maximal members of $\mathcal{P}$ are, of course, the deterministic processes $\overline{\mathcal{D}}$.

Now it is easy to show that if a monotonic function f over $\mathcal{U}$ has a 'post-fixed' point (one such that $f(x) \sqsubseteq_\mathcal{U} x$) then it has a least fixed point. For we can use the proof of Tarski's theorem for complete lattices on page 472: the crucial point here is that the set of post-fixed points (upon which the proof is based) has a greatest lower bound as it is non-empty and every non-empty subset of $\mathcal{U}$ has one.

Barrett proved that every CSP definable function f has a pre-deterministic post-fixed point by finding a monotonic function f' from $\mathcal{P}$ to itself such that $f(P) \sqsubseteq_\mathcal{U} f'(P)$ for all $P \in \mathcal{P}$. This has the desired consequence because then f' (being a monotonic function from a cpo to itself) has a fixed point $\mu f'$, and

$$f(\mu f') \sqsubseteq_\mathcal{U} f'(\mu f') = \mu f'$$

He built the f' by replacing each CSP operator by a refinement that preserves determinism in a systematic way. Essentially, he modified the operators so that each way described on page 219 for them to introduce nondeterminism was avoided. For example, $P \sqcap' Q = P$ and $P \square' Q$ always behaves like P where an ambiguous first event is chosen.

EXERCISE 10.2.1   Show that any process $P \in \mathcal{N}$ such that $Traces(P)$ consists only of finite traces can either deadlock or terminate. Hence prove from I2 that if $s \in traces_\perp(Q)$ for $Q \in \mathcal{U}$, then *either* there is $u \in infinites(Q)$ with $s < u$, *or* Q can either deadlock or terminate on some $s' \geq s$.

EXERCISE 10.2.2   Recall the R_{ab} recursion on page 251. Find a set of infinite traces I that is consistent with F_{ab} but such that $(F_{ab}, \{\}, I)$ is not a fixed point of the recursion.

EXERCISE 10.2.3   If u is any infinite trace in $\{a, b\}^\omega$, let $\Delta(u)$ be the subset of $\{a, b\}^*$ consisting of those sequences obtainable by a finite sequence of additions and deletions from u: $\{s\hat{\ }v \mid s \in \{a, b\}^* \wedge \exists t \in \{a, b\}^*.u = t\hat{\ }v\}$. Even though there are infinitely many members of each $\Delta(u)$ and $v \in \Delta(s) \Leftrightarrow u \in \Delta(v)$, there are infinitely[4] many *different* $\Delta(u)$ and each satisfies the identity $\Delta(u) = \{\langle a \rangle\hat{\ }v, \langle b \rangle\hat{\ }v \mid v \in \Delta(u)\}$.

Show that, for any u, $N_{\Delta(u)}$ (as defined on page 252) is a solution to the R_{ab} recursion.

Find a sequence I_n of subsets of $\{a, b\}^\omega$ such that $(R_{ab}, \{\}, I_n) \in \mathcal{U}$ for all n, $I_n \supseteq I_{n+1}$, but $\bigcap\{I_n \mid n \in \mathbb{N}\} = \{\}$. This leads to a $\sqsubseteq_\mathcal{U}$ increasing sequence of members

---

[4]There are, in fact, *uncountably* many since $\{a, b\}^\omega$ is uncountable and each $\Delta(u)$ is countable. Since any union of countable sets is countable, there must be uncountably many different such sets.

of $\mathcal{U}$ which differ only in their infinite traces, but which has no upper bound. This shows that the strong order $\leq$ (defined in a footnote on page 256) is incomplete.

EXERCISE 10.2.4   Prove that the deterministic processes are precisely the $\sqsubseteq_{\mathcal{U}}$ maximal elements of $\mathcal{U}$. *Hint: use the characterization of $\mathcal{U}$ as the nondeterministic compositions of closed processes, and the corresponding result over $\mathcal{N}$.*

10.3   Using infinite traces

It is controversial whether an infinitely nondeterministic system could really be (fully) implemented. Any implementation would have to include a mechanism which guaranteed to select between an infinity of choices in a finite time. You cannot do this by repeatedly performing a finitely nondeterministic activity such as tossing a coin or throwing dice, since König's lemma implies that any such procedure that has infinitely many outcomes can go on for ever. For example, if you toss a coin and count how many successive heads are seen before the first tail, there remains the possibility that the series of heads will go on for ever. On the other hand, if a system made a choice dependent on the value of some infinitely varying physical quantity such as time ...

Whatever you believe about this, the ability to model infinite nondeterminism has a number of practical applications. Many of these occur when we want either to specify or to assume some property, which requires infinite nondeterminism to express it, of a process even though the process may well only be finitely nondeterministic. This can quite legitimately lead to us reasoning about infinitely nondeterministic processes, even if you take a conservative position in the debate above. This having been said, you should always bear in mind that there is no need to use $\mathcal{U}$ when you are dealing with a finitely nondeterministic CSP term and want to prove a property of it that can be expressed in one of the weaker models.

10.3.1   Infinitary specifications and fairness

Recall the specification of a buffer B from Section 5.1: $divergences(B) = \{\}$ and

(i) $s \in traces(B) \Rightarrow s \in \{|\ left, right\ |\}^* \wedge s \downarrow right \leq s \downarrow left$

(ii) $(s, X) \in failures(B) \wedge s \downarrow right = s \downarrow left \Rightarrow X \cap \{|\ left\ |\} = \{\}$

(iii) $(s, X) \in failures(B) \wedge s \downarrow right < s \downarrow left \Rightarrow \{|\ right\ |\} \not\subseteq X$

This allows a buffer to input infinitely without ever outputting. We might wish to insist that our buffer is always finite, in the sense that it never accepts an infinite sequence of inputs without outputting. To express this naturally requires an infinite trace specification:

(iv) $u \in infinites(B) \Rightarrow u \setminus \{| \; left \; |\}$ is infinite

Clearly each of the explicitly bounded buffer processes $BUFF_{\langle\rangle}^{N}$ meets this specification, but the infinite buffer $B_{\langle\rangle}^{\infty}$ does not. It remains true, of course, that any satisfiable behavioural specification can be identified with the most nondeterministic process satisfying it (its characteristic process, the nondeterministic choice of all processes satisfying it). Naturally, $BUFF_{\langle\rangle}$, the characteristic process of the basic buffer specification, does not satisfy the stronger finite buffer specification. It is interesting to construct an explicit CSP representation $FinBUFF_{\langle\rangle}$ of this process: see Exercise 10.3.6.

Even if you believe it is impossible actually to *build* an infinitely nondeterministic system, it can still be sensible to include an infinitely nondeterministic component in a model of an implementation. For there may be a component process which is either outside your control or which you may wish to vary: in either case it is appropriate to replace the component by a specification it is assumed to meet, and this specification may well be infinitely nondeterministic.

A good example of this can be found in the Alternating Bit Protocol as discussed in Sections 5.3 and 8.4. Recall that this protocol is designed to work (i.e., transmit successive pieces of data correctly) provided that neither of the two error-prone channels used either loses an infinite sequence of consecutive messages or duplicates any message infinitely. In the first discussion (Section 5.3) we had to choose some fixed bound on the number of consecutive errors, while in the second we saw that the protocol could be proved correct for arbitrary loss/duplication conditional on any refinement that removes the divergence. The channel processes we really want (which are, indeed, refinements of those $C(in, out)$ used in Section 8.4) can only be modelled accurately in models incorporating infinite traces.

What we want to assert about the channels is that they cannot output infinitely without inputting (for that would constitute infinite duplication), nor input infinitely without outputting (which would be infinite loss). We call such a condition a *fairness* assumption. A *fair arbiter* between two non-empty and usually disjoint sets A and B of events is a process which repeatedly chooses between allowing A and B, but which never chooses either side infinitely without the other. The most general fair arbiter between A and B is

$$
\begin{aligned}
Fair(A, B) &= LFair(A, B) \sqcap RFair(A, B), \quad \text{where} \\
LFair(A, B) &= \textstyle\bigsqcap\{NLeft(n, A, B) \mid n \in \{1, 2, \ldots\}\} \\
RFair(A, B) &= \textstyle\bigsqcap\{NRight(n, A, B) \mid n \in \{1, 2, \ldots\}\} \\
NLeft(n, A, B) &= RFair(A, B) \mathbin{\langle\!\!\!\mid} n = 0 \mathbin{\mid\!\!\!\rangle} ?x : A \to NLeft(n - 1, A, B) \\
NRight(n, A, B) &= LFair(A, B) \mathbin{\langle\!\!\!\mid} n = 0 \mathbin{\mid\!\!\!\rangle} ?x : B \to NRight(n - 1, A, B)
\end{aligned}
$$

since this repeatedly chooses one of A and B a non-zero finite number of times, and then goes back and starts on the other. $Fair(A, B)$ is divergence-free, has as its finite traces $(A \cup B)^*$ and for each trace has (when $A \cap B = \{\}$) maximal refusals $\Sigma^\checkmark \setminus A$ and $\Sigma^\checkmark \setminus B$. What makes it special is its set of infinite traces, which can be written, in a natural extension of existing notation,

$$A^*(B\,B^*\,A\,A^*)^\omega$$

The asymmetry in this expression is immaterial, since switching all A's and B's leaves the set unchanged.

You can use processes like $Fair(A, B)$ to add fairness into systems by making them replace existing (unfair) choice mechanisms like those in $C(in, out)$. The definition of $C_*(in, out)$ below simply replaces the nondeterministic choices of $C(in, out)$ by external choices, thus leaving them to be made by the parallel composition with the arbiter.

$$
\begin{aligned}
C_*(in, out) &= in?x \rightarrow C'_*(in, out, x) \\
C'_*(in, out, x) &= out!x \rightarrow C'_*(in, out, x) \\
&\quad \square\ in?y \rightarrow C'_*(in, out, y) \\
C_{fin}(in, out) &= C_*(in, out) \underset{\Sigma}{\parallel} LFair(\{|\ in\ |\}, \{|\ out\ |\})
\end{aligned}
$$

Notice that we use the version of the arbiter that guarantees that its first choice will go to the left, because C_* needs to input first.

$C_{fin}(in, out)$ has identical failures to $C(in, out)$, but has just the restriction on its infinite traces we want. Using it to model the channels in the alternating bit protocol eliminates the divergences that occur when you use $C(in, out)$, though of course you need the power of $\mathcal{U}$ to express this formally. The mathematical argument would just paraphrase the informal one for lack of divergence in Section 5.3. One could then either prove directly in $\mathcal{U}$ that the resulting system is equivalent to $COPY$, or deduce it from the analysis done in Section 8.4 over $\mathcal{F}$.

What we have managed to capture over $\mathcal{U}$ are the 'real' assumptions on the communication medium that are required to make the protocol work. Of course, having done this, any medium that refines the C_{fin} model is also guaranteed to work.

Fairness is a difficult subject, both because it is inextricably linked with unbounded nondeterminism and because interpretations of what it means for a system to be 'fair' vary widely depending on just how one has chosen to model systems and on authors' opinions. See, for example, [15, 36, 70, 80]. Different notions of fairness are couched in terms:

- of one or more specific internal decisions inside the program, as was the one above;

- of the complete pattern of internal decisions, one example being 'angelic nondeterminism': if, whatever decisions are made, it always remains *possible* to attain some desirable state, then eventually that state *must* be reached;

- of the pattern of 'enabled actions' – if an action is enabled infinitely then it will occur; or

- of 'fair parallel': ensuring that each side of a parallel composition is treated fairly in terms of being allowed to make progress.

In CSP one has to be careful about how to define fairness because of the basic model of communication: no action can occur unless the environment is willing to perform it. Thus a process like $\mu\, p.(a \to p) \;\square\; (b \to p)$ cannot enforce fairness between a and b, even though each is always enabled, and nor does it make sense to say that the equivalent process $\mu\, p.a \to p \;|||\; \mu\, p.b \to p$ necessarily behaves as a fair parallel construct, since in either case the environment can insist on an unfair trace such as $\langle a, a, a, \ldots \rangle$.

For clarity, and because it corresponds directly to perhaps the most widely used notion of fairness in the literature, the only form we will consider directly is the first. The most natural way to introduce this into CSP would seem to be a fair nondeterministic choice operator $\sqcap_F$ that behaves like $\sqcap$ except that it guarantees to make its choices fairly. There is no reason why you should not use this as a shorthand, but it cannot be treated as a CSP operator like all others. One problem is that, as a binary operator over CSP models, $\sqcap$ and $\sqcap_F$ are indistinguishable, and yet in a recursive context they mean very different things.

Where there are multiple fair choices in a program, these have to be treated as *separately* fair, in the sense that if any one of the choices is made infinitely often it is made fairly, but there is no linking property between the ways in which combinations of choice are made. This creates curious programs like

$$(\mu\, p.(a \to p) \;\sqcap_F\; (b \to p)) \underset{\{a,b\}}{\|} (\mu\, p.(a \to p) \;\sqcap_F\; (b \to p))$$

Obviously this *can* deadlock, for the two sides can immediately, or after any finite trace, pick different actions. The interesting question is whether it *must* eventually deadlock. On a global view of fairness (perhaps along the lines of angelic fairness) one is tempted to say 'yes' (it being too much of a coincidence if they always pick the same event), but actually the two sides of the parallel are allowed to make exactly the same fair decisions (behaving, perhaps, like $\mu\, p.a \to b \to p$) since there is no link between the fairness conditions. Indeed it is quite likely that if we take a fair choice mechanism off the shelf it will, in fact, always follow the same pattern such as strict alternation. Thus the answer under our model of fairness is 'no'.

A very similar phenomenon creates a second problem in trying to view $\sqcap_F$ as an ordinary operator. Consider the 'identity'

$$(P \sqcap Q); (R \sqcap_F S) = (P; (R \sqcap_F S)) \sqcap (Q; (R \sqcap_F S))$$

which should be provable by the left distributive law of ; . But the right-hand side has two $\sqcap_F$ operators while the left-hand side has one, and this makes a big difference to how the two sides behave when put in a context such as the infinite iteration P^* that forces infinitely many choices to be made.

- If the ordinary nondeterministic choice on the left-hand side alternates between P and Q, there is nothing to stop the fair choice alternating between R and S, so that R always follows P and S always follows Q.

- On the other hand, the different pattern of $\sqcap_F$'s on the right-hand side means that *each* of P and Q, if picked infinitely often, must be followed by a fair choice between R and S. The alternating pattern $\langle P; R, Q; S \rangle^\omega$ is thus not allowed.

Fair choices are thus much more context sensitive than other CSP constructs. As said above, $\sqcap_F$ should really be thought of as shorthand rather than as an operator in its own right. To implement processes involving this 'operator' we simply delegate the choices to separate fair arbiters for each occurrence of $\sqcap_F$, rather like the modelling of C_{fin} above. This can be done by transforming the CSP definition of your process. Invent two new events for each occurrence of $\sqcap_F$ ($a.i$ and $b.i$ for the ith, say) and replace the ith $P \sqcap_F Q$ by $a.i \rightarrow P \square b.i \rightarrow Q$. The new events should not be synchronized, hidden or renamed in the transformed definition. Then take the final transformed process T and place it in parallel with fair arbiters for each choice:

$$(T \underset{\{|a,b|\}}{\|} (Fair(\{a.1\}, \{b.1\}) \,|||\, \ldots \,|||\, Fair(\{a.n\}, \{b.n\}))) \setminus \{|\, a, b \,|\}$$

This transformation is incorrect if there is any possibility of the original process terminating ($\checkmark$), since the fair arbiter(s) prevent the transformed one terminating. A more elaborate transformation is then required (see Exercise 10.3.3).

We might well want fair choices between more than two options. When there are finitely many (the only case we consider here) it can accurately be done by composing the binary version: executing a program with the construct

$$P_1 \sqcap_F (P_2 \sqcap_F \ldots (P_{n-1} \sqcap_F P_n) \ldots)$$

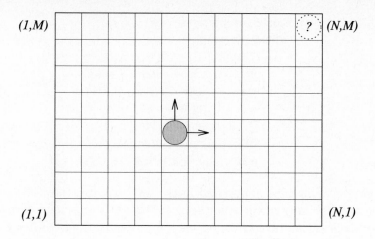

Figure 10.1 A counter moving across an $N \times M$ board.

implemented as above, allows just those behaviours in which all of the P_i are chosen infinitely often if any is. Obviously one could define a more than two-way fair arbiter and use it to implement a multi-way fair choice more directly. For example,

$$Fair(A, B) \parallel_{B} Fair(B, C)$$

has (for A and C disjoint) exactly the behaviour we want of $Fair(A, B, C)$. Make sure you understand why the asymmetry of this definition does not matter.

EXAMPLE 10.3.1 (FAIR COUNTER) Fairness is generally used to ensure progress of some sort in a system. For example, imagine a counter sitting on a rectangular board as in Figure 10.1. The counter c, when sitting at co-ordinates (i, j), can do one of three things:

- It can choose not to move, and communicate the event *procrastinate.c*.

- It can try to move up (to $(i, j{+}1)$) by communicating with the target square.

- It can try to move right (to $(i + 1, j)$) by communicating with the target square.

Let's assume that after requesting permission to move to a square it receives either an *ok* or *ref* signal, indicating that it can move or not, and that we ensure that if it asks to leave the board (off the top or right edges) then it always gets the refusal (*ref*) response.

$$
\begin{aligned}
CTR(c,i,j) \;=\; & procrastinate.c \to CTR(c,i,j) \\
& \sqcap\, (req.i.j+1.c \to \\
& \quad (ref.i.j+1.c \to CTR(c,i,j) \\
& \quad \square\; ok.i.j+1.c \to enter.i.j+1.c \to \\
& \qquad leave.i.j.c \to CTR(c,i,j+1))) \\
& \sqcap\, (req.i+1.j.c \to \\
& \quad (ref.i+1.j.c \to CTR(c,i,j) \\
& \quad \square\; ok.i+1.j.c \to enter.i+1.j.c \to \\
& \qquad leave.i.j.c \to CTR(c,i+1,j)))
\end{aligned}
$$

Clearly if no fairness is assumed in the way it makes these choices, then it need never move, no matter where it starts, since it can always take the first option. If the board is programmed in the obvious way so that a square, when empty, will allow a counter to move onto it, etc., then if these choices are made fairly a system consisting of a single counter on an $N \times M$ board will eventually have the counter reach the top right-hand corner (N, M) no matter where it starts.

This naturally leads to the question of how one specifies the concept of 'eventually' in CSP. To specify that a system P must eventually (unless deadlocked by the environment) communicate a specific event a, all you have to specify is

$$
a \to \mathbf{div} \sqsubseteq P \setminus (\Sigma \setminus \{a\})
$$

over either $\mathcal{N}$ or $\mathcal{U}$ as appropriate to the constructs used. For this says that the process P can neither diverge nor engage in an infinite sequence of non-a actions before communicating a, and neither can it deadlock or terminate before doing so. This has much in common with the timing consistency check described on page 386. One can obviously compose variations on this theme.

In this case you can either show that eventually our counter seeks to move to $(N+1, M)$ or $(N, M+1)$ (since it has to be on (N, M) to do so), or, better, to look for the event the counter communicates when entering (N, M). In other examples you might well have to add a 'success' event explicitly into the program, and look for that.

It is interesting to consider the case where there are two or more tokens on the board. At first sight you would probably expect that the fair counter definition will inevitably result in the counters becoming huddled together at and around (N, M). But this is not so, since no fairness is imposed regarding the speed of different counters. If there are, initially, counters at $(1, M)$ and $(2, M)$ then there is nothing to say that the left-hand one cannot perform infinitely many actions while the right-hand one does nothing. This, of course, would lead to no counter moving since the left-hand one is blocked by the top edge and the right-hand one. What is required is essentially the fair parallel composition discussed briefly earlier. This only makes sense if we remove from the environment the ability to choose which counter communicates next. The appropriate way to do this is to place the system in parallel with a fair arbiter whose job it is to choose which counter acts. If

$$choices(c) = \{procrastinate.c, req.i.j.c \mid i, j \in \mathbb{N}\}$$

then for counters c_1 and c_2, you can use the arbiter $Fair(choices(c_1), choices(c_2))$. *(End of example)*

EXERCISE 10.3.1   Complete the programming of the system in the example above by defining a $Square(i, j)$ process, any others you need, and putting the complete network together.

EXERCISE 10.3.2   If instead of moving just up and right, the counter chooses fairly between trying to move up, down, left and right, need it ever leave the board?

EXERCISE 10.3.3   The implementation of $\sqcap_F$ given in the text does not work for potentially terminating processes. Put this right as follows:

(a) Revise the definition of $Fair(A, B)$ to produce a process $TFair(A, B, tk)$ (for $tk \in \Sigma \setminus (A \cup B)$) whose behaviour is identical except that it is always willing to communicate tk (as an alternative to its current choice of A or B), upon which it terminates.

(b) In transforming a program with $\sqcap_F$'s in, as on page 262, sequentially compose the previous result with $tk \to SKIP$ for some new event tk.

(c) Put together the resulting process with $TFair$ processes, synchronizing appropriately, and explain why the result behaves as you would wish.

EXERCISE 10.3.4   The process $C_{fin}(in, out)$ can both lose and duplicate messages. Define (in CSP) the most general process $E_{fin}(in, out)$ that acts like a one-place buffer except that it can lose any message as long as it does not lose an infinite consecutive sequence of them (i.e., it behaves like $C_{fin}(in, out)$ except that it never duplicates). What refinement relation, if any, holds between the $C_{fin}(in, out)$ and $E_{fin}(in, out)$? *Hint: define the process using $\sqcap_F$ and then use the transformation implementing this.*

EXERCISE 10.3.5   The process

$$SemiFair(A, B) = RUN_A \;|||\; Fair(A, B)$$

always allows any event in A and need never allow B, but specifically does not permit an infinite trace unless it contains infinitely many events from A. Compute its sets of failures and infinite traces and find a *direct* definition of this process in the style of that of $Fair(A, B)$ on page 259.

Construct the process which, for three disjoint sets A, B and C, may at any time select between them, and which does not allow infinitely many of either A or B without the other, and which does not allow infinitely many C without infinitely many each of A and B.

EXERCISE 10.3.6   Use a fair arbiter (using the $\sqcap_F$ to introduce it, if you wish) to construct the most general finite buffer $FinBUFF\langle\rangle$ discussed on page 259.

10.3.2   Fixed-point induction over $\mathcal{U}$

As we saw on page 250, it is not possible to use restriction functions to generate complete metrics over models incorporating infinite traces, and indeed constructive functions often have multiple fixed points. These facts are as true over $\mathcal{U}$ as over $\mathcal{I}$. This is a great pity since the UFP rule and fixed point induction (whose proofs in Section 9.2 depend on constructiveness and the uniqueness of fixed points) are very important tools for establishing facts about recursively defined processes.

It is possible to establish weak versions of fixed point induction and the 'unique' fixed point rule over $\mathcal{U}$ and $\mathcal{I}$. To do this we have to define what a constructive function is via a family of restriction functions: over $\mathcal{U}$ these are defined $(F, D, I) \downarrow n = \overline{(F, D) \downarrow n}$ where the restriction on the right-hand side is that defined over $\mathcal{N}$, with a similar definition over $\mathcal{I}$. Though these do not generate a metric (there are pairs of distinct processes they cannot separate), we can still define 'constructive' and 'non-destructive' functions exactly as before, and exactly the same collections of the standard operators are respectively one or the other (see, for example, Lemma 8.2.3).

While a constructive function over $\mathcal{U}$ may not have a unique fixed point, it is easy to show that all fixed points have identical projections into $\mathcal{N}$. This is because you can inductively prove that if P and Q are two fixed points then $P \downarrow n = Q \downarrow n$ for all n. This argument leads to the following result.

LEMMA 10.3.1 *Suppose* $F : \mathcal{U} \to \mathcal{U}$ *is constructive, monotonic and has a least fixed point* μF, *and* $P \in \overline{\mathcal{N}}$ *(a closed member of* $\mathcal{U}$*) is such that* $P \sqsubseteq_{\mathcal{U}} F(P)$. *Then* $P \sqsubseteq_{\mathcal{U}} \mu F$

PROOF   By induction on n it is easy to prove that

$$P \sqsubseteq_{\mathcal{U}} F^n(P) \quad \text{and} \quad F^n(P) \downarrow n = (\mu F) \downarrow n$$

Suppose b is a finite-length behaviour of μF (i.e., a failure or divergence). Choosing n to be any number greater than its length we thus have that b is a behaviour of

$F^n(P)$ and hence of P. Hence

$$failures_\perp(\mu F) \subseteq failures_\perp(P) \qquad (+)$$
$$divergences(\mu F) \subseteq divergences(P)$$

We thus have

$$
\begin{aligned}
infinites(\mu F) &\subseteq \overline{traces_\perp(\mu F)} & (1) \\
&\subseteq \overline{traces_\perp(P)} & (2) \\
&= Traces(P) & (3)
\end{aligned}
$$

Here, (1) is a consequence of axiom I1, (2) is by $(+)$, and (3) is because of our assumption that $P \in \overline{\mathcal{N}}$. This implies that

$$infinites(\mu F) \subseteq infinites(P)$$

completing the proof that $P \sqsubseteq_{\mathcal{U}} \mu F$. ∎

This result means that the rule of fixed point induction (Sections 5.1 and 9.2) is valid over $\mathcal{U}$ provided the property you are proving is finitely nondeterministic and the function is constructive.

Of course, both the above lemma and the conclusion regarding fixed point induction extend easily to mutual recursions (i.e., functions in $\mathcal{U}^\Lambda \to \mathcal{U}^\Lambda$). It also leads to the following weak analogue of the UFP rule since under the assumptions of the following rule we have $\underline{P} \sqsubseteq_{\mathcal{U}} \mu F$ by the lemma, but μF is the *least* fixed point.

UNIQUE CLOSED FIXED POINT RULE   *Suppose $F : \mathcal{U}^\Lambda \to \mathcal{U}^\Lambda$ is a constructive, CSP definable function, and that $\underline{P} \in (\overline{\mathcal{N}})^\Lambda$ is such that $F(\underline{P}) = \underline{P}$. Then $\underline{P} = \mu F$.*

Thus, if a finitely nondeterministic process satisfies a constructive recursion, it is always the value of the recursion. There are, of course, recursions that do not have a closed solution like this, an example is $\mu q.(a \to q) \underset{\{a\}}{\|} A^*$ which we studied earlier.

10.4   Notes

The role of infinite traces in modelling unboundedly nondeterministic constructs such as fairness was well understood before CSP was invented. They were not incorporated into the semantic models for some years, however, because of technical difficulties they introduce such as incompleteness and discontinuity.

$\mathcal{U}$ was introduced in [95], which also is the main reference for the basic properties of this model. It proves the existence of fixed points of recursions via operational congruence. Barrett's alternative proof can be found in [5, 7], and is analyzed further in [77]. Some finer properties of the model can be found in [6, 12]. Our understanding of the axioms of $\mathcal{U}$ (especially I2) owes much to the work of Stephen Blamey.

Chapter 11

Algebraic semantics

11.1   Introduction

Throughout the introductory chapters we used algebraic laws to help explain the meanings of the various operators of CSP. Laws of this type have historically played an important role in the field of process algebra (the very name of which suggests this).

An *algebraic* semantics for a programming language is one where the notion of process equivalence is derived from a set of laws. Some authors proposing process algebras have regarded algebraic semantics as the most basic means of defining process equality, in that they propose a given set of laws and set about investigating what equivalence they produce. The theory most closely associated with this approach is ACP (see, for example, [9, 10]). This gives a remarkable degree of freedom, since essentially any set of laws will create an equivalence on the set of process terms. There is no constraint on one's choices that is nearly as sharp as the requirement that a denotational model induce a congruence.

Simply quoting a set of laws does bring the dangers of not identifying processes that you had intended should be equal, or, more worryingly, identifying far too many. See Exercises 11.1.1, 11.4.5 and 11.5.3 for examples of the latter. Therefore the equivalence induced by a proposed set of laws must be thoroughly investigated to make sure it has the intended effect.

Since we already have a well-established concept of equivalence between CSP processes, our approach will be to attempt to characterize that. In other words, we will attempt to capture the equivalences induced by the various denotational models for CSP described in Chapter 8. Obviously all laws used must be theorems of the equivalence under consideration: if the semantics we are attempting to duplicate is written $\mathcal{S}[\![\cdot]\!]$, this just involves proving a series of simple lemmas such as

$$\mathcal{S}[\![P \,\square\, Q]\!] \;=\; \mathcal{S}[\![Q \,\square\, P]\!]$$

$$\mathcal{S}[\![SKIP;\, P]\!] \;=\; \mathcal{S}[\![P]\!]$$

$$\mathcal{S}[\![P \,|||\, (Q \,|||\, R)]\!] \;=\; \mathcal{S}[\![(P \,|||\, Q) \,|||\, R]\!]$$

(in each case for all processes P, Q and R). It is usually not hard to find a large number of true laws with respect to a sensible notion of equivalence. Provided all your laws satisfy this basic 'sanity' stipulation, and all rules which you use in conjunction with them are valid also, it is plain that they can never prove a pair of inequivalent processes equal. In the usual logical sense of the word, such a theory is *sound*.

The real challenge is in finding, and being able to show you have found, enough laws to be able to prove any pair of equivalent processes equal; in other words, creating a *complete* algebraic theory. This chapter shows how you can do this. We will deal only with the semantics of finitely nondeterministic CSP with Σ finite. We will also, for now, deal only with the fragment of the CSP language without *SKIP* or sequential composition since these require special cases that would unnecessarily complicate an introductory view of the way algebraic methods work. Most attention is given to the equivalence induced by $\mathcal{N}$, since that is the main denotational model for finitely nondeterministic CSP.

All the laws given names (e.g., '⟨hide-dist⟩ (3.1)') in earlier chapters are true under all the equivalences generated by the models described in Chapters 8 and 10. Since each of our models equates some pairs of processes that are discriminated in at least one of the others, a set of laws true in all three models cannot be sufficient to capture any one of the model-based equivalences completely, but, as we will see, they require very few additions.

Examples of such pairs of processes are

$$P \;=\; \mathbf{div}$$

$$P' \;=\; \mathbf{div} \,|||\, a \to STOP \quad \text{(equivalent to P in $\mathcal{N}$ but not in $\mathcal{T}$)}$$

$$Q \;=\; STOP$$

$$Q' \;=\; STOP \,\sqcap\, \mathbf{div} \quad \text{(equivalent to Q in $\mathcal{T}$ and $\mathcal{F}$ but not in $\mathcal{N}$)}$$

Our existing laws thus cannot prove the equivalences

$$P =_{\mathcal{N}} P' \quad \text{and} \quad Q =_{\mathcal{T}} Q'$$

since any such proofs would contradict the inequivalences

$$Q \neq_{\mathcal{N}} Q' \quad \text{and} \quad P \neq_{\mathcal{T}} P'$$

EXERCISE 11.1.1   A certain text ($[48]$[1]) proposes the following laws for CSP (amongst many others)

(1) $\qquad P \parallel \perp \ = \ \perp$
(2) $\quad P \parallel STOP \ = \ STOP$
(3) $\quad P \square STOP \ = \ P$
(4) $\qquad P \square \perp \ = \ \perp$

Which of these are true, and which false, over $\mathcal{N}$ on the assumption that $\perp$ is identified with **div**? Show that these laws alone (and hence any superset) are sufficient to prove that $P = Q$ for all processes P and Q.

EXERCISE 11.1.2   Prove that the following laws are all valid in the semantics of CSP over $\mathcal{N}$:

(a) $\langle ; \text{-assoc} \rangle$ (6.3), (b) $\langle \text{hide-step} \rangle$ (3.6), (c) $\langle \text{hide-combine} \rangle$ (3.3).

11.2   Operational semantics via algebra

An operational semantics does not have to follow the pattern set out in Chapter 7: all we require is a formally-based method of implementing a language. You can do this via systematic algebraic transformations: a *reduction* strategy very much like those used for functional programming. A way of implementing CSP in this fashion is to calculate the selections of initial actions a process can communicate by transformation to a process of the form[2]

$$\bigsqcap_{i=1}^{N} ?x : A_i \to P_i$$

where, of course, the P_i are terms that can depend on the identifier x. By analogy with functional programming, an appropriate name for this is *head normal*

---

[1] An amazing proportion of the 'laws' stated in [48] are false, and it is possible to find many distinct combinations which prove all processes equal. Three disjoint such sets can be found in this exercise and Exercises 11.4.5 and 11.5.3 in this chapter. Some of the laws given in that book make even less sense than simply being false: for example '$P \ ||| \ Q \wedge Q \ ||| \ R \Rightarrow P \ ||| \ R$' which is trivially ill-typed since processes are not truth values.

[2] Here, $\bigsqcap_{i=1}^{N} Q_i$ is an abbreviation for $Q_1 \sqcap (Q_2 \sqcap \ldots (Q_{N-1} \sqcap Q_N) \ldots)$, though in what follows we will not go explicitly through the transformations required to turn more arbitrarily constructed nondeterministic compositions into this precise, right-associated, form. This can, of course, be done with the laws $\langle \sqcap\text{-assoc} \rangle$ (1.6), $\langle \sqcap\text{-sym} \rangle$ (1.4) and $\langle \sqcap\text{-idem} \rangle$ (1.2) in such a way as to guarantee that all the Q_i are different.

form (hnf)[3]. To execute a process, you thus transform it into this form and make an arbitrary selection from the nondeterministic choice of initial selections A_i of actions which are thereby displayed. If the environment picks one of these, it is communicated and we can repeat the procedure on the result process, and so on.

There are four types of laws required to do this:

- the *distributive* laws, for removing nondeterministic choices to the outside;

- the *step* laws, which calculate the first-step actions of constructs like $P \oplus Q$ in terms of those of P and Q;

- the unwinding law of recursion; and

- manipulations of the expressions within processes.

Just as in earlier chapters we have avoided going into details about the syntax and semantic details of sub-process expressions, here we will generally assume that one of these can always be replaced by an equivalent expression without comment. The only law as such we will need is one to change the names of input identifiers:

$$?x : A \to P \ = \ ?y : A \to P[y/x]$$
$$\text{if } y \text{ is not free in } P$$

$\langle \text{input } \alpha\text{-cnv} \rangle$ (11.1

While this is frequently needed to perform the transformations below, in describing them we will simply assume it has been used to unify the names of inputs where necessary without further comment.

The strategy for reducing an arbitrary process P into hnf is quite simple, and is as follows:

- If P has the form $?x : A \to P'$, it is already in the required form so we need do nothing.

- If P has the form $P' \sqcap P''$, then reduce each of P' and P''. The resulting process ($P_1' \sqcap P_1''$, say) is in the required form.

- If P is *STOP*, then apply the law $\langle STOP\text{-step} \rangle$ (1.15).

- If P has the form $P' \oplus P''$, where $\oplus$ is any other standard binary operator (i.e., $\Box$, $\|$, $\|\|$ or $_X\|_Y$), then first reduce each of P' and P'', to $P^\dagger$ and $P^\ddagger$, say. Next, use the left and right distributive laws of $\oplus$ (in each case the right distributive law is proved using the left distributive law and the symmetry

---

[3]The formal definition of hnf will appear on page 276 and be a little more general than this.

law) to move all the top-level nondeterminism from $P^\dagger$ and $P^\ddagger$ to the outside. The result then has the form

$$\bigsqcap_{i=1}^{N}(?x : A_i \rightarrow P_i^\dagger) \oplus (?x : B_i \rightarrow P_i^\ddagger)$$

In each case the respective step law ($\langle\Box\text{-step}\rangle$ (1.14), $\langle\|\text{-step}\rangle$ (2.10), $\langle\|\|\text{-step}\rangle$ (2.6) or $\langle_X\|_Y\text{-step}\rangle$ (2.2)) transforms this into the required form.

- If P has the form $P'[\![R]\!]$, then very much the same procedure (using $\langle[\![R]\!]\text{-dist}\rangle$ (3.13) and $\langle[\![R]\!]\text{-step}\rangle$ (3.15)) is followed.

- If P has the form $P' \setminus X$, then applying the same procedure (using $\langle\text{hide-dist}\rangle$ (3.1) and $\langle\text{hide-step}\rangle$ (3.6)) will result in a process of the form $\bigsqcap_{i=1}^{N} Q_i$ where the Q_i either have the form $?x : A_i \rightarrow (Q_i' \setminus X)$, which is what we want, or

$$(?x : A_i \rightarrow (Q_i' \setminus X)) \triangleright \bigsqcap\{P_{i,j}'' \setminus X \mid j \in \{1, \ldots, M_i\}\}$$

which is not. The second case occurs, evidently, when some of the initial actions of P' are hidden and so do not create initial *visible* actions of P (in the operational semantics of Chapter 7 they would have become τ's).

The strategy in the second case is to reduce the processes $P_{i,j}'' \setminus X$, and then use the definition of $P \triangleright Q = (P \Box Q) \sqcap Q$ and $\langle\Box\text{-step}\rangle$ (1.14) to organize the result into the correct shape. (*)

- If P is recursively defined, simply apply $\langle\mu\text{-unwind}\rangle$ (1.23) and reduce the result. (**)

There is a significant problem with this strategy, namely it need not terminate. The problem is that the clauses for reducing $P \setminus X$ and $\mu\, p.P$ can both result in infinite regression: the reduction-based operational semantics diverges rather than produces a term of the required form. In fact, this is just as well, because of course there are CSP terms in the language we are considering that are not equivalent in $\mathcal{N}$ to any process in head normal form: the ones that can diverge immediately.

The reduction strategy must therefore certainly fail on any term mapped by the semantics to $\perp_\mathcal{N}$. This can easily be demonstrated on divergent terms such as

$$(\mu\, p.a \rightarrow p) \setminus \{a\} \qquad \mu\, p.p \qquad \mu\, p.STOP \sqcap p$$

The converse (i.e., the strategy succeeds on any other term) is also true, because it is easy to show that any infinite regression contains an infinite number of uses of (*) and (**), the application of either of which generates a τ in the original operational semantics.

EXAMPLE 11.2.1 Consider the process $(COPY \; ||| \; COPY) \setminus \{| \; left \; |\}$. To transform this to hnf we first expand the two recursions: this immediately brings each of them into the hnf

$$left?x \rightarrow right!x \rightarrow COPY$$

The law $\langle |||\text{-step} \rangle$ (2.6) then brings the interleaving to the hnf

$$
\begin{aligned}
& left?x \rightarrow (\;\; (right!x \rightarrow COPY) \; ||| \\
& \qquad\qquad\qquad (left?x \rightarrow right!x \rightarrow COPY)) \\
\sqcap \;\; & left?x \rightarrow (\;\; (left?x \rightarrow right!x \rightarrow COPY) \; ||| \\
& \qquad\qquad\qquad (right!x \rightarrow COPY))
\end{aligned}
$$

which (thanks to $\langle |||\text{-sym} \rangle$ (2.7) and $\langle \sqcap\text{-idem} \rangle$ (1.2) and re-folding the recursion) can be simplified to the hnf

$$left?x \rightarrow ((right!x \rightarrow COPY) \; ||| \; COPY)$$

(Such simplifications are not a necessary part of the procedure, but help.)

We then apply $\langle \text{hide-step} \rangle$ to this to transform the complete process (incorporating the external hiding) to

$$\bigsqcap \{((right!x \rightarrow COPY) \; ||| \; COPY) \setminus \{| \; left \; |\} \mid x \in T\}$$

This, of course, is not in hnf since the hiding takes away the visible guard. We therefore have to re-apply our strategy to the processes

$$((right!x \rightarrow COPY) \; ||| \; COPY) \setminus \{| \; left \; |\} \qquad (\S)$$

which yields

$$
\begin{aligned}
& right!x \rightarrow (COPY \; ||| \; COPY) \\
\square \;\; & left?y \rightarrow ((right!x \rightarrow COPY) \; ||| \; (right!y \rightarrow COPY))
\end{aligned}
$$

for the process inside the hiding. (Bear in mind that in practice it is a lot clearer to use an appropriate mixture of prefix choices such as $left?y$ and external choices of these to represent a given initial set of actions of a given branch of an hnf, rather than using the pure prefix-choice form used in the definition, though the latter could easily be recovered using $\langle \square\text{-step} \rangle$ (1.14).) Thus (via $\langle \text{hide-step} \rangle$ again) the process ($\S$) becomes

$$
\begin{aligned}
& right!x \rightarrow (COPY \; ||| \; COPY) \setminus \{| \; left \; |\} \\
\rhd \;\; & \bigsqcap \{((right!x \rightarrow COPY) \; ||| \; (right!y \rightarrow COPY)) \setminus \{| \; left \; |\} \mid y \in T\}
\end{aligned}
$$

This is *still* not hnf, since we have once again lost some of the guards to the hiding. We now have to re-apply our strategy once more to

$$((right!x \rightarrow COPY) \ ||| \ (right!y \rightarrow COPY)) \setminus \{| \ left \ |\}$$

which fortunately does now yield an hnf:

$$right!x \rightarrow (COPY \ ||| \ (right!y \rightarrow COPY)) \setminus \{| \ left \ |\}$$
$$\Box \ right!y \rightarrow ((right!x \rightarrow COPY) \ ||| \ COPY) \setminus \{| \ left \ |\}$$

(It would really be purer to separate the cases of $x = y$ and $x \neq y$ as would be done by $\langle\Box\text{-dist}\rangle$, but it would be even more complex!) We can now collect together an hnf for (§): after a little manipulation it is

$$\sqcap\{right!x \rightarrow \ \ (COPY \ ||| \ COPY)$$
$$\sqcap (COPY \ ||| \ right!y \rightarrow COPY)$$
$$\Box \ right!y \rightarrow (right!x \rightarrow COPY \ ||| \ COPY)$$
$$| \ y \in T\}$$

and the hnf for the original process is then just the nondeterministic choice over this as x varies.

Obviously if we had hidden $\{| \ left \ |\}$ in a buffer with no initial bound on how many inputs it can take, such as $BUFF_{\langle\rangle}$, then the strategy would not terminate. (*End of example*)

EXERCISE 11.2.1   Reduce the following processes to hnf:

(a) $COPY \setminus \{| \ right \ |\}$

(b) $((a \rightarrow P_a) \sqcap (b \rightarrow P_b)) \ ||| \ ((b \rightarrow Q_b) \sqcap (c \rightarrow Q_c))$

(c) $COPY \setminus \{left.0\}$ where the type T of the channels is $\{0, 1\}$

11.3   The laws of $\perp_{\mathcal{N}}$

Our attempts to reduce divergent processes to hnf failed in the previous section because the divergence translated itself into non-termination of the reduction algorithm. It is a good idea to include an explicit representation of a divergent process in the language we reason about algebraically: let **div** represent this as it did in Section 3.1. We can then see how a term that is equivalent to a diverging process behaves algebraically.

As one might expect from the discussions in Chapter 8, it is in the handling of **div** that $\mathcal{N}$ differs from the models without an explicit representation of divergence

($\mathcal{F}$ and $\mathcal{T}$). The laws for **div** (equalling $\perp_{\mathcal{N}}$) over $\mathcal{N}$ are thus often not valid over these other models: with the exception of prefixing and the right-hand side of sequencing, all operators are strict (in the sense defined on page 472). Notice that the names of these laws reflect their selective validity. They are called *zero* laws because of their similarity to the arithmetic equivalence $0 \times x = 0$.

$$\textbf{div} \sqcap P = \textbf{div} \qquad\qquad \langle \sqcap\text{-zero}^{\mathcal{N}} \rangle \quad (11.$$

$$\textbf{div} \,\square\, P = \textbf{div} \qquad\qquad \langle \square\text{-zero}^{\mathcal{N}} \rangle \quad (11.$$

$$\textbf{div} \parallel_X P = \textbf{div} \qquad\qquad \langle \parallel_X\text{-zero}^{\mathcal{N}} \rangle \quad (11.$$

$$\textbf{div} \,_X\|_Y\, P = \textbf{div} \qquad\qquad \langle _X\|_Y\text{-zero}^{\mathcal{N}} \rangle \quad (11.$$

$$\textbf{div} \,|||\, P = \textbf{div} \qquad\qquad \langle |||\text{-zero}^{\mathcal{N}} \rangle \quad (11.$$

$$\textbf{div} \setminus X = \textbf{div} \qquad\qquad \langle \text{hide-zero} \rangle \quad (11.$$

$$\textbf{div}[\![R]\!] = \textbf{div} \qquad\qquad \langle [\![R]\!]\text{-zero} \rangle \quad (11.$$

$$\textbf{div}; P = \textbf{div} \qquad\qquad \langle ;\text{-zero-l} \rangle \quad (11.$$

These laws mean it makes sense to add the term **div** as an alternative head normal form: we can now formally define a process to be in hnf if

- it is **div**, or
- it has the form $?x : A \to P$, or
- it is $\sqcap_{i=1}^{N} Q_i$ for processes Q_i in hnf.

The laws mean that if either **div** appears explicitly in a program or you can recognize and replace[4] some divergent term by it, then you can extend the reduction strategy to deal with this. Essentially, if **div** is encountered at any level in reducing a process P to calculate its initial behaviour, then these laws (together with symmetry laws to derive the right-zero laws for binary operators other than ;) will reduce the process itself to **div**.

The definition of hnf above makes it optional whether to reduce a process in which **div** appears as a choice, such as

$$(?x : A \to P) \sqcap \textbf{div}$$

---

[4]If the replacement is going to form part of our algebraic semantics, then it is clear that the means of performing it would have to be formalized, justified, and incorporated within the semantics.

to **div** using $\langle \sqcap\text{-zero}^{\mathcal{N}} \rangle$. For simplicity, let us assume that we always do make this reduction.

The possible outcomes of the reduction strategy are then (i) the original type of hnf, (ii) the term **div** and (iii) non-termination of the strategy. There is no complete algorithm for telling if a given CSP term diverges[5] or not, and so no effective procedure which will tell us which terms our strategy will fail to terminate on.

There is a simple and powerful[6] algebraically-based method for detecting divergence, namely:

Loop$^{\mathcal{N}}$ If, during an attempt to reduce a process P to head normal form the (syntactic) process P is encountered other than at the root of the reduction, then P is divergent and may be replaced by **div**.

This is not, of course, a *law* in the conventional sense of the word, rather a *rule*. To implement this rule it is necessary to keep a record of the tree structure that results from the attempt to reduce a process, and look for loops (nodes identical to predecessors). The notation **Loop**$^{\mathcal{N}}$ indicates that this is a valid rule over $\mathcal{N}$, but not over $\mathcal{T}$ or $\mathcal{F}$.

11.4 Normalizing

It is our objective to be able to prove *any* pair of equivalent processes equal using an algebraic theory. An obvious approach to this is to identify a *normal form*: a highly restricted syntax for processes meeting the following requirements.

- A pair of normal form programs are only semantically equal if they are either syntactically identical, or perhaps differ in a well-defined and trivial way such as the name of a bound variable or the order of terms composed under a symmetric and associative operator.

- Every program is equivalent to one in normal form.

- This equivalence can be demonstrated by the algebraic theory.

Let us restrict ourselves, for the time being, to processes that are finitely transformable to hnf, as are all successors reached when executing their algebraic

---

[5]This would solve the halting problem.

[6]Inevitably, given the previous discussion, it is not *complete* in the sense of detecting all divergence. It is, however, complete provided the process is finite state. It then corresponds to a depth-first search for loops in the graph of nodes reachable from the chosen root.

operational semantics. (In other words, processes in which all divergences are either syntactically explicit, **div**, or detectable using a rule such as **Loop**$^{\mathcal{N}}$.)

Our approach will be to refine the concept of head normal form into a full normal form, and to show how a program in head normal form can be transformed using the laws of $\square$ and $\sqcap$ into this restricted form.

Given that Σ is finite, the first-step behaviour $P \downarrow 1$ of any process P is completely characterized by the following information:

- Does P diverge immediately? If not,

- what is P's set of initial actions $initials(P)$, and

- what are P's maximal refusals?

The divergent case of head normal form evidently captures the first of these precisely, but the non-divergent one is too loose in that there are typically many different sets $\{A_1, \ldots, A_N\}$ of initial actions that would give rise, in

$$\sqcap_{i=1}^{N} x : A_i \to P_i$$

to exactly the same sets of initial actions and maximal refusals, bearing in mind that the complements of the A_i are the refusals. For example,

$$\{\{a, b, c\}, \{a\}, \{b\}\}$$
$$\{\{b, c\}, \{a\}, \{b\}\}$$
$$\{\{a, b, c\}, \{a, b\}, \{a\}, \{b\}\}$$
$$\{\{a, b, c\}, \{a, b\}, \{a, c\}, \{b, c\}, \{a\}, \{b\}\}$$

all give the same result, and are by no means the only sets that give this particular one. We need to decide on a unique representation of any given collection of *acceptance* sets[7] A_i and provide a way of transforming any non-**div** head normal form

---

[7]The concept of an acceptance set is obviously very closely related to that of a refusal set. If we define an acceptance set just to be the complement of a refusal set (in $\Sigma^{\checkmark}$) then clearly we could have replaced all uses of refusal sets in our models with them, subject to systematic changes in definitions. This would, however, imply that acceptance sets were superset-closed (as an analogy to axiom F2), implying there were members of 'acceptance sets' that a process could never accept. Thus an acceptance is arguably better defined to be a set of events which is (a) the complement of some refusal and (b) contained in $initials(P)$. This modification means that the translation from refusal sets to acceptance sets is not so direct and means that model, operator, etc. definitions work better with failures rather than with their acceptance-set analogues. So it seems that in order to create acceptance-based analogues of the models $\mathcal{N}$ and $\mathcal{F}$ one either has to compromise on naturalness or on ease of manipulation. Perhaps the most natural acceptance-set model is that proposed in [79], which has no superset closure condition at all: modulo divergence, an acceptance set is the set of all events offered by some stable state. This gives a subtly different (and less abstract) congruence which fails the law $\langle \sqcap\text{-}\square\text{-}\textbf{dist} \rangle$ (1.13).

to this. There are various sensible choices one could make, but the one we opt for here is to specify that the set $\{A_1, \ldots, A_N\}$

- has the property that $A_1 \supset A_j$ for all $j > 1$ (i.e., A_1 is the union of all A_i and represents *initials(P)*), and

- if $i, j > 1$ are distinct then $A_i \not\subseteq A_j$ (i.e., all these A_i represent minimal acceptances, and hence their complements, the maximal refusals).

Note that in the case where *initials(P)* is a (necessarily the only) minimal acceptance, $N = 1$ and A_1 plays a double role.

A simple procedure, which is described below, transforms an arbitrary non-**div** head normal form to this format. It rests almost entirely on the laws of $\square$, $\sqcap$, prefixing and conditionals.

You can ensure that each set A_i only appears once in the result by applying the law $\langle$input-dist$\rangle$ (1.11) repeatedly till all pairs of identical ones are eliminated.

If there is only one A_i remaining after this, there is nothing further to do. If there are more than one, we have to ensure the collection contains the union and that all the rest are minimal. Observe that, for any processes P and Q,

$$P \sqcap Q \;=\; (P \sqcap Q) \,\square\, (P \sqcap Q)$$
$$\text{by } \langle\square\text{-idem}\rangle \text{ (1.1)}$$

$$=\; (P \,\square\, Q) \sqcap P \sqcap Q$$
$$\text{by } \langle\square\text{-dist}\rangle \text{ (1.7)}, \langle\sqcap\text{-idem}\rangle \text{ (1.2), etc.}$$

This argument can (see Exercise 11.4.1) be extended, by induction, to show that for any N and processes Q_i,

$$\textstyle\bigsqcap_{i=1}^{N} Q_i \;=\; (\square_{i=1}^{N} Q_i) \sqcap (\bigsqcap_{i=1}^{N} Q_i)$$

In the case where $Q_i =?x : A_i \to P_i$, the extra process $Q_1 \,\square\, \ldots \,\square\, Q_N$ can be transformed using $\langle\square\text{-step}\rangle$ (1.14) to the form

$$?x : A^\dagger \to R$$

where $A^\dagger = \bigcup_{i=1}^{N} A_i$ and such that, for any $a \in A_j$, we have

$$P_j[a/x] \sqcap R[a/x] \;=\; R[a/x]$$

Any $a \in A^\dagger$ may appear in several different A_i, and the processes $P_i[a/x]$, which are the possible results of performing it, may all be different from each other and $R[a/x]$. What the above does ensure is that $R[a/x]$ is the most nondeterministic of these choices. Consider the transformation:

$$
\begin{aligned}
& (?x : A^\dagger \to R) \\
& \sqcap (?x : A_i \to P_i)
\end{aligned}
\quad = \quad
\begin{aligned}
& (?x : A^\dagger \setminus A_i \to R \;\square\, ?x : A_i \to R) \\
& \sqcap (?x : A_i \to P_i) \\
& \text{by } \langle \square\text{-step} \rangle \text{ and } \langle \text{\textctreversedglotstop} \cdot \text{\textrevtailtee-idem} \rangle \; (1.17)
\end{aligned}
$$

$$
\begin{aligned}
= \quad
& (?x : A^\dagger \setminus A_i \to R \;\sqcap\, ?x : A_i \to P_i) \\
& \square \, (?x : A_i \to R \;\sqcap\, ?x : A_i \to P_i) \\
& \text{by } \langle \sqcap\text{-}\square\text{-dist} \rangle \; (1.13)
\end{aligned}
$$

$$
\begin{aligned}
= \quad
& (?x : A^\dagger \setminus A_i \to R \;\sqcap\, ?x : A_i \to P_i) \\
& \square \, (?x : A_i \to (R \sqcap P_i)) \\
& \text{by } \langle \text{input-dist} \rangle \; (1.11)
\end{aligned}
$$

$$
\begin{aligned}
= \quad
& (?x : A^\dagger \setminus A_i \to R \;\sqcap\, ?x : A_i \to P_i) \\
& \square \, (?x : A_i \to R) \\
& \text{by what we established about } R \text{ above}
\end{aligned}
$$

$$
\begin{aligned}
= \quad
& (?x : A^\dagger \setminus A_i \to R \;\square\, ?x : A_i \to R) \\
& \sqcap \, (?x : A_i \to P_i \;\square\, ?x : A_i \to R) \\
& \text{by } \langle \square\text{-dist} \rangle
\end{aligned}
$$

$$
\begin{aligned}
= \quad
& (?x : A^\dagger \to R) \sqcap (?x : A_i \to P_i \sqcap R) \\
& \text{by } \langle \square\text{-step} \rangle, \text{ etc.}
\end{aligned}
$$

$$
\begin{aligned}
= \quad
& (?x : A^\dagger \to R) \sqcap (?x : A_i \to R) \\
& \text{by what we established about } R \text{ above}
\end{aligned}
$$

What this does is to show we can replace all the old result processes P_i by R in the process we are transforming, making all the possible results of performing a given a identical. This is both a vital part of the normalization process itself and is helpful for the next and final part of transforming it to our target shape of hnf, which is the removal of any non-minimal A_i (other than $A^\dagger$). This makes use of the following identity, which is essentially that proved in the last part of Exercise 3.1.5.

$$
(P \,\square\, Q \,\square\, S) \sqcap P = (P \,\square\, Q \,\square\, S) \sqcap (P \,\square\, Q) \sqcap P
$$

since we can then, for any $A_i \subset A_j$, set

$$
\begin{aligned}
P &= \; ?x : A_i \to R \\
Q &= \; ?x : A_j \setminus A_i \to R \\
S &= \; ?x : A^\dagger \setminus A_j \to R
\end{aligned}
$$

and apply the identity from right to left.

What we have managed to do is transform our process P into a *one-step normal form*: a hnf which is either **div** or satisfies the restrictions on its acceptance-set pattern set out above and furthermore has a unique successor process for each initial action. This gives a complete characterization of the first-step behaviour of the original process P, and has the property that (provided P does not equal **div**) for each $a \in initials(P)$ we have $P/\langle a \rangle = R[a/x]$. If P' were another process equivalent to P in $\mathcal{N}$ then it would reduce to a one-step normal form with exactly the same shape (pattern of A_i, except that the A_i for $i > 1$ may be re-ordered) and such that its successor process R' is equivalent to R in $\mathcal{N}$ (in the sense that $R[a/x] = R'[a/x]$ for all a in the initials set $A^\dagger$).

This notion of a one-step normal form extends naturally to a full normal form: the definition is exactly the same except that, in addition, we insist that each of the result processes $R[a/x]$ is also in normal form. (It is in doing these lower-level normalizations of the leaf processes of a one-step normal form that we need the assumption that all successor processes can be reduced to hnf.) The argument in the previous paragraph can easily be extended by induction to show that any pair of normal form programs which are equivalent in $\mathcal{N}$ have equivalent normal form structures and can trivially be inter-transformed by laws. The only things that can differ are things like the order of A_i's and the names of input variables.

It would seem that we have attained our goal of completely capturing the denotational equivalence via algebra. Essentially we have, but not as simply as it appears on the surface. The problem is how to handle processes that can go on communicating for ever and which therefore fail to have a finite-depth normal form. It is evident that we can attempt fully to normalize a process P by first transforming it to one-step normal form and then normalizing each of the result processes $R[a/x]$, but this transformation will only terminate and produce a finite-depth normal form program if the set $traces_\perp(P) \setminus divergences(P)$ is finite (which, under our assumptions, is equivalent to there being a bound on the length of its members). There are several ways around this difficulty, but all mean we have to abandon any hope that all pairs of equivalent CSP processes are inter-transformable by a finite sequence of law applications.

The first approach we can take is to incorporate into our theory the fact that processes P and Q are equivalent in $\mathcal{N}$ if, and only if, $P \downarrow n = Q \downarrow n$ for all $n \in \mathbb{N}$, where the restriction functions $\downarrow n$ are as defined on page 196. We can express $P \downarrow n$ directly in CSP[8], it is $P \underset{\Sigma}{\parallel} Rest(n)$ where

$$
\begin{aligned}
Rest(0) &= \textbf{div} \\
Rest(n) &= ?x : \Sigma \to Rest(n-1) \quad \text{for } n > 0
\end{aligned}
$$

---

[8] The expression given here is dependent on our assumption that P never terminates. For how to extend this idea to processes that can communicate $\checkmark$, see Exercise 11.5.4.

Since each $P \downarrow n$ always has a finite normal form, the rule

Equiv$^{\mathcal{N}}$ If P and Q are any processes in finitely nondeterministic CSP, defined
without *SKIP* or sequential composition, then they are equivalent in $\mathcal{N}$
if and only if, for all $n \in \mathbb{N}$,

$$P \underset{\Sigma}{\parallel} Rest(n) \;=\; Q \underset{\Sigma}{\parallel} Rest(n)$$

leads directly to a decision procedure for equivalence which involves converting
infinitely many processes into finite normal form and seeing if you get the same
results for each pair. It is complete on processes satisfying our assumptions about
reducibility to hnf.

Another approach is to transform the program into a potentially infinite
normal form tree. It is perhaps easiest to understand this in terms of deriving,
from a process P, a recursive definition of a vector of processes which turns out
to be indexed by T, the set of members of $traces_{\perp}(P)$ other than non-minimal
divergences. If s is such a trace, we can compute R_s, the result process (equivalent
to P/s) derived from applying the one-step normal form transformation down s as
follows.

$$
\begin{aligned}
R_{\langle\rangle} &= P \\
R_{s^\frown\langle a\rangle} &= Q[a/x], \quad \text{where applying the one-step normal form trans-}
\end{aligned}
$$

formation to R_s yields something of the form
$$\bigsqcap_{i=1}^{N} ?x : A_i \to Q$$

Along with this derivation you have produced an expression for each R_s in terms
of the $R_{s^\frown\langle a\rangle}$: the one-step normal form of R_s. If you now replace the processes
R_s by the corresponding components of a vector $\underline{N}$ of process variables, the result
is a constructive one-step tail recursion whose unique fixed point in $\mathcal{N}^T$ is clearly
$\langle R_s \mid s \in T\rangle = \langle P/s \mid s \in T\rangle$. If P' is a process equivalent to P then the recursion
produced will be exactly the same, since the one-step normal form of P'/s has the
same shape as that of P/s for all s. So we have managed to transform P and P' to
the same process definition, albeit using in many cases an infinite number of steps.

When deriving this 'tree' expression for the normal form, it may very well
be the case that the number of distinct values of P/s visited is actually finite. This
is always so if P is finite state and even sometimes when it is not, for example

$$\mu\, p.a \to (p \,|||\, p) \quad \text{(equivalent to } \mu\, p.a \to p)$$

If you can recognize these equivalences (by transformation, for example), then you
can produce a more compact representation of the normal form tree as a finite graph

or as a recursion with a finite indexing set. Thus you can represent the process

$$P_0 = \mu\, p.(a \to a \to p) \sqcap (a \to STOP)$$

as the two-state recursion

$$N_{\langle\rangle} = a \to N_{\langle a \rangle}$$

$$N_{\langle a \rangle} = a \to N_{\langle\rangle} \\ \sqcap STOP$$

rather than having a component for each member of $\{a\}^*$.

The problem with this is that it re-introduces an element of flexibility into the way normal form processes are structured: flexibility is just what you do not want of a normal form. The main source of flexibility is the fact that one may or may not spot an equivalence between a pair of processes. Consider, for example, the process

$$P_1 = P_0 \underset{\{a,b\}}{\parallel} (\mu\, p.a \to a \to ((a \to p) \,\square\, (b \to STOP)))$$

This is, in fact, equivalent to P_0, but the finite-state normal form you would be most likely to derive for it is

$$N'_{\langle\rangle} = a \to N'_{\langle a \rangle}$$

$$N'_{\langle a \rangle} = a \to N'_{\langle a,a \rangle} \\ \sqcap STOP$$

$$N'_{\langle a,a \rangle} = a \to N'_{\langle a,a,a \rangle}$$

$$N'_{\langle a,a,a \rangle} = a \to N'_{\langle a,a,a,a \rangle} \\ \sqcap STOP$$

$$N'_{\langle a,a,a,a \rangle} = a \to N'_{\langle a,a,a,a,a \rangle}$$

$$N'_{\langle a,a,a,a,a \rangle} = a \to N'_{\langle\rangle} \\ \sqcap STOP$$

because the structures of, for example, $P_1/\langle\rangle$ and $P_1/\langle a,a \rangle$ are sufficiently different that it is unlikely one would spot or easily prove their equality while transforming to normal form.

If the above were computed for P_1, then one can no longer establish its equivalence with P_0 by the identity of their normal forms. The way around this, though it is not in any obvious sense an algebraic operation, is to factor each normal form you compute by the maximal bisimulation computed over it[9] (see Section 7.2). In the case above this identifies $\{N'_{\langle\rangle}, N'_{\langle a,a\rangle}, N'_{\langle a,a,a,a\rangle}\}$ and $\{N'_{\langle a\rangle}, N'_{\langle a,a,a\rangle}, N'_{\langle a,a,a,a,a\rangle}\}$ resulting in a structure identical to the normal form of P_0 (which has no interesting equivalences between its nodes).

These bisimulated normal forms are in some ways less attractive from a purely algebraic standpoint than the ones with separate components for all traces, but they are a lot more practical since they are so often finite. Though they are derived via direct manipulation of the underlying LTS rather than by algebraic transformations, the normal forms which play a crucial part in FDR's operations are essentially the same objects. See Appendix C for more details.

The reader might have noticed the great similarity between the normal forms described in this section and the recursion defined on page 231 to demonstrate the coverage of $\mathcal{N}$ by the CSP notation. This should not come as a surprise, since in each case our task was to find a standard way of representing a given semantic value, even if we did have to approach this problem from opposite ends. Except for the fact that we have, in this chapter, yet to deal with *SKIP* and sequencing, the only difference between the recursions N_s defined above and $Int^{\mathcal{N}}_{(F,D)}$ defined on page 231 is the indexing sets used. In the second case this is, for a given value $(F, D) \in \mathcal{N}$,

$$\{(F, D)/s \mid s \in T\}$$

where T is, again, the set of traces other than non-minimal divergences. Naturally, in comparing this with the normal form of a process P such that

$$(F, D) = (failures_{\perp}(P), divergences(P)) = \mathcal{S}_{\mathcal{N}}[\![P]\!]$$

it is not hard to prove that the relation over T defined

$$s \equiv s' \iff \mathcal{S}_{\mathcal{N}}[\![P]\!]/s = \mathcal{S}_{\mathcal{N}}[\![P]\!]/s'$$

corresponds precisely to the maximal bisimulation over the processes N_s derived from P. This demonstrates nicely that the result of quotienting the maximal bisim-

---

[9]This bisimulation can be computed in two ways. The first is to use the ordinary bisimulation relation over the LTS you get from the standard operational semantics of the normal form recursion. Before bisimulating you would then start with distinct nodes for all the normal form states, and also extra states (reachable under τ actions from this first sort) for the *initials* sets and maximal refusals. The second, and much more elegant, way is to consider only the normal form states as nodes of the transition system. The nodes are marked with divergence or with maximal refusal information which is taken into account when computing the maximal bisimulation: no two nodes with different markings are ever identified. See Section C.2 for more discussion of this idea.

ulation into any 'normal form' of the sort represented by the N'_s above gives a true normal form. In other words, it demonstrates the 'completeness' of the method.

To summarize, we have shown that the algebraic laws completely characterize the semantics of CSP over $\mathcal{N}$, though the procedures we have provided for deciding equivalence are infinitary. The only remaining issue is our assumption that we can detect all divergent terms and replace them with **div**. The procedure for reducing a process to hnf does, of course, provide an infinitary complete method for this, and we could argue reasonably that if we are to accept an infinitary procedure for one thing then it will do for this too! The unfortunate feature is that it leads to one infinitary procedure (divergence detection) being a frequently-used subroutine in another. You can get round this (i.e., back to a single level of infinity) by several methods, perhaps the most frequently used of which is the concept of *syntactic approximation* where, instead of comparing the desired pair of processes algebraically, you compare pairs of recursion-free approximations (where recursions have been unwound a finite number of times, and those that remain are replaced by **div**). For more details of this, see [40], for example.

It is well worth commenting that the normalization procedure uses a surprisingly small proportion of the laws set out in earlier chapters. The laws of prefixing and choice have been used extensively in normalization, but the only laws used for other operators have been unwinding and their distributive, step and zero (strictness) laws (with the exception that some symmetry laws are needed to derive symmetric versions, such as right distributive laws from left ones). The only possible conclusion is that the rest of the laws must be implied by the ones we used, examples being $\langle \|\|\text{-assoc} \rangle$ (2.8), $\langle {}_X\|_Y\text{-assoc} \rangle$ (2.5), $\langle \text{hide-}\|\text{-dist} \rangle$ (3.8), $\langle \text{hide-combine} \rangle$ (3.3) and $\langle f[\cdot]\text{-}\underset{X}{\|}\text{-dist} \rangle$ (3.9). None of these is a trivial consequence of the ones we used in the same sense that $\langle \text{hide-sym} \rangle$ follows from $\langle \text{hide-combine} \rangle$. It is usually possible to prove them from the algebraic theory, but the proofs are generally much harder than those directly using the underlying models. The proofs often make use of the rule **Equiv**$^{\mathcal{N}}$ and inductions such as

$$((P \;|||\; Q) \;|||\; R) \downarrow n \;=\; (P \;|||\; (Q \;|||\; R)) \downarrow n$$

in which, for the inductive step, the two sides are reduced to hnf. See Exercise 11.4.2.

Algebraic semantics also give us (as discussed earlier) the freedom to ask the question of what equivalence is induced if we drop one or more of the laws that actually were necessary to characterize failures/divergences equivalence. The most interesting ones to consider dropping are $\langle \sqcap\text{-}\square\text{-dist} \rangle$ (1.13), which plays a crucial role in normalization and which is, as discussed at the point of its definition on page 32, somewhat hard to justify on intuitive grounds, and the step laws of parallel operators. But all of this is beyond the scope of this text, and in any case the occupation of experimenting with sets of laws for its own sake is a great deal more fascinating theoretically than it is practically useful.

EXERCISE 11.4.1   Prove, using the laws and induction on N, that for any $P_1, \ldots, P_N$

$$\sqcap_{i=1}^{N} P_i = (\square_{i=1}^{N} P_i) \sqcap (\sqcap_{i=1}^{N} P_i)$$

EXERCISE 11.4.2   Using the expression for $P \downarrow n$ given in the statement of the rule **Equiv**$^{\mathcal{N}}$, show by induction on n that for any processes P, Q and R

$$((P \;|||\; Q) \;|||\; R) \downarrow n = (P \;|||\; (Q \;|||\; R)) \downarrow n$$

by computing the hnf's of the right- and left-hand sides in terms of hnf's of P, Q and R. Do you think this form of induction would work as easily for proving the law ⟨hide-combine⟩?

EXERCISE 11.4.3   Compute finitely mutual recursive normal forms for $(COPY \;|||\; COPY) \setminus \{| \; left \; |\}$, dealt with in Example 11.2.1 and the process of Exercise 11.2.1 part (c).

EXERCISE 11.4.4   Recall the interrupt operator described on page 235. $P \; \triangle_a \; Q$ behaves like P except that at any time a may occur and the process subsequently behave like Q. Give the failures/divergences semantics of $P \; \triangle_a \; Q$. Is it strict in P? and in Q?

Now give a step law that allows the reduction strategy to hnf to be extended to processes involving $\triangle_a$ constructs together with the strictness properties above and distributive laws.

Notice that these laws completely determine the semantics of this new operator. Do you think a similar principle applies to any new operator?

EXERCISE 11.4.5   Repeat Exercise 11.1.1 for the following 'laws' (also taken from [48]), though this time only showing all divergence-free processes equal.

(1)	$P \;\|\; RUN$	$=$	P	
(2)	$P \;\|\; SKIP$	$=$	P	
(3)	$P \;\|\; Q$	$=$	$Q \;\|\; P$	
(4)	$P \;|||\; SKIP$	$=$	P	
(5)	$P \;|||\; RUN$	$=$	$RUN \Leftrightarrow divergences(P) = \{\}$	

11.5   Sequential composition and *SKIP*

We have not dealt with *SKIP*, and hence sequential composition, so far because it necessarily adds cases to the reduction/normalization strategies and to the definitions of the normal forms. This is not only because we are not permitted to include $\checkmark$ in choice sets A_i but also because $\checkmark$ is, as seen in earlier chapters, not treated like other actions. The law $\langle\Box\text{-}SKIP$ resolve$\rangle$ (6.6) was crucial in explaining the difference earlier, and it has a large impact on how the algebraic semantics are affected by $\checkmark$.

The crux of the problem is that we now have processes like $(a \to STOP) \Box SKIP$ which can offer an event in Σ transiently before they terminate. In many ways the behaviour of this process is similar to

$$((a \to STOP) \Box (b \to c \to STOP)) \setminus \{b\}$$

in that both can independently make the decision to remove the choice of doing a in favour of something else. This latter process has hnf (indeed, normal form)

$$(?x : \{a, c\} \to STOP) \sqcap c \to STOP$$

In other words, the process with the transient event a has been replaced by a process definition without transients which has identical observed behaviour. This is not possible with the first process, because it involves the trick of offering the external choice of the transient a and the result of the internal choice, and we do not permit process definitions like

$$(?x : \{a, \checkmark\} \to STOP) \sqcap SKIP$$

which would be the translation.

There are two reasonable ways to incorporate termination into hnf. In some ways the more pleasing is to bring the sliding choice/timeout operator $P \rhd Q$ into the syntax of hnf, thinking of it as a primitive operator implemented as in the direct operational semantics for it on page 165 rather than as $(P \Box Q) \sqcap Q$ (though the equality over denotational models with this representation would still hold). However, because some people might find this 'doublethink' about $\rhd$ confusing, and because it is probably simpler overall, we will add termination by allowing $(?x : A \to P) \Box SKIP$ to be considered an hnf.

The definition of hnf now becomes:

- **div** is in hnf;

- $SKIP$ is in hnf;

- $?x : A \to P$ is in hnf;

- $(?x : A \to P) \Box SKIP$ is in hnf;

- if each Q_i is a hnf, then $\sqcap_{i=1}^{N} Q_i$ is;

When we want to distinguish this extended form we will refer to it as $\checkmark$-hnf.

The idea that reducing to hnf provides an operational semantics easily extends to this larger class. Obviously $SKIP$ terminates, whereas $(?x : A \to P) \;\square\; SKIP$ may offer the choice of A for a short time before terminating.

Imagine you are reducing a construct like $P \oplus Q$ ($\oplus$ being any binary operator other than $\sqcap$ or, with the obvious modifications, renaming or hiding) to $\checkmark$-hnf. The recipe given earlier calls for us first to reduce P and Q. Clearly you need to deal with the extra cases that arise when one or both of the results, P' and Q', are of the form $SKIP$ or $(?x : A \to R) \;\square\; SKIP$. The laws of $SKIP$ given in Section 6.3 easily deal with all combinations of $SKIP$ with itself and prefix choices. And $SKIP$; Q' and $((?x : A \to P) \;\square\; SKIP)$; Q' reduce, for any Q', via $\langle$; -unit-l$\rangle$ (6.4) and $\langle$; -step$\rangle$ (6.7).

The remaining cases for $\square$ can be dealt with using existing laws, and the case of $((?x : A \to P) \;\square\; SKIP)[\![R]\!]$ by $\langle [\![R]\!]$-$\square$-dist$\rangle$ (3.14) and $\langle SKIP$-$[\![R]\!]$-Id$\rangle$ (6.10). The corresponding case for $\backslash X$ requires a new law which is closely based on its existing step law:

$$((?x : A \to P) \;\square\; SKIP) \backslash X \;=$$
$$(?x : A \to (P \backslash X)) \;\square\; SKIP$$
$$\blacktriangleleft A \cap X = \{\} \blacktriangleright \qquad \qquad \langle \text{hide-}SKIP\text{-step}\rangle \;(11.10)$$
$$((?x : A \backslash X \to (P \backslash X)) \;\square\; SKIP$$
$$\sqcap \bigsqcap \{P[a/x] \backslash X \mid a \in A \cap X\}$$

Parallel operators require three new laws each: one each for an input/$SKIP$ combination in parallel with a different type of $\checkmark$-hnf. (There is no need to introduce a law to deal with the cases where the other process is a nondeterministic choice or **div** since these are reducible by distributive and zero laws respectively.) Because of this multiplicity we only give those for $\underset{X}{\|}$, since each of $\||$ and $_X\|_Y$ are expressible in terms of it. The second and third of these are better and more succinctly expressed as general principles involving the $\triangleright$ construction (bearing in mind the law $\langle \square$-$SKIP$ resolve$\rangle$). These laws make it straightforward to extend the strategy so that it can reduce CSP processes possibly involving $SKIP$ and sequential composition to $\checkmark$-hnf.

$$((?x : A \to P) \;\square\; SKIP) \underset{X}{\|} SKIP \;=$$
$$(?x : A \backslash X \to (P \underset{X}{\|} SKIP)) \;\square\; SKIP \qquad \qquad \langle \underset{X}{\|}\text{-}\square\; SKIP\rangle \;(11.11)$$

$$(P \triangleright Q) \underset{X}{\|} (R \triangleright S) \;=$$
$$(P \underset{X}{\|} R) \triangleright ((Q \underset{X}{\|} (R \triangleright S)) \sqcap ((P \triangleright Q) \underset{X}{\|} S)) \qquad \qquad \langle \underset{X}{\|}\text{-}\triangleright\text{-split}\rangle \;(11.12)$$

$$(P \rhd Q) \parallel_X (?x : A \to R)) \; =$$

$$?x : A \setminus X \to ((P \rhd Q) \parallel_X R)$$

$$\Box \, ((P \parallel_X ?x : A \to R) \rhd (Q \parallel_X ?x : A \to R)) \qquad \langle \parallel \text{-}\rhd\text{-input} \rangle \quad (11.13)$$

if x is not free in P or Q

Given its similarity to the normal form in the *SKIP*-free case, it is natural to look to the full abstraction recursion on page 231 for guidance about how to extend the definitions of one-step and full normal forms. The first-step behaviour of any non-divergent process is now characterized by its initial actions (which may now include $\checkmark$) and the minimal acceptance sets which are subsets of Σ. Minor extensions to the strategy given in the previous section can transform any $\checkmark$-hnf to one of the following forms:

(a) **div**

(b) $?x : A \to R$

(c) $(?x : A \to R) \, \Box \, SKIP$

(d) $(?x : A \to R) \sqcap (\bigsqcap_{i=1}^{N} ?x : A_i \to R)$ where the A_i are incomparable proper subsets of A

(e) $((?x : A \to R) \, \Box \, SKIP) \sqcap (\bigsqcap_{i=1}^{N} ?x : A_i \to R)$ where the A_i are incomparable subsets (not necessarily proper subsets) of A.

Here, (a) is the representation of a divergent process, (b) of a process which cannot terminate or behave nondeterministically on its first step and (c) of a process which can terminate immediately and must do so if no member of A is accepted quickly enough. (d) and (e) add the possibilities of nondeterministic offers of proper subsets of the initials to the cases in (b) and (c).

The most important new transformation required to bring the manipulation of an arbitrary $\checkmark$-hnf to one of these forms is developed in Exercise 11.5.1 below.

The above is the extended definition of one-step normal form, and the methods and problems associated with converting this to a full normal form are exactly as for the smaller language in the previous section.

EXERCISE 11.5.1   Show algebraically that for any P and Q,

$$(P \, \Box \, SKIP) \sqcap (Q \, \Box \, SKIP) = (P \, \Box \, Q \, \Box \, SKIP)$$

Why is this useful for transforming a $\checkmark$-hnf process to one-step normal form?

EXERCISE 11.5.2   Our dealings with the combinations involving $P \,\square\, SKIP$ and parallel operators would have been simplified if the distributive law

$$(P \rhd Q) \parallel_X R = (P \parallel_X R) \rhd (Q \parallel_X R)$$

were true. Give an example to show that it is not.

EXERCISE 11.5.3   Repeat Exercises 11.1.1 and 11.4.5 for the following 'laws' (also taken from [48]), proving all processes equal.

> (1) $STOP; P = STOP$
> (2) $P; STOP = P$
> (3) $SKIP; P = P$
> (4) $P; (Q; R) = (P; Q); R$

It can be done with, or without, the associative law (4), which is, of course, true.

EXERCISE 11.5.4   Recall that on page 281 we showed how to define restriction over $\mathcal{N}$ for $\checkmark$-free processes via a process context. Assuming that there is some event $a \in \Sigma$ that P never communicates on a non-divergent trace, find a corresponding way of defining $P \downarrow n$ when P can terminate.

Hint: consider $P; (a \rightarrow SKIP)$ in parallel with a well-chosen process.

11.6   Other models

We will not deal with the algebraic characterization of the other models for finitely nondeterministic CSP in as much detail, since many of the basic principles are the same and, as we will see, in some ways the algebraic approach does not work quite as cleanly for $\mathcal{T}$ and $\mathcal{F}$ as for $\mathcal{N}$.

Over both $\mathcal{F}$ and $\mathcal{T}$ we have the law

$$P \sqcap \mathbf{div} = P \qquad\qquad\qquad \langle\sqcap\text{-unit}^{\mathcal{T},\mathcal{F}}\rangle \;\; (11.14)$$

which is, of course, radically different from the corresponding law over $\mathcal{N}$ (namely $\langle\sqcap\text{-zero}^{\mathcal{N}}\rangle$). The characteristic law of $\mathcal{T}$ is

$$P \,\square\, Q = P \sqcap Q \qquad\qquad\qquad \langle\text{trace-equiv}^{\mathcal{T}}\rangle \;\; (11.15)$$

which, together with $\langle\sqcap\text{-unit}^{\mathcal{T},\mathcal{F}}\rangle$, $\langle\square\text{-unit}\rangle$ (1.16) and symmetry, can establish that $\mathbf{div} =_T STOP$. The fact that $\mathbf{div}$ can be replaced by $STOP$ means that the lack of all the $\mathbf{div}$-strictness laws true over $\mathcal{N}$ is no handicap over $\mathcal{T}$ when it comes to transforming processes involving $\mathbf{div}$ to hnf.

The situation over $\mathcal{F}$ is more complex because the processes **div**, P and $P \;\square\; $ **div** are all, in general, different. This leads to the need for a variety of new laws in much the same way we needed laws to deal with processes of the form $P \;\square\; SKIP$ in the previous section. We do not enumerate them here.

An essential ingredient of demonstrating that you have captured one of the other models is, as with $\mathcal{N}$, the creation of normal forms which capture all possible semantic values in exactly one way. This is always done by creating what is essentially a picture in syntax of the semantic model, but we are still left with choices, which generally increase in weaker models like $\mathcal{T}$.

Given the close correspondence between the normal form for $\mathcal{N}$ and the construction used for full abstraction in Section 9.3, you might expect the same to be true for $\mathcal{T}$ and $\mathcal{F}$. While their representations in Section 9.3 are perhaps the starkest imaginable syntactic pictures of the representations of processes, they do have disadvantages as normal forms. One is the fact that finitely nondeterministic processes over finite Σ would often require a $\sqcap S$ construct, with infinite S, in their normal forms. Another is the fact that the highest-level syntactic structure now depends not on the first-step behaviour of the target process (as it did for $\mathcal{N}$) but on all levels. The crucial difference is in the place where nondeterministic choices are made: in the $\mathcal{N}$ normal form (and its construction in Section 9.3) all choices are left as late as possible, whereas in the Section 9.3 constructions for $\mathcal{T}$ and $\mathcal{F}$ a choice is made immediately which effectively determines what the process will do through all time.

There is no need for any nondeterministic choices in a normal form for $\mathcal{T}$: a process is in one-step normal form if it is either

$$?x : A \to P \quad \text{or} \quad (?x : A \to P) \;\square\; SKIP$$

since all we have to specify of a process is what its initial actions are, and how it behaves after each. You can build full normal forms from this one-step form in just the same way as over $\mathcal{N}$.

The normal form for $\mathcal{F}$ is like that for $\mathcal{N}$, though heavily influenced by the radically different role of **div**: see Exercise 11.6.1.

When we were reducing a process to hnf over $\mathcal{N}$, we could be sure that either we would succeed or the process was equivalent to **div** (with this frequently detectable via the rule **Loop**$^{\mathcal{N}}$). How helpful this is can be seen when we look at the contrasting situation in models such as $\mathcal{T}$ which are not divergence-strict.

In $\mathcal{T}$, the fact that a process can diverge does not mean it is identified with **div**. For example, even though you can immediately deduce that it diverges, the process

$$\mu\, p.(a \to Q) \sqcap p[\![R]\!]$$

needs its recursion unwound potentially many times (infinitely if Σ is infinite) just to reveal its first-step behaviour (its initial actions being the smallest set which contains a and is closed under the renaming relation R). The real problem is that the procedure for reducing this process to hnf diverges without the simple answer this inevitably leads to over $\mathcal{N}$.

This means that reduction to hnf (at least, the same hnf) cannot be at the core of a reduction-based operational semantics which faithfully reflects all possible behaviours predicted by $\mathcal{T}$ and $\mathcal{F}$ beyond points of possible divergence. In essence, the strategy is certain to diverge on processes like the above which these models suggest have alternative behaviours. The operational semantics described in Section 11.2 would, if the behaviours they predicted for processes were abstracted into these other models, yield sometimes proper refinements of the denotational semantics of the processes.

The possibility of divergence on reducing a process to hnf also creates problems in reducing an arbitrary process to one-step normal form, since we previously relied on conversion to hnf first. Since these problems do not arise for recursion-free processes, probably the best way of completing the algebraic characterizations of $\mathcal{T}$ and $\mathcal{F}$ is via the concept of syntactic approximations discussed on page 285.

EXERCISE 11.6.1   Show that every member of $\mathcal{F}$ can be expressed in one, and only one, of the following four ways

(i) $(?x : A \to P) \,\square\, \mathbf{div}$

(ii) $(?x : A \to P) \,\square\, SKIP$

(iii) $((?x : A \to P) \,\square\, \mathbf{div}) \sqcap (\sqcap_{i=1}^{N} ?x : A_i \to P)$

(iv) $((?x : A \to P) \,\square\, SKIP) \sqcap (\sqcap_{i=1}^{N} ?x : A_i \to P)$

where in (iii) and (iv) the A_i are all incomparable subsets of A.

Hence define a normal form for $\mathcal{F}$.

Calculate the normal form of the process

$(\mathbf{div} \,\square\, (SKIP \sqcap a \to SKIP)); STOP$

11.7   Notes

Algebraic laws have played an important part in the definition of CSP from its earliest beginnings, and many of those presented here can be found in [17].

The algebraic semantics for the language was first given in Brookes's thesis [14]. The version presented here deals with a wider range of operators (consequently requiring more laws) and deals with recursion differently, but is in most important respects the same.

A closely related algebraic semantics is that of OCCAM [105], which deals with parallel language based on CSP with the added complexity of assignable state. Algebraic approaches to other process calculi may be found in [1, 9, 10, 46, 74] (amongst many other works).

The concept of algebraic reduction as an operational semantics has its origins in the λ-calculus and similar. Hoare and He have advocated their use on more general languages, see [42, 43].

Chapter 12

Abstraction

One view of systems is said to be more abstract than another if it hides more detail, thereby identifying more processes. Greater or lesser abstraction can result from the choice of model used, where, for example, the traces model $\mathcal{T}$ is more abstract thana the stable failures model $\mathcal{F}$. What we will be studying in this chapter are ways in which one can deliberately abstract detail away from a process by applying CSP constructs. We will then apply these ideas to formulating a variety of specifications, including fault tolerance. Perhaps the most important of these is characterizing information flow across processes and hence security.

What we will be doing, in other words, is learning both how to build carefully designed fuzzy spectacles which let us see just that aspect of process behaviour that may seem relevant and, equally importantly, why this activity can be useful.

One such abstraction mechanism is many-to-one renaming, which allows us to ignore distinctions between events which may be irrelevant for some purpose. A typical example of such a renaming might be to ignore the data that passes along a channel by mapping all communications over the channel to a single value. Though we will be using renaming occasionally in the rest of this chapter, the effects of renaming, in itself, as an abstraction are covered in Sections 3.2.2 and 13.6.1 (see Deadlock Rule 15 on page 377 in particular) and we will study the concept of *data-independence*, which in some respects is similar, in Section 15.2.2.

It is worth remarking that many-to-one renaming often introduces nondeterminism, as is well shown by the routeing node example on page 377. In this it has something in common with just about all imaginable abstraction mechanisms: in forming an abstraction you deliberately obscure some detail about how a process behaves and therefore risk losing information about how some choice is made, though the effects of the choice remain visible. Any example of many-to-one renaming introducing nondeterminism illustrates this, such as

$$((a \to c \to STOP) \mathbin{\square} (b \to d \to STOP))[\![^b/a]\!]$$
$$= a \to ((c \to STOP) \mathbin{\sqcap} (d \to STOP))$$

The rest of this chapter is devoted to abstraction mechanisms with one specific aim: taking a process P and a set of events $X \subseteq \Sigma$ and working out what P looks like to a user who can only see the events X (though there may be other users interacting with P in the complement of X).

12.1 Modes of abstraction

Throughout this section we will assume that P is a divergence-free, finitely nondeterministic process with two users, Hugh and Lois, who respectively communicate with P in the disjoint sets of events H and L which contain between them all the events P ever uses, with each user only being able to see his or her own events. If P could ever terminate ($\checkmark$) we would have to worry about which of our two users could see this; to avoid special cases of limited practical use we will assume that P never does terminate. (This does not, of course, exclude the possibility that the definition of P might internally use *SKIP* and sequential composition.)

12.1.1 Lazy and eager abstraction

Given a process P and set of events L, it is tempting to believe that the abstracted view of P in L is given by $P \setminus (\Sigma \setminus L)$. In the traces model $\mathcal{T}$ this is the right answer, but over the richer models the situation is more complex since this definition does not necessarily deal with refusal sets and divergences appropriately. The problem is that the hiding operator $P \setminus X$ assumes that X has passed out of sight and control of the entire environment and hence that events from H become τ actions and thus 'eager'. We will thus identify hiding with *eager* abstraction[1]:

$$\mathcal{E}_H(P) = P \setminus H$$

though we will find that, outside $\mathcal{T}$, this is of rather limited use as a means of abstraction.

If, on the other hand, we believe that the events H are under the control of some other part of P's environment (the other user Hugh) but happen to be

---

[1]When choosing the notation for abstraction there is an important choice we have to make, namely whether to make the set parameter either the events we are abstracting *from*, as done here, or *to*, which would have led us to replace the subscript H here by L. Obviously this is arbitrary.

invisible to *us* (looking at P through Lois's eyes), then when an event in H becomes available it may be either accepted or refused by Hugh. Thus Hugh, from Lois's perspective, gets to introduce nondeterminism into the system both by the choice of *which* action to communicate and also by *whether* to communicate at all. If, for example, Hugh decides to refuse absolutely all communications offered to him, P will appear to act like $P \parallel_H STOP$.

The most general behaviour of the abstracted environment (Hugh) is $Chaos_H$, accepting or refusing any event available to him. This suggests that the right way to form the abstraction is

$$(P \parallel_H Chaos_H) \setminus H$$

and indeed this has a lot to recommend it. However, in the failures/divergences model $\mathcal{N}$, this construction will introduce a divergence whenever P can perform an infinite sequence of events in H even though P is not itself diverging. While you can imagine that this corresponds to the real possibility of Hugh continuously offering events to the process which are accepted, thereby excluding Lois from doing anything, it is, particularly in conjunction with the severe way $\mathcal{N}$ treats divergence, too strong an abstraction for most practical purposes: the divergences typically mask much L behaviour we should really want to see. It is usually better to assume either that Hugh is always sufficiently lazy not completely to use up the process, or equivalently that the implementation is sufficiently *fair* between Hugh and Lois that neither is infinitely excluded simply because of the eagerness of the other. There are three, largely equivalent but stylistically different, ways of constructing a *lazy* abstraction $\mathcal{L}_H(P)$ which behaves like the above except for not introducing the divergences.

Our assumptions about P mean that its representations in the three models $\mathcal{N}$, $\mathcal{U}$ and $\mathcal{F}$ are essentially the same (entirely characterized in each case by the set of stable failures $failures(P)$). The following versions of the abstraction exist, respectively, in these models.

The $\mathcal{N}$ version is best defined by direct manipulation of the failures of P. As P is a divergence-free process, the *projection* of P into the alphabet L is the divergence-free process $P@L$ with failure-set

$$\{(s \setminus H, X) \mid (s, X \cap L) \in failures_\perp(P)\}$$

The main difference between this and the definition of the hiding operator $P \setminus H$ (see page 199) is that it does not insist that the whole of H is refused before generating a failure. This is because Hugh can always refuse all the events in $H \setminus X$. $\mathcal{L}_H^{\mathcal{N}}(P)$ is defined to be $P@L$.

For example, if $L = \{l1, l2\}$ and $H = \{h\}$, we might define P by

$$
\begin{aligned}
P \;=\; & l1 \rightarrow P \\
& \square \; l2 \rightarrow h \rightarrow P \\
& \square \; h \rightarrow P
\end{aligned}
$$

$\mathcal{L}_H^{\mathcal{N}}(P)$ is then equivalent to Q where

$$
\begin{aligned}
Q \;=\; & l1 \rightarrow Q \\
& \square \; l2 \rightarrow (STOP \sqcap Q)
\end{aligned}
$$

Notice that the (finite) traces of $\mathcal{L}_H^{\mathcal{N}}(P)$ are precisely $\{s \setminus H \mid s \in traces(P)\}$, which is what we might have expected and coincides with the abstraction mechanism for $\mathcal{T}$, namely hiding.

The second version, using the infinite traces/failures/divergences model $\mathcal{U}$, can be expressed directly using CSP operators, since in that model we can express fairness properties, as seen in Section 10.3.1. As discussed in Exercise 10.3.5,

$$
SemiFair(A, B) \;=\; RUN_A \;|||\; Fair(A, B)
$$

is a process which never refuses events in A, allows any finite combination of A's and B's, but only allows infinitely many B events to occur if infinitely many A's do as well.

$$
\mathcal{L}_H^{\mathcal{U}}(P) \;=\; (P \;\underset{\Sigma}{\parallel}\; SemiFair(L, H)) \setminus H
$$

cannot diverge unless P can, as the structure of the infinite traces of $SemiFair(L, H)$ prevents new divergences being introduced by the hiding here. The failures of $\mathcal{L}_H^{\mathcal{U}}(P)$ are exactly the same as those of $P@L$. The infinite traces are precisely those infinite traces of P with infinitely many L events, with all H events hidden. (Obviously the other infinite traces of P cannot be mapped sensibly onto infinite traces in L^{ω}, since $u \setminus H$ is then finite. Naturally, it is then a finite trace of $\mathcal{L}_H^{\mathcal{U}}(P)$. This is because u will have a finite prefix s such that $u \setminus H = s \setminus H$ and $SemiFair(L, H)$ does not prevent P performing s.)

It should be remarked that abstraction in $\mathcal{U}$ distinguishes more processes than abstraction in $\mathcal{N}$, since the infinite traces component of the model can vary when the abstraction construct (which is, itself, infinitely nondeterministic) is applied to finitely nondeterministic processes whose $\mathcal{L}_H^{\mathcal{N}}$ abstractions are identical. Examples are $Q1$ and $(Q2; STOP)$, where

$$Q1 \;\; = \;\; l1 \rightarrow Q1$$
$$\sqcap\, h \rightarrow Q1$$

$$Q2 \;\; = \;\; h \rightarrow (Q2; \; l1 \rightarrow SKIP)$$
$$\sqcap\, SKIP$$

Each of $\mathcal{L}_H^{\mathcal{U}}(Q1)$ and $\mathcal{L}_H^{\mathcal{U}}(Q2; \; STOP)$ can perform any number of $l1$'s before refusing this event, but only the abstraction of $Q1$ can perform an infinite trace of $l1$'s, since the only infinite trace of $Q2; \; STOP$ is $\langle h, h, h, \ldots \rangle$. This is a very reasonable distinction to make, but it is one which is only possible over $\mathcal{U}$.

The above discussion shows that lazy abstraction should be added to the list of operators which can have the effect of introducing infinite nondeterminism, and therefore require $\mathcal{U}$ as opposed to $\mathcal{N}$ for full precision. In fact the extra distinctions only become an issue if *either* we need to place lazy abstractions into contexts in which they affect the divergence-set via hiding as discussed in Section 8.3.2, *or* if we want to prove that they meet specifications which constrain infinite traces. None of the examples we will see in the rest of this chapter does either of these things, so the extra precision of $\mathcal{L}_H^{\mathcal{U}}(P)$ is not something we will need.

As we will see later in this chapter, the case where $\mathcal{L}_H(P)$ is deterministic is very important. If the failures of $\mathcal{L}_H^{\mathcal{U}}(P)$ show it to be deterministic then we know (see page 252) that only one set of infinite traces (all those that are limits of finite ones) is possible. Thus, if $\mathcal{L}_H^{\mathcal{N}}(P1) = \mathcal{L}_H^{\mathcal{N}}(P2)$ and this value is deterministic, then also $\mathcal{L}_H^{\mathcal{U}}(P1) = \mathcal{L}_H^{\mathcal{U}}(P2)$.

The third, and for practical purposes the best, way of computing the lazy abstraction is the one over the stable failures model $\mathcal{F}$ where divergence is not a concern for the simple reason that it is not recorded in the model: the value of

$$\mathcal{L}_H^{\mathcal{F}}(P) \;\; = \;\; (P \parallel_H Chaos_H) \setminus H$$

in this model is precisely

$$(traces(P) \setminus H, failures(P@L))$$

because $(s, X \cap L) \in failures(P)$ implies that $(s, X \cup H) \in failures(P \parallel_H Chaos_H)$ and hence

$$(s \setminus H, X) \in failures((P \parallel_H Chaos_H) \setminus H)$$

Since, under our basic assumptions, the traces of $\mathcal{L}_H^{\mathcal{F}}(P)$ are exactly those of its failures, this form of abstraction is identical in strength to $\mathcal{L}_H^{\mathcal{N}}(P)$: these two values being trivially inter-translatable. In fact, it is best to think of $\mathcal{L}_H^{\mathcal{F}}(P)$ as an alternative way of computing $\mathcal{L}_H^{\mathcal{N}}(P)$. Under our assumptions about P,

- the determinism of $\mathcal{L}_H^{\mathcal{F}}(P)$ is equivalent to that of the other two versions, and

- if S is a divergence-free and finitely nondeterministic (specification) process, then the three refinements

$$S \sqsubseteq_F \mathcal{L}_H^{\mathcal{F}}(P) \quad S \sqsubseteq_{FD} \mathcal{L}_H^{\mathcal{N}}(P) \quad S \sqsubseteq_U \mathcal{L}_H^{\mathcal{U}}(P)$$

are all equivalent.

$\mathcal{L}_H^{\mathcal{F}}(P)$ is the best form of lazy abstraction in *practice* simply because it is directly computable by FDR for finite-state P, and the above equivalences mean that in most cases we are free to choose whichever we want. Together with its application to the specification and automated analysis of deadlock discussed around page 213 it provides the main ways of applying $\mathcal{F}$ to tell us things about divergence-free processes P by putting them in contexts $C[P]$ which could introduce divergence if analyzed over $\mathcal{N}$.

Throughout the rest of this chapter we will only use lazy abstraction in circumstances where all three are equivalent, and therefore cease to distinguish between them in our notation: henceforth we will normally simply refer to $\mathcal{L}_H(P)$. Equally, the refinement relation $\sqsubseteq$ will denote any one of the three generally equivalent versions referred to above (i.e., *not* $\sqsubseteq_T$).

The following results are both easy to prove and show the extent to which lazy abstraction really does capture an accurate one-sided view of a process.

LEMMA 12.1.1 *If Σ is partitioned by $\{H, L\}$ and $P = P_L \mathbin{|||} P_H$ where P_L and P_H are processes satisfying the assumptions of this section whose finite traces are respectively contained in L^* and H^*, then $\mathcal{L}_H(P)$ and $\mathcal{L}_L(P)$ respectively equal P_L and P_H.*

A process that can be factored into two components with disjoint alphabets like this is called *separable*. Invariably, separability will be considered relative to a specific pair of alphabets.

The proof of this lemma is left as an exercise.

THEOREM 12.1.2 *If Σ is partitioned by $\{H, L\}$ and P is any process satisfying the basic assumptions of this section, then*

$$P \sqsupseteq \mathcal{L}_L(P) \mathbin{|||} \mathcal{L}_H(P)$$

in any of the three models over which lazy abstraction is defined. Additionally, over the traces model $\mathcal{T}$ we have the analogous result:

$$P \sqsupseteq_T P \setminus H \;|||\; P \setminus L$$

PROOF   We deal with the result over $\mathcal{N}$, which is equivalent to that over $\mathcal{F}$ and implies that over $\mathcal{T}$. Suppose $(s, X) \in failures_{\perp}(P)$. Then, by definition of $P@A$, $(s \setminus H, X) \in failures_{\perp}(\mathcal{L}_H^{\mathcal{N}}(P))$ and $(s \setminus L, X) \in failures_{\perp}(\mathcal{L}_L^{\mathcal{N}}(P))$. Since plainly $s \in (s \setminus H) \;|||\; (s \setminus L)$ for any $s \in \Sigma^*$ (where $|||$ is the trace version of the operator defined on pages 67 and 144), it follows from the definition of $|||$ over $\mathcal{N}$ (see page 199) that

$$(s, X) \in failures_{\perp}(\mathcal{L}_H^{\mathcal{N}}(P) \;|||\; \mathcal{L}_L^{\mathcal{N}}(P))$$

which establishes our result.

The result for $\mathcal{U}$ follows because if u is any infinite trace of P, then $u \setminus H$ and $u \setminus L$ are respectively traces (which may be either finite or infinite) of $\mathcal{L}_H^{\mathcal{U}}(P)$ and $\mathcal{L}_L^{\mathcal{U}}(P)$. u is then an interleaving of these two.   ∎

The above theorem cannot be extended to equivalence: the refinement is often proper, as it is if

$$P \quad = \quad l \to h \to P$$

when $\mathcal{L}_{\{h\}}(P) = l \to Chaos_{\{l\}}$ and $\mathcal{L}_{\{l\}}(P) = Chaos_{\{h\}}$ so that the interleaving of the two abstractions contains *all* traces in $\{l, h\}^*$ rather than the highly restricted set of P. This is hardly surprising, since we would rather expect the behaviour of P visible to Lois to depend on what Hugh does, and *vice-versa*, and the interleaving into two abstractions removes all such influences and hence all linkage between what they see. The lemma above shows that the refinement turns into equality when there demonstrably is no linkage because P is separable. The following result gives an interesting partial converse to this, allowing us to determine when deterministic processes are separable.

COROLLARY 12.1.3 *P is deterministic and separable (over $\{H, L\}$) if and only if the processes $\mathcal{L}_H(P)$ and $\mathcal{L}_L(P)$ are both deterministic.*

PROOF   The '$\Longrightarrow$' half of this result follows from the lemma and properties of determinism. For the '$\Longleftarrow$' half, suppose both the abstractions are deterministic. Then, as the alphabetized parallel operator $_A\|_B$ preserves determinism (see page 219), so is

$$\mathcal{L}_H(P) \;_L\|_H\; \mathcal{L}_L(P) \;=\; \mathcal{L}_H(P) \;|||\; \mathcal{L}_L(P)$$

But we know that P refines this process, so the two must be equal by maximality of deterministic processes under refinement. ∎

For example, this shows that the deterministic process $P = l \to h \to P$ considered above is *not* separable, since its two abstractions are both nondeterministic. On the other hand, the process $Q(n)$ defined

$$Q(n) = h \to Q(n)$$
$$\quad\quad \Box \left((l \to Q(n-1)) \blacktriangleleft n > 0 \blacktriangleright STOP\right)$$

is separable, since its abstractions are respectively

$$\overbrace{l \to \ldots \to l}^{n} \to STOP \quad \text{and} \quad \mu\, p.h \to p$$

The above series of results, and especially the last, hints at one of the most important uses of abstraction: characterizing when one user of P can influence what another user sees. We will return to this in Section 12.4.

12.1.2   Mixed abstraction

While lazy abstraction is the one truest to the underlying philosophy of CSP, it is sometimes necessary to weaken the assumption that the abstracted user Hugh can delay all events he sees. One quite often builds models of systems in CSP whose alphabets contain some events that the environment really can delay – typically inputs to the system – and some, perhaps outputs, that it would be more comfortable to picture as not *really* delayable. If Hugh is sitting at a workstation, his keystrokes would naturally be thought of as delayable actions, but outputs displayed on the VDU would not. In many respects, undelayable *signal* events have much in common with the way the termination signal $\checkmark$ is thought of (see Chapter 6).[2] As long as such events remain visible, this is not much of a concern since we can take account of the differences between events in specifying and animating the process. But, if they are to be abstracted, one can get undesirable results if the signal events are abstracted lazily.

---

[2] It would be possible to take this analogy further and develop models in which Σ was partitioned into delayable events and signals; the semantic treatment of signals would then be very like that we have developed for $\checkmark$. We have not done so in this book in the interests of purity (sticking close to Hoare's original concept of CSP) and simplicity. Without this special modelling, signals only really make sense at the external interface of a process with its environment unless one is extremely careful to make sure that whatever process context they are placed in does not delay them. There are close connections between these ideas and some of those we will meet when we model timed processes in Chapter 14.

The right abstraction to use is then a *mixed* one, with delayable events treated lazily and signal events abstracted eagerly (i.e., by ordinary hiding). If S are P's signal events then we define

$$\mathcal{M}_H^S(P) \; = \; \mathcal{L}_H(P \setminus (H \cap S))$$

Essentially, this treats the events in $H \cap S$ exactly as though they are internal actions of the abstracted process. This is reasonable since they are invisible to Lois and cannot be delayed by anyone. There is a potential problem in this definition, namely that the hiding $P \setminus (H \cap S)$ might either introduce divergence or (if the hidden set is infinite) unbounded nondeterminism; either of these take it outside the domain over which we have defined lazy abstraction. While one should be aware of the second problem, it will rarely occur in practice since in practical examples process alphabets are usually finite, and all it would mean in any case is that we would be forced to compute the two abstractions over $\mathcal{U}$.

Divergence of $P \setminus (H \cap S)$ corresponds to an infinite unbroken sequence of signal events from P to Hugh. We might well think that this sort of behaviour, which gives Hugh no opportunity to be lazy and gives Lois a slice of P's attention, is more compellingly identified with divergence, from her perspective, than the type we so carefully avoided when defining lazy abstraction. Whatever one thinks, the process produced by this hiding is not one to which lazy abstraction can be applied, and so we have to stipulate that mixed abstraction is only used for processes where the inner hiding does not introduce divergence. In any case where this is a danger, you should, if using FDR, establish this divergence freedom separately before computing the abstracted process $\mathcal{M}_H^S(P)$ which, as with $\mathcal{L}_H(P)$, is then evaluated over $\mathcal{F}$. Over this model it equals

$$(P \parallel_{H \setminus S} Chaos_{H \setminus S}) \setminus H$$

EXAMPLE 12.1.1 This form of abstraction is often the appropriate one for processes in which each transaction with a user comprises an input from the user followed by some finite sequence of responses. Consider, for example, a memory device with the following specification:

$$
\begin{aligned}
Mem(s) \;\; = \;\; & write?user?a?v \rightarrow \\
& \quad (ok.user \rightarrow Mem(update(s, a, v)) \\
& \quad \triangleleft a \in WriteAddresses(user) \triangleright \\
& \quad (reject.user \rightarrow Mem(s))) \\
\square \;\; & read?user?a \rightarrow \\
& \quad (value.user!fetch(s, a) \rightarrow Mem(s) \\
& \quad \triangleleft a \in ReadAddresses(user) \triangleright \\
& \quad (reject.user \rightarrow Mem(s)))
\end{aligned}
$$

The functions *update* and *fetch* respectively modify the state s to execute a write, and look up the value for a read.

Here, we would expect the events in $\{| \; write, read \; |\}$ to be delayable, and $S = \{| \; ok, reject, value \; |\}$ to be the signals. We will, naturally, assume that the set of users is $\{Hugh, Lois\}$. If you use lazy abstraction on this, then the abstracted views can both deadlock immediately because it is assumed that the hidden user might initiate a read or write and then refuse the response it gets.

Mixed abstraction does not predict these deadlocks. The only way (it says) that either user can affect the other is by writing to variables readable by the other: if L is the set of Lois's events, then $\mathcal{M}_H^S(Mem(s))$ is equivalent to the process $M_L(s)$, where

$$
\begin{aligned}
M_L(s) \quad = \quad & write.Lois?a?v \to \\
& \quad (ok.Lois \to M_L(update(s, a, v)) \\
& \quad \mathord{<\!\!\!\!\!\!<} a \in WriteAddresses(Lois) \mathord{>\!\!\!\!\!\!>} \\
& \quad (reject.Lois \to M_L(s))) \\
\square \quad & read.Lois?a \to \\
& \quad ((value.Lois!fetch(s, a) \to M_L(s) \\
& \quad \quad \mathord{<\!\!\!\!\!\!<} a \notin WriteAddresses(Hugh) \mathord{>\!\!\!\!\!\!>} \\
& \quad \quad \sqcap \{value.Lois!v \to M_L(s) \mid v \in T\}) \\
& \quad \mathord{<\!\!\!\!\!\!<} a \in ReadAddresses(Lois) \mathord{>\!\!\!\!\!\!>} \\
& \quad (reject.Lois \to M_L(s)))
\end{aligned}
$$

Here, T is the (finite, to avoid difficulties with unbounded nondeterminism) type of the values stored in the memory. The nondeterminism in this abstraction relates to the fact that Lois has no way of knowing, when she reads a value that is writeable-to by Hugh, what the value will be. On the assumption that T has more than one member, this process will be deterministic if, and only if,

$$ReadAddresses(Lois) \cap WriteAddresses(Hugh) \; = \; \{\}$$

It might have been preferable, in formulating the above, to have restricted the range of memory locations held in the parameter s of $M_L(s)$ relative to the original (i.e., only retaining those accessible by Lois). The semantics of the result would not, however, differ from the version where the full range is retained, provided of course that everything was done appropriately. *(End of example)*

EXERCISE 12.1.1   Find as simple as possible representations, as CSP processes, of the following lazy abstractions.

(i) $\mathcal{L}_{\{down\}}(COUNT_0)$ (see page 16)

(ii) $\mathcal{L}_{\{up\}}(COUNT_0)$

(iii) $\mathcal{L}_{\{up,down\}}(Counter(0,0))$ (see page 26)

(iv) $\mathcal{L}_A(COPY)$, where $A = \{left.a, right.a \mid a \in V\}$ for $\{\} \neq V \subset T$, T being the type of *left* and *right*.

Which of these processes is separable (in each case relative to the partition of its alphabet implied by the abstraction quoted above)?

EXERCISE 12.1.2   Show that $\mathcal{L}_\Sigma(P) = STOP$ and $\mathcal{L}_{\{\}}(P) = P$ for every P satisfying the assumptions quoted at the start of this section.

Show that $\mathcal{L}_A^{\mathcal{F}}(\mathcal{L}_B^{\mathcal{F}}(P)) = \mathcal{L}_{A\cup B}^{\mathcal{F}}(P)$ for any A, B and P.

EXERCISE 12.1.3   Let V and A be as in Exercise 12.1.1 (iv) above. Describe the behaviour, respectively, of the mixed abstractions

(i) $\mathcal{M}_A^{\{|right|\}}(COPY)$

(ii) $\mathcal{M}_A^{\{|right|\}}(COPY \gg COPY)$

Which of these is deterministic? How would you expect the same abstraction to behave applied to an N-fold chaining of $COPY$ (i.e., an N-place deterministic buffer)?

EXERCISE 12.1.4   Suppose we were to replace the formulation of $\mathcal{L}_H^{\mathcal{U}}(P)$ on page 298 by the following:

$$\hat{\mathcal{L}}_H^{\mathcal{U}}(P) = (P \parallel_H FINITE_H) \setminus H$$

where $FINITE_H$ is the process (defined as on page 254) which can communicate any finite trace of events from H, but no infinite trace. Show that this always has exactly the same set of failures as the other lazy abstractions, but can differ from $\mathcal{L}_H^{\mathcal{U}}(P)$ in its set of infinite traces. Find a process P which demonstrates this difference.

Does any refinement relation hold between the two versions (for all allowable P)? Find a reason why $\mathcal{L}_H^{\mathcal{U}}(P)$ is the better of the two.

EXERCISE 12.1.5   Prove Lemma 12.1.1 for the failures/divergences model $\mathcal{N}$.

EXERCISE 12.1.6   Show that, for any P, Q and X, the equivalence

$$(P \parallel_X Q) \parallel_H Chaos_H = (P \parallel_H Chaos_H) \parallel_X (Q \parallel_H Chaos_H)$$

holds in $\mathcal{F}$. Deduce that, if $H \cap X = \{\}$, then

$$\mathcal{L}_H(P \parallel_X Q) = \mathcal{L}_H(P) \parallel_X \mathcal{L}_H(Q)$$

and hence that

$$\mathcal{L}_H(P \vertiii Q) = \mathcal{L}_H(P) \vertiii \mathcal{L}_H(Q)$$

12.2   Reducing specifications

It is very common to want to prove that a process P meets a specification S which refers only to a subset of its events. It makes no sense to ask the direct question '$S \sqsubseteq P$?', since we know it will fail. We have either to extend S so that it allows the extra events of P, without specifying anything about them, or to abstract the extra events away from P.

With *traces* specifications, there is little difficulty about achieving this either way. If X are the events of P that we want to ignore, then we should establish either

$$S \;|||\; RUN_X \sqsubseteq_T P \quad \text{or} \quad S \sqsubseteq_T P \setminus X$$

For example, to prove that a pair a and b of actions alternate, irrespective of any other events P might do, we could establish the refinement

$$\mu\, p.a \to b \to p \;\sqsubseteq_T\; P \setminus (\Sigma \setminus \{a, b\})$$

On the whole it is better to take the hiding approach rather than the one of boosting the specification. It is arguably clearer, especially when examining any failure of the specification, but the main argument is in terms of efficiency when running FDR. If the set X is large, the process $S \;|||\; RUN_X$ may be slow to normalize, whereas the act of hiding X in P frequently enables the result to be compressed (as described in Section C.2), thereby substantially speeding up the check.

When the specification S involves failures, we have to worry not only about how to abstract away from events that P may perform outside the alphabet of S, but also how to deal with its refusals. Perhaps the most spectacular example of a failures specification abstracted has already been seen in Section 8.4, where we found that, over $\mathcal{F}$, P is deadlock-free if and only if $P \setminus \Sigma$ is. Thus, apparently, we can reduce deadlock freedom to a specification with an empty alphabet! What turns out to be important here is the way the (many) irrelevant events are abstracted: by doing so eagerly, we have said that the only relevant refusal sets are those where *all* the abstracted events are refused.

To generalize this, over $\mathcal{F}$, with X being the 'extra' events as before,

$$S \sqsubseteq_F P \setminus X$$

means that, in addition to $S \sqsubseteq_T P \setminus X$, whenever $(s, Y \cup X) \in \textit{failures}(P)$ then $(s \setminus X, Y) \in \textit{failures}(S)$. But this says nothing whatsoever about P's refusals in any state where it does not reject the whole of X. This may or may not be what we want. For example, it does not allow us to make the specification 'P always offers either a or b', since in fact

$$\mu\, p.(a \to p) \sqcap (b \to p) \sqsubseteq_F P \setminus (\Sigma \setminus \{a, b\})$$

is (for $\checkmark$-free P) another equivalent of 'P is deadlock-free'.

The obvious alternative is to replace eager abstraction by lazy abstraction and, indeed,

$$\mu\, p.(a \to p) \sqcap (b \to p) \sqsubseteq \mathcal{L}_{\Sigma \setminus \{a, b\}}(P)$$

says exactly what we wanted, namely that every stable state of P can perform either a or b. Thus,

- we should *eagerly* abstract X if, as with the deadlock specification, we are only interested in those refusals which occur when *every* member of X is impossible, and

- we should *lazily* abstract X if, as is more likely in other situations, we are concerned about P's refusals in the alphabet of S at other times as well.

Given our discussion in the previous section, one would expect that $\mathcal{L}_{\Sigma \setminus X}(P)$ will normally give the right abstraction into the alphabet of S and therefore be the correct process to test. Of course, if some of the events in X were signals and therefore not delayable by the environment, it would be appropriate to use mixed abstraction instead. We will see some important examples of this in Chapter 14. Perhaps the right way of looking at the deadlock specification is as an extreme example of this: it is not that we are assuming that the environment *cannot* delay any event, only that if it is testing for deadlock then it is reasonable to assume that it *chooses* not to.

As discussed in Section 8.4, one of the main advantages of the abstracted proof of deadlock freedom is the compression it often makes possible when performing a check using FDR. This is brought about by pushing the hiding as far into a parallel system as possible. The formulation of $\mathcal{L}_H^{\mathcal{F}}(P)$ on page 299 does not directly show how to extend these manipulations of lazy abstraction: $\langle$hide-$\|$-dist$\rangle$ (3.8) is X no longer directly applicable since the entire hidden set P is synchronized (with *Chaos*$_H$) immediately below the hiding. Fortunately, however, it is possible to combine $\langle$hide-$\|$-dist$\rangle$ with properties of *Chaos* to establish rules for pushing lazy X abstraction down through a process: see Exercise 12.2.1.

EXAMPLE 12.2.1 A *token ring* is a parallel network organized as a ring. It is designed so that there are a fixed number of tokens that exist in the ring, each conveying some privilege on the node containing it. For example, if there is only one, ownership of the token might permit the node to perform some critical operation which must not be simultaneously executed in more than one place at once. (This is another view of the mutual exclusion problem, discussed briefly on page 4.)

A very simple implementation of this might be

$$
\begin{aligned}
Empty(i) &= ring.i \rightarrow Full(i) \\
Full(i) &= ring.i \oplus 1 \rightarrow Empty(i) \\
&\quad \Box\; start\text{-}cr.i \rightarrow end\text{-}cr.i \rightarrow Full(i) \\[4pt]
Ring &= \big\|_{i=0}^{N-1} (Full(i) \blacktriangleleft i = 0 \blacktriangleright Empty(i), A_i) \\
&\quad \text{where } A_i = \{ring.i, ring.i \oplus 1, start\text{-}cr.i, end\text{-}cr.i\}
\end{aligned}
$$

and the events $start\text{-}cr.i$ and $end\text{-}cr.i$ respectively represent the start and end of i executing a critical region. The intention is that at all times exactly one process has the token.

We might want to specify this in the alphabet $CR = \{|\; start\text{-}cr, end\text{-}cr\; |\}$ as follows:

$$
Spec = \bigsqcap \{ start\text{-}cr.i \rightarrow end\text{-}cr.i \rightarrow Spec \mid i \in \{0, \ldots, N-1\} \}
$$

Interpreted as a failures specification, this says that the ring is always able to perform some event in CR, and furthermore the events in this set that do occur comprise the sequencing of a number of disjoint critical regions. Of course, exactly *which* process is allowed to perform $start\text{-}cr.i$ will depend on where the token is.

We can test this specification of the ring by the abstracted check

$$
Spec \sqsubseteq \mathcal{L}_{\{|ring|\}}(Ring)
$$

This is true, and essentially says that however the passing of tokens round the ring is managed, *Spec* holds.

There will be further discussion of token rings in Exercise 13.2.4 and elsewhere. *(End of example)*

EXERCISE 12.2.1   Use the results of Exercises 12.1.2 and 12.1.6 to prove that

$$
\mathcal{L}_H^{\mathcal{F}}(P \;_A\|_B Q) = \mathcal{L}_{(A\cap B\cap H)}^{\mathcal{F}}(\mathcal{L}_{(H\cap A)\setminus B}^{\mathcal{F}}(P) \;_A\|_B \mathcal{L}_{(H\cap B)\setminus A}^{\mathcal{F}}(Q))
$$

where $L' = L \cup (A \cap B) \cup (\Sigma \setminus (A \cup B))$. Secondly, prove algebraically that

$$
\mathcal{L}_H^{\mathcal{F}}(P \setminus X) = (\mathcal{L}_{L\setminus X}^{\mathcal{F}}(P)) \setminus X
$$

Combine these two principles to produce a rule for pushing $\mathcal{L}_H^{\mathcal{F}}$ into processes of the form $(P \;_A\|_B\; Q) \setminus A \cap B$.

This question is formulated in terms of $\mathcal{F}$ because $\mathcal{L}$ has the easiest CSP formulation over this model.

EXERCISE 12.2.2   Let S be a divergence-free, finitely nondeterministic and $\checkmark$-free process.

(a)   Show that $S \sqsubseteq \mathcal{L}_H(P)$ if, and only if,

$$S \;|||\; Chaos_{\Sigma \setminus L} \sqsubseteq P$$

Hint: use the series of results beginning on page 300 and monotonicity properties.

(b)   Show that $S \sqsubseteq \mathcal{L}_H(P)$ if, and only if,

$$S \;|||\; RUN_{\Sigma \setminus L} \sqsubseteq P \;|||\; RUN_P$$

Hint: use a similar argument to part (a), plus the result of Exercise 12.1.6.

12.3   Abstracting errors: specifying fault tolerance

CSP is often used for modelling systems with unreliable or potentially faulty components, the intention being to overcome these errors and preserve all, or a defined subset, of their functionality. The main examples we have seen so far have been unreliable communication media in Chapter 5, as well as subsequent further investigations of the alternating bit protocol in Sections 8.4 and 10.3.1.

The approach to error modelling used so far has been the most obvious one: namely to make the occurrence of each error a nondeterministic choice introduced by $\sqcap$: see, for example, the definitions of E_0 on page 118 and $C(in, out)$ on page 130. In systems with potential faults it is usually the case that, if errors happen in a totally unrestricted way, then at least some of the intended behaviour is lost. This is certainly true of the example designed to overcome message corruption on page 119, where we built our model of the medium so that it commits at most one error for every three transmissions: if we had allowed the corruption of any message, then neither the transmitter and receiver defined there nor any others could overcome this. Even the alternating bit protocol relies on there not being so many errors as to create an infinite sequence of consecutive losses or duplications. A fault-tolerant system created (as is common) by replicating functionality (such as processors) and using a voting mechanism will only be immune to some finite limit of errors which disable individual elements: plainly it will not function if *all* the processors are disabled.

It is often easier to understand the relationship between the pattern of errors that occur and the behaviour of the entire system if the errors appear in traces. In other words, each fault, when it occurs, is signposted by some event. It is usually simple to adapt CSP models of faults to reflect this: instead of being selected by a nondeterministic choice, errors are triggered by special events placed in the alphabet specially and not confused with the 'ordinary' events of the processes concerned. Thus the loss/duplication medium $C(in, out)$ for the alternating bit protocol would become:

$$
\begin{aligned}
C_E(in, out) &= in?x \rightarrow \quad (out!x \rightarrow C'_E(in, out, x) \\
&\qquad\qquad\qquad \Box \; loss \rightarrow C_E(in, out)) \\
C'_E(in, out, x) &= dup \rightarrow out!x \rightarrow C'_E(in, out, x) \\
&\qquad \Box \; C_E(in, out)
\end{aligned}
$$

Each time a message is input it can be lost if *loss* occurs, and once it has been output once it can be duplicated arbitrarily often if *dup* is communicated.

You should imagine that the events $E = \{loss, dup\}$ are under the control of some dæmon that can choose whether or not to introduce errors. We could get back to the original medium by abstracting away these events:

$$
\mathcal{L}_E(C_E(in, out)) = C(in, out)
$$

When building a model of a faulty process where the errors are controlled by extra events, you should aim to create one where the lazy abstraction, as above, is equivalent to the version in which the errors occur nondeterministically. Conversely, if you prevent the errors from occurring by synchronizing with $STOP$, as in $C_E(in, out) \underset{E}{\|} STOP$, you should get a process equivalent to perfect behaviour of the component in question. In this case it is a suitably renamed version of $COPY$.

When the components with these visible errors are put into the entire network, we can fulfil our wish to see directly how the occurrence of faults affects runs of the system. One simply places the erroneous processes into the system and leaves the error events unsynchronized. In cases like the alternating bit protocol, where there are several erroneous components, it is a good idea to ensure that the error events of each are distinct. This is so that the errors in the different components can be distinguished when analyzing the behaviour later. Thus the alternating bit protocol might become

$$
ABP_E = ((S \underset{\{|a,d|\}}{\|} (C1_E \; ||| \; C2_E)) \underset{\{|b,c|\}}{\|} R) \setminus \{|\, a, b, c, d \,|\}
$$

where S and R are as previously and

$$C1_E = C_E(a, b)$$
$$C2_E = C_E(c, d)[\![loss', dup'/loss, dup]\!]$$

We thus extend E to be $\{loss, loss', dup, dup'\}$.

Having constructed a system with visible errors like this, we can either abstract them immediately or put bounds on the circumstances in which they occur before doing so. It turns out that the first of these options is what is required for the alternating bit protocol. The lazy abstraction $\mathcal{L}_E(ABP_E)$ is the natural one to look at: it is well-defined since ABP_E is finitely nondeterministic and is, provided R and S are correctly defined as in Section 5.3, divergence-free. This form of abstraction correctly reflects our expectations of this protocol, namely that an error can happen at any time but we should never *rely* on one happening. The fairness assumptions built into lazy abstraction also correspond closely to the fact that the protocol works provided the channels are not permitted to commit an infinite series of errors. If S and R are as defined in Section 5.3, it is true that

$$COPY \sqsubseteq \mathcal{L}_E(ABP_E)$$

What this establishes precisely is that the alternating bit protocol refines this specification *provided* only finitely many errors of any sort occur between each pair of visible actions. Another way of saying the same thing is that, whatever errors have occurred in the past, if whatever dæmon is selecting them stops doing so for long enough, the protocol will come into a state where it can make the progress required by the specification.

This lazy abstraction into non-error events gives what is probably the best general-purpose picture of the way a system with potential errors can behave under the assumption that errors do not exclude everything else. However, what we have shown in this case is not precisely the same as was proved in Section 10.3.1 where we looked directly at how infinite traces can analyze the protocol. There the infinitary relation was directly over the two internal channels, whereas here it is between the errors and the external communications of the entire protocol. While the difference does not appear to be of great importance in this example, this is not always so: see Exercise 12.3.3. It teaches us one general lesson, namely that *if* you want to relate the errors that occur to some internal events of your system, then you *must* delay hiding the latter until after the comparison has been made.

The best way to assume a stronger bound on error behaviour than that expressed implicitly by lazy abstraction is by putting a constraining process in parallel with either the whole system or an appropriate part of it. Such a bound is likely to take one of two forms: either a limit on the total number of errors that can occur through all time (perhaps with separate limits for different types of errors) or a limit on how many errors can occur relative to some other behaviour, in which case, of course, the limitation must be imposed before any of the comparative actions have been hidden.

Imagine, for example, a supposedly fault-tolerant processor built out of four identical units enclosed in a context which feeds them all identical inputs and gathers all their results.[3] There are at least two different modes of failure of one of the processors: they might simply die in such a way that they never communicate again (i.e., behave like *STOP*) or might become corrupted so that they can be relied on for nothing, not even not communicating (the most appropriate model then being *Chaos*$_A$ where A is the failing processor's alphabet). In this latter case we are assuming that a corrupted processor might, either through luck or, in some applications, malice, do whatever it can to make the surrounding hardware's job as difficult as possible. A fault of this second sort is usually termed a *Byzantine* failure.

If *Proc* is a process modelling the correct (and deterministic) behaviour of a processor without faults, then

$$(Proc \, \triangle_{halt} \, STOP) \, \triangle_{byzantine} \, Chaos_A$$

gives a natural way of adding the potential for faulty behaviour. ($P \, \triangle_a \, Q$ is the *interrupt* operator defined on page 235.)

Suppose that the result of composing the entire system, together with these faulty components and the harness used to manage the distribution and collection of data to and from the four processors, is *FTP* (fault-tolerant processor).[4] The important thing from our point of view is that the four sets of fault events are permitted to occur freely (i.e., they do not synchronize with each other or anything else). We will assume that the error events have become

$$E = \{halt.i, byzantine.i \mid i \in \{0, 1, 2, 3\}\}$$

You would not expect *FTP* to work once all four processors have been brought down by faults. And Byzantine faults are likely to be harder to over-

---

[3]In any application like this it is vital that the programs running on the processors are deterministic, since otherwise there might be several valid answers that the various copies could produce, almost certainly leading to confusion in the surrounding voting hardware!

[4]The mechanisms used to do this in the general case are really quite complex and would take too long to describe for this book. One of the major issues is the extent to which the harness itself has to be fault tolerant, since the advantages of running multiple copies of a processor are clearly reduced significantly if you are dependent on some unreplicated piece of hardware to achieve 'fault tolerance'. The mechanisms for achieving fault tolerance frequently use the timed dialect of CSP described in Chapter 14. Some references can be found at the end of this chapter.

come than halting faults. It is, for example, reasonable to expect it to continue working when all but one processor has halted, but it could not work when even two chaotic faults have appeared since the pair of faulty processors might agree on a different answer to a problem than the pair of correct ones; plainly there is no way for a voting system to distinguish which is right. If we wanted to prove that *FTP* was tolerant of one Byzantine, or three halting, faults, the way to do this would be to prove that

$$\mathcal{L}_E(FTP \underset{E}{\parallel} Halt(3)) \quad \text{and} \quad \mathcal{L}_E(FTP \underset{E}{\parallel} Byzantine(1))$$

both meet an appropriate specification (see later), where, for example

$$Halt(n) \quad = \quad halt?i \rightarrow Halt(n-1)$$
$$\langle n > 0 \rangle STOP$$

One of the major applications of the style of error modelling where the number of faults is limited relative to some other set of events is in *timed* modelling, which we will meet in Chapter 14 and where you can express a bound on how many errors occur in a given interval. For example, you could state that no more than 3 errors occur in any 13 time units. See page 409 for more on this.

In general, if you are imposing limits on how many errors occur, it will almost *never* be appropriate to make an implicit assumption that errors *definitely* occur. This means that if the limit is expressed via the parallel composition

$$System_E \underset{A \cup E}{\parallel} Limiter$$

where A is part of the alphabet of $System_E$, then the process *Limiter* should never restrict which members of A occur. In other words,

$$\mathcal{L}_{\Sigma \setminus A}(Limiter) \ = \ RUN_A$$

A process which satisfies this condition is said to be a *monitor* for A: its E behaviour can depend on what it sees in A, but it will never refuse any communication in A.

If, for example, you want *Limiter* to express the condition that no more than N errors occur for every M events in A, an appropriate process to use would be

$$Limit(E, A, N, M) \ = \ Bound(E, A, N) \underset{E}{\parallel} \ldots \underset{E}{\parallel} Bound(E, A, N) \quad (M \text{ copies})$$

where

$$Bound(E, A, n) \quad = \quad ?a : A \rightarrow Bound(E, A, N)$$
$$\square \left((?e : E \rightarrow Bound(E, A, n-1)) \langle n > 0 \rangle STOP \right)$$

is the process which prevents more than N error events happening for every A event. This subtle parallel composition expresses exactly the right condition on traces via the way it synchronizes only on E: it acts as a monitor on A because each $Bound(N)$ does. See Exercise 12.3.4.

The most extreme limitation on errors is to ban them outright. If E is the set of error events in a process $System_E$ modelled with visible errors (perhaps limited in a less severe way), then

$$NoFaults = System_E \underset{E}{\parallel} STOP$$

represents its behaviour under the assumption that no error ever occurs. There is no need to abstract error events in this process since they never occur. The refinement check

$$NoFaults \sqsubseteq \mathcal{L}_E(System_E)$$

has a very interesting interpretation: it says that the system, with error events permitted to the extent allowed by the definition of $System_E$, behaves no worse than the error-free version. In other words, it asserts that $System_E$ is fault tolerant to the extent that it assumes faults can occur. The definition of lazy abstraction implies that the reverse refinement relation holds for any process $System_E$ at all, so proving the above relation actually implies equivalence.

This gives a very clean *definition* of what it means for a process to be fault tolerant, and it is invaluable when faced with a system for which it is difficult to give a complete functional specification in a more abstract way. In using it you should, however, realize that simply proving a system is fault tolerant does not mean it does what you intended. All it means is that any misbehaviour which is present in the version with faults is also there without. For example, the process $Chaos_{A \cup E}$ (which is, of course, refined by any divergence-free process with this alphabet) is fault tolerant because it behaves no worse when faults are allowed than without. Thus it is not, in general, the case that if P is fault tolerant and $P \sqsubseteq Q$ then Q is fault tolerant: fault tolerance is not a *behavioural* specification. (Unlike determinism it does satisfy a distributive law – see Exercise 12.3.5.)

Thus, if faced with the problem of developing a system which combines complex external behaviour with the need for fault tolerance, you should combine the above refinement check with tests of whatever basic functional specifications (such as freedom from deadlock and safety checks) seem appropriate. Of course, it would only be necessary to prove these of the *NoFaults* version.

In conclusion to this section, it is the author's opinion that the approach to modelling faults as controlled by visible actions, subsequently regulated and

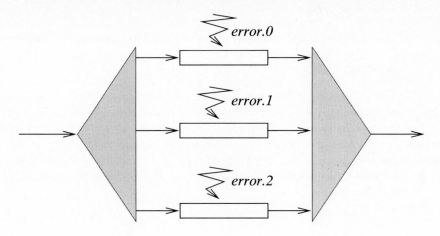

Figure 12.1 Replicating data over multiple lanes (see Exercise 12.3.1).

abstracted, gives a more flexible and usually superior method than simply using nondeterministic choices. The exceptions to its superiority are cases, such as over-coming a specified level of message corruption by replicating messages on page 119, where (i) there is no need to specify patterns of errors above a very low level, (ii) the occurrence of errors is sufficiently bounded to avoid problems with divergence and (iii) the overall system behaviour is sufficiently simple so as to make the abstract specification of fault tolerance above unnecessary.

By their nature, interesting complete examples of fault tolerance are moder-ately complex. Thus it was not possible to give as many examples in this section as we might have wished. The interested reader can, however, find various analy-ses based on the methods described in this section at the associated web site (see Preface for details).

EXERCISE 12.3.1   Define a buffer of bits ($\{0, 1\}$) which uses three error-prone channels as shown in Figure 12.1. Channel i, after communicating the event *error.i*, may corrupt (but, for simplicity, does not lose) any bit it subsequently receives. Each bit is sent separately through the channels and voted on at the other end.

Describe such a system and formulate a refinement check that asserts it is tolerant of one such error.

EXERCISE 12.3.2   Let P be any deterministic process with alphabet A. We can define a process

$$reboot(P) \; = \; P \, \triangle_{error} \, reboot(P)$$

which reboots itself (back to initial state) each time the event *error* ($\notin A$) occurs. Define a context *rebuild*($\cdot$) which, though allowing all *error* events to occur, is such that

$$P = \mathcal{L}_{\{error\}}(rebuild(reboot(P)))$$

Hint: rebuild(Q) should record the external trace. Whenever an error event occurs it should communicate that trace to Q so as to bring it back from its rebooted state to the one it was in before the error. Be careful to take account of any errors that occur during this rebuilding. It is helpful to use $1 \to 2$ renaming on the argument Q so that some of the events it communicates are visible, but a second copy of them is available to be used while resetting, and hidden. Specifically, you do not want to hide the 'normal' actions of Q, but need to hide the rebuilding actions.

Why is it important that P is deterministic?

EXERCISE 12.3.3   Define a process *Alt* which alternately outputs 0 and 1 on channel c, and another *Switch* which inputs values on channel d and communicates the event *switch* each time it inputs a consecutive pair of values that are different. Show that, as defined in this section, with C_E as defined on page 310, the process

$$((Alt \underset{\{|c|\}}{\|} C_E(c,d)) \underset{\{|d|\}}{\|} Switch) \setminus \{| c, d |\}$$

is fault tolerant.

Show that this behaviour is not preserved when $C_E(c, d)$ is replaced by the medium process $C_N(c, d)$ defined on page 130 used in the original version of the alternating bit protocol which guarantees to transmit at least one of each N messages and to duplicate each no more than N times. How does the misbehaviour manifest itself?

This is an illustration of the effect mentioned in the text by which a system is considered fault tolerant, using the lazy abstraction definition, if it works provided there are no more than finitely many faults between consecutive visible actions.

EXERCISE 12.3.4   Prove that the traces of *Limit*(E, A, N, M) (page 313) are precisely those members s of $(A \cup E)^*$ satisfying

$$s = s1\hat{}s2\hat{}s3 \wedge \#(s2 \upharpoonright E) > N \Rightarrow \#(s2 \upharpoonright A) \geq M$$

EXERCISE 12.3.5   Suppose P and Q are both fault tolerant (in the sense defined using *NoFaults*) with respect to the same set E of error events. Show that $P \sqcap Q$ is also fault tolerant.

12.4   Independence and security

In the first section of this chapter we imagined the existence of two users, and formed views of how some process P looks to one of them with the other abstracted away.

Suppose they are working in a security conscious environment, and that Hugh has a higher security classification than Lois. It is a problem of considerable practical importance to understand when information about what Hugh is doing can get to Lois via their joint use of P. You can imagine the following scenarios:

(a) Lois, a spy, attempts to find out about Hugh's interactions with P, the assumption here being that Hugh is unaware of Lois's presence.

(b) Hugh is a 'mole', namely an agent working in the high security levels of his enemies. He is trying to set up a 'covert channel' with Lois, who is his friend on the outside, so that the information he has learned can be relayed back to their spy-masters. Therefore they try to use P to get information from one to the other, and may well have agreed some code in advance.

Though the second of these is, on the face of it, the more challenging problem for the process designer from the point of view of counter-espionage, in an absolute sense they are the same. If no information about what Hugh does ever leaks through to Lois (i.e., P is secure in the sense (a)) then automatically no covert channel can exist since anything a malicious Hugh does under (b) to pass information, an innocent one under (a) might have done 'by accident'. It is only when considering imperfect systems that the two modes should perhaps be differentiated.

Clearly what is important is Lois's abstracted view of P. She can only see what Hugh is doing if what he does affects what she sees. What we are trying to specify is what one can either view *non-interference* (i.e., what Hugh does does not interfere with what Lois sees) or *independence* (i.e., what Lois sees is independent of Hugh). The latter of these two terms is more appropriate for the applications we now have in mind. A very clear specification of this is simply that Lois's view is deterministic: you can think of Hugh as a nondeterminism resolving dæmon within an abstraction such as $\mathcal{L}_H(P)$, so if the abstraction is actually deterministic then none of his choices is reflected in what she sees. You should use either lazy or mixed abstraction depending on the nature of the interface between Hugh and P.

For a finitely nondeterministic, divergence and $\checkmark$-free process P we can thus *define*

- P is *lazily* independent from H (written $\mathcal{L}\mathrm{IND}_H(P)$) if and only if $\mathcal{L}_H(P)$ is deterministic, and

- P is *mixed*, or *transaction*[5] independent from H, with respect to the set of signals S (written $\mathcal{M}\mathrm{IND}_H^S(P)$) if and only if $\mathcal{M}_H^S(P)$ is deterministic.

---

[5]The term *transaction* independence (used by Wulf [122]) derives from the most common use of mixed abstraction: interpreting the output phases of transactions such as those seen in the memory example on page 303 correctly.

There is a clear connection between this definition and Corollary 12.1.3, since it is evident that the condition of *separability* is closely related to security. After all, a process which is built as the parallel composition of two processes which do not synchronize and respectively serve only Hugh and only Lois is self-evidently secure. Indeed, some authors have used it as one definition of non-interference/ independence. It has two disadvantages: the easier to understand is that it is clearly symmetric whereas independence is not. We do not mind Hugh being able to see what Lois can do, since we have not banned information flowing that way. We will discuss the second disadvantage later.

The best way to understand our definitions is to see some examples. Let $L = \{l, l1, l2, ls1, ls2\}$, $H = \{h, h1, h2, hs1, hs2\}$ and $S = \{ls1, ls2, hs1, hs2\}$ (the set of signal events). The following simple processes show the main ways security and insecurity manifest themselves.

1. Let $P1 = h \to l \to P1$. This is insecure because $\mathcal{L}_H(P1) = Chaos_{\{l\}}$, which is nondeterministic. Intuitively, this process is insecure because Lois can see exactly how many events Hugh has performed.

2. On the other hand, $P2 = (h \to l \to P2) \,\square\, (l \to P2)$ is secure, since $\mathcal{L}_H(P2) = \mu\, p.l \to p$. It is not, however, separable since the abstraction into H is nondeterministic. The fact that l can always occur means that Lois can no longer count h's by counting l's.

3. Define

$$
\begin{aligned}
P3 &= l1 \to P3' \\
&\quad \square\; h1 \to P3
\end{aligned}
$$

$$
\begin{aligned}
P3' &= l2 \to P3 \\
&\quad \square\; h2 \to P3'
\end{aligned}
$$

   $P3$ is secure since $\mathcal{L}_H(P3) = \mu\, p.l1 \to l2 \to p$. It is not secure in the reverse direction since

$$
\mathcal{L}_L(P3) = \mu\, q.(h1 \to q) \sqcap (h2 \to q)
$$

   The point is that only Lois controls which state ($P3$ or $P3'$) it is in, but Hugh can detect the state by looking which of $h1$ and $h2$ is permitted. Thus information can pass from Lois to Hugh but not back.

4. The following process, unlike those seen so far, uses signal events:

$$
\begin{aligned}
P4 &= l1 \to ls1 \to P4 \\
&\quad \square\; l2 \to ls2 \to P4 \\
&\quad \square\; h1 \to hs1 \to P4 \\
&\quad \square\; h2 \to hs2 \to P4
\end{aligned}
$$

You can think of this process as one that both Hugh and Lois can ask questions of by inputting values, and it gives them the appropriate answer back as a signal. The lazy abstraction of this process is nondeterministic, since if Hugh could delay the events $hs1$ and $hs2$ then Lois could tell he was doing so (and had input some value). The mixed abstraction $\mathcal{M}_H^S(P4)$ is, however, deterministic and so this process satisfies $\mathcal{MIND}_L^S(\cdot)$. This is appropriate, since its behaviour towards Lois does not depend on what Hugh has done.

5. If Hugh is certain to receive a signal at some point then the fact that he does does not convey information to Lois. Thus the following process satisfies $\mathcal{MIND}_L^S(\cdot)$, since to Lois it looks exactly like $\mu\, p.l \to p$.

$$P5 \;=\; hs1 \to l \to P5$$

6. On the other hand, if Lois can tell something about *which* signal Hugh received, then we get an insecure process, and indeed

$$
\begin{aligned}
P6 \;=\;\; & hs1 \to l1 \to P6 \\
& \sqcap\, hs2 \to l2 \to P6
\end{aligned}
$$

fails the mixed condition. This only applies when, as in this example, the value Hugh gets is not predictable on the basis of what Lois legitimately knows.

Now look back to the memory example on page 303. The work we did there shows that this is secure, for $\mid T \mid > 1$, if and only if there is no location that Hugh can write to and Lois can read. This is, of course, exactly what one might expect. This is perhaps the simplest of a wide range of situations where our two users are both reading and writing to some system. Some extensions that can lead to further security difficulties are listed below.

- They might be reading and writing to files, which have to be *created* using some name. It is possible for information to flow by Lois testing, by trying to create a file with a given name, whether Hugh has one of the same name open. (This assumes that either user will have a request to create a file refused if the other has one with the chosen name.)

- There might be contention for resources: if what Hugh does affects whether there is room (in memory, on disk etc.) for an action of Lois to be executed, then information can flow.

- Instead of the transactions on the data being only atomic reads and writes, they may comprise series of actions which require *locks* to be placed on some data items (usually non-exclusive read locks or exclusive write locks). If

Hugh were to place a read lock on a location Lois wants to write to, then it is possible for information to flow.

All of these situations have been dealt with successfully via the methods described in this chapter. For more details, see [107, 122] and the worked examples on the web site (see Preface).

EXAMPLE 12.4.1 (SHARING A COMMUNICATION MEDIUM) Interference, and hence information flow, can also appear in other applications where high-level and low-level processes share resources. One of these is shared communication media. Suppose Hugh and Lois respectively want to send messages to Henry and Leah, who share their security clearances. Consider the network

$$Comm_1 = ((SendH \;|||\; SendL) \underset{\{|in|\}}{\|} Medium) \underset{\{|out|\}}{\|} (RecH \;|||\; RecL)$$

where

$$
\begin{aligned}
SendL &= send.lois?x \to in.lois.leah!x \to SendL \\
SendH &= send.hugh?x \to in.hugh.henry!x \to SendH \\
RecL &= out.leah?x \to rec.leah!x \to RecL \\
RecH &= out.henry?x \to rec.henry!x \to RecH \\
Medium &= in?s?t?x \to out!t!x \to Medium
\end{aligned}
$$

Even though the high-level processes cannot send messages to the low-level ones through this system, it does not satisfy the obvious lazy security property. Despite the buffering provided at the two ends, it is possible for the high-level processes to block up the network if Henry refuses to accept the messages that arrive for him. This means that the low-level lazy abstraction is nondeterministic: the low-level processes can detect certain high-level activity via their own messages being blocked.

The following two solutions illustrate much more widely applicable methods for overcoming security problems which arise, like this one, from contention for resources.

The first solution is simply to give the low-level users priority in access to resources: we could replace the process *Medium* by

$$
\begin{aligned}
Medium2 &= in.lois?t?x \to out!t!x \to Medium2 \\
&\quad\; \Box \; in.hugh?t?x \to Medium2'(t, x) \\
Medium2'(t, x) &= in.lois?t'?x' \to out!t'!x' \to Medium2 \\
&\quad\; \Box \; out!t!x \to Medium2
\end{aligned}
$$

This simply throws away any high-level communication that is sitting in the medium when a low-level one comes along. In the revised system, $Comm_2$, the low view becomes deterministic (it is a 3-place buffer), but there is the great disadvantage of losing some high level messages. That in turn can be got around by a further revised medium informing a modified *SendH* whether each message got through successfully or not, with each thrown-away message being resent.

$$SendH3 \quad = \quad send.hugh?x \to in.hugh.henry!x \to SendH3'(x)$$

$$SendH3'(x) \quad = \quad ok.hugh \to SendH3$$
$$\square \ ref.hugh \to in.hugh.henry!x \to SendH3'(x)$$

$$Medium3 \quad = \quad in.lois?t?x \to out!t!x \to Medium3$$
$$\square \ in.hugh?t?x \to Medium3'(t, x)$$

$$Medium3'(t, x) \quad = \quad in.lois?t'?x' \to ref.hugh \to out!t'!x' \to Medium3$$
$$\square \ out!t!x \to ok.hugh \to Medium3$$

This addition, producing $Comm_3$, preserves security and re-establishes the link between Hugh and Henry as a trace-correct buffer (with capacity reduced from 3 to 2). Except for this reduction in capacity, the system now gives essentially the same behaviour towards Hugh and Henry as did the original system, but Lois and Leah cannot now detect what the high-level users are doing.

Attaining security by giving priority to low-level users will not be an ideal solution in many cases. The system designer has to decide, on pragmatic grounds, whether it is better or worse than the other solution, which is to limit individual users' access to the system sufficiently that low-level users are never *further* restricted by high-level activities. In a file system one might, with an overall disk capacity of N, allocate M units to high-level users and $N - M$ to the low-level ones. The analogy in our communication example is to use flow-control to prevent either user deadlocking the system. We reprogram the sender and receiver processes so that the sender waits until it gets a message back from the receiver before it next accepts an input on *send*, and the receiver does not send such a message until it knows it will be able to accept another message. The following processes can be combined with the original *Medium* (from $Comm_1$): the *content* of the reverse messages is irrelevant.

$$SendL4 \quad = \quad send.lois?x \to in.lois.leah!x \to out.lois?x \to SendL4$$

$$SendH4 \quad = \quad send.hugh?x \to in.hugh.henry!x \to out.hugh?x \to SendH4$$

$$RecL4 \quad = \quad out.leah?x \to rec.leah!x \to in.leah.lois.Zero \to RecL4$$

$$RecH4 \quad = \quad out.henry?x \to rec.henry!x \to in.henry.hugh.Zero \to RecH4$$

The resulting $Comm_4$ is not only secure, it is separable and equivalent to the composition of a one-place buffer (i.e., $COPY$) between each of the two pairs of processes. Note that the medium is used more than previously, since two internal messages are required for each external one, but it is used more carefully as each time one of the four processes around it sends a communication to it on *in*, it is impossible for the resulting *out* to be refused. *(End of example)*

We have seen that the natural specifications of both security and fault tolerance involve similar ideas. They are, in fact, closely related specifications. Suppose $\mathcal{L}\text{IND}_H(P)$ holds. The determinism of $\mathcal{L}_H(P)$ easily implies that it equals

$$\mathcal{L}_H(P \underset{H}{\parallel} Q)$$

for any divergence-free process Q with alphabet H. This is reassuring, since it means that what Lois sees does not depend on what high-level process we put in parallel with P. It also means that

$$\mathcal{L}_H(P) = P \underset{H}{\parallel} STOP$$

and so P is 'fault tolerant' if you think of the high-level actions as the errors. This is not surprising, since if there is no way of telling, by looking at the pattern of a process's behaviour in its non-error alphabet, what, if any, errors have occurred, then it must be fault tolerant!

On the other hand, a process can be fault tolerant without the abstraction

$$\mathcal{L}_E(P)$$

being deterministic, so the reverse implication does not hold. The difference is that, when considering fault tolerance we have an inbuilt standard to judge the process against, namely the way it behaves without errors. If it should happen that some error resolves a nondeterministic choice which would have had to be made anyway, this does not matter in judging fault tolerance, but it might convey information to the user about the pattern of errors. See Exercise 12.4.2 for a class of examples.

In real applications one will frequently have more than just the two security levels we have modelled in this section. One could have any number with a partial order *security policy* relating them: user U_i's behaviour can affect U_j if and only if $clearance(i) \leq clearance(j)$. There is, however, no need to extend our theory further since all you have to do is to show that, for each security level λ, the collection of all users with this level or below is independent of the collection of all the others. Thus you simply look at a series of two-way partitions of the overall alphabet. For example, if there is another user Mhairi with alphabet M whose clearance is midway between Hugh's and Lois's, then to establish security of a process P you should prove

$$\mathcal{L}\mathrm{IND}_{H \cup M}(P) \quad \text{and} \quad \mathcal{L}\mathrm{IND}_{H}(P)$$

i.e., neither Hugh nor Mhairi can influence what Lois sees, and Hugh cannot influence what Lois and Mhairi see.

The limitations of security modelling

Security modelling is a subject full of philosophical difficulties, and just about all specifications of what it means for a process to be 'secure' can be criticized in one way or another. A general text is not the place to go into this in detail, but it is as well to understand just what our particular specification can and cannot do.

First and foremost, a security specification couched in a particular model can only reflect information flow via the sort of behaviour the model records. The most obvious thing missing from the models we have used is timing information, and it is certainly possible to construct examples which appear secure over $\mathcal{N}$ which one would suspect might contain 'timing channels' if implemented in the obvious way. The various secure communication examples above, such as $Comm_4$, come into this category as the low users will presumably get a variable bandwidth depending on the level of activity of Hugh and Henry.

By and large, the more detailed a model one chooses, the more complex both process modelling and security analysis become, and (presumably) the more likely we are to find small flaws in security. All one can do is to pick one's model intelligently and be aware of the limitations built into the choice.

As we will see in Chapter 14, it is possible to take time into account in modelling CSP. There is no reason in principle why the determinism-based specification could not be used to specify security over that sort of model too.

There is a clear sense in which the determinism-based condition can be viewed as too strong. It only defines as secure those processes whose low view-point is deterministic. However, it is undoubtedly possible to build a secure process whose low-level abstraction is nondeterministic, since the mechanism resolving the nondeterminism has nothing to do with how the high interface behaves. For example, there are many separable processes whose low-level abstraction is nondeterministic, and clearly any process *implemented* as an interleaving of entirely disjoint high and low-level processes is secure. In this sense,

$$Chaos_{H \cup L} = Chaos_H \;|||\; Chaos_L$$

is secure.

The point you should try to understand, however, is that just because one implementation of a given process is secure, this is no guarantee that all are. For example, if *LEAK* is any divergence-free process whatsoever, for example

$$\mu\, p.hugh?x \rightarrow lois!x \rightarrow p$$

you would not naturally think of

$$Chaos_{H \cup L} \sqcap LEAK$$

as secure since it is free to behave like *LEAK* every single time it is used. The above process is, however, equivalent to $Chaos_{H \cup L}$, and we thus have two process definitions that none of our semantic models can tell apart, one being plainly secure and one insecure. Perhaps the problem is that our models go to great lengths to represent nondeterminism as abstractly as possible, and specifically do not give us information about whether a given nondeterministic decision is resolved innocently or in a way that allows information to flow.

A number of authors have attempted to define conditions to decide whether a general CSP process is secure in the sense we have being trying to capture. Invariably these conditions are satisfied by $Chaos_{H \cup L}$, even though this process is refined by many others which do not satisfy them. We might call this the *refinement paradox*. The idea that P can be secure and $Q \sqsupseteq P$ insecure is contrary to all our understanding of what refinement means. Reassuringly, it is true that if $\mathcal{L}\text{IND}_H(P)$ and $P \sqsubseteq Q$ then $\mathcal{L}\text{IND}_H(Q)$, because by construction

$$P \sqsubseteq Q \;\Rightarrow\; \mathcal{L}_H(P) \sqsubseteq \mathcal{L}_H(Q)$$

and the only refinement of a deterministic process is itself. In truth, it simply is not possible to determine whether a general process is secure by looking at its value in the standard denotational models of CSP.

A good analogy is provided by deadlock freedom: if P is deterministic you can tell if it can deadlock by looking at its value in $\mathcal{T}$, but for general processes you need a richer model like $\mathcal{N}$. Similarly, if P is *low-deterministic*[6] in the sense that for all traces s and $a \in L$

$$s^\smallfrown\langle a \rangle \in traces_\perp(P) \;\Rightarrow\; (s, \{a\}) \notin failures_\perp(P)$$

then you can accurately decide whether or not it is secure from its value in $\mathcal{N}$. For values outside this class, like $Chaos_{H \cup L}$, they do not give enough information.

---

[6]Any deterministic process is low-deterministic, as is any process satisfying $\mathcal{L}\text{IND}_H(\cdot)$.

Just how much finer a model is required to deal with the general case is debatable: certainly you need something about as fine as that provided by the operational semantics in Chapter 7, and arguably you should incorporate probability as well. In any case it is very unlikely that such an attractive, persuasive, or practical (thanks to FDR's ability to check determinism: see page 221) definition can be found.

EXERCISE 12.4.1   Recall from page 313 that a *monitor* for a set A of events is one that never refuses any member of A. Say that P is *semi-separable* with respect to (H, L) if there is a monitor M for L and a process P_L using only events from L such that $P = M \parallel_L P_L$.

(a) Show that if P is separable then it is semi-separable.

(b) Suppose P is semi-separable (into (M, P_L) as above) with respect to (H, L). Show that $\mathcal{L}_H(P) = P_L$ for such P. Deduce that if P_L is deterministic then $\mathcal{L}\text{IND}_H(P)$ holds.

(c) Now suppose that P is such that $\mathcal{L}\text{IND}_H(P)$. Let M be the process whose failures are

$$\{(s, X \cap H) \mid (s, X) \in \mathit{failures}(P)\}$$

$$\cup \{(s^\frown\langle l\rangle^\frown t, Y) \mid s \in \mathit{traces}(P) \wedge \langle l\rangle^\frown t \in L^* \wedge l \notin \mathit{initials}(P/s)\}$$

Show that M is a monitor such that $P = M \parallel_L \mathcal{L}_H(P)$ and hence that P is semi-separable.

EXERCISE 12.4.2   Let P be any divergence-free process with alphabet $H \cup L$. Show that $P' = P \sqcap \mathit{Chaos}_L$ satisfies the definition of fault tolerance

$$P' \parallel_H STOP \sqsubseteq \mathcal{L}_H(P')$$

but need not be secure.[7]

12.5   Tools

With the exception of the fine distinctions made at the start by the interpretation of abstraction over infinite traces, just about everything in this chapter is relevant to FDR. The ways of structuring the checking of specifications using abstraction both helps in formulating the properties you want of processes and in using the tool's compression functions (see Section C.2).

---

[7]There are a number of definitions of 'security' in the literature which would define such P' to be secure for all P, even though if with $P = LEAK$ from page 324, for example, you can guarantee that if Hugh communicates anything with P', then Lois gets to hear it.

We have seen various applications of determinism checking in this chapter, in the sense that it has been used to characterize security and separability. FDR's ability to check determinism was included mainly because of these results. Note that because of the way lazy and mixed abstraction are formulated it will often be necessary to use the stable failures model $\mathcal{F}$ for these determinism checks, just as it is used for refinement checks involving abstraction. For the only formulation of lazy abstraction which can be rendered in finitely nondeterministic CSP is the one on page 299 which, if interpreted over $\mathcal{N}$, often introduces false divergences that would confuse FDR. This means that you are, in fact, checking a process that might well diverge for $\mathcal{F}$-determinism as discussed on page 217. This is only a technicality, however, since the $\mathcal{F}$-determinism of $\mathcal{L}_H^{\mathcal{F}}(P)$ is equivalent to the (true) determinism of the other two formulations of $\mathcal{L}_H(P)$.

All the significant examples from this chapter, and several larger applications of the definitions of fault tolerance and security, can be found on the web site.

12.6   Notes

The work in this chapter has developed over the past three years, with many of the results arising from Lars Wulf's doctoral studies with the author: his thesis provides by far the most extensive study of the compositional properties of abstraction and its application to security. Jim Woodcock was very influential on the early phases of this work.

The precise formulations of lazy and mixed abstractions in this chapter are new. They are direct descendants of the versions used in [99, 107, 108] which were based on a definition of lazy abstraction using interleaving:

$$\mathcal{L}_H^{|||}(P) \;=\; P \;|||\; RUN_H$$

The intuitive justification for that form of abstraction is that the process RUN_H camouflages events in H: you can never get any information about P from such an event occurring since it could always have come from RUN_H.

The one advantage of the earlier version is that it is easily definable using standard operators over $\mathcal{N}$, while we have had to compute ours over $\mathcal{F}$ (in the knowledge that the $\mathcal{N}$ version is, in fact, the same). It has at least three disadvantages. The first is that it is not natural to have an abstraction into L performing lots of events in H, with the consequence that many of the results and definitions we have formulated do not work as neatly since they have to take account of the camouflage events. The second is that the corresponding way of lifting a specification on L to one on the whole alphabet (implied by the second part of Exercise 12.2.2) does not lend itself nearly as well to facilitating compression.

The third and main disadvantage is that $\mathcal{L}_H^{|||}(P)$ is not quite abstract enough: it identifies strictly less processes than $\mathcal{L}_H(P)$. If the event $l \in L$ is only possible after $h \in H$ this is still true of the interleaving abstraction. Thus if

$$
\begin{aligned}
P_1 &= STOP \sqcap l \to STOP \\
P_2 &= h \to l \to STOP \\
P_3 &= h \to h \to l \to STOP
\end{aligned}
$$

we have that $\mathcal{L}_H(P_i)$ are all the same, but $\mathcal{L}_H^{|||}(P_i)$ are all different. The interleaving-based abstraction of P_1 has the trace $\langle l \rangle$, whereas the shortest traces of the other abstractions containing an l are respectively $\langle h, l \rangle$ and $\langle h, h, l \rangle$. Intuitively, the interleaving definition gets this wrong since surely all these three processes actually do look the same in L.

Having seen this example you might wonder why the interleaving definition was ever used, but in fact this difference does not show up in three of the most important applications of lazy abstraction. Thanks to the result contained in the second part of Exercise 12.2.2, noting that

$$
NoFaults = P \underset{E}{\|} STOP
$$

never communicates in E, we get that P is fault tolerant in the sense described earlier if and only if

$$
\mathcal{L}_E^{|||}(NoFaults) \sqsubseteq \mathcal{L}_E^{|||}(P)
$$

So it yields an identical definition of fault tolerance.

It can be shown that $\mathcal{L}_H(P)$ is deterministic if and only if $\mathcal{L}_H^{|||}(P)$ is. This is left as an (interesting) exercise. It follows that independence defined in terms of the determinism of either abstraction is identical, and that a deterministic process is separable if and only if both $\mathcal{L}_H^{|||}(P)$ and $\mathcal{L}_L^{|||}(P)$ are deterministic.

An example of the use of abstraction in formulating fault tolerance properties can be found in [125]. Earlier fault tolerance case studies such as [13] have used specifications crafted to the examples under consideration. .

There have been numerous definitions of security, in the sense of independence/non-interference, over CSP models. Several of these, namely those of [109, 2, 39] turn out to be equivalent to ours for deterministic P, though they usually make the mistake of extending their definitions over all processes rather than restricting them to the low-deterministic processes or a subset. Though we have, of course, couched our determinism-based definition of security in the models of CSP, one can argue that it is largely independent of which process algebra equivalence is used. This is explained in [99] and illustrated in [34].

Part III

Practice

Chapter 13

Deadlock!

We have already met several examples of deadlock, which is certainly the best-known pathology of concurrent systems. It is also – probably for this reason – the most feared. A system becomes deadlocked when no further progress can be made. We distinguish it from livelock, where an infinite amount of internal progress is being made without any interaction with the external environment, even though from the outside a deadlocked and a livelocked system look similar. *Internally* the two phenomena are quite unalike, meaning, for example, that different techniques are needed for analyzing when they can appear.

In the first section we find out how deadlock arises, how to eliminate deadlocks arising for local reasons, and hence how to eliminate deadlock in *tree* networks. There are various useful *ad hoc* conditions on networks, many based on orderings, which can be used to eliminate deadlock; these are surveyed in the second section. The third section looks at some more general global techniques for deadlock avoidance. The fourth shows how the construction and topology of a network can sometimes allow us to factor its deadlock analysis into a number of smaller parts. The fifth section looks at the limitations of the style of local analysis we advocate.

13.1 Basic principles and tree networks

13.1.1 Assumptions about networks

We cannot detect or reason about deadlock using traces alone. After all, for any process P,

$$traces(P) = traces(P \sqcap STOP)$$

and the right-hand side can deadlock immediately whether or not the left-hand side can. Deadlock is best described in the stable failures model of CSP, where it is represented by the failure $(s, \Sigma \cup \{\checkmark\})$ for s any trace in Σ^*. (The fact that a process does nothing after it terminates should not be regarded as deadlock.) In fact, systems in which both deadlock and termination are simultaneously an issue are (at least in the author's experience) very rare and it would be an unnecessary complication to have to deal at every turn with the case of processes or networks terminating. This leads us to make the first of a number of assumptions about the sorts of network we are dealing with. These are all things we will assume throughout the first four sections of this chapter, since they all help in pinning down and reasoning about deadlock in realistic systems.

(A) Throughout this chapter we will assume that none of the component processes of our networks can terminate (though this does not preclude them being constructed out of sub-processes that can).

Deadlock is a static condition: when it happens no process is making progress and, in particular, both the shape of the network and the states of all the processes in it are, from that moment, fixed. This leads to our second assumption about the networks we are considering:

(B) We will consider only statically-defined networks $\left\|_{i=1}^{n} (P_i, A_i)\right.$, where the communications of P_i are entirely within A_i.

This does not mean we are excluding dynamically-growing networks such as those we can build with piping and enslavement, merely that one would have to take a snapshot of such a network at the moment of deadlock and think of it in our new terms. The use of the alphabetized parallel operator means we have excluded uses of $|||$ and $\|_{X}$ where there are some events that can be communicated independently (i.e., without synchronization) by more than one process. We want to know exactly which process or processes participate in each event. The majority of practical uses of $\|_{X}$ and $|||$ could be written in this way since they do not use the power of those operators to introduce ambiguity about which process performs an event. In practice we will allow the use of these operators as long as the network *could* have been built using the alphabetized parallel operator. What we have done is to concentrate on 'realistic' style compositions, at the expense of forms of parallel composition which are mainly used for establishing specification effects. This is equally true of our next assumption:

(C) We will consider only networks that are *triple-disjoint*, meaning that there is no event that requires the synchronization of more than two processes. In

other words, if P_i, P_j and P_k are three distinct nodes in the network, then
$A_i \cap A_j \cap A_k = \{\}$.

Thus all events are either communications between a pair of processes, or are simple interactions between a single process and the environment. All interaction within the network must be point-to-point. The main thing that this excludes is the use of parallel composition as the many-way conjunction of trace specifications.[1]

Implicit in assumption (B), but sufficiently important that it should be stated directly, is the following:

(D) We consider only networks built using parallel composition from their component processes. In particular, they contain no renaming or hiding.

Since the majority of networks one meets in practice violate this, especially because of the hiding of internal communications, this looks like an over-strong assumption. The reason why we make it is to allow us to concentrate on a single central case and to see the communications of all the component processes of a network directly. Two basic facts and a series of laws mean that we can always transform any reasonable network into one which is, from the point of view of deadlock, equivalent and which meets condition (D). The two facts are:

- P is deadlock-free if, and only if, $P \setminus X$ is for any $X \subseteq \Sigma$. ($P \setminus X$ may be able to *diverge* when P cannot, but see Section 8.4.)

- P is deadlock-free if, and only if, $P[\![R]\!]$ is for any alphabet transformation R which contains all of P's events in its domain.

Intuitively these are both obvious: since deadlock means reaching a state where no action of whatever name and whether visible or invisible is possible, it does not matter if the actions are renamed or hidden.

The laws referred to are just $\langle \text{hide-}_X \|_Y \text{-dist} \rangle$ (3.7), $\langle f[\cdot]\text{-}_X \|_Y \text{-dist} \rangle$ (3.10), $\langle f[\cdot]\text{-hide-sym} \rangle$ (3.11), and $\langle f[\cdot]\text{-hide-null} \rangle$ (3.12).

These usually allow us to move all the hiding to the outside of a parallel composition, and all the renaming onto the individual component processes. The hiding is then irrelevant from the point of view of deadlock, and the renaming simply creates new (and necessarily busy if the originals were) component processes. (Two of these laws are restricted to 1–1 renaming, but fortunately it is that sort of renaming which is generally used in the construction of realistic models of implementations – typically modularized into operators like $\gg$ and $/\!/$.) An example is given at the end of this chapter in Section 13.7.

---

[1]In that case, deadlock is likely to arise because of 'inconsistency' in the specifications: they allow a trace s but no continuation of s.

Our final assumption is much easier to understand than the one above:

(E) We assume the network is *busy*, defined to mean that each component process
is deadlock-free.

While there are many deadlock-free networks that do not satisfy this, the deadlocks
occurring in their individual processes usually fall into one of the following two
categories:

- states (often error states) which in fact – and often because of the correct
functioning of the network – the component process never reaches; and

- the component process that is deadlocking is one (most often the process
STOP itself) which is an 'extra' process designed to prevent some undesirable
event from happening in the main network.

In the second case one can usually (and always when the offending process is *STOP*)
just redesign the individual processes so that they simply avoid the offending behaviour rather than require an externally imposed ban. To expect a deadlock analysis technique to be able to handle the first case is like using a screwdriver to hammer
in a nail – one should not expect it to be able to analyze trace conditions of individual component processes. Thus this assumption of *busy-ness* is a reasonable
starting point for examining deadlock behaviour *per se*.

Finally we make an assumption about the way we describe processes rather
than about the processes themselves. The concept of a *channel* in CSP is rather
broad, and in general many processes may share events from the same channel (i.e.,
the events $c.x$ for the name c) even when the network is triple-disjoint. This is
typically because the name c really represents an *array* of 'real' channels. Throughout our discussions of deadlock, the word *channel* will be restricted to this 'real'
sense: a collection of events used either by a single process to communicate with
the environment, or by a pair of processes to talk to each other. In other words,
any channel that intersects the alphabet of a process is contained in it. There is
also the implication in the word 'channel' that communications over it are somehow
well-behaved and co-ordinated. This is an idea we will be able to make clearer at
the end of the next section.

This completes our base assumptions. Though they may seem severe, the
intention is only to concentrate on the central cases of deadlock and to give ourselves
a common language to talk about the systems we are considering. In fact we will
find that the methods used to combat deadlock are often phrased in a way that is
not specific to our tightly-defined class of networks, merely to the class of networks
that could be transformed into it in the ways described above.

13.1.2   Ungranted requests and conflicts

The assumption of triple-disjointness gives particular importance to the concept of a *communication graph*, something we first discussed in Section 2.2, for this graph (a node for each process and an edge between a pair if their alphabets intersect) now 'shows' all the interactions between processes. The essence of any deadlock state will be the collection of requests for communication that processes are making to each other along the edges of this graph.

We might as well assume that this graph is connected (i.e., that there is a path through the edges between any chosen pair of nodes). If it were not connected the various connected components into which it divides can be thought of as completely independent processes from the point of view of deadlock analysis.

Since deadlock is a static phenomenon, we can examine the fixed state in which it occurs. Each component process is in a state which we can add to the communication graph. Because of our assumption of busy-ness, each process must be able to perform some action. In general this might be either one which does not require the agreement of any other process or (because of triple-disjointness) one which requires the agreement of exactly one other process. The first of these (which breaks into two cases: internal (τ) actions and 'external' communications) cannot be the case in a deadlock state since there would be nothing in the network preventing the action – meaning that it was not deadlocked. Therefore every process must have one or more *requests* to other processes – necessarily ones that do not agree to any of the requested actions.

Thus, all of the interest in a deadlock state is concentrated on the set of communications that are shared by two processes: we will call this set

$$\bigcup\{A_i \cap A_j \mid i \neq j\}$$

the *vocabulary* of the network.

Suppose P and Q, with alphabets A and B, are processes in the network which can communicate with each other (i.e., $A \cap B \neq \{\}$). We define an *ungranted request* to exist from P to Q in the state σ (the details of which we will discuss later), written $P \stackrel{\sigma}{\Longrightarrow}\bullet Q$, if neither process can communicate outside the vocabulary of the network; P can communicate in B but they cannot agree on any communication in $A \cap B$.

Ungranted requests are the building blocks of a deadlock. We can form a *snapshot graph* of a deadlock by superimposing the (directed) arcs representing them onto the communication graph. A possible example is shown in Figure 13.1 (where the dotted lines represent edges of the communication graph with no ungranted request). We should notice that any ungranted request which appears between a

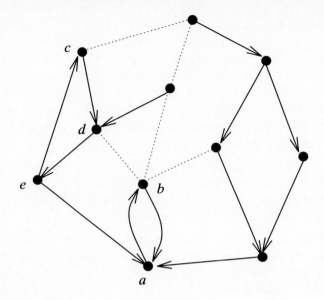

Figure 13.1 Typical snapshot graph of a deadlock state.

pair (P_i, P_j) of processes in the entire network can also appear when P_i and P_j are put in parallel (only) with each other.

There are very good reasons why as much as possible of the analysis (whether for deadlock or anything else) of a large network should be done locally rather than considering the whole system all the time. The patterns of behaviour that occur between small and localized collections of processes are much easier to understand both for humans and computer tools – the latter because of the state-space explosion which occurs as networks grow. The various assumptions (A)–(E) above are all conditions that apply to an individual process (i.e., are local in the strongest sense), and it is clear that enumerating the ungranted requests between pairs of processes is also very local.

Start from any process P_0 in a deadlocked network. It has an ungranted request to another process P_1, which in turn has an ungranted request to some P_2, and so on. Since the network we are looking at is finite this sequence must repeat, giving a cycle of processes

$$\langle P_r, P_{r+1}, \ldots, P_{r+s-1} \rangle$$

where $P_r = P_{r+s}$. This simple argument, and the chains and cycles of processes it creates, are central in deadlock analysis.

Look again at Figure 13.1. Wherever you start here, and whatever choices

Two nodes in conflict (both may have external requests)

Strong conflict (at most one may have external requests)

Figure 13.2 Illustrations of conflict and strong conflict.

are made about which requests to follow, the sequence leads to one of two cycles: either $\langle a, b \rangle$ or $\langle c, d, e \rangle$. The latter is very much what we might have expected, but one might well regard the former as rather peculiar: an adjacent pair of processes each waiting for the other. This can, of course, happen when the intersection of a pair's alphabets has size greater than 1 (consider the processes $\mu\, p.a \to b \to p$ and $\mu\, q.b \to a \to q$ placed in parallel). There are two variants of this situation that need to be studied separately.

- We say that a pair of processes are in *conflict* if each has an ungranted request to the other, no matter what other requests they may have.

- They are in *strong conflict* if, additionally, one of the two processes in conflict has its only ungranted request to the other. (Note that the pair $\langle a, b \rangle$ are in strong conflict.)

These two situations are illustrated in Figure 13.2.

One can search for potential conflicts and strong conflicts between a pair of neighbours by looking at their binary parallel composition. They are said to be free of conflict (respectively free of strong conflict) if the appropriate situation never occurs. (Note that the vocabulary of the entire network is necessary to judge these things since it affects whether a given state is formally an ungranted request. In practice the escape clause this can provide is rarely used, though it certainly can prove invaluable.) A network is free of (strong) conflict if all its constituent pairs are. Notice that this is another example of a locally-checkable property.

As we will see in the rest of this chapter, these are extremely useful properties for a network to have. Most well-designed systems, except ones with rather symmetric communication patterns, are (or can readily be made) conflict-free. For example, any pair of processes connected by a single channel will be conflict-free (except in unusual circumstances where the inputter can select which inputs it wants), as will any pair where both sides agree on the sequence of channels/events to be communicated (with the same caveat).

Note that freedom from strong conflict is a weaker condition than conflict freedom. (It is better to avoid the potentially ambiguous phrase 'strong conflict freedom' so as not to get confused about this.) Since to fail it there must be one process Q which is willing to communicate only with another one, P, which strangely offers some communication to Q but none that Q can accept, this is a condition which is met by the great majority of practical networks. And the few correctly functioning networks that fail to satisfy it can invariably (at least in the author's experience) be redesigned so that they do satisfy it without changing the behaviour of the network at all. The author believes it should be adopted as a design principle for parallel networks.

EXAMPLE 13.1.1 (DINING PHILOSOPHERS) One of the first examples of deadlock we saw (in Section 2.2.1), and certainly the best known generally, is the five dining philosophers (the number of philosophers, as it turns out, being immaterial). We look at it again here because it turns out to be an excellent example for illustrating the design principle discussed above.

The basic example described earlier is easily shown to be conflict-free. The only pairs of processes we have to examine are adjacent $FORK_j$ and $PHIL_i$ processes ($i \in \{j, j \oplus 1\}$), and both of these agree that the sequence of communications between them will be a potentially unbounded alternating sequence of $picksup.i.j$ and $putsdown.i.j$ events. Since they always agree on what their next communication will be, they can never be in conflict.

The situation becomes much more interesting if we adopt one of the standard ways of avoiding the deadlock: the introduction of a $BUTLER$ process whose duty it is to prevent all the philosophers sitting down simultaneously. Perhaps the most obvious definition of this process is $BUTLER_0$, where

$$BUTLER_n = (sits?i \rightarrow BUTLER_{n+1} \triangleleft n < 4 \triangleright STOP)$$
$$\square (getsup?i \rightarrow BUTLER_{n-1} \triangleleft n > 0 \triangleright STOP)$$

This process just keeps a count of how many philosophers there are at the table, allowing another as long as there are no more than three already there, and allowing one to leave as long as there is any there. This process works: if it is put in parallel

with the network described in Section 2.2.1, synchronizing on $\{| \ sits, getsup \ |\}$, the
result is deadlock-free.

This solution has much more the feeling of a patch put on to cure the observed
deadlock than of a network designed from first principles to be deadlock-free. It is
relatively easy to find the right patch for this example since there really is only one
deadlock possible in the original system (as well as there only being one cycle in the
communication graph), but on more complex systems it would be relatively harder.
For that reason we will, in the rest of this chapter, concentrate on ways of building
systems that are intrinsically deadlock-free rather than on removing deadlocks after
they have been introduced.

The network augmented by this definition of *BUTLER*, perhaps surprisingly, contains strong conflicts between the new process and philosophers. These
arise when four philosophers are sitting down and the fifth ($PHIL_0$ say) *wants* to
sits down. The *BUTLER* quite correctly refuses, but also (on close examination,
bizarrely) is quite happy to let $PHIL_0$ get up from the table (the event $getsup.0$),
an event that this philosopher in turn refuses, not being at the table! Because these
two processes each have an ungranted request to the other, this is a conflict; because
$PHIL_0$ has no other request it is a *strong* conflict.

We can remove this by a slightly more careful definition of *BUTLER*: it
becomes $BUTLER'(\{\})$, where

$$
\begin{aligned}
BUTLER'(X) \quad = \quad & (sits?i : (\{0,1,2,3,4\} \backslash X) \to BUTLER'(X \cup \{i\}) \\
& \triangleleft \ | \ X \ | < 4 \triangleright \ STOP) \\
& \square \ getsup?i : X \to BUTLER'(X \backslash \{i\})
\end{aligned}
$$

This is designed so that it does not make offers to philosophers that it should know
they cannot accept. The behaviour of the network with *BUTLER'* is identical
to that with the other; the new network is, however, more amenable to deadlock
analysis. *(End of example)*

We can easily transfer the notion of conflict freedom to a single channel
connecting two processes. This will be when the two processes cannot both offer
communication on the channel without agreeing at least one event in the channel. This definition is more focused than simply saying that the two processes are
conflict-free since it ignores the other channels they may have and their external
communication. However, we can say that if two processes are only connected by a
single conflict-free channel then they are conflict-free.

Channels that are *not* conflict-free, while easy to give examples of, are a
somewhat counter-intuitive concept. From the point of view of deadlock analysis it
will sometimes be helpful to assume all channels are conflict-free.

Formal definitions

Many of the concepts in this section have been defined more in words than in mathematical notation. Though hopefully these words have clearly expressed what we wanted, it is important that we can formalize our reasoning within our mathematical models. While the concepts and definitions in this section may help clarify things for the mathematically inclined reader, it is only necessary to understand the concepts below if it is intended to pursue deadlock proofs at a very formal level. The rest of this chapter does not depend significantly on the precise definitions below; other readers can safely proceed to the next section.

As discussed earlier, the model we are using here is the stable failures model $\mathcal{F}$ where (except for the special case of $\checkmark$ actions which is irrelevant to this chapter because of assumption (A)) a process is identified with the sets

(i) of pairs (s, X) such that it can perform the trace s and then reach a stable state where it cannot perform any action from X, and

(ii) of its finite traces.

The network $V = \left\|\right._{i=1}^{n}(P_i, A_i)$ is deadlocked when it has the failure (s, Σ) for some $s \in \Sigma^*$. (Our assumption that no P_i can terminate means that we can ignore the refusal of $\checkmark$, which must now be refused in every stable state.) We know (from the failures definition of the parallel operator) that $s \in (\bigcup_{i=1}^{n} A_i)^*$, that $s_i = s \restriction A_i \in traces(P_i)$ and that there are refusal sets X_i such that $(s_i, X_i) \in failures(P_i)$ and

$$\bigcup_{i=1}^{n} A_i = \bigcup_{i=1}^{n} A_i \cap X_i$$

(In general there may be many different combinations of X_i that work here.) A *deadlock state* is the pair $(s, \langle X_1, \ldots, X_n \rangle)$: it allows us to see how each P_i contributed to the deadlock. Except in quite exceptional circumstances, where both Σ is infinite and the definitions involve unbounded nondeterminism, we can assume that all the component failures (s_i, X_i) are maximal in the sense that there is no $Y \supset X_i$ with $(s, Y) \in failures(P_i)$. We can and will always assume that $X_i \supseteq \Sigma \setminus initials(P/s_i)$.

In the common case that a P_i is deterministic, the only option is to set $X_i = \Sigma \setminus initials(P_i/s)$.

We can generalize the above notion of deadlock state to look at how any failure of a parallel composition arises:

DEFINITION   A *state* of $\left\|\right._{i=1}^{n}(P_i, A_i)$ is a pair $(s, \langle X_1, \ldots, X_n \rangle)$ where

- $s \in (\bigcup_{i=1}^{n} A_i)^*$,

- $(s \restriction A_i, X_i) \in failures(P_i)$,
- $X_i \supseteq \Sigma \setminus initials(P_i/s \restriction A_i)$

A state is *maximal* if all the X_i are maximal refusals as described above. It is a deadlock state if

$$\bigcup_{i=1}^n A_i = \bigcup_{i=1}^n A_i \cap X_i$$

Note that from any state we can deduce a state for each subnetwork, in particular all adjacent pairs of processes.   ∎

The notions of request, ungranted request, conflict, etc. are now straightforward to define formally.

DEFINITION   If $(s, X) \in failures(P_i)$ and $X \supseteq \Sigma \setminus initials(P/s)$, then we say P_i is making a *request* to P_j $(i \neq j)$ if $A_j \cap (\Sigma \setminus X) \neq \{\}$.   ∎

DEFINITION   There is an *ungranted request* from P to Q in the composition $P \,_A\|_B Q$, with respect to vocabulary $C \supseteq A \cap B$ if it has a state $(s, \langle X_P, X_Q \rangle)$

- $(\Sigma \setminus X_P) \cup (\Sigma \setminus X_Q) \subseteq C$
- $B \cap (\Sigma \setminus X_P) \neq \{\}$
- $B \cap (\Sigma \setminus X_P) \subseteq X_Q$.

There is an ungranted request from P_i to P_j in the deadlock state σ (written $P_i \stackrel{\sigma}{\Longrightarrow}\bullet P_j$) if the corresponding state of the parallel composition of P_i and P_j is an ungranted request with respect to the vocabulary of the whole network V.   ∎

DEFINITION   A *conflict* (with respect to vocabulary $C \supseteq A \cap B$) in the parallel composition $P \,_A\|_B Q$ is a state $(s, \langle X_P, X_Q \rangle)$ which is simultaneously an ungranted request (with respect to C) in both directions.   ∎

DEFINITION   A *strong conflict* of the pair $P \,_A\|_B Q$ with respect to C is a conflict $(s, \langle X_P, X_Q \rangle)$ with respect to C such that *either* $\Sigma \setminus X_P \subseteq B$ or $\Sigma \setminus X_Q \subseteq A$.   ∎

DEFINITION   The network V is free of conflict (respectively strong conflict) if each pair of adjacent processes in its communication graph are, in the sense that no state of their pairwise composition is a conflict (respectively strong conflict) with respect to the vocabulary of V.   ∎

13.1.3   The Fundamental Principle and tree networks

If a network is free of strong conflict, we can make an important assumption about the sequence of nodes $\langle P_0, P_1, P_2 \ldots \rangle$ constructed when developing the Fundamental

Principle, namely that $P_n \neq P_{n+2}$ for any n. This is because, even though P_{n+1} may have an ungranted request to P_n, we can guarantee that it has one to at least one other node, for otherwise P_n and P_{n+1} would be in strong conflict. We can immediately deduce that the cycle of ungranted requests produced by the sequence must be a *proper* cycle, namely one which is a sequence of at least three distinct nodes. This is the fundamental result which underpins all of our deadlock analysis techniques.

FUNDAMENTAL PRINCIPLE OF DEADLOCK   *If V is a network which satisfies our basic assumptions (A)–(E)[2] and which is free of strong conflict, then any deadlock state of V contains a proper cycle of ungranted requests.*

It has one immediate consequence, since no tree network (i.e., one whose communication graph is a tree) can contain a proper cycle of ungranted requests.

DEADLOCK RULE 1   *If V is a tree network which is free of strong conflict, then V is deadlock-free.*

This is likely to be the only rule you ever need for proving deadlock freedom in tree networks. What it shows is that deadlock is not a real concern in well-designed tree networks.

Since the dynamic networks produced by recursing though operators like $\gg$ and $/\!/$ (see Chapter 4) are almost invariably trees, it is worth noting here that even though these do not fit directly within assumptions (A)–(E) set out earlier, the remarks and transformations set out with those assumptions mean that to all intents and purposes Rule 1 still applies. Thus, so long as basic principles (such as busy-ness and freedom from strong conflict) are adhered to, deadlock is rarely a problem in this type of network.

One could generalize Rule 1 a little to deal with the case where the communication graph is not a tree, but where there are enough (directed) edges between nodes over which ungranted requests are impossible to exclude proper cycles of them. Obviously one should bear this in mind if there are such edges, but it does not seem to be a very common situation.

EXERCISE 13.1.1   Let us suppose we need to pass messages in either direction between a pair of users separated by a chain of intermediate nodes. Someone proposes the following design for a node:

$$Node \quad = \quad leftin?m \to rightout!m \to Node$$
$$\square \; rightin?x \to leftout!m \to Node$$

where, in composing the network, these channels are renamed so that each adjacent pair is connected by a pair of channels, one in each direction. He argues that this must be deadlock-free because the communication graph is a tree.

[2]In subsequent results we will, for brevity, omit these assumptions, which will be implicit.

Show that he is wrong and that it can deadlock, and explain why in terms of the analysis in this section.

What modification would you suggest so that the system meets its intended purpose but is deadlock-free?

EXERCISE 13.1.2   Sketch a proof that the dynamic network described on page 108 for implementing the quicksort algorithm is deadlock-free. To do this you should show that any deadlock state is equivalent, from the point of view of deadlock, to one of a conflict-free tree network satisfying our assumptions. (Unless you are keen to do this, there is no need to go into details of the transformations that manipulate the renaming and hiding introduced by enslavement.)

EXERCISE 13.1.3   A token ring, as previously discussed on page 307, is a network in which a fixed number of tokens are passed round the processes in a ring network. We are not yet in a position to prove one these deadlock-free since it is evidently not a tree network! One can, however, produce an interesting variant on this which is.

Suppose we are presented with an arbitrary connected tree structure of processes, and we want to ensure that exactly one of these has a token at any time. Design a node process which achieves this, and additionally allows any node to issue a request for the token which will normally result in it being sent. (The resulting network should have the given tree as its communication graph.) It should be deadlock-free by Rule 1.

It is helpful to note that (with correct initialization) each node can always either have the token or know which of its neighbouring processes is the right one to ask for the token. After our node has seen the token, this is simply the neighbour to whom it most recently passed the token.

13.2   Specific ways to avoid deadlock

If the communication graph of V is not a tree (i.e., it contains cycles) we need to find ways of showing that the sort of cycle produced by the Fundamental Principle cannot appear, even though there is now 'room' for it to do so.[3] In this section we meet a number of design rules which, when they are followed, guarantee that no such cycle can appear. Each of these rules tends to apply to only a certain class of system.

---

[3]Though in fact there are cases of deadlock-free networks that can contain proper cycles of ungranted requests, all our rules are based on removing them. In fact the careful reader may notice that a few of our later rules do not exclude the possibility of there being some, provided that ones that 'matter' in some sense are not there.

13.2.1 Node orderings

Our first few rules and examples are based on the existence of some partial ordering on the nodes which represents something like the direction in which data, or perhaps some decision process, flows. A *node ordering* on a network is a partial order on its nodes where every pair of processes whose alphabets intersect (i.e., have an edge between them in the communication graph) are comparable. We will use these orderings to break symmetry and eliminate the possibility of cycles.

DEADLOCK RULE 2 *Suppose V is conflict-free and has a node ordering < such that whenever node P_i has a request to any P_j with $P_j < P_i$ then it has a request to all its neighbours P_k such that $P_k < P_i$. Then V is deadlock-free.*

The proof of this particular rule is very easy: if there were a cycle of ungranted requests $\langle P_0, P_1, \ldots, P_n \rangle$ then necessarily this contains at least one P_i which is maximal (under $<$) among the members of the cycle. Necessarily P_i has an ungranted request to P_{i+1}, a process less than itself; the assumptions of the rule mean that it therefore has a request (necessarily ungranted) to each Q such that $Q < P_i$. But the predecessor P_{i-1} of P_i in the cycle is necessarily one of these, and so (in contradiction to the assumption of conflict freedom) these two processes are in conflict. This completes the proof.

Notice that the assumptions of Rule 2 imply that when a node P_j has an ungranted request to a P_i with $P_j < P_i$, then P_i must have a request to a P_k with $P_i < P_k$ (for, by busy-ness, P_i must have a request somewhere and it cannot have a request to any of its predecessors). This fact alone is enough to imply deadlock freedom since it would imply that any deadlock state contains an ever-increasing sequence of nodes, each with an ungranted request to the next. This is impossible because the network is finite. This rule would be slightly more general than Rule 2 but also it would also be harder to verify its conditions, since one has to look at how pairs of processes behave in parallel rather than at the construction of individual processes.

EXAMPLE 13.2.1 (LAYERED ROUTEING) An elegant example of the use of this Rule is provided by a routeing algorithm invented by Yantchev [124], which he calls 'virtual networks'.[4] Suppose we have a rectangular[5] grid of nodes $\{N_{i,j} \mid 0 \le i \le A, 0 \le j \le B\}$ and might want to send a message packet from any one of these nodes to any other. On the face of it, this system is too symmetric to apply the above rule: messages can be sent in any direction so there is no obvious partial

---

[4]He also invented a clever hardware-level packet propagation mechanism which minimizes propagation latency in this network. He called this the *mad postman* algorithm, but the details are not relevant to the present discussion.

[5]In fact the algorithm works equally well in any number of dimensions.

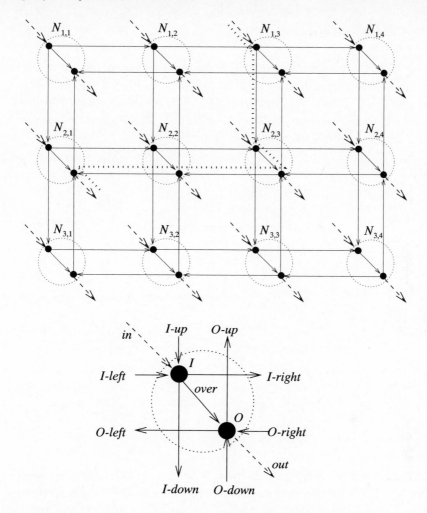

Figure 13.3 Virtual network routing and detail of a node.

ordering on the nodes that we could begin to use for Rule 2. The trick is to divide each node $N_{i,j}$ into the parallel composition of two processes $I_{i,j}$ and $O_{i,j}$ and to put the following ordering on the resulting network:

$$
\begin{aligned}
I_{i,j} &\leq I_{i',j'} && \text{iff } i \leq i' \wedge j \leq j' \\
O_{i,j} &\leq O_{i',j'} && \text{iff } i \geq i' \wedge j \geq j' \\
I_{i,j} &\leq O_{i',j'} && \text{for all } i,j,i',j'
\end{aligned}
$$

This implies (following the intuition of the order) that data flows into the $I_{i,j}$;

through these in increasing index order; over to a $O_{i',j'}$, and then through these in decreasing index order before leaving the network.

In fact it is possible to route from any $N_{i,j}$ to any other $N_{i',j'}$ in this way: data is input into $I_{i,j}$; routed to $I_{i'',j''}$ where $i'' = max\{i, i'\}$ and $j'' = max\{j, j'\}$; passed over to $O_{i'',j''}$ and then routed to $O_{i',j'}$ before being output. A picture of the 4×3 version of this network is shown in Figure 13.3, with the routeing technique illustrated by the path a message takes from $N_{1,3}$ to $N_{2,1}$.

One implementation of this is given by the following process descriptions:

$$
\begin{aligned}
I_{i,j} \quad &= \quad in?x?y?m \to I'_{i,j}(x, y, m) \\
&\quad\ \square\ I\text{-}up?x?y?m \to I'_{i,j}(x, y, m) \\
&\quad\ \square\ I\text{-}left?x?y?m \to I'_{i,j}(x, y, m) \\[4pt]
I'_{i,j}(x, y, m) \quad &= \quad I\text{-}right!x!y!m \to I_{i,j} \\
&\quad\ \langle\!\langle i < x \rangle\!\rangle \\
&\quad\ (I\text{-}down!x!y!m \to I_{i,j} \\
&\quad\ \langle\!\langle j < y \rangle\!\rangle\ over!x!y!m \to I_{i,j}) \\[4pt]
O_{i,j} \quad &= \quad over?x?y?m \to O'_{i,j}(x, y, m) \\
&\quad\ \square\ O\text{-}down?x?y?m \to O'_{i,j}(x, y, m) \\
&\quad\ \square\ O\text{-}right?x?y?m \to O'_{i,j}(x, y, m) \\[4pt]
O'_{i,j}(x, y, m) \quad &= \quad O\text{-}left!x!y!m \to O_{i,j} \\
&\quad\ \langle\!\langle i > x \rangle\!\rangle \\
&\quad\ (O\text{-}up!x!y!m \to O_{i,j} \\
&\quad\ \langle\!\langle j > y \rangle\!\rangle\ out!x!y!m \to O_{i,j})
\end{aligned}
$$

Here, *X-up*, *X-down*, *X-left* and *X-right* (with $X \in \{I, O\}$) are the channels connecting $I_{i,j}$ or $O_{i,j}$ to the process of the same sort in the chosen direction in the *X*-plane, *over* is the channel connecting $I_{i,j}$ and $O_{i,j}$, and *in*, *out* are the channels connecting $N_{i,j}$ to the environment. (All of these need to be renamed when composing the complete network so as to get the synchronizations right.) These processes transparently satisfy the requirements of Rule 2 with respect to the given order. *(End of example)*

Rule 2 applies to networks where, whatever nodes are doing with the data they are taking in, they do not mind what order it arrives on the various input channels (i.e., the neighbours that precede them). There is no restriction on which output channels are used and when. The rule applies to systems where (like the example above) each input is in some sense complete and atomic. It does not really deal with situations where a pair of neighbours have a related series of communications, since the greater one in the partial order is obliged to deal with all its other neighbours every time it offers a communication to the lesser one of the pair: it cannot concentrate temporarily on one predecessor. Rule 3 below, a direct extension of Rule 2, specifically allows for this in a way that is frequently useful.

DEADLOCK RULE 3   *Suppose V is conflict-free and has a node ordering $<$. Further, suppose that the state space of each process P_i of V breaks into two parts A and B in such a way that*

- *when P_i is in a state of type A it obeys the assumptions of Rule 2;*

- *when P_i is in a state of type B it has a request to some P_j with $P_j < P_i$;*

- *the parallel composition of each pair of neighbours P_j and P_i with $P_j < P_i$ is such that whenever P_i, in a state of type B, has an ungranted request to P_j, then P_j is also in a state of type B.*

Then V is deadlock-free.

The proof of this is almost as easy as Rule 2: we can ensure that the cycle of ungranted requests picked by the Fundamental Principle has the property that the ungranted request from any node in a B-state is to another, lesser node in a B-state. It follows that if one of the nodes in the cycle is in a B-state then they all are, in a sense that is incompatible with the node ordering; so they are all in an A-state and the Rule 2 argument applies.

In this rule, a node is in a B-state just when it is waiting for a communication from the (usually) unique predecessor to whom it is temporarily engaged. The rule says that we must only allow such a request to be ungranted when the predecessor is simultaneously engaged with one of *its* predecessors and waiting for communication on that session. In this way, chains (or occasionally more complex patterns) of these engagements can build up through the network. The wormhole routeing example below shows how these arise.

Networks of the form amenable to this rule are often termed *client/server* networks, the idea being that each process acts as a *server* for some activity for those processes less than it in the order, which are its *clients*. The conditions of the rule can then be paraphrased:

- A server process is either engaged by one of its clients or is available to them all.

- A client and server never get into conflict, and the only way an ungranted request can arise from a server to a client it is currently engaged by is when that client is itself a server to another process and has itself a request to that process.

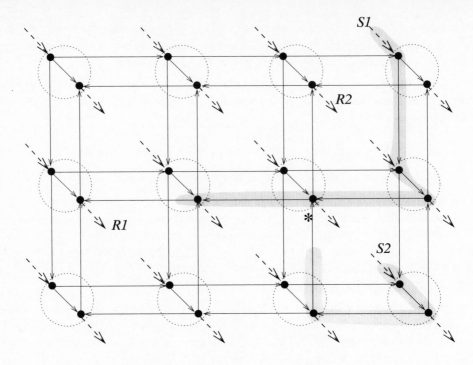

Figure 13.4 Wormhole routeing in action.

EXAMPLE 13.2.2 (WORMHOLE ROUTEING) A typical example of the type of network supported by Rule 3 is an extension of the class of network seen in our previous example. Suppose a typical message is large: it may be that they can be too large to fit into a single node in our routeing system; even if not, the time taken to transmit a message step-by-step across the network may be substantial if the whole message has to enter a node before the node can begin to send it out.

What we do is to break up each message into a variable number of packets where the first one (the header) contains all of the routeing information and each node can tell when it has received the last packet (either by counting relative to some earlier figure contained in the header or by a marker).

When a node is not currently engaged in transmitting a message it behaves very much like one of the nodes in the earlier example. After receiving and passing on a message header it will only accept input from the node which sent it the header (passing on the packets one at a time) until the message is complete. Thus a complete message, at any one time, occupies a connected chain of nodes which, when the message is completely within the network, is at least as long as the number of packets it comprises. The way it works leads to this method being given the name *wormhole routeing.*

Figure 13.4. shows how this might look, with two messages currently in transit. The two messages are from $S1$ to $R1$ and $S2$ to $R2$ respectively. Notice that the second message is temporarily blocked by the first: it will only be able to progress when the first message clears the node labelled $*$.

The actual coding of wormhole routeing in CSP is left as an exercise. *(End of example)*

13.2.2   Cyclic communication networks

There is a large class of calculations that can be performed on (usually) regular networks where data and partially-computed results flow through, and where each processor regularly inputs one collection of values before performing a calculation and then outputting another collection on another set of channels. These are often referred to as *systolic* arrays, though that term more properly applies to the case where the calculations and communications in the network are regulated by a global clock rather than being self-timed. These networks are perhaps the most common example of a rather different class of ordered networks to those treated by Rules 2 and 3: ones where each node communicates in a fixed cyclic pattern with its neighbours.

DEFINITION   A *cyclic communication network* is a network V in which

- Every node is connected to each of its neighbours by one or more distinct, conflict-free channels.

- The communications of each node P_i are divided into *cycles*.

- On each cycle P_i communicates exactly once on each of its channels in a fixed order.

The following two rules show how to design these networks to be deadlock-free.

DEADLOCK RULE 4   *A cyclic communication network is deadlock-free if and only if there is a linear (total) ordering of all the channels linking the nodes such that each P_i addresses its neighbours in order on each cycle.*

DEADLOCK RULE 5   *If there is exactly one channel connecting each pair of neighbours in a cyclic communication network V (i.e., no pair of processes communicate twice in any one cycle), and there is a linear node ordering on V such that each node addresses its neighbours in this order, then V is deadlock-free.*

Rule 5 is just a somewhat simplified version of Rule 4: it is easy to show that it is a corollary of it since under the assumptions of Rule 5 one can find an ordering on the channels satisfying Rule 4 – see the exercises.

The proof that Rule 4 works is rather like those of earlier rules. It depends on the following two facts, both of which are easy to see when you consider how the parallel composition of a pair of neighbouring processes communicate in a cyclic communication network:

- If $P_i \overset{\sigma}{\Longrightarrow}\bullet P_j$ then the number of cycles completed by P_i either equals the corresponding number for P_j or exceeds it by exactly 1.

- If $P_i \overset{\sigma}{\Longrightarrow}\bullet P_j$ and they have completed the same number of cycles, then the channel currently offered by P_j (there is always exactly one) precedes that offered by P_i (to P_j) in the order on channels.

From the first of these we get that all the nodes in a cycle of ungranted requests have completed the same number of communication cycles. The second then shows the cycle cannot exist because the order on channels decreases all the way round. Showing that deadlock freedom actually implies the existence of such an order (the other half of this if-and-only-if result) is rather harder.

Often the way this type of network is built makes it natural for the nodes to perform a group of communications within a cycle *in parallel.* In other words, instead of enforcing a fixed order between the communications $a_1, \ldots, a_k$, say, they are all made available, and as each is performed it is removed from the set until they have all happened. These communications are termed parallel because it is equivalent to writing

$$(a_1 \to SKIP \;|||\; \ldots \;|||\; a_k \to SKIP); \; P'$$

where P' is the subsequent behaviour (though there are likely to be identifier binding problems if this style is used for parallel inputs).

We can liberalize the definition of cyclic communication networks to take this into account.

DEFINITION   A *generalized cyclic communication network* is a network V in which

- every node is connected to each of its neighbours by one or more distinct, conflict-free channels;

- the communications of each node P_i are divided into *cycles*;

- each P_i partitions its channels into a number of subsets and offers these each of these sets in parallel in turn, the order of the sets being fixed.   ∎

It is a good idea to make the communications in one of these networks as parallel as possible. Putting communications in parallel can substantially reduce the computation time because nodes are not blocked from communicating for so long. It is important to know that this 'parallelization' does not interfere with deadlock freedom: this is captured in the following rule.

DEADLOCK RULE 6   *If V is a deadlock-free generalized cyclic communication network, and V' is identical except that one or more groups of consecutive communications in nodes of V have been made parallel, then V' is still deadlock-free.*

The proof of this result can be found in [102].

EXAMPLE 13.2.3 (MATRIX MULTIPLICATION) The rows and columns of two matrices we want to multiply together can flow, respectively, along the rows and columns of a rectangular grid. As pairs of values meet, their product is added to a value that is accumulating in the node where they meet. Recall that the product of the $p \times q$ and $q \times r$ matrices $[a_{i,j}]$ and $[b_{j,k}]$ is the $p \times r$ matrix whose terms are

$$c_{i,k} = \sum_{j=1}^{q} a_{i,j} b_{j,k}$$

The top left-hand corner of the array is shown in Figure 13.5, including an example configuration of data.

We will first code this without parallel communication. Since the nodes all communicate once with each neighbour per cycle, we can do this by selecting a linear node ordering and using Rule 5. Since we expect our node to input (up and left) on each cycle before outputting (right and down), the order must make the two nodes that a given one inputs from less than the two it outputs to. This still gives a great deal of freedom in the choice of order, but there are only a few natural ones, one of which is

$$N_{i,j} \leq N_{i',j'} \quad \Leftrightarrow \quad \begin{aligned} & i + j < i' + j' \quad \text{or} \\ & i + j = i' + j' \wedge i \leq i'. \end{aligned}$$

The resulting code for a node (omitting whatever method is used to access the final value) is $N(0)$, where

$$N(x) = up?a \rightarrow left?b \rightarrow right!b \rightarrow down!a \rightarrow N(x + a \times b)$$

since, for any fixed node, the surrounding ones are ordered in the way implied by these communications.

It is rather unnatural to impose an order on the two inputs and the two outputs of a node in this example. Knowing that the above system is deadlock-free

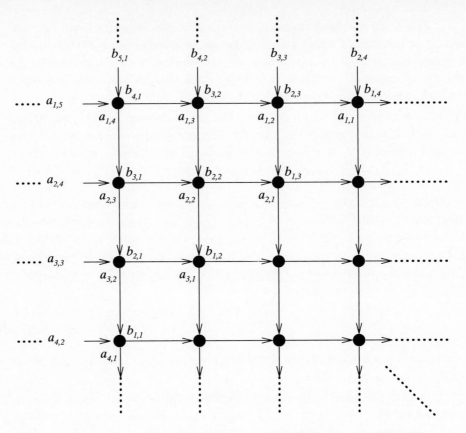

Figure 13.5 Matrix multiplication on a rectangular array.

we can use Rule 6 to observe that the system where the inputs and outputs are both put in parallel is still deadlock-free:

$$N'(x) \quad = \quad up?a \to left?b \to N''(x, a, b)$$
$$\square \ left?b \to up?a \to N''(x, a, b)$$
$$N''(x, a, b) \quad = \quad (down!a \to SKIP \ ||| \ right!b \to SKIP); \ N'(x + a \times b)$$

Notice that inputs have been 'put in parallel' by giving explicit alternatives to allow the values of a and b to carry over. *(End of example)*

It is worth noting that the generalized cyclic communication network produced over *any* node-ordered network in which each node communicates with all the preceding processes in parallel, and then with all the following processes in parallel, is bound to be deadlock-free.

Finally, if it is possible to put *all* the communications of each cycle in parallel then the network is guaranteed to be deadlock-free without the need to consider any orders at all. This could well be possible in a network iterating the solution to an equation[6] by a method in which the $(n{+}1)$th value at a given point is some function of the nth values at that point and the four surrounding ones.

13.2.3 Resource sharing

Many classic deadlocks, not least the dining philosophers, occur because of contention for resources. The basic set-up is that the network consists of two separate classes of process: *users* and *resources*. For simplicity we will assume that the only communications are between a user and a resource[7] (i.e., the alphabets of any two users, or any two resources, are disjoint). Each resource can be acquired by a user U, and then cannot be acquired by any other until it is released by U. Notice how this describes the dining philosophers, where the resources are the fork processes and each fork can only be acquired by the two neighbouring philosophers.

More formally, the user processes will be enumerated $\{U_x \mid x \in \Upsilon\}$ and the resource processes are $\{R_n \mid n \in \{1, \ldots, k\}\}$. The resource processes each allow themselves to be acquired by one user at a time ($acq.x.n$ represents the acquisition of R_n by U_x), and have to be released ($release.x.n$) before being available to others:

$$R_n = acq?x{:}X_n!n \to release.x.n \to R_n$$

Here $X_n \subseteq \Upsilon$ is the non-empty set of users that R_n can be acquired by.

Notice that this definition of R_n completely abstracts away from whatever the users do with the resources once they have them. In a real example it is likely that there would be other communications, but eliminating them here allows us to concentrate on the central issue of contention.[8]

Our objective is to understand how the users must behave to prevent deadlocks like that in the dining philosophers. We must obviously assume that the users interact properly with the individual resources: any trace of a user alternates acquiring and releasing a specific R_n. For simplicity we will assume that, initially, no user holds any resource so that the first event of each of these alternating sequences is the appropriate $acq.x.n$. Notice that this assumption means that our network is certainly conflict-free.

---

[6]Perhaps an elliptic partial differential equation like Poisson's equation.

[7]Technically, the communication graph is *bipartite*.

[8]From the point of view of eliminating deadlock when communications between users and currently-held resources are allowed, it should be very helpful to observe that at all times these clusters are all rather simple tree networks.

If *tr* is any trace of a user process U_x, we can easily compute the set of resources held after *tr*:

$$resources_x(tr) \; = \; \{n \mid tr \downarrow acq.x.n > tr \downarrow release.x.n\}$$

Because there will never be an ungranted request from a user to an unused resource, or from a user to a resource which it currently has possession of, it follows that any cycle of ungranted requests in such a network is bound to look essentially like the one in the dining philosophers. It will alternately consist of users and resources; with a given user waiting for the next resource on the cycle while holding the previous one with the resources waiting to be released.

The classic way to prevent this, which you will see is very like the methods we have already developed for other types of network, is to follow the principle set out in the following rule.

DEADLOCK RULE 7   *Suppose we have a network V of users and resources as set out above, and each U_x follows the principle that it never tries to acquire a resource of lower index than one it presently holds, i.e.,*

$$tr^\smallfrown\langle acq.x.n \rangle \in traces(U_x) \Rightarrow resources_x(tr) \cap \{m \mid m > n\} \; = \; \{\}$$

then V (under our usual assumptions such as busy-ness) is deadlock-free.

Of course this assumption about the users would imply that the indexes of the resources increase as we move round the cycle of ungranted requests discussed above, which is clearly impossible, hence the deadlock freedom.

EXAMPLE 13.2.4 (ASYMMETRIC DINING PHILOSOPHERS) Given the above rule it is simple to apply it to the dining philosophers example. We would not expect it to matter to a philosopher in which order he or she picks up the forks, but the above rule shows that this order is the key to eliminating deadlock. All we have to do is pick any enumeration whatsoever of the forks and to program the philosophers so that each of them picks up the one with lower index first. Using the obvious enumeration (the one used to define them) we get the following definition of a philosopher: if $i \in \{0, 1, 2, 3\}$ then

$$\begin{aligned}
PHIL_i \;\; = \;\; & thinks.i \rightarrow sits.i \rightarrow picksup.i.i \rightarrow picksup.i.i + 1 \rightarrow \\
& eats.i \rightarrow putsdown.i.i + 1 \rightarrow putsdown.i.i \rightarrow getsup.i \rightarrow PHIL_i
\end{aligned}$$

while

$$\begin{aligned}
PHIL'_4 \;\; = \;\; & thinks.4 \rightarrow sits.4 \rightarrow picksup.4.0 \rightarrow picksup.4.4 \rightarrow \\
& eats.4 \rightarrow putsdown.4.4 \rightarrow putsdown.4.0 \rightarrow getsup.4 \rightarrow PHIL'_4
\end{aligned}$$

If the network is otherwise constructed as in Section 2.2.1, it satisfies all the conditions of Rule 7, and so this very slight adjustment has made it deadlock-free. What we have in essence done is to break the symmetry of the original example by varying the order (in the sense of the ring) in which the philosophers pick up their forks. We end up with four left-handed ones and one right-handed (say). *(End of example)*

13.2.4   Communication order

The rules introduced so far have certainly not covered all the possible ways of eliminating cycles of ungranted requests. Any reader who cannot make a network fit any of the rules given here is encouraged to try to capture *why* it is deadlock-free and to attempt to formulate it either in the same way or to translate it into the methods described in the rest of this chapter.

To illustrate this process we will give an example which does not fit into any of the categories shown so far, and then show how this motivates another class of rule.

EXAMPLE 13.2.5 (NON-BLOCKING MESSAGE RING) The objective here is to create a ring network where messages may be input at any node, addressed to any other node. They are to be transported in one direction (clockwise, say) round the ring until they get to their destination, and are then output.

It is very easy to build such a system that deadlocks: this is the fate, for example, of just about the simplest possibility, described below.

$$
\begin{aligned}
D_i &= \quad in.i?m \rightarrow D_i'(m) \\
&\quad \Box \; ring.i?m \rightarrow D_i'(m) \\
D_i'(m) &= \quad out.i!m \rightarrow D_i \\
&\quad \langle destination(m) = i \rangle \\
&\quad ring.(i \oplus 1)!m \rightarrow D_i
\end{aligned}
$$

Here every node has one 'slot' for a message: this can be occupied either by a message input from the local user over *in.i* or by one from the ring. One way to deadlock the resulting ring is for all the users simultaneously to transmit a message for another node. All the processes are then stuck waiting to output to the next member of the ring.

One's first reaction to this might be to add more buffering capacity to the nodes. But this in itself does not help, since however large a finite capacity we give each node we cannot stop them becoming full if the external users are very keen to send messages.

What we need is a mechanism to prevent the ring getting filled up. There are several ways to do this. The first way, which is unacceptable[9] for practical reasons, is to take the approach of the *BUTLER* process for the dining philosophers: a single process, put in parallel, which counts how many messages are present (i.e., input but not yet output) and prevents ones being inserted over a given limit.

A second approach (which is in some respects just a distributed implementation of the first) is to implement a *token ring* alongside the communication ring. This ring contains a number (again, less than the number that could deadlock the communication ring) of tokens. A message can only be input to the communication ring by a node that has a free token, and the message then occupies the token for as long as it is in the ring. There has to be some mechanism for nodes seeking to input but without a token to obtain one (if available), in this sense one would have to produce a more sophisticated ring than that seen in Section 12.2: see Exercise 13.2.4.

The third approach, which is much simpler to describe in CSP than the second, is to make each node responsible for making sure that *it* is not the one to complete the deadlock. This is done by increasing the buffering capacity of each node to at least two, picking a limit for each node that is at least one and strictly less than its total capacity, and programming the nodes so that they only accept new messages from their own user when this would not make the total content exceed this limit. We can easily modify the earlier definition to get the required node process (which is now parameterized by the sequence of message it currently holds):

$$
\begin{aligned}
D_i(s) \;\; = \;\; & (in.i?m \rightarrow D_i(s^\frown\langle m\rangle)\,\lessdot\#s < limit(i)\gtrdot STOP) \\
& \square\; (ring.i?m \rightarrow D_i(s^\frown\langle m\rangle)\,\lessdot\#s < capacity(i)\gtrdot STOP) \\
& \square\; (STOP \lessdot s = \langle\rangle\gtrdot \\
& \quad (out.i!head(s) \rightarrow D_i(tail(s)) \\
& \quad \lessdot destination(head(s)) = i\gtrdot \\
& \quad ring.(i \oplus 1)!head(s) \rightarrow D_i(tail(s))))
\end{aligned}
$$

(where $1 \leq limit(i) < capacity(i)$).

We would intuitively expect a ring of these processes to be deadlock-free because

- The ring can never become full, in the sense that every node is full to its *capacity*. Therefore there is at least one node that is not full.

---

[9]It is unacceptable because one would normally expect the ring to be moderately well distributed. Having a process which has to synchronize with every input and output is therefore not practical.

- A node that is not full will accept input from its ring predecessor.

- The said predecessor can at all times either communicate with its own user or output to our node.

The crux of this argument is, of course, the first line. To turn it into a formal proof we would have to define and prove this statement, which itself requires understanding every state the ring can reach. (One would probably go about this by formulating and proving a suitable *invariant* – something we will discuss later.) We will shortly find that the proof of deadlock freedom can be cast in rather different terms, much more akin to the methods seen hitherto.

A substantial case study (most of which is cast in OCCAM rather than CSP) of how this ring mechanism can be extended to a deadlock-free routeing protocol for use on an arbitrarily connected network can be found in [93]. *(End of example)*

The only cycle of ungranted requests that could arise in the ring above is of each node blocked from outputting to its clockwise neighbour. (The reverse cycle of each node waiting for input does not arise because then all the nodes are prepared to input – i.e., communicate outside the vocabulary of the network, which means this is not formally an ungranted request.) Consider the state of an individual node in this cycle: it is certainly full, and the last communication it performed was the one that filled it. But that communication must have been from its anticlockwise neighbour rather than from its external user, because of the way it is defined. We can deduce that our node has communicated more recently with its anticlockwise neighbour than with its clockwise one.

This brings us right back into familiar territory: as we progress clockwise round the cycle of ungranted requests we find that the most recent communications on the channels were earlier and earlier, creating the usual contradiction when we have gone all the way round. Thus the cycle, and consequently deadlock, are impossible. This is formalized in the following.

DEADLOCK RULE 8 *Suppose V is a network which is free of strong conflict and such that, for each pair P, Q of neighbouring processes, it can be shown that, whenever $P \Longrightarrow_\bullet Q$,*

(i) *Q has previously communicated with P and*

(ii) *Q has done so more recently than with at least one other process to which Q has a request,*

then V is deadlock-free.

This rule allows us to prove our ring deadlock-free by local analysis (since, like all of our rules, the conditions underlying this one are checked by looking at the behaviour of individual processes or small collections of them). Another, larger example that uses Rule 8 can be found in Section 15.2.1.

Of course, once we have discovered this rule, other related rules immediately occur to us. We could, for example, turn the above rule around and specify that Q must have communicated with another neighbour (to which it has a current request) more recently than any communication with P. This looks less likely and the author is not aware of any natural applications.

EXERCISE 13.2.1   Recall the treatment of the alternating bit protocol in Section 5.3. We argued on page 132 that it is deadlock-free. That argument can be re-cast in terms of one of the rules in this section: do so.

EXERCISE 13.2.2   Suppose V is a cyclic communication network satisfying the assumptions of Rule 5. Show how to build an ordering on the edges that satisfies the conditions of Rule 4, showing that Rule 5 is a consquence of its predecessor. *Hint: identify each edge with the two-element set of the nodes at each end.*

EXERCISE 13.2.3   Define a version of the 'virtual network' on page 344 that operates in three dimensions rather than two. You still only require 2 layers. Define the node ordering with respect to which Rule 2 applies to your network.

EXERCISE 13.2.4   Recall Exercise 13.1.3. Now design a token ring proper, in the sense that you have a single token passing clockwise round a ring network. When a node wants the token (but does not have it), it issues a request to its anticlockwise neighbour and then waits for it to arrive. It should be a cyclic communication network that is deadlock-free by Rule 4.

EXERCISE 13.2.5   Provide definitions of the nodes in a wormhole routeing network based (like that in Figure 13.4) on a two-dimensional virtual routeing network. Assume that each message consists of a series of packets, with a special one representing the end of the message. Identify which of the states of these processes are types A and B for Rule 4, and check that they satisfy the necessary conditions to make this rule work.

13.3   Variants

13.3.1   Introduction

The arguments underlying the various principles in the previous section seem to be variations on a common theme: we follow a putative cycle of ungranted requests and find that some ordering property gives a contradiction once we have gone all the way round.

We can unify the rules under a single theory, which gives perhaps the most general practical tool for proving deadlock freedom in networks with cycles. The idea is related to a well-known method of proving loop termination in sequential programming, namely *variants*. In sequential programming a variant function is a usually natural-number valued function of state, with the property that every time the loop body is executed the value of the function decreases. The fact that such a function cannot decrease for ever means that the loop must terminate after a finite number of iterations.

The corresponding idea in deadlock analysis is to make sure a variant function decreases round a cycle of ungranted requests. We associate a value – its variant – with the state of each process. Showing this decreases once round the cycle is enough since the variant of each process is then less than itself *in the same state*, which gives exactly the sort of contradiction we were getting in the arguments in the previous section. Because this type of argument is essentially finitary, there is no need to restrict ourselves to orders which, like the natural numbers, have no infinite descending sequences.

The first thing we have to do to use variants is to define the functions themselves. Usually these depend on two things: the node's position in the network and its current trace. But there is no particular limitation on what is included – it may be necessary, for example, to include internal process parameters or to take account of the way an internal nondeterministic choice is resolved. All that matters is that the variant can be calculated in terms of the node's own state and history.

The reason why this last condition is necessary is the requirement that the preconditions to our proof rules are locally checkable. We need to be sure that the fact that variants decrease across ungranted requests between P and Q when we examine their parallel composition implies that the same is true when they are part of a large network.

Given a network $\{(P_i, A_i) \mid 1 \leq i \leq N\}$ the associated variant functions will usually be written $\{f_i \mid 1 \leq i \leq N\}$. The f_i are all functions into the same partial order Z, and as discussed above will usually be functions of the traces of the corresponding P_i. For clarity, many of the rules and arguments below assume that they *are* functions of traces but can be modified easily to take account of other circumstances. The objective in defining these functions is to make the value decrease over any ungranted request. In many – perhaps a majority of – practical cases it is possible to make the variant decrease *strictly* over every ungranted request, which gives the easiest-to-understand case.

DEADLOCK RULE 9   *A network V is deadlock-free if it has a system of variant functions such that, for every pair (P_i, P_j) of neighbouring processes and every state σ of their parallel composition*

$$P_i \overset{\sigma}{\Longrightarrow}\!\bullet P_j \;\Rightarrow\; f_i(tr_\sigma \restriction A_i) > f_j(tr_\sigma \restriction A_j)$$

Notice that we did not explicitly assume the network to be free of strong conflict: in fact the assumptions of the rule *imply* conflict freedom since two processes with an ungranted request to each other would both need to have variants less than the other.

Most of the rules in the previous section can be reduced to this one. Two examples of this are given below, and others are included as exercises at the end of this section.

EXAMPLE 13.3.1 (RULE 4 IN TERMS OF RULE 9) We can more or less translate the proof that Rule 4 (concerning cyclic communication networks) guarantees deadlock freedom into a system of variant functions. Notice that the proof uses two levels of order: a cycle count and then events. This suggests that the partial order should compound these two ideas together: $\mathbb{N} \times L$, where the first component is the natural number of cycles a node has completed and the second is the linear order from the statement of the rule. The order on this structure is

$$(n, a) \leq (m, b) \Leftrightarrow n \leq m \vee (n = m \wedge a \leq b)$$

The variant of process P_i after trace s is then just the pair (n, c) where n is the number of cycles completed (i.e., the natural number $\#s$ div k_i where k_i is the number of events P_i communicates each cycle) and c is the channel on which it is due to communicate on next. The statement that, for each state σ of the parallel composition of P_i and P_j,

$$P_i \stackrel{\sigma}{\Longrightarrow} \bullet P_j \Rightarrow f_i(tr_\sigma \upharpoonright A_i) > f_j(tr_\sigma \upharpoonright A_j)$$

then follows by exactly the arguments we put forward earlier when justifying Rule 4. We have simply translated the original proof to the framework of variants rather than found a genuinely different proof.

We can, of course, use orders (for the range of the variant functions) that are less contrived. For example, if we enumerate the channels in the order of L: $c_1, c_2, \ldots, c_M$ then, for sufficiently large K the variant functions

$$f_i(s) = K \times (s \text{ div } k_i) + nextindex(s)$$

work, where $nextindex(s)$ is the index in this enumeration of the channel that P_i is due to communicate on next. (K has to be sufficiently large so that any pair of neighbouring processes with one a cycle behind the other always give the smaller variant to that one. M is certainly large enough.)

Slightly simpler variant functions than these can be found for many examples of this type: see the exercises for ones that work on the matrix multiplication examples. *(End of example)*

EXAMPLE 13.3.2 (RULE 2 IN TERMS OF RULE 9) The two things we have to build the variant from in Rule 2 are a node's position in the node ordering, and what it is doing. So far as the rule is concerned there are really only two possibilities for the latter: either it is making a request to all processes less than itself (call this an α state), or it is not making a request to any of them (a β state). There are four sorts of ungranted requests we can get in one of these networks:

1. A process in an α state can have an ungranted request to a predecessor in an α state.

2. A process in an α state can have an ungranted request to a predecessor in a β state (because the latter is waiting for a different successor).

3. A process in an α state *might* (if able to output as well as input) have an ungranted request to a successor in a β state.

4. A process in a β state can have an ungranted request to a successor in a β state.

The other four cases are impossible because of the assumptions of the rule: a process in a β state has no requests to its predecessors, and no process can have an ungranted request to a successor in an α state (here we are using the assumption of conflict freedom from the rule).

The partial order we use is thus $\{\alpha, \beta\} \times W$, where W is the node ordering, and

- $(\alpha, x) > (\beta, y)$ for all x and y

- $(\alpha, x) > (\alpha, y)$ if, and only if, $x > y$

- $(\beta, x) > (\beta, y)$ if, and only if, $x < y$ (note that the sense of the node ordering is reversed for this clause).

The variants are then obvious: a process maps to the pair of the type of its state and its position in the node ordering. That these satisfy the requirements of Rule 9 follows directly from the analysis above.

It is worth remarking that these variant functions may have to be thought of as functions on (maximal) failures rather than traces: in the general case it may not be possible to tell from the trace alone whether a process is in an α or β state. *(End of example)*

13.3.2   Cycle-cutting sets

Having established the basic idea of a variant function, we can develop a few variations which give it a little more power. The first of these is based on the realization that making the variant decrease *strictly* all the way round a cycle contains an element of overkill. It would be just as effective if we were to guarantee the variant is non-strictly decreasing (i.e., $\geq$) over each ungranted request, in such a way that there is always at least one strict decrease in every cycle.

The easiest-to-understand way to obtain this is to nominate a set C of directed edges such that every proper cycle in the communication graph contains one of them. Then we simply have to insist that ungranted requests over an edge in C always have a strictly decreasing variant. Such a set will be called a *cycle-cutting set* for obvious reasons.

As an example, consider a rectangular grid network like that defined for the matrix multiplier array earlier in this chapter. A possible C for this network is the set of all directed edges leading in any one of the four directions up, down, left or right – since any cycle is bound to contain at least one of each.

DEADLOCK RULE 10   *If the network V is free of strong conflict and has a system of variant functions f_j and a cycle-cutting set C such that, for every pair (P_i, P_j) of neighbouring processes and every state σ of their parallel composition*

$$P_i \overset{\sigma}{\Longrightarrow}\bullet P_j \Rightarrow \quad \begin{aligned} f_i(tr_\sigma \restriction A_i) &\geq f_j(tr_\sigma \restriction A_j) \quad \text{and} \\ f_i(tr_\sigma \restriction A_i) &> f_j(tr_\sigma \restriction A_j) \quad \text{if } (i,j) \in C \end{aligned}$$

then V is deadlock-free.

We have had to bring in the explicit assumption of freedom from strong conflict, since the non-strict variant decrease is not enough to exclude it.

The more liberal requirements for variant functions can be used both to create simpler variants for networks that could have been dealt with by Rule 9, and to deal with some that could not. Below there is an example of each.

EXAMPLE 13.3.3 (MATRIX MULTIPLICATION AGAIN)   We once again deal with the first – purely cyclic – array of processes defined for matrix multiplication. Choose as C the set of *downward*-pointing edges. It turns out that with this choice we can simplify the variant functions to just the cycle-count: i.e.,

$$f_{i,j}(s) = \#s \text{ div } 4$$

Work previously done implies that this variant is non-increasing over all ungranted requests in any cyclic communication network. The important thing to notice about the cyclic order we chose (guided by a linear order) – $\langle up, left, right, down \rangle$ – is that because the first thing a node does on each cycle is look *up*, the existence of an ungranted request on a downward-pointing edge (i.e., one in C) implies that the upper node is one cycle ahead of the lower one. In other words the simplified variants decrease and the conditions of Rule 10 are satisfied. *(End of example)*

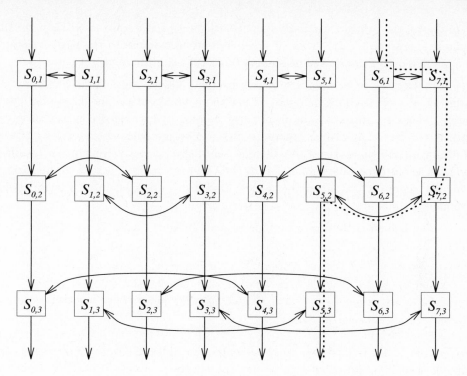

Figure 13.6 Binary switching network.

EXAMPLE 13.3.4 (BINARY SWITCHING NETWORK) Suppose there are a number of potential senders and receivers of messages, each of whom might wish to send a message to any one of a class of receivers. With a carefully chosen network structure one can connect 2^n of each with the average path length only being as long (to within a small constant factor) as that of the n^2 nodes connected by a square version of the virtual routeing network we saw earlier.[10]

The network, shown for $n = 3$ in Figure 13.6, has 2^n columns of n 'switch' processes, with a sender and a receiver connected at each end. Each is connected to exactly one process in a different column: the one in column i and row j is connected to the one in row k and column $\overline{i}^j$, the natural number with the same binary representation as i except that the jth least significant bit has been complemented.

The routeing algorithm is very simple: it is the duty of the processes in row j to make sure that the jth least significant bit in the address of the message matches that of the place it is sent to. In other words, if the (i, j) process receives a message

[10]Though that network certainly has compensating advantages.

from above, the jth bit of i is compared with that of the address. If they are the same the message is sent down, if not it is switched across to the node's partner $(\overline{i}^j, j)$. The path from 6 (110 in binary) to 5 (101) is illustrated in Figure 13.6.

In fact the precise nature of this routeing algorithm is irrelevant from the point of view of deadlock analysis, as are the contents of the messages communicated. Thus, we *abstract* away from these details. All we need concern ourselves with is the fact that a node might receive a message from above or its partner. A message from the partner (on channel *swin*, say) is always sent down (channel *out*), while one from above (channel *in*) is either sent down or across to the partner (channel *swout*). From our point of view, under this abstraction, this latter choice is nondeterministic.

The behaviour of a typical node is given below:

$$
\begin{aligned}
Sw &= in \rightarrow (Sw' \sqcap out \rightarrow Sw) \\
&\quad \square\ swin \rightarrow out \rightarrow Sw \\
Sw' &= swout \rightarrow Sw \\
&\quad \square\ swin \rightarrow out \rightarrow Sw'
\end{aligned}
$$

Notice that, when this process contains a message which it has decided to send over its link (i.e., is in state Sw'), it retains the ability to accept a message from the linked process. This is to avoid the strong conflict which would otherwise have arisen if both of a pair of partners decided simultaneously to relay messages to each other. The network is free of strong conflict, but not of conflict, since when each of a pair of partners is empty they have ungranted requests to each other. This last fact implies that Rule 9 does not apply, but it is straightforward to apply Rule 10 with C the set of all vertical edges (i.e., all except the ones linking partner nodes). The variant function $f_{i,j}$ of node $Sw_{i,j}$ is defined:

$$
f_{i,j}(s) = \begin{cases} j & \text{when the node contains no message} \\ -j & \text{when it contains one or more messages} \end{cases}
$$

These work because, in our network, no node that contains a message can have an ungranted request to one that is empty. Notice that when a pair of partners are either both empty or both non-empty, their variants are equal.

The node process above is what you would get if you started with a definition in which all the information necessary for routeing were included, and the decisions made accordingly, and then applied a forgetful many-to-one renaming which omitted the address and data components of communications. This abstraction mechanism will be re-examined in Section 13.6.1 *(End of example)*

13.3.3 Selective requests

The rules seen so far insist that *all* ungranted requests a process makes have a reducing variant across them. Looking back at how we derived the Fundamental Principle, this is a little more than we really need. All we require is that the ungranted requests which we happen to have chosen for the processes in the cycle have this property. And of course we are free to select any ungranted request for the process P_n in the sequence as long as it is not back to P_{n-1}.

In just about all the examples we have seen to date (the nearest thing to an exception among the concrete examples being the binary switching network), all the requests a process makes in any one state have been similar to each other. There was no particular reason why the process should single one out. But in less symmetric examples one can imagine a process might be making several very different requests at once, and of course it (and we) might have different expectations about the processes at the other ends of these requests. Since we only need to follow a single path to find the cycle for the Fundamental Principle, it may be sensible in such circumstances to nominate which request to follow from a given one (selected from the set of requests it is making in its current state). Ordinarily one would expect to select the one (or one of those) that we are relying on eventually being able to satisfy the request.

So as well as having a variant function of each process's state, we will also have a *request selector* function. For each state σ of process P_i which is (i) stable and (ii) refuses all events not in the vocabulary of the network, $c_i(\sigma)$ must choose a process to which P_i has a request in σ (the assumption of busy-ness implying there is at least one to choose from). The advantage of this is that the variant only has to decrease across *chosen* ungranted requests: $P_i \overset{\sigma}{\Longrightarrow}\bullet P_j$ where $c_i(\sigma) = j$.

We state here the rule that corresponds to Rule 9 – i.e., the variant functions always decrease strictly. One could similarly produce an analogue of Rule 10, but in that case care has to be taken to ensure that a pair of nodes in conflict do not select each other.

DEADLOCK RULE 11   *If the network V has a system of variant functions such that, for every pair (P_i, P_j) of neighbouring processes and every state σ of their parallel composition*

$$P_i \overset{\sigma}{\Longrightarrow}\bullet P_j \wedge j = c_i(\sigma) \ \Rightarrow\ f_i(tr_\sigma \restriction A_i) > f_j(tr_\sigma \restriction A_j)$$

then V is deadlock-free.

It is possible to modify some of the rules of Section 13.2 in the same way to allow for explicit selection, notably Rule 8 (which already contains an element of it).

One of the best uses of selection functions is to liberalize communications in a network that has been carefully engineered to be deadlock-free, but where a seemingly heavy penalty has been paid for this. The approach is to extend the range of requests a process makes – adding some 'optimistic' ones – but in such a way that the variant functions continue to be defined and to work for the old requests. The selection functions then choose the old requests.

One example of this – relaxing the constraints imposed by Rule 7 on resource acquisition – can be found in the exercises below.

13.3.4 Weak variants

A *weak* set of variants is one where there is never the requirement of a strict decrease over an ungranted request. All we insist on is a non-strict reduction. (While there may be some use for ones equipped with selection functions as discussed above, we will assume that this decrease occurs over all ungranted requests.) Weak variants do not in themselves prove absence of deadlocks – after all if we simply choose the same constant function for each process in a network, the non-decreasing requirement is satisfied whether the network deadlocks or not.

What they can do is refine our understanding of where a deadlock might be in a network, allowing us to concentrate our search. In some cases it may be possible to refine the weak variants into a set that does prove deadlock freedom by one of our earlier rules, or to establish deadlock freedom by some other method. In other words, weak variants are an analytic tool.

The following rule captures the main analytic principle using weak variants.

DEADLOCK RULE 12   *If the network V is free of strong conflict, and has a system of variant functions such that for every pair (P_i, P_j) of neighbouring processes and every state σ of their parallel composition*

$$P_i \stackrel{\sigma}{\Longrightarrow}\!\bullet P_j \;\Rightarrow\; f_i(tr_\sigma \upharpoonright A_i) \geq f_j(tr_\sigma \upharpoonright A_j)$$

(a weak set of variant functions) then every deadlock state of V has a proper cycle of ungranted requests in which all the variant values are equal.

EXAMPLE 13.3.5 (CYCLIC COMMUNICATION AGAIN) Good examples of the analytic power of weak variants can be found in the area of cyclic communication networks and, more generally,[11] conflict-free networks where each process communicates exactly once each cycle on each channel.

---

[11]The generalization comes from not assuming that the communications are in the same order each cycle.

The natural weak variants for such systems are just cycle counts: in the notation of earlier discussions of similar networks:

$$w_i(s) \ = \ s \operatorname{div} k_i$$

No process can have an ungranted request to a neighbour that has completed more cycles, because this would imply that the requesting process has communicated on the requested channel less times than the other process (contradicting the fact that the two processes synchronize on such events and so have at all times communicated on the channel exactly the same number of times).

Thus, by Rule 12, any deadlock state must contain a cycle of ungranted requests with every process having completed the same number of cycles. This means, for example, that the fact that a process can vary its order from cycle to cycle is irrelevant: all that matters is the particular order they have chosen for this cycle. One can, by examining how this cycle can arise, deduce that there is a cycle of processes $\langle Q_0, \ldots, Q_{r-1} \rangle$ and one (with the same length) of channels $\langle c_0, \ldots, c_{r-1} \rangle$ where c_i and $c_{i \oplus 1}$ are both in the alphabet of P_i which insists (in the offending cycle) on communicating $c_{i \oplus 1}$ before c_i.

If we had not already seen Rules 4, 5 and 6 we would have been in a much better position to deduce them after the above analysis.

We now turn to a fascinating specific example, where we can refine the weak variants a little. Imagine a network which behaves like the rectangular matrix multiplication array except that nodes are allowed to choose nondeterministically in which order to communicate the two inputs and in which order to communicate the two outputs. (We still insist that inputs precede outputs.) Ignoring the data values and calculations, the resulting node then behaves like

$$
\begin{aligned}
NDN \quad = \quad & ((\textit{left} \rightarrow \textit{up} \rightarrow SKIP) \\
& \sqcap (\textit{up} \rightarrow \textit{left} \rightarrow SKIP)); \\
& ((\textit{right} \rightarrow \textit{down} \rightarrow SKIP) \\
& \sqcap (\textit{down} \rightarrow \textit{right} \rightarrow SKIP)); \\
& NDN
\end{aligned}
$$

Now consider the number of *half*-cycles a node has completed when it has an ungranted request to its neighbour.

- When it has an ungranted output (*down* or *right*) request it must have completed at least one more half-cycle than the process it is requesting to.

- When it has an ungranted input (*left* or *in*) request it must have completed at least the number that is one less than the half-cycle count of the process it is requesting.

If we therefore define a set of weak variants

$$w_{i,j}(s) = i + j + (s \text{ div } 2)$$

we find that these satisfy the conditions of Rule 12. For a process such that $i+j = K$ (level K) outputs to ones at level $K + 1$ and inputs from ones at level $K - 1$.

We can thus infer that any deadlock state of the resulting network must have a cycle of nodes whose variants $w_{i,j}(s)$ are equal. Closer examination shows this to be impossible, for

- If a process (in level K, say) has an ungranted request to one in level $K + 1$ and their variants are equal (i.e., the first process has completed exactly one more half-cycle than the second) then the second process itself has all its ungranted requests to other processes in level K. (In other words, it must be waiting for its other input first.)

- If a process (in level K, say) has an ungranted request to one in level $K - 1$ and their variants are equal, then the second process itself has all its ungranted requests to other processes in level K.

- If follows that the cycle of ungranted requests lies in the nodes on two adjoining levels: K and $K + 1$, say. But there is no cycle amongst these nodes (which actually form a chain when thought of as a graph).

In other words, from the point of view of deadlock, it actually does not matter what order the nodes choose to input and output in on each cycle (and they may choose independently) so long as they make all their inputs before their outputs.

Exactly the same analysis applies when we move up to higher-dimensional grids of processes (e.g., three-dimensional) and allow the processes to order their inputs and outputs nondeterministically (there being as many of each as there are dimensions). *Except*, that is, the very last part, for in three or more dimensions the set of processes in two consecutive layers does contain cycles, and the system can actually deadlock (see exercises). This difference between two and three dimensions is most surprising and the fact that we can discover it so easily illustrates the power of weak variants in focusing in on the essentials of a deadlock analysis. *(End of example)*

EXERCISE 13.3.1   Show that the variants

$$f_{i,j}(s) = 2 \times (i + j) + \#s$$

work for Rule 9 for the matrix multiplier array.

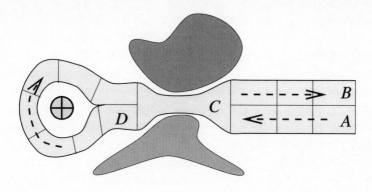

Figure 13.7 Road with a narrow section: see Exercise 13.3.5.

EXERCISE 13.3.2   On page 361 we showed how Rule 2 could be shown to be a consequence of Rule 9 by constructing a set of variant functions. Do the same thing for Rule 3.

EXERCISE 13.3.3   Take your solution to Exercise 13.2.4 (token ring with request messages). Find a set of variant functions for Rule 9, and a simplified set (together with a set of cycle-cutting edges) for Rule 10.

EXERCISE 13.3.4   (a)   Show that Rule 7 (resource acquisition) can by proved via Rule 9, again by defining a suitable set of variants.

(b)   Use the variant functions defined in (a) and Rule 11 to liberalize Rule 7: users can be given the additional ability to acquire any resource they want at any time provided they follow rules about there being at least one 'legitimate' request in each state. Formulate these rules.

EXERCISE 13.3.5   Figure 13.7 shows a road layout allowing visitors to drive round a monument. Cars all enter the road at *A* and pass round the loop until they exit at *B*. As you can see, a pair of rocks have meant that one stretch of road is too narrow for cars to pass each other: it is single lane there and two-lane elsewhere.

Code CSP processes which implement this layout, with one process per lane segment with the assumption that no more than one car can occupy each with, for the moment, no other restriction on who can move forward onto the next segment on their route. (Except for segment *C*, each should have two states, *Empty* and *Full*; *C* should have three states, *Empty*, *Leftwards* and *Rightwards*.) Show that this can lead to deadlock.

It is then decided to give out-going (i.e., rightward in our picture) cars priority over in-coming ones, in the sense that an in-coming car is not allowed to enter the single-lane segment (*C*) until segment *D* is empty. Modify your coding to achieve this, it will require extra communication between *C* and *D*. Your aim should be to produce a system that is now deadlock-free via a rigorous argument. The following is a suggested argument.

Use a set of weak variants (taking values in $\{0, 1\}$) to show that, in any state with a deadlock, either all segments are empty or there is a cycle of ungranted requests involving full segments only. Show that the first of these is not deadlocked.

Now show that, when full, segment C can never have an ungranted request to D nor *vice-versa*, and that therefore the cycle of full processes cannot arise.

How would your coding and argument be affected if there were more than one single lane segment (all separated by two-lane stretches)? Would it work to give in-coming traffic priority rather than out-going?

EXERCISE 13.3.6   Find the deadlock discussed on page 368 that appears in a three-dimensional version of a nondeterministic input/output systolic array.

13.4   Network decomposition

Remember Rule 1, which shows how simple deadlock analysis is for tree networks. We might hope to inherit some of this simplicity in cases where the network, though not a tree itself, can be decomposed into a number of components (probably not trees themselves) which are connected to each other like a tree. Specifically, we might hope that the proof of deadlock freedom can be broken down into a separate proof for each component.

First, we have to decide on exactly what it means for a graph to break down into a number of components. There are really two sensible answers to this question, both of which turn out to be relevant to decomposing deadlock analyses. For simplicity we will concentrate on the coarser factorization (i.e., the one that divides a network into fewer pieces), but will later indicate where the other one could have been used.

Define a *disconnecting edge* to be one whose removal would disconnect the communication graph. Such an edge can never be part of any cycle since the rest of the cycle provides an alternative path between its two ends. These edges can be thought of as the edges of a tree whose nodes are the components they leave behind when they are all removed. These components might be termed *essential components* since we hope to concentrate our deadlock analysis on these.

This gives a very pleasing decomposition of our network: if $C_1, C_2, \ldots, C_k$ are the partition of the nodes (or rather their indexes) into essential components, and $A_1^*, A_2^*, \ldots, A_k^*$ are the unions of the alphabets of the members of these components, we have

$$\left\|{}_{i=1}^{n}\right.(P_i, A_i) \;=\; \left\|{}_{i=1}^{k}\right.(P_i^*, A_k^*) \quad \text{where} \quad P_j^* \;=\; \left\|{}_{i \in C_j}\right.(P_i, A_i)$$

is the composition of the processes in the component C_j. The communication graph of this re-construction of the network is, of course, a tree and the intersection in the alphabets of two neighbouring components is just the intersection of the alphabets of the unique pair of processes in them that are adjacent in the original graph (across a disconnecting edge).

Since we have a tree (the network V^* comprising the (P_j^*, A_j^*)), the obvious hope is that we can apply Rule 1. There are two requirements of Rule 1 that we need to be careful are satisfied:

- The new network has to be *busy*. In other words, the subnetworks defining the P_j^* must all be deadlock-free. This is hardly surprising: the individual proofs of deadlock freedom for the P_j^* are just the parts our overall analysis gets factored into.

- The new network has to be free of strong conflict. This creates more of a problem since it turns out that even if the original network V was free of strong conflict, V^* need not be. If, however, each of the (disconnecting) edges in V linking two of the P_j^* is free of conflict, then it is easy to see that V^* is also free of conflict, which is of course enough.

DEADLOCK RULE 13   *If each of the essential components of the network V is free of deadlock, and each of the disconnecting edges in V is free of conflict, then V is deadlock-free.*

This rule is pleasingly general except for the requirement that the disconnecting edges are conflict-free. This more or less excludes the nodes at either end getting into a state where each is waiting for some stimulus (e.g., a message packet) from the other. Its use is therefore largely restricted to cases where, either naturally or by careful design (e.g., the introduction of to-and-fro polling across such edges), the two processes at the ends of a disconnecting edge agree which channel their next communication will be on.

Of course we are still left with the problem of proving the essential components deadlock-free. It is quite likely that we will use some of the methods seen in this chapter which work by proving the non-existence of cycles of ungranted requests. If this is done, then the restriction that the disconnecting edges are conflict-free can be dropped.

DEADLOCK RULE 14   *If the network V is free of strong conflict, and such that none of the essential components can contain a cycle of ungranted requests (judged relative to the vocabulary of V, not those of the components) then V is deadlock-free.*

This is, of course, a trivial consequence of the Fundamental Principle since the cycle of ungranted requests this generates must lie entirely within one of the

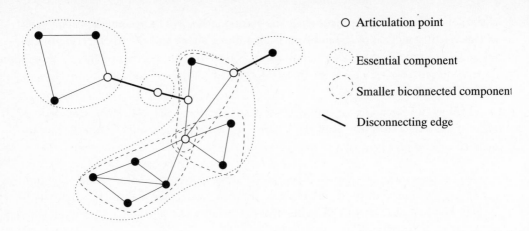

Figure 13.8 Two ways of decomposing graphs.

essential components. Of our rules so far, Rules 2, 3, 4, 5, 7, 9 and 10 all exclude cycles entirely.

For example, we can choose the variant functions (if Rule 9 or 10 is to be our chosen method) for the different essential components independently: there is no need for variants to decrease across disconnecting edges.

We mentioned above that there are two natural ways to decompose a network. The difference between these comes from so-called *articulation points*: *nodes* rather than *edges* whose removal would disconnect the graph. The *biconnected components* of a graph are the largest subsets of a graph such that any two different points belong to a proper cycle. In general one essential component[12] may divide into several biconnected components: the divisions coming at articulation points like the one shown in Figure 13.8 which belongs to three different biconnected components. To find out more about this, consult a book on graph theory such as [41].

Rule 14 applies if essential components are replaced by biconnected components, since any proper cycle always lies completely inside one of these (which are the smallest regions of which this can be said). This can lead to the curious situation where we have to define two (or even more) different variant functions for a single node: one for each biconnected component it belongs to!

EXERCISE 13.4.1   Suppose there are two adjacent tables of dining philosophers, each individually made deadlock-free as in Example 13.2.4. A pair of them (one from each table) make a pact that they will always eat at the same time: how is this situation described in

---

[12]In graph theoretic terms essential components are termed *edge biconnected components*.

CSP? Show that it does not harm deadlock freedom. What can happen if there are two, disjoint, pairs of philosophers like this?

13.5   The limitations of local analysis

Deadlock is a global phenomenon over a network and sometimes arises – or fails to arise – for extremely subtle reasons. There is probably no complete method for deciding whether or not a network deadlocks other than brute-force state exploration. And yet all the methods described in this chapter so far have relied entirely on *local* analysis: establishing properties of the behaviour of small collections – usually no more than 2 – of processes. Such methods can never hope to decide all cases, though they do seem to work in a large proportion of the examples that we humans are cunning enough to devise.

If faced with the problem of designing a network that had to be deadlock-free, you should look first to the principles already established in this chapter, including concepts not emphasized much such as building some of the pairs of processes so that an ungranted request can never arise in one or both directions.

There is a rather precise sense in which all of our existing methods produce networks that are *robustly* deadlock-free. It is this: all of the existing rules which themselves guarantee deadlock freedom (Rules 1–11) actually guarantee the stronger condition of *hereditary* deadlock freedom, meaning that the network and all its subnetworks are deadlock-free.

What this does mean is that there can be no hope of using them to prove the deadlock freedom of networks where one subnetwork relies on the behaviour of other processes to prevent it reaching a deadlock state it might otherwise find itself in. The archetypal example of this is the dining philosophers with butler we saw earlier: this is not hereditarily deadlock-free since the network can deadlock if the *BUTLER* process is removed.

That was a case where it was very easy to do things properly, but there are other examples where this is much harder and/or unreasonable. An example of this is shown in Figure 13.9 which shows a picture of a small railway layout, in which each of the pieces of track is one-way and there are two sets of points. The rules are that a train can only move onto an empty section of track (where, if relevant, the points are not against it) and that each set of points can only be switched when the segment of track containing it is empty. Unlike some other codings of railways in this book, the only processes in this network are the track segments, with adjoining ones communicating with each other to represent the movement of a train, rather than there being separate train processes.

If we happen to know that there are only two trains running round this picture we will probably quickly come to believe it is deadlock-free. On the other

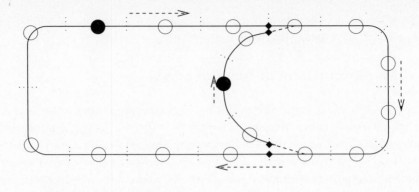

●   Full track segment

○   Empty track segment

Figure 13.9 A simple railway layout with two trains.

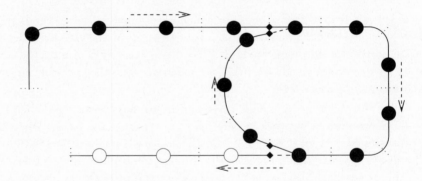

Figure 13.10 A subnetwork that deadlocks.

hand, it is not hereditarily deadlock-free: as soon as we look at a proper subnetwork such as that shown in Figure 13.10 there is nothing to prevent what is left becoming filled up with trains. We have to rely on the fact that the overall network is closed to prevent any more getting in. And this can lead to deadlocks: the configuration in Figure 13.10 (in which one track-segment process has been removed) is deadlocked because the lower 'exit' set of points on the small loop cannot move to let out any of the trains that are clogging this loop.

     In this particular case a substantial re-coding to make trains explicit processes would help, but the more natural way to go is probably to prove an *invariant* of the network (namely that the total number of trains is 2) and then use this to contradict the existence of cycles of ungranted requests. This specific sort of invariant, which can be written

$$\sum_{i=1}^{n} f_i(\sigma_i) = K$$

where $f_i(\sigma_i)$ is a function of the state σ_i of the ith process, can itself be established by local analysis: what we have to show is that each action of a single process P_i leaves its contribution unchanged, and that each communication between a pair of processes leaves their joint contribution $f_i(\sigma_i) + f_j(\sigma_j)$ invariant.

13.6   Deadlock and tools

We already know how to test a process for deadlock via refinement checking[13]: test it against one of the specifications

$$DF \quad = \quad \bigsqcap_{a \in \Sigma} a \to DF$$

$$DF^{\checkmark} \quad = \quad (\bigsqcap_{a \in \Sigma} a \to DF^{\checkmark}) \sqcap SKIP$$

depending whether or not it has the potential to terminate. When a system is within the scope of this type of check, this is usually the easiest way to analyze for deadlock. It has the added advantage that none of the basic assumptions such as busy-ness and triple-disjointness made at the start of this chapter is required. In the first part of this section we look at ways of bringing relatively complex networks within the scope of this form of checking; in the second we discuss tools which implement techniques more like those seen hitherto in this chapter.

13.6.1   Direct mechanical checking of deadlock freedom

The direct approach to analyzing systems for deadlock: simply testing for refinement of *DF* has two main drawbacks. The first, which we can do little about, is that any check of a system on FDR requires us to define a specific network. There is no sense in which we can directly prove that a particular structure of network is deadlock-free whatever its size. We can only attack N dining philosophers for a particular N, not for all N at once.

---

[13]FDR has a specific deadlock-checking function. At the time of writing all this does is to perform this refinement check; everything discussed in this section about improving the efficiency of the said check therefore applies to the FDR deadlock check.

The second problem is one of state-space size. Many problems of interest have (at least in non-trivial instances) very large state-spaces and quickly get out of the range that FDR can deal with by enumerating one state at a time. There are two main tricks that can be used to bring a problem down to the size where its deadlock behaviour can be analyzed on FDR.

The first is *abstraction*. Usually our intended use of a network will involve it in handling data values; for example, passing messages around or processing numbers. Certainly we would expect the values passed along channels to depend on this data. It may or may not be the case that which channels the process communicates on also depends on data. Good examples to consider here are the matrix multiplication nodes, where the values passed along channels depend on data, but the choices of which channels do not, and our various routeing networks, where both the contents of messages and where they are sent depend on data (i.e., address fields).

Assume that communication on a given channel is straightforward (specifically, conflict-free). In the first case above – where the only thing that depends on input data is output data – it is clear that the data being passed is quite irrelevant from the point of view of deadlock analysis. Thus, for deadlock analysis, the matrix multiplication node process

$$N(x) = up?a \rightarrow left?b \rightarrow right!b \rightarrow down!a \rightarrow N(x + a \times b)$$

is equivalent to one with all the data values removed:

$$N^\dagger = up \rightarrow left \rightarrow right \rightarrow down \rightarrow N^\dagger$$

This process of abstraction has reduced a process with an infinite state space (assuming the values are real numbers) to one with four states.[14]

Now consider a node from the virtual routeing network (Section 13.2.1). The data it transmits is in two parts: address and message contents. We would expect to be able to abstract away from the contents field in exactly the same way, since the only thing that depends on what is input is the value later output in the same field. The address field is, however, used in a crucial way to decide *where* (in each case of three options) to send the data, so we cannot eliminate that so easily.

Whether we can eliminate it at all depends on whether we believe (and this is a belief we can test using the following) that the precise choice between the available options is important from the point of view of deadlock. Unless you are sure it is

---

[14]This form of abstraction – removing detail which is irrelevant to the internal operation of component processes – is very closely linked to the topic of *data-independence* which we will study in Section 15.2.2.

important, you should turn all the choices, made on the basis of the data you are trying to abstract, into nondeterministic ones. Thus, the two types of node in the virtual network will become

$$I^\dagger \quad = \quad in \to I'^\dagger$$
$$\square\ I\text{-}up \to I'^\dagger$$
$$\square\ I\text{-}left \to I'^\dagger$$

$$I'^\dagger \quad = \quad I\text{-}right \to I^\dagger$$
$$\sqcap\ I\text{-}down \to I^\dagger$$
$$\sqcap\ over \to I^\dagger$$

$$O^\dagger \quad = \quad over \to O'^\dagger$$
$$\square\ O\text{-}down \to O'^\dagger$$
$$\square\ O\text{-}right \to O'^\dagger$$

$$O'^\dagger \quad = \quad O\text{-}left \to O^\dagger$$
$$\sqcap\ O\text{-}up \to O^\dagger$$
$$\sqcap\ out \to O^\dagger$$

This abstraction procedure is one you can check: if *forget* is the renaming function that forgets whatever data values we are abstracting from channel communication (e.g., $forget(in.i.j.m) = in$), you should find that

$$I^\dagger \sqsubseteq forget(I)$$

In other words, every behaviour that I might make is reflected in the abstracted process.

You should then use the processes $I^\dagger$ and $O^\dagger$ in place of the originals when checking for deadlock freedom. In this case it would work: in fact the proof of deadlock freedom in terms of Rule 2 works just as well for the abstracted network as it did for the original. If it does work this guarantees deadlock freedom for the unabstracted network. If it does not, and a deadlock is found, you have to decide whether the offending behaviour was one that the unabstracted network could have produced or not. Bear in mind that just because a single deadlock of the abstracted network could not appear in the original, this does *not* imply the original is deadlock-free.

The formal basis of this abstraction procedure is captured in the following rule.

DEADLOCK RULE 15 (ABSTRACTION RULE)   *Suppose 'forget' is the function that abstracts away the data contents of one or more conflict-free channels (each of which is contained in each process alphabet it intersects) in the network* $V = \{(P_i, A_i)\ |$

$1 \leq i \leq n\}$. *Then*

$$\left\|\right._{i=1}^{n}(P_i^{\dagger}, A_i^{\dagger}) \sqsubseteq forget(\left\|\right._{i=1}^{n}(P_i, A_i))$$

where $(P_i^{\dagger}, A_i^{\dagger}) = (forget(P_i), forget(A_i))$. *Hence if the left-hand side of the above refinement is deadlock-free, so is* V.

Notice that we already performed the same sort of abstraction in the binary switching network (page 363). It can, of course, also be applied to wormhole routeing.

The second method of making the state spaces of explicit checks manageable is the combination of hiding and compression. In the stable failures model a CSP process P can deadlock if and only if $P \setminus \Sigma$ can (see Section 8.4 for technical details). This is of interest because it is generally the case that the more hiding is present in a process definition, the more susceptible it is to hierarchical compression. The objective of hierarchical compression (which is discussed in more detail in Section C.2) is to build up processes in stages, at each one trying to minimize the number of states in their representations. The effectiveness of this technique is demonstrated by several of the example files on the web site (see Preface).

13.6.2 Automated checking of rule-based proofs

While the methods described above frequently allow one to investigate automatically whether a network is deadlock-free, it will certainly sometimes occur that, even using compressions, addressing the state space of the entire network is too great a problem.

It is then natural to ask whether automation can help in the sort of deadlock analysis addressed in the rest of this chapter. All of the basic conditions on networks we have used, such as busy-ness and freedom from (strong) conflict, as well as the preconditions to Rules 1–8, can quickly be checked for any network of finite-state processes, though it sometimes requires a good deal of ingenuity to do so with a refinement checker like FDR. The reason for this problem is that in conditions relating to how a pair of processes evolve (such as strong conflict) it is necessary to examine the inner workings of the pair (such as whether they have requests to each other) as well as their outward appearance as a process. It is really better, particularly because of this need to examine how pairs evolve, to build a specialized tool for checking the preconditions for deadlock rules. This has been done by Jeremy Martin, whose tool is called the *Deadlock Checker*.[15]

The later, variant-based, rules are a little more problematic to automate because we need some way to represent the variant function. It must be recognized

---

[15]See the Bibliography for the availability of this tool.

that sometimes adding a variant function can turn a finite-state process into an infinite-state one: this obviously happens when, as in the variants used for cyclic communication networks, the variant has an infinite range.

Martin's tool incorporates an additional method of analyzing for deadlock which is arguably very close to the concept of variant, but has the advantage of being completely automatic. This is based on the *State Dependency Digraph* (SDD), something which is usually too unwieldy to work out by hand but which is well within the scope of an automated tool even for very large networks. The SDD of a network has one node for each state of an individual process in the network V – thus its size is the sum of the state space sizes of the component processes. It has an edge from (i, σ) (P_i in state σ) to (j, ρ) if, and only if, P_i and P_j can simultaneously reach σ and ρ when put in parallel and then P_i has an ungranted request to P_j.

It is possible to show that the SDD is acyclic if, and only if, there is a set of variant functions for V satisfying the preconditions of Rule 9 and such that the functions are all based purely on the position the processes are in their finite state machine representations. (It should be noted that not all the variant functions used earlier have this latter property. The exceptions are those relating to cyclic communication networks and similar.) Thus an acyclic SDD implies deadlock freedom. Martin's thesis [71] and tool both contain extensions of this technique to allow SDDs to be used for proving deadlock freedom in wider classes of network such as networks with conflict.

Clearly any cycle of ungranted requests in the network implies the existence of a cycle in the SDD. It is tempting to believe the reverse, but there are two reasons why the existence of a cycle in the SDD does not necessarily imply the possibility of a cycle of ungranted requests in V.

Firstly, just because the processes round some cycle in V can reach some assignment of states when we consider their parallel compositions pairwise does not mean that the same combination can be reached in the parallel composition of the entire network.

Secondly, and more interestingly, it is entirely possible for different states of the same process to appear in the same cycle in the SDD. Obviously no such cycle can correspond to a cycle of ungranted requests. It is this possibility that generates the restriction above that the variant functions have to be based on the specific states used in constructing the SDD. Clearly one can look only for those cycles that involve all different processes, but this appears to be much more time consuming.

Despite these drawbacks, methods based on analyzing SDD graphs appear to be perhaps the most interesting and powerful class for building deadlock analysis tools.

13.7   Notes

The definitions and results in this chapter are largely taken from the author's papers with Dathi and Brookes [102] and [20] together with the theses of Dathi [25] and Martin [71], as are many of the examples. These are probably the best sources to pursue for further details. Earlier work on the analysis of deadlock in CSP networks can be found in [91] and [19]. There have been various applications of this type of analysis, especially in the OCCAM community, see [93, 120], for example.

The fact that tree networks are a special and easy case in deadlock analysis has been long known and it is hard to pin down where it originates. The conditions and definitions in Section 13.1 can be thought of as an attempt to capture formally the circumstances under which the result 'trees are deadlock-free' is true.

The concept of a cyclic communication network was described by Dijkstra and Scholten in [30], and Deadlock Rule 4 is essentially derived from that source.

It should be appreciated that none of the combinatorial techniques described in this chapter is complete, in the sense of guaranteeing to establish deadlock freedom whenever it is true. It seems almost certain that no tractable locally-based technique could do this, since in general the problem of deciding whether a CSP network can deadlock is NP complete. All one can hope for is that the methods we have described, and other similar ones, are sufficient to deal with the majority of practical deadlock analyses. Provided one is prepared to espouse the principle discussed on page 339 that we should build our systems to be inherently deadlock-free rather than adding patches later, this seems a much more reasonable desire.

The author hopes that the wide range of deadlock analysis techniques in this chapter will deal with many of the examples readers want to handle, and also give them ideas about how to formulate and prove their own rules to deal with other examples.

Example transformation

A typical transformation using algebraic laws to manipulate hiding and renaming as discussed when introducing assumption D in Section 13.1.1 is given below. The example considered is the parallel/hiding/renaming combination

$$(P \gg Q) \gg R$$

We wish to move all hiding to the outside, and all renaming on to the component processes.

First we observe that the name of the channel *mid* used in defining $\gg$ is irrelevant, because, for any other name n (apart from *left* and *right*),

$$
\begin{aligned}
P \gg Q \;=\;& (P[\![right, mid/mid, right]\!] \,_{\{|left,mid|\}}\|_{\{|mid,right|\}} \\
& Q[\![mid, left/left, mid]\!]) \setminus \{|\ mid\ |\} \\
\;=\;& ((P[\![right, mid/mid, right]\!] \,_{\{|left,mid|\}}\|_{\{|mid,right|\}} \\
& Q[\![mid, left/left, mid]\!]) \setminus \{|\ mid\ |\})[\![n/mid]\!] \\
\;=\;& (P[\![right, n/n, right]\!] \,_{\{|left,n|\}}\|_{\{|n,right|\}} \ P[\![left, n/n, left]\!]) \setminus \{|\ n\ |\}
\end{aligned}
$$

(Here the second line follows by $\langle f[\cdot]\text{-hide-null}\rangle$, and the final one by a combination of $\langle f[\cdot]\text{-hide-sym}\rangle$, $\langle f[\cdot]\text{-}_X\|_Y\text{-dist}\rangle$ and $\langle [\![R]\!]\text{-combine}\rangle$ (3.16).) Note that the last line above is identical to the definition of $P \gg Q$ except that the name n replaces *mid*.

This shows that $(P \gg Q) \gg R$ can be written:

$$
\begin{aligned}
& (((P[\![right, n/n, right]\!] \,_{\{|left,n|\}}\|_{\{|n,right|\}} \\
& Q[\![left, n/n, left]\!]) \setminus \{|\ n\ |\})[\![right, mid/mid, right]\!] \\
& _{\{|left,mid|\}}\|_{\{|mid,right|\}} \ R) \setminus \{|\ mid\ |\}
\end{aligned}
$$

This is important because it allows us to push the renaming of the inner combination down to P and Q (using $\langle f[\cdot]\text{-hide-sym}\rangle$ and $\langle f[\cdot]\text{-}_X\|_Y\text{-dist}\rangle$) without changing the name of the channel hidden at the intermediate level:

$$
\begin{aligned}
& (((P[\![right, n/n, right]\!][\![mid, right/right, mid]\!] \,_{\{|left,n|\}}\|_{\{|n,mid|\}} \\
& \qquad Q[\![left, n/n, left]\!][\![mid, right/right, mid]\!]) \setminus \{|\ n\ |\}) \\
& _{\{|left,mid|\}}\|_{\{|mid,right|\}} \ R) \setminus \{|\ mid\ |\}
\end{aligned}
$$

And equally importantly it then lets us move this intermediate-level hiding, using $\langle \text{hide-}_X\|_Y\text{-dist}\rangle$, to the outside since the events hidden do not intersect the alphabet of the right-hand process.

$$
\begin{aligned}
& ((P[\![right, n/n, right]\!][\![mid, right/right, mid]\!] \,_{\{|left,n|\}}\|_{\{|n,mid|\}} \\
& \qquad Q[\![left, n/n, left]\!][\![mid, right/right, mid]\!]) \\
& _{\{|left,mid,n|\}}\|_{\{|mid,right|\}} \ R) \setminus \{|\ n\ |\} \setminus \{|\ mid\ |\}
\end{aligned}
$$

Finally, we can collect all the renamings of each component, and all the hiding at the outside, together.

$$
\begin{aligned}
& ((P[\![right, n/n, right]\!][\![mid, right/right, mid]\!] \,_{\{|left,n|\}}\|_{\{|n,mid|\}} \\
& \qquad Q[\![left, n/n, left]\!][\![mid, right/right, mid]\!]) \\
& _{\{|left,mid,n|\}}\|_{\{|mid,right|\}} \ R) \setminus \{|\ n\ |\} \setminus \{|\ mid\ |\}
\end{aligned}
$$

Chapter 14

Modelling discrete time

14.1 Introduction

All of the modelling we have done so far has been done without measuring the passage of time. We have cared about what order events happen in, but not how long there is between them or at what time any specific one happens. When our correctness criteria are independent of time (as have been all we have seen to date, of course) and our implementations do not rely on internal timing details to meet their specifications, this abstraction is very useful since it simplifies both the description of, and reasoning about, processes. Nevertheless, it is in the nature of the sort of interactive systems we describe using CSP that sometimes it is desirable to be able to reason about their timed behaviour.

There are two distinct approaches to this. The more elegant is to re-interpret the CSP language over time, and record the exact time at which each event occurs. A trace thus consists of a series of time/event pairs rather than just events. This leads to a range of semantic models incorporating time, just as we have seen a variety of models for the untimed version. This theory of *Timed CSP*, though its models are sometimes surprisingly different to those we have seen (and generally more complex), has elegant links into the untimed theory allowing development and verification to be carried out in both. This will typically allow the developer to use the more complex timed models only for those parts of his or her work which require it.

There is a substantial literature on Timed CSP (see Section 14.8) and, in particular, a textbook (by S.A. Schneider) mainly based on it is in preparation at the time of writing. We will not, therefore, go into the details of it here.

In Timed CSP, the times associated with events are non-negative real numbers. In other words, it adopts a *dense, continuous* model of time. This has an intuitive appeal, since it corresponds with the standard way in which we think about measuring time. It is unfortunately true that using continuous time substantially complicates the problem of automating verification and, except in very restricted circumstances, makes decision procedures based on state enumeration infeasible or impossible. For continuous time adds an extra infinite dimension both to the recording of events and to the evolving process state, and it is only by imposing severe restrictions and using clever equivalences that this infinity can be avoided.

The most obvious alternative model of time is of an infinite series of discrete instants, equally separated. This results in a time domain which looks like the natural numbers, though the interval between successive beats of the drum might be any size, from nanoseconds (as would typically be the case for a clocked circuit) upwards. In most computer applications where all of the component processes are ultimately controlled by a single clock, such as clocked VLSI or scheduler-based systems, a discrete clock is closer to the spirit of the system than a continuous time model. In any case it is often possible to give a good enough approximation to other systems using sufficiently fine discrete models.

There is a considerable variety of ways in which we could include a discrete time model into CSP. Many of these would involve incorporating time explicitly into semantic models, as described above for Timed CSP. The subject of this chapter, however, is how to model timed systems in ordinary, 'untimed' CSP by including the drum-beat of the passage of time as an explicit event. This event is conventionally called *tock* (rather than *tick* since that is easily – especially on tools – confused with $\checkmark$). All of the processes with timing constraints must synchronize on the event *tock*: this allows us to regulate and reason about the amount each process and the overall system does in given time intervals.

Advantages of this approach are:

- As we will see, it gives considerable flexibility about how to model and reason about timed systems.

- The human user can understand timed systems without having to learn another model.

- Existing tools can be applied to timed systems.

14.2   Meeting timing constraints

Having taken the decision to include the *tock* event in a process's alphabet, one is forced to make detailed decisions about what its actions mean and how they occur in time. This is illustrated by a timed version of *COPY*. Suppose it takes one unit of time for a data value to pass through this one-place buffer, and that a further unit of time is required between the output and the next input. The obvious definition, given this, is

$$TCOPY1 \;=\; left?x \to tock \to right!x \to tock \to TCOPY1$$

But there is a big difference between this process and the original *COPY*, because this one *insists* on performing an action each unit of time: it does not allow time to pass until it has done something on each and every cycle. The original *COPY* will wait as long as you like either to input or output. The correct translation of this (with the same timing assumptions) is actually

$$
\begin{aligned}
TCOPY2 \;&=\; left?x \to tock \to TCOPY2'(x) \\
&\quad \Box\ tock \to TCOPY2 \\[4pt]
TCOPY2'(x) \;&=\; right!x \to tock \to TCOPY2 \\
&\quad \Box\ tock \to TCOPY2'(x)
\end{aligned}
$$

since this process says that there has to be *at least* one time unit between input and output events, without expressing an upper bound.

An interesting hybrid between these processes is one which will wait to input, but not to output:

$$
\begin{aligned}
TCOPY3 \;&=\; left?x \to tock \to right!x \to tock \to TCOPY3 \\
&\quad \Box\ tock \to TCOPY3
\end{aligned}
$$

By slight modifications one can come up with versions which expect one or other of their communications to occur within any fixed N time units, or which can nondeterministically select when (and for how long) a communication is available.

Clearly, then, we can be much more expressive about how a process behaves in this timed world than previously. This makes it possible to describe paradoxical networks which must meet inconsistent timing constraints. Imagine, for example, placing $TCOPY1$ in parallel with a process expressing the constraint that there cannot be more than M communications in the first N time units: $TLimiter(N, M)$, where

$$
\begin{aligned}
TLimiter(n, m) \;&=\; RUN \Leftapprox n = 0 \Rightapprox \\
&\quad ((STOP \Leftapprox m = 0 \Rightapprox ?x : \Sigma \backslash \{tock\} \to TLimiter(n, m-1)) \\
&\quad \Box\ tock \to TLimiter(n-1, m))
\end{aligned}
$$

If $M < N$ then our two sets of timing requirements are inconsistent, which manifests itself in the combination deadlocking. This is what happens when one puts together a combination whose timing requirements do not match, which gives us an easy way of testing for this. This situation is called a *time-stop*. If we can place a process like $TCOPY1$ or $TCOPY3$ into a system without creating a time-stop, it essentially means that the timing assumptions on the availability of communication that are built into these processes are consistent with the system.

As a further example to illustrate this idea, we can modify $TCOPY3$ so that it is parameterized by the channels it uses and, more importantly, by the delay between the input and output of a datum:

$$
\begin{aligned}
TCOPY4(left, right, D) &= left?x \rightarrow TCOPY4'(left, right, D, D, x) \\
&\quad \Box \; tock \rightarrow TCOPY4(left, right, D) \\
TCOPY4'(left, right, D, N, x) &= tock \rightarrow TCOPY4'(left, right, D, N - 1, x) \\
&\quad \langle\!\langle N > 0 \rangle\!\rangle \\
&\quad right!x \rightarrow tock \rightarrow TCOPY4(left, right, D)
\end{aligned}
$$

Let us think about what happens if we 'pipe' two of these together:

$$
TCOPY4(a, b, D_1) \underset{\{|b, tock|\}}{\|} TCOPY4(b, c, D_2)
$$

If $D_2 \leq D_1$, all is fine: we can guarantee that the right-hand process will not be expected to make its $(n+1)$th input until at least $D_1 + 1$ time units after its nth, and it is therefore ready. On the other hand, if $D_2 > D_1$, then if (though it need not) the left-hand process makes its second input as soon as it can, this will lead to a 'time-stop' when it needs to output D_1 units later and the right-hand process is not ready. If, on the other hand, the environment is sufficiently slow in putting inputs into the combination, the problem will not arise.

In most examples it would be ridiculous to have infinitely many ordinary actions between two *tock*s, since this would mean that infinitely many actions occur in a finite time interval. This is equally easy to check for, all we have to do is look for divergence in

$$
P \setminus (\Sigma \setminus \{tock\})
$$

Indeed, the most basic 'sanity check' on this sort of model of a timed system is to verify that the above process equals (which is equivalent, because the following process is deterministic, to saying that it refines)

$$
TOCKS = tock \rightarrow TOCKS
$$

in the failures/divergences model. This shows that infinitely many actions cannot occur in any finite time interval, and that no matter what happens it is possible (provided the environment communicates appropriately) for time to progress – in other words, there are no reachable inconsistencies in the timing constraints. If there were any possibility of our process terminating ($\checkmark$) we would have generalized this to proving refinement of

$$TOCKS^{\checkmark} = (tock \to TOCKS^{\checkmark}) \sqcap SKIP$$

though this will never be necessary for any of the examples we deal with in this chapter.

As said above, a process can satisfy this check when, in order to let time pass, it is necessary for the environment to engage in suitable communications with the process. Both $TCOPY1$ and $TCOPY3$ satisfy it, for example. It may well be that we need the process to be tolerant of not receiving some or all communications instantly – the most obvious distinction here being between *input* and *output* events.[1] (It may well be reasonable to assume that the environment is always willing to accept an output, but it may be unreasonable to assume that the environment is always waiting to send an input.)

If there is a set of events D which the environment is assumed to be allowed to delay indefinitely, but may still allow, the above test should be modified to showing that

$$(P \parallel_{D} Chaos_{D}) \setminus (\Sigma \setminus \{tock\})$$

refines $TOCKS$. If $D = \{| \ left \ |\}$, we will have that $TCOPY3$ satisfies this that $TCOPY1$ does not. The point is that $Chaos_{D}$ may either allow or prevent actions from D, so the process can neither discount the occurrence of these events nor rely on them happening. Setting D equal to $\Sigma \setminus \{tock\}$ would correspond to *all* normal events being arbitrarily delayable by the environment – the conventional CSP view of communication.

It would also be possible to allow for an environment that will guarantee intermediate levels of acceptance of communication, such as guaranteeing to accept any communication in a set B if offered for at least N units. There might well be a role for such tests when we know that the component in hand will ultimately be put in a system that makes such guarantees (because, for example, of scheduling). But in specifying a 'complete' system, events will tend to come into the category that are simply observed by the environment, which it cannot delay, and those which the environment can delay indefinitely.

---

[1]There are similarities between this distinction and the one between ordinary and signal events discussed in Section 12.1.2. Indeed, the process defined here for testing timing constraints is exactly the mixed abstraction defined in that section. Setting $D = \Sigma \setminus \{tock\}$ reduces it to lazy abstraction.

EXERCISE 14.2.1   Define a version of *TCOPY* which outputs at a time it nondeterministically chooses between A and B time units from the corresponding input. It is then ready to input again C units later. What might happen when two of these are connected together?

EXERCISE 14.2.2   Give trace specifications for the following: (i) no more than N ordinary events occur between any two *tock*s, (ii) no more than M *tock*s occur between consecutive occurrences of the event a. Give definitions for the characteristic processes of these specifications.

EXERCISE 14.2.3   Recall the cash-point machine examples in Part I. Define a version in which the machine will wait only M time units for the correct insertion of the PIN, and otherwise will retain the card. It should wait indefinitely for all its other communications.

14.3   Case study 1: level crossing gate

A level crossing is where a road crosses a railway track (without a bridge or tunnel). The road direction is usually controlled by a gate that is meant to stop cars getting onto the railway line when a train is passing. In this example we consider a simple model of this, in which timing is used to establish basically untimed safety properties (e.g., when a train is near or on the gate, the gate is down) and to specify timing properties of the system (e.g., the gate goes up within K units when there is no train near or approaching).

We describe this system as a parallel combination consisting of a number of parts:

- processes representing track segments;
- processes representing trains;
- processes describing timing constraints on these things;
- a process representing the gate;
- a controller process which monitors sensors, etc., and sends control signals to the gate.

For simplicity we will model the case of a single line along which trains only move in one direction. The track is broken into segments (which are at least as long as any train). They are numbered, with this sensor in segment 1 and the crossing in segment *GateSeg*.

We are not going to rely on timing for anything other than the properties of the gate. Other safety requirements obviously apply to our little system, such as that there are never two trains on the same track segment, but these will not be our primary concern here. Our method of system development will be to describe the track segments and trains as untimed processes, and later put processes in parallel with them to describe their timed behaviour.

The following gives an untimed description of train t on track segment j. Note that a train enters the next segment $(j + 1)$ before it leaves segment j, and that there is a 'track segment' 0 which represents the outside world. SC denotes the number of segments including this segment 0. We will assume that the level crossing itself is in segment $GateSeg$, which lies between 1 and $SC - 1$. For timing reasons it should never, in fact, be either the first or last segment.[2] Here, t ranges over a set $TRAINS$ of train names and $\oplus$ represents addition modulo SC.

$$Train(t, j) \quad = \quad enter.t.j{\oplus}1 \to leave.t.j \to Train(t, j{\oplus}1)$$

The track segments can be occupied by one train at a time, and each time a train enters segment 1 or leaves $GateSeg$ the appropriate sensor fires.

$$
\begin{aligned}
Track(j) \quad &= \quad (enter?t!j \to sensor.in \to Trackf(t,j)) \\
&\qquad \langle\!\langle j = 1 \rangle\!\rangle \\
&\qquad (enter?t!j \to Trackf(t,j)) \\[6pt]
Trackf(t,j) \quad &= \quad leave.t.j \to sensor.out \to Track(j) \\
&\qquad \langle\!\langle j = GateSeg \rangle\!\rangle \\
&\qquad leave.t.j \to Track(j)
\end{aligned}
$$

It makes sense to consider the combination of the $SC - 1$ track segment processes with as many trains as we wish to consider. The processes within each of these classes do not communicate with each other, but the collection of all trains synchronizes with the tracks on all *enter* and *leave* events apart from those relating to the notional 'outside' segment 0.

$$
\begin{aligned}
Tracks \quad &= \quad Track(1) \;|||\; \ldots \;|||\; Track(SC - 1) \\[4pt]
Trains \quad &= \quad Train(Duncan, 0) \;|||\; \ldots \;|||\; Train(Thomas, 0) \\[4pt]
Network \quad &= \quad Trains \underset{IFace}{\parallel} Tracks
\end{aligned}
$$

$$\text{where} \quad IFace \quad = \quad \{enter.t.j, leave.t.j \mid t \in TRAINS \wedge j \in \{1 \ldots SC{-}1\}\}$$

It would, of course, be possible to prove various safety properties of this system, such as the fact that there are never two trains on the same track segment.

---

[2] If it were the first then it would not be possible to get the gate down in time and if it were the last then the way we later arrange our timing constraints means there would be no guarantee a train would ever leave $GateSeg$, thus preventing the gate from rising. The best value for $GateSeg$ is probably $SC - 2$.

None of these processes uses the time event *tock*, but since our eventual goal is to ensure *via timing* that the gate is up and down at appropriate moments, we have to make some assumptions about the relative timing of the events in the above system. What we do in this case is to introduce one or more timing processes to regulate the behaviour of each of the component processes that needs it.

We can make assumptions about the speed of the trains as they pass through our system by regulating how many units of time are taken over a track segment. Let us suppose there are identifiers *MinTocksPerSeg* and *MaxTocksPerSeg* which represent our assumptions about the minimum and maximum number of time units a train can spend per track segment. This could be expressed either as a constraint on trains or on track segments. In the former case one might set out the range of times a train can spend between successive *enter* events (in which case it is necessary to special-case the behaviour when outside the system). In the latter case one might express a bound on the time between any train entering and leaving a segment, or between them entering a segment and entering the next. While the enter/leave approach has obvious attractions, it has the disadvantage that the length of a train affects how fast it can travel – presumably the *enter* event is triggered by the front of the train and the *leave* event by the back. This would also mean that the same *tock*s can apply to the train's passage through two different segments: the time taken to pass through several would not be the sum of the times apparently taken for the individual ones. The approach we take is therefore the first alluded to above: expressing upper and lower speed limits on all the real track segments via consecutive *enter* events.

$$
\begin{aligned}
SpeedReg(j) \;=\;& enter?t!j \;\rightarrow\; SpeedReg'(j,0) \\[2mm]
SpeedReg'(j,n) \;=\;& (tock \;\rightarrow\; SpeedReg'(j,n+1) \triangleleft n < MaxTocksPerSeg \triangleright STOP) \\
& \square\, (enter?t!j{\oplus}1 \;\rightarrow\; SpeedReg(j) \\
& \quad \triangleleft n \geq MinTocksPerSeg \triangleright STOP)
\end{aligned}
$$

Slight modifications would allow the speed limits to vary from segment to segment, or to change from this 'track-centred' constraint to a 'train-centred' one (with one process per train).

The only other timing constraints we need are on the firing of the sensors: we specify that these must fire within one unit of a train entering the first segment or leaving the last, as appropriate.

$$
\begin{aligned}
InSensorTiming \;=\;& enter?t!1 \;\rightarrow\; sensor.in \;\rightarrow\; InSensorTiming \\
& \square\, tock \;\rightarrow\; InSensorTiming \\[2mm]
OutSensorTiming \;=\;& leave?t!GateSeg \;\rightarrow\; sensor.out \;\rightarrow\; OutSensorTiming \\
& \square\, tock \;\rightarrow\; OutSensorTiming
\end{aligned}
$$

Thus we end up with timing regulators only on the track segments. Thanks to the associative properties of parallel operators, there are two equivalent ways of adding in these constraints:

- We could rebuild the process *Network* by adding the timing constraints individually onto the component processes before combining them together (bearing in mind that all the ones this is done to – in this case the track segments – need to be synchronized on *tock*). This approach is complicated in our example by the fact that most *SpeedReg(j)*'s overlap the alphabets of two *Track(j)*'s.

- We could combine all the timing constraints together as a single process and put it in parallel (synchronizing on all relevant events) with the existing *Network*.

Using the second of these approaches, we get the additional process structure

$$SpeedRegs \quad = \quad \Big\|_{j=1}^{SC-1}(SpeedReg(j), \alpha SR(j))$$

$$\text{where } \alpha SR(j) \quad = \quad \{tock, enter.t.j, enter.t.j\oplus 1 \mid t \in TRAINS\}$$

$$SensorTiming \quad = \quad InSensorTiming \underset{\{tock\}}{\|} OutSensorTiming$$

$$NetworkTiming \quad = \quad SpeedRegs \underset{S}{\|} SensorTiming$$

$$\text{where } S \quad = \quad \{tock\} \cup \{enter.t.1 \mid t \in TRAINS\}$$

$$TimedNetwork \quad = \quad Network \underset{T}{\|} NetworkTiming$$

$$\text{where } T \quad = \quad \{leave.t.GateSeg \mid t \in TRAINS\} \cup \{\mid enter, sensor \mid\}$$

The gate is operated by a controller process. In terms of CSP modelling, we could either build our assumptions about the timing behaviour of the gate into the controller process itself, or have a separate gate process. It is probably better to do the latter, particularly if there is any nondeterminism about the gate timing. Therefore we will define separate controller and gate processes. There are then four basic states of the controller, some of them parameterized by a count of trains (the number currently in the domain).

To illustrate a different way of constructing timed processes, we include the rather simple timing constraints on the operation of the controller into its basic definition rather than add them in later.

When the gate is up we allow time to pass or the inward sensor to fire, which immediately (i.e., before the next *tock*) causes the *godown* command to be sent to the gate. The first of the four states is thus:

$$ControllerUp \quad = \quad sensor.in \rightarrow gate!godown \rightarrow ControllerGoingDown(1)$$
$$\Box \ tock \rightarrow ControllerUp$$

This raises an interesting question about our model: what happens if the *sensor.out* event occurs in state *ControllerUp*? Now of course we do not *want* this to happen, since it would mean that a train was on the segment including the crossing while the gate is up. The process above, as written, would simply refuse the sensor event – a refusal that does not really correspond to reality since simply refusing to look at a problem does not mean it is not there! There are at least three ways one could resolve this:

1. Remember that our description is not accurate in this eventuality but prove later that it never happens. (One of our aims will be to show that the gate is always down when there is a train nearby.)

2. Note that the process *OutSensorTiming* implies that the event in question *must* happen within one unit of time from the one that causes it, and that the refusal of it when possible would cause a time-stop, since the basic timing consistency check would have failed.

3. Add a clause to the above definition of *ControllerUp* which accepts the event. It might then either cause an error/alarm condition or simply ignore it.

Of these, the author prefers the last since it avoids using either assumptions or the subtleties of timing to ensure our definitions make sense. And while we can later verify quite independently that the basic safety condition holds, it is useful for debugging purposes explicitly to catch obvious error conditions, so we modify the above definition to

$$ControllerUp \quad = \quad sensor.in \rightarrow gate!godown \rightarrow ControllerGoingDown(1)$$
$$\Box \ sensor.out \rightarrow ERROR$$
$$\Box \ tock \rightarrow ControllerUp$$

On the whole, if a process is one that simply observes an event (as the controller observes various sensors) rather than being able to refuse it, it is good practice to write the definition of the process in such a way that this pattern is obviously adhered to.[3]

The two states *ControllerGoingDown* and *ControllerDown* both keep a record of how many trains have to pass before the gate may go up. Each time the sensor

---

[3]This is related to the concept of a *monitor* that was defined on page 313.

event occurs this count is increased. In order to keep the controller finite state, we put in a clause to ensure that the count should not get greater than the number of trains that can legally be in the domain (which equals the number of track segments). The *ControllerGoingDown* state comes to an end when the *gate.down* event occurs. It is no more legitimate for the *sensor.out* event to occur in this state than the previous one, so the same solution is adopted.

$$
\begin{aligned}
ControllerGoingDown(n) \;=\; & (ERROR \blacktriangleleft n > GateSeg \blacktriangleright \\
& sensor.in \rightarrow ControllerGoingDown(n{+}1)) \\
& \square\; tock \rightarrow ControllerGoingDown(n) \\
& \square\; gate.down \rightarrow ControllerDown(n) \\
& \square\; sensor.out \rightarrow ERROR
\end{aligned}
$$

When the gate is down, either sensor event may occur, incrementing or decrementing the train count as appropriate (subject to the same finite state limitation). When there are no trains left in the system the gate is signalled to go up.

$$
\begin{aligned}
ControllerDown(n) \;=\; & (ERROR \blacktriangleleft n > GateSeg \blacktriangleright \\
& sensor.in \rightarrow ControllerDown(n{+}1)) \\
& \square\; tock \rightarrow ControllerDown(n) \\
& \square\; sensor.out \rightarrow \\
& ((gate!goup \rightarrow ControllerGoingUp) \\
& \blacktriangleleft n = 1 \blacktriangleright ControllerDown(n{-}1))
\end{aligned}
$$

When the gate is going up, the inward sensor may still fire, which means that the gate must be signalled to go down again. Any occurrence of the other sensor event is an error, as previously. Of course this state may get the signal confirming the gate is up, and will then return to its initial state.

$$
\begin{aligned}
ControllerGoingUp \;=\; & sensor.in \rightarrow gate!godown \rightarrow ControllerGoingDown(1) \\
& \square\; sensor.out \rightarrow ERROR \\
& \square\; tock \rightarrow ControllerGoingUp \\
& \square\; gate.up \rightarrow ControllerUp
\end{aligned}
$$

In the above definitions, you can take *ERROR* to be any process whose activation would make itself felt in the complete network, in the sense that it is trivial to check that it never occurs. The two obvious possibilities for *ERROR* are the divergent process **div** (which requires the full failures/divergences model to detect it), and a process that raises an alarm via an error event (which should not, of course, be synchronized with any other error events there may be in other processes).

$$
ERROR \;=\; error \rightarrow STOP
$$

If the latter approach is taken, one should assert that the *error* event never appears by proving that the ultimate system refines $Chaos_{\Sigma \setminus \{error\}}$.

Neither *ERROR* nor **div** makes any allowance for how the system behaves after an error occurs. This is fine when, as in this case, our objective is to prove that errors never occur; but when errors can occur and have to be handled, a more careful treatment would be required.

The gate process can always be commanded to go up or down, and will obey the command in some nondeterministically chosen time within assumed bounds. When it reaches either the up or down state it sends a signal indicating this.

$$
\begin{aligned}
GateUp \ = \ & gate.goup \rightarrow GateUp \\
& \Box \ gate.godown \rightarrow GateGoingDown(0) \\
& \Box \ tock \rightarrow GateUp
\end{aligned}
$$

$$
\begin{aligned}
GateGoingDown(n) \ = \ & gate.goup \rightarrow GateGoingUp(0) \\
& \Box \ gate.godown \rightarrow GateGoingDown(n) \\
& \Box \ (((gate.down \rightarrow GateDown) \\
& \qquad \sqcap \ tock \rightarrow GateGoingDown(n{+}1)) \\
& \qquad \mathbf{\triangleleft} n < DownTime \mathbf{\triangleright} (gate.down \rightarrow GateDown))
\end{aligned}
$$

$$
\begin{aligned}
GateDown \ = \ & gate.goup \rightarrow GateGoingUp(0) \\
& \Box \ gate.godown \rightarrow GateDown \\
& \Box \ tock \rightarrow GateDown
\end{aligned}
$$

$$
\begin{aligned}
GateGoingUp(n) \ = \ & gate.goup \rightarrow GateGoingUp(n) \\
& \Box \ gate.godown \rightarrow GateGoingDown(0) \\
& \Box \ (((gate.up \rightarrow GateUp) \\
& \qquad \sqcap \ tock \rightarrow GateGoingUp(n{+}1)) \\
& \qquad \mathbf{\triangleleft} n < UpTime \mathbf{\triangleright} (gate.up \rightarrow GateUp))
\end{aligned}
$$

This completes the definition of the component processes, and we can now add the last two processes to the network:

$$
GateAndController \ = \ ControllerUp \underset{\{|tock,gate|\}}{\|} GateUp
$$

$$
SYSTEM \ = \ TimedNetwork \underset{\{|sensor,tock|\}}{\|} GateAndController
$$

It is worth noting that all the components of the system have been initialized to indicate that there are no trains in the domain and the gate is up. This is much the simplest (both to define and to understand) initialization, but it would be possible to deal with other situations as long as care were taken to make sure that all of the components were initialized consistently.

The reason why timing analysis is necessary in this system is that there is no interlock that prevents a train getting onto the level crossing when the gate is not down: note that *TimedNetwork* and *GateAndController* only synchronize on *tock* and the sensor events. We are relying simply on the relative times that the train takes to get from being sensed, to reaching the gate, and from the firing of the sensor to the gate being fully down. Whether the basic safety requirement is satisfied will depend on just what parameters (number of track segments, speed limits and gate timings) are used.

Before looking at this issue in detail we need to establish, on the pattern discussed earlier, that the timing descriptions in our code are consistent. Most of the events in our system are ones which are observed by, rather than controlled by, the external environment. The only events that the system does not rely on happening within some bound are those representing trains' entries into segment 1. Beyond that it does make various progress assumptions. So the only events that are considered to be delayable by the environment are $D = \{enter.t.1 \mid t \in TRAIN\}$ in the check that

$$(SYSTEM \parallel_D Chaos_D) \setminus (\Sigma \setminus \{tock\})$$

failures/divergences-refines *TOCKS*.

Given the chosen initialization, the assertion that the gate is always down when there is a train on the same segment as the crossing comes down to two things:

- When a train enters *GateSeg*, the gate is down, in that the most recent (non-*tock*) event communicated by the gate process is *gate.down*. (Note that the gate is initially up.)

- The gate never goes up when there is a train on *GateSeg*, in that no *gate* event occurs between a train entering *GateSeg* and leaving it.

These are both elementary safety specifications which can be expressed as follows. Let A, B and C be disjoint sets of events. We can define a general trace specification *BetweenSets*(A, B, C) stating that events in C only happen between being enabled by any element of A and the next element of B (which disables C). *OutsideSets*(A, B, C) is the same except that elements of C are initially enabled (becoming disabled by the first member of B). We define two processes representing trace specifications of these things over the events $A \cup B \cup C$, and then lift[4] these

---

[4]This is a case where we are specifying the behaviour of a process in what is potentially a proper subset of its alphabet. See Section 12.2 for alternative ways to formulate such checks.

to specifications that allow other events as well.

$$
\begin{aligned}
BetweenSets'(A, B, C) \;=\; & ?x : A \to OutsideSets'(A, B, C) \\
& \square\, ?x : B \to BetweenSets'(A, B, C)
\end{aligned}
$$

$$
\begin{aligned}
OutsideSets'(A, B, C) \;=\; & ?x : C \to OutsideSets'(A, B, C) \\
& \square\, ?x : A \to OutsideSets'(A, B, C) \\
& \square\, ?x : B \to BetweenSets'(A, B, C)
\end{aligned}
$$

$$
BetweenSets(A, B, C) \;=\; BetweenSets'(A, B, C) \underset{A \cup B \cup C}{\|} Chaos_{\Sigma}
$$

$$
OutsideSets(A, B, C) \;=\; OutsideSets'(A, B, C) \underset{A \cup B \cup C}{\|} Chaos_{\Sigma}
$$

The two requirements described above can thus be formalized as specifications to test for the refinement of:

$$
\begin{aligned}
EnterWhenDown \;=\; & BetweenSets(\{gate.down\}, \\
& \{gate.up, gate.goup, gate.godown\}, \\
& \{enter.t.GateSeg \mid t \in TRAINS\})
\end{aligned}
$$

$$
\begin{aligned}
GateStillWhenTrain \;=\; & OutsideSets(\{leave.t.GateSeg \mid t \in TRAINS\}, \\
& \{enter.t.GateSeg \mid t \in TRAINS\}, \{\mid gate \mid\})
\end{aligned}
$$

Since these are trace specifications we can take their conjunction by placing them in parallel:

$$
Safety \;=\; EnterWhenDown \parallel GateStillWhenTrain
$$

Whether or not this is satisfied will depend on the timing details, as discussed above, even though the specification itself does not mention time.

This is a *safety* specification in more than one sense of the word! Another safety, in the technical sense only, specification we might want is that the gate does not go down unless there is a train in the domain. The most natural way of expressing this one is as a pure trace property:

$$
tr = tr'^{\frown}\langle gate.godown \rangle \;\Rightarrow\; \#(tr \upharpoonright INS) > \#(tr \upharpoonright OUTS)
$$

where

$$
\begin{aligned}
INS \;&=\; \{enter.t.1 \mid t \in TRAINS\} \\
OUTS \;&=\; \{leave.t.GateSeg \mid t \in TRAINS\}
\end{aligned}
$$

This can be expressed as a process to refine, but since that process involves a count of the number of trains presently in the domain, in order to make it finite-state one has to assume a limit (just as in the controller process).

It is also possible to express safety conditions involving time, typically expressing some limitation on the times certain events can happen. In the present case one could, for example, assert that the event *gate.up* only happens within a certain interval of an event of the form *leave.t.GateSeg*.

There are two distinct varieties of liveness conditions that appear in this sort of timed reasoning: those which assert that some set of events is *offered* by the process in appropriate circumstances (very possibly involving time in the conditions) and those that assert that things definitely *occur* within some time. The first sort corresponds best to untimed liveness conditions, and we will shortly look at an important class of these in detail. The second sort is made possible by our ability to define processes that insist on certain communications before allowing the event *tock*. They are, in fact, trace conditions, since they make statements such as 'no more than three *tock*s occur before an output' and depend on our model of time: we *know* that *tock*s appear regularly, so if the only way for four *tock*s to happen is for an output to appear, then it *does*. Thus any trace condition which expresses a limit on when the event *tock* can occur is, in fact, a liveness condition of this second variety.

The following expresses a condition of this sort, namely that the gate rises within K units of the last train leaving unless some other train appears before that time limit expires. Once again we express it as a pure trace condition, the same considerations applying to the construction of a process-style specification as in the earlier case.

$$
\left(
\begin{array}{l}
\quad ((tr = tr'^\smallfrown\langle leave.t.GateSeg\rangle^\smallfrown tr'') \\
\wedge \quad (\#(tr' \upharpoonright INS) = \#(tr' \upharpoonright OUTS) + 1) \\
\wedge \quad \#(tr'' \upharpoonright INS) = 0 \wedge tr'' \downarrow tock > K)
\end{array}
\right)
\implies tr'' \downarrow gate.up > 0
$$

Again, whether or not this is satisfied will depend on the parameters. An example file to allow you to experiment with them for this and all the other specifications relating to this example can be found on the web site (see Preface).

EXERCISE 14.3.1   How should the system be adapted to handle two or more railway tracks running over our crossing gate? *Hint: different tracks are independent of each other, and the total number of trains present is the total of those on the individual tracks.*

EXERCISE 14.3.2   Give the controller the responsibility of turning on and off a red traffic light that must always be on when the gate is down and for some defined time beforehand. You should both modify the *ControllerUp* process to do this, and formulate appropriate specifications for the new events used by the light.

14.4   Checking untimed properties of timed processes

It will often be the case that we want to compare a process in our timed style against an untimed specification (which could be simply an untimed version of the same process). Where the specification is of traces only, there is no real problem in comparing a timed process against it: all one has to do is modify the specification so it ignores *tock* events – something we did without thinking about it several times in the level crossing gate example and which could be done simply by hiding *tock*.

Divergence (except for cases where an infinite number of events appear in a finite time) is a rather different phenomenon in the timed world than in the untimed one. In many ways it is less dangerous because of the fact that timed ways of looking at processes tell you what they are doing at each moment, rather than only giving an accurate picture when internal activity has stopped (which never happens in a diverging process). It is sufficiently different that, except for the case of infinitely many actions in a finite time, it is difficult to formulate a general method for approaching the question in our timed formulation. Indeed, in many cases timed analysis can make sense of, and prove well-behaved, systems that the untimed models would regard as divergent.

What we will concentrate on in this section is how to prove untimed failures specifications of timed systems. In other words, we want to place limits on what traces a process can perform, and specify things about what the process offers after each trace. (This is distinct from the extremely strong liveness properties illustrated in Section 14.3 which asserted that events were not only offered, but definitely happened.) The crucial issue with this type of property is deciding what we mean by the word 'offer'. An untimed failure (s, X) means that the process can get into a state after the trace s where it can refuse X and will refuse it for ever after because it has become *stable*. The best timed analogue of what is intended by a failures specification that precludes a particular refusal X is that, after some time beyond the end of the trace, the process will get into a state where it must accept an element of X, and will do so for ever after until some (non-*tock*) visible event occurs.

What we will in fact attempt to do in this section is to prove this statement, but with the additional demand that the (permanent) offer occurs within some fixed time bound. For the timed model gives us ability to see how long it takes for an offer to be made and makes it impossible to say that an offer will eventually be made without a limit of this sort.

The specification methods we use will be developed using an example. This particular example is one where the internal timing behaviour is needed to establish that the specification is met: the corresponding untimed process would not meet the specification.

It simply consists of a pipeline of two processes, feeding data items from left to right.

The sender process waits for an input, and then outputs it on the next time interval (i.e., after exactly one *tock*). It then waits three *tock*s before being able to input again.

$$TS \;=\; tock \to TS$$
$$\square\; left?x \to tock \to mid!x \to tock \to tock \to tock \to TS$$

The receiver waits for an input, then outputs and returns to its initial state on the next two time intervals.

$$TR \;=\; tock \to TR$$
$$\square\; mid?x \to tock \to right!x \to tock \to TR$$

The system is put together by synchronizing and hiding the shared data channel and synchronizing on *tock*.

$$TIMP \;=\; (\,TS \underset{\{\mid tock,mid\mid\}}{\parallel} TR\,) \setminus \{\mid mid \mid\}$$

Thinking about this system, it is clear that the output must have occurred before three *tock*s have happened since the corresponding input. This is before the next input is possible and therefore this process behaves, in an untimed sense, like the one-place buffer *COPY*

$$COPY \;=\; left?x \to right!x \to COPY$$

even though the untimed analogues of S and R would behave like a two-place buffer if piped together. Note we are assuming that the external output is not refusable by the environment.

Since *COPY* is an untimed specification that does not mention *tock*, and our proposed implementation is a system that certainly does communicate this event, it is clear that we cannot simply ask the question

$$COPY \sqsubseteq TIMP?$$

and expect a sensible answer. We will have to do one of two things:

- Build an understanding of time, and of our requirements for when offers need to be made, into the specification.

- *Abstract* away the time event *tock* from the implementation in an appropriate way.

In fact, either of these is possible. The obvious argument against the first is that we have negated the objective of this section: if internal manipulation to bring time into the specification is needed, it is no longer an untimed specification! In fact we can do better than that and one can devise rather precise recipes for doing the check in ways that do not require *internal* manipulation of either the untimed specification or the timed implementation. Since they are both quite interesting in their own right and give insight into the problem and each other, we will describe both in the following subsections.

14.4.1 Abstracting time

We know two basic ways to abstract away from a set of events: *lazy* and *eager* abstraction (see Chapter 12). Since the *tock* event is interpreted rather differently from other events, it is worth while investigating what it would mean to abstract it in these two ways.

In lazy abstraction we are placing no reliance on the abstracted events ever happening. Thus the refinement test appropriate for the use of lazy abstraction:

$$COPY \sqsubseteq_F (TIMP \underset{\{tock\}}{\parallel} Chaos_{\{tock\}}) \setminus \{tock\}$$

asserts that the process *TIMP* does what is required of it by *COPY* no matter how many *tock*s it has done. In particular, it can never refuse whatever event *COPY* says it must accept next, no matter how short a time has passed since the last action. Clearly, then, this refinement does not hold because our system takes some time before it is able to move from one communication to the next.

In eager abstraction, where the corresponding check would be

$$COPY \sqsubseteq_{FD} TIMP \setminus \{tock\}$$

we are assuming that the abstracted events are never resisted by the environment. While this is true (hopefully) of the *tock* event, the different interpretation we make of this event means that eager abstraction's consequences for failures refinement testing are wrong. For any process which can let time pass indefinitely (i.e., communicate infinitely many *tock*s without other intervening communication) will give rise to divergence under this form of abstraction (which is just hiding) so that no assertion can be made about what the process accepts or refuses between these *tock*s. In other words, eager abstraction will only pick up refusal information when and if the process has run out of *tock*s to perform.

What we want to achieve is a mixture of the two. We want to allow a fixed interval to pass during which the process can offer what it likes, but after that we want to specify what it must offer irrespective of whether it can perform another *tock*. We need to apply eager abstraction to the first few *tock*s after an event, and lazy abstraction to the rest.

A certain amount of subterfuge is required to achieve this hybrid abstraction (which is not the same as the *mixed* abstraction used in Chapter 12). We transform the timed implementation process by allowing either of two sorts of *tock* events when the original communicates the original one:

$$RTIMP = TIMP[\![tock1, tock2/tock, tock]\!]$$

Having got two sorts of *tock*, we then constrain the process so that exactly one of them is possible whenever the original process can perform a *tock*. Specifically, the first N after the start of time or a non-*tock* event become *tock*1's while the rest become *tock*2's.

$$REG(n) = nontock \to REG(N)$$
$$\qquad\qquad \Box\ (tock2 \to REG(n) \triangleleft n = 0 \triangleright tock1 \to REG(n-1))$$

$$Reg = REG(N)[\![x/nontock \mid x \in \Sigma \backslash \{tock, tock1, tock2\}]\!]$$

$$RegTIMP = RTIMP \parallel_\Sigma Reg$$

The effect of this complex procedure is to give the classes of *tock*'s that we want to treat differently different names. We can therefore apply eager abstraction to the *tock*1's and lazy to the *tock*2's to get the effect we want. The appropriate test is then

$$COPY \sqsubseteq_F (RegTIMP \parallel_{\{tock2\}} Chaos_{\{tock2\}}) \setminus \{tock1, tock2\}$$

This establishes that the refusal of the implementation process is correct when either (i) at least N time units have passed either from the beginning or the last non-*tock* event or (ii) the process insists on a communication before allowing time to pass. In general, increasing N weakens this test, and decreasing it until it fails will reveal the longest time one might have to wait before the underlying timed process is ready to accept whatever is required by the specification.

A larger example of this technique can be found in Section 14.5.

14.4.2   Untimed specifications in a timed harness

In the first method we essentially put a harness around the implementation which understood the timing requirements we were putting on the process, and did appropriate things to *tock* events to allow for these. We will now deal with the dual approach: putting a similar harness round the untimed specification so as to transform it into one which allows for the occurrence of *tock* and makes the same statement about the relationship between the untimed specification and the timed implementation as was made by the first method.

The check set out above in terms of the first method seeks to establish the following:

- The untimed traces of the implementation are correct.

- If it is within N time units of the last non-time event or the start, then *either* time can pass *or* the set of events offered by the specification meets the current requirements of the untimed specification.

- If at least N time units have passed then the set of events offered meets these requirements *whether time can pass further or not*.

This careful statement takes account of the fact that our processes sometimes insist on communicating before *tock* occurs. What we will do is construct a process *SpecReg* which, put in parallel with any untimed specification (synchronizing on all non-*tock* events), transforms it so that it says the above:

$$SpecReg \quad = \quad RSpec(N, N)[\![x/anyother \mid x \in (\Sigma \setminus \{tock\})]\!], \quad \text{where}$$

$$
\begin{aligned}
RSpec(M, r) \quad = \quad & (tock \to RSpec(M, r-1) \\
& \sqcap anyother \to RSpec(M, M)) \\
& \langle\!\langle r > 0 \rangle\!\rangle \\
& (anyother \to RSpec(M, M)) \\
& \Box (STOP \sqcap tock \to RSpec(M, 0))
\end{aligned}
$$

We can now 'lift' our untimed specification to a timed one by putting this process in parallel with it:

$$TSpec = SpecReg \parallel_{\Sigma \setminus \{tock\}} Spec$$

(where $Spec = COPY$ in the example we are considering). This achieves the goals set out above since *SpecReg* allows any trace of *Spec* with arbitrary insertions of *tock*, and when *RSpec* offers *anyother* the renamed version *SpecReg* offers all non-*tock* events and hence *TSpec* offers whatever of these events that *Spec* does.

The refinement check *TSpec* $\sqsubseteq_F$ *System* makes exactly the same statement about *System* as the check developed using abstraction in the previous section. This second version is easier to implement, since the amount of process transformation is less, but arguably required a closer understanding of exactly what we wanted to say about such things as the passage of time.

One possible reason for proving an untimed specification *UTS* of a timed process *TC* is because you want to include it as a component in an otherwise untimed system. It would then be natural to develop the untimed system with the specification in the place of *TC*, before developing *TC* to meet *UTS* in the sense discussed in this section. One important thing that should be borne in mind if you do this is that we have here considered processes to meet untimed specifications even though they may place upper time bounds on when some visible communications occur: for example the outputs of the buffers above must happen within one time unit even though the untimed *COPY* process would wait. It is therefore necessary to perform a second check on the process *TC* which is developed to fill the slot left by *UTS*: any event of its interface with the rest of the system, which you are not totally confident will never be delayed, must be included in the *Delayable* set for a timing consistency check on *TC*.

EXERCISE 14.4.1   Modify *SpecReg* so that it never refuses *tock*, but otherwise behaves as before. Comment on how the revised timed specification it produces (when combined with an untimed one) is relevant to the discussion above about *TC* and *UTS*. How would the *TIMP* process above fare when checked against it?

EXERCISE 14.4.2   The example in this section shows how what is apparently a two-place buffer might become a one-place one thanks to timing. Find an example of an apparently deadlocking system which is deadlock-free because of timing.

14.5   Case study 2: the alternating bit protocol

In this section we give a slightly larger example of the sort of reasoning introduced in the previous section, namely proving what are largely untimed specifications of a system which depends on timing for its correct functioning. This is a version of the alternating bit protocol which relies on time-outs to decide when it resends messages and acknowledgements, rather than the mechanisms described in Section 5.3.

The overall specification we want it to satisfy will still be the same, namely that it is a one-place buffer.

Unlike the untimed example, this version does not rely on the eventual correct transmission of data to avoid CSP divergence, but we do need some bound on the loss if we are to prove that data does eventually get through, and how long this takes. Rather than make the occurrence of *error*'s explicitly nondeterministic as in the earlier treatments of communications protocols, here we use the more sophisticated coding where *error*'s are prompted by external actions as discussed in Chapter 12. This has the advantage that the limits on errors do not have to be coded into the basic system definition, and we can thus construct a single system and analyze it under a variety of assumptions rather than having to reconstruct the system each time. The only error modelled here is message loss; duplication could easily be added.

$$TE \;=\; a?tag?data \to tock \to (b!tag!data \to TE \;\square\; error \to TE)$$
$$\square\; tock \to TE$$

$$TF \;=\; c?tag \to tock \to (d!tag \to TF \;\square\; error \to TF)$$
$$\square\; tock \to TF$$

Note that we have specified that all messages take precisely one unit of time to get through and that an arbitrary time then passes before the next input. Clearly one could make this more nondeterministic.

The implementation of the protocol consists of a sender process and receiver process, linked by E and F above.

14.5.1   Describing time-outs

The crucial feature of the sender and receiver processes in this presentation is their use of *time-outs*. A time-out is a sort of choice operator between two processes (like $\square$ and $\sqcap$), that only fully makes sense in a timed model. A time-out gives one process the chance to communicate for some length of time (which is a parameter to the time-out operator) and then, if no such communication has occurred, gives up and behaves like the other process. In Timed CSP it is written

$$P \rhd \{t\}\, Q$$

meaning the process which times-out to Q if P has not communicated within t time units. It looks very like the untimed operator $P \rhd Q$ that we have seen from time to time, since in its most natural implementation the latter essentially behaves like a time-out though without the control over exactly when the decision to time-out is made.

In the style of CSP discussed in this chapter we will obviously have to tie the occurrence of time-outs to the *tock* event. Unless we are thinking that *tock* has some real existence, like a broadcast clock signal, it is better not to make the time-out (i.e., the transition from P to Q) occur precisely at some *tock* (counted, presumably, from when the time-out combination was started). This would create a potential synchronization between time-outs in different parallel processes when there is no mechanism to achieve it. As a simple example, consider $P \rhd \{t\} \; Q \parallel Q \rhd \{t\} \; P$, where $P = a \to P$ and $Q = b \to Q$. If the time-outs are triggered by the same *tock*, this combination is certain to deadlock while, assuming that in reality they are managed by unsynchronized clocks, we would have the possibility (though not the certainty) of being able to communicate one of a or b for a short interval.

It is usually preferable, therefore, to specify an interval (amongst the *tock*s) during which a time-out will occur, without forcing it to occur *at* a tock. Thus a time-out will be an event whose occurrence is tied to a specific interval, very like many of the other events we have seen in this chapter.

Perhaps the most elegant way of achieving this is to delegate the firing of the time-out to a separate parallel process which, rather like a kitchen timer, can be set up to 'ring' at a given time in the future. In general the time-out controller process might, like the more sophisticated kitchen timers,[5] be programmable with a variety of intervals. It should therefore have an input channel *setup* over which this data is communicated, an event it communicates back when it fires, plus the *tock* event. Because any time-out is abandoned if the left-hand process communicates before the set time, the time-out controller has to be programmed so that it can be reset.

$$
\begin{aligned}
TOC \quad &= \quad setup?n \to Armed(n) \\
&\quad\; \square \; tock \to TOC \\
&\quad\; \square \; reset \to TOC \\
Armed(n) \quad &= \quad ((timesout \to TOC) \mathbin{\triangleleft} n = 0 \mathbin{\triangleright} (tock \to Armed(n-1))) \\
&\quad\; \square \; reset \to TOC
\end{aligned}
$$

The main process then sends *TOC* the *setup* signal to arm the time-out function, and includes the event *timesout* amongst the choices it offers during the period while the time-out might fire. It is combined with the *TOC* process (of which there is one for every separate component that needs one, since it is possible for the network to have more than one time-out running at once) with the *setup* and *timesout* events hidden.

The structure of the complete process is then either

$$
(Main \underset{\Sigma}{\parallel} TOC[\![a/reset \mid a \in R]\!]) \setminus \{\mid setup, timesout \mid\} \qquad \text{or}
$$

$$
(Main \underset{\Sigma \setminus \{tock\}}{\parallel} TOC[\![a/reset \mid a \in R]\!]) \setminus \{\mid setup, timesout \mid\}
$$
$$
\text{where } R = \Sigma \setminus \{tock, setup, timesout\}
$$

---

[5]Ones that are not egg timers!

depending on whether or not (respectively) the process *Main* is timed.

For example, if P and Q are the processes described earlier when discussing the consequences of synchronized time-outs, we can describe $P \rhd \{t\}\ Q$ by defining *Main* (in the first line above) to be $setup.t \to (S \ ||| \ RUN_{\{tock\}})$, where

$$S \quad = \quad \begin{array}{l} timesout \to Q \\ \square\ P \end{array}$$

(This is a timed process because it insists on sending the $setup.t$ signal immediately – before any *tock*s. The subsequent interleaving with $RUN_{\{tock\}}$ means there are no further timing constraints apart from the ones introduced by *TOC*.)

If $Q \rhd \{t\}\ P$ is defined similarly, it is now possible for

$$P \rhd \{t\}\ Q \ ||\ Q \rhd \{t\}\ P$$

to synchronize on either a or b between *tock*s number t and $t+1$.

14.5.2   The sender and receiver

In this treatment of the alternating bit protocol we have factored the sender process into three parallel components: one for transmitting data, one for managing the time-outs for retransmissions, and one for receiving acknowledgement signals and filtering out repeats. By doing this it is easier to ensure that signals are sent and received at appropriate times. It is, of course, possible to do the same thing with a sequential process: see Exercise 14.5.1.

$$\begin{array}{rcl} Send(bit) & = & \begin{array}{l} left?x \to tock \to Snd1(bit, x) \\ \square\ tock \to Send(bit) \end{array} \\[2ex] Snd1(bit, x) & = & a!bit!x \to setup!sto \to Snd2(bit, x) \\[2ex] Snd2(bit, x) & = & \begin{array}{l} timesout \to Snd1(bit, x) \\ \square\ tock \to Snd2(bit, x) \\ \square\ ack \to Send(1{-}bit) \end{array} \end{array}$$

sto is a constant defining how long the process waits between successive outputs of the same piece of data. The following process sends the *ack* signal just when it gets each new, rather than repeated, acknowledgement on channel d.

$$\begin{array}{rcl} SAck(bit) & = & \begin{array}{l} d.bit \to ack \to SAck(1{-}bit) \\ \square\ d.(1{-}bit) \to SAck(bit) \\ \square\ tock \to SAck(bit) \end{array} \end{array}$$

Note below that this *ack* event is used to reset the time-out timer.

$$SEND \;=\; ((Send(0) \underset{\{tock,ack\}}{\|} SAck(0))$$
$$\underset{A}{\|}\; TOC[\![ack/reset]\!]) \setminus \{|\; ack, setup, timesout \;|\}$$
$$\text{where} \quad A = \{|\; tock, setup, ack, timesout \;|\}$$

The receiver has one main component plus a timer, which is only reset (now explicitly) when a new (rather than repeat) input is received. In this sense its behaviour is not a classic time-out, since there are events the main process does that do not reset the timer. (This illustrates the flexibility of this approach of using parallel timers.) *rto* is the interval between successive sendings of the same acknowledgement. Note that, in both the sender and receiver processes, it is only elapsed time which determines how many times each message and acknowledgement are sent.

$$Rec(bit) \;=\; b?tag?data \rightarrow$$
$$(reset \rightarrow tock \rightarrow right!data \rightarrow c!bit \rightarrow$$
$$setup!rto \rightarrow Rec(1-bit)$$
$$\langle\!\langle tag = bit \rangle\!\rangle$$
$$Rec(bit))$$
$$\square\; timesout \rightarrow c!(1-bit) \rightarrow setup!rto \rightarrow Rec(bit)$$
$$\square\; tock \rightarrow Rec(bit)$$

$$REC \;=\; (Rec(0) \underset{\{|tock|\}\cup\alpha TOC}{\|} TOC) \setminus \alpha TOC$$
$$\text{where } \alpha TOC = \{|\; setup, timesout, reset \;\}$$

$$TABP \;=\; SEND \underset{\{|a,d,tock|\}}{\|}$$
$$((TE \underset{\{tock\}}{\|} TF) \underset{\{|b,c,tock|\}}{\|} REC) \setminus \{|\; a, b, c, d \;|\}$$

Aside from *tock*, the external alphabet of this system is $\{|\; left, right, error \;|\}$. Of these events we are relying on the environment accepting the system's outputs (on *right*) promptly. Therefore the timing consistency check deems the delayable events to be the complement of this set. It is appropriate to include the event *error* in this set since not to do so would mean that we could not exclude the possibility that the process is relying on some *error*'s happening to ensure correct behaviour! (Essentially we are lazily abstracting the error events, as recommended in Section 12.3.)

$$D \;=\; \{|\; left, error \;|\}$$
$$TimingConsistency \;=\; (TABP \underset{D}{\|} Chaos_D) \setminus (\Sigma \setminus \{tock\})$$

As ever, this check simply shows there are no contradictory timing requirements in our system. The main check, that our system behaves like a one-place buffer, follows the pattern set out in the previous section. The checks set out below attempt to show that the system meets the untimed specification *COPY* with all required communications being offered within a specified number of time units since the last external communication.

With *Reg* defined as on page 401:

$$RTIMP \quad = \quad TABP[\![^{tock1,\,tock2}/_{tock,\,tock}]\!]$$

$$RegTIMP \quad = \quad RTIMP \parallel Reg$$

This can now be checked against *COPY* by eagerly abstracting *tock1* and lazily abstracting *tock2* and *error*:

$$RHS \;=\; (RegTIMP \underset{\{tock2,error\}}{\parallel} Chaos_{\{tock2,error\}}) \setminus \{tock1, tock2, error\}$$

This check, if successful (which depends on the timing parameters used), shows something quite interesting because of the way it deals with errors. Since the process *Reg* (which chooses between *tock1*'s and *tock2*'s) allows an *error* event to reset its clock, what we are showing is that the offers required by *COPY* are made by the time that a fixed interval has passed since the last input or output, and the last error. This is the advantage of keeping the errors visible: we allow any number of errors but only insist that the system makes progress when there have not been any errors recently. If the thing which decides whether or not errors occur was an invisible nondeterministic choice operator, there is no way such a statement could be made.

Having put the system together in such a way as to leave errors (or, at least, events that give us control over when these happen) visible, one can, if one chooses, make assumptions about the error rate and see what effect this has on system performance. The typical assumption it might be appropriate to make would be 'there are no more than L errors in any T time units': something it is easy to specify using the *tock* style of CSP. If $L = 1$ we can define

$$ER_1(T) \quad = \quad ER_1'(T, 0), \quad \text{where}$$

$$ER_1'(T, j) \quad = \quad tock \to ER_1'(T, j{-}1) \mathbin{\lessdot} j > 0 \mathbin{\gtrdot}$$
$$(tock \to ER_1'(T, 0) \mathbin{\square} (STOP \mathbin{\sqcap} error \to ER_1'(T, T)))$$

and $ER_{L+1}(T) = ER_L(T) \underset{\{tock\}}{\parallel} ER_1(T)$. (This definition has a lot in common with that of *Limit* on page 313.) The last line in the definition of $ER_1'(T, j)$ includes the nondeterministic choice between *error* and *STOP* because we do not want processes to be able to rely on errors happening.

The appropriate thing to do with one of these assumptions is to use it to constrain *TABP* and then to hide the *error* event.

$$CSYSTEM = (TABP \quad \underset{\{tock, error\}}{\|} \quad ER_L(T)) \setminus \{error\}$$

One would then seek to prove that *CSYSTEM* meets the untimed specification *COPY* using the same methods as above, though this time there is no need to put in the abstraction of *error* and the fact that *error* has already been hidden means that it does not reset the specification clock. One would expect to find that the time one needs to wait before this version of the system makes the offers required of it will be longer than in the version where *error* is allowed to reset the waiting period for this, and also that there would be critical error rates beyond which no 'settle time' is long enough because there are enough errors to prevent real progress.

When this check succeeds it establishes that, *provided* the error pattern is within the limits specified, the system meets the specification in a way independent of exactly when the errors happen. This shows how one can elegantly extend to timed systems the concepts of fault tolerance described in Chapter 12. Thus, one might prove that, provided there are no more than L errors every T time units, the system meets the *COPY* specification with settle-time (since the last proper input or output) of N units.

EXERCISE 14.5.1   Write an alternative version of *Send(bit)* that does not require the special acknowledgement handler *SAck(bit)* in parallel with it (though it should still use *TOC* to handle its time-outs). Be careful that, whenever *TOC* wants to perform the event *timesout*, your *Send* does not deadlock it.

EXERCISE 14.5.2   Use the time-out mechanism provided by *TOC* to re-work your answer to Exercise 14.2.3. Then produce a further version where the *TOC* is also used to place limits on the time the user has to perform each of his or her other actions.

14.6   Urgency and priority

Recall the process *TCOPY2*, the timed version of *COPY* from the start of this chapter that behaves most like the original. It will wait indefinitely for either an input or an output. Now, preferably without looking ahead in this text, think how you would expect the result of piping two copies of this together to behave:

$$(TCOPY2[\![mid/right]\!] \quad \underset{\{|mid, tock|\}}{\|} \quad TCOPY2[\![mid/left]\!]) \setminus \{| \ mid \ |\}$$

The issue you have to decide is: when does the hidden communication on *mid* happen? One time unit after the corresponding input by the left-hand process, both processes (assuming the right-hand one is not full) are willing and able to do this action, but are also able to wait. A hidden action is one that the environment has no control over, so the implementation (and our modelling) has to decide which route to follow.

In all the timed examples seen so far we have carefully avoided this ambiguity. Whenever a hidden communication occurred between two parallel processes, one of them (invariably the one doing the 'outputting') specified exactly when it happened. This puts us under the obligation to ensure that these communications are accepted at precisely the specified moments, for otherwise the *TimingConsistency* checks fail.

In reasoning about untimed CSP we made the assumption that when a process had a hidden action (a τ) available then the τ always happens unless some other action occurs quickly. Certainly the process could not wait for ever in a state with a τ available. The problem we have to face in modelling the passage of time by *tock* events is that the untimed models of CSP do not understand the special nature of this event. They would model the system of two *TCOPY*2's shown above in such a way that the hidden *mid* event can nondeterministically happen after any number of *tock*s or never, in the sense that the infinite trace

$$\langle left.0, tock, tock, tock, \ldots \rangle$$

is possible without the transfer on *mid* occurring. Thus, this attempt at modelling a timed system in untimed CSP fails in an important way to model accurately our understanding of how this system ought to behave.

Imagine the state this system is in one time unit after the input event *left*.0 (which we can assume is the first event the combination does). The internal communication (*mid*.0) is available; if it does not happen before the next *tock* then, unless we are to keep some timer running, the state the system is in after the *tock* is identical to that before it. This means that if one *tock* is possible then, without special treatment, it must be possible for there to be any finite number before the hidden action occurs, and even for the hidden action never to happen at all. This would mean that the interpretation we were putting on this internal event in this world of *tock*s would be different to the usual untimed models, where we have assumed that a process cannot sit waiting for ever when there is an internal action possible. The cleanest solution to this problem is to assert that a *tock* never happens when there is an internal event available. In other words, internal events are *urgent* in the sense that time does not pass when they are enabled. This is often called the assumption of *maximal progress* and is common across a variety of models of timed concurrency, including conventional Timed CSP.

Looking at a timed system in this way gives a (possibly strict) refinement of the way we would interpret it over the usual models of CSP, thinking of *tock* as any other event. This is because these models (in particular the failures/divergences one) *allow* the implementation to choose internal events that are available in preference to any or all others (including *tock*), while our new view simply asserts that in some circumstances it is *obliged* to do this.

It is perfectly clear how to simulate a system running under these new rules: we have to give internal events *priority* over *tock*. (Other events are not affected by this.) In terms of operational semantics, what we are doing is describing a new transition rule $\xrightarrow{x}_T$ in terms of the old one $\xrightarrow{x}$: here T is a set of *time-like* actions (usually $\{tock\}$). Unless $x \in T$ we have

$$P \xrightarrow{x}_T Q \Leftrightarrow P \xrightarrow{x} Q$$

If $x \in T$, then

$$P \xrightarrow{x}_T Q \Leftrightarrow P \xrightarrow{x} Q \wedge \neg \exists\, Q'.P \xrightarrow{\tau} Q' \vee P \xrightarrow{\checkmark} Q'$$

Here, τ is the usual internal action we are familiar with.

The consequences of this re-interpretation for our system of two $TCOPY2$'s is that the data moves across as soon as both sides are willing, namely, one time unit after the later of the corresponding input and the output of the previous datum (if any) by the right-hand process.

In almost all circumstances this new, prioritized, view is the right way of looking at timed systems and the cases where the conventional semantics provides the right answer (like all those in previous sections of this chapter) are written so that the above rules are, to all intents and purposes, followed by the standard transition rule $\xrightarrow{x}$ without the need to impose them. In other words, in those cases the semantic values of the standard and prioritized views coincide.

As discussed above, this will be true whenever one of the participants in each internal action is unwilling to let time pass until it has occurred. Fortunately, since the new prioritized view always gives a refinement of the old one, checking a timed system against a specification[6] will never give a false positive.

14.6.1   Consequences for semantic models

While the prioritized view of time is easy to understand in terms of operational semantics, it presents rather more difficulties if you want to get a denotational theory

---

[6]Necessarily a specification that does not depend on the prioritized interpretation of time to deduce its own behaviour.

for predicting process behaviour (like the traces model, or the failures/divergences model). The problem is that our usual models conceal all details of internal τ actions, so there is no way of imposing the new interpretation on a process once we have reduced it to its description in one of them. Whole new models, giving much more detail about what was refused by a process *during* a trace as well as *after* it, are required. While these are interesting, they are also complex and this is not the place to describe them. The issues which arise are essentially the same as those as in modelling (continuously) Timed CSP, and there is extensive discussion of these in the literature.

It is possible, under the prioritized view, to have two processes that are equivalent in all the denotational models of untimed CSP which are inequivalent when put in a simple CSP context. What this means from a practical point of view is that the compression functions described in Section C.2 are unsafe for prioritized analysis, and that techniques for proving properties of processes by putting them in contexts should be considered carefully before use. Basically, you should regard the primary means of understanding a prioritized program as being its operational semantics, rather than the denotational models which dominate for the standard interpretation.

We need to understand how this new prioritized view interacts with the methods described in Section 14.4 for proving a timed process meets an untimed specification. The answer is very simple: the first method creates problems because of the way time is abstracted by hiding. The problem is that once one hides a *tock* event, it becomes a τ and so is put into precisely the category of events we are giving priority to over *tock*s. Thus, once this hiding is done, we have lost the mechanism to impose priority of more normal τ's over the passage of time. Thus this method should not be used for systems with priority.

On the other hand, the second method, where the specification was transformed and the implementation left unaltered, creates no problems and should be used in preference.

The lazy abstraction of error events in this type of analysis does not appear to cause any problems since, by construction, it allows the abstracted events to be refused at any time.

14.7   Tools

The style of CSP presented in this chapter was developed specifically to meet the demand for a mechanism for analyzing timed systems with FDR. Probably because of the practical importance of timing analysis it has become widely used for that purpose.

Except where priority is required, no special considerations apply to using tools. The main thing anyone intending to use CSP tools for timing analysis should do is get a good grasp of the principles of modelling time set out in this chapter.

It is possible[7] to add an operator `prioritize(P)` to FDR as a function applied to processes: the process the function is applied to is given a revised operational semantics of the sort described above.

Potential users of the prioritized implementation of timing are warned to ensure they understand just what this construction achieves and the limitations on when it is safe to use it.

All the examples in this chapter, plus further examples of the style of CSP it describes, can be found on the associated web site.

14.8   Notes

As we have said previously, the techniques presented in this chapter are not Timed CSP in the sense described in the work of the author, Reed, Schneider, Davies and others [26, 27, 28, 87, 88, 89, 111] because we do not use the continuous time model used there. It has more in common, in terms of timing, with work on other flavours of timed copncurrency. A good survey can be found in [3], and the rest of the papers in that conference proceedings are also useful. The primary reason for advocating the discrete approach here is pragmatic: while it is not as mathematically elegant, it is easier to automate its analysis and, in many respects, easier to program in. David Jackson has played an important role in the development of the style and in promoting it.

There have been several papers published applying the `tock`-timed style of CSP [13, 44], but no widely available general introductions to this style before. The level crossing example was originally proposed in [63] and was the example used in [44].

---

[7]This operator was present in later versions of FDR1. At the time of writing it has not yet been included in FDR2.

Chapter 15

Case studies

We have already seen some moderately large examples of systems described and specified in CSP in relation to protocols (Chapter 5), information flow (Chapter 12), deadlock (Chapter 13) and timing (Chapter 14). In this chapter we look at some more which illustrate some different ideas and methods, and the notation's power in a wide variety of applications, some of which are by no means obvious at first sight.

All of the examples in this chapter are drawn from case studies developed as applications of FDR by the author and his colleagues. The definitions of more realistically-sized processes such as those we use here are often easier to read in the ASCII-based syntax used by FDR with its slightly lower emphasis on 'algebraic' constructs. This syntax also helps in presenting the functional programs[1] for manipulating data which form a vital part of most realistic FDR examples and, hopefully, will assist the reader to get used to the machine-readable version of the language (details of which can be found in Appendix B).

In each case all the process definitions are included in the text, as are sufficient subsidiary definitions to make these clear and to show what is involved in setting up a realistic system description in CSP. Copies of the complete files from which they are drawn are obtainable on the Internet (see Preface). Where possible, readers are encouraged to run these files in conjunction with studying this chapter.

The author hopes that readers will gain both ideas and confidence in the expressive power of CSP from looking at these examples.

---

[1] These programs are frequently simple and self-explanatory, as the ones in this chapter hopefully are. However, an understanding of functional programming such as can be obtained from [11] is undoubtedly useful for dealing with some types of example using FDR.

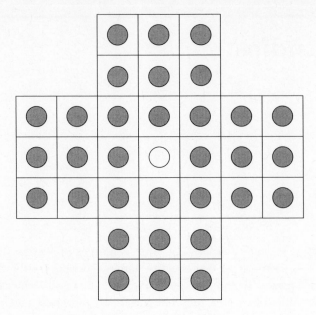

Figure 15.1 Peg solitaire.

15.1   Combinatorial systems: rules and tactics

CSP can be used to describe systems quite unlike the obvious applications to networks of communicating parallel processes. There are a great many types of system
which evolve according to rules based on their states' structures and where there is
a designated set of states which either one wishes to prove unreachable, or perhaps
one is simply interested in finding out whether the set is reachable and if so how.
An example of the former might be a railway signalling system, where we would
hope to prove that, provided some set of rules were applied, no two trains end up
on the same segment of track (amongst other properties of a similar flavour).

Examples of the latter are provided by the class of puzzles where the objective
is to reach one of a set of target states (frequently this set has only one member)
from a fixed starting state. The example we use in this section is one of the best-
known puzzles of this sort: *peg solitaire*. The starting position of the usual version
of this puzzle is shown in Figure 15.1. Thus initially there are 32 slots with a peg
in, plus an empty slot in the middle.

The rules are very simple: in any one of the four horizontal and vertical
directions (up, down, left, right) you can hop any peg over another peg into an
empty slot, after which you remove the hopped-over peg. The objective is to remove

all but one of the pegs and leave the remaining one in the slot that was initially empty. Most human beings find this a very difficult puzzle.

Evidently the initial configuration can be varied, thus creating an infinity of different puzzles, some of which are soluble and some of which are not.[2] The CSP script on which this section is based supports a simple notation which allows the user to design his or her own puzzles and try them out.

This is done by writing each puzzle as a rectangular list of lists (i.e., a list of rows) in which the standard version is shown

```
Board = <<X,X,P,P,P,X,X>,
        <X,X,P,P,P,X,X>,
        <P,P,P,P,P,P,P>,
        <P,P,P,E,P,P,P>,
        <P,P,P,P,P,P,P>,
        <X,X,P,P,P,X,X>,
        <X,X,P,P,P,X,X>>
```

Here, X is a non-slot (there just to fill up the rectangle), P is a slot with a peg and E is an empty slot. (These are members of a data type which is declared in the script.)

The rest of the script just compiles a parallel network out of the above notation. To do this we need the dimensions of the board:

```
Height = #Board
Width = #(head(Board))
```

and a function which extracts the value of the (i, j)th member of the array. The following definition allows for the fact that the above picture is inverted because the 0th row is at the top, whereas it is easier to think of the origin (point $(0,0)$) as being at the bottom left-hand corner.

```
init(i,j) = nth(j,nth(Height-1-i,Board))
```

The following set then consists of all the co-ordinates of slots on the board.

```
BoardCoords = {(i,j) | i <- {0..Height-1},
                       j <- {0..Width-1}, init(i,j)!=X}
```

---

[2]The puzzle can be analyzed mathematically and a theory developed which helps predict which boards can be solved, and in some cases how to solve them. See [8] for an extensive treatment of this. We will, however, treat the puzzle 'blind' to its theory.

When using FDR you have to declare the types of all channels used. The main events we will use are ones representing moves, with the indexing of the events corresponding to the co-ordinates of the slot the move is *to* (rather than *from* or *over*). For reasons that will become apparent later we declare the possible indexes of these events to range over an area a little bigger than the actual board:

```
Ycoords = {(-2)..Height+1}
Xcoords = {(-2)..Width+1}

channel up,down,left,right:Ycoords.Xcoords
channel done
```

We next define a process for each slot with just two states: full and empty. These record the effects of the various moves and also permit the special event done just when the state is correct for a solution (as recorded in the parameter target using one of the values P and E used in the list-picture).

When a slot is full it can become empty in two basic ways: either the peg that is in it hops out, or another hops over it. Since either of these can happen in four directions, there are eight move events it can participate in.

```
Full(i,j,target) = (target==P) & done -> Full(i,j,target)
                [] up.i+2.j -> Empty(i,j,target)
                [] down.i-2.j -> Empty(i,j,target)
                [] right.i.j+2 -> Empty(i,j,target)
                [] left.i.j-2 -> Empty(i,j,target)
                [] up.i+1.j -> Empty(i,j,target)
                [] down.i-1.j -> Empty(i,j,target)
                [] right.i.j+1 -> Empty(i,j,target)
                [] left.i.j-1 -> Empty(i,j,target)
```

When it is empty, the slot cannot allow any of the above moves, but does allow four new ones, namely the four directions of a peg hopping in.

```
Empty(i,j,target) = (target==E) & done -> Empty(i,j,target)
                 [] up.i.j -> Full(i,j,target)
                 [] down.i.j -> Full(i,j,target)
                 [] right.i.j -> Full(i,j,target)
                 [] left.i.j -> Full(i,j,target)
```

The initial value of the process at co-ordinates (i,j) is determined by the picture: note the target is always the opposite.

```
Slot(i,j) = if init(i,j) == E then Empty(i,j,P)
                              else Full(i,j,E)
```

We are going to put all the various slot processes in parallel. To do so we need an expression for the alphabet of each: it is just **done** plus all the moves the slot is involved in.

```
Alpha(i,j) = Union({{done},
                    {up.i+k.j    | k <-{0,1,2}},
                    {down.i-k.j  | k <-{0,1,2}},
                    {left.i.j-k  | k <-{0,1,2}},
                    {right.i.j+k | k <-{0,1,2}}})
```

Placing **done** in all the alphabets like this will mean that it can only occur when every process is in its target state.

In a sense the definitions of the **Full** and **Empty** states, and also the alphabets, are too general. They assume that all slots have a full complement of moves, ignoring the fact that ones within two units of an edge of the board (in any direction) have fewer. For example, a slot on the left-hand edge has no moves hopping over it to left or right, none hopping in from the left and none hopping out to the left. For a move to be a 'real' move, all of the from-, over- and to-slots need to be on the board. This calculation is performed by the following:

```
JumpTos = {up.i.j, down.i.j, left.i.j,
           right.i.j | (i,j) <- BoardCoords}

JumpOvers = {up.i+1.j, down.i-1.j, left.i.j-1,
             right.i.j+1 | (i,j) <- BoardCoords}

JumpFroms = {up.i+2.j, down.i-2.j, left.i.j-2,
             right.i.j+2 | (i,j) <- BoardCoords}

RealMoves = inter(JumpTos,inter(JumpOvers,JumpFroms))

OffBoardMoves = diff({|up,down,left,right|},RealMoves)
```

The following definition of the complete puzzle comprises the parallel composition of one process for each slot, which is put in parallel with *STOP* to prevent the moves **OffBoardMoves** from occurring:

```
Puzzle = (|| (i,j):BoardCoords @ [Alpha(i,j)] Slot(i,j))
         [|OffBoardMoves|] STOP
```

Notice that each move in `RealMoves` appears in the alphabets of exactly three slots, and that `done` is, as discussed above, in the alphabets of them all.

We now have a perfect model of the puzzle in CSP: the traces are precisely the legal sequences of moves, with the additional possibility of `done` when and if a solution is reached. There is a solution, indeed, if and only if this event can occur, and this fact leads to an obvious refinement check which we can give to FDR to look for one: it is failed if `Puzzle` can perform `done`. The following is the syntax used to pre-load a (traces) refinement check into FDR.

```
assert STOP [T= Puzzle \ {|up,down,left,right|}
```

This is all very well, but for the standard board the check[3] created is very substantial indeed and beyond the implementations of FDR in existence at the time of writing, when running on ordinary workstations.

An interesting way round this is to impose further rules on the puzzle in such a way as to restrict the number of states, and then see if this constrained version has a solution. This can be done by placing another process in parallel which limits the patterns of `up`, `down`, `left` and `right` events. In this case it is best to regard these as *tactics* for solving the puzzle, but in other games you could use exactly the same programming structure to add in standard rules, and when analyzing a more real-life combinatorial system it could be used both for rules and to make assumptions about the system's environment.

Two examples are given below. The first simply says that moves in the four directions rotate:

```
Tactic1 = left?x -> Tactic1'
Tactic1' = up?x -> Tactic1''
Tactic1'' = right?x -> Tactic1'''
Tactic1''' = down?x -> Tactic1
```

```
Puzzle1 = Puzzle [union(RealMoves,{done})||RealMoves] Tactic1
```

This fails to find a solution (i.e., the refinement check succeeds), establishing that the puzzle has no solutions of the form implied by the tactic. If this tactic is weakened so that the rotation only applies for the first 24 moves, a solution is found: the coding of this is left as an exercise!

A second tactic is to make some of the pegs 'sticky' and forbid them being moved until most of the others have gone. The best way to do this is to extend the

---

[3]It must have approximately 10^9 states, and because of its highly coupled nature it does not yield well to the intermediate compressions described in Section C.2.

notation used to define the puzzle to include a sticky peg S as well as an ordinary
one P. An arrangement that works well for the standard puzzle is

```
Board1 = <<X,X,P,P,P,X,X>,
          <X,X,P,P,P,X,X>,
          <S,S,P,P,P,P,P>,
          <P,P,P,E,P,P,P>,
          <S,S,P,P,P,P,P>,
          <X,X,S,P,S,X,X>,
          <X,X,S,P,S,X,X>>
```

Adopting this extended notation does not change the network produced by the
earlier definition of Puzzle, because of the way the process Slot(i,j) was defined
above. It does, however, allow us to define a tactic process to implement our
restricted search for a solution. The following constants (derived from this new
board) represent the number of pegs that are not to be delayed, and the moves
which are respectively in the alphabets of any sticky peg and those which are not.

```
NoDelays = card({(i,j) | (i,j) <- BoardCoords, init(i,j) == P})
```

```
DelayMoves = diff( Union({Alpha(i,j) | (i,j) <- BoardCoords,
                                          init(i,j)==S}),
                   {done})
```

```
NoDelayMoves = diff(RealMoves,DelayMoves)
```

To define the tactic fully we need to know how many moves need to happen
before a sticky peg can move. Perhaps the cleanest way to do this is to define a
constant NonStickiesLeft which defines how many other pegs are left when the
first peg marked S can move. This can be used, in conjunction with NoDelays, to
compute the initial parameter for a process that runs in parallel with the system to
implement the tactic.

```
Tactic2(n) = if n==0 then []x:RealMoves @ x -> Tactic2(0)
                     else []x:NoDelayMoves @ x -> Tactic2(n-1)
```

```
Puzzle2 = Puzzle [|RealMoves|]
          Tactic2(NoDelays-NonStickiesLeft)
```

Provided this allowance is set to be at least 4, the configuration given above
(the first one the author tried, and the one described in [98], where the implied
NonStickiesLeft is 5) finds a solution.

Solving puzzles like this is great fun, and several times we have found solutions to other ones which are shorter than the best previously known. (Evidently all solutions to solitaire have the same length!) The serious points of this example are firstly to show how the constructs of CSP (especially its ability to synchronize an arbitrary number of processes on a given event) allow us to model combinatorial systems which evolve according to rules, secondly how to add further rules, tactics or assumptions via parallel composition, and finally to show that model-checking tools such as FDR really can discover things that are at or beyond the limit of what the unassisted human can do.

Most of the exercises in this chapter require FDR or some similar tool.

EXERCISE 15.1.1   Modify `Tactic1` so that it allows any move after 24 rotating ones and find a solution to the puzzle that follows this pattern.

EXERCISE 15.1.2   A farmer has to ferry a wolf, a goat and a cabbage across a river using a boat that is only big enough for him and one of his charges. Unfortunately, without the farmer to control then, the goat would eat the cabbage and the wolf would eat the goat. Devise a CSP program to find the way the farmer can get all across safely.

Use your program to demonstrate that his task would become impossible if he had even one more of any of the cargo items. Would it help him, in that case, to have an island in the middle of the river?

EXERCISE 15.1.3   Produce a version of the solitaire script which uses a hexagonal grid like the two example puzzles shown in the upper part of Figure 15.2, with the pieces now able to hop in any one of six directions along the lines. Are the puzzles shown soluble, in the sense that you can end up with a single peg left, in the initially empty slot?

Hint: you might find adapting the script easier if you transform the hexagonal grid to a rectangular one with moves allowed on one set of diagonals, as shown in the bottom of the figure.

15.2   Distributed data and data-independence

Many of the applications CSP is best suited to are systems that handle data items without altering them. Rather they manage data values, and input and output them – hopefully at appropriate times on the desired channels. We have seen many examples in buffers and communication protocols, stacks and bags. Some of the most striking examples are systems that store multiple copies of data (either for security against failure or speed of access) but seek to maintain the appearance of a single copy which can be accessed for reading and writing.

In this section we see two of these: one where copies of a store are held at every node on a ring, and a model of a cache not unlike those used on most

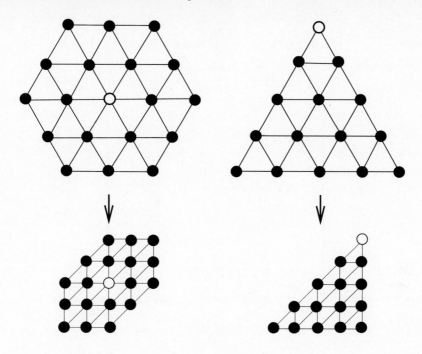

Figure 15.2 Hexagonal solitaire (see Exercise 15.1.3).

microprocessors. One of our main objectives is to explain and illustrate the theory of *data-independence*, whereby it is often possible to prove facts about processes of the type described in the previous paragraph for *any* data type by showing they hold for a particular finite data type.

15.2.1   A ring database

Imagine that you have a ring of processes, each holding a copy of a selection of registers, and that you want each node to be able to update any of these. An update is first executed locally, and then transmitted around the other nodes in turn until it arrives back home. See Figure 15.3. If two nodes at opposite sides (*A* and *D*, say) of the ring choose to update the same register at very nearly the same time, it is evident that the resulting updates will be seen in different orders if they both simply pass all the way round the ring. This, in turn, might lead to a situation where even after all updates have completed their journeys, nodes *B* and *F* disagree on the value of the register.

Unless some sort of locking mechanism is employed – inevitably expensive in time and effort – it is certain that we must put up with there being instants

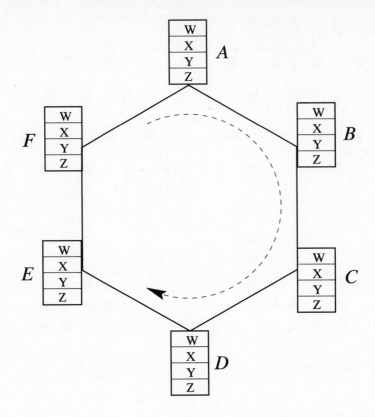

Figure 15.3 The ring database.

where simultaneous reads to the same register will yield different results. What we cannot tolerate is any inconsistency which persists, like the one described above, even when the system is quiescent. The author proposed several related algorithms in [96][4] which guarantee at least this degree of consistency under various scenarios: the simplest one is described below.

Let the nodes on the ring be N_i for $0 \leq i < M$, with indexes increasing in the direction messages pass round. The user of any node may read or write any of a set of registers locally. When a local write has occurred, N_i will generate an update that is entered into the ring to carry the new value round the other nodes.

---

[4]In that paper they are proved mathematically. The mathematical arguments have the advantage that they apply to any size of ring, and yield rather more detail about the pattern of values visible than we do here: provided the priorities are restructured to follow a logical time regime, a form of *sequential consistency* can be proved. They have the disadvantage of being very far from trivial, and also do not address questions such as deadlock and livelock freedom as we will here.

If otherwise uninterrupted, an update passes round until it arrives back at the node that generated it; updates thus carry the identity of their origins with them, and each node keeps a list E_i of the updates it has generated that are expected back.

In order to resolve the inconsistencies that can arise due to simultaneously existing updates to the same register, the nodes are all assigned unique priorities: let p_i be the priority of N_i. These affect what happens when an update u originated by N_i arrives at N_j:

- If $i = j$ then u is removed from the head of E_j provided it is there. Its absence is an error: we can deal with it any way we please. In the implementation below we do not notice it belongs to the node if E_j is empty, and so it just gets executed and passed round. Other options would be to STOP locally or transmit some error event.

- If $i \neq j$ and there is no clashing update (i.e., an update of the same location) in E_j, u is executed locally and passed on round the ring.

- If $p_i < p_j$, and E_j contains any updates that clash with it, then u is *stopped*: it is neither passed on round the ring nor executed locally.

- If $p_i > p_j$, and E_j contains any updates that clash with it, then u is executed locally and passed on round the ring, and the clashing updates are *cancelled* (removed from E_j).

In studying this algorithm it is plainly sufficient to consider only a single register (i.e., each node has a copy of this register), since, while updates to the same location interfere with each other in a complex way, ones to different locations do not. Thus, in building our implementation we will restrict ourselves to that case. This has the twin advantages of somewhat simplifying the programming and reducing the size of the state space, though it would not be difficult to adapt the definitions to deal with any number of registers.

It is clearly desirable that the system we build is free of deadlock and livelock as well as satisfying consistency results. There would be no hope of achieving this if the underlying mechanism that transports updates round the ring could deadlock or livelock. We therefore base this aspect of our system on sound principles, namely Deadlock Rule 8 (see page 357) in a way similar to the message-passing ring described with the rule. Specifically we give each node the capacity to hold two (travelling, as opposed to expected-back) updates, but only allow it to become full due to an input from the ring.

Our later specifications will be predicated on what the system looks like when it is *quiescent* (no updates circulating and none expected). This is the role of the event quiet: each node can communicate it when it is locally quiescent; we force them all to synchronize on it so that the event can happen when, and only when, the whole system truly is quiescent. This event is not one that would be part of a real implementation; it is simply something we will need for the purpose of specification and verification. It actually has a lot in common with the event **done** from the previous section, since they are both synchronized over all processes to identify a particular global state.

The processes defined below do not actually hold the local copy of the register: we will later combine each of them in parallel with a process that does. What they do is handle updates according to the above algorithm, assuming that any that are input have already been executed on local data and that any output are immediately applied (at the point of output).

Below, N0(i,E,T) represents the node N_i which presently holds no travelling updates, and which is expecting the list E of updates back from the ring. The parameter T is the type which is being stored in the register: the reasons for making this explicit will become apparent later. We impose a limit on the length of E since this is necessary to keep the process finite state.

```
N0(i,E,T) = (#E<limit) & in.i?x:T -> N1(i,E^<x>,i,x,T)
          [] #E==0 & quiet -> N0(i,E,T)
          [] ring.i?j?x:T -> (if #E==0
                            then (out.i.j!x -> N1(i,E,j,x,T))
                            else (if i==j
                                   then N0(i,tail(E),T)
                                   else (if priority(i)<priority(j)
                                          then (out.i.j!x -> N1(i,<>,j,x,T))
                                          else N0(i,E,T) )))
```

The connections of the channels when these are put in parallel are shown in Figure 15.4. Since there is only one register, there is no need to name it when passing updates round the ring. The communication `ring.i.j.x` means the passing to N_i round the ring of an update to the register originated by N_j of value x. In the above state our node can (subject to the **limit** on E) accept inputs either from its environment or the ring. When it already holds an update `j.x` which it is ready to output on the ring, then because of the requirements of Deadlock Rule 8, it will only accept a ring input, but otherwise it behaves similarly.

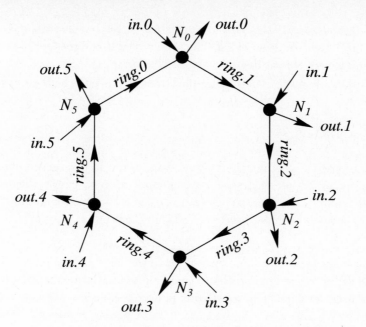

Figure 15.4 Communications in the implementation.

```
N1(i,E,j,x,T) = ring.((i+1)%M)!j!x -> N0(i,E,T)
           [] ring.i?k?y:T ->
             (if #E==0
             then (out.i.k!y -> ring.((i+1)%M)!j!x -> N1(i,E,k,y,T))
             else (if k==i
                     then N1(i,tail(E),j,x,T)
                     else (if priority(i)<priority(k)
                             then (out.i.k!y -> ring.((i+1)%M)!j!x ->
                                     N1(i,<>,k,y,T) )
                             else  N1(i,E,j,x,T) )))
```

Since the capacity of these nodes is 2, whenever they are full they insist on outputting on the ring before accepting any more inputs. The ring can then be assem-
bled as follows.

```
Alpha(i) = {|in.i, out.i, ring.i, ring.(i+1)%M, quiet|}

RING(T) = (|| i:NodeNames @ [Alpha(i)] N0(i,<>,T))\{|ring|}
```

It is natural to split the desired properties of this system into *safety* (traces) and *liveness* (failures/divergences) specifications. For this basic ring without registers, one can identify three different liveness checks.

The first and most obvious is deadlock freedom, established, for example, via the check[5]

$$\text{DF } [\text{F= RING(T)}] \tag{1}$$

It is not too hard to see that the ring as constituted is divergence-free, because each time a hidden action occurs (i.e., a communication on `ring`), this is preceded by either the input (`in`) or an output (`out`) of the relevant update. It is, however, interesting to ask whether the process `RING(T)\{|out|}` can diverge.

$$\text{CHAOS(Events) } [\text{FD= RING(T)}\backslash\{|\text{out}|\}] \tag{2}$$

Such a divergence would correspond to one or more updates circulating endlessly without the need for further input; this is plainly not meant to happen but could if an update ever arrived back home to find the relevant E_j empty (i.e., it was not expected).

Assuming that both deadlock freedom and this extended form of livelock freedom have been proved as they can be (for given implementations) with FDR, the final liveness check we use is to establish that, on the assumption that nodes are never prevented by the environment from outputting updates, they inevitably stabilize in the quiescent state. In other words, left to its own devices, the ring will eventually come back to the state where no updates are active and none is expected back. We need to show that, eagerly abstracting the output events and lazily abstracting the input events, the ring *failures* refines the process

```
QS = quiet -> QS
```

The abstracted process can be represented and checked as follows:

$$\text{QS } [\text{F= MixedAbstraction}(\{|\text{in}|\},\{|\text{out}|\},\text{RING(T)})] \tag{3}$$

where the mixed abstraction operator is defined

```
MixedAbstraction(D,E,P) = (P[|D|]CHAOS(D)) \(union(D,E))
```

See Section 12.2 for more details of this style of specification using abstraction. This particular check has much in common with the style of timing consistency check described on page 407. A more direct and equivalent check is to show that

---

[5]The checks in this section are numbered so we can refer to them later.

```
CHAOS({|in|})  |||  QS
```

is failures or, equivalently, failures/divergences, refined by `RING(T)\{|out|}`.

Now that we know that our system always returns to the quiescent state, a natural way of formulating the basic safety specification (namely, consistency) is to assert that whenever it is quiescent all the copies of the register are equal. One can do this directly on the process `RING(T)` described above by carefully monitoring the pattern of updates that occur in each node *within the specification*. This is done as an alternative in the example file which illustrates this section, but here we concentrate on the more obvious method, which is to add the actual registers into the network. The following definition adds a new channel `read`, but identifies writes to the register at node *i* with the communications `in.i.x`. There is nothing essential about this approach and writes could also take place on a separate channel provided the register process carried a flag which indicates whether an update needs to be sent to the ring. (It would be set just when a local write had occurred more recently than the last communication on `in.i` or `out.i`.)

```
VAR(i,x,T) =  (out.i?j?v:T -> VAR(i,v,T))
           [] (in.i?v:T -> VAR(i,v,T))
           [] read.i!x -> VAR(i,x,T)


VARS(x0,T) = ||| i:NodeNames @ VAR(i,x0,T)

DDB(x0,T) = (RING(T) [|{|in,out|}|] VARS(x0,T))\{|out|}
```

Here x0 (ranging over the type T) represents the initial value of the register.

The appropriate trace specification is then simply that whenever a `quiet` has occurred more recently than a write (i.e., in this case an `in` event), two reads will give the same answer. This can be established by showing that

$$ \text{SS} \ [\text{T}= \ |\tilde{\ }| \ \text{x0:T} \ @ \ \text{DDB(x0,T)} \tag{4} $$

where the specification process SS is defined

```
SS  =  quiet -> Q0
    [] read?j?x -> SS
    [] in?j?u -> SS


Q0 =  read?j?x -> Q1(x)
    [] quiet -> Q0
    [] in?j?u -> SS
```

```
Q1(x) =  read?k!x ->  Q1(x)
      [] quiet -> Q1(x)
      [] in?j?u -> SS
```

Note that Q1(x) only permits one value to be read (any other leading to a failure
of refinement) whereas the other two states permit any. This is because Q1(x)
represents the case where at least one read (giving value x) has occurred since a
quiet event and before any further input on in.

15.2.2   Data-independence

Processes often have one or more *parameters*, namely quantities or objects that can
vary giving different instances of the system. Only the very simplest CSP processes
are usually defined without using parameterization at all. Parameters are typically
used to help capture the states of individual processes or to create a number of
similar components to include in a network (e.g., $PHIL_i$), but often a complete
network will still depend on one or more parameters (such as the total number of
philosophers). The parameters of the distributed database in the previous section
are:

1. The data type T of stored values.

2. The number of nodes.

3. The limit on the sizes of expected-back queues.

4. The ordering on nodes used to determine priority.

In addition, one could address the question of whether it was buffer tolerant (as
discussed in Section 5.2) and regard the sizes of the buffers as parameters.

What we would really like to do is prove all the results about liveness and
consistency of the database independently of these parameters. However, tools like
FDR generally only address one specific instance at a time and are usually only capable of handling ones with relatively small values for variable-sized parameters such
as the first three above. The general *Parameterized Verification Problem* (PVP), of
whether a system satisfies a correctness condition for all parameter values, is certainly formally *undecidable* [4] (it being easy to reduce other undecidable problems
such as the halting problem to it), but the subject of looking for specific classes
of problems where it might be made tractable is an active area of research (over a
much wider range of theories than simply CSP) and will probably remain one for
many years to come.

At the time of writing the most progress, by far, has been made with parameters of the first sort described above, namely data types, and this section is
devoted to presenting the most accessible and useful results about these.

A data type T used in a program P can fairly be said to be a parameter if
P treats it *data-independently*: it can input and output values of type T along its
channels, store them for later use, but never perform any 'interesting' computations
on them that constrain what T might be. (For example, if members of T were added
to each other, they would have to be numbers, ...) With one or two exceptions,
the criteria for deciding whether a type is data-independent are identical to those
for deciding whether it is a free *polymorphic* type variable in the sense of languages
such as ML. Precise criteria for this, which are readily automatable, can be found
in [60], but the following are the main principles:

(i)   Concrete values from T (such as 0, *true*, etc.) may not appear in the program
      text of P.

(ii) You may use basic polymorphic operations on T such as tupling, list forma-
      tion and suitable operations for extracting members of structures built out of
      T in these ways. Intuitively these can be thought of as operations which pass
      members of T around without looking inside them *at all*. No other functions
      which involve T either in the types of their arguments or result may be used.

(iii) No predicate (in a conditional) used in the program can depend on values
      from T. The only exception to this rule is that we allow equality (and
      inequality) tests between members of T. We do not, however, allow order
      comparisons such as $\leq$ and $>$.

(iv) Operations such as `card(S)` (the size of a set) may not be applied to any set
      involving set T. (This would give a way of extracting information from T
      that could be used to influence how P behaved.)

(v)   No replicated constructs except nondeterministic choice ($|\tilde{\ }|$ `x:S @ Q(x)`)
      can appear in the process *if their indexing set depends in any way on* T.
      Thus, parallel and external choice constructs indexed over T are banned,
      though the effect of the latter can, in practical circumstances, almost always
      be recovered using input (`c...?x:S...`), which is allowed.

Typical data-independent processes are *COPY* (in the type communicated)
and all the processes in the section on the distributed database (in the parameter
type T).

A data-independent program over type T makes sense whatever non-empty
set is substituted for T. If `Spec` and `Impl` are two of them, then it makes sense to
ask questions such as

- Spec $\sqsubseteq_T$ Impl?

- Spec $\sqsubseteq_F$ Impl?

- Spec $\sqsubseteq_{FD}$ Impl?

- is Impl deterministic?

for any specific T. Anybody performing many checks of this sort quickly comes to the conclusion that there must be a strong relationship between the answers to these questions for different sizes of T (it being relatively easy to see that the answer for any pair of T's of the same size *must* be the same). Fortunately this intuition is true and in almost all cases there is a *threshold*: an integer N such that the answer to one of the above questions for a type of size $M \geq N$ is independent of M. In other words, one can prove or refute a result for all sufficiently large[6] T via one check on FDR.

It is obviously of great practical importance to determine when these thresholds exist, and to find as small a threshold value as possible for each question we are presented with. There is a recently developed theory, too complex to present here, which allows the computation of thresholds by an extension of the theory of *logical relations* (or *parametricity*) to processes, by augmenting the operational semantics and CSP normalization to encompass terms with free variables as symbols for members of the independent type, and by using techniques for exploiting symmetry in state spaces. For details of this theory, see Section 15.4 and [62, 59]. References to related work can be found in these papers and in Section 15.4. What we can present here are the main conclusions.

There are four main factors which influence the size (and in some cases the existence) of a threshold for a given refinement check. These are

- the extent to which the specification constrains which members of T are communicated,

- the kinds of equality checks between members of T that are present in the specification and implementation,

- the subtlety of any nondeterminism in the specification, and

- the extent to which any values of type T which the specification uses are recorded in its traces (rather than only having some 'behind the scenes' effect)

---

[6]Where there is such a threshold N the answer for sufficiently large finite T also applies to all infinite T.

Lazić has proved a wide variety of results for calculating thresholds for refinement and determinism checks, falling into four main categories. The following
sections present the central ideas and results from each. Often the result presented
can be improved (e.g., by weakening its assumptions or strengthening its conclusions) if, for example, we are interested only in traces refinement: the interested
reader should consult [60, 62, 59].

When $\mid T \mid = 1$ is enough

One frequently wants to prove specifications of data-independent processes that do
not say anything of significance about how they are permitted to handle members
of T. Examples are deadlock and divergence freedom and any trace specification
that is always happy to allow any member of T in an event when it allows one.
It turns out that in many cases it is sufficient to prove such specifications for the
simplest possible T: a one-element type. In other words, the threshold is just 1.

Equality tests over T are banned altogether from both the specification and
implementation[7]:

NoEqT   A data-independent process P satisfies this when it contains *no* test of
equality between members of T.

All the processes of the distributed database example satisfy **NoEqT**, as do *COPY*
and all the other buffer and similar examples we have seen.

NoEqT effectively rejects the liberal side of condition (iii) in the definition
of data-independence. To ensure that the specification basically ignores T we assert
that the only way a member of T can occur in a communication of the specification
process Spec is via a *nondeterministic selection* of the form a$x:T -> P which is
introduced as an abbreviation for

|~| x:T @ a.x -> P

(For the purpose of trace specification, this is equivalent to a?x:T -> P.) In other
words, Spec can never specify *which* member of T is communicated or that any

---

[7]It should be pointed out that there are ways of introducing 'hidden equality tests' into CSP
programs via some operations and predicates on sets and sequences, and via communication. The
communication effect appears when we synchronize on two output events: c!x -> P [|{|c|}|]
c!y -> Q contains an implicit equality check between x and y and therefore violates **NoEqT**.
These problems do not appear in the great majority of practical programs and can be avoided
provided the only set constructs used involving T are unioning of straightforward channel alphabets
(for synchronization and hiding), and each synchronization over channels of type T only has one
output. If you are in doubt about the legitimacy of some construct you should consult one of
[60, 59].

more than one arbitrary member of T is offered. We will only use the $ form on the specification side of refinement, since it will always be permissible to re-write ones in the implementation using the more general |˜| as above.

The characteristic processes DF of deadlock freedom and $Chaos_\Sigma$ of divergence freedom satisfy these criteria, as do processes like

```
ALT = a$x:T -> b$x:T -> ALT
```

This particular example just says that communications over a and b alternate without placing any constraint on which members of T appear.

We can now state the first of a number of results establishing exact criteria for data-independent reasoning.

THEOREM 15.2.1 *Suppose we have processes* Spec(T) *and* Impl(T), *each data-independent with respect to the type parameter T and additionally satisfying condition* **NoEqT**. *Suppose further that* Spec *is restricted to nondeterministic selections over T as described above. Then, with $\sqsubseteq$ representing any of $\{\sqsubseteq_T, \sqsubseteq_F, \sqsubseteq_{FD}\}$ the result of the refinement check*

$$\text{Spec}(T) \sqsubseteq \text{Impl}(T)$$

is independent of which non-empty T is used. In particular, the answer for all T is answered by the check when $T = \{0\}$ is a one-element type.

What this result says, in essence, is that if we have a program whose control-flow does not depend on which members of T it holds, and a specification which ignores how it handles members of T relative to each other, then we can collapse T to a single value without affecting the result of a refinement check. Obviously this will usually give a significant advantage in state space size. It applies to checks (1–3) from the distributed database example.

In fact, essentially the same result holds when Impl is, in addition, allowed to use arbitrary functions whose result is of type T. These processes, which we can term *weakly* data-independent, can thus calculate values in T in non-trivial ways, but still cannot let T affect their control-flow. See [61, 62, 60, 59] for details.

When $| T |= 2$ is enough

If we build a system which is data-independent in some type T then it is likely that we will want to prove things about how it handles members of T as well as specifications that ignore T like those dealt with above. It turns out that, provided we make the same assumptions about the implementation as in the previous section (i.e., it is data-independent and satisfies **NoEqT**), and follow a set of conditions on the specification designed to remove ambiguity about what state it is in after a given trace, then we can assume that T has just two elements. In other words, the threshold is then 2.

The following condition states, in essence, that the specification is already nearly in the normal form for CSP used in the algebraic semantics (Section 11.4) and in refinement checking (Appendix C).

Norm   A process Spec meets this condition if

   (i)   its definition contains no hiding or renaming;

  (ii)   the only parallel operators allowed are alphabetized parallel P[X||Y]Q and its replicated version;

 (iii)   other than the nondeterministic selection construct[8] a$x:S -> P described above, no indexed nondeterministic choice is used whose indexing set depends on T;

  (iv)   all internal and external choice constructs (Q |~| R, Q [] R, indexed versions of these, and [> (the 'time-out' operator)) have the initial events of each argument disjoint (i.e., once one event has occurred we must know which branch was chosen) and

   (v)   any uses of the operators ; and /\ ($\triangle$, the interrupt operator) conform to some technical conditions given in [60] which essentially ensure that (iv) is not broken implicitly.

The main role of this condition is to avoid the introduction of any nondeterminism except when its effects are immediately apparent. Almost all natural specification processes one ever builds satisfy this condition, or could easily be transformed to ones that do, since in order for us to know what a specification says it should be clear what state it is in after a given trace. In other words, **Norm** can be regarded almost as a well-formedness condition on specifications in a wider sense.[9]

THEOREM 15.2.2 *Suppose* Spec *and* Impl *are data-independent processes, both satisfy* **NoEqT** *and* Spec *satisfies* **Norm**. *Let* $\sqsubseteq$ *be any of* $\{\sqsubseteq_T, \sqsubseteq_F, \sqsubseteq_{FD}\}$.

---

[8]It is legitimate to use complex prefixes such as cxy?z, but for technical reasons (see [62, 59]) you may not mix (either here or anywhere else the nondeterministic selection construct is used in the study of data-independence) nondeterministic selections over T with inputs over types other than T.

[9]The only major class of specifications we have seen that do not fall within this category are the fault-tolerance specifications such as *NoFaults* on page 314. These, being derived from implementations, may very well contain hiding, etc.

- If $\mathtt{Spec}(2) \sqsubseteq \mathtt{Impl}(2)$ *holds (i.e., for* T *of size 2) then* $\mathtt{Spec}(m) \sqsubseteq \mathtt{Impl}(m)$ *holds for all finite and infinite* $m \geq 1$.

- If *the refinement* $\mathtt{Spec}(2) \sqsubseteq \mathtt{Impl}(2)$ *fails then* $\mathtt{Spec}(m) \sqsubseteq \mathtt{Impl}(m)$ *fails for all finite and infinite* $m \geq 2$.

The difference between this result and the previous one is that here there is nothing to prevent the specification restricting which of the values of T it knows about is communicated after a given trace. Also, in the case of failures and failures/divergences specifications, it can specify much more about which refusal sets involving members of T are acceptable. Thus, for example, any of the processes $BUFF^N_{\langle\rangle}$ and $WBUFF^N_{\langle\rangle}$ from Section 5.1 would be acceptable for $\mathtt{Spec}$ in this result but not for Theorem 15.2.1.

Intuitively, this result says that if we have both an implementation and a specification which pass members of T around without letting them determine the control-flow, then in order to check whether a refinement holds it is sufficient to look at T of size 2. What you have to check in these cases is that each value input into an implementation is output in just the right places. In [61, 62, 60, 59] it is shown that in many cases you can restrict the state space of the check further: although it still requires a data type of size 2, one can assume that all but one of the values input into the implementation are equal. These references also contain (i) significant strengthenings of Theorem 15.2.2 which depend on definitions we have not had space for here, and (ii) discussion of the extent to which specifications that do not satisfy the condition **Norm** can be transformed into ones that do via an equivalent of the normalization procedures described in Section 11.4 and Appendix C.

The consistency check (4) of the distributed database, as well as most of the earlier correctness conditions of communications protocols and similar processes, come directly within the scope of the above theorem, however. Thus all the checks in the previous section have, as far as the type parameter T is concerned, a threshold of 1 or 2.

The general case

The definition of data-independence quoted at the start of this section allowed for equality tests between members of T. Thus the process

```
RemDups = left?x -> right!x -> RemDups'(x)

RemDups'(x) = left?y -> if x==y then RemDups'(x)
                        else right!y -> RemDups'(y)
```

which removes adjacent duplicates from a stream of values is data-independent even though its control-flow depends on the values of T it uses. Evidently, however, this does not satisfy the condition **NoEqT**, and so neither of the earlier results applies to it. In cases like this it is still, under appropriate conditions, usually possible to find thresholds, but they vary with the complexity of the processes under consideration. For example, a process which inputs N values and then communicates a only if they are all different plainly needs a threshold of at least N in order to show that it can sometimes communicate a.

Lazić has shown how to compute thresholds in terms of the following quantities. Bear in mind that we are going to assume that the specification `Spec` satisfies **Norm** whereas no such assumption will be made of `Impl`.

$W^{\texttt{Impl}}$ is the maximum number of values of type T that the implementation `Impl` ever has to store for future use. This number can be computed by going through the operational semantics of the process in such a way that members of T are treated as 'symbolic' identifiers and counting how many of them are required in any state. For the `RemDups` example above, this number is 1 because in any state it only has to store 'x' or 'y'. (It might appear that the point in `RemDups'(x)` just before the equality test has to store two values, but in fact the operational semantics merges the effect of any conditional with the preceding action. The fork produced by the conditional thus occurs as part of the `left?y` action, with some values of y leading one way and some the other.)

$W^{\texttt{Spec}}$ is the corresponding number for the specification.

$L_?^{\texttt{Impl}}$ is the largest number of values of type T that can be input in any *single* visible event of `Impl`. This can be greater than one when dealing with channels with multiple components and/or components that are tuples, lists and similar.

$L^{\texttt{Spec}}$ is the corresponding number for the specification, except that it additionally takes into account nondeterministic selections (using $) which may be present in `Spec`.

$L_{\sqcap}^{\texttt{Impl}}$ is the largest number of values from T that can be nondeterministically chosen in any single nondeterministic choice made over sets involving T in `Impl`. Thus the choice `|~| p:(T,T) @ Q(p)` requires this quantity to be (at least) 2.

All of these quantities *can* be infinite in some circumstances, for example, through the use of unrestricted-length sequences of type T. When a constant necessary for computing a given threshold is infinite, it essentially means that no useful one can be obtained in this way.

The following results show the thresholds. We get a lower one for traces refinement because it is not necessary to worry about how the members of T get involved in the creation of refusal sets. There are examples (see [62, 60, 59]) which show that neither of the thresholds given in the following pair of results can be improved under the stated assumptions.

THEOREM 15.2.3 *Suppose* Spec *and* Impl *are data-independent processes,* Spec *satisfies* **Norm***, and*

$$B \geq W^{\text{Spec}} + W^{\text{Impl}} + max(L_?^{\text{Impl}}, L_\sqcap^{\text{Impl}})$$

Then for all $N \geq B$, the following traces refinements are equivalent:

Spec$(B) \sqsubseteq_T$ Impl(B)

Spec$(N) \sqsubseteq_T$ Impl(N)

THEOREM 15.2.4 *Suppose* Spec *and* Impl *are data-independent processes,* Spec *satisfies* **Norm***, and*

$$B \geq W^{\text{Spec}} + W^{\text{Impl}} + max(L^{\text{Spec}}, L_?^{\text{Impl}}, L_\sqcap^{\text{Impl}})$$

Then for all $N \geq B$ and $\sqsubseteq$ either of $\sqsubseteq_F$ or $\sqsubseteq_{FD}$, the refinements

Spec$(B) \sqsubseteq$ Impl(B)

Spec$(N) \sqsubseteq$ Impl(N)

are equivalent.

For example, we might define a dual process to RemDups which, instead of removing duplicates, only keeps the members of a sequence of values that do duplicate their immediate predecessors.

```
OnlyDups = left?x -> OnlyDups'(x)

OnlyDups'(x) = left?y -> if x==y then right!y -> OnlyDups'(y)
                        else OnlyDups'(y)
```

Obviously we would expect the process

```
FilterAll = RemDups [right <-> left] OnlyDups
```

(the machine-readable version of `RemDups` $\gg$ `OnlyDups`) not to transmit any value at all. In other words, it should refine

```
Sink = left?x -> Sink
```

The various parameters for the refinement check `Sink` $\sqsubseteq$ `FilterAll` are $W^{\text{Sink}} = 0$, $W^{\text{FilterAll}} = 2$, $L^{\text{FilterAll}}_? = L^{\text{Sink}} = 1$ and $L^{\text{FilterAll}}_\sqcap = 0$. Thus the threshold value for both Theorem 15.2.3 and Theorem 15.2.4 is 3. Similarly, the process

```
Partition = RemDups [|{|left|}|] OnlyDups
```

can be shown to refine `COPY` with a threshold of 4 (since W^{COPY} is 1 rather than 0).

In fact, the threshold for this last check can be lowered to 3 by observing that, in `Partition`, the two component processes always hold the same member of T so that, in fact, $W^{\text{Partition}}$ is 1 rather than 2.

A bigger application of these results can be found in the next section.

Though this has not been done at the time of writing, there is an obvious potential for the creation of tools that check the various conditions of data-independence and calculate thresholds. It should also be possible to do two further things:

- Transformation of more arbitrary specifications into ones satisfying **Norm**.

- The theory that Lazić developed to prove the theorems in this section also anticipates the possibility of proving a refinement parameterized by a data type by carrying out the check symbolically, in the sense that members of the type are kept as symbols during the check which is otherwise performed not unlike the method described in Appendix C. This should be automatable and, in many cases, should be significantly more efficient than checks derived from thresholds calculated using general formulae. (One can argue that in many cases the 'real' threshold of a given check is often lower than the values predicted by Theorems 15.2.3 and 15.2.4.)

Determinism checks

It is natural to ask whether versions of the results we have seen for refinement checks also exist for determinism checking, as this is a condition of processes that is not readily characterized as a refinement check. In other words, can we compute thresholds which are sufficient to prove that a given data-independent process `Impl`(N) is deterministic for all larger N? We have already seen the practical importance of this question, particularly in Chapter 12 where determinism was the key to deciding issues of security.

As with refinement checking, there are a number of results depending on the complexity of the use of T within Impl. We quote two here, respectively for processes that do, and do not, satisfy **NoEqT**. In the first case, perhaps surprisingly given Theorem 15.2.2, we get a variable threshold rather than the fixed value of 2. It is, however, equal to 2 in most simple cases since the following constant is usually then 1:

L_{Occur}^{Impl} is the largest number of distinct values of type T that can appear in any *single* visible event of Impl.

THEOREM 15.2.5 *Suppose* Impl *is data-independent and satisfies* **NoEqT**. *Then*

(a) *If* $\text{Impl}(L_{Occur}^{Impl} + 1)$ *is deterministic, then* $\text{Impl}(N)$ *is deterministic for all* $N \geq 1$.

(b) *If* $\text{Impl}(L_{Occur}^{Impl} + 1)$ *is nondeterministic, then* $\text{Impl}(N)$ *is nondeterministic for all* $N \geq L_{Occur}^{Impl} + 1$.

This result applies to all the versions of Example 12.4.1 (page 320 *et seq*), in each case giving threshold 2 (in the type of messages).

The second result covers the same class of Impl as Theorem 15.2.3, namely general data-independent processes, and uses the same quantities to compute thresholds. The assumption about renamings should hold in the great majority of cases: a threshold can still be computed when it does not hold, see [59].

THEOREM 15.2.6 *Suppose* Impl *is data-independent and contains no renaming which conceals the value of any member of* T *input in a communication, then the threshold for determinism is given by*

$$2 \times W^{Impl} + \max(L_?^{Impl}, L_\sqcap^{Impl})$$

in the sense that $\text{Impl}(N)$ *is deterministic if and only if* $\text{Impl}(M)$ *is, for* M, N *at least this value.*

Both these results apply equally[10] to true determinism (decided in $\mathcal{N}$) and to the weaker notion of $\mathcal{F}$-determinism discussed on page 217. The latter is relevant since the recommended way of of deciding the determinism of lazy abstractions $\mathcal{L}_H(P)$ (as discussed in Chapter 12) is via the $\mathcal{F}$-determinism of the potentially divergent process $(P \parallel_H Chaos_H) \setminus H$.

---

[10]In fact, at the time of writing, the quoted threshold in Theorem 15.2.6 is known to be tight for $\mathcal{F}$-determinism but not for true determinism. It is conjectured that, for the latter, the factor of 2 on W^{Impl} can be removed.

15.2.3   Cache coherency

Imagine your computer has a large memory which is relatively slow to access compared to the clock-speed of the process that is accessing it. The standard solution to this is to use a *cache*: a relatively small piece of fast memory through which the processor makes all accesses and which always keeps part of the main memory in it, in the hope that the addresses which are required will be already there. Modern computers may have several levels of cacheing, for example:

- Virtual memory (on disk) *versus* 'real' (i.e., RAM) memory.

- Slow (often DRAM) memory *versus* an off-processor (often SRAM) cache.

- Cache which is an integral part of the processor chip *versus* off-processor memory.

Though the technology of these different levels may be different, the logical problems are the same, namely ensuring that, though there are in fact several copies of some memory locations around, this does not affect the values the processor reads relative to any writes that may have occurred. Logically, the combination of the cache and the memory which it uses must be equivalent to the memory itself. You can think of the memory as being enslaved to the cache:

$$Memory \quad = \quad Cache /\!/ m : Memory$$

Since enslavement is not supported directly in machine-readable CSP (see Section 4.3) we will re-write this as

```
Memory = Cache [m_ra <-> ra, m_rv <-> rv, m_w <-> w] Memory
```

where the memory has three channels respectively for read requests, read values and writes, and the cache has the same three channels (for its processor interface) and separate versions (`m_ra` etc.) for communicating with the memory.

```
channel ra, m_ra:address
channel rv, m_rv:value
channel w, m_w:address.value
```

In order to prove this equivalence it will be sufficient to prove that the right-hand side refines `Memory`, since the latter will be deterministic. (There should be no need to apply the data-independence results above to establish this determinism: Lemma 9.1.4 on page 220 should apply.) We will therefore concentrate on establishing this refinement.

At any time the cache keeps a list of triples (a,(v,b)) where a is an address[11] presently resident in the cache, v is the value stored in that address and b is a bit which records whether or not the address has been written to since it was brought into the cache. b is necessary because it lets us tell, when the address is eventually removed from the cache, whether or not the stored value has to be written-back to the main memory. The four parameters of the process Cache are this list, the types of addresses and storable values in use, and the maximum number of addresses that can be stored in the cache at once.

The cache starts off empty and fills itself up as the processor asks to read and write to addresses. Such reads evidently require a fetch from memory. Any read or write to a location already in the cache is done without any interaction with the main memory. When the cache is full and a *miss* occurs (i.e., an attempt to access a location not presently held) it is necessary to flush one thing out of the cache in order to make room for the new member. There are a number of *cache replacement policies* used to do this, such as FIFO (first in, first out), random, and *least recently used*. It is the last of these which is implemented below since each time an address is used it moves up to the front of the queue.

The following definition captures all the behaviour of such a cache except what happens when a flush is required. Note how the boolean flags that control write-backs are set to true whenever a write to the given location occurs.

```
Cache(ps,A,V,N) = ra?a:A ->
            (if elem(a,<a' | (a',_) <- ps>) then
                (rv!val(a,ps) -> Cache(tofront(a,ps),A,V,N))
            else if #ps < N then
                m_ra!a -> m_rv?v:V -> rv!v ->
                    Cache(<(a,(v,false))>^ps,A,V,N)
            else FlushAndRead(ps,a,A,V,N))
        [] w?a:A?v:V ->
            if elem(a,<a' | (a',_) <- ps>) then
                Cache(update(a,v,ps),A,V,N)
            else if #ps < N then
                Cache(<(a,(v,true))>^ps,A,V,N)
            else FlushAndWrite(ps,a,v,A,V,N)
```

The following three functions used above respectively fetch a value from the cache, move a just-read address to the front of ps and perform a write to an address already in the cache.

---

[11] In practice, data tends to be stored in blocks of more than one address. This would have a minor impact on what follows.

```
val(a,ps) = head(<v | (a',(v,_)) <- ps, a'==a>)

tofront(a,ps) = <(a',x) | (a',x) <- ps, a'==a>^
                <(a',x) | (a',x) <- ps, a'!=a>

update(a,v,ps) = <(a,(v,true))>^<(a',x) | (a',x) <- ps, a'!=a>
```

The following two processes flush the last member of the queue (i.e., the least recently used member) out, performing a write-back to memory if necessary. They then fill up the vacant space with a new location either read-from or written-to.

```
FlushAndRead(ps^<(a',(v',wr_bk))>,a,A,V,N) =
                if wr_bk then
                    m_w!a'!v' -> m_ra!a -> m_rv?v:V -> rv!v ->
                    Cache(<(a,(v,false))>^ps,A,V,N)
                else
                    m_ra!a -> m_rv?v:V -> rv!v ->
                    Cache(<(a,(v,false))>^ps,A,V,N)

FlushAndWrite(ps^<(a',(v',wr_bk))>,a,v,A,V,N) =
                if wr_bk then
                    m_w!a'!v' -> Cache(<(a,(v,true))>^ps,A,V,N)
                else
                    Cache(<(a,(v,true))>^ps,A,V,N)
```

There are various ways in which one can provide a model of the memory that the cache is intended to interact with. Perhaps the obvious one is to model it as a simple shell around a function from addresses to values.

```
Memory(A,V,f) = ra?a:A -> rv!f(v) -> Memory(A,V,f)
            [] w?a:A?v:V -> let f'(a') = if a==a' then v else f(a')
                            within Memory(A,V,f')
```

This does not work with FDR at the time of writing since the tool, for very good reasons, does not detect the equalities between the functions that arise as it explores the states of this process. The above definition can easily be modified so that it does work by replacing the function with, for example, a set of address/value pairs.

The check that the Memory/Cache combination refines the Memory alone has interesting data-independence properties in the types V of storable values and A of addresses. The processes concerned are data-independent in both types, and satisfy **NoEqT** in V. The process Memory satisfies **Norm** with respect to both. They do not, however, satisfy **NoEqT** with respect to A since the behaviour of `Cache` depends quite explicitly on comparisons between addresses, and `Memory` needs, whatever the details of its definition, to be able to compare addresses to know which internal value to read or modify.

Theorem 15.2.2 tells us that, whatever A is, it is sufficient to prove refinement with V of size 2. If we can find a threshold for A with such V, we can then guarantee that refinement holds for all larger instances of both types.

Unfortunately there is no useful threshold deducible from Theorems 15.2.3 and 15.2.4 in the type A for the refinement check involving the cache coupled with the whole memory, since the process `Memory` has every member of A in its state: there is no bound on either W^{Impl} or W^{Spec}.

This can be remedied in an interesting way: we can concentrate on a single but arbitrary address. Instead of proving that all interactions with the cache are as expected for a well-behaved memory, we show that for any particular location each read from the cache gives the right answer purely on the assumption that the reads that the cache itself makes for the chosen location are well-behaved. The following process behaves like a reliable memory for whatever address is chosen (together with initial value) in the first communication. On the other locations it selects the value of a read nondeterministically rather than by reference to previous writes: this means that it only has to remember a single address rather than them all.

```
OneLoc(A,V) = loc?a:A?v:V -> OneLoc'(a,v,A,V)

OneLoc'(a,v,A,V) = w?a':A?v':V -> (if a==a' then OneLoc'(a,v',A,V)
                                            else OneLoc'(a,v,A,V))
            [] ra?a':A ->
                 (if a==a' then rv!v -> OneLoc'(a,v,A,V)
                  else |~| v':V @ rv!v' -> OneLoc'(a,v,A,V))
```

We can then check to see if this process is refined by a combination of the cache and itself, which takes the form below to prevent any communications between the environment and the cache before the special location is chosen:

```
Test(A,V,N) = loc?a:A?v:V ->
              (Cache(<>,A,V,N)
                 [m_ra <-> ra, m_rv <-> rv, m_w <-> w]
               OneLoc'(a,v,A,V))
```

In a sense, the fact that `OneLoc(A,V)` is refined by `Test(A,V,N)` proves a stronger correctness condition than the more obvious one involving `Memory`, since it shows that the reads made from the cache of address **a** only depend on the reads the cache makes of the memory at **a** being correct.

Theorems 15.2.3 and 15.2.4 can be applied to this check since all the quantities they use are finite with respect to the type **A**: $W^{\text{Test}} = 2 + N$, $W^{\text{OneLoc}} = L^{\text{OneLoc}} = L_?^{\text{Test}} = 1$ and $L_\sqcap^{\text{Test}} = 0$. Thus, for a cache of size N it is sufficient to prove the refinement for $N + 4$ addresses (and 2 storable values).

It should not come as a surprise that the required size of **A** increases with N, since the control-flow of the cache depends crucially on whether it is full or not, and obviously it could not get full if it had more slots than there were addresses! The size of the cache is, of course, another parameter that we would like to dispense with within the scope of the PVP. It is not, however, one that can be dealt with via data-independence. At the time of writing there is no technique of comparable generality to handle variation in N. We have to resort to *ad hoc* (i.e., application specific) arguments. It can be shown without too much difficulty that the possible behaviours relating to any given address are independent of cache size since any behaviour of a small cache corresponds to a behaviour of a large one with more accesses to other addresses between accesses to the chosen one.

Three different arguments have thus shown that our cache works for any[12] **V**, **A** and **N** provided it does for them respectively being of sizes 2, 5 and equalling 1.

EXERCISE 15.2.1   Recall the buffer defined on page 119 which worked by majority voting over groups of three bits, and was tolerant of no more than one corrupted bit in any three. Define a version of this in which bits are replaced by an arbitrary type. We then have to deal, when programming the receiver, with a group of three all being different: you should make it deadlock in that case.

Your complete program, including a revised version of the corrupting channel, should be data-independent and a buffer refining $BUFF_{\langle\rangle}^3$. What threshold for the data-independent type do the results predict for this (failures/divergences) refinement check?

EXERCISE 15.2.2   In the previous section we briefly discussed cache replacement policies. One such policy is FIFO, where the value in the cache to be replaced is always the one that has been there longest (irrespective of how recently it has been used). It can happen with this policy that adding to the size of the cache increases the number of cache misses in a given series of reads and writes.

Build a CSP model that allows you to find an example of this behaviour with FDR: it will probably consist of two different-sized caches to allow you to compare how they behave on each possible run.

---

[12]In fact, the data-independence theorems do not always allow us to conclude refinement below the threshold from refinement at it, and so it is actually necessary to deal separately with smaller values of **A**.

Although it is about caches, this fairly difficult question has much more in common with the puzzles of Section 15.1 than with the cache model seen in this section. In particular, the values stored in the memory and caches are irrelevant. All that matters is how the addresses in the two FIFO queues of the large and small caches correspond.

EXERCISE 15.2.3   In books such as [24] you will find many intriguing distributed algorithms for a wide variety of tasks, generally expressed at a lower level of formality than those we have seen in this section. It is a fascinating practical exercise to take one of these, re-work it in CSP and analyze versions with FDR, as we did for the database and cache algorithms. Clearly these vary significantly in difficulty: suggestions taken from [24] are the *Bully algorithm*, *Two-phase commit* and concurrency control techniques. Many will require timing to be built into the model in the style of Chapter 14.

15.3   Breaking crypto-protocols

One sometimes needs to achieve secure interactions between individuals over a medium which is untrustworthy and subject to tampering by potential intruders. These interactions, and the consequent need for security, vary widely from application to application, and several possibilities are given below.

1. The most obvious is to make communications between parties secret. No information which Alice sends confidentially to Bob should become known to an intruder.

2. Parties should be able to *authenticate* others: if Bob thinks he has been talking to Alice, then he should have been (and Alice should think she has been talking to Bob).

3. We might want to authenticate that a message is precisely the one issued by Alice, even when we are not concerned about confidentiality.

4. In contexts where financial transactions are being implemented, we clearly need to protect their integrity from interference and fraud.

To do these things in a context where an intruder can overhear messages, stop messages from reaching their intended destinations, and even potentially fake messages, for example, to Bob purporting to be from Alice, you need to make use of encryption and related methods which limit:

(a) an intruder's ability to understand the messages he or she hears, and equally importantly,

(b) the potential for the intruder to create fake messages which can convince someone else that they are genuine.

CSP is not an appropriate vehicle either for describing encryption algorithms or for devising methods of deciphering coded messages. That involves a lot of sophisticated mathematics in number theory, algebra, etc. However, it is often the case that a use of encryption fails not because of vulnerability of the cipher in use, but because of the way it is used. Frequently it is possible to defeat protocols using and supporting encryption even under the assumption that the encryption method used is unbreakable.

A *cryptographic protocol* is a series of carefully defined messages, often encrypted, between two or more participants designed so that when it is complete, they can be sure that a specified goal has been achieved, even in the presence of an intruder who can perform the malicious acts described above. The only restriction we place on the intruder is that it is unable to decrypt coded messages without the appropriate key or to generate faked messages when it does not possess the necessary information. Many cryptographic protocols are concerned with establishing a connection between two nodes, often involving the trading or generation of a key for use during the resultant session. CSP and FDR have proved to be excellent tools for modelling and analyzing cryptographic protocols, using symbolic representations of encryption.

The following is an authentication protocol known as the *Needham–Schroeder Public-Key* protocol. It is intended to authenticate a pair of nodes to each other (so that each is aware that the other is willing to talk to it), and to ensure that each possesses the other's public key.[13] We assume that there are potentially many nodes

---

[13]Public-key encryption is based on the idea that it is possible to find algorithms where (i) the key required to decrypt a message is different from the one used for encryption, and (ii) it is computationally infeasible to construct one of this pair of keys from the other. Any node may thus publish one of a pair of keys like this as its *public key*, retaining the other for itself as its *secret key*. Then anyone holding the public key can send it a private message that only our node can understand.

A more subtle use is for the node to send a message encrypted with its secret key: anyone can decrypt this on the assumption that (as is true with some algorithms such as RSA), the decryption key for the secret key is the public key. But when they do they will realize that the only person who could have sent it is the node holding the secret key. This is an example of a cryptographic *signature*. In fact it is generally considered good practice to use separate pairs of keys for signing messages and confidentiality, but the same ideas still apply.

There are several problems in the use of public-key encryption in transmitting information between nodes. An important one on practical grounds is that the algorithms used tend to be computationally significantly more complex than symmetric algorithms (ones where the encryption and decryption keys are the same). A second, and more directly security-related problem, is that one has to guard against the situation where it is possible for an intruder to guess that a message is going to be a member of a small set such as {*yes*, *no*}, since all the intruder has to do is to encrypt each member of the set using the public key and compare them against the one actually sent. Therefore public-key encryption is often used only during the establishment of a session, and is replaced by a symmetric algorithm once it is possible to give the participants a key known only to them (the session key).

that might want to talk to each other, and that they do not necessarily remember all other's public keys, but do remember that of a server S from which they can request other users' keys. (Servers are a common, though by no means universal, feature of cryptographic protocols, and play a wide range of roles in them.) The protocol proceeds as follows when node A wants to establish communication with B:

1. $A \rightarrow S : B$

2. $S \rightarrow A : \{pk(B), B\}_{sk(S)}$

3. $A \rightarrow B : \{N_A, A\}_{pk(B)}$

4. $B \rightarrow S : A$

5. $S \rightarrow B : \{pk(A), A\}_{sk(S)}$

6. $B \rightarrow A : \{N_A, N_B\}_{pk(A)}$

7. $A \rightarrow B : \{N_B\}_{pk(B)}$

Here $\{X\}_Y$ means the public-key encryption of the message X under the key Y. A commentary on this protocol follows:

1. A asks the server for B's public key.

2. S sends it, signed. There is no need for this information to be encrypted, but it has to be signed (as a combination with B's name) to prevent, for example, a malicious node substituting its own public key so it can impersonate B to A. The body of this message can be regarded as a *certificate* that B's public key is $pk(B)$.

3. A can then send a message to B, which has the purpose of requesting a session set-up. N_A represents a *nonce*, which is a piece of random information which has just been made up by A so that when it gets a response containing N_A it knows it must have been generated for *this* message 3.

4. B then requests A's public key from the server,

5. and is sent it exactly as with message 2.

6. B can then reply to message 3, acknowledging it with the nonce N_A and a new nonce of its own, which

7. A then sends back to B so that B knows that the message 3 it has been acting on was genuine (bearing in mind that, from B's point of view until it receives message 7, anyone could have made message 3 up, and the confirmation to B that it is real is when A understands and acts on message 6).

Apparently, when the run is complete, both A and B are reassured that the other exists and is willing to talk to it, and the nonces N_A and N_B that have been created are secrets known only to these two.

Note that messages 1 and 4 of this protocol are completely unsecured, merely being indications to the server that a particular sort of information would be appreciated. There is nothing to stop an intruder preventing one or both of these getting through and then replaying old messages 2 and 5 it may have recorded much earlier, but the signature mechanism means that they would be identical to the ones the server actually would have sent, and no fundamental security problem is created. (However, if a node's public key ever changes, this would create a problem and the protocol would have to be improved.)

In fact, the mechanism for distributing public keys in messages 1, 2, 4 and 5 is largely independent of the authentication mechanism contained in messages 3, 6 and 7, which still makes sense as a protocol if we assume that nodes do not need to communicate with a server to discover each others' public keys. For simplicity we will concentrate henceforth on the three-message version, re-numbering the messages accordingly.

To test a protocol like this one with CSP we have to build models of well-behaved nodes and an intruder and see how the latter can interfere with the former. There is usually no need to create more than two well-behaved nodes (plus a well-behaved server, if one is used in the protocol, which it is not in the abbreviated Needham–Schroeder protocol). Rather, we give the intruder the ability to behave like other nodes and to interact properly as well as improperly with the good ones. The basic facts we then aim to prove are that the security of a session between the well-behaved nodes is intact whatever else happens, and that neither of them can be fooled into thinking it has a session with the other when it does not. Both of these things should hold even though one or both nodes may previously have had sessions with other, possibly corrupt, users.

An *attack* on a protocol is a series of messages that the intruder can bring about in which each trustworthy node carries out its role properly but which brings the network into an insecure state. Essentially our job in analyzing a protocol is to capture this concept precisely and find out if attacks are possible.

15.3.1 Data types for symbolic encryption

What follows is a coding of this network. As we have already said, the encryptions and similar will be modelled as symbolic objects: we create an appropriate data type to contain them which consists of various constants we will need, public-key (PK) and symmetric-key encryption constructions and a sequencing construct.

```
datatype fact = Sq. Seq(fact) |
                PK. (fact , fact) |
                Encrypt. (fact, fact) |
                Alice | Bob | Cameron |
                Na | Nb | Nc |
                pkA | pkB | pkC |
                skA | skB | skC |
                AtoB | BtoA | Cmessage
```

The type fact contains various collections of constants, which can be collected together into sets for later use. The three identities used are those of two nodes we will later treat as reliable, plus one (Cameron) for the intruder to assume when it acts as another party.[14]

```
agents = {Alice, Bob, Cameron}

publickey = {pkA, pkB, pkC}

secretkey = {skA, skB, skC}

nonces = {Na, Nb, Nc}

sessmess = {AtoB, BtoA, Cmessage}
```

The roles of these sets will become apparent later.

We can tie the keys to these identities as follows, thereby defining functions for determining the public and secret keys of each node and for mapping a key to its inverse or dual.

```
keybindings = {(Alice,pkA,skA), (Bob,pkB,skB),
                              (Cameron, pkC, skC)}

pk(a) = pick({k | (a',k,_) <- keybindings, a==a'})

sk(a) = pick({k | (a',_,k) <- keybindings, a==a'})

dual(k) = pick(Union({{k'' | (_,k',k'') <- keybindings, k==k'},
                      {k' | (_,k',k'') <- keybindings, k==k''}}))
```

---

[14]With the great majority of protocols it would not improve the intruder's prospects to have any more identities (Donald, Eve, etc.) to play with. This is because any attack which involved more than one of these identities acting would also work with them all being Cameron.

Here `pick` is a function that maps a singleton set {x} to its member x (see also page 504). The following definitions allow us to make the symbolic encryption operations into functions.

```
pke(k,m) = PK . (k , m)
encrypt(k,m) = Encrypt . (k , m)
```

15.3.2   Defining reliable nodes

We are now in a position to define processes representing the behaviour of a reliable node implementing the protocol. The following defines the node with identity `id` which has the supply of nonces `ns` to use in sessions: we have to keep these lists finite and fairly small if the size of checks generated on FDR is to be reasonable. Evidently the definition below, which gives up when the list is empty, is not adequate if we expect the resulting system to satisfy liveness[15] but in this treatment we will only worry about safety (traces) properties and so the only real concern is whether the size of system used is sufficient to reveal any pathologies in the protocol. A node can either act as an initiator of the protocol (**Send**) or as the responder (**Resp**).

```
User(id,ns) = if ns == <> then STOP else
              Send(id,ns) [] Resp(id,ns)
```

When acting as an initiator, the node chooses a target to start up a session with, and then communicates the three messages of the protocol in turn with it. Note that any nonce is accepted as N_B in the second message. When the three messages are complete, it enters a state (which is discussed below) in which it is happily in a session with its partner.

```
Send(id,ns) = |~| b:diff(agents,{id}) @
                  comm.id.b.pke(pk(b),Sq.<head(ns),id>) ->
                  ([] nb:nonces @
                  comm.b.id.pke(pk(id),Sq.<head(ns),nb>) ->
                  comm.id.b.pke(pk(b),nb) ->
                  Session(id,b,nb,tail(ns)))
```

---

[15]The coding that follows is, for quite separate reasons, insufficient to achieve liveness. In order to stop the intruder deadlocking well-behaved nodes in a protocol like this, very careful use of constructs like time-outs is required, which produces a system too complex to include here. In any case, the presentations of crypto-protocols in the literature generally ignore issues of liveness and so, to analyze them in their own terms, it is probably better to restrict the implementations to simple ones that allow only safety properties to be addressed.

The responder process performs the same three messages, only from the opposite perspective regarding who chooses nonces, etc. Note that each side, by accepting only those events in an appropriate set, performs a check on the message it gets from its partner containing its own nonce. Because we are only studying the three-message version of the protocol, we assume each node has a (true) knowledge of the public key it must use to communicate with the other.

```
Resp(id,ns) = [] a:diff(agents,{id}) @
              [] na:nonces @
                    comm.a.id.pke(pk(id),Sq.<na,a>) ->
                    comm.id.a.pke(pk(a),Sq.<na,head(ns)>) ->
                    comm.a.id.pke(pk(id),head(ns)) ->
                    Session(id,a,head(ns),tail(ns))
```

There is nothing in the protocol description which says what the nodes do once their sessions are set up. They may very well send each other messages either under their public keys or under a symmetric *session key* constructed out of the secrets established in the protocol run. Clearly the design of the code that does this has to be as careful as that of the protocol itself, since for example:

- there is no way of knowing who has sent a public-key encrypted message unless it is either signed or contains a secret known only to the sender and recipient;

- a symmetrically encrypted message can potentially be replayed at the node who sent it, who will (unless is contains something to securely authenticate its origin) believe it has come from its partner; and

- in either case the intruder can trap, duplicate or reorder messages.

The `Session` state below uses the second nonce as a key for symmetric encryption, but you should bear in mind that our purpose in designing this process is not really to pass messages, but to test the correct behaviour of the main protocol. Namely, we wish to show that when a node behaving like either the initiator or responder has completed the protocol and entered the `Session` state then its partner has also engaged in the protocol in the opposite mode and the secrets of the run (namely the two nonces) really are secret.

When connected to another node, a process in state `Session` uses the (arbitrarily chosen) second nonce as the key and sends appropriately chosen messages to its partner. Alice and Bob send messages that are symbols introduced to represent secrets, when they believe they are connected to each other (namely `AtoB` and

BtoA) but do not use these when connected to Cameron.[16] We add a clause (one made possible by the special choice of messages) which checks to see whether, if one trustworthy node (Alice, say) receives a message which is apparently part of a session with the other one (Bob), it really is. If, in this case, Alice receives anything other than BtoA then something must have gone wrong.

```
Session(id,a,n,ns) =  comm.id.a.encrypt(n,mess(id,a)) ->
                                    Session(id,a,n,ns)
              [] ([] m:sessmess @
              comm.a.id.encrypt(n,Sq.<id,m>) ->
              (if ok(id,a,Sq.<id,m>) then Session(id,a,n,ns)
                                    else error -> STOP))
              [] close.id -> User(id,ns)
```

```
ok(a,b,m) = (mess(b,a)==m) or (b==Cameron)
```

Equally, we would expect the intruder to be unable to learn the secrets AtoB and BtoA, since these are never revealed to Cameron deliberately.

We are going to plumb the system together as shown in Figure 15.5. The spy or intruder can hear whatever passes between Alice and Bob, can interact with them as Cameron, and can intercept and fake messages.

- An *intercepted* message must look to its sender no different to one that got through successfully, but obviously it should not be received by its intended recipient.

- A *faked* message should be indistinguishable at its destination from an identical message that was sent from its supposed sender (who, of course, should never have seen it).

We have programmed our nodes so all communications use a channel called comm (labelled with sender and address fields). An elegant way of implementing interception (abbreviated take) and faking is to introduce two 'shadow' channels with the same type, and then put a shell around each node that doubles each communication by renaming:

```
channel comm,take,fake:agents.agents.messages
```

---

[16]There is no sense in which Cmessage, AtoB and BtoA are real messages that Alice, Bob, and Cameron might wish to send to each other. Rather, they are tangible ways of demonstrating and testing their beliefs about who they are connected to.

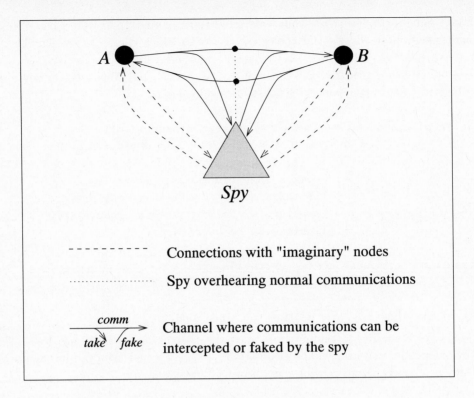

Figure 15.5 Network to test a simple crypto-protocol.

```
RenUser(id,ns)  = User(id,ns)[[comm.id <- comm.id,
                               comm.id <- take.id]]
                           [[comm.a.id <- comm.a.id,
                             comm.a.id <- fake.a.id |
                                           a <- agents]]
```

Each output `comm` can now either happen (so far as the outside world is concerned)
either as itself or as the corresponding `take`, and similarly each input `comm` can now
happen as the result of an external `comm` or `fake`. It is important to realize that the
`User` process inside has no way of knowing which way any of its communications
appears to the outside. The following parallel connection thus synchronizes Alice
and Bob on their mutual `comm` channels, but leaves the corresponding `take` and `fake`
channels to be manipulated by the spy. The resulting system actually gives the spy
two routes to and from each node when it acts as the third identity Cameron:
the divisions of the channels are unnecessary there. The final line below simply

removes this ambiguity: all communications with Cameron are (from the external perspective) along `take` and `fake` rather than `comm`.

```
Network = (RenUser(Alice,<Na>)
          [|{|comm.Alice.Bob,comm.Bob.Alice|}|]
          RenUser(Bob,<Nb>))
          [|union({|comm.Cameron|},
           {|comm.a.Cameron | a <- agents|})|] STOP
```

15.3.3   Creating a set of deductions

All that remains is to build the spy process. At first thought, you might expect this to be a process endowed with great ingenuity and cunning to allow it to break protocols. The great disadvantage of following this approach is that if, eventually, it proves that your spy cannot break the protocol, all you have established is that the particular tactics employed by the spy you happen to have created do not succeed.

There is no real evidence about the possible effects of other tactics, some of which you might not even have imagined. As we saw in Section 15.1, the effect of adding a tactic is to narrow a search making the finding of a solution (in the case of a protocol, an attack) less likely. It is far better, unless prevented by a combinatorial explosion as we were in Section 15.1, to create a definition which models *all possible tactics*: we simply build a process that can perform any trace that a spy reasonably ever could, and incorporate that into our network. If, after doing this, the result is a system where the protocol remains intact in the sense that it satisfies appropriate safety specifications, then you can be sure that no spy, however cunning, could have broken it.

The most general spy can always overhear (`comm`) and intercept (`take`) any message available to it. The limitation comes in what it can `fake`, since we are making basic assumptions about the cryptographic devices used, such as the undecipherability of encryptions without appropriate keys and the non-guessability of nonces. The entire coding that follows is devoted to the problem of creating a process whose message generation ability is determined by what it initially knew, what it has overheard or intercepted since, and a set of rules governing deducibility of messages through encryption.

The rules of deducibility have to be programmed into our spy. We can work out what deductions are relevant to a given finite subset X of the data type `fact` using the following clauses. In them, a deduction is a pair (Y, a) where Y is a finite set of facts and a is a fact which anyone in possession of the whole of Y can construct. Below, we set up three types of deduction, each of which operates in two directions, one 'constructing' and the other 'destructing'. The first type says that

if one knows a sequence one can extract any of its members, and if one knows all
its members one can build the sequence:

```
deductions1(X) = {(({Sq . m}, nth(j,m)) ,
                    ({nth(i,m) | i <-{0..#m-1}}, Sq . m) |
                    Sq.m <- X, j<-{0..#m-1}}
```

The other two types of deduction are based on encryption, one on symmetric-
key encryption and the other on public-key encryption. In each case they say that
anyone in possession of a message and the appropriate key can build an encryption,
and that someone holding an encryption and the key necessary to decrypt it (the
detail of which differs between the two cases) can know the contents. Finally, we
can put together all three sorts of deductions into a single set.

```
deductions2(X) = {({m, k}, encrypt(k,m) ) ,
                   ({encrypt(k,m), k}, m) |
                   Encrypt.(k,m) <- X}
```

```
deductions3(X) = {({m, k}, pke(k,m) ) ,
                   ({pke(k,m), dual(k)}, m) |
                   PK.(k,m) <- X}
```

```
deductions(X) = Union({deductions1(X),deductions2(X),
                       deductions3(X)})
```

We omit here the definition of the finite set `messages`: it is the subset of `fact`
consisting of all message bodies which could form part of any protocol run or session
between two of our three nodes. It is finite because the sets of agents, nonces, etc.
are finite. `messages` obviously forms the basis of what the spy might ever learn or
want to construct for faking. However, since the spy might build or learn messages
in parts it helps to have a way of taking a subset X of `fact`, and creating from it
a larger set consisting of all objects which are of direct relevance to members of X.
Applied to `messages`, this gives the set of facts which it might be sensible for the
spy to construct *en route* to building a message. The final clause of the following,
which is present to deal with all the constants (such as `Alice` and `pkC`) from `fact`,
exploits the convention that where a function is 'over-defined' on a particular value,
the textually first definition applies.

```
explode(Sq.xs) = union({Sq.xs},
                        Union({explode(x) | x <- set(xs)}))
explode(PK.(k,m)) = union({PK.(k,m),k,dual(k)},explode(m))
```

```
explode(Encrypt.(k,m)) = Union({{Encrypt.(k,m)},explode(k),
                                  explode(m)})
explode(x) = {x}


AllFacts = Union({explode(m) | m <- messages})


AllDeductions = deductions(AllFacts)
```

AllFacts is a finite set, unlike the full data type `fact`, which is infinite.

The spy will have an initial basic knowledge: public facts such as agent names and public keys, and the private facts necessary to enable it to act as the agent Cameron.

```
Known' = Union({agents, publickey,
              {sk(Cameron)}, {Nc,Cmessage}})
```

Our spy can initially construct a number of legitimate messages (such as initial messages asking for sessions with either Alice or Bob, acting as Cameron) from this set. The full initial knowledge can be found by closing up `Known'` under the deductions.

```
Close(S) = let
           S' = {f | (X,f) <- AllDeductions, diff(X,S)=={}}
           within
           if diff(S',S)=={} then S else Close(union(S,S'))


Known = Close(Known')
```

There remain many messages that the spy does not initially know, so we need to describe how its state of knowledge evolves as it overhears more things. An obvious coding of the spy which says exactly what we want is `Spy1(Known)` where

```
Spy1(X) = learn?x -> Spy1(Close(union(X,{x})))
        [] say?x:X -> Spy1(X)
```

In other words, it can always create any message it knows, and each time it learns a new one it adds in all the resultant deductions. Here, `learn` and `say` are two channels of type `messages` which would subsequently be plumbed by renaming so that they respectively took the roles of overhearing and intercepting, and of faking (see below).

This would be a perfect definition, as well as being delightfully simple, if it were not for one practical problem. This is that there are, for a typical protocol model, between 50 and 1000 messages and perhaps 50% more other facts of relevance to the spy (in the example presented here, there are respectively 90 and 42). The state space of the spy when defined as above becomes impossibly large, given FDR's desire to pre-compute the state spaces of all 'low-level' processes such as this that it encounters. In fact Spy1's state space, when measured like this, is generally exponential in the number of interesting facts. Most of these states are never actually reached when the spy is eventually explored as part of the complete system, but this only adds to the frustration of having computed them in the first place.

15.3.4 The lazy spy

We need to find an equivalent process definition that avoids this impossible amount of pre-computation. We will do this by creating a parallel network which has one process for every fact that the spy (i) does not initially know and (ii) could conceivably learn during a run. These are the facts contained in the set LearnableFacts defined below, since the spy can never know anything outside what can be deduced from its initial knowledge and all the messages it could ever hear. (In the present example this set has 96 members.)

```
PossibleBasicKnowledge = union(Known,messages)

KnowableFacts = Close(PossibleBasicKnowledge)

LearnableFacts = diff(KnowableFacts,Known)
```

We can discard all those deductions whose conclusion is something the spy knows already, or where either the conclusion or one of the assumptions is never knowable by him. For different reasons we know that these will never be relevant to the spy in any run.

```
Deductions = {(X,f) | (X,f) <- AllDeductions,
                member(f,LearnableFacts),
                not member(f,X),
                diff(X,KnowableFacts)=={}}
```

For each fact in LearnableFacts we can then create a component of our spy: it only has two states, respectively representing ignorance and knowledge of the fact. It can always learn its fact, but can say it only when the fact is known. Since these actions are only relevant when the fact is a complete message these actions are limited to this case. Inferences are carried out by a channel infer of type Deductions: each one can only occur when all its assumptions are known (either

because they are in the set `Known` or because the relevant process is in state `knows`)
and the conclusion is not known. Thus each `infer.(X,f)` action may have many
different components synchronize on it.

```
ignorantof(f) = member(f,messages) & learn.f -> knows(f)
          [] infer?t:{(X,f') | (X,f') <- Deductions, f'==f}
                          -> knows(f)


knows(f) = member(f,messages) & say.f -> knows(f)
       [] member(f,messages) & learn.f -> knows(f)
       [] infer?t:{(X,f') | (X,f') <- Deductions, member(f,X)}
                        -> knows(f)
       [] member(f,Banned) & spyknows.f -> knows(f)
```

The last line above assumes we have defined a set `Banned` of events which the spy is
not allowed to know. For our example we define this to be `{AtoB, BtoA}` since we
know that these two facts will never properly be sent to Cameron. The respective
alphabets `AlphaL(f)` of these processes are the sets of events they can perform.

    The spy is then constructed by putting all the component processes in parallel
and hiding the `infer` events, since these are internal actions of this parallel inference
system. It is important to note that, by definition of `Deductions`, any assumption
of an `infer.(X,f)` which is not in `LearnableFacts` is initially `Known` to the spy.
Thus, whenever this event occurs in the following process, all the assumptions are
known.

```
Spy = (|| f:LearnableFacts @  [AlphaL(f)] ignorantof(f))
                    \{|infer|}
      ||| SayKnown


SayKnown = say?f:inter(Known,messages) -> SayKnown
        [] learn?f:inter(Known,messages) -> SayKnown
```

Note that `Spy` incorporates a process which can always communicate any message in
`Known`, since evidently the spy can generate these messages and we did not include
them in the set `LearnableFacts`.

    This version of the spy process is equivalent to `Spy1(Known)`, but does not
suffer the same problems. As it runs the `infer.(X,f)` actions which occur (hidden)
within it have the same effect as the `Close` function used in `Spy1`. Whenever it learns
a new fact it can carry out just those inferences which extend its present state of
knowledge (defined to be `Known` plus the set of facts `f` whose component process is in
state `knows(f)`) appropriately. We have christened this model the *lazy spy* because

it avoids the eager pre-computation of inferences, most of which are unnecessary, present in Spy1.

To use the spy in the network proper, we rename it so that the messages it learns come from communications it has overheard or intercepted, and what it says becomes a fake. Obviously the messages it overhears and fakes in actual runs have sender and address fields, but since these are irrelevant to the issue of knowing what the spy can generate[17] we left these off when building the spy processes for reasons of efficiency.

```
RenSpy = Spy[[learn.f <- comm.a.a'.f,
              learn.f <- take.a.a'.f |
            a <- agents, a'<- agents]]
          [[say.f <- fake.a.a'.f |
            a <- agents, a'<- agents]]


System = Network [|{|comm,take,fake|}|] RenSpy
```

We can then test for attacks on the protocol by checking for occurrence of the events error and spyknows.f, since none of them should be possible. Essentially, the first represents a failure of authentication and the second a failure of confidentiality. In the particular case we are looking at, either of these checks reveals a striking attack (discovered by Gavin Lowe[18] [65] many years after the protocol was published and despite the fact that it had been analyzed with various logics without revealing problems). The bottom line of this attack is that if one trustworthy node (Alice, say) chooses to communicate with a node (Cameron) who proves to be corrupted, then the intruder can impersonate Alice in opening a session (learning all the secrets therein) with any other trustworthy node (Bob). Thus Bob thinks he has a session with Alice, even when she may never have heard of him. We might doubt Alice's *judgement* in talking to Cameron, but she always behaves *honestly*. It is clearly unacceptable for the security of sessions between a pair of honest nodes to depend on the set of nodes with whom they have previously interacted.

The attack proceeds as follows: it contains two interleaved runs of the protocol, labelled α and β. Where you see $C(A)$ below it means a situation where C intercepts a message for A or fakes one apparently from A, as appropriate. Each

---

[17]The address fields never contain information unknown to the spy, and whenever the spy can generate a message it can send it to whomever, and 'from' whomever, it pleases.

[18]Lowe was the first person to apply the combination of FDR and CSP to crypto-protocols. The CSP model Lowe developed for the Needham–Schroeder Public-Key protocol in [65] differs from the one presented here mainly in its relatively *ad hoc* spy model. The lazy spy model presented here, with its power and easy adaptation to new protocols, has since become the standard method and has been integrated into Lowe's protocol compiler Casper: see below.

message is shown in two ways, with the right-hand one being the literal output from FDR.[19]

$\alpha.1 \quad A \to C : \{N_A, A\}_{pk(C)}$ `take.Alice.Cameron.(pkC.Sq.<Na,Alice>)`

$\beta.1 \quad C(A) \to B : \{N_A, A\}_{pk(B)}$ `fake.Alice.Bob.(pkB.Sq.<Na,Alice>)`

$\beta.2 \quad B \to C(A) : \{N_A, N_B\}_{pk(A)}$ `take.Bob.Alice.(pkA.Sq.<Na,Nb>)`

$\alpha.2 \quad C \to A : \{N_A, N_B\}_{pk(A)}$ `fake.Cameron.Alice.(pkA.Sq.<Na,Nb>)`

$\alpha.3 \quad A \to C : \{N_B\}_{pk(C)}$ `take.Alice.Cameron.(pkC.Nb)`

$\beta.3 \quad C(A) \to B : \{N_B\}_{pk(A)}$ `fake.Alice.Bob.(pkB.Nb)`

The spy uses node A in run α to decode the message it receives (but cannot at that stage understand) in message $\beta.2$, since because of the way the protocol works A assumes the nonce N_B was generated by C in run α and so sends it back to C in message $\alpha.3$. Upon receipt of message $\beta.3$ node B has completed a run apparently with A, as claimed.

The methods described in this section have been employed to analyze a wide variety of protocols, dealing with a range of protocol features and specification techniques we have not had time to cover here. Many of the analyses have involved timing analysis along the lines set out in Chapter 14. Frequently they have discovered attacks which were in no way imagined at the time of creating the CSP model. Gavin Lowe has produced a compiler (Casper, [67]), which inputs protocols described in a notation close to the one used to describe the Needham–Schroeder protocol on page 448, and outputs a CSP file which can be used to check various forms of correctness. See the Bibliography for how to obtain this tool. All of this has made FDR into arguably the most powerful tool available at the time of writing for checking properties of crypto-protocols.

There are two main lessons to get out of this example aside from the intrinsic interest of security protocols. The first of these is the way renaming has been used at various points to achieve subtle effects in plumbing the network together. In fact this idea can be taken a stage further to allow crypto-protocol analyses to take account of any algebraic equivalences that may relate encrypted terms, such as

$$\{\{M\}_a\}_b = \{\{M\}_b\}_a$$

(the statement that if a message is encrypted twice, the order of the encryptions does not matter). The second is how we managed to code what is effectively an

---

[19] The trace continues `take.Bob.Alice.Encrypt.(Nb,Sq.<Alice,BtoA>)` which enables the event `spyknows.BtoA`.

inference system as a parallel process,[20] exploiting the multi-way synchronizations allowed in CSP.

This example is also illuminating because it shows how very large networks of CSP processes (almost exactly 100 processes in the present example, and quite a lot larger in the case of other protocols we have worked with) can have a practical use on FDR. The way it stores states means that it gets 32 one-bit spy components into each word of memory.

15.3.5   Cutting corners

Initially the spy process used above does not know the nonce Na. It can easily learn this nonce by being sent the message

```
comm.Alice.Cameron.pke(pk(Cameron),Sq.<Na,Alice>)
```

This immediately allows it to generate many more messages than it could before: 9 new message 1's (of the abbreviated protocol), 9 new message 2's and 3 more message 3's. In all, there are 31 facts which can be inferred from this new one. They cannot be deduced in *any* order. For example, the deduction of Sq.<Na,Alice> from the body of the above message (and the spy's knowledge of sk(Cameron)) via a Deduction3 must be done first, and the subsequent deduction of Na from this is necessary for almost all the others. However, there is an enormous number of alternatives for the order in which these inferences are performed (certainly greater than 24^{12}), and similarly a huge number of states that the spy process can pass through *en route* to the state where it knows all 31 new things (more than 2^{24}).

This combinatorial explosion is unfortunate since it considerably slows up checks of protocols on FDR, and severely limits the sizes of protocols and depths of checks it can manage. Fortunately, however, there is a way round the problem. When our spy performs an inference it never loses the ability to perform any other action (either visible or inference) it could already do. If we simply force all available inferences to be performed in the spy, in an arbitrarily chosen order, before any other action is allowed, then the observable behaviour of the spy is unchanged but the state explosion is completely avoided. In the example above, it will simply be forced through 30 inferences ('appearing' externally as τ actions) before coming to rest in the state corresponding to

```
Spy1(Close(union(Known,pke(pk(Cameron),Sq.<Na,Alice>))))
```

---

[20]It would be interesting to try the techniques of the lazy spy on other applications where one wants an inference system as part of a network.

A function has been incorporated into FDR for this purpose: `chase(P)` behaves like `P` except that whenever `P` reaches a state where it can perform a τ action, this operator executes τ's until no more are possible. The other behaviour paths are not explored. Thus this operator has, in general, the right to select from a range of states since it may have many paths of τ's to follow. In the case of the spy (or any similar inference system) there is a unique final state which any path reaches, but this is certainly not true for general processes.

Unlike the other compression operators (see Section C.2) defined in FDR, `chase` sometimes changes the value of the process it is applied to and should only be used when, as with the `Spy` example, we are confident it does not. It is always true that

$$P \sqsubseteq_{FD} \text{chase(P)}$$

since the `chase` operator only takes decisions which an implementation is free to make. Thus `chase(P)` is equivalent to `P` whenever `P` is deterministic (as our spy is, since it is equivalent to the process `Spy1(Known)`), but in most cases the above refinement is proper when `P` is nondeterministic. (It need not be since `chase` does not remove nondeterminism other than that introduced by τ actions. It will not remove the nondeterminism created by the initial ambiguity in $(a \to P) \,\square\, (a \to Q)$.) You should note that `chase` is an operator which is properly thought of as being applied to a transition system, not to an abstract process, and that, for nondeterministic P, different transition system implementations of P may well produce different results when the operator is applied.

In principle you can, of course, use the determinism checking capability of FDR (see Section 9.1) to test if a process is one suitable to `chase`. Indeed, the determinism checking algorithm has a lot in common with `chase`. But since a determinism check involves visiting each state of the process under examination, this is rarely a sensible option with processes we want to `chase`, since the whole point of the exercise is to avoid visiting them all! Thus most applications will probably involve a more mathematical proof of determinism.

The use of the `chase` operator has an enormously beneficial effect on protocol checks in FDR. For the one described above, running on the version of FDR2 current at the time of writing, it cut the number of states visited in finding the attack from several million to 325. The reduction is even greater in cases where no attack is found, since finding the above attack takes fewer actions than would allow an unchased version to go through the complete combinatorial explosion detailed above, while a complete refinement check inevitably explores it all. For example, if the second message of the abbreviated protocol is changed from

$$B \to A : \{N_A, N_B\}_{pk(A)} \qquad \text{to} \qquad B \to A : \{N_A, N_B, B\}_{pk(A)}$$

Lowe's attack is avoided and (subject to various assumptions we do not have time to detail here) the protocol appears to be secure. Certainly the corresponding checks now succeed, using about 300 states with the use of `chase` and being well out of reach on the present tool without it. Thus, the lazy spy model only really makes sense as a practical proposition on FDR with the `chase` operator, and fortunately, with it, one is able to model protocols significantly more complex than the one we have seen here.

The `chase` operator is an extreme – and by far the clearest applying to CSP at the time of writing – example of a model-checking technique known as *partial order methods*. These can be defined as methods for avoiding complete state explorations in model-checking runs by the knowledge that certain actions can be performed in any order (when available) without affecting the check, so that not all orders need be explored. More examples of these as applied to other notations can be found in [115, 86], amongst many others. (This is a regular topic for papers in the annual proceedings of CAV, for example.)

15.4   Notes

The solitaire example presented here is a slightly updated version of the one described in [98]. A number of similar puzzles can be found on the web site described in the Preface.

The algorithm for managing a distributed database presented in Section 15.2 is taken, as stated there, from one of the author's earlier papers [96] where it is proved mathematically. The main reason for including it in this chapter is that it shares one important quality with the examples from Sections 15.1 and 15.3, namely that it is far from obvious on first encountering it whether it works or not. It is only one of a large number of interesting distributed algorithms that have been invented for a variety of purposes. An extensive general survey can be found in [24]: certainly many of the algorithms and methods presented there would translate into interesting case studies for CSP and FDR, and, indeed, a few of them already have been.

The concept of data-independence, or something like it, has occurred independently to many people. This is probably because of the amount of time they have wasted watching their respective tools analyzing successively larger versions of some system in which, in some sense, all the 'interesting' behaviours really ought to have been caught using relatively small examples. The first person to have studied it formally is Wolper [121], other references being [45, 53, 56].

Some of the data-independence rules for CSP set out in this chapter were conjectured by the author in [106] (an earlier version of the distributed database case study). These conjectures were proved, and many further results found, by Ranko Lazić [60, 59, 61, 62], who established, amongst other things, a formal connection with the theory of *parametricity*, or *logical relations* from functional programming [16, 57, 78, 83, 90, 118] and developed versions of the operational semantics and normal forms that differ from those seen in Chapters 7 and 11 in that they use symbolic representations of data values (parts of this work are similar to work on other process algebras, for example [47]). This work also exploits techniques, related to those in [23, 31, 32, 53, 54] for exploiting symmetry in state spaces. The data-independence results in this chapter were produced by Lazić specifically for this book, and are mainly consequences of more complex results that you can find in [60, 59, 61, 62]. The cache example in this chapter is adapted from the one presented in [61]. See [37, 85] for other examples of how techniques related to data-independence can be applied to caches. Many more references to work on data-independence and related topics can be found in [59, 61, 62].

There is a large literature on the subject of crypto-protocols, fascinating because of the remarkable proportion of protocols which are proposed with highly plausible rationale for, or formal proofs in some logic of, their security, only to have an attack found on them in a subsequent paper. There can be no other area of computer science where such short programs are so frequently wrong. It is also interesting how little consensus there is on how this security should be specified in the abstract. Usually, though not invariably, researchers will agree on whether a specific 'attack' is real; it is much harder to get them to agree on what constitutes an attack in general. Some references to applications of CSP to these protocols are [65, 66, 67, 68, 100, 101]; for more general references the reader should follow up some of the citations in these papers or look through publications such as the *Journal of Computer Security* and the annual proceedings of the IEEE Computer Security Foundations workshop.

A natural question that may well have arisen in the minds of readers who have studied both Section 12.4 and Section 15.3 is how the rather different views of computer security seen in them are related. The non-interference/independence discussed in the first of these is an absolute notion and is best applied to analyze the security of systems whose internal details are assumed to be inaccessible to potential intruders. We look for ways in which one user can affect another, when both are using 'natural' (generally unencrypted) interfaces to the system. Encryption is necessary, in essence, when it is assumed that an intruder might well have an *entrée* to some information being stored or passed around the interior of a system. (You should think of networks over which encrypted messages pass as being highly distributed systems in which the intruder can see and manipulate much of the internal state, namely the messages.) It does not seem, at the time of writing, to be possible to make the independence conditions properly understand the fact that encrypted traffic is incomprehensible without the relevant key. The problem is that the definition of independence does not understand that the distinctions between the intruder seeing the encrypted messages $\{X\}_K$ and $\{Y\}_K$ are of less significance than those between it seeing X and Y. Therefore the notions of independence and non-interference are of limited used when dealing with the security of any encrypted view of a system. So even though at an intuitive level one might characterize our requirements of crypto-protocols as achieving two-way non-interference between legitimate users and the intruder (i.e., the intruder cannot disrupt the users and cannot detect what they are doing), the two approaches are not as closely related as one might immediately expect. In fact, the level at which it is traditional to analyze crypto-protocols (and is the level in Section 15.3) rarely achieves absolute non-interference in either direction.

Appendix A

Mathematical background

Much of our work on semantics requires knowledge of the mathematics that underlies the models we build. This appendix is designed to provide a tutorial introduction to two theories which go beyond the basic mathematics of sets, relations and functions we have used throughout this book and which are essential to a full understanding of Chapters 8, 9 and 10. These are *partial orders* and *metric spaces*. Naturally, we concentrate on those aspects of these things which are most needed elsewhere in this book, in particular the fixed-point theories derivable in each. The intention is that each of the two sections is, however, freestanding (in particular, being independent of the other). Examples are drawn both from conventional mathematics and from the world of CSP.

A.1   Partial orders

A.1.1   Basics

A partial order is a relation that describes when one member of a set is less than another in some sense. It is generally written either something like $x < y$, indicating a *strict* order where an element is not less than itself, or like $x \leq y$, indicating a 'less-than-or-equal-to' style order where each element is comparable to itself. The following are some examples.

- The usual order on numbers.
- The 'divides' relation on natural numbers: $n \mid m \equiv \exists r.n \times r = m$.
- The subset relation $\subseteq$ on any set of sets.
- The prefix order $\leq$ on Σ^* ($s \leq t \equiv \exists u.s\hat{\ }u = t$).

There are two properties a relation must have to be a partial order. It must be *transitive*:

$$x \leq y \wedge y \leq z \Rightarrow x \leq z$$

(Here, x, y, z are arbitrary members of the underlying set X.) This simply says that if x is less than y and y is less than z then x is less than z. The statement of the other property, that no pair of distinct objects are less than each other, is different depending on whether we are looking at a strict or non-strict order, namely

$$x \leq y \wedge y \leq x \Leftrightarrow x = y$$
$$x < y \Rightarrow \neg(y < x)$$

These are called *anti-symmetry* properties, with the former encompassing *reflexivity* (meaning that everything is related to itself) and the second *anti-reflexivity*.

There is no requirement that any two objects are comparable, and indeed only the first of the four examples above satisfies the following property which, when it is true in addition to the other properties, defines a *total* order:

$$x < y \ \vee \ y < x \ \vee \ x = y$$

As a relation, $\leq$ is always the (disjoint) union of the corresponding $<$ and the identity relation $\{(a, a) \mid a \in X\}$. When discussing an order we will feel free to move between $<$, $\leq$ and the reverse versions $>$ and $\geq$ when discussing a given order, even though they are all different relations in a formal mathematical sense.

It is often convenient to represent partial orders (especially finite ones) as pictures: Figure A.1 is an example of a *Hasse diagram* which shows the subset order on $\mathbb{P}(\{a, b, c\})$.

Two partial orders with the same Hasse diagram are said to be *order isomorphic*. This generalizes to infinite orders: $(X, \leq_1)$ is order isomorphic to $(Y, \leq_2)$ if and only if there is a bijection f from X to Y such that $x \leq_1 x' \Leftrightarrow f(x) \leq_2 f(x')$ for all $x, x' \in X$.

A number of branches of mathematics and theoretical computer science have been built on top of partial orders, each of them generating its own set of special conditions on orders to generate appropriate results about them. Two well-known examples are lattice theory and domain theory. In the rest of this section we will introduce just the relatively small portions of these theories that are important to the study of CSP.

If a partial order has a least element (one that is less than all others), it is conventionally written $\bot$ (pronounced 'bottom'). Similarly, a greatest element is

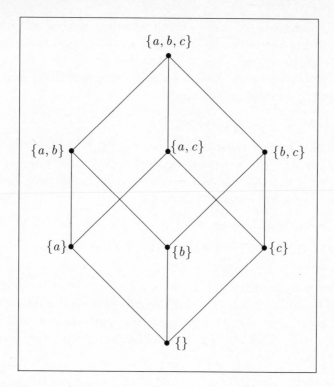

Figure A.1 Hasse diagram of a simple partial order.

written ⊤ ('top'). Clearly, an order can have at most one ⊥ or ⊤, though, if it does not have one or other of these, it can have many minimal or maximal elements (ones that have no other element less than, or respectively greater than, them). For example, the set ℕ (natural numbers) with its usual order has a bottom (0) but no top. ℙ(X), under the subset order, has both a bottom ({}) and a top (X). The set ℕ\\{1} = {0, 2, 3, ...} under the divisibility order described above has a top element (0, since $n \mid 0$ for all n) and all prime numbers as its minimal elements.

Suppose P is a partial order. If $X \subseteq P$ and $a \in P$ then a is an *upper bound* for X if $x \leq a$ for all $x \in X$. Similarly it is a *lower bound* if $a \leq x$ for all $x \in X$. It is the *least upper bound* of X (written $\bigsqcup X$) if it is an upper bound and $a \leq b$ for all upper bounds b of X, and is the *greatest lower bound* (written $\bigsqcap X$) if a lower bound and greater than all others. The following remarks should help to explain these concepts:

- Since a (least) upper bound is just a (greatest) lower bound in the reverse order, everything that is said about one can, with suitable modifications to take account of the switch, be said about the other.

- A set X can have many upper (lower) bounds or none at all. For example, if the set Σ^* is given the prefix order and $s, t \in \Sigma^*$, then the set $\{s, t\}$ always has at least one lower bound ($\langle\rangle$) and perhaps many, but only has upper bounds if s is a prefix of t or *vice-versa*. Note that if P has a $\bot$ ($\top$), then every set has a lower (upper) bound.

- If $\bigsqcup X$ exists it is unique, and similarly for $\bigsqcap X$.

- Even when a set has upper bounds, there may be no least one. The simplest example to show this is a four-point order $\{a, b, c, d\}$ where $a < c$, $a < d$, $b < c$, $b < d$ and the pairs a, b and c, d are incomparable. Here, $\{a, b\}$ has two upper bounds (c and d) but no least one.

- Note the similarity between the pairs of symbols $\bigsqcap, \bigcap$ and $\bigsqcup, \bigcup$. Over the powerset $\mathbb{P}(A)$ (with subset order) they correspond exactly: $\bigsqcap X = \bigcap X$ and $\bigsqcup X = \bigcup X$ for all $X \subseteq \mathbb{P}(A)$.

- Since every $x \in P$ is both an upper and a lower bound for the empty set $\{\}$, $\bot = \bigsqcup\{\}$ and $\top = \bigsqcap\{\}$ (these two bounds existing just when $\bot$ and $\top$ do). If they both exist and P has at least two points we have the odd situation that $\bigsqcup\{\} < \bigsqcap\{\}$: something that can be true for no other set since $x \in X$ implies that

$$\bigsqcap X \leq x \leq \bigsqcup X$$

- Similarly, $\bot = \bigsqcap P$ and $\top = \bigsqcup P$ whenever these objects exist.

It will often be important to us to understand which sets X have $\bigsqcap X$ and $\bigsqcup X$ existing, and how these operators behave. Just about the strongest possible assumption that could be made in this department is that *every* set has both. An order with this property is called a *complete lattice*.[1] Good examples of complete lattices are the powerset $\mathbb{P}(A)$ and the traces model $\mathcal{T}$ of CSP (the non-empty, prefix-closed subsets of $\Sigma^{*\checkmark}$), both ordered by $\subseteq$. That the latter is a complete lattice is seen from the following observations.

- If X is any non-empty subset of $\mathcal{T}$ then $\bigcup X$ is necessarily non-empty and prefix closed. It follows that $\bigsqcup X = \bigcup X$.

- If $X \subseteq \mathcal{T}$ is non-empty then $\bigcap X$ is non-empty (it contains $\langle\rangle$) and prefix closed (if $s < t$ and $t \in \bigcap X$ then necessarily s belongs to all $x \in X$).

- $\bigsqcup\{\} = \{\langle\rangle\}$ (the bottom element) and $\bigsqcap\{\} = \Sigma^{*\checkmark}$ (the top).

[1] A *lattice* is a partial order in which all finite sets X have $\bigsqcap X$ and $\bigsqcup X$ existing.

In fact, there is an interesting proof that if every set has a greatest lower bound, then every set also has a least upper bound. Of course, the reverse is also true by symmetry. Thus an order is a complete lattice if each set has a least upper bound or if each set has a greatest lower bound.

LEMMA A.1.1   *If $\sqcap X$ exists for every set X, then so does $\bigsqcup X$.*

PROOF   Let $X \subseteq P$, and define $Y = \{y \mid y \text{ is an upper bound for } X\}$. Clearly $x \leq y$ whenever $x \in X$ and $y \in Y$, so we can deduce that each $x \in X$ is a lower bound for Y. It follows that $x \leq \sqcap Y$, since the latter is the *greatest* lower bound. Thus $\sqcap Y \in Y$, by definition of Y, and it is clear that $\sqcap Y$ is necessarily the *least* member of Y, i.e., the least upper bound of X.   ∎

Note that any complete lattice L necessarily has both a $\top$ ($\sqcap\{\}$ and $\bigsqcup L$) and a $\bot$ ($\bigsqcup\{\}$ and $\sqcap L$). It tends to be the case in computer science that we use orders where $x < y$ means that y is in some way better than, or more defined than, x. It is usually possible and realistic to arrange that there is a worst process, or $\bot$, but it is often inconceivable that any process could exist that was better than all others. For this and other reasons we frequently have to deal with orders that have $\bot$'s but do not have such rich structures of $\sqcap$ and $\bigsqcup$ as complete lattices.

There are two main reasons why we will frequently need CSP models to have interesting structures of least upper bounds and greatest lower bounds. These are the finding of fixed points to yield the semantics of recursive terms, and the semantics of nondeterministic choice. The latter requirement comes from the fact that very often the order on the models corresponds to refinement: $P \sqsubseteq Q$ if, and only if, Q refines P. In that case it is natural to expect that the nondeterministic choice $\sqcap S$ of the set of processes S is the *most* refined process that is refined by *all* the members of S, i.e., the greatest lower bound of S. This explains the coincidence in symbols between greatest lower bound and nondeterministic choice. In a model like this, greatest lower bounds have to exist for all sets of processes over which we expect to be able to take nondeterministic choices. Depending on whether or not you expect to be able to handle unbounded nondeterminism, these will either be all the non-empty sets, or all the non-empty finite sets.

EXERCISE A.1.1   There are two essentially different partial orders with two elements: one where they are comparable and one where they are not. How many are there with 3 and 4 elements respectively? Draw Hasse diagrams of all the possibilities. For higher numbers than 4 elements it is better to use a computer to enumerate the number of different orders.

A.1.2   Functions and fixed points

If P and Q are partial orders with least elements $\perp_P$ and $\perp_Q$, then the function $f : P \to Q$ is said to be *strict* if $f(\perp_P) = \perp_Q$.

A function from one partial order to another is called *monotonic* (or monotone) if

$$x \leq y \Rightarrow f(x) \leq f(y)$$

In other words, the larger the input to the function, the larger the output. It turns out that, provided a partial order with a $\perp$ has a reasonably rich structure of least upper bounds, any monotone function from a partial order to itself has a fixed point. Indeed, it has a *least* fixed point, and this is in most cases the correct one to assign as the value of a recursively defined program. Note that the least fixed point of any strict function from a partial order to itself has least fixed point $\perp$.

There are numerous versions of this theorem proved by many people, but they are all traditionally collected together under the name 'Tarski's theorem', or sometimes 'Knaster-Tarski'. The strongest possible assumption we could make about an order is that it is a complete lattice; in this case the theorem has a simple if clever proof.

THEOREM A.1.2 (TARSKI'S THEOREM FOR COMPLETE LATTICES) *If P is a complete lattice and $f : P \to P$ is monotonic, then f has a least fixed point.*

PROOF   The least fixed point is given by the following formula

$$x = \sqcap \{ y \in P \mid f(y) \leq y \}$$

Call the set on the right-hand side above Y: the set of all points that are mapped down by f. (Though this is not important for the proof, this set is clearly non-empty since it contains $\top$.) If $y \in Y$ then $x \leq y$, so

$$
\begin{aligned}
f(x) &\leq f(y) &&\text{as } f \text{ is monotonic} \\
     &\leq y   &&\text{by definition of } Y
\end{aligned}
$$

It follows that $f(x)$ is a lower bound of Y, and hence

$$
\begin{aligned}
       f(x) &\leq x   &&\text{as } x \text{ is the } greatest \text{ lower bound} \\
\Rightarrow f(f(x)) &\leq f(x) &&\text{as } f \text{ is monotonic} \\
\Rightarrow f(x) &\in Y
\end{aligned}
$$

We can thus conclude that $f(x) \geq x$ and, putting this together with the above, that $x = f(x)$. The *least-ness* of x is an easy consequence of the fact that Y contains every fixed point.   ∎

We need to weaken the assumption that the underlying order is a complete lattice, since we will often need to find fixed points in orders that do not satisfy it. It turns out that we can still prove Tarski's theorem provided that certain subsets that look as though they *ought* to have least upper bounds actually do.

DEFINITION A subset D of P is said to be *directed* if each finite subset F of D has an upper bound in D; in other words, there is $y \in D$ such that $x \leq y$ for all $x \in F$. ∎

The concept of a directed set generalizes that of a *chain*, a subset in which every pair of elements is ordered, i.e., a totally ordered subset. Every chain C is directed, since a finite subset F of C necessarily has a greatest element. There are many directed sets that are not chains, for example

- in $\mathbb{P}(\mathbb{N})$ with the subset order, the set of all finite subsets is directed;

- any set with a greatest element is directed (whether a chain or not).

You should think of a directed set D as an abstract picture of how a system of elements of P 'converges' from below to a limit (that may or may not actually exist in P). The higher an element is in D, the closer it is to the place we are converging to. This is easiest to understand for an increasing sequence

$$x_0 \leq x_1 \leq x_2 \leq \ldots$$

which simply converges upwards towards a supposed limit. A directed set with a greatest element is just like a converging sequence that is eventually constant.

The limit of a directed set is thus its least upper bound, where this exists. Not all directed subsets of partial orders have limits, since for example the natural numbers $\mathbb{N}$ have no least upper bound in $\mathbb{R}$. Putting the condition on a partial order that all directed sets *do* have limits is therefore a definite restriction. It characterizes an extremely important class of partial orders.

DEFINITION   A *complete* partial order (often abbreviated cpo) is one in which every directed set[2] has a least upper bound, and which has a $\bot$. ∎

Clearly every complete lattice is a cpo, but the reverse does not hold. The most obvious distinction is that cpo's need not have $\top$'s. For example, since every *finite* directed set D has a greatest element (the one in D that bounds the whole of D), which is necessarily $\bigsqcup D$, any finite partial order with a $\bot$ is complete.

---

[2] Directed sets are sometimes replaced by chains in this definition. It is possible, but far from easy, to show that this substitution does not matter, in the sense that an order is directed-set closed if and only if it is chain closed. These equivalent concepts are both strictly stronger than another definition one frequently encounters, namely *ω-completeness*, in which only countable increasing sequences $x_0 \leq x_1 \leq \ldots$ are obliged to have limits. For example, the set of all countable subsets of an uncountable set such as $\mathbb{R}$ is (under the subset order) ω-complete but not complete.

Σ^* is not complete under the prefix order, since directed sets such as

$$\{\langle\rangle, \langle a\rangle, \langle a, a\rangle, \langle a, a, a\rangle, \ldots\}$$

have no upper bound. It becomes complete, however, if we add in the infinite traces: $Seq = \Sigma^* \cup \Sigma^\omega$. Each infinite trace u is then *maximal* in the order, in the sense that there is no v such that $v > u$.

Two interesting examples of cpo's are (i) the set F_{XY} of all partial and total functions from X to Y (arbitrary sets) and (ii) the set O_X of all strict (i.e., $<$ rather than $\leq$) partial orders on any set X. In each case the order is subset ($\subseteq$) on the respective representation as a set of pairs. Both of these have least elements (the empty set, representing respectively the partial function with no mappings and the order in which no distinct objects are comparable). The arguments why these two orders are closed under the limits of directed sets depend crucially on directedness. If $\Delta \subseteq F_{XY}$ is directed, then $\bigcup \Delta$ is its least upper bound, because it is a function. This is because the only way it could fail to be a function would be if there were x and y, y' with $y \neq y'$ such that $(x, y), (x, y') \in \bigcup \Delta$; but then there would be $f, g \in \Delta$ such that $(x, y) \in f$ and $(x, y') \in g$. Directedness of Δ then tells us that there is $h \in \Delta$ such that $f, g \subseteq h$, contradicting the fact that h, as a function, cannot contain both (x, y) and (x, y'). The very similar argument for O_X is left as an exercise.

Both F_{XY} and O_X have interesting classes of maximal elements. The maximal elements of F_{XY} are precisely the total functions (as any non-total function can clearly be extended, and a total function cannot be extended without losing the property of being a function) and those of O_X are the total orders (see Exercise A.1.5).

Not all partial orders have maximal elements: this happens when, as in $\mathbb{N}$ and $\mathbb{R}$, we can find a way of moving upwards through the order so that there is no element greater than all the ones we pass through. This means we are 'converging' out of the top of the order with some chain or perhaps other directed set. This cannot happen in a cpo since every directed set has an upper bound in the order, meaning that however far we move up through it we can never find this sort of behaviour. Thus, we would expect every cpo to have maximal elements. This principle, which is known as *Zorn's lemma*, is a subtle and important result of advanced mathematics.[3] Clearly it is extremely important in understanding the structures of cpo's. For proofs of Zorn's lemma and discussion of its position in

---

[3]It is one of the standard equivalents of the Axiom of Choice. Zorn's lemma is usually quoted as the statement that any partial order in which every chain has a (not necessarily least) upper bound has maximal elements. The version given here (that every cpo has maximal elements) can readily be shown equivalent.

mathematics, the interested reader should consult a book on set theory such as [33].

   We are now in a position where we can state and prove perhaps the most general version of Tarski's theorem.

THEOREM A.1.3 (TARSKI'S THEOREM FOR COMPLETE PARTIAL ORDERS)
Suppose P is a cpo and $f : P \to P$ is monotonic. Then f has a least fixed point.

PROOF   We begin this proof with two observations that are frequently useful when reasoning about monotonic functions between cpo's:

- If D is a directed set, then $f(D) = \{f(x) \mid x \in D\}$ is also directed, since any finite subset of $f(D)$ is $f(F)$ for some finite subset of D, and monotonicity implies that $f(y)$ is an upper bound for $f(F)$ where $y \in D$ is chosen to be an upper bound for F.

- If X is any set for which both $\bigsqcup X$ and $\bigsqcup f(X)$ are defined (something that is true for any directed X by the above), then $\bigsqcup f(X) \leq f(\bigsqcup X)$. This is because $x \leq \bigsqcup X$ for all $x \in X$, which implies $f(x) \leq f(\bigsqcup X)$ by monotonicity.

   Now, let *Fix* be the set of f's fixed points in P. For all we know so far, this might be empty. This is used to define a subset Q of P:

$$Q = \{x \in P \mid x \leq f(x) \wedge \forall y \in \mathit{Fix}.\, x \leq y\}$$

Q is the set of all points that are mapped up by f and are less than or equal to every fixed point of f. Q is non-empty, since it contains $\bot$. If we look at the partial order structure Q inherits from P, it is actually complete. To show this, it is enough to establish that whenever $D \subseteq Q$ is directed then $\bigsqcup D \in Q$ (where the upper bound is taken in P). Since each $y \in \mathit{Fix}$ is an upper bound for D, it follows that $\bigsqcup D \leq y$ also. And $f(D)$ is a directed set such that

$$
\begin{aligned}
\bigsqcup D \;\; &\leq \;\; \bigsqcup f(D) \quad \text{as } x \leq f(x) \text{ for } x \in D \\
&\leq \;\; f(\bigsqcup D) \quad \text{by the second observation above}
\end{aligned}
$$

These two things show $\bigsqcup D \in Q$.

   If $x \in Q$ then $f(x) \in Q$ since (i) $x \leq f(x) \Rightarrow f(x) \leq f(f(x))$ by monotonicity and (ii) if $y \in \mathit{Fix}$ then $x \leq y \Rightarrow f(x) \leq f(y) = y$. So if we choose x to be one of the maximal elements of Q that Zorn's lemma tells us exist, then necessarily $x = f(x)$ since $x < f(x)$ would contradict x's maximality. Thus x is a fixed point and, by definition of Q, is plainly the least one. (Incidentally, this proves that Q actually only has one maximal element.)   ∎

The least fixed point of a function f is frequently written μf.

The two proofs of versions of Tarski's theorem we have seen to date are stylistically rather similar, though understandably the second required a little more machinery. In essence they are clever manipulations of the ordering that give little or no idea why it might be reasonable to use the least fixed point as the natural denotation of recursively defined programs. This can be remedied for an important subclass of the monotonic functions, to which we can frequently restrict our attention. The concept of a function whose value at a limit point can be determined from its values on a sequence converging to that point is familiar to students of real analysis and topology: it is said to be *continuous*. Recalling that we are thinking of a directed set in a cpo as being a generalized convergent sequence, we can extend the idea of continuity to partial orders.

DEFINITION   If P and Q are two cpo's and $f : P \to Q$, then f is said to be *continuous* if, whenever $\Delta \subseteq P$ is directed, $\bigsqcup\{f(x) \mid x \in \Delta\}$ exists and equals $f(\bigsqcup \Delta)$.   ∎

Notice that this definition does not assume f is monotonic. It does, however, *imply* this, for if $x \leq y$ then $\bigsqcup\{x, y\} = y$, so if f is continuous $\bigsqcup\{f(x), f(y)\}$ exists and equals $f(y)$, which of course implies that $f(x) \leq f(y)$. (If this had not been provable, we would certainly just have added a condition that f was monotone into the definition of continuity. Almost invariably the first thing one does when trying to prove that a function is continuous is to prove it is monotone.)

Because we already know that monotone functions preserve directedness, this shows that continuous functions map 'convergent sequences' to 'convergent sequences', and by definition map the limit of one to the limit of the other.[4] Not all monotonic functions are continuous: consider $P = \mathbb{P}(\mathbb{N})$ under the subset order, and the function $f : P \to P$ defined

$$f(x) = \begin{cases} \{\} & \text{if } x \text{ is finite} \\ \mathbb{N} & \text{if } x \text{ is infinite.} \end{cases}$$

Continuity fails for this function whenever Δ is an infinite directed set of finite sets, for example $\Delta = \{X \in P \mid X \text{ is finite}\}$.

Figure A.2 illustrates the definitions of monotonicity and continuity by three simple examples. The partial orders with 'and so on' dots (ellipsis) all consist of an infinite increasing sequence below a single limit point.

Both monotonicity and continuity are preserved under function composition, in the sense that if $f : Q \to R$ and $g : P \to Q$ both have one of these properties, then the composition $f \circ g : P \to R$ has the same one.

---

[4]These properties define what it means for a function to be continuous in real analysis or over metric spaces.

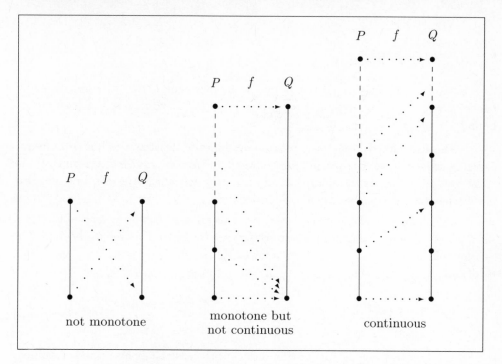

Figure A.2 Monotonicity and continuity.

Since continuous functions are all monotone, the theorem proved above establishes that they have least fixed points. There is, however, a very different proof that is highly suggestive of how to build the fixed point, as might be done by a recursive definition.

PROOF OF TARSKI'S THEOREM FOR CONTINUOUS FUNCTIONS ON A CPO P Since $\bot$ is the least element, we have $\bot \leq f(\bot)$. Now suppose $f^n(\bot) \leq f^{n+1}(\bot)$. It follows immediately from the fact that f is monotone that $f^{n+1}(\bot) \leq f^{n+2}(\bot)$. We have thus proved by induction that $\langle f^n(\bot) \mid n \in \mathbb{N} \rangle$ is an increasing sequence in P.

But f is continuous, so

$$f(\bigsqcup \{f^n(\bot) \mid n \in \mathbb{N}\}) = \bigsqcup \{f^{n+1}(\bot) \mid n \in \mathbb{N}\} .$$

It is obvious that if Δ is any directed set then $\bigsqcup \Delta = \bigsqcup (\Delta \cup \{\bot\})$. (Clearly any upper bound of one set is an upper bound of the other!) Therefore $\bigsqcup \{f^{n+1}(\bot) \mid n \in \mathbb{N}\} = \bigsqcup \{f^n(\bot) \mid n \in \mathbb{N}\}$, and it follows that $x = \bigsqcup \{f^n(\bot) \mid n \in \mathbb{N}\}$ is a fixed point of f.

Now, if y is any other fixed point then clearly $\bot \leq y$. Suppose $f^n(\bot) \leq y$.

Then

$$f^{n+1}(\bot) \le f(y) = y$$

as f is monotone and y is a fixed point. It follows that $f^n(\bot) \le y$ for all n and hence that y is an upper bound for $\{f^n(\bot) \mid n \in \mathbb{N}\}$. But x is the least upper bound, so $x \le y$. ∎

The least fixed point of a continuous function is thus the limit of the increasing sequence we get by applying f over and over to $\bot$. This is a much more constructive picture of μf than that produced by the earlier proofs, but unfortunately it only applies to continuous functions.[5]

There are a great many ways in which we can establish properties of the least fixed point. Some of the simplest are described below and more can be found in Section 9.2.

If x is any point in a cpo P then it is easy to see that the sets

$$
\begin{aligned}
U_x &= \{y \in P \mid x \le y\} \\
L_x &= \{y \in P \mid y \le x\}
\end{aligned}
$$

are themselves both cpo's (under P's order) with least elements x and $\bot$ respectively. Thus, if the monotone function $f : P \to P$ maps either of these sets to itself (i.e., $f(U_x) \subseteq U_x$ or $f(L_x) \subseteq L_x$) then f has a fixed point in the given set. If $f(x) \le x$ then $f(L_x) \subseteq L_x$ (by monotonicity), so f has a fixed point less than x (meaning, of course, that the least fixed point is less than x). Such an x is called a *post-fixed point*. Similarly if $f(x) \ge x$ then $f(U_x) \subseteq U_x$ so f has a fixed point greater than x, and x is termed a *pre-fixed point*.

If it is known, for whatever reason, that f has a unique fixed point, and $x \le f(x)$, the above of course implies that $x \le \mu f$. The main way of showing the uniqueness of fixed points is discussed in Section A.2 below, but there are others, such as the simple observation that if the least fixed point is maximal in P then it is necessarily unique.

EXERCISE A.1.2   Suppose $f : A \times B \to P$, where A and B are sets and P is a partial order, such that

- $\bigsqcup\{f(a, b) \mid a \in A \land b \in B\}$ exists, and
- $F(b) = \bigsqcup\{f(a, b) \mid a \in A\}$ exists for all $b \in B$.

---

[5] In fact, the more usual proof of the monotone function on cpo version works on the same principle with potentially much longer sequences than these merely infinite ones! It requires some advanced mathematical concepts such as ordinal numbers, which is why we gave the less constructive but easier to understand Zorn's lemma proof.

Show that $\bigsqcup\{F(b) \mid b \in B\}$ exists and equals $\bigsqcup\{f(a, b) \mid a \in A \wedge b \in B\}$. *(This shows that it does not matter whether one takes a complex upper bound 'all at once' or takes the upper bounds of suitable cross-sections first and then bounds these. Of course, if the opposite cross-sectional upper bounds $F'(a) = \bigsqcup\{f(a, b) \mid b \in B\}$ also exist, the above result establishes*

$$\bigsqcup\{\bigsqcup\{f(a, b) \mid b \in B\} \mid a \in A\} = \bigsqcup\{\bigsqcup\{f(a, b) \mid a \in A\} \mid b \in B\}$$

or, in other words, we can take upper bounds with respect to a and b in either order.)

EXERCISE A.1.3   Which of the following partial orders are complete lattices or cpo's?

(a) The natural numbers $\mathbb{N} = \{0, 1, 2, 3, \ldots\}$ under the divisibility order $n \leq m \equiv n \mid m$.

(b) The closed interval $[0, 1] = \{x \in \mathbb{R} \mid 0 \leq x \leq 1\}$.

(c) $[0, 1] \backslash \{\frac{1}{2}\}$

(d) $C = \{X \subseteq \mathbb{N} \mid a, b \in X \wedge a \neq b \Rightarrow gcd(a, b) = 1\}$ under the subset order, where $gcd(\cdot a, b)$ is the greatest common divisor of a and b. $C \subset \mathbb{P}(\mathbb{N})$ is the set of coprime subsets of $\mathbb{N}$.

EXERCISE A.1.4   Find a complete partial order that has a $\top$ but is not a complete lattice. *Hint: find a finite partial order with $\top$ and $\bot$ where not all subsets have least upper bounds.*

EXERCISE A.1.5   Recall that O_X is the set of all strict partial orders of a set X.

(a) Show that O_X is a cpo under the subset order.

(b) Show that the maximal elements of O_X are precisely the total orders on X. *Hint: show that if $<$ is a partial order and x, y are incomparable under $<$ ($x \neq y$, $x \not< y$ and $y \not< x$) then there is an order $<'$ which extends $<$ and in which $x <' y$. Be careful to ensure that the $<'$ you build is transitive.*

EXERCISE A.1.6   Consider the complete partial order $\Sigma^* \cup \Sigma^\omega$. Let a and b be distinct members of Σ. Show carefully that the functions

$$
\begin{aligned}
f(s) &= \langle a \rangle \hat{\ } s \\
g(s) &= \langle a \rangle \hat{\ } (s[a, b/b, a])
\end{aligned}
$$

are continuous, where $s[a, b/b, a]$ means the trace s with all a's replaced by b's and vice-versa.

What are μf and μg?

A.1.3   Product spaces

A product space is one where objects have a number of components, each from some smaller space. The simplest product space is the Cartesian product $P \times Q$ of the sets P and Q – consisting of all pairs (x, y) where $x \in P$ and $y \in Q$.

If P and Q are both partially ordered then $P \times Q$ can be given an order in several different ways. The standard order (which we will always use except, perhaps, in a few exercises) is defined

$$(x, y) \leq (x', y') \iff x \leq x' \land y \leq y'.$$

It is sometimes called the component-wise order because one pair is less than another if and only if each of its components is less than the corresponding component of the other pair.

We will sometimes need to use product spaces where there are many or even infinitely many components. The elements of such a space can be thought of as vectors or tuples with the appropriate number of components, or alternatively as functions from an indexing set to the union of the sets from which the components are taken. Thus, for ordered pairs in $P \times Q$, we would choose an indexing set with two elements (say $\{1, 2\}$) and think of pairs as being functions from $\{1, 2\}$ to $P \cup Q$, where the image of 1 is in P, and the image of 2 is in Q.

The most obvious case where this need arises is in defining the semantics of a mutual or parameterized recursion, since instead of defining a single process as a fixed point, we have to compute a whole system of processes.

A typical example of an infinite product space is P^ω, the infinite sequences of elements of P; this is identified with the functions from $\mathbb{N}$ to P. Another is the $\{0, 1\}^X$ for any set X – this is naturally isomorphic to the powerset $\mathbb{P}(X)$ since we can identify a tuple with the set of all components with value 1, and the product order becomes the usual subset order $\subseteq$.

Note that we have used the 'to-the-power-of' notation X^Y to denote the function space $Y \to X$ where this means the product of Y copies of X. This is justified by the observation that if X has n elements and Y has m elements, then the product space X^Y has n^m elements. A more general notation is

$$\prod_{\lambda \in \Lambda} P_\lambda$$

which denotes the product space with indexing set Λ in which λth components of tuples are picked from P_λ.

It is often convenient to use vector notation for product spaces (especially large ones): a typical element of P^Λ will be underlined, $\underline{x}$ and its λ component is x_λ. In 'tuple' notation we then have $\underline{x} = \langle x_\lambda \mid \lambda \in \Lambda \rangle$.

The partial order on an arbitrary product space is a straightforward extension of the one above:

$$\langle x_\lambda \mid \lambda \in \Lambda \rangle \leq \langle y_\lambda \mid \lambda \in \Lambda \rangle \Leftrightarrow \forall \lambda . x_\lambda \leq y_\lambda \,.$$

With the exception of total ordering, which is *not* preserved (for example, the product of a two-point total order with itself has two incomparable points), almost all of the properties identified in earlier sections are preserved by product. This is shown by the following result.

THEOREM A.1.4 *If each of P_λ has (the same) one of the following properties, then $\prod_{\lambda \in \Lambda} P_\lambda$ also has that property.*

  (a) *complete*

  (b) *lattice*

  (c) *complete lattice*

PROOF   Suppose that $X \subseteq \prod_{\lambda \in \Lambda} P_\lambda$ and that, for each $\lambda \in \Lambda$, the set $X_\lambda = \{x_\lambda \mid \underline{x} \in X\}$ has a least upper bound y_λ. Then $\underline{y} = \langle y_\lambda \mid \lambda \in \Lambda \rangle$ is an upper bound for X – since if $\underline{x} \in X$ we know $x_\lambda \leq y_\lambda$ for all λ – and if $\underline{z}$ is any other upper bound then z_λ is an upper bound for X_λ for all λ, and so $\underline{y} \leq \underline{z}$. In other words, $\underline{y}$ is the least upper bound of X.

The same component-wise construction also works for greatest lower bounds.

These observations essentially prove each of (a), (b) and (c) since if $X \subseteq \prod_{\lambda \in \Lambda} P_\lambda$ is (a) directed or (b) finite then it is clear that all X_λ also have the corresponding property. The only thing left to show is that the product of cpo's has a bottom element: this is obviously $\langle \perp_\lambda \mid \lambda \in \Lambda \rangle$ where $\perp_\lambda$ is the bottom of P_λ.   ∎

Clearly a function such as $f(x, y)$ that has more than one argument drawn from partial orders can be thought of as a function with a single argument drawn from some product space. This identification defines what it means for such a function to be monotone or continuous. The following result shows that where there are two (and hence, inductively, any finite number of) arguments, there is a straightforward test for these properties.

LEMMA A.1.5 *Suppose P, Q, R are partial orders and $f : P \times Q \to R$. Then we may define two functions $f'_x : Q \to R$ and $f''_y : P \to R$ for any $x \in P$ and $y \in Q$ by*

$$f'_x(y) = f''_y(x) = f(x, y) \,.$$

The continuity and monotonicity of f is related to that of f'_x and f''_y as follows.

(a) *f is monotone if and only if all f'_x and f''_y are (i.e., if f is monotone in each argument separately).*

(b) *f is continuous[6] if and only if all f'_x and f''_y are (i.e., if f is continuous in each argument separately).*

PROOF   The fact that f being monotone implies all f'_x and f''_y are is trivial, so suppose that all f'_x and f''_y are monotone and that $(x, y) \leq (x', y')$. Then $x \leq x'$ and $y \leq y'$, so

$$
\begin{aligned}
f(x, y) &= f'_x(y) \\
&\leq f'_x(y') \qquad \text{as } f'_x \text{ monotone} \\
&= f''_{y'}(x) \\
&\leq f''_{y'}(x') \qquad \text{as } f''_{y'} \text{ monotone} \\
&= f(x', y')
\end{aligned}
$$

This proves part (a).

If Δ_1, Δ_2 are directed subsets of P and Q respectively then $\{(x, y) \mid x \in \Delta_1\}$ and $\{(x, y) \mid y \in \Delta_2\}$ are directed in $P \times Q$ with respective limits $(\bigsqcup \Delta_1, y)$ and $(x, \bigsqcup \Delta_2)$. It follows immediately that if f is continuous then all f'_x and f''_y are. So suppose all f'_x and f''_y are continuous and that $\Delta \subseteq P \times Q$ is directed. Define

$$
\Delta_1 = \{x \mid (x, y) \in \Delta\} \quad \text{and} \quad \Delta_2 = \{y \mid (x, y) \in \Delta\} .
$$

We know already from the proof of Theorem A.1.4 that $\bigsqcup \Delta = (\bigsqcup \Delta_1, \bigsqcup \Delta_2)$. It is clear that $\Delta^* = \Delta_1 \times \Delta_2$ is directed with the same limit as Δ, and that $\Delta \subseteq \Delta^*$. If $(x, y) \in \Delta^*$ then there are x', y' such that (x, y') and (x', y) are in Δ and hence, by directedness, there is $(x'', y'') \in \Delta$ with $(x, y) \leq (x'', y'')$ and so by monotonicity of f:

$$
\bigsqcup \{f(x, y) \mid (x, y) \in \Delta^*\} \leq \bigsqcup \{f(x, y) \mid (x, y) \in \Delta\}
$$

and the reverse inequality holds because $\Delta \subseteq \Delta^*$, so that in fact the terms are equal. But we then have

$$
\begin{aligned}
\bigsqcup \{f(x, y) \mid (x, y) \in \Delta\} &= \bigsqcup \{f(x, y) \mid (x, y) \in \Delta^*\} \\
&= \bigsqcup \{f(x, y) \mid y \in \Delta_2 \wedge x \in \Delta_1\} \\
&= \bigsqcup \{\bigsqcup \{f(x, y) \mid y \in \Delta_2\} \mid x \in \Delta_1\} \quad (1) \\
&= \bigsqcup \{f(x, \bigsqcup \Delta_2)\} \mid x \in \Delta_1\} \quad (2) \\
&= f(\bigsqcup \Delta_1, \bigsqcup \Delta_2) \quad (3) \\
&= f(\bigsqcup \Delta^*)
\end{aligned}
$$

---

[6]Continuity only makes sense if P, Q and R are cpo's.

Line (1) is an application of the result established in Exercise A.1.2. Lines (2) and (3) follow respectively from the continuity of f'_x and $f''_{\sqcup \Delta_2}$. This completes the proof. ∎

This result does not generalize to the case of infinite product spaces: if $f : \{0,1\}^\omega \to \{0,1\}$ is defined

$$f(\underline{x}) = \left\{ \begin{array}{ll} 0 & \text{if infinitely many } x_n \text{ equal } 1 \\ 1 & \text{otherwise} \end{array} \right.$$

then f is not monotone but all the f_n are (being constant functions, since the value of $f(\underline{x})$ is unaffected by a change to a single component of $\underline{x}$). A trivial modification to this example (defining $g(\underline{x}) = 1 - f(\underline{x})$) produces a monotone but discontinuous function all of whose 'sections' g_n are continuous.

However, the corresponding result for functions *to* product spaces is not restricted in this way. All parts of the following result are easy to prove.

LEMMA A.1.6 *The function* $f : P \to \prod_{\lambda \in \Lambda} Q_\lambda$ *is (a) monotone or (b) continuous if and only if all of the component functions* $f_\lambda : P \to Q_\lambda$ *are (a) monotone or (b) continuous, where* $f_\lambda(x) = f(x)_\lambda$. ∎

Function spaces as product spaces

We have already seen how product spaces can be thought of as the sets of functions from some indexing set to a partial order (or several partial orders). These spaces pay no attention to any partial order structure that may be present in the indexing set, but we have already met two classes of functions that do, namely the monotonic ones and the continuous ones. In this subsection we will examine the partial orders these restricted function spaces inherit from the full product space. Notice that the partial order can be written

$$f \leq g \iff \forall x . f(x) \leq g(x) .$$

DEFINITIONS   If P and Q are two cpo's, define $P \xrightarrow{m} Q$ and $P \xrightarrow{c} Q$ respectively to be the sets of all monotone and continuous functions from P to Q. ∎

Both of these constructions preserve the two main categories of cpo's we have defined:

LEMMA A.1.7 *Both of the spaces* $P \xrightarrow{m} Q$ *and* $P \xrightarrow{c} Q$ *are cpo's if P and Q are. If Q is, in addition, a complete lattice, then both function spaces are, too.*

PROOF The least upper bound of a set Φ of functions (directed in the case where Q is a cpo rather than a complete lattice) is, in all cases we have to consider, the same as that in the full product space, namely

$$(\bigsqcup \Phi)(x) \;=\; \bigsqcup \{f(x) \mid f \in \Phi\} \,.$$

To prove the result we must simply prove that if all elements of Φ are respectively monotone or continuous then so is $\bigsqcup \Phi$.

The monotone case is very straightforward since, if $x \leq y$, then $f(x) \leq f(y)$ for all $f \in \Phi$, so certainly

$$\bigsqcup \{f(x) \mid f \in \Phi\} \;\leq\; \bigsqcup \{f(y) \mid f \in \Phi\} \,.$$

For the continuous case, suppose $\Delta \subseteq P$ is directed. Then we have

$$
\begin{aligned}
(\bigsqcup \Phi)(\bigsqcup \Delta) \;&=\; \bigsqcup \{f(\bigsqcup \Delta) \mid f \in \Phi\} \\
&=\; \bigsqcup \{\bigsqcup \{f(x) \mid x \in \Delta\} \mid f \in \Phi\} \quad &(1) \\
&=\; \bigsqcup \{\bigsqcup \{f(x) \mid f \in \Phi\} \mid x \in \Delta\} \quad &(2) \\
&=\; \bigsqcup \{(\bigsqcup \Phi)(x) \mid x \in \Delta\} \quad &(3)
\end{aligned}
$$

where line (1) is by continuity of the f's, line (2) is a general property of partial orders (see Exercise A.1.2) and line (3) is by definition of $\bigsqcup \Phi$. ∎

The final result of this section is important because it is needed to justify the application of versions of Tarski's theorem to functions which have themselves been defined using least fixed points (i.e., finding the value of a recursive construct which has another recursion nested within it). For example, in order to show that

$$F(p) \;=\; \mu\, q.(a \to (p \underset{\{a\}}{\parallel} q))$$

is a continuous function, you need to have not only that the operations of prefixing and parallel composition are continuous over the chosen semantic model, but also that the very process of extracting fixed points is continuous.

LEMMA A.1.8 *Let P be a cpo. Then (a) the least fixed point operator $\mu : (P \xrightarrow{m} P) \to P$ on the space of monotonic functions is itself monotonic, and (b) restricted to the space of continuous functions $\mu : (P \xrightarrow{c} P) \to P$ it is continuous.*

PROOF For part (a), we note that if f is any monotone function then

$$\mu f \;=\; \bigsqcap \{x \mid f(x) \leq x\}$$

since we know that μf belongs to the set on the right-hand side and have already observed that if y belongs to this set then $\mu f \leq y$. But now if $f \leq f'$ in the function-space order, then trivially

$$\{x \mid f(x) \leq x\} \supseteq \{x \mid f'(x) \leq x\}$$

so the greatest lower bound of the left-hand side is necessarily less than or equal to the greatest lower bound of the right-hand side, which is what we require.

For part (b), suppose $\Phi \subseteq P \xrightarrow{c} P$ is directed. We know from the proof of Tarski's theorem on page 477 that, for any continuous f,

$$\mu f = \bigsqcup \{f^n(\bot) \mid n \in \mathbb{N}\}\,.$$

Claim that for all n we have

$$(\bigsqcup \Phi)^n(\bot) = \bigsqcup \{f^n(\bot) \mid f \in \Phi\}\,.$$

This is certainly true when $n = 0$ (both sides are $\bot$), so suppose it holds for n. Then by induction, the definition of $\bigsqcup \Phi$ and the continuity of all $g \in \Phi$ we have

$$(\bigsqcup \Phi)^{n+1}(\bot) = \bigsqcup \{g(f^n(\bot)) \mid g, f \in \Phi\}\,.$$

But since all $f, g \in \Phi$ have $k \in \Phi$ with $k \geq f, g$ this is in turn equal to

$$\bigsqcup \{k^{n+1}(\bot) \mid k \in \Phi\}$$

as claimed.

Given this, we have

$$
\begin{aligned}
\mu(\bigsqcup \Phi) &= \bigsqcup \{(\bigsqcup \Phi)^n(\bot) \mid n \in \mathbb{N}\} \\
&= \bigsqcup \{\bigsqcup \{f^n(\bot) \mid f \in \Phi\} \mid n \in \mathbb{N}\} \\
&= \bigsqcup \{\bigsqcup \{f^n(\bot) \mid n \in \mathbb{N}\} \mid f \in \Phi\} \\
&= \bigsqcup \{\mu f \mid f \in \Phi\}
\end{aligned}
$$

which proves the lemma.   ∎

EXERCISE A.1.7   Suppose P, Q and R are cpo's. Prove that the following pair of partial orders are order isomorphic when $\to$ is interpreted as (i) the full function space (equivalently product space) operator, (ii) $\xrightarrow{m}$ and (iii) $\xrightarrow{c}$.

$$(P \times Q) \to R \qquad \text{and} \qquad P \to (Q \to R)$$

This is the identity underlying the functional programming construct of Currying;[7] to prove these isomorphisms you should show that the maps

$$curry: \quad ((P \times Q) \to R) \to (P \to (Q \to R)) \quad \text{and}$$
$$uncurry: \quad (P \to (Q \to R)) \to ((P \times Q) \to R)$$

are (well-defined) order isomorphisms in each of the three cases.

EXERCISE A.1.8   If X is any partial order, show that X^ω and $(X^\omega)^\omega$ are order isomorphic.

EXERCISE A.1.9   Let $P = \mathbb{N} \cup \{a, b\}$ be ordered with the usual order on $\mathbb{N}$ and such that $n < a < b$ for all $n \in \mathbb{N}$. Construct a directed set Δ of functions in $P \overset{m}{\to} P$ such that $\bigsqcup \{\mu f \mid f \in \Delta\} \neq \mu(\bigsqcup \Delta)$. What does this demonstrate?

EXERCISE A.1.10   Suppose P and Q are cpo's. The mutual recursion

$$p_0 = F(p_0, q_0)$$
$$q_0 = G(p_0, q_0)$$

for monotonic functions $f : P \times Q \overset{m}{\to} P$ and $g : P \times Q \overset{m}{\to} Q$ is naturally identified with the least fixed point of the composite function $H(p, q) = (F(p, q), G(p, q))$. We can alternatively interpret the recursion as an *iterated fixed point*: let

$$p_1 = \mu p.F(p, \mu q.G(p, q))$$
$$q_1 = \mu q.G(p_1, q)$$

Show that (p_1, q_1) is a fixed point of H and hence that $(p_0, q_0) \leq (p_1, q_1)$. Next, show that $q_0 \geq \mu q.G(p_0, q)$ and hence that

$$F(p_0, \mu q.G(p_0, q)) \leq q_0$$

Deduce that $p_1 = p_0$ and $q_1 = q_0$,

A.2   Metric spaces

The concept of distance should be familiar to readers, both through everyday experience and through the mathematical study of ordinary Euclidean space. For

---

[7]Currying (named after H.B. Curry) involves taking a function $f(x, y)$ of two arguments and turning it into a function which takes them separately: $curry(f)(x)$ is the function which takes any y and returns the value $f(x, y)$. Thus, if *plus* is the function that adds two numbers, $curry(plus)(1)$ is the function that adds one to any number.

example, if $\mathbf{a} = (x, y, z)$ and $\mathbf{a}' = (x', y', z')$ are two members of $\mathbb{R}^3$ (Euclidean 3-space), the distance between them would ordinarily be defined to be

$$d_e(\mathbf{a}, \mathbf{a}') = \sqrt{((x - x')^2 + (y - y')^2 + (z - z')^2)}$$

As with many other phenomena, mathematicians have sought to identify and axiomatize the essential properties which make a distance function like this one work. A *metric* is a function from any two points in a space X to $\mathbb{R}^+$ (the non-negative real numbers) which satisfies the following three laws:

$$
\begin{array}{lll}
d(x, y) = 0 & \Leftrightarrow \quad x = y & \text{diagonal} \\
d(x, y) & = \quad d(y, x) & \text{symmetry} \\
d(x, z) & \leq \quad d(x, y) + d(y, z) & \text{triangle inequality}
\end{array}
$$

These just say that the distance from any point to itself is 0 but the distance between any two distinct points is strictly positive; that the distance from y back to x is the same as that from x to y; and that the distance from x to z *via* y must be at least that of the direct route.

All of these are either obvious or well known for d_e.

It is possible to have many different metrics on the same space. For example, if d is any metric then so is any multiple of d, and if X is any set then the following *discrete* metric always satisfies the axioms:

$$
d(x, y) = \begin{cases} 0 & \text{if } x = y \\ 1 & \text{otherwise} \end{cases}
$$

A *metric space* is just the pair (X, d) for a space X and metric d on X. Just as with partial orders, we will usually be happy to refer to X alone as a metric space as long as the metric d can be understood from the context.

EXAMPLE A.2.1 The metric spaces used in CSP (and other process algebras) bear remarkably little resemblance to ordinary Euclidean space. In many ways they are simpler to reason about. Consider the example of finite and infinite traces over a set Σ:

$$Seq = \Sigma^* \cup \Sigma^\omega$$

We can define a distance function on this set by examining how far down the sequences we have to look to tell two of them apart. This can conveniently be done by defining restriction functions $\downarrow n$ that give a standardized view of any sequence to a chosen depth $n \in \mathbb{N}$:

$$
\begin{array}{llll}
s \downarrow n & = & s & \text{if } s \in \Sigma^* \text{ and } \#s \leq n \\
s\hat{\ }t \downarrow n & = & s & \text{if } s \in \Sigma^n \text{ and } t \in Seq
\end{array}
$$

The important features of these functions are

(a) $s \downarrow 0 = t \downarrow 0$ for all s, t;

(b) $s \downarrow n \downarrow m = s \downarrow min(n, m)$ for all s, n, m;

(c) if $s \neq t$, then there is n such that $s \downarrow n \neq t \downarrow n$

Together, these imply that whenever $s \neq t$ there is $n \in \mathbb{N}$ such that $s \downarrow m = t \downarrow m$ if and only if $m \leq n$. A set together with a family of restriction operators satisfying (a), (b) and (c) will be called a *restriction space*.

The distance between two points of a restriction space can be defined to be

$$ inf\{2^{-n} \mid s \downarrow n = t \downarrow n\} $$

(the choice of 2 being arbitrary). This is just 2^{-n} where n is the length of their longest common prefix when $s \neq t$, and 0 when $s = t$. This is a strange measure of distance, not least since the range of possible distances is restricted to powers of $\frac{1}{2}$. It obviously satisfies the first two conditions for a metric, so the only remaining thing we have to check is the triangle inequality. This is trivial to check in the case that any two of the points x, y and z are equal, so we can assume

$$ d(x, y) = 2^{-n} \quad \text{and} \quad d(y, z) = 2^{-m} $$

If $k = min(n, m)$, it follows that $x \downarrow k = y \downarrow k$ and $y \downarrow k = z \downarrow k$, and hence that $x \downarrow k = z \downarrow k$. Thus

$$ d(x, z) \leq 2^{-k} = max(d(x, y), d(y, z)) \ (\leq d(x, y) + d(y, z)) $$

which is actually a much stronger inequality than the triangle law.[8] This inequality is very hard to visualize since it says that the distance from x to z is no longer than the greater of the two legs of this journey via y, for arbitrary y!

The metrics used for CSP models are almost invariably derived from restriction spaces in this way.

Metric spaces allow us to transfer understanding about things like *convergence* – derived from distance over Euclidean space – to a more general setting where we have any well-behaved distance function. Firstly, it is simple to define what it means for a sequence of points $\langle x_i \mid i \in \mathbb{N} \rangle$ to *converge* to a point y: for any

---

[8]Metrics satisfying it are sometimes called either *ultra-metrics* or *non-Archimedean* metrics.

positive distance $\epsilon > 0$, if we go far enough down the sequence the entire remainder of the sequence must lie within ϵ of y:

$$\epsilon > 0 \ \Rightarrow \ \exists N. \forall n \geq N. d(y, x_n) < \epsilon$$

The limit point y is unique, because if there were another, say y', then you could set $\epsilon = d(y, y')/2$ which would lead quickly to a contradiction.

Notice that the only convergent sequences under the discrete metric are those that are eventually constant, since otherwise there would be no way of getting ϵ below 1. This is also true of sequences with a finite trace as limit in *Seq*, since if $\#s = n$ then the only point within $2^{-(n+1)}$ of s is s itself. However, all members of Σ^ω have many 'interesting' sequences converging to them. For example, the sequences

$$\langle \rangle, \langle a \rangle, \langle a, a \rangle, \langle a, a, a \rangle, \ldots \quad \text{and}$$
$$\langle b, b, \ldots \rangle, \langle a, b, b, \ldots \rangle, \langle a, a, b, b, \ldots \rangle, \langle a, a, a, b, \ldots \rangle$$

both converge to $\langle a, a, a, \ldots \rangle$.

The subset C of a metric space X is said to be *closed* if, whenever $\langle x_i \mid i \in \mathbb{N} \rangle$ is a sequence of points in C that converges to a point y of X, then $y \in C$. In other words, the process of convergence cannot take us outside C. Closed sets have the following crucial properties:

- The empty set $\{\}$ is closed (having no convergent sequences); the whole space X is closed, and any one-point set $\{x\}$ is closed as the sequence $\langle x, x, x, \ldots \rangle$ converges to x.

- If C and D are closed, then so is $C \cup D$ since if $\langle x_i \mid i \in \mathbb{N} \rangle$ is a convergent sequence of points in it then an infinite subsequence must belong either to C or D. It is easy to see that any infinite subsequence of a convergent sequence is convergent with the same limit; and since C and D are closed it follows that the limit of our sequence is contained in one of them.

- If $\mathcal{C}$ is any non-empty set of closed sets, then $\bigcap \mathcal{C}$ is closed, because the limit of each infinite sequence in this set clearly belongs to each $C \in \mathcal{C}$.

An *open set* U is one whose complement is closed. This is equivalent to saying that whenever $x \in U$ there is no convergent sequence in $X \setminus U$ with limit x. An elegant way of re-phrasing this is to say that for each $x \in U$ there is a ball (of sufficiently small positive radius ϵ) about x contained in U:

$$B_\epsilon(x) \ = \ \{ y \in X \mid d(x, y) < \epsilon \} \subseteq U$$

Just as the set of closed sets is closed under finite union and arbitrary intersection, the open sets are closed under finite intersection and arbitrary union.[9] (This follows, amongst other things, from de Morgan's laws.)

Every subset of the discrete metric space is closed (and open). A prefix-closed subset C of *Seq* is closed if, and only if, each $s \in \Sigma^{\omega}$ is in C whenever all its finite prefixes are.

A sequence of points $\langle x_i \mid i \in \mathbb{N} \rangle$ is said to be a *Cauchy sequence* if it looks as though it *ought* to be converging in the following tightly defined sense: for every positive distance $\delta > 0$, if we go far enough down the sequence the points are all within ϵ of each other. And this means all points beyond some N, not just consecutive ones:

$$\delta > 0 \;\Rightarrow\; \exists N . \forall n, m \geq N . d(x_n, x_m) < \delta$$

Every converging sequence is a Cauchy sequence: this follows by taking the N obtained for $\epsilon = \delta/2$ in the definition of convergence, and using the symmetry and triangle properties of a metric.

Cauchy sequences play exactly the same role in metric spaces as directed sets do in partial orders: they are the 'formally convergent' structures, and we judge completeness by seeing if they really all do converge.

DEFINITION   A metric space is said to be *complete* if, and only if, all Cauchy sequences converge to some point.   ∎

Not all metric spaces are complete: a good example is the set of all *rational* numbers ($\frac{n}{m}$ where $n \in \mathbb{N}$ and $m \in \mathbb{Z} \backslash \{0\}$) with its usual distance function ($\mid x - y \mid$). If you take the decimal expansion of any irrational number such as π (a number being irrational when it is not rational, of course), then the sequence of finite truncations of this, for example

3,   3.1,   3.14,   3.141,   3.1415,   3.14159,   3.141592,   ...

is a Cauchy sequence of rationals that fails to converge to a rational.

Seq is complete: if $\langle x_i \mid i \in \mathbb{N} \rangle$ is a Cauchy sequence then for any r we can find N_r such that $n, m \geq N_r$ implies $x_n \downarrow r = x_m \downarrow r$. The limit of the sequence is constructed as the unique sequence which agrees with x_{N_r} up to depth r for all r.

---

[9]Mathematicians' love of abstraction is shown by the fact that, just as metric spaces put distance into a general setting, a whole subject has been built up from these properties of open and closed sets. A *topology* on a set X is any collection of subsets containing $\{\}$ and X, and closed under finite intersection and arbitrary union. This is just a yet-more-abstract way of looking at the idea of convergence and, in fact, it is sufficiently general to encompass the partial order notions of convergence we have previously seen. We do not pursue this subject here, since it is not needed for a basic treatment of the theory of CSP.

In general we say a restriction space is complete if its associated metric is also complete, which turns out to be equivalent to the property that for every sequence of points $\langle x_0, x_1, x_2, \ldots \rangle$ such that $x_{n+1} \downarrow n = x_n$, there is a (necessarily unique) point x such that $x \downarrow n = x_n$ for all n.

The most important property of complete metric spaces, at least for us, bears a striking similarity to the corresponding property of complete partial orders: a useful class of functions can be shown always to have fixed points.

Suppose $f : X \to Y$ is a function between two metric spaces. f is said to be

- *non-expanding* if $d(f(x), f(y)) \leq d(x, y)$ for all $x, y \in X$, and

- a *contraction map* if there is a positive constant $\alpha < 1$ such that

$$d(f(x), f(y)) \leq \alpha d(x, y)$$

for all $x, y \in X$. (α must be independent of x and y.)

Thus a non-expanding function is one that guarantees not to increase the distance between points, and a contraction is one that decreases the distance in a uniform way. Obviously

- each contraction map is non-expanding;

- the composition $f \circ g$ of two non-expanding functions is non-expanding, and

- if f and g are both non-expanding and one is a contraction, then $f \circ g$ is a contraction.

The following result is certainly the most widely-used fixed point theorem in mathematics, even though it is not quite as frequently used as Tarski's theorem in computer science. The proof has much in common with that for the continuous function version of Tarski's theorem, since both involve constructing the fixed point as the limit of a sequence formed by iterating the function we are extracting the fixed point from.

THEOREM A.2.1 (CONTRACTION MAPPING THEOREM *or* BANACH'S THEOREM)
Suppose X is a complete metric space and $f : X \to X$ is a contraction map. Then f has a unique fixed point (i.e., exactly one $y \in X$ such that $f(y) = y$).

PROOF   It turns out that sequence obtained by applying f over and over to any point converges to a fixed point: if we choose any $x_0 \in X$ and define $x_{n+1} = f(x_n)$, then if α is the contraction factor of f, we have

$$d(x_{n+2}, x_{n+1}) = d(f(x_{n+1}), f(x_n)) \leq \alpha d(x_{n+1}, x_n)$$

and hence $d(x_{n+1}, x_n) \leq \alpha^n d(x_1, x_0)$ for all n. Thus the distance between consecutive points in this series decreases (at least) like powers of α starting from whatever happens to be the distance $K = d(x_1, x_0)$ between the first two. The series $K, K\alpha, K\alpha^2, \ldots$ is known as a *geometric progression* and has a finite sum: $K/(1-\alpha)$. This easily leads to the conclusion that $\langle x_i \mid i \in \mathbb{N} \rangle$ is a Cauchy sequence:

$$
\begin{aligned}
d(x_r, x_{r+n}) &\leq d(x_r, x_{r+1}) + \ldots + d(x_{r+n-1}, x_{r+n}) \\
&\leq \sum_{j=r}^{r+n-1} K\alpha^j \\
&\leq \sum_{j=r}^{\infty} K\alpha^j \\
&= \frac{K\alpha^r}{1-\alpha}
\end{aligned}
$$

The first line of the above follows from the triangle inequality, and the last line can be made as small as we please by choosing large enough r. Thus this sequence converges on a point y. This is certain to be a fixed point: to show this we suppose the contrary, i.e., $d(y, f(y)) > 0$. The fact that $\langle x_i \mid i \in \mathbb{N} \rangle$ converges to y implies we can find r such that $d(x_r, y)$ and $d(x_r, x_{r+1})$ are both strictly less than $d(y, f(y))/3$. Then

$$
\begin{aligned}
d(y, f(y)) &\leq d(y, x_r) + d(x_r, x_{r+1}) + d(x_{r+1}, f(y)) \\
&\leq d(y, x_r) + d(x_r, x_{r+1}) + \alpha d(x_r, y) \\
&< (2 + \alpha) d(y, f(y))/3
\end{aligned}
$$

which is a contradiction. Here, the first line is just the triangle inequality and the second follows as $x_{r+1} = f(x_r)$.

We can thus conclude $y = f(y)$. If z is any fixed point, then

$$
\begin{aligned}
d(y, z) &= d(f(y), f(z)) \qquad \text{as } y \text{ and } z \text{ are fixed points} \\
&\leq \alpha d(y, z) \qquad \text{as } f \text{ is a contraction}
\end{aligned}
$$

which implies $d(y, z) = 0$, proving that $y = z$. Thus y is the *unique* fixed point. $\blacksquare$

A particularly simple example is given over the complete metric space $\mathbb{R}$ by the contraction map $x \mapsto x/2$. Wherever we start iterating this function from we end up with a sequence converging to 0, for example $\langle 1, 1/2, 1/4, 1/8, \ldots \rangle$.

Notice that it was much easier to show in the proof that the fixed point is unique than to show it exists in the first place. All we really need, to show that there is no more than one fixed point, is that $d(f(x), f(y)) < d(x, y)$ whenever $x \neq y$: neither the uniformity of α nor the completeness of X is required. Both of these are necessary to get us a fixed point: in the incomplete space $\{x \in \mathbb{R} \mid x > 0\}$ (with the usual metric $\mid x - y \mid$), the contraction map $f : x \mapsto x/2$ has no fixed point. And similarly, in the complete space $\{x \in \mathbb{R} \mid x \geq 1\}$, again with the usual metric, the function $g : x \mapsto x + 1/x$ has no fixed point even though $\mid g(x) - g(y) \mid < \mid x - y \mid$ when $x \neq y$.

The structure of the metric on *Seq* means that $d(f(x), f(y)) < d(x, y)$ implies that $d(f(x), f(y)) \leq d(x, y)/2$, so that any function that brings distinct points closer together is bound to be a contraction. Remembering that the distance between two points is determined by the depth up to which they look the same, for a function f to be a contraction over *Seq* it must be that, to whatever depth x and y look identical, $f(x)$ and $f(y)$ must look the same to a strictly greater depth. If $x \downarrow n = y \downarrow n$, then $f(x) \downarrow n{+}1 = f(y) \downarrow n{+}1$. This is the formal definition of f being a *constructive* function over any restriction space. Similarly, non-expanding functions correspond to *non-destructive* functions: ones such that if $x \downarrow n = y \downarrow n$, then $f(x) \downarrow n = f(y) \downarrow n$.

A simple example of a constructive function over *Seq* is the one defined

$$f(s) \;=\; \langle a \rangle\char`^s$$

We can infer from the proof of the fixed point theorem that from wherever you begin to construct the sequence $\langle x_i \mid i \in \mathbb{N} \rangle$, a sequence will be found that converges to the same fixed point. If we iterate this from the starting points $\langle \rangle$ and $\langle b, b, b, \ldots \rangle$ we get precisely the two sequences seen earlier that converge to $\langle a, a, a, \ldots \rangle$, which is obviously this function's fixed point.

The structure of the metric means that any constructive function whose fixed point is a finite sequence with length n *must* reach this fixed point after no more than $n + 1$ iterations.

Non-destructive functions might have many fixed points (for example, the identity function fixes all points) or none at all. An example of the latter for *Seq* when $\Sigma = \{a, b\}$ is given by

$$
\begin{aligned}
f(\langle \rangle) &= \langle a \rangle \\
f(\langle a \rangle\char`^s) &= \langle b \rangle\char`^s \\
f(\langle b \rangle\char`^s) &= \langle a \rangle\char`^s
\end{aligned}
$$

Thus constructiveness is clearly required to get us the unique fixed point result.

The great advantage of the contraction mapping theorem over Tarski's theorem, where both can be applied, is the uniqueness of the fixed point it generates. It is, of course, the justification of the UFP rule that we have used to good effect over several CSP models.

A good general introduction to the simpler topics in metric spaces and topology can be found in [112].

EXERCISE A.2.1   Show that a closed, non-empty subset Y of a complete metric space X is itself a complete metric space under the restriction of X's metric to Y.

Now suppose that f is a contraction mapping on X such that $f(Y) \subseteq Y$. Show that the unique fixed point of f lies in Y.

EXERCISE A.2.2   Show that the infinite traces Σ^ω are a closed subset of *Seq*. Use the result of the previous question to show that if $f : Seq \to Seq$ is a constructive function that maps infinite traces to infinite traces (i.e., $f(s) \in \Sigma^\omega$ when $s \in \Sigma^\omega$) then its fixed point is infinite.

Can Σ^ω be replaced by Σ^* in this result. If not, why not?

EXERCISE A.2.3   Find a constructive function from *Seq* to itself which is *not* monotonic in the sense described in Section A.1.2.

A guide to machine-readable CSP

B.1   Introduction

The machine-readable dialect of CSP (CSP$_M$) is one result of a research effort[1] with the primary aim of encouraging the creation of tools for CSP. FDR was the first tool to utilize the dialect, and to some extent FDR and CSP$_M$ continue to evolve in parallel, but the basic research results are publicly available (see later for more details). The language described here is that implemented by the 2.1 release of FDR and has many features not present in FDR1.

CSP$_M$ combines the CSP process algebra with an expression language which, while inspired by languages like Miranda/Orwell and Haskell/Gofer, has been modified to support the idioms of CSP. The fundamental features of those languages are, however, retained: the lack of any notion of assignment, the ability to treat functions as first-class objects, and a lazy reduction strategy.

Scripts

Programming languages are used to describe algorithms in a form which can be executed. CSP$_M$ includes a functional programming language, but its primary purpose is different: it is there to support the description of parallel systems in a form which can be automatically manipulated. CSP$_M$ scripts should, therefore, be regarded as defining a number of processes rather than a program in the usual sense.

---

[1]This Appendix was written by Bryan Scattergood, of Formal Systems (Europe) Ltd. He is the main developer and implementor of this version of CSP. Comments and queries about the notation, and potential tool developers who wish to use his results, should contact him by email: bryan@fsel.com.

B.2   Expressions

At a basic level, a CSP$_M$ script defines processes, along with supporting functions and expressions. CSP draws freely on mathematics for these supporting terms, so the CSP$_M$ expression-language is rich and includes direct support for sequences, sets, booleans, tuples, user-defined types, local definitions, pattern matching and lambda terms.

We will use the following variables to stand for expressions of various types.

m, n	numbers
s, t	sequences
a, A	sets (the latter a set of sets)
b	boolean
p, q	processes
e	events
c	channel
x	general expression

When writing out equivalences, z and z' are assumed to be fresh variables which do not introduce conflicts with the surrounding expressions.

Identifiers

Identifiers in CSP$_M$ begin with an alphabetic character and are followed by any number of alphanumeric characters or underscores optionally followed by any number of prime characters ('). There is no limit on the length of identifiers and case is significant. Identifiers with a trailing underscore (such as `fnargle_`) are reserved for machine-generated code such as that produced by Casper [67].

CSP$_M$ enforces no restrictions on the use of upper/lower-case letters in identifiers (unlike some functional languages where only data type constructors can have initial capital letters.) It is, however, common for users to adopt some convention on the use of identifiers. For example

- Processes all in capitals (`BUTTON, ELEVATOR_TWO`)

- Types and type constructors with initial capitals (`User, Dial, DropLine`)

- Functions and channels all in lower-case (`sum, reverse, in, out, open_door`)

Note that while it is reasonable to use single character identifiers (`P, c, T`) for small illustrative examples, real scripts should use longer and more descriptive names.

Numbers

Syntax

12	integer literal
m+n, m-n	sum and difference
-m	unary minus
m*n	product
m/n, m%n	quotient and remainder

Remarks

Integer arithmetic is defined to support values between -2147483647 and 2147483647 inclusive, that is those numbers representable by an underlying 32-bit representation (either signed or twos-complement.) The effect of overflow is not defined: it may produce an error, or it may silently wrap in unpredictable ways and so should not be relied upon.

The division and remainder operations are defined so that, for $n \neq 0$,

$$m \ = \ n * (m/n) + m\%n$$
$$| \, m\%n \, | \ < \ | \, n \, |$$
$$m\%n \ \geqslant \ 0 \ (\text{provided } n > 0)$$

so that, for positive divisors, division rounds down and the remainder operation yields a positive result.

Floating point numbers (introduced experimentally for Pravda [64]) are not currently supported by FDR. Although the syntax for them is still enabled, it is not documented here.

Sequences

Syntax

<>, <1,2,3>	sequence literals
<m..n>	closed range (from integer m to n inclusive)
<m..>	open range (from integer m upwards)
s^t	sequence catenation
#s, length(s)	length of a sequence
null(s)	test if a sequence is empty
head(s)	the first element of a non-empty sequence
tail(s)	all but the first element of a non-empty sequence
concat(s)	join together a sequence of sequences
elem(x,s)	test if an element occurs in a sequence
<x_1,..., x_n | x<-s, b>	comprehension

Equivalences

$$\texttt{null}(s) \;\equiv\; s\texttt{==<>}$$

$$\texttt{<}m\texttt{..}n\texttt{>} \;\equiv\; \texttt{if } m\texttt{<=}n \texttt{ then <}m\texttt{>^<}m\texttt{+1..}n\texttt{> else <>}$$

$$\texttt{elem}(x,s) \;\equiv\; \texttt{null(< z | z<-}s\texttt{, z==}x \texttt{ >)}$$

$$\texttt{< } x \texttt{ | > } \;\equiv\; \texttt{< } x \texttt{ >}$$

$$\texttt{< } x \texttt{ | } b\texttt{, ...> } \;\equiv\; \texttt{if } b \texttt{ then < } x \texttt{ | ...> else <>}$$

$$\texttt{< } x \texttt{ | } x'\texttt{<-}s\texttt{, ...> } \;\equiv\; \texttt{concat(< < } x \texttt{ | ...> | } x'\texttt{<-}s \texttt{ >)}$$

Remarks

All the elements of a sequence must have the same type. `concat` and `elem` behave as if defined by

```
concat(s)      = if null(s) then <> else head(s)^concat(tail(s))
elem(_, <>)    = false
elem(e, <x>^s) = e==x or elem(e,s)
```

The following function tests if a sequence reads the same forwards and backwards

```
palindrome(<x>^s^<y>) = x==y and palindrome(s)
palindrome(_)         = true
```

Sets

Syntax

`{1,2,3}`	set literal
`{`m`..`n`}`	closed range (between integers m and n inclusive)
`{`m`..}`	open range (from integer m upwards)
`union(`a_1,a_2`)`	set union
`inter(`a_1,a_2`)`	set intersection
`diff(`a_1,a_2`)`	set difference
`Union(`A`)`	distributed union
`Inter(`A`)`	distributed intersection (A must be non-empty)
`member(`x,a`)`	membership test
`card(`a`)`	cardinality (count elements)
`empty(`a`)`	check for empty set
`set(`s`)`	convert a sequence to a set
`Set(`a`)`	all subsets of a (powerset construction)
`Seq(`a`)`	set of sequences over a (infinite if a is not empty)
`{`$x_1,\ldots,\ x_n$`|` x`<-`a`, ` b`}`	comprehension

Equivalences

$$\begin{aligned}
\texttt{union}(a_1,a_2) &\equiv \texttt{\{ z,z' | z<-}a_1\texttt{, z'<-}a_2 \texttt{ \}} \\
\texttt{inter}(a_1,a_2) &\equiv \texttt{\{ z | z<-}a_1\texttt{, member(z,}a_2\texttt{) \}} \\
\texttt{diff}(a_1,a_2) &\equiv \texttt{\{ z | z<-}a_1\texttt{, not member(z,}a_2\texttt{) \}} \\
\texttt{Union}(A) &\equiv \texttt{\{ z | z'<-}A\texttt{, z<-z' \}} \\
\texttt{member}(x,a) &\equiv \texttt{not empty(\{ z | z<-}a\texttt{, z==}x \texttt{ \})} \\
\texttt{Seq}(a) &\equiv \texttt{union(\{<>\}, \{<z>\^{}z' | z<-}a\texttt{, z'<-Seq(}a\texttt{)\})} \\
\texttt{\{ }x\texttt{ | \}} &\equiv \texttt{\{ }x\texttt{ \}} \\
\texttt{\{ }x\texttt{ | }b\texttt{, ...\}} &\equiv \texttt{if }b\texttt{ then \{ }x\texttt{ | ...\} else \{\}} \\
\texttt{\{ }x\texttt{ | }x'\texttt{<-}a\texttt{, ...\}} &\equiv \texttt{Union(\{ \{ }x\texttt{ | ...\} | }x'\texttt{<-}a\texttt{ \})}
\end{aligned}$$

Remarks

In order to remove duplicates, sets need to compare their elements for equality, so only those types where equality is defined may be placed in sets. In particular, sets of processes are not permitted. See the section on pattern matching for an example of how to convert a set into a sequence by sorting.

Sets of negative numbers (`{ -2}`) require a space between the opening bracket and minus sign to prevent it being confused with block comment.

Booleans

Syntax

`true, false`	boolean literals
b_1 `and` b_2	boolean and (shortcut)
b_1 `or` b_2	boolean or (shortcut)
`not` b	boolean not
x_1`==`x_2, x_1`!=`x_2	equality operations
x_1`<`x_2, x_1`>`x_2, x_1`<=`x_2, x_1`>=`x_2	ordering operations
`if` b `then` x_1 `else` x_2	conditional expression

Equivalences

$$\begin{aligned}
b_1 \texttt{ and } b_2 &\equiv \texttt{if } b_1 \texttt{ then } b_2 \texttt{ else false} \\
b_1 \texttt{ or } b_2 &\equiv \texttt{if } b_1 \texttt{ then true else } b_2 \\
\texttt{not } b &\equiv \texttt{if } b \texttt{ then false else true}
\end{aligned}$$

Remarks

Equality operations are defined on all types except those containing processes and functions (lambda terms).

Ordering operations are defined on sets, sequences and tuples as follows

$$x_1 \; \texttt{>=} \; x_2 \quad \equiv \quad x_2 \; \texttt{<=} \; x_1$$
$$x_1 \; \texttt{<} \; x_2 \quad \equiv \quad x_1 \; \texttt{<=} \; x_2 \; \textbf{and} \; x_1 \; \texttt{!=} \; x_2$$
$$a_1 \; \texttt{<=} \; a_2 \quad \equiv \quad a_1 \; \text{is a subset of} \; a_2$$
$$s_1 \; \texttt{<=} \; s_2 \quad \equiv \quad s_1 \; \text{is a prefix of} \; s_2$$
$$(x_1, y_1) \; \texttt{<=} \; (x_2, y_2) \quad \equiv \quad x_1 \; \texttt{<} \; x_2 \; \textbf{or} \; (x_1 \; \texttt{==} \; x_2 \; \textbf{and} \; y_1 \; \texttt{<=} \; y_2)$$

Ordering operations are not defined on booleans or user-defined types.

```
if b then {1} else <2>
```

is an error[2] because both branches of a conditional expression must have the same type.

Tuples

Syntax

```
    (1,2), (4,<>,{7})    pair and triple
```

Remarks

Function application also uses parentheses, so functions which take a tuple as their argument need two sets of parentheses. For example the function which adds together the elements of a pair can be written either as

```
plus((x,y)) = x+y
```

or as

```
plus(p) = let (x,y) = p within x + y
```

The same notation is used in type definitions to denote the corresponding product type. For example, if we have

---

[2]At the time of writing no type-checker has yet been produced for CSP_M (though the development of one is undoubtedly desirable). The parser does some limited type checking (it would reject the above example), but sometimes type errors are only caught at run-time in FDR.

```
nametype T = ({0..2},{1,3})
```

then T is

```
{ (0,1), (0,3), (1,1), (1,3), (2,1), (2,3) }
```

Local definitions

Definitions can be made local to an expression by enclosing them in a 'let within' clause.

```
primes =
  let
    factors(n)  = < m | m <- <2..n-1>, n%m == 0 >
    is_prime(n) = null(factors(n))
  within < n | n <- <2..>, is_prime(n) >
```

Local definitions are mutually recursive, just like top-level definitions. Not all definitions can be scoped in this way: channel and datatype definitions are only permitted at the top-level. Transparent definitions can be localized, and this can be used to import FDR's compression operations on a selective basis. For example,

```
my_compress(p) =
  let
    transparent normal, diamond
  within normal(diamond(p))
```

Lambda terms

Syntax

> \ x_1, ...x_n @ x lambda term (nameless function)

Equivalences

The definition

```
f(x,y,z) = x+y+z
```

is equivalent to the definition

```
f = \ x, y, z @ x+y+z
```

Remarks

There is no direct way of defining an anonymous function with multiple branches. The same effect can be achieved by using a local definition and the above equivalence. Functions can both take functions as arguments and return them as results.

```
map(f)(s) = < f(x) | x <- s >
twice(n)  = n*2
assert map(\ n @ n+1)(<3,7,2>) == <4,8,3>
assert map(map(twice))(< <9,2>, <1> >) == < <18,4>, <2> >
```

B.3 Pattern matching

Many of the above examples made use of pattern matching to decompose values. The version of CSP_M used by FDR2.1 introduced much better support for pattern matching; for example, we can write

```
reverse(<>)    = <>
reverse(<x>^s) = reverse(s)^<x>
```

as well as

```
reverse(s) = if null(s) then <> else reverse(tail(s)) ^ <head(s)>
```

The branches of a function definition must be adjacent in the script, otherwise the function name will be reported as multiply defined.

Patterns can occur in many places within CSP_M scripts

- Function definitions (reverse above)
- Direct definitions (x,y) = (7,2)
- Comprehensions { x+y | (x,y) <- {(1,2),(2,3)} }
- Replicated operators ||| (x,y):{(1,2),(2,3)} @ c!x+y->STOP
- Communications d?(x,y)->c!x+y->STOP

The patterns which are handled in these cases are the same, but the behaviour in the first two cases is different. During comprehensions, replicated operators and communications we can simply discard values which fail to match the pattern: we have a number of such values to consider so this is natural. When a function fails to match its argument (or a definition its value) silently ignoring it is not an option so an error is raised. On the other hand, functions can have multiple branches (as in the case of **reverse**) which are tried in top to bottom order while the other constructs only allow a single pattern. For example,

```
f(0,x) = x
f(1,x) = x+1
print f(1,2) -- gives 3
print f(2,1) -- gives an error
print { x+1 | (1,x) <- { (1,2), (2,7) } } -- gives {3}
```

The space of patterns is defined by

1. Integer literals match only the corresponding numeric value.

2. Underscore (_) always matches.

3. An identifier always matches, binding the identifier to the value.

4. A tuple of patterns is a pattern matching tuples of the same size. Attempting to match tuples of a different size is an error rather than a match failure.

5. A simple sequence of patterns is a pattern (`<x,y,z>`) matching sequences of that length.

6. The catenation of two patterns is a pattern matching a sequence which is long enough, provided at least one of the sub-patterns has a fixed length.

7. The empty set is a pattern matching only empty sets.

8. A singleton set of a pattern is a pattern matching sets with one element.

9. A data type tag (or channel name) is a pattern matching only that tag.

10. The dot of two patterns is a pattern. (`A.x`)

11. The combination of two patterns using `@@` is a pattern which matches a value only when both patterns do.

12. A pattern may not contain any identifier more than once.

For example, `{}`, `({x},{y})` and `<x,y>^_^<u,v>` are valid patterns. However, `{x,y}` and `<x>^s^t` are not valid patterns since the decomposition of the value matched is not uniquely defined. Also `(x,x)` is not a valid pattern by rule 12: the effect that this achieves in some functional languages requires an explicit equality check in CSP_M.

When a pattern matches a value, all of the (non-tag) identifiers in the pattern are bound to the corresponding part of the value.

The fact that tags are treated as patterns rather than identifiers can cause confusion if common identifiers are used as tags. For example, given

```
channel n : {0..9}
f(n) = n+1
```

attempting to evaluate the expression f(3) will report that the function \ n @ n+1 does not accept the value 3. (It accepts *only* the tag n.)

Only names defined as tags are special when used for pattern matching. For example, given

```
datatype T = A | B
x = A
f(x) = 0
f(_) = 1
g(A) = 0
g(_) = 1
```

then f is not the same as g since f(B) is 0 while g(B) is 1.

The singleton-set pattern allows us to define the function which picks the unique element from a set as

```
pick({x}) = x
```

This function is surprisingly powerful. For example, it allows us to define a sort function from sets to sequences.

```
sort(f,a) =
  let
    below(x)  = card( { y | y<-a, f(y,x) } )
    pairs     = { (x, below(x)) | x <- a }
    select(i) = pick({ x | (x,n)<-pairs, i==n })
  within < select(i) | i <-<1..card(a)> >
```

where the first argument represents a <= relation on the elements of the second. Because pick works only when presented with the singleton set, the sort function is defined only when the function f provides a total ordering on the set a.

B.4   Types

Simple types

Types are associated at a fundamental level with the set of elements that the type contains. Type expressions can occur only as part of the definition of channels or other types, but the name of a type can be used anywhere that a set is required.

For example, the type of integer values is `Int` and the type of boolean values
is `Bool`, so

```
{0..3} <= Int
{true, false} == Bool
```

In type expressions the tuple syntax denotes a product type and the dot
operation denotes a composite type so that

> ({0,1},{2,3})   denotes   {(0,2),(0,3),(1,2),(1,3)}
>
> {0,1}.{2,3}   denotes   {0.2, 0.3, 1.2, 1.3}

The `Set` and `Seq` functions which return the powerset and sequence space of
their arguments are also useful in type expressions.

Named types

Nametype definitions associate a name with a type expression, meaning that '.'
and '(, ,)' operate on it as type constructors rather than value expressions. For
example,

```
nametype Values = {0..199}
nametype Ranges = Values . Values
```

has the same effect as

```
Values = {0..199}
Ranges = { x.y | x<-Values, y<-Values }
```

If, on the other hand, we had left `Values` as an ordinary set, `Values . Values`
would have had the entirely different meaning of two copies of the set `Values`
joined by the infix dot. Similarly the expression (`Values`,`Values`) means *either*
the Cartesian product of `Values` with itself *or* a pair of two sets depending on the
same distinction.

Data types

Syntax

```
    datatype T = A.{0..3} | B.Set({0,1}) | C    definition of type
    A.0, B.{0}, B.{0,1}, C                       four uses of type
```

Remarks

Data types may not be parameterized (T may not have arguments).

The `datatype` corresponds to the variant-record construct of languages like Pascal. At the simplest level it can be used to define a number of atomic constants

```
datatype SimpleColour = Red | Green | Blue
```

but values can also be associated with the tags

```
Gun = {0..15}
datatype ComplexColour = RGB.Gun.Gun.Gun | Grey.Gun | Black | White
```

Values are combined with '.' and labelled using the appropriate tag, so that we could write

```
make_colour((r.g.b)@@x) =
  if r!=g or g!=b then RGB.x else
  if r==0 then Black else
  if r==15 then White else Grey.r
```

to encode a colour as briefly as possible.

Note that while it is possible to write

```
datatype SlowComplexCol = RGB.{r.g.b | r<-Gun, g<-Gun, b<-Gun} | ...
```

this is less efficient and the resulting type must still be rectangular, that is expressible as a simple product type. Hence it is *not* legal to write

```
datatype BrokenComplexColour = -- NOT RECTANGULAR
  RGB.{r.g.b | r<-Gun, g<-Gun, b<-Gun, r+g+b < 128 } | ...
```

Channels

Syntax

```
    channel flip, flop          simple channels
    channel c, d :  {0..3}.LEVEL  channels with more complex protocol
    Events                      the type of all defined events
```

Remarks

Channels are tags which form the basis for events. A channel becomes an event when enough values have been supplied to complete it (for example `flop` above is an event). In the same way, given

```
datatype T = A.{0..3} | ...
```

we know that `A.1` is a value of type `T`, given

```
channel c : {0..3}
```

we know that `c.1` is a value of type Event. Indeed, the channel definitions in a script can be regarded as a distributed definition for the built-in `Events` data type.

Channels must also be rectangular in the same sense as used for data types. It is common in FDR2 to make channels finite although it is possible to declare infinite channels and use only a finite proportion of them.

Channels interact naturally with data types to give the functionality provided by variant channels in occam2 (and channels of variants in occam3.) For example, given `ComplexColour` as above, we can write a process which strips out the redundant colour encodings (undoing the work performed by `make_colour`)

```
channel colour : ComplexColour
channel standard : Gun.Gun.Gun

Standardize =
    colour.RGB?x -> standard!x -> Standardize
  []
    colour.Grey?x -> standard!x.x.x -> Standardize
  []
    colour.Black -> standard!0.0.0 -> Standardize
  []
    colour.White -> standard!15.15.15 -> Standardize
```

Closure operations

Syntax

`extensions(`x`)`	The set of values which will 'complete' x
`productions(`x`)`	The set of values which begin with x
`{|`x_1`,`x_2`|}`	The productions of x_1 and x_2

Equivalences

$$\text{productions}(x) \;\equiv\; \{ \; x.z \;|\; z\texttt{<-extensions}(x) \; \}$$
$$\{|\, x \;|\; ...|\} \;\equiv\; \text{Union}(\; \{ \; \text{productions}(x) \;|\; ...\} \;)$$

Remarks

The main use for the {| |} syntax is in writing communication sets as part of the various parallel operators. For example, given

```
channel c : {0..9}
P = c!7->SKIP [| {| c |} |] c?x->Q(x)
```

we cannot use {c} as the synchronization set; it denotes the singleton set containing the channel c, not the set of events associated with that channel.

All of the closure operations can be used on data type values as well as channels. They are defined even when the supplied values are complete. (In that case extensions will supply the singleton set consisting of the identity value for the '.' operation.)

B.5   Processes

Syntax

STOP	no actions
SKIP	successful termination
c->p	simple prefix
c?x?x':a!y->p	complex prefix
p;q	sequential composition
p/\q	interrupt
p\a	hiding
p[]q	external choice
p|~|q	internal choice
p[>q	untimed time-out
b & p	boolean guard
p[[a<- b]]	renaming
p|||q	interleaving
p[|a|]q	sharing
p[a||a']q	alphabetized parallel
p[c<->c']q	linked parallel
;x:s@p	replicated sequential composition
[]x:a@p	replicated external choice
|~|x:a@p	replicated internal choice (a must be non-empty)
|||x:a@p	replicated interleave
[|a'|]x:a@p	replicated sharing
||x:a@[a']p	replicated alphabetized parallel
[c<->c']x:s@p	replicated linked parallel (s must be non-null)

Equivalences

As a consequence of the laws of CSP,

$$p|||q \;\equiv\; p[| \{\} |]q$$
$$;x:\langle\rangle@p \;\equiv\; \texttt{SKIP}$$
$$[]x:\{\}@p \;\equiv\; \texttt{STOP}$$
$$|||x:\{\}@p \;\equiv\; \texttt{SKIP}$$
$$[|a|]x:\{\}@p \;\equiv\; \texttt{SKIP}$$
$$||x:\{\}[a]p \;\equiv\; \texttt{SKIP}$$

By definition

$$p[>q \;\equiv\; (p[]q)|\tilde{}\,|q$$

Remarks

The general form of the prefix operator is cf->p where c is a communication channel, f a number of communication fields and p is the process which is the scope of the prefix. A communication field can be

$!x$	Output
$?x:A$	Constrained input
$?x$	Unconstrained input

Fields are processed left to right with the binding produced by any input fields available to any subsequent fields. For example, we can write

```
channel ints : Int.Int
P = ints?x?y:{x-1..x+1} -> SKIP
```

Output fields behave as suggested by the equivalence

$$c\ !x\ f\ \text{->}\ p \;\equiv\; c.x\ f\ \text{->}\ p$$

The proportion of the channel matched by an input fields is based only on the input pattern. There is no lookahead, so if

```
channel c : {0..9}.{0..9}.Bool
P = c?x!true -> SKIP -- this will not work
Q = c?x.y!true -> SKIP -- but this will
```

then P is not correctly defined. The input pattern x will match the next complete value from the channel ({0..9}) and true will then fail to match the next copy of {0..9}. In the case of @@ patterns, the decomposition is based on the left-hand side of the pattern.

If an input occurs as the final communication field it will match any remaining values, as in

```
channel c : Bool.{0..9}.{0..9}
P = c!true?x -> SKIP -- this will work
Q = c!true?x.y -> SKIP -- this will also work
```

This special case allows for the construction of generic buffers.

```
BUFF(in,out) = in?x -> out!x -> BUFF(in, out)
```

is a one place buffer for any pair of channels.

Dots do not directly form part of a prefix: any which do occur are either part of the channel c, or the communication fields. (FDR1 took the approach that dots simply repeated the direction of the preceding communication field. This is a simplification which holds only in the absence of data type tags.)

The guard construct 'b & P' is a convenient shorthand for

```
if b then P else STOP
```

and is commonly used with the external choice operator ([]), as

```
COUNT(lo,n,hi) =
  lo < n & down -> COUNT(lo,n-1,hi)
[]
  n < hi & up -> COUNT(lo,n+1, hi)
```

This exploits the CSP law that $p[]\text{STOP} = p$.

The linked parallel and renaming operations both use the comprehension syntax for expressing complex linkages and renamings. For example,

```
p [ right.i<->left.((i+1)%n), send<->recv | i<-{0..n-1}] q
p [[ left.i <- left.((i+1)%n), left.0<-send | i<-{0..n-1} ]]
```

Both the links (c<->c') and the renaming pairs (c<-c', read 'becomes') take channels of the same type on each side and extend these pointwise as required. For example

```
p [[ c <- d ]]
```

is defined when `extensions(c)` is the same as `extensions(d)` and is then the same as

```
p [[ c.x <- d.x | x<-extensions(c) ]]
```

The replicated operators allow multiple generators between the operator and the @ sign in the same way as comprehensions. The terms are evaluated left to right, with the rightmost term varying most quickly. So

```
; x:<1..3>, y:<1..3>, x!=y @ c!x.y->SKIP
```

is the same as

```
c.1.1->c.1.2->c.2.1->c.2.3->c.3.1->c.3.2->SKIP
```

The linked parallel operator generalizes the chaining operator $\gg$. For example, if `COPY` implements a single place buffer,

```
COPY(in,out) =
  in?x -> out!x -> COPY(in,out)
```

then we can implement an n-place buffer by

```
BUFF(n,in,out) =
  [out<->in] i : {1..n} @ COPY(in, out)
```

The precedence rules for operators (both process and expression level) are set out in Table B.1. The replicated versions of the process operators have the lowest precedence of all. The @@ pattern operator has a precedence just below that of function application.

B.6 Special definitions

External

External definitions are used to enable additional 'magic' functions supported by a specific tool. Requiring a definition, rather than silently inserting names into the initial environment, has two advantages: any dependencies on such functions are made explicit and there is no possibility that users will introduce conflicting definitions without being aware of it. For example, to make use of an (imaginary) `frobnicate` external function, we might say

Class	Operators	Description	Associativity
Application	`f(0)`	function application	
	`[[ <- ]]`	renaming	
Arithmetic	`-`	unary minus	
	`*, /, %`	multiplication	left
	`+, -`	addition	left
Sequence	`^`	catenation	
	`#`	length	
Comparison	`<, >, <=, >=`	ordering	none
	`==, !=`	equality	none
Boolean	`not`	negation	
	`and`	conjunction	
	`or`	disjunction	
Sequential	`->`	prefix	
	`&`	guard	
	`;`	sequence	
Choice	`[>`	untimed time-out	
	`/\`	interrupt	
	`[]`	external choice	
	`|~|`	internal choice	
Parallel	`[| |], [ || ], [ <-> ],`	parallel	none
	`|||`	interleave	
Other	`if then else`	conditional	
	`let within`	local definitions	
	`\ @`	lambda term	

Table B.1   *Operator precedence.*: the operators at the top of the
table bind more tightly than those lower down.

```
external frobnicate
P(s) = c!frobnicate(s^<0>, 7) -> STOP
```

Without the external definition, `frobnicate` would be reported as an unde-
clared identifier. Tools should report as an error any attempt to define an external
name which they do not recognize.

Transparent

As described in Section C.2, FDR uses a number of operators that are used to
reduce the state space or otherwise optimize the underlying representation of a

process within the tool. While these could be defined using external definitions, they are required to be semantically neutral. It is thus safe for tools which do not understand the compression operations to ignore them. By defining them as transparent, tools are able to do so; unrecognized external operations would be treated as errors. As an example,

```
transparent diamond, normal
squidge(P) = normal(diamond(P))
```

enables the diamond and normal compression operators in FDR2, while other tools see definitions of the identity functions, as if we had written

```
diamond(P) = P
normal(P) = P
squidge(P) = normal(diamond(P))
```

Assert

Assertions are used to state properties which are believed to hold of the other definitions in a script. (FDR1 scripts adopted a convention of defining two processes SPEC and SYSTEM, with the understanding that the check SPEC[=SYSTEM should be performed. This has weaknesses: the correct model for the check is not always apparent, and some scripts require multiple checks.) The most basic form of the definition is

```
assert b
```

where b is a boolean expression. For example,

```
primes       = ...
take(0,_)    = <>
take(n,<x>^s) = <x> ^ take(n-1,s)
assert <2,3,5,7,11> == take(5, primes)
```

It is also possible to express refinement checks (typically for use by FDR)

```
assert p [m= q
```

where p and q are processes and m denotes the model (T, F or FD for trace, failures and failures/divergences respectively.) Note that refinement checks cannot be used in any other context. The (refinement) assertions in a script are used to initialize the list of checks in FDR2.

Similarly, we have

```
assert p : [ deterministic [FD] ]
assert p : [ deadlock free [F] ]
assert p : [ divergence free ]
```

for the other supported checks within FDR. Only the models F and FD may be used with the first two, with FD assumed if the model is omitted.

Note that process tests cannot be used in any other context. The process assertions in a script are used to initialize the list of checks in FDR2.

Print

Print definitions indicate expressions to be evaluated. The standard tools in the CSP$_M$ distribution include 'check' which evaluates all (non-refinement) assertions and print definitions in a script. This can be useful when debugging problems with scripts. FDR2 uses any print definitions to initialize the list of expressions for the evaluator panel.

B.7   Mechanics

CSP$_M$ scripts are expressible using the 7-bit ASCII character set (which forms part of all the ISO 8859-x character sets.) While this can make the representation of some operators ugly, it makes it possible to handle the scripts using many existing tools including editors, email systems and web-browsers.

Comments can be embedded within the script using either end-of-line comments preceded by '--' or by block comments enclosed inside '{-' and '-}'. The latter nest, so they can be safely used to comment out sections of a script.

If it is necessary to exploit an existing library of definitions, the 'include' directive performs a simple textual inclusion of another script file. The directive must start at the beginning of a line and takes a filename enclosed in double quotes. Block comments may not straddle file boundaries (comments cannot be opened in one file and closed in another.)

Definitions within in a script are separated by newlines. Lines may be split before or after any binary token and before any unary token. (There are exceptions to this rule, but they do not occur in practice.)

The `attribute`, `embed`, `module` and `subtype` keywords are currently reserved for experimental language features.

B.8 Missing features

Those familiar with functional languages such as Haskell will notice several omissions in CSP_M.

Floating point

Floating point numbers are a natural part of the timed and probabilistic variants of CSP, and the machine-readable dialect has a syntax to support them. However, as the current generation of tools have concentrated on the simpler variants of the notation, the underlying semantics have not been implemented.

Strings

Real programming languages have string and character types, along with an input/output system. CSP_M is not a programming language: input and output introduce unnecessary complications when performing analysis of scripts.

Characters and strings could be useful for modelling some problem domains, but no compelling example has yet to be demonstrated. Integers and sequences provide workable alternatives.

Sections and composition

Operator sections and functional composition are a convenient shorthand allowing the terse expression of some powerful constructs. This terseness conflicts with the need for CSP process descriptions to be readable, often by new users of the language. For now, it is felt that their utility is outweighed by their unreadability.

B.9 Availability

The research into tools for CSP has been sponsored by the US Office of Naval Research under N00014-87-J1242 and as such the basic results from that research are freely available on request. It is hoped that this will help encourage a common input syntax between CSP-based tools. The results include the machine-readable form of CSP complete with both denotational and operational semantics, a congruence proof between the two semantic models using a bridging semantics, an implementation of a parser for the language using flex and bison to produce a syntax-tree in C++ and methods defined over that tree which are sufficient to implement the operational semantics.

The operation of FDR

Though the basic concept of what FDR does, namely refinement checking, is simple, the mechanisms it uses to make this efficient are much more complex. Understanding them undoubtedly helps one to use the tool effectively. This appendix, therefore, seeks to give the interested user some insight, frequently guided by the theory developed in Part II, about how it works. It is in no sense, however, a manual. The first part looks at the basic principles; the second deals with the compression functions FDR provides to enable the user to check larger networks of processes than would otherwise be in range.

C.1 Basic operation

C.1.1 Running the operational semantics efficiently

With the exception of its potential support for the prioritized view of time (as discussed in Sections 14.6 and 14.7) everything FDR does is rooted in the denotational models of CSP described in Chapter 8. These are refinement checking, determinism checking and looking for deadlocks and divergences. There is, however, no direct sense in which the tool calculates sets of traces, failures etc.; it manipulates processes at the level of operational semantics and labelled transition systems, borrowing one important idea (normalization) from the algebraic semantics. Thus all three of the semantic methods described in Part II of this book are involved in its design.

While the operational semantics presented in Chapter 7 allow one to calculate the transitions of any process at all, any implementation which treats all processes the same is likely to be more inefficient than one would like in both space and time when running checks involving millions of states. The problem is, that in order to treat such features as unfolding recursions properly, it is necessary to use a symbolic representation of each state (probably as a syntax tree) and to use a method probably not unlike the basic inference system over syntax seen in Chapter 7 in order to calculate transitions.

FDR therefore uses a two-level approach to calculating operational semantics; it is important to appreciate the differences between these levels if you want to use it effectively. The low level is fully general but relatively inefficient, whereas the high level is restricted (specifically, it cannot handle recursion) but much more efficient in space and time. When you ask FDR to perform a check it analyzes the structure of the process or processes it is given and decides on an appropriate cut-off point between the low and high levels. Everything below this level is fully evaluated using the low-level compiler (i.e., each individual low-level component has its full operational semantics evaluated). What the compiler outputs for the high-level structure is a series of recipes for combining together the transitions of these low-level components into transitions of the whole.

At the time of writing the division between low and high levels is decided by a complex algorithm which is closely approximated by the following.

- All true recursions are low level. A true recursion is a process name (possibly parameterized) whose value depends (possibly through other recursive expansions) on itself (where parameterized, with *the same* arguments). Thus the recursion

  ```
  P(n) = a -> P(if n==0 then N else n-1)
  ```

  is low level (for $0 \leq n \leq N$) but

  ```
  Q(n) = a -> if n==0 then STOP  else Q(n-1)
  ```

  is not.

- Subject to the above over-riding principle, as many 'high-level' operators (all parallel operators, renaming and hiding) as possible are high level, but any other operators are treated at low level unless they are forced to high level[1] by being outside one of these. Thus, in the unlikely combination

  ```
  LevelExample = a -> ((b -> STOP)
                      |~|
                      ((c -> STOP) ||| Q))
  ```

  (where the identifier `LevelExample` does not appear in `Q`), the processes `b -> STOP` and `c -> STOP` are both compiled at low level, while the internal

---

[1] At the time of writing there is no high-level implementation of $\Box$, so this forces a process to low level irrespective.

choice |~| and the a -> construct are both high level because they are outside the |||.

The first principle arises from necessity: the high-level approach only works where the set of basic structures a process might have is predictable and finite. The second is pragmatic and designed to keep the number of these structures generated as small as possible for typical examples.

Indeed, for a majority of practical examples this approach will produce just one structure. These well-behaved examples fall into two categories: processes (often designed as specifications) with no high-level operators which are entirely compiled at low level, and combinations of low-level processes using parallel, hiding and renaming operations. The crucial point about a combination using only these operators is that the overall process structure is unaffected by any action it performs. Consider, for example, the solitaire board described in Section 15.1: for the standard board, the process Puzzle on page 419 is a parallel composition of 34 processes at the outset, and keeps the same basic structure throughout. It is only the states of the individual components that change: every single state it goes through is equivalent to

```
(|| (i,j):BoardCoords @ [Alpha(i,j)] Slot'(i,j))
[|OffBoardMoves|] STOP
```

where Slot'(i,j) is one of the states of the original process Slot(i,j). In this case, of course, most of the processes have just two states[2] and the other one, STOP, has only one.

For this example, and any other with a single structure, the compiler in FDR works out the complete state spaces of the component processes and the rules under which actions of the components combine to give actions of the whole. In this case you would get a rule that allowed a τ action of any individual process to be promoted to a τ action of the whole, and rules for each visible action. For each move in RealMoves the rule would simply say that it can happen just when the three processes whose alphabet it is in can. (The introduction of hiding and renaming operators can make these relationships more complex.) Except in rare pathological cases the number of rules has the same order of magnitude[3] as the alphabet of actions being used (including any hidden actions).

---

[2]The operational semantics in Chapter 7 would give them four, the extra ones being created by τ actions introduced on unfolding recursions. By default these are omitted by FDR since they serve no purpose except in making sense of very badly defined recursions as described on page 161.

[3]In particular, this approach, based on combinations of *events* as opposed to *states* of the component processes, works well for many-way synchronization. The earlier version, FDR1, used the latter approach which frequently caused a combinatorial explosion on timed systems (as described in Chapter 14) where many processes have to synchronize on tock.

If there is more than one structure the system could go through as it evolved, the rules have to encompass the transitions from one to another. For example, on the assumption that Q is a process compiled at low level, the process LevelExample defined above would give four structures: the initial one (prefix), one in which the choice is unresolved, and one each for after it has been resolved each way. Then, for example, the second of these would have two available τ actions, which resolve it into the third or fourth.

Within the terminology of FDR, the individual structures the system can go through are termed *configurations*, or *formats* and the rules which allow it to infer the actions of one of these from those of its components are called *supercombinators*. In the version of the tool current at the time of writing it is possible to switch off the use of supercombinators, whereupon a mechanism rather closer to the basic operational semantics is used to derive transitions. The slow-down this creates is generally spectacular.

Because all the low-level processes have been fully evaluated at compile time, as have all the potential structures, a single state of the complete system can be represented by an indication of which structure this is and the indexes of the states the components are in. Since in a typical run you may encounter a huge number of states, it is desirable to store them as compactly as possible. Therefore FDR packs this information so that each component process P_i with S_i states only occupies k bits, where k is minimal such that $2^k \geq S_i$. Thus each of the two state Slot processes in Puzzle occupies one bit. Some versions of the tool offer further compressions which exploit similarities between collections of states.

Once a process has been compiled the recipe for running it (i.e., the state spaces of its components, its configurations and supercombinators, and of course its initial state) are passed to another program which runs it. This might be to evaluate it for normalization, to check it against a specification, or for compression. The later sections of this appendix describe all of these possibilities.

A recipe like this is an *implicit* representation of an LTS, since it gives the initial state and sufficient information to calculate all the transitions and all the other states. This is in contrast to the compiled low-level components, which are included as *explicit* LTSs (i.e., a list of states and transitions). It does not, of course, matter to such a recipe how its components were generated, only that they are explicit LTSs. You can think of such a recipe as some CSP context applied to some processes represented as explicit LTSs.

In deciding how to structure a process for input into FDR, you should bear in mind the distinction between how it deals with high- and low-level state evaluation. High level is many times more efficient. At the time of writing a reasonable limit on the size of a low-level component to compile is in the range 1,000–5,000 states depending on example.

The most likely source of problems in compiling (as opposed to any of the post-compilation functions) a process on FDR is an over-large (perhaps infinite) low-level component. Bear in mind that since these components are evaluated in full, the fact that the context they are put in means they never reach most states would not help in this (the archetypal example of this is the sequential coding of the Spy1 process on page 457). It is also possible, but much rarer, for combinatorial problems to arise in the enumeration of configurations or supercombinator rules.

C.1.2   Normalization

Suppose we have asked FDR to check the refinement $P \sqsubseteq Q$ (the precise model is more or less irrelevant). The first thing it does is to compile P and Q, as described in the previous section. It cannot do the refinement check directly on the raw state machines these would give when run: it has to transform P (only) into a *normal form*. The normal form it aims at is essentially of the type described on page 283, i.e., a state machine in which all states are semantically distinct (thanks to the factorization by bisimulation) and which follows normal form structure rules. The exact shape of the nodes varies depending on which model is being used, but they always satisfy the basic principles that (i) there are no τ actions and (ii) each node has a unique successor on each visible initial action it can perform.

The crucial point about normal form state machines is that they have a unique state for each trace: once we are told the present trace, there is only one state it can be in.

There are two main differences with the normal forms seen in Chapter 11. Firstly, they are now stored as state machines, with a node represented solely by its index, its transitions, and perhaps refusal/divergence information, rather than as highly stylized pieces of syntax. Secondly, rather than normalizing a process by algebraic transformation using laws, FDR performs this function (rather more efficiently) by directly manipulating the transition diagram of the process.

If you carry out a normalization as described in Chapter 11 you will find that the process you are left with to normalize after a trace s, namely P/s, ends up being the nondeterministic choice of a number of states P can get into – namely, all those states it can be in after s. When we directly normalize an LTS, this corresponds to the decision below to form a graph whose nodes are sets of nodes of the original. Each set node of the normal form behaves like the nondeterministic choice of the original nodes it contains. The normalization algorithm that FDR uses comes in two stages.

Stage 1   Given a finite labelled transition system $L = (V, E, v_0)$, we form a graph $\mathcal{P}_L$ whose nodes are members of $\mathbb{P}(V)$ as follows

- The initial node is $\tau^*(v_0)$, where $\tau^*(v)$ is defined to be $\{w \mid v \stackrel{\langle\rangle}{\Longrightarrow} w\}$, the nodes reachable under some sequence of τ's from v_0.

- For each node generated we have (if using the failures/divergences model $\mathcal{N}$) to decide whether it is divergent: this is true if and only if it contains a divergent node of L. Techniques for deciding this are discussed in the next section. A divergent normal form node over $\mathcal{N}$ has no successors. (Over other models divergence is ignored.)

- If a node N is not divergent, we determine the set of non-τ actions possible for $v \in N$. For each such action a we form a new node, the set $\bigcup\{\tau^*(w) \mid \exists v \in N.v \stackrel{a}{\longrightarrow} w\}$, the set of all nodes reachable after action a and any number of τ's from members of N.

- The search is completed when all 'new' nodes generated are ones that have been previously expanded.

The resulting graph will be termed the *pre-normal* form of L. It coincides with the output of the procedure for looking for a finite algebraic normal form described on page 283, but it suffers from the same drawback, namely (as was the case with the normal form $\underline{N}'$ derived for P_1 there) that it may have equivalent nodes. FDR uses the same solution as adopted there, namely to factor the pre-normal form by a strong bisimulation calculated taking account of divergence and refusal information (where relevant to the model). This strong bisimulation calculation comprises **Stage 2**.

The possible refusals of a pre-normal form node v are just the sets refused by the stable $v \in N$. (Refusals are represented by the set of *minimal acceptances*, the complements of maximal refusals.)

The normalization process of an LTS corresponding to a data-free version of $COPY \gg COPY \gg COPY$ is shown in in Figure C.1. The left-hand graph shows the states and transitions of the basic process, and the sets of nodes identified by pre-normalization. These are mapped to the normal form transition diagram on the right. Each node on the right is marked with its set of minimal acceptances (in this case, as this is a deterministic process, there is just one of these for each node, namely its set of initials).

In this case the pre-normal form nodes are all semantically distinct, and so the final bisimulation makes no further identification.

The complexity of normalization

Given that the pre-normalization process builds a transition system over the power-space of the original one, there is the possibility that the normal form will be exponential in the size of the original system. This can indeed occur, as is shown

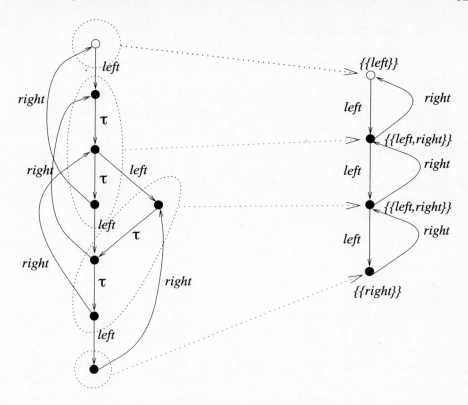

Figure C.1 Normalizing a transition system.

by the example below. This possibility is to be expected given the result [58] that checking failures/divergences refinement of transition systems is PSPACE-hard (a complexity class at least as hard as NP).

Fortunately there are two mitigating factors that work in our favour, making this particular obstacle more or less disappear.

1. 'Real' process definitions simply do not behave as badly as the pathological example below. In practice it is rare for the normal form of a naturally occurring process to have more states than the original transition system. Indeed, the normal form is frequently significantly *smaller*, offering scope for intermediate compression. It seems that deciding refinement is one of that large class of NP-complete and similar problems where the hard cases are rare.

2. It is only the *specification* end of the refinement that we have to normalize.

In practice the simpler process is usually that one rather than the implementation. Frequently, indeed, the specification is a representation of an abstract property such as two events alternating or deadlock freedom, and has a trivial number of states.

One would usually expect that a process playing the role of a 'specification' is reasonably clearly and cleanly constructed, with understandable behaviour. These aims are more-or-less inconsistent with the sort of nondeterminism that leads to an explosion in the normal form.

EXAMPLE C.1.1 The potential for state explosion on normalization is shown in extreme form by the following pathological system, defined for any $n > 0$. We construct a transition system with $n + 1$ states and n events $\{1, \ldots, n\} = B$. If the kth state is P_k we define

$$
\begin{aligned}
P_0 &= STOP \\
P_k &= ?r : B \to P_{k+1} \quad k \in \{1, \ldots, n-1\} \\
P_n &= ?r : B \to P_0 \\
&\quad \square ?r : B \to P_1 \\
&\quad \square ?r : B \to P_r
\end{aligned}
$$

This system is illustrated in Figure C.2. The pre-normal and normal forms of this system (with initial state P_1) both have precisely $2^n - 1$ states (one for each non-empty subset A of the states $P_1, \ldots, P_n$ since, as can be proved by induction on the size of A, there is for each such subset a trace s_A such that the states reachable on s_A are A and perhaps P_0). The role of the state P_0 is to allow us to distinguish between these sets: if it is in the set reachable after a given trace, then P_1 can deadlock after that trace, otherwise not. If the state P_0 is removed we get a system with the same number of pre-normal form states but only *one* normal form state, since every one is then semantically equal to RUN_B. *(End of example)*

The pragmatics of normalization

While you are never likely to happen upon a system which behaves as badly as the one above by accident, you are likely to come across some where normalization is slow and expands rather than contracts the process it is applied to. Fortunately this happens much more often when normalization is being used as a compression function (as described in the Section C.2) where it is optional, rather than when it is being used on a specification, where it is compulsory and automatic.

The size of system it is possible to normalize depends on the size of the underlying system, the size of the sets comprising the pre-normal form nodes, and the number of transitions and minimal acceptance sets, amongst other things. Thus while you may have no problem normalizing a 50,000-state process, another one

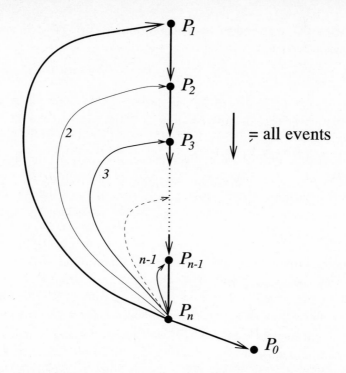

Figure C.2 Transition system with pathological normalization.

of 5,000 can turn out to be too slow or demanding of memory. In any case the substantial transformation performed by normalization means that it can only be applied to systems which are, at best, one or two orders of magnitude smaller than those which can be used on the right-hand sides of refinement checks.

Bear in mind that hierarchical compression, as described in the next section, is at least as useful in helping the normalization of complex specifications as it is on the implementation side.

C.1.3   Checking refinement

Given that determinism checking is reduced by the algorithm given on page 221 to refinement checking, and both divergence freedom and deadlock freedom are naturally expressed as refinement checks, the only basic function of FDR we have to detail further is refinement checking.

Once the specification end of a refinement check has been normalized, the following two phases are necessary to establish failures/divergence refinement.

- Establish which states of the implementation transition system are divergent, marking them as such.

- Model-check the implementation, thus marked, against the normal form.

Only the latter is necessary for refinement checks over $\mathcal{F}$ and $\mathcal{T}$. For $\mathcal{N}$ these two phases can (as was the case in early versions of FDR) be done one after the other, or interleaved.

A state P of a finite LTS is divergent if, and only if, the directed graph formed by considering only τ actions has a cycle reachable from P. There are two standard algorithmic approaches to this problem: computing the transitive closure of the graph or taking advantage of the properties of depth-first search (DFS). A DFS algorithm can be used to find the *strongly connected components* of the directed graph formed by an LTS under τ actions: the maximal collections of nodes which are mutually reachable. Subject to various assumptions about speed of array access, etc., there are algorithms to do this, such as Tarjan's algorithm, which are essentially linear. Since any cycle is necessarily contained in a single strongly connected component, this easily yields a method for identifying divergent nodes.

In the main, model-checking phase we have to discover whether all the behaviours of each implementation state are allowable in all the normal form states such that they have a trace in common. This is done by exploring the Cartesian product[4] of the normal form and implementation state machines as follows. (Here we describe what is done for the failures/divergences model $\mathcal{N}$; the other models do essentially the same on the behaviours relevant to them. For simplicity we do not cover here the special cases required to deal with $\checkmark$ actions.)

We maintain a set of checked pairs and a set of *pending* pairs; initially the former is empty and the latter is the singleton set of the pair of initial states of the two systems. Until it is empty, we repeatedly inspect pairs from *pending*. The pair $\langle \nu, w \rangle$ checks if (i) the normal-form state ν is divergent *or* (ii) the implementation state w is non-divergent *and*

- the set of initial actions of w is a subset of those of ν *and*

- either w is unstable (has a τ-action) *or* the set of actions it refuses (the complement of its initials) is a subset of one of the maximal refusals of ν.

The set of all pairs reachable from $\langle \nu, w \rangle$ and not in *checked* is added to *pending*. A pair $\langle \nu', w' \rangle$ is *reachable* from $\langle \nu, w \rangle$ if either

---

[4]The fact that you are exploring the Cartesian product means that occasionally the model-checking phase visits more 'states' than there are states in the implementation. This happens when proving refinement demands that a single implementation state refines more than one specification state. This is relatively rare in practice.

(a) $w \xrightarrow{\tau} w'$ and $\nu = \nu'$, or

(b) $w \xrightarrow{a} w'$ and $\nu \xrightarrow{a} \nu'$ for $a \neq \tau$; noting that whenever $w \xrightarrow{a} w'$, then this ν' must exist and be unique.

If a pair is found which fails to check, then the proposed refinement does not hold. If the above process completes without finding such a pair, then refinement does hold.

The first case (failure of refinement) is easy to see: the implementation has a trace (the sequence of visible actions used to bring the Cartesian product to the failing state-pair), which can bring it into a state with behaviours not possible for the normal form. This means there is a divergence, a trace or a refusal of the implementation that is not allowed in the specification. Provided we have a way of finding the trace that led to a specific pair $\langle \nu, w \rangle$ being considered, it is thus possible to report not only the failure of refinement but also a reason.

Conciseness being a virtue, it is as well to report the shortest possible sequence of actions that can lead to an error. This is achieved if we perform a breadth-first search (BFS) during the model-checking phase. We will see later that this brings other advantages.

The case of successful proof is a little more subtle. One can justify the claim that refinement always holds in these circumstances either operationally or abstractly. If refinement fails then, from an operational perspective, this is because the implementation has some behaviour that is banned by the normal form. There is therefore some sequence of actions which exhibit this, potentially bringing the implementation into some state w where it can (a) diverge illegally, (b) perform an event that takes the traces outside the set permitted by the normal form or (c) refuse a set not refused by the normal form. It is clear that the unique normal form state ν corresponding to this trace is such that $\langle \nu, w \rangle$ will be found in the search above, leading to a failure to check.

Abstractly, one can show that the refinement-checking process is simultaneously formulating and proving a sort of mutual recursion induction over the state space of the implementation akin to those analyzed in Section 9.2.

Breadth-first searching

In a large refinement check you may have to search through state spaces with many millions of states, with similar numbers of transitions being found for the states at each level. It is of vital importance to manage these efficiently.

The algorithms FDR uses show an interesting difference between the DFS used for divergence checking and the BFS used for model checking. Both of these algorithms rely on the maintenance of sets of which states have been visited before.

In a DFS we need a constantly updated representation of this set so that we can discover whether the state we are looking at has been visited before. Since we immediately look at the children of the most recently visited node, there is no potential for grouping these tests. In order to perform this you either need a much larger and more complex representation of the LTS (such as that generated by the explicate function described in the next section) or a hash table.

In performing a BFS there is a high latency between generating a pending state and actually visiting it, if it is new. The test of whether it is new can be performed at any time during this interval. A natural way of doing this is to look at all successor states generated during a particular 'layer' of the search. If the current list of visited states is stored as a sorted list, then we can find out which of the successors are new by sorting the successors (naturally, removing duplicates) and then merging them into the established list. Obviously the successors of each genuinely new state can be generated as it is merged in.

This latter method has been found to be faster and more memory-efficient than the former. The greatest benefit appears when the set of states becomes too large to fit within the physical memory of the computer. Hash table representations of sets map so badly onto virtual memory that they are effectively unusable at this level. The sorted list representation maps onto virtual memory extremely well: all access into the lists is sequential (depending on which sorting routine is used during that phase). We have found very little degradation in performance in checks when they are forced to use virtual memory.

This fact has meant that it is often significantly quicker to perform the model-checking phase than the divergence-checking, and indeed the former can frequently be performed on systems when the latter is not within reach. This is why it is frequently better to factor a $\sqsubseteq_{FD}$ check in FDR into a proof (perhaps not automated) of divergence freedom and a failures-only refinement check.

C.2   Hierarchical compression

The state spaces of systems described in CSP or any similar notation can grow very quickly as the number of parallel components increases. In the worst case – one that is unfortunately often experienced – this growth is exponential. Anyone who experiments with many variable-sized systems on FDR will quickly encounter it and discover that it is all too easy to build networks which exceed the order 10^6–10^7 states that can conveniently be handled on a typical workstation or PC.

If one wants to deal with larger state spaces then it is necessary to find some way of avoiding visiting each state explicitly. Several clever approaches have been taken to this in the model-checking community as a whole; the ones that have been successfully used for refinement checking CSP are *Binary Decision Diagrams* (BDDs), and *hierarchical compression*. BDDs provide a radically different method of refinement checking to the one outlined in the previous section: in it, the state machines and refinement relations are encoded as logical formulae and checked in that form. BDDs have proved very successful in many hardware design applications, see [22], for example. Several people have developed BDD-based tools for CSP, for example [123]: it is hoped to include an up-to-date list of these in the web site site referenced in the Preface.

At the time of writing, FDR does not include BDD capability, though this may change in the long term. It does, however, support hierarchical compression, which is a technique directly rooted in the semantic theory of CSP[5]. The basic idea is to take the description of a complex CSP process, say $P \parallel_X Q$, and instead of calculating the state space given it by the operational semantics, finding smaller LTSs representing P and Q and combining these. This is done by calculating the complete state spaces of P and Q and applying a compression function. If, for example, P and Q are both 1,000 state processes but can be compressed to 100 each, this may have reduced the states of the complete system from 10^6 to 10^4. The crucial results which support this technique are the congruences between the operational and denotational semantics (see Section 9.4), since that means that the overall denotational semantics of any context $C[P_1, P_2, \ldots, P_k]$ depends only on the denotational semantics of $P_1, \ldots, P_k$, not on the precise LTSs chosen to represent them. Thus, if you have evaluated the operational semantics of the P_i, in building a recipe for an implicit machine to represent the complete context you can replace the resulting component LTSs with any smaller ones which happen to have equivalent semantics.

C.2.1   Methods of compression

At the time of writing, FDR2 uses five different methods of taking one LTS and attempting to compress it into a smaller one. Each of these is called by simply applying a function to the process you want to compress. Since these do not change the semantic value of the process they are applied to, FDR terms them *transparent* functions. Each one you want to use has to be declared as such.

1. Normalization (`normal(P)`) is as discussed in Section C.1.2. It can give significant gains, but it suffers from the disadvantage that by going through powerspace nodes it can be expensive and lead to expansion.

---

[5]It is possible to base similar compression methods on congruences for other languages than CSP, as shown, for exmaple, in [38], and we were by no means the first people to point out the advantages of CSP equivalences for this purpose [117].

2. Strong bisimulation (`sbisim(P)`): the standard notion defined in Section 7.2 enriched (as necessary) by any labellings of minimal acceptances and/or divergences found on the nodes. FDR computes this relation by using explicit iteration based on the proof of Tarski's theorem for continuous functions (see page 477) to find the maximal bisimulation on the input LTS, which is then factored by this relation. Ordinarily, bisimulation is faster than normalization and can be applied to larger systems. The size of system it can be applied to still depends somewhat an the application, though less so than with normalization.

   Applied to the process shown in Figure C.1, strong bisimulation would give no compression at all: it would not identify any nodes. The sort of behaviour it can compress is shown in Figure 7.4 on page 156.

3. τ-loop elimination (`tau_loop_factor(P)`): since a process may choose automatically to follow a τ action, it follows that all the processes on a τ-loop (or, more properly, a strongly connected component under τ-reachability) are equivalent. Therefore all the nodes on such a component can be identified. As discussed in the previous section, this calculation is done via depth-first search algorithms.

   Since this can only compress divergent processes, its stand-alone uses are necessarily rather specialized. It exists mainly as a precursor to `diamond`, described below.

4. Diamond elimination (`diamond(P)`): this carries out a transformation which cuts out all τ actions from an LTS. Like normalization, it produces an LTS with explicitly marked minimal acceptance and divergence information, but unlike normalization it never increases the number of nodes. (It can, on occasion, have the drawback of creating large numbers of transitions between states.)

   It applies τ-loop elimination as its first step. A detailed description of the `diamond` transformation can be found in [103].

   Applied to the system of Figure C.1, diamond compression will produce identical results to *normal*, i.e., the four-state process.

   It is often a good idea to apply strong bisimulation to the result of a diamond compression.

5. Factoring by semantic equivalence (`model_compress`): the compositional models of CSP we are using all represent much weaker congruences than bisimulation. Therefore if we can afford to compute the semantic equivalence relation over states it will be at least as good a compression as bisimulation to factor by this equivalence relation. A formal justification of this method can be found in [103]. As with `normal`, the degree of compression this function gives depends on which model is being used.

The algorithm used to compute these equivalences is based on an extension to normalization. On the basis of our experience so far the cost of this function (it is the slowest of all the compressions to compute) is not usually worth the usually small extra benefits. Therefore we will not discuss it further here.

Some of these functions, if given an ordinary LTS, will return a *Generalized* LTS, an LTS where nodes may be marked with divergence or minimal acceptance information. In fact, therefore, the whole of FDR is programmed to operate with these GLTSs rather than the basic sort.

The range of options is supplied because the one that is most effective varies with example. In the author's experience, the most effective is usually either `normal(P)` or `sbisim(diamond(P))`. Normalization tends to work well where the internal choices present in P do not result in a lot of externally visible nondeterminism arising for subtle reasons. Diamond elimination, and to a lesser extent normalization, work best on processes with many τ actions.

None of the compression techniques will affect a normalized process: not only the semantic value but also the transition system will be identical.

There is another `transparent` function supported by FDR that should be mentioned, though not a compression function in the sense described above:

- `explicate(P)` takes any description FDR can understand of a (G)LTS and turns it into an explicit list of states, transitions and minimal acceptance/ divergence markings. This is usually applied to any machine implemented as an implicit supercombinator machine as described on page 520 before carrying out other transformations. All of the compressions above explicate their arguments before doing anything else.

    It is typically benificial to explicate a transition system when, like the compressions, you need to perform a reasonably complex calculation or transformation of it.

Though `chase`, described on page 463, is used as a compression function, it does not (as discussed there) preserve the semantics of nondeterministic processes. It is therefore declared as `external` rather than `transparent`. The same is true of the `prioritize` function discussed on page 413, where implemented.

C.2.2   Using compression

The purpose of using these compression functions is to reduce the number of states explored when checking or normalizing a complete system. Since the cause of state explosion is almost invariably the multiplication that arises from parallel composition, the right place to apply compression is to a process that is to be put in parallel with another. These might either be individual sequential components or subnetworks consisting of a number of these in parallel. You can of course compress subnetworks built up of smaller ones that have themselves been compressed, and so on.

It is difficult to give any hard and fast rules about when compression techniques will work effectively. The author has frequently been surprised both at how well they work on some examples and at how badly they work on others. Some examples are given below and the reader will find many more in the files to be found on the web site, but there is no real substitute for personal experience.

Broadly speaking, you have a reasonable chance of success when the following are all true:

(a) Part of the alphabet of the process you are compressing has been hidden, either because the hidden events are true internal actions or because they have been abstracted as irrelevant to the specification (following the principles set out in Section 12.2).

(b) It sometimes helps if these hidden actions represent progress within the process, as opposed to the resolution of nondeterminism.

(c) It is not the case that a large part of the state space of the process you are compressing is never visited when it is put into the complete system. (The danger here is that you will expend too much effort compressing irrelevant states, or that the irrelevant states will make the subsystems too large to compress. Some tricks for getting round this type of problem are illustrated in example files.)

The following principles[6] should generally be followed when you are structuring a network for compression:

1. Put together processes which communicate with each other together early. For example, in the dining philosophers, you should build up the system out of consecutive fork/philosopher pairs rather than putting the philosophers all together, the forks all together and then putting these two processes together at the highest level.

---

[6]The second of these principles is easy to automate if the description of a network is input into FDR in a format that allows it to apply the necessary laws. The best choices to follow in automating the first are rather more subjective, and the success in getting a program to make what turn out to be the 'right' decisions consequently more variable.

2. Hide all events at as low a level as is possible. The laws of CSP allow the movement of hiding inside and outside a parallel operator as long as its synchronizations are not interfered with. In general, therefore, any event that is to be hidden should be hidden the first time that (in building up the process) it no longer has to be synchronized at a higher level. The reason for this is that the compression techniques all tend to work much more effectively on systems with many τ actions.

We give three examples here, each of which indicates a different class of network where compression can be used with considerable success.

EXAMPLE C.2.1 Compression is likely to work well if some subcomponent of a network is relatively self-contained. It may have complex internal behaviour, while its external functionality is comparatively simple.

Imagine, for example, a communication service which uses a number of copies of the alternating bit protocol to overcome an error-prone medium. We might have a ring of nodes N_i ($i \in \{0, \ldots, K-1\}$) with a channel between N_i and $N_{i\oplus1}$ being implemented by an ABP. There would thus be K copies of this process.

Each copy of the alternating bit protocol would have many fewer states once compressed: if the type it operates over has size 2 (as is frequently justifiable by data-independence as discussed in Section 15.2.2) the reduction (on applying `normal`) will typically be from some 100's or 1000's of states to just 3 states. Thus the overall reduction in state-space size is by a factor of perhaps 100^K. The structure of this compression is illustrated in Figure C.3. For obvious reasons we might term this strategy *modular compression*.

This specific case is, in a sense, *too* good in that it is easy to find a direct representation of the process an ABP compresses to (namely *COPY*) and use properties of refinement effectively to perform the compressions by hand (simply substituting a *COPY* for each ABP in the program text). One does frequently, however, come across cases where the reduced components are, while significantly more complex than this, still a great improvement on the originals.

The whole concept of hierarchical compression, but especially modular compression, has a lot in common with the idea of compositional development described on page 46. The only difference is that here the intermediate specification is computed automatically.

EXAMPLE C.2.2 A second class of example which tends to work well is provided by networks whose communication graph is basically one-dimensional, in the sense that it either is a chain of processes or is built in a simple way by joining a few chains together. These frequently, though not invariably, compress well provided

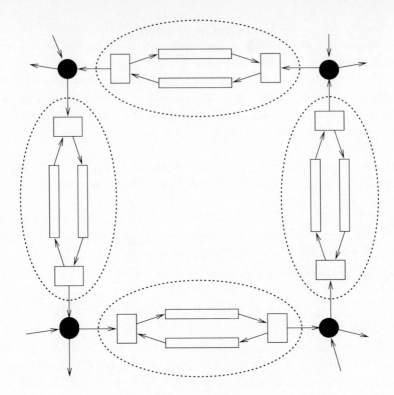

Figure C.3 Modular compression strategy.

it is possible to build up the chains in a way that hides all or nearly all of the alphabets of the processes that are not at the ends of partially constructed chains.

A typical example of this is provided by the deadlock analysis of the dining philosophers which can, of course, be built up as a chain until the two ends are joined together. We use the fact, discussed in Section 8.4, that over the stable failures model $\mathcal{F}$ a process P is deadlock-free if and only if $P \setminus \Sigma$ is. The dining philosophers network with all events hidden can be structured

$$(\|_{i=0}^{K-1}(PandF_i, AP_i)) \setminus \Sigma$$

where $PandF_i$ is the combination

$$PHIL_i \underset{AF_i}{\|} FORK_i$$

We can take the process definitions to be either those used in Section 2.2.1 (which deadlock) or as revised in Section 13.2.4 (made asymmetric so they do not). The

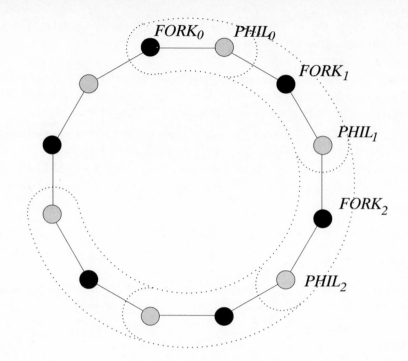

Figure C.4 Inductive compression strategy applied to dining philosophers.

law $\langle$hide-$_X \| _Y$-dist$\rangle$ (3.7) is then used to push the hiding into the parallel network, which can then be defined with compression:

$$C_1 \quad = \quad PandF_0$$
$$C_{n+1} \quad = \quad compress(C_n \setminus (\Sigma \setminus I_n)) \;_{I_n}\|_{AP_n} PandF_n \quad \text{for } n < K$$

Here, I_n are the events that the chain C_n of the first n philosopher/fork pairs has to synchronize with other processes, namely

$$\{picksup.K-1.0, putsdown.K-1.0, picksup.n-1.n, putsdown.n-1.n\}$$

This leaves only AP_{K-1} to hide at the outside. As mentioned earlier, in practice the manipulation of hiding is done automatically.

If *compress* is chosen to be normalization, each C_n for $n < K$ reduces to just four states independent of n (basically one state for each combination of the fork at either end being up or down). Thus K philosophers can be checked in time linear[7] in K, though the uncompressed network has exponentially many states. The *inductive* compression structure used here is shown in Figure C.4.

EXAMPLE C.2.3 Our final example is taken from Milner's text [75]. Like the dining philosophers, it is a ring network, but it turns out to have rather different characteristics. The code given here is translated (trivially) from CCS.

It is a 'scheduler' which has the job of arranging two classes of event: $a.i$ and $b.i$ for $i \in \{0, \ldots, N-1\}$. It lets the $a.i$ happen in strict rotation and (for every i) insists on precisely one $b.i$ occurring between each pair of $a.i$'s. Milner's network achieves this with a ring of simple cell processes connected using an extra, internal channel c:

$$Cell(0) \;=\; a.0 \to c.1 \to b.0 \to c.0 \to Cell(0)$$
$$Cell(i) \;=\; c.i \to a.i \to c.i \oplus 1 \to b.i \to Cell(i) \quad \text{if } i > 0$$

The different case for 0 reflects that the rotation of the $a.i$ starts with $a.0$. The alphabet AC_i is just the four events $Cell(i)$ uses, in the network description

$$Scheduler \;=\; (\big\|_{i=0}^{N-1}(Cell(i), AC_i)) \setminus \{| \; c \; |\}$$

There are various specifications one might wish to prove of this: that it is deadlock-free,[8] that the $a.i$ do in fact rotate, and something about the relationships between a's and b's. Like the dining philosophers, the number of states in this network grows exponentially with its size (it is, in fact, $N2^N$), so in order to deal with a large one it is necessary to use compressions.

Essentially the same inductive strategy as over the dining philosophers works reasonably well for proving deadlock freedom: one adds a *Cell* at a time while hiding all events not needed for external synchronization. (The external events of the cells from 0 to $n-1$ are $\{c.0, c.n\}$.) In this case the number of states of a partially constructed network grows linearly with size, resulting in an overall quadratic (i.e., $O(N^2)$) check.

To prove that the $a.i$ rotate we use a trace specification with alphabet $\{| \; a \; |\}$: $ASpec(0)$ where

$$ASpec(n) \;=\; a.n \to ASpec(n \oplus 1)$$

---

[7]In fact, using a doubling-up technique rather than adding one at a time, you can check 2^K philosophers in $O(K)$ time: see [103].

[8]Note that it is, in fact, a cyclic communication network of the type described in Section 13.2.2. The methods given there easily establish deadlock freedom, should you wish to follow that approach.

leading to the refinement check

$$ASpec(0) \sqsubseteq_T Scheduler \setminus \{| \, b \, |\}$$

Interestingly, in this case, the inductive strategy fails badly with the state spaces of the partially constructed networks growing exponentially. The reason for this turns out to be a possibility we mentioned earlier: it is actually the case that with the network *Scheduler*, properties of the entire network prevent partially constructed chains getting into many of the states they could reach if working by themselves. The operation of this system is rather like a token ring (as discussed, for example, on page 307), with the token currently being held by the $Cell_i$ that has communicated $c.i$ more recently than $c.i \oplus 1$. The complete ring maintains the invariant that there is only one token, and this simplifies its state space considerably. The problem is that, rather like the incomplete railway network in Figure 13.10, the partial networks built up in the inductive approach do not enjoy this simplifying property.

Fortunately, a simpler approach, which one might term *leaf compression* works very well in this case. The only compressions are applied to the individual components of the network after distributing the abstraction of irrelevant events. In this case this gives the check:

$$ASpec(0) \sqsubseteq_T (\|_{i=0}^{N-1} (normal(Cell(i) \setminus \{b.i\}), AC_i)) \setminus \{| \, c \, |\}$$

This gives a linear time check (with $2N$ states), and in fact the same approach (where the set hidden on $Cell_i$ becomes $\{a.i, b.i\}$) works better than inductive compression for deadlock freedom, since it is now a linear time check (with N states).

If presented with a specification involving all the events in $\{| \, a, b \, |\}$, such as the assertion that the total number of b's lies between the number of a's and that number minus N, there seems to be no compression of *Scheduler* which will do much good. Too many essentially different states exist with respect to the alphabet we need to see to decide the specification. You can, however, successfully deal with checks involving only a few events, such as showing that the number of $a.i$ and $b.j$ (for any chosen pair (i, j)) never differ by more than 2. *(End of example)*

Leaf compression, thanks to its simplicity and the fact that it is very unlikely to lead to computational problems in the calculation of the compressions themselves, is probably the first thing you should try on a system for which it is possible to abstract a reasonable number of events that are specific to individual components (i.e., unsynchronized with others). This approach would have produced a substantial reduction in the number of states checked in the dining philosophers from the uncompressed version, but the number of states would still have grown exponentially.[9] Thus different methods work well in different circumstances: the examples given here are indicative of the type of places where you can expect the various strategies to succeed or fail, but as we said earlier it is not possible at the time of writing to give any hard and fast rules.

The example files contain these examples and more, and include general-purpose high-level functions for implementing inductive and leaf compression, generalizations of them using mixed abstraction rather than just hiding, and further strategies we have not had space to describe here.

---

[9]The growth slows from approximately 6^N to approximately 2^N.

Notation

This glossary sets out some of the mathematical notation in this book. Descriptions marked thus^I have a reference in the main index, and those marked thus^P have one in the process index; in either case further information can be obtained by referring to that. For notation, such as *initials*(P), with an obvious alphabetical place in the indexes, you should refer directly there.

Many pieces of notation whose use is relatively localized (to a single chapter or section) are not included below.

Sets and numbers

$a \in x$	set membership (true iff a is in x)
$x \subseteq y$	subset ($\forall\, a.a \in x \Rightarrow a \in y$)
$\{\}$	the empty set
$\{a_1, \ldots, a_n\}$	set containing these elements
$x \cup y,\quad \bigcup X$	union
$x \cap y,\quad \bigcap X\ (X \neq \{\})$	intersection
$x \setminus y$	difference ($= \{a \in x \mid a \notin y\}$)
$\mathbb{P}(x)$	powerset ($= \{y \mid y \subseteq x\}$)
$x \times y$	Cartesian product ($= \{(a, b) \mid a \in x \wedge b \in y\}$)
$x \to y$	the space of all functions from x to y
$\mathbb{N}$	natural numbers ($\{0, 1, 2, \ldots\}$)
$\mathbb{Z}$	integers ($\{\ldots, -2, -1, 0, 1, 2, \ldots\}$)
$\mathbb{R}$	real numbers
$\mathbb{R}^+$	non-negative real numbers
$\oplus, \ominus$	addition and subtraction *modulo* the appropriate base

Logic

$x \wedge y$	conjunction (x and y)
$x \vee y$	disjunction (x or y)
$\neg x$	negation (not x)
$x \Rightarrow y$	implication ($\equiv (\neg x \vee y)$)
$x \Leftrightarrow y$	double implication (($x \Rightarrow y) \wedge (y \Rightarrow x)$)
$\forall x.\chi$	universal quantification (χ holds for all x)
$\exists x.\chi$	existential quantification (χ holds for at least one x)

Communications

Σ	(Sigma[I]): alphabet of all communications
$\checkmark$	(tick) termination[I] signal
τ	(tau[I]): the invisible action
$\Sigma^{\checkmark}$	$\Sigma \cup \{\checkmark\}$
$\Sigma^{\checkmark,\tau}$	$\Sigma \cup \{\checkmark, \tau\}$
$a.b.c$	compound event (see page 26)
$c?x$	input[I]
$c!e$	output[I]
$\{\mid a, b \mid\}$	events associated with channels (see page 27)

Sequence/trace notation (see pages 36 and 43)

A^*	set of all finite sequences over A
$A^{*\checkmark}$	$A^* \cup \{s^\frown \langle \checkmark \rangle \mid s \in A^*\}$
A^ω	set of all infinite sequences over A
$\langle \rangle$	the empty sequence
$\langle a_1, \ldots, a_n \rangle$	the sequence containing $a_1, \ldots, a_n$ in that order
$s^\frown t$	concatenation of two sequences
$s \setminus X$	hiding: all members of X deleted from s
$s \upharpoonright X$	restriction: $s \setminus (\Sigma^{\checkmark} \setminus X)$
$\# s$	length of s
$s \downarrow a$	(if a is an event) number of a's: $\#(s \upharpoonright \{a\})$
$s \downarrow c$	(c a channel) sequence of values communicated on c in s
$s \leq t$	($\equiv \exists u.s^\frown u = t$) prefix order
$s \parallel_X t \ (\subseteq \Sigma^{*\checkmark})$	generalized parallel[I]
$s \mathbin{\vert\vert\vert} t \ (\subseteq \Sigma^{*\checkmark})$	interleaving[I]
$\overline{S}$	closure[I] of S ($= S \cup \{u \in \Sigma^\omega \mid \forall s < u.s \in S\}$)

Note that sequence-like notation is also used to denote vectors indexed by arbitrary sets, usually with reference to mutual recursion, for example $\langle B_s^\infty \mid s \in T^* \rangle$.

Processes

For `machine-readable` CSP, see Appendix B.

$\mu\,p.P$	recursion[I]
$a \to P$	prefixing[I]
$?x : A \to P$	prefix choice[I]
$(a \to P \mid b \to Q)$	guarded alternative[I]
$P \,\square\, Q$	external choice[I]
$P \sqcap Q, \quad \bigsqcap S$	nondeterministic choice[I]
$P \mathbin{\triangleleft} b \mathbin{\triangleright} Q$	conditional choice[I]
$P \parallel Q$	synchronous parallel[I]
$P \mathbin{_X\!\parallel_Y} Q$	alphabetized parallel[I]
$P \mathbin{\underset{X}{\parallel}} Q$	generalized parallel[I]
$P \mathbin{\vert\vert\vert} Q$	interleaving[I]
$P \setminus X$	hiding[I]
$f[P]$	renaming[I] (functional)
$P[\![R]\!]$	renaming[I] (relational)
$P[\![a/b]\!]$	renaming[I] (relational, by substitution)
$a.P$	process naming[I]
$P;\, Q$	sequential composition[I]
$P \gg Q$	piping[I] (or chaining)
$P \mathbin{/\!/_X} Q$	enslavement[I]
$P \mathbin{/\!/} m : Q$	enslavement[I] (of a named process)
$P \rhd Q$	'time-out' operator (sliding choice)[I]
$P \mathbin{\triangle_a} Q$	interrupt[I]
$P[x/y]$	substitution (for a free identifier x)
P/s	'after'[I] operator
$P \downarrow n$	restriction[I] to depth n (model dependent)
$\mathcal{L}_H(P)$	lazy abstraction[I]
$\mathcal{E}_H(P)$	eager abstraction[I]
$\mathcal{M}_H^S(P)$	mixed abstraction[I]

Transition systems (see Section 7.2)

$P \xrightarrow{a} Q$ $(a \in \Sigma^{\checkmark, \tau})$ single action transition

$P \xRightarrow{s} Q$ $(s \in \Sigma^{*\checkmark})$ multiple action transition with τ's removed

$P \xmapsto{t} Q$ $(t \in (\Sigma^{\tau})^{*\checkmark})$ multiple action transition with τ's retained

$\tau^*(P)$ $(\{Q \mid P \xRightarrow{\langle\rangle} Q\})$ τ-expansion of P (see page 521)

$P \; ref \; B$ P refuses B

$P \; div$ P diverges

Semantic models

$\mathcal{T}$ traces model[I]

$\mathcal{N}$ failures/divergences model[I]

$\mathcal{F}$ stable failures model[I]

$\mathcal{I}$ infinite traces/divergences model[I]

$\mathcal{U}$ failures/divergences/infinite traces model[I]

$\bot_{\mathcal{N}}$ (etc.)   bottom elements of models[P]

$\top_{\mathcal{F}}$ (etc.)   top elements of models[P]

$\sqsubseteq_T$ traces refinement

$\sqsubseteq_{FD}$ failures/divergences refinement

$\sqsubseteq_F$ failures refinement (i.e., over $\mathcal{F}$)

$\sqsubseteq_{\mathcal{I}}$ refinement over $\mathcal{I}$

$\sqsubseteq_{\mathcal{U}}$ refinement over $\mathcal{U}$

$\sqsubseteq$ refinement over whatever model is clear from the context (with a special meaning in parts of Chapter 12, and with a default of $\sqsubseteq_{FD}$)

$P \leq Q$ strong order[I] (over $\mathcal{N}$ or $\mathcal{U}$)

$\mathcal{D}$ set of deterministic[I] processes

$\mathcal{T}^d$ possibly deterministic members of $\mathcal{T}$ (see page 218)

Partial orders

$\bigsqcup X$ least upper bound

$\bigsqcap X$ greatest lower bound

μf least fixed point of f

Bibliography

[1] L. Aceto and M. Hennessy, *Termination, deadlock and divergence*, Proceedings of MFPS89, Springer LNCS 442, 1989.

[2] P.G. Allen, *A comparison of non-interference and non-deducibility using CSP*, Proceedings of the 1991 IEEE Computer Security Workshop, IEEE Computer Society Press, 1991.

[3] R. Alur and T. Henzinger, *Logics and models of real time: a survey*, in 'Real time: theory in practice' (de Bakker *et al, eds*), Springer LNCS 600, 1992.

[4] K.R. Apt and D.C. Kozen, *Limits for automatic verification of finite-state concurrent systems*, 307–309, Information Processing Letters **22**, 6, 1986.

[5] G. Barrett, *The fixed-point theory of unbounded nondeterminism*, Formal Aspects of Computing, **3**, 110–128, 1991.

[6] G. Barrett and M.H. Goldsmith, *Classifying unbounded nondeterminism in CSP*, in 'Topology and category theory in computer science' (Reed, Roscoe and Wachter, *eds*), Oxford University Press, 1991.

[7] G. Barrett and A.W. Roscoe, *Unbounded nondeterminism in CSP*, Proceedings of MFPS89, Springer LNCS 442, 1991.

[8] J.D. Beasley, *The ins and outs of peg solitaire*, Oxford University Press, 1985.

[9] J.A. Bergstra and J.W. Klop, *Process algebra for synchronous communicaction*, Information and Control, **60**, 109–137, 1984.

[10] J.A. Bergstra and J.W. Klop, *Algebra for communicating processes with abstraction*, Theoretical Computer Science, **37**, 1, 77–121, 1985.

[11] R.S. Bird and P.L. Wadler, *Introduction to functional programming*, Prentice Hall, 1988.

[12] S.R. Blamey, *The soundness and completeness of axioms for CSP processes*, in 'Topology and category theory in computer science' (Reed, Roscoe and Wachter, *eds*), Oxford University Press, 1991.

[13] N.A. Brock and D.M. Jackson, *Formal verification of a fault tolerant computer*, Proceedings of 1992 Digital Aviation Systems Conference, IEEE Computer Society Press, 1992.

[14] S.D. Brookes, *A model for communicating sequential processes*, Oxford University D.Phil thesis, 1983. (Published as a Carnegie-Mellon University technical report.)

[15] S.D. Brookes, *Fair communicating processes*, in 'A classical mind: essays in honour of C.A.R. Hoare', Prentice Hall, 1994.

[16] S.D. Brookes, *The essence of Parallel Algol*, Proceedings of the 11th IEEE LICS, 1996.

[17] S.D. Brookes, C.A.R. Hoare and A.W. Roscoe, *A theory of communicating sequential processes*, Journal of the ACM **31**, 3, 560–599, 1984.

[18] S.D. Brookes and A.W. Roscoe, *An improved failures model for CSP*, Proceedings of the Pittsburgh seminar on concurrency, Springer LNCS 197, 1985.

[19] S.D. Brookes and A.W. Roscoe, *Deadlock analysis in networks of communicating processes,* in 'Logics and models of concurrent systems' (K.R. Apt, *ed.*) NATO ASI series F, Vol. 13, Springer, 1985.

[20] S.D. Brookes and A.W. Roscoe, *Deadlock analysis in networks of communicating processes,* Distributed Computing, **4** 209–230, 1991.

[21] S.D. Brookes, A.W. Roscoe and D.J. Walker, *An operational semantics for CSP*, Technical report, 1988.

[22] J.R. Burch, E.M. Clarke, K.L. McMillan, D.L. Dill and L.J. Hwang, *Symbolic model checking:* 10^{20} *states and beyond*, 142–170, Information and Computation **98**, 2, 1992.

[23] E.M. Clarke, R. Enders, T. Filkorn and S. Jha, *Exploiting symmetry in temporal logic model checking*, Formal Methods in System Design, **9**, 77–104, 1996.

[24] G. Colouris, J. Dollimore and T. Kindberg, *Distributed systems, concepts and design*, Addison-Wesley, 1994.

[25] N. Dathi, *Deadlock and deadlock-freedom*, Oxford University D.Phil thesis, 1990.

[26] J.W.M. Davies, *Specification and proof in real-time CSP*, Cambridge University Press, 1993.

[27] J.W.M. Davies, D.M. Jackson, G.M. Reed, A.W. Roscoe and S.A. Schneider, *Timed CSP: theory and applications*, in 'Real time: theory in practice' (de Bakker *et al*, *eds*), Springer LNCS 600, 1992.

[28] J.W.M. Davies and S.A. Schneider, *A brief history of Timed CSP*, Oxford University Computing Laboratory technical monograph PRG-96, 1992.

[29] R. de Nicola and M. Hennessy, *Testing equivalences for processes*, Theoretical Computer Science **34**, 1, 83–134, 1987.

[30] E.W. Dijkstra and C.S. Scholten, *A class of simple communication patterns,* in 'Selected writings on computing', EWD643, Springer-Verlag, 1982.

[31] E.A. Emerson and A.P. Sistla, *Utilizing symmetry when model checking under fairness assumptions: an automata-theoretic approach*, 309–324, Proceedings of the 7th CAV, Springer LNCS 939, 1995.

[32] E.A. Emerson and A.P. Sistla, *Symmetry and model checking*, Formal Methods in System Design, **9**, 105–131, 1996.

[33] H.B. Enderton, *Elements of set theory*, Academic Press, 1977.

[34] R. Focardi and R. Gorrieri, *Comparing two information-flow properties*, Proceedings of 1996 IEEE Computer Security Foundations Workshop, IEEE Computer Society Press, 1996.

[35] Formal Systems (Europe) Ltd, *Failures-Divergence Refinement: FDR2 Manual*, 1997.

[36] N. Francez, *Fairness*, Springer, 1986.

[37] S. Graf, *Verification of a distributed cache memory by using abstractions*, Proceedings of the 6th CAV, Springer LNCS 818, 1994.

[38] S. Graf and B. Steffen, *Compositional minimisation of finite-state systems*, Proceedings of CAV '90, Springer LNCS 531, 1990.

[39] J.C. Graham-Cumming, *The formal development of secure systems*, Oxford University D.Phil thesis, 1992.

[40] I. Guessarian, *Algebraic semantics*, Springer LNCS 99, 1981.

[41] F. Harary, *Graph theory*, Addison-Wesley, 1969.

[42] He Jifeng and C.A.R. Hoare, *From algebra to operational semantics*, Information Processing Letters, **46**, 2, 1993.

[43] He Jifeng, C.A.R. Hoare and A. Sampaio, *Normal form approach to compiler design*, Acta Informatica, **30**, 701–739, 1993.

[44] C.L. Heitmeyer and R.D. Jeffords, *Formal specification and verification of real-time system requirements: a comparison study*, U.S. Naval Research Laboratory technical report, 1993.

[45] A. Hojati and R.K. Brayton, *Automatic datapath abstraction in hardware systems*, 98–113, Proceedings of the 7th CAV, Springer LNCS 939, 1995.

[46] M. Hennessy, *Algebraic theory of processes*, MIT Press, 1988.

[47] M. Hennessy and H. Lin, *Symbolic bisimulations*, 353–389, Theoretical Computer Science, **138**, 2, 1995.

[48] M.G. Hinchey and S.A. Jarvis, *Concurrent systems: formal development in CSP*, McGraw-Hill, 1995.

[49] C.A.R. Hoare, *Communicating sequential processes*, Communications of the ACM, **21**, 8, 666–677, 1978.

[50] C.A.R. Hoare, *A model for communicating sequential processes*, in 'On the construction of programs' (McKeag and MacNaughten, *eds*), Cambridge University Press, 1980.

[51] C.A.R. Hoare, *Communicating sequential processes*, Prentice Hall, 1985.

[52] Inmos Ltd., OCCAM2 *reference manual*, Prentice Hall, 1988.

[53] C.N. Ip and D.L. Dill, *Better verification through symmetry*, Formal Methods in System Design, **9**, 41–75, 1996.

[54] K. Jensen, *Condensed state spaces for symmetrical coloured Petri nets*, Formal Methods in System Design, **9**, 7–40, 1996.

[55] G. Jones and M.H. Goldsmith, *Programming in* OCCAM2, Prentice Hall, 1988.

[56] B. Jonsson and J. Parrow, *Deciding bisimulation equivalences for a class of non-finite-state programs*, Information and Computation **107**, 2, 272–302, 1993.

[57] A. Jung, *ed, Domains and denotational semantics: history, accomplishments and open problems*, 1996.

[58] P.C. Kanellakis and S.A. Smolka, *CCS expressions, finite state processes and three problems of equivalence*, Information and Computation **86**, 43–68, 1990.

[59] R.S. Lazić, *A semantic study of data-independence with applications to the mechanical verification of concurrent systems*, Oxford University D.Phil thesis, to appear in 1997.

[60] R.S. Lazić, *Theorems for mechanical verification of data-independent CSP*, Oxford University Computing Laboratory technical report, 1997.

[61] R.S. Lazić and A.W. Roscoe, *Using logical relations for automated verification of data-independent CSP*, Proceedings of the Workshop on Automated Formal Methods (Oxford, U.K.), Electronic Notes in Theoretical Computer Science 5, 1997.

[62] R.S. Lazić and A.W. Roscoe, *A study of data-independence in CSP*, Submitted for publication, 1997.

[63] N.G. Leveson and J.L. Stolzy, *Analyzing safety and fault tolerance using timed Petri nets*, Proceedings of TAPSOFT, Springer, 1985.

[64] G. Lowe, *Pravda: a tool for verifying probabilistic processes*, Proceedings of the Workshop on Process Algebra and Performance Modelling, 1993.

[65] G. Lowe, *Breaking and fixing the Needham-Schroeder public-key protocol using FDR*, Proceedings of TACAS '97, Springer LNCS 1055, 1996.

[66] G. Lowe, *Some new attacks upon security protocols*, Proceedings of 1996 IEEE Computer Security Foundations Workshop, IEEE Computer Society Press, 1996.

[67] G. Lowe, *Casper: a compiler for the analysis of security protocols*, Proceedings of 1997 IEEE Computer Security Foundations Workshop, IEEE Computer Society Press, 1997.

[68] G. Lowe and A.W. Roscoe, *Using CSP to detect errors in the TMN protocol*, University of Leicester Dept. of Mathematics and Computer Science techical report 1996/34, and to appear in the Journal of Computer Security.

[69] W.F. McColl, *Scalable computing*, in 'Computer science today: recent trends and developments', Springer LNCS 1000, 1995.

[70] K. McMillan, *Symbolic model checking*, Kluwer Academic Publishers, 1993.

[71] J.M.R. Martin, *The design and construction of deadlock-free concurrent systems*, University of Buckingham D.Phil thesis, 1996.

[72] R. Milner, *Fully abstract models of typed lambda-calculi*, Theoretical Computer Science **4**, 1–22, 1977.

[73] R. Milner, *A calculus of communicating systems*, Springer LNCS 92, 1980.

[74] R. Milner, *Lectures on a calculus for communicating systems*, Proceedings of the Pittsburgh seminar on concurrency, Springer LNCS 197, 1985.

[75] R. Milner, *Communication and concurrency*, Prentice Hall, 1989.

[76] R. Milner, J. Parrow and D. Walker, *A calculus of mobile processes, I and II*, Information and Computation **100**, 1, 1–77, 1992.

[77] M.W. Mislove, A.W. Roscoe and S.A. Schneider, *Fixed points without completeness*, Theoretical Computer Science **138**, 2, 273–314, 1995.

[78] J.J. Mitchell, *Type systems for programming languages*, in 'Handbook of theoretical computer science' (van Leeuwen, *ed*), Elsevier, 1990.

[79] E.R. Olderog, and C.A.R. Hoare, *Specification-oriented semantics for communicating processes*, Acta Informatica, **23**, 9–66, 1986.

[80] D. Park, *On the semantics of fair parallelism*, in 'Abstract software specifications' (Bjorner, *ed*), Springer LNCS 86, 1980.

[81] W.W. Peterson and E.J. Weldon, Jr., *Error-correcting codes*, M.I.T. Press, 1972.

[82] G.D. Plotkin, *LCF considered as a programming language*, Theoretical Computer Science **5**, 223–255, 1977.

[83] G.D. Plotkin, *Lambda-definability in the full type hierarchy*, in 'To H.B. Curry: essays on combinatory logic, lambda calculus and formalism' (Seldin and Hindley, *eds*), Academic Press, 1980.

[84] G.D. Plotkin, *A structured approach to operational semantics*, DAIMI FN–19, Computer Science Dept., Aarhus University, 1981.

[85] A. Pnueli and E. Shahar, *A platform for combining deductive with algorithmic verification*, 184–195, Proceedings of the 8th CAV, Springer LNCS 1102, 1996.

[86] D.K. Probst and H.F. Li, *Using partial order semantics to avoid the state explosion problem in asynchronous systems*, Proceedings of CAV '90, Springer LNCS 531, 1990.

[87] G.M. Reed, *A uniform mathematical theory for real-time distributed computing*, Oxford University D.Phil thesis, 1988.

[88] G.M. Reed and A.W. Roscoe, *A timed model for communicating sequential processes*, Theoretical Computer Science **58**, 249-261, 1988.

[89] G.M. Reed and A.W. Roscoe, *Analysing TM_{FS}: a study of nondeterminism in real-time concurrency*, in 'Concurrency: theory, language and architecture' (Yonezawa and Ito, *eds*), Springer LNCS 491, 1991.

[90] J.C. Reynolds, *Types, abstraction and parametric polymorphism*, Information Processing 83, 513–523, North-Holland, 1983.

[91] A.W. Roscoe, *A mathematical theory of communicating proceses*, Oxford University D.Phil thesis, 1982.

[92] A.W. Roscoe, *Denotational semantics for* OCCAM, Proceedings of the Pittsburgh seminar on concurrency, Springer LNCS 197, 1985.

[93] A.W. Roscoe, *Routing messages through networks: an exercise in deadlock avoidance*, Proceedings of 7th OCCAM User Group technical meeting, IOS B.V., Amsterdam, 1987.

[94] A.W. Roscoe, *An alternative order for the failures model*, in 'Two papers on CSP', technical monograph PRG-67, Oxford University Computing Laboratory, July 1988. Also Journal of Logic and Computation **2**, 5, 557–577, 1992.

[95] A.W. Roscoe, *Unbounded nondeterminism in CSP*, in 'Two papers on CSP', technical monograph PRG-67, Oxford University Computing Laboratory, July 1988. Also Journal of Logic and Computation, **3**, 2 131–172, 1993.

[96] A.W. Roscoe, *Maintaining consistency in distributed databases*, Oxford University Computing Laboratory technical monograph PRG-87, 1990.

[97] A.W. Roscoe, *Topology, computer science and the mathematics of convergence*, in 'Topology and category theory in computer science' (Reed, Roscoe and Wachter, *eds*), Oxford University Press, 1991.

[98] A.W. Roscoe, *Model checking CSP*, in 'A classical mind: essays in honour of C.A.R. Hoare', Prentice Hall, 1994.

[99] A.W. Roscoe, *CSP and determinism in security modelling*, Proceedings of 1995 IEEE Symposium on Security and Privacy, IEEE Computer Society Press, 1995.

[100] A.W. Roscoe, *Modelling and verifying key-exchange protocols using CSP and FDR*, Proceedings of 1995 IEEE Computer Security Foundations Workshop, IEEE Computer Society Press, 1995.

[101] A.W. Roscoe, *Intensional specifications of security protocols*, Proceedings of 1996 IEEE Computer Security Foundations Workshop, IEEE Computer Society Press, 1996.

[102] A.W. Roscoe and N. Dathi, *The pursuit of deadlock freedom*, Information and Computation **75**, 3, 289–327, 1987.

[103] A.W. Roscoe, P.H.B. Gardiner, M.H. Goldsmith, J.R. Hulance, D.M. Jackson and J.B. Scattergood, *Hierarchical compression for model-checking CSP or how to check* 10^{20} *dining philosophers for deadlock*, Proceedings of the 1st TACAS, BRICS Notes Series NS-95-2, Department of Computer Science, University of Aarhus, 1995. (Also Springer LNCS 1019.)

[104] A.W. Roscoe and M.H. Goldsmith, *The perfect 'spy' for model-checking crypto-protocols*, Proceedings of DIMACS workshop on the design and formal verification of cryptographic protocols, 1997.

[105] A.W. Roscoe and C.A.R. Hoare, *The laws of* OCCAM *programming*, Theoretical Computer Science, **60**, 177-229, 1988.

[106] A.W. Roscoe and H. MacCarthy, *Verifying a replicated database: A case study in model-checking CSP*, Formal Systems technical report, 1994.

[107] A.W. Roscoe, J.C.P. Woodcock and L. Wulf, *Non-interference through determinism*, Journal of Computer Security **4**, 1, 27–54, 1996 (revised from Proceedings of ESORICS 94, Springer LNCS 875).

[108] A.W. Roscoe and L. Wulf, *Composing and decomposing systems under security properties*, Proceedings of 1995 IEEE Computer Security Foundations Workshop, IEEE Computer Society Press, 1995.

[109] P.Y.A. Ryan, *A CSP formulation of non-interference*, Cipher, 19–27. IEEE Computer Society Press, 1991.

[110] J.B. Scattergood, *Tools for CSP and Timed CSP*, Oxford University D.Phil thesis, forthcoming 1997.

[111] S.A. Schneider, *Correctness and communication in real-time systems*, Oxford University D.Phil thesis, 1989.

[112] W.A. Sutherland, *Introduction to metric and topological spaces*, Oxford University Press, 1975.

[113] H. Tej and B. Wolff, *A corrected failure-divergence model for CSP in Isabelle/HOL*, To appear in the Proceedings of FME97.

[114] L.G. Valiant, *A bridging model for parallel computation*, Communications of the ACM, **33**, 8 103–111, 1990.

[115] A. Valmari, *Stubborn sets for reduced state space generation*, Proceedings of 10th International conference on theory and applications of Petri nets, 1989.

[116] A. Valmari, *The weakest deadlock-preserving congruence*, Information Processing Letters **53**, 341–346, 1995.

[117] A. Valmari and M. Tienari *An improved failures equivalence for finite-state systems with a reduction algorithm*, Protocol Specification, Testing and Verification XI, North-Holland, 1991.

[118] P.L. Wadler, *Theorems for free!*, 347–359, Proceedings of the 4th ACM FPLCA, 1989.

[119] D.J. Walker, *An operational semantics for CSP*, Oxford University M.Sc. dissertation, 1986.

[120] P.H. Welch, G.R.R. Justo and C.J. Willcock, *High-level paradigms for deadlock-free high-performance systems*, Transputer Applications and Systems '93, IOS Press, 1993.

[121] P. Wolper, *Expressing interesting properties of programs in propositional temporal logic*, 184–193, Proceedings of the 13th ACM POPL, 1986.

[122] L. Wulf, *Interaction and security in distributed computing*, Oxford University D.Phil thesis, 1997.

[123] J.T. Yantchev, *ARC – A tool for efficient refinement and equivalence checking for CSP*, IEEE 2nd Int. Conf. on Algorithms and Architectures for Parallel Processing, 1996.

[124] J.T. Yantchev and C.R. Jesshope, *Adaptive, low latency, deadlock-free packet routing for processor networks*, IEE Proc. E, May 1989.

[125] I. Zakiuddin, *An FDR analysis of a fault-tolerant information system*, Proceedings of AAS '97, ACM, 1997.

How to obtain the tools mentioned in this book

The following details are believed to be correct at the time of writing, but potential users are advised in the case of difficulty to consult the web site given in the Preface. The web site should also contain details of further tools.

- FDR: this is a product of Formal Systems (Europe) Ltd. At the time of writing the release is 2.11. Much of what is described in this book does not apply to the earlier FDR 1. For details please email `enquiries@fsel.com`.

- ProBE: at the time of writing this animator is under beta-test by Formal Systems (Europe) Ltd, with a formal release expected later in 1997. For details please email `enquiries@fsel.com`.

- Jeremy Martin's *Deadlock Checker* (see Section 13.6) operates (at the time of writing) on the more restricted syntax used by FDR 1. It is hoped to rectify this. You can obtain it through the web site with URL

  `http://users.ox.ac.uk/~jeremy/Deadlock/index.html`

- Gavin Lowe's *Casper* (a security protocol compiler, as discussed in Section 15.3) can be obtained through the web site with URL

  `http://www.mcs.le.ac.uk/~gl7/Security/Casper/index.html`

Main index

Entries in **bold face** are the primary reference(s) to the item concerned, while *italic* entries denote references in exercises. Note that processes have a separate index, following this one.

Index of named processes

This book contains many CSP process definitions, some of which are used many times. The following index is a reference to the main uses of a selection of the processes that we have given distinctive names. The notational conventions are as in the main index.

SPIVEY, J.M., *The Z Notation: A reference manual (2nd edn)*
TENNENT, R.D., *Semantics of Programming Languages*
WATT, D.A., *Programming Language Concepts and Paradigms*
WATT, D.A., *Programming Language Processors*
WATT, D.A., *Programming Language Syntax and Semantics*
WATT, D.A., WICHMANN, B.A. and FINDLAY, W., *ADA: Language and methodology*
WELSH, J. and ELDER, J., *Introduction to Pascal (3rd edn)*
WOODCOCK, J. and DAVIES, J., *Using Z: Specification, refinement and proof*